9/04

THE GUARDIANS

THE GUARDIANS

KINGMAN BREWSTER, HIS CIRCLE,
AND THE RISE OF THE LIBERAL
ESTABLISHMENT

GEOFFREY KABASERVICE

HENRY HOLT AND COMPANY, INC.

NEW YORK

Henry Holt and Company, LLC
Publishers since 1866
115 West 18th Street
New York, New York 10011

Henry Holt® is a registered trademark of Henry Holt and Company, LLC.

Library of Congress Cataloging-in-Publication Data
Kabaservice, Geoffrey M.
  Guardians : Kingman Brewster, his circle, and the rise of the liberal establishment /
Geoffrey Kabaservice—1st ed.
    p. cm.
  ISBN 0-8050-6762-0
  1. Brewster, Kingman, 1919– 2. Yale University—Presidents—Biography. 3. College
presidents—Connecticut—New Haven—Biography. 4. Liberalism—United States—
History—20th century. I. Title.
LD6330.1963.B74 K23 2004
378.1'11—dc22
[B]   20033057142

First Edition 2004

Designed by Fritz Metsch

Printed in the United States of America
1   3   5   7   9   10   8   6   4   2

To my parents,
Marcia and Thomas Kabaservice

If we want the best among our Guardians, we must take those naturally fitted to watch over a commonwealth. They must have the right sort of intelligence and ability; and also they must look upon the commonwealth as their special concern—the sort of concern that is felt for something so closely bound up with oneself that its interests and fortunes, for good or ill, are held to be identical with one's own.

—The Republic of Plato

CONTENTS

THE GUARDIANS

INTRODUCTION

T HE STAGE was ready, the actors in place. Nearing midnight on the first of May, 1970—May Day, the day of revolution and apocalypse—Kingman Brewster looked out on a scene not unlike others playing out, in various renditions, across the United States. From a second-story window of his secret command post fronting the New Haven Green, Brewster, the president of Yale University, saw a mob of radicals who were banging drums and waving banners, swarming around the Green's three ancient churches. Black Panthers shouted obscenities through bullhorns.

To Brewster's left stood the stately columns of the Superior Court Building, where the Panthers' national leader Bobby Seale was on trial for the torture-murder of an alleged police informant. Two companies of the National Guard braced themselves in front of the building, brandishing bayonets. On the Green's northern edge loomed the ivy-covered ramparts and battlements of the Old Campus, the historic heart of the university over which Brewster had presided for seven years. Tear gas drifted across the quadrangle where Beat poet Allen Ginsberg sat in lotus position on a bandstand in the middle of the quad, clinking finger cymbals and chanting *om*. Colorful parachutes hung from the elms, and a huge sign draped from Gothic windows proclaimed THINK, EDUCATE, BE NONVIOLENT.

Earlier that day, the Green's grassy expanse had been filled with thousands of demonstrators from around the country protesting Seale's trial. At one point, the Yippie anarchist Jerry Rubin, garbling Brewster's proud New England name, had tried to get the crowd to chant "Fuck Kingston Brewer." Now a file of police and National Guardsmen stood, rifles at the ready, in front of the courthouse and City Hall as ragged, self-proclaimed revolutionaries in motorcycle helmets came streaming toward them through darkness and clouds of tear gas, hurling rocks. Peacekeeping marshals from town and university tried to interpose themselves between street fighters and guardsmen. Crews from every major media outlet in the country jostled for position. If this was the revolution, it most certainly would be televised.

In Yale's courtyards, beneath Gothic spires and turrets, students mingled with thousands of strangely garbed demonstrators, including some of the nation's most feared and hated radicals. Among the event's sponsors were the Chicago Seven "conspirators," including Yippie spokesman Abbie Hoffman, who had predicted "the biggest riot in history."[1] Young people everywhere had been urged, through rallies, posters, and word of mouth, to burn Yale and "free Bobby."

New Haven's police chief warned that violent provocations could come from the extreme left or right. Rumors circulated that the Hell's Angels motorcycle gang was camped outside town, poised to pillage, and that a fleet of trucks had been rented to transport the expected corpses. Mayor Bartholomew Guida declared that "the eyes of the nation will be on New Haven this weekend," then fled town. Many residents and merchants had followed his example, leaving behind boarded-up windows and storefronts now covered with political slogans and stencils of the Yale bulldog and the Black Panther. President Richard Nixon, acting on FBI predictions of massive destruction, had alerted four thousand marines and paratroopers to be ready to storm into the anticipated bloodbath.

The pressure on Brewster was keen. One of the last university presidents to be a highly visible national figure, he was controversial despite his intelligence and charm. His outspoken views on a variety of issues would make him the first and only university president to appear simultaneously on the covers of *Time* and *Newsweek.*

The social upheavals of the 1960s had flared earliest and most intensely in the universities, in the wake of the civil rights, antiwar, and feminist movements. Campuses had become the front lines of the battles that were breaking down long-established divisions between whites and blacks, men and women, teachers and students, parents and children, authorities and their subjects. By the late 1960s, as these battles spread far beyond the universities, Brewster had emerged as one of a handful of leaders who were not baffled or frightened by youthful unrest. A former student protester himself, who had helped found the America First movement against United States participation in World War II, he wanted to show young, disaffected Americans that the establishment heard their voices, shared some of their concerns, and was open to change. Until the May Day drama, Yale had been strengthened rather than damaged by the turmoil of the times, in large part because of Brewster's deft responses and bold actions.

Brewster inevitably would be judged on May Day's outcome because he had opened his university to the demonstrators, even offering them food and shelter. Brewster had persuaded the faculty to "modify" academic expectations during the strike, partly to show that Yale was also concerned about social justice. Class attendance would be optional for students and faculty alike. Brewster even told the faculty that although the institution had to remain politically neutral, he personally was "skeptical of the ability of black revolutionaries to achieve a fair trial anywhere in the United States."[2] This statement, leaked to the press, produced a firestorm of conservative backlash. Vice President Spiro Agnew called for Yale's alumni to remove Brewster from the presidency.

Despite the swirling tension of the May night, the handsome, fifty-year-old Brewster managed to look dashing even though he had been operating on minimal sleep for days. Tall and commanding in his Savile Row suit, Brewster appeared energized by the tension, pacing past a table with dozens of phones linking him to military and civil authorities and to the rest of the campus. Occasionally he sat down on a couch to listen to reports from the police scanner. At his side was Cyrus Vance, a dapper, silver-haired patrician in a rumpled but well-tailored three-piece suit. A member of the Yale Corporation (the university's governing board) and a longtime friend, Vance provided Brewster with advice and counsel. Brewster had wanted his friend to be present so that he could testify on Brewster's behalf if the demonstration surged out of control. Knowing that the potential for havoc was high, Brewster realized that he could easily find himself under indictment if violence erupted, and Vance was an old hand at crisis management. Before Nixon took office, he had served as Lyndon Johnson's troubleshooter in emergencies ranging from war in Cyprus to riots in Detroit to the Vietnam peace talks in Paris. A Wall Street lawyer, Vance had ascended through the foreign policy ranks on the strength of his wisdom, courtliness, and discretion. He cultivated a presence marked by a dignified gravitas, after the fashion of the previous generation of lawyer-statesmen, yet his sober bearing was slightly undercut by his boyish features and whimsical half-moon glasses.

THE MAY DAY demonstration had come upon Brewster like a forest fire. Making matters worse, President Nixon had gone on television the night before with the news that United States troops had invaded Cambodia, widening the seemingly endless Indochina war in an attempt to wipe out North Vietnamese sanctuaries. Within minutes of the speech, campus demonstrations had ignited from coast to coast. News commentators anticipated that the Cambodian invasion would hit the New Haven demonstration like gasoline on a blaze. Radical journalists envisioned "the fall of the American Winter Palace."

An era of student protest, which could plausibly be said to have begun a decade earlier when black students staged a sit-in at Woolworth's lunch counters, now appeared likely to come to a bloody finale in the symbolic heart of the establishment. But Brewster wanted to show that student protest—and the rebelliousness of the era—didn't have to lead to violence. He was well aware that if disaster struck, his critics would rejoice at his downfall. He had enemies in some very high places. Key members of the Nixon administration hated him. Agnew and Attorney General John Mitchell had denounced him, and the president himself had become a foe. "Nixon would have loved to see Yale humiliated," one of Brewster's allies remembered.[3] A self-made man from a modest background, the President despised the East Coast establishment world of privilege and culture. He believed that the unrest at Yale was actively encouraged by Brewster and other irresponsible elites. When he appeared on television the night before, grimacing and stabbing at a map of Cambodia, Nixon had warned: "We live in an age of anarchy both abroad and at home. We see mindless attacks on all the great institutions which have been created by free civilizations in the past 500 years. Even here in the United States, great universities are being systematically destroyed."[4] Brewster was told that an early draft of Nixon's speech made reference to the anticipated devastation of Yale.[5]

TEN MINUTES BEFORE midnight, three bombs detonated simultaneously in the Yale hockey rink, the setting of a rock concert and dance. Explosions shook the building and echoed across the campus.

Brewster heard the wail of sirens as fire trucks, ambulances, and police cars converged on the shattered rink, where early reports had estimated that about a thousand were in attendance. The university police chief radioed in, announcing, "We're moving in to look for survivors." One of Brewster's aides remembered that the words "[gave] you a sense of mangled bodies all over the place."[6] Brewster and Vance sat on the couch in silence. If Brewster was thinking that his gamble had failed, that people had been killed, and that he was about to become internationally infamous, he gave no indication. He remained poised and self-contained.

Brewster knew that, in the face of potential catastrophe, he had the support of other leaders cast from the same mold, friends and colleagues who shared his background and outlook. Like him, they had started life as promising sons of the WASP upper class, the standouts at prep schools and Ivy League colleges. They served as junior officers in World War II and, in the postwar era, as younger partners to the "Wise Men," eminent statesmen like Dean Acheson and Averell Harriman. They had both brains and breeding; they were the best of the brightest, the brightest of the best. Their backgrounds and ambitions had conditioned them to carry on a tradition of gentlemen elites in the public service that traced back to Theodore Roosevelt—perhaps even, some said, to the Founding Fathers. By the early 1960s, they had become pillars of the establishment in their own right, and all looked forward to glittering futures.

But the years between John F. Kennedy's assassination and the end of the 1960s proved to be more revolutionary than anyone could have anticipated. By May 1970, the successors to the Wise Men had to deal with social realities undreamed of by their elders. Their backgrounds had hardly prepared them for the problems of race, social mobility, and the challenges to established authority they were contending with now. And although they had once assumed that America, united in a supposed liberal consensus, would defer to their authority, they had acquired enemies on the left and on the right.

ANOTHER MEMBER OF Brewster's circle was Nixon's undersecretary of state, Elliot Lee Richardson. He and Brewster had met as undergraduates (as heads of their respective literary societies at Harvard and Yale), and Richardson, like Brewster, was an upper-crust Bostonian and liberal New England Republican. With his dark hair, chiseled jawline, and black-rimmed glasses, he looked remarkably like Superman's alter ego Clark Kent. The historian Stephen Ambrose observed that Richardson's heroic political independence may have stemmed from World War II and the fact that he "was one of those junior officers at Utah Beach who led the way up and over. No man who had been through that experience ever had anything again to fear."[7]

Richardson and Brewster also overlapped at Harvard Law School after World War II, and were part of the same social circuit in Boston during the 1950s. Richardson moved between law practice and public service, first as an aide to established liberal Republican politicians, then as an appointee to federal office, then as a political candidate in his own right. As Massachusetts lieutenant governor and attorney general in the 1960s, he built a reputation as a brilliant, hardworking Mr. Clean, a scourge of criminals, corrupt pols, and fixers. Despite his privileged background, he had a genuine concern for the education and welfare of the nation's disadvantaged citizens. Like Brewster, Richardson had been seriously discussed as a dark-horse candidate for the Republican nomination for the presidency in 1968; his stature may have influenced Nixon's decision to offer him the position at State when the new administration came into office.

Liberal Republicans were a rapidly vanishing breed, and Richardson, again like Brewster, was regarded with suspicion by conservatives in the Nixon administration. On May first, he had been ordered to the Capitol to brief Republican senators on Nixon's reasons for invading Cambodia. Although Richardson privately told friends that the invasion was a mistake, the briefing was Nixon's test of loyalty; if Richardson passed, it was whispered in Washington corridors, he would soon be named secretary of health, education, and welfare. But if the May Day protest at Yale turned violent, he inevitably would be involved in the fallout.

THE NIGHT BEFORE May first, Brewster's best friend, McGeorge Bundy, the president of the Ford Foundation, had addressed the Yale Club of Boston. Blue eyes flashing behind his spectacles, "Mac" Bundy assured his fellow alumni that "one of the things I have observed about my friend Brewster is that he will deal with anybody and surrender his responsibilities to nobody." Responsibility, Bundy said, "rests where legitimacy has placed it"—an oddly aristocratic statement for 1970, a time when talk of legitimacy and aristocracy was likely to conjure up images of tumbrels and guillotines.[8] Still, Bundy's remark would have reminded his Boston audience that he and Brewster were descendants of New England's oldest families.

Widely known as the brightest boy of his generation at Groton and Yale, protégé of mentors like Henry Stimson and Dean Acheson, Bundy became dean of the faculty at Harvard at age thirty-four. Foreign policy had been the usual preserve of the Wise Men, and Bundy followed their example by serving as national security advisor under Presidents Kennedy and Johnson. In that capacity he had been one of the principal architects of American intervention in Vietnam, as to a lesser extent were his brother William and Cyrus Vance. His brilliance and arrogance made him a natural metaphor for journalists trying to explain the failure of "the best and brightest" in Indochina.

By May Day, McGeorge Bundy and his once-confident friends were as troubled by social upheaval at home as they were by Communism abroad. Bundy had attempted to put the resources of the nation's largest philanthropic enterprise, the Ford Foundation, behind the task of improving the American social structure. His support of bold, controversial activism in the ghetto and in New York City's public school system made him a favorite target of the political right, while his Vietnam involvement automatically made him suspect to the left.

IN HIS PREPARATIONS for May Day, Brewster had relied heavily on the counsel of the Yale Corporation members. He reached out not only to Vance but to other patrician liberals on the board, including Paul Moore Jr., the Episcopal bishop of New York, and the city's mayor, John Lindsay.

Moore was also on the Yale campus that day, partly because his son and daughter had been students at the university who were involved in the protests that led up to May Day. Tall, blue-eyed, and imposing, his silver hair modishly long, Moore had been a childhood playmate of McGeorge Bundy's and a Yale classmate of Brewster's. He came from one of America's richest families. A hero in World War II, he received a Purple Heart, Silver Star, and Navy Cross; he nearly died on Guadalcanal. After training at the General Theological Seminary, he was part of a new breed of idealistic Episcopal priests seeking to reclaim parishes in inner cities abandoned by white flight. His priesthood in decaying Jersey City during the 1950s gave him a decade's head start on understanding civil rights grievances, and, as head of the Episcopal Church in Washington and in New York, he used what he had learned to prick the consciences of the nation's elite.

Moore appreciated that the May Day protests were about more than just the Panther trial or protest against the war. He felt that just as World War II had begun the breakup of colonialism, now "the domestic equivalent of colonialism, namely the domination of society by old established institutions, was being resisted as well."[9]

SIX FOOT, FOUR inches tall, blue-eyed, and athletic, John Lindsay was charismatic in the extreme. A graduate of St. Paul's School (with Moore), he had entered Yale a few years behind Brewster. After war service and Yale Law School, Lindsay plunged into liberal Republican politics.

Like Richardson, Lindsay moved back and forth between corporate law and Washington before being elected to Congress as the representative of the "Silk Stocking" district on Manhattan's Upper East Side. He won national admiration as well as the enmity of Republican Party regulars for his idealism and unshakable independence. In 1965, the widespread belief that he would someday contend for the presidency had propelled him into the New York mayoralty—"the second toughest job in the nation," it was said. But by 1970, it was clear that Lindsay's expertise and charisma were no match for the problems that beset America's cities—although Lindsay had prevented major riots in New York during the long, hot summers of the late 1960s.

As a member of the presidentially appointed Kerner Commission on urban unrest, Lindsay had authored the famous warning that "our nation is moving toward two societies, one black, one white—separate and unequal."[10] He had applauded Brewster's decision to open Yale to the May Day demonstrators; the decision echoed his own policy of trying to convince disaffected youth and minorities that the system worked and that its leaders were willing to listen. But Lindsay was also under attack on May first. Two days earlier, he told a college audience that he had "unending admiration" for those willing to go to prison rather than serve in Vietnam. Soon Agnew would vilify Lindsay along with Brewster, assailing the New York mayor as a "well-born elitist." "There are men now in power in this country," Agnew told his heartland audiences, "who do not represent authority, who cannot cope with tradition, and who believe that the people of America are ready to support revolution as long as it is done with a cultured voice and a handsome profile."[11]

The vice president had, in so many words, charged the liberal establishment with treason. Brewster and his friends had heard this before; such talk reminded them of Senator Joseph McCarthy's attacks on their mentors like Acheson a generation earlier. This time around, however, the establishment was also under siege from the left. Conservative populists like Agnew saw the small group of men and institutions as an elite acting to frustrate the will of the people. Ironically, many leftists shared that view. They saw Brewster and Yale as pillars of an oppressive order. Brewster himself recognized that some of the demonstrators in New Haven "were so fed up with the establishment of which Yale was a part that they were going to try to destroy Yale as a symbol of the establishment."[12]

It was a measure of America's polarization that as Brewster sat in his command post in the waning minutes of May first, waiting for news from the shattered rink, he considered it equally likely that the bomb could have been set by a provocateur from the left or the right. Considering that presidential aide John Dean had been spotted in town earlier that day, it was not completely paranoid to wonder whether the government itself may have been involved.

JUST BEFORE MIDNIGHT the police scanner in Brewster's command post crackled with the news that there were no casualties in the rink. Most of the crowd, drawn by the excitement on the Green, had left the building just minutes before the explosion. The few remaining had suffered only minor cuts from flying glass. Brewster and his assistants began to speak again, although, as one recalled, "it was that kind of talk that you have after you have just avoided an accident and your adrenaline has been pumping."[13]

As Brewster and Vance left the command post and walked back to the president's house sometime after two in the morning, Brewster turned to his friend and said, "You know what this is all about? It is a test as to whether we are right or they are right."[14] In other words, was authority best served by Agnew's and Mitchell's brand of divisiveness, force, and hard-line tactics? Or was it best served by the liberal establishment's tolerance, openness, and flexibility, which Brewster called "taking the risk of latitude for freedom"? Two and a half days later, an answer of sorts came when National Guardsmen opened fire on a crowd of students at Kent State University, killing four.

At this moment in American history, some leaders were aware that the nature of authority was changing. Brewster had moved Yale away from its deeply conservative New England roots, transforming it into a modern, international institution. The university's culture, reflected in its policies in administration, faculty hiring, and undergraduate admissions, had long stressed the superiority of white Anglo-Saxon Protestant leadership. Brewster reshaped Yale to emphasize merit rather than background. He redefined leadership to include individuals from nonprivileged circumstances, minorities, and women. Yet he did not turn his back on Yale's heritage, its hallowed tradition of community, or its distinctive reputation for producing leaders and achievers. He sought a middle course through the Sturm und Drang of the era—a difficult balancing act—and found himself pressed between impatient students and angry conservative alumni.

KINGMAN BREWSTER'S STORY exemplifies the experiences of the leadership class of "the greatest generation." Brewster and most of his friends and associates traced their ancestry to the New England colonists, and they shared backgrounds of at least modest privilege. Educated at a handful of private schools and colleges, they were brought together from an early age and throughout their lives. And they achieved leadership positions in careers and in institutions that historically had been tilted in favor of their class.

It is striking how often people referred to Brewster as someone who seemed born to leadership. When pressed for specifics, they would point to cultural markers such as his lineal male descent from Elder William Brewster of the *Mayflower,* his education at a private school and Yale College and Harvard Law School, his handsome patrician features, his sonorous New England accent, his tailored English suits, and his closetful of sailing trophies from summers on Martha's Vineyard. He was a member of the Council on Foreign Relations and tony metropolitan clubs. He had close, longtime friendships with powerful men: Washington fixers, Wall Street lawyers and bankers, presidents of the major universities and foundations. They not only tended to uphold the status quo; they *were* the status quo.

Yet the establishment was not a monolith of ideas shared by a group of identically minded individuals. The dominant strain undoubtedly was the rock-ribbed Republicanism for which New England had been known. Men who inclined toward this view—including most of the leaders of Brewster's father's generation—generally tried to preserve the social and political privileges that their class enjoyed. This is to be expected; ruling classes typically attempt to reproduce themselves.

Yet, surprisingly, the establishment leaders of Brewster's generation were mostly liberals, who in different ways set out to reform the institutions and the society that had given them their advantages. In matters of appearance and custom, they were much like the older generation. They belonged to the right clubs, accepted the settled canons of dress and behavior, upheld the old ideals of honor and patriotism and integrity, internalized the Cold Warrior code, sailed off Cape Cod and Martha's Vineyard, tanned on the shores of the Bahamas and Antigua, and followed the East Coast family rituals. But they sensed and responded to the new generation's desire for a more just social order, what Brewster in his inaugural address called the yearning of the young "to be involved in something more meaningful than inherited patterns of success."[15]

Like their predecessors, Brewster and his peers found themselves in the same company again and again, not just at upper-class watering holes and old-school reunions, but in government, on university and corporate and foundation boards, and on presidential commissions and associations of concerned citizens. They served as a nexus between government, media, and academia, shuttling along the East Coast between the often-separate worlds of power, opinion, and knowledge. Also like their predecessors, they exerted a disproportionate influence on public opinion. Unlike their mentors, however, they struggled to modernize what might be called the nation's operating system, the social order that had placed power in their hands.

When the members of this new, liberal establishment came to positions of responsibility in the 1960s, their background conditioned their responses to the urban and racial crises, the trauma of the Vietnam War, and the alienation of the younger generation. None of them could have kept aloof from the problems of the 1960s even if they had wanted to. The disruptions provoked by the era kept bubbling up into their spheres of politics, education, administration, diplomacy, philanthropy, and religion. Their responses followed similar patterns, for reasons that had to do with background and temperament, and the interactions among the elites.

Most important, perhaps, was the fact that Brewster and his friends thought of themselves as society's guardians: modern leaders of the country's institutions, who had national responsibilities and tried to take a national perspective. As their conception of the national interest changed during the 1960s, they responded in ways that many other leaders, and people who shared their background, did not. At their best, these men held out the promise that they could overcome the flaws and prejudices of their fathers' generation while retaining the positive attributes of that old WASP elite. Their supporters praised them as pragmatic idealists, while their enemies damned them as oppressors or as traitors to their class.

Guardianship is a useful metaphor for understanding Brewster and his circle. The guardians, in Plato's *Republic*, are the ideal rulers of the ideal state. They serve no interest other than the good of the state and are indifferent to money or celebrity. While Plato called his state an aristocracy (i.e., "rule by the best"), the Platonic system of the guardians was not a conventional aristocracy, because it did not rest on inherited advantage. The guardians' responsibility was not only to defend the state and its interests but to enforce equal opportunity. If the offspring of the upper class proved inferior, it was the guardians' duty to "assign to each one a status appropriate to his nature and not hesitate to thrust him out among the farmers and craftsmen." At the same time, talented members of the lower classes should be "honored and raised up."[16]

Brewster and his peers oversaw that process of social churning in the 1960s, guiding a movement toward meritocracy and greater equality for minorities. The peaceful transition of the United States from a system much like aristocracy to a more open society was one of the epochal changes in the nation's history, yet the role of the guardians who made it possible has been curiously understudied. Subsequent years have not been kind to the reputations of the members of Brewster's establishment. When they are remembered at all, it is largely by their enemies, who recall them either as villains who promoted the Vietnam War or as social engineering elitists. Despite their best intentions, Brewster and his circle were divisive figures. They infuriated even some of the people they helped simply because of who they were, with their funny names, ingrained upper-class traits, polished intellects, high-minded liberalism, and aura of natural superiority that derived, ironically, from the tradition of WASP leadership they helped undermine. "Vote for Elliot Richardson," read a bumper sticker printed by the Bostonian's electoral opponents, "he's better than you." Guardianship is an alien concept to most Americans, and the members of the establishment provoked a fierce resentment of liberals, intellectuals, and the elite that continues to drive current politics. Perhaps as a result, their milieu has gone unexamined, their ideas forgotten, their speeches unread, their contributions ignored. And yet they were an important part of the dynamic that shaped the society we live in today. The history of twentieth-century America will never be properly understood until the establishment is written back into history.

EXAMINING THE LIBERAL establishment from the standpoint of Brewster and his circle—men like Cyrus Vance, McGeorge Bundy, Elliot Richardson, Paul Moore, and John Lindsay—inevitably presents a portrait drawn from a particular perspective. Like a fishing net, a human network looks a certain way if it is picked up by a single strand. Even if another strand of the social fabric is examined, however—such as that of the liberal establishment's nemesis, William F. Buckley Jr.—Brewster's circle would remain the heart of the network.

Buckley gave the name "liberal establishment" to the interlocking directorate of individuals, institutions, and ideas that he fought in his quest to revive conservatism in postwar America. As an undergraduate at Yale, Buckley locked horns with the American Veterans Committee, a liberal, internationalist group led by Brewster at Harvard Law School and by William Sloane Coffin Jr. (later chaplain of Yale under Brewster) in New Haven. Buckley rose to national fame with his 1951 *God and Man at Yale*, an attack on academic freedom and the alleged betrayal of conservatism at his alma mater. The book met a bitter rebuttal from McGeorge Bundy, who insinuated that Buckley's nonestablishment background (Irish, Catholic, son of a Texas oilman) disqualified him from criticizing a WASP institution like Yale; Bundy's attack helped get him named dean of the faculty at Harvard. Buckley became an advocate of and informal assistant to Joseph McCarthy, whose populist, anti-Communist crusade was aimed at the establishment in all but name. In 1965, Buckley ran for mayor of New York against John Lindsay. Three years later, he ran for trustee of the Yale Corporation against Cyrus Vance. He castigated Coffin's involvement in civil rights and antiwar protest—and Brewster's support of the chaplain's activism. Buckley charged that Brewster himself, in helping to convert one of America's most conservative universities into one of the most progressive, had become "a Kerensky . . . wooing the cheers of the mob."[17]

The legacy of Brewster's liberal establishment, and of the 1960s as a whole, is a continuing source of political debate, involving not only ideas but personalities. Bill Clinton and Hillary Rodham met at the Yale Law School during Brewster's presidency, and Rodham was part of the committee of support for the Black Panthers during the May Day 1970 demonstrations. Several members of President Clinton's brain trust were former Brewster protégés, including Strobe Talbott, Gregory Craig, Joseph Lieberman, and Derek Shearer. The cartoonist Garry Trudeau, whose *Doonesbury* series began as a satire of life at Yale in the late 1960s and early 1970s, continues to memorialize Brewster through his affectionate characterization of the wise but world-weary President King. On the other hand, George W. Bush, who matriculated at Yale shortly after Brewster was inaugurated, saw the Yale president as one of those leaders who had betrayed the institution's conservative tradition and turned the university over to leftists and intellectual snobs.

The story of the rise and fall of the liberal establishment, as told through Kingman Brewster's life and times, does more than shed light on the actions and motivations of one of the twentieth century's most famous university presidents. It provides a broad view of the United States, complete with individuals and movements and debates—some well known, some forgotten—that changed a nation. Many of the issues that raise passions today emerged from the actions of liberal establishment figures, like Brewster, who applied the lessons of their heritage (as they saw it) and their experiences of depression, war, and Cold War to the unexpected challenges of a new era. These were the last of the Wise Men. Their legacy is still with us.

ORIGINS

Kingman Brewster spent the last days of the summer of 1937 sailing off Martha's Vineyard. At age eighteen, he had established himself as one of the country's top young sailors. Straight-backed and intent, he was the image of assurance and command at the tiller. As a racer, he won through competence, aggression, and élan. He was nervy, relied on a gambler's instinct, and was especially good at match racing, which called for a chess-like ability to anticipate a competitor's moves. In August he had, for the second time, been crowned the best young small-boat racer in North America by winning the Prince of Wales Cup in Nova Scotia.[1] Brewster was not a particularly methodical or shipshape sailor, and he didn't spend much time grooming his boat or poring over navigational charts to see where rocks and shoals might lurk. But he was lucky, and he knew it. He counted on his luck.

Even as a teenager, Brewster had the hallmarks of one whom the gods had ordained to be a leader. The very name Kingman suggested he had been born to rule, although it was, in fact, the patronymic of a distant branch of his family. Tall and tanned from sailing, with wavy brown hair swept over a high forehead, he had a noticeably large, well-formed head. When serious, Brewster could look as imposing as a marble bust of one of his Puritan forebears. His more usual expression, though, was a wry grin, one side of his mouth turning up while the other turned down, laugh lines crinkling at the edges of his dark eyes. His was the face of authority: patrician, somehow aristocratic, yet at the same time relaxed, amused, and approachable.

Brewster spoke in a rolling and sonorous baritone, with a Connecticut Valley accent that sounded vaguely British. No one who talked to him could miss the marks of his privileged background and upbringing, but he wore them lightly. More striking were his intelligence and curiosity, his idealism, and his deep connection to the New England places and traditions in which he was born and raised. Sailing around Martha's Vineyard through sunlight and fog, around the dunes of Lambert's Cove and the cliffs of Gay Head, past the whaling captains' mansions in Edgartown, Brewster felt rooted in America in a way that he found hard to convey. Martha's Vineyard, he wrote as a youth, "is much more than a place to me. . . . I know it had an influence in my make-up, in an almost spiritual way. Perhaps my deepest attachment is to that island. It stands for the essential harmony and eternity of the world to me."[2]

Brewster's ancestors had been sailing the waters of the Vineyard and Cape Cod since the Pilgrims made harbor at Provincetown and Plymouth in 1620. Kingman Brewster was an eleventh-generation lineal male descendant of Elder William Brewster, the spiritual head of the *Mayflower* and chief religious prefect of the Plymouth Colony. If he had wanted, Brewster could have traced his roots back to a signer of the Magna Carta and an assortment of European royalty. But he was skeptical of all forms of inherited success, and he regarded his family heritage with mild self-deprecation. When one of his distant cousins sent him an encomium to the Elder Brewster, he replied that he was "grateful that you and I had the wisdom to select such a magnificent ancestor."[3]

Nonetheless, Kingman took pride in the Pilgrims' legacy of independence and freedom under law, and was conscious of the blood ties that linked him to a range of prominent men including the poet Archibald MacLeish, diplomat George Kennan, and the Rockefellers. He wore a signet ring on his right hand bearing the Brewster family crest and motto, "Vérité soyez ma garde," Norman French for "Truth be my shield." He was well aware that others were also conscious of this background, and that it could do certain things for him. A friend observed that "for all of Kingman's diffidence, for all the uncertainty he sometimes felt . . . there was behind it all the assurance that came from being a direct descendant of Elder Brewster. And it gave him an inner serenity even when he was feeling taxed . . . on which in the end he could fall back, because he was a Brewster."[4]

Elisha Brewster, Kingman's great-great-grandfather, was an officer in the light dragoons in the Revolutionary War. The Brewsters belonged to the rural gentry; Elisha was one of the officers who crushed the populist rising of farmers in western Massachusetts known as Shays's Rebellion.[5] Five successive generations of Brewsters were gentleman farmers and Republicans who served in the state legislature. Brewster's grandfather Charles Kingman Brewster was a merchant and farmer who at various times had been a selectman, town clerk and treasurer, postman, county commissioner, and member of the State House of Representatives from the Second Berkshire District. When he died, in the summer of 1908, his obituary noted his "pleasing personality, his integrity, his loyalty to his friends and his faithful public service."[6]

Brewster's father, Kingman Brewster Sr., was born in Worthington, Massachusetts, in 1882, the youngest of five surviving children. He graduated Phi Beta Kappa from Amherst College in 1906. While there, he came under the spell of professor Charles Edward Garman, whose belief that the privileged had responsibility for the moral and physical welfare of the poor influenced Brewster to spend a year and a half, after graduation, in New York City, doing social work with the intercollegiate Young Men's Christian Association. (Kingman Jr. recalled that his less-than-liberal father abandoned social work for Harvard Law School after his hat was stolen at the New York YMCA.[7]) He received his LL.B. degree from Harvard in 1911, and moved to Oregon to begin law practice.

While public attention focused on Kingman Brewster Jr.'s paternal ancestry, his upbringing was far more influenced by his maternal family. The Besses, of French Huguenot descent, had become a prominent family in Springfield, Massachusetts, since their move there in 1888. Brewster's mother, born in 1885, was one of the six children of Lyman Waterman Besse and Eleanor Pass. Her father, though not born rich, became wealthy by starting one of the country's first clothing store chains, the Besse System, which would boast of shops in twenty-seven cities, from Maine to Missouri.[8]

Florence Besse grew up in the family's Victorian mansion at 29 Ingersoll Grove, a massive home with baronial fireplaces and elegant stained-glass windows, an entire floor for servants, a porte cochere, and one of New England's largest carriage houses at the edge of a ravine in back. The Besse children had a formal upbringing common to the provincial nouveau riche in the Gilded Age. Lyman and his wife dressed for dinner every night and ate separately from their children. The family summered on Martha's Vineyard in the town of Cottage City, which later became Oak Bluffs. Their home, which still survives, is a substantial gingerbread-Gothic house overlooking what remains unspoiled land to the beach and Nantucket Sound beyond. The family sailed along the south shores of Cape Cod in their large yacht *Uneeda,* for which Lyman employed a professional captain and crew.[9]

Florence, a brilliant, dark-haired beauty, graduated Phi Beta Kappa from

Wellesley in 1907, an English major and president of the student government. She soon enrolled as one of the first students at the Simmons School of Social Work, graduating in 1909. Through mutual friends connected with Harvard Law School, Florence met Kingman Brewster in 1911 on one of his trips back east from Oregon. In December they became engaged, and they were married in Springfield in November 1912. The couple moved to Portland but returned to Springfield the next year. Mary, their first child, was born in September 1914. Another daughter, Ann, arrived in 1916 but died in 1918 of pneumonia. Her death was never spoken of in the family.

Kingman Jr. was born in Longmeadow, a suburb of Springfield, in June 1919. His sister recalled that he had a buoyant sense of humor even as a little boy, and it was hard to discipline him when he got into trouble because he would always think of something that made everyone laugh.[10] He was also a good mimic from an early age, and imitating people and accents gave him a great deal of pleasure.

Kingman Jr. grew up in close contact with the Besse clan, whose members crowded the house at Ingersoll Grove at holidays and for Sunday lunches. A photo from the time shows sixteen children at such a gathering. The youngsters were allowed to sit with the adults at the table, legs dangling from their chairs, as long as they did not fidget or interrupt the grownups' discussion. There were annual touch football games in the side yard, baseball games in the backyard, and hide-and-seek in the house and carriage house.[11] Lyman Besse had once taken great pride in his matched pairs of horses, but by the 1920s, the horses had long since been replaced by Packards and Cadillacs.

In Brewster's early years, his father moved restlessly. In 1921, he relocated the family to Washington, D.C., where he worked for several government agencies. The family briefly returned to Springfield in 1923, then went back to Washington, where Kingman Sr. went into practice and sped through a variety of law partners. Not long thereafter, the Brewsters separated and began proceedings for divorce.

The split was painful and drawn out but not acrimonious. In many ways husband and wife were an unlikely match from the start. Kingman wrote that his father "was an arch-conservative lawyer-lobbyist in Washington, wheeling and dealing with equally conservative wheelers and dealers. He was brilliant, charming, and fiercely, bitterly impatient with the New Deal and the brain trusts (most of whom had done better than he at Harvard Law School)." His mother, on the other hand, was "a marvellously speculative and philosophical type," a "free-thinking spirit . . . given to far-out enthusiasms and delighting in sprightly argument with her more intellectually conventional friends."[12]

Kingman was raised by his mother, who was a formidable influence but never overbearing. One of Brewster's friends characterized her as "one of those people whose presence you always felt when she was in the room."[13] Another remembered that "she knew poetry, she knew music, she knew art, she knew architecture, and believe me, she knew Kingman."[14]

After the separation, mother and children returned to Springfield. Three years later, after Florence's mother died, she moved into 29 Ingersoll Grove to take care of her father. Florence Brewster stayed active and independent. In the mid-1920s she was president of the Springfield Women's Club, a group that attempted to interest women in current events and ideas. From an early age, her children took part in what Brewster remembered as "an atmosphere of uninhibited but rational discourse."[15] Freud and Marx were debated in lively exchanges, and some of Florence's friends protested the execution of Sacco and Vanzetti. While Florence had not been a suffragist like many of her friends, she opposed restrictions on women's freedom and intellectual development. But her rebellions were mild: she dared to drive an automobile. Still, she was a divorcée when such status was scandalous. Her family remained loyal, though, and she had the support of close women friends.

Kingman Brewster occasionally called himself "a loyal son of Springfield," although he lived there only until he was eleven. Still, it was here that he acquired his accent, here that he first attended school (at the Longmeadow School for Boys, where he was usually driven by his grandfather's chauffeurs), and here that he first enjoyed popularity among his peers. Both the Brewster and Besse families were nominally Congregationalist, and Kingman occasionally attended the Congregational church on Mount Vernon Street, but neither he nor his sister was baptized. Florence positively forbade her children to go to Sunday school, her daughter recalled: "Mother thought that having to color those dreadful pictures of Christ performing one miracle after another was poor religion and worse art."[16] Florence herself wrote: "I find I do not believe in the personal or father image of God nor in the exclusive divinity of Jesus. I do not believe in the Virgin birth and I regret its implication that there is a lesser holiness in the universal process of propagation."[17]

The children's English governess, Mrs. Goodall, subscribed to the Victorian notion that boys had to be hardened physically. Every day, summer or winter, she put Kingman in a bath of cold water straight from the tap.

Whether through birth or this regimen, he grew up to have an enormously strong constitution and was rarely ill.

In the summer of 1927, when Kingman was eight, the children and their mother went to Europe, traveling through Britain, France, and Switzerland. Brewster later recalled that "I had been exposed to stories about William Wallace and was full of Scottish romanticism, so I . . . was greatly impressed by Stirling Castle—exactly what a boy's castle should be. [But] what I remember most vividly about that visit was the trip to Paris. I've always been bug-eyed about aviation. . . . We flew on Imperial Airways in a big trimotor biplane, and that seemed to me the most *dramatic* thing that life could afford."[18] In the same year, 1927, Charles Lindbergh soloed across the Atlantic, and he became Brewster's early hero.

Although he grew up in a female-headed household, Brewster was "never very far removed from the shelter of my wealthy 'substantial' conservative grandfather," he remembered. "Unconsciously I probably absorbed some of the strict conservative proper environment."[19] Lyman Besse was remote in a Victorian way, and the relationship, while proximate, was never close. Kingman Sr. would appear about once a year bearing gifts, but Kingman was without a real father figure until his uncle Arthur Besse stepped into the role.

That connection evolved in Martha's Vineyard, where the extended family rented houses in and around Vineyard Haven and visited grandfather Besse at Oak Bluffs. All the children swam, roamed along the beach, played tennis, and rode horseback. When Kingman expressed a particular interest in sailing, Arthur Besse and Florence rented the Whitney House, a large, red-roofed, Spanish-style structure overlooking Vineyard Haven Harbor, and bought eighteen-foot Cape Cod knockabouts for Kingman and the three Besse boys. Since they were too small to handle the boats by themselves, a Harvard student was hired to help teach them to sail.

The boys would sail practically from dawn to dusk; even their lunchtime conversation concerned winds, tides, and sail ratios. Brewster's cousin Richard Besse recalled that "Kingman was very much the ringleader of our early days at the Whitney House. On rainy days he taught us all the songs from *H.M.S. Pinafore* and a number of other nautical Gilbert and Sullivan songs—he had an incredible repertoire of Gilbert and Sullivan songs. He sang with great gusto and flavor." Brewster was "full of energy, bright, creative, always thinking of things to do, always making things happen." He devised games using the intercom system of the Whitney House, and another summer he got the group into designing and building balsa models of flying gliders. His constant companion at the Whitney House was a large, powerful German shepherd named Fritz. Richard Besse felt that Fritz's relationship to Brewster was an early indication of the visceral loyalty that Brewster would later inspire: "That was a one-man dog. His whole life was for King."[20]

Brewster's uncle Arthur Besse, a liberal Republican who had attended Lawrenceville and Harvard College, was a partner in a New York brokerage firm until 1933, when the firm collapsed in the depression. From then until his death, he was president of the National Association of Wool Manufacturers.[21] One of his sons described him as "a man of tremendous warmth and honesty, a generous and wonderfully moral person."[22] When his brokerage firm dissolved, he cut deeply into his own capital by personally paying off as many of his clients as he could. He was by all accounts a very good surrogate father to Kingman.

Lyman Besse died in 1930, leaving a fortune that in early-twenty-first century terms would be worth more than forty million dollars—enough to provide his children and grandchildren with an extremely comfortable lifestyle in the midst of the depression.[23] Florence relocated to Cambridge, Massachusetts, buying a house in the blue-blooded Brattle Street neighborhood. Kingman was eleven years old at the time, and for the next thirty years, Cambridge would be his home territory. The primary reason for the family's move was Florence's engagement to Edward Ballantine, a childhood friend and a music professor at Harvard. They "reached an understanding," in the parlance of the time, in 1930, and lived around the corner from each other in Cambridge until they were married in 1932.

Kingman described his stepfather as "marvelous, and sensitive to the point of vulnerability."[24] He had no children of his own and did not want to play a fatherly role—the children called him Edward—but he was rather avuncular. He spoke French, German, Italian, and Spanish, read a great deal, and had wide cultural interests. He taught classes in the history of music at Harvard, and was an accomplished pianist and witty composer whose most famous piece was "Variations on 'Mary Had a Little Lamb,'" a series of playful renditions of the children's song in the style of different composers. Ballantine was more worldly than his aesthetic nature might suggest. His father had been president of Oberlin College. His brother Arthur, a founding partner of the powerful Wall Street law firm Root, Clark, Howland & Ballantine, served as undersecretary of the Treasury under Hoover and Franklin Roosevelt; he brought Dean Acheson into government in 1933. Edward himself was a member of the Century Association, perhaps the most prestigious of Manhattan's gentlemen's clubs.

The Cambridge house that Edward shared with Florence and her children was very large; it had, in fact, once been used as a girls' school. Two grand pianos dominated the living room, which had a high vaulted ceiling, clerestory windows, and glorious acoustics. A small greenhouse was built onto the side, where Florence cultivated camellias, jasmine, acacias, and other exotic blooms. She also brought with her two Irish maids from her father's household, sisters who had immigrated to Holyoke, Massachusetts, as girls and who had once worked in the mills. While Brewster rarely mentioned the maids later in life, he did on occasion draw on a repertoire of Irish sayings, noting that "there are more Irish in Holyoke than there are in Boston."[25] Perhaps the two sisters helped immunize him against the characteristic prejudice against Irish and Catholics of the Boston Brahmins (the blue bloods who were so named because they formed the city's highest caste).

Florence Ballantine continued to involve herself in civic work, but her main outlet was the musical world. She and Edward went to concerts in Boston and New York, and were highly connected in musical circles. Their house became a well-known musical and intellectual salon. Parties, dances, and concerts were often held in the living room, attended by a variety of interesting people. Stravinsky was an occasional visitor, and Rudolph Serkin liked to practice on the living room pianos before his Boston concerts. Although Kingman was interested in music, he was for the most part an appreciative rather than a critical listener. As he grew into his teens, he came to recognize the cultural atmosphere of Boston, and the quality and richness of the museums, musical offerings, libraries, and educational institutions of the "American Athens."[26]

In the fall of her first year in Cambridge, Florence began taking Radcliffe graduate seminars in English literature and philosophy with such professors as Robert Hillyer and Alfred North Whitehead. Brewster particularly remembered that on one of his mother's papers, Whitehead added the wry compliment "Very good, much clearer than the truth."[27] Florence received her M.A. from Radcliffe in 1932. Kingman had no doubt that his mother's return to study at a mature age had sharpened her intellectually. Her experience lay behind his later observation that universities could "revive the sense of a second choice in mid-career."[28]

Not long after the move to Cambridge, the children began to spend a week of their Christmas and Easter vacations with Kingman Sr. in Washington. Kingman Jr. finally got to know his father. Brewster, whom the newspaper columnist Drew Pearson called a "blue-stockinged tax lobbyist," was the author of several books on tax law.[29] In 1932, at about the time of Kingman's first visit, his firm was representing the Sioux Nation in its suit against the United States government. It was a case Brewster particularly enjoyed because of his love of the American West; his extensive art collection included a number of valuable bronzes and paintings by Frederic Remington; his daughter, Mary, remembered how he proudly displayed a huge war bonnet the Sioux gave him.[30]

A memo to the Sioux Nation from its attorneys commented that "Mr. Kingman Brewster . . . is an organizer and an executive of outstanding ability, and as we would say on our Dakota prairies, 'he is a hard driver.'"[31] Several accounts confirm that the senior Brewster was a hard- and high-charging lawyer, whose policies toward his underlings were Scrooge-like and whose ruthlessness was felt by competitors, clients, and partners. Perhaps because he was so difficult to work with, his fortunes fluctuated drastically. "He was always either very rich or completely on the rocks, with nothing in between," Mary recalled. "He was never on an even keel."[32]

Brewster Sr. owned a hunting lodge and a two-thousand-acre tract of forest and farm in the Catoctin Mountains in Maryland, between Herbert Hoover's lodge and what is now Camp David. He was a voracious reader, a collector of Lincolniana, a snappy dresser, a good athlete, an excellent shot, and an enthusiastic sportsman. He enjoyed golf, fishing, riding, and similar outdoor activities, and made numerous hunting trips to the western United States, Alaska, and Austria. He liked to get away to the Catoctins to enjoy country living: fishing from a well-stocked trout stream, hunting, raising wild turkeys, and running his horses up the mountains.

Brewster, described by one acquaintance as "a crustacean McKinleyite Republican," entertained many members of Congress at his Catoctin retreat.[33] According to his son, he "did enjoy a bit of wheeling and dealing in Washington circles; but I wouldn't say he was a 'power' or a lion under the throne."[34] Brewster's politics, however, were too extreme to be openly expressed in the mainstream GOP. His anti-Communism was so rabid and sweeping that his son remembered that "if I were considerate enough to visit him in Washington with a friend whose parents were somehow associated with the Roosevelt administration, it was natural that he should refer quite regularly to my 'Communist friends.'"[35] The senior Brewster believed that Roosevelt was secretly a Jew named Rosenfeld, and that Smith College (where his daughter, Mary, was a student) was a hotbed of communism. Brewster's political opinions and his business contacts with Germany led the FBI to start a file on him. While various informers testified that he admired the Nazi system and claimed to have met personally with Hitler on visits to Germany, the FBI's investigation revealed little aside from the fact that "BREWSTER possessed a great hatred for Jews and regarded them with suspicion at all times."[36]

Brewster's views on race and religion were perhaps most fully expressed in the works of his good friend the eugenicist Lothrop Stoddard, who believed that Anglo-Saxon civilization and America's ancestral purity were under threat from inferior races. Stoddard was, like Brewster, a Harvard Law School graduate and sometime resident of Brookline, Massachusetts. (Brookline was, not coincidentally, the location of the nation's first country club.) Stoddard's works included evocative titles such as *The Rising Tide of Color Against White World Supremacy* and *The Revolt Against Civilization: The Menace of the Under-Man.*

American society, according to Brewster and Stoddard, was a racial aristocracy under threat not only from degenerate races but also from the idea that merit rather than birth should determine an individual's lot in life. If all gifted people could be identified and elevated, Stoddard conceded, "the immediate result would be a tremendous display of talent and genius." But it "would be but the prelude to utter racial impoverishment and irreparable racial and cultural decline." Many upper-class East Coast gentlemen shared the view that snobbery and racial exclusion were necessary to preserve their elite culture, even if they stopped short of Stoddard's conclusion that "race cleansing is the obvious starting-point for race betterment."[37] Although Brewster's virulent racial opinions were welcome in polite society, most of his peers expressed themselves in more decorous terms.

Brewster's investigation by the FBI did not prevent him from maintaining a warm friendship with the bureau's director, J. Edgar Hoover. Other close friends included CIO head John L. Lewis and the Louisiana demagogue Huey Long. His daughter, Mary, remembered that she was "terribly humiliated" when, accompanying her father on a visit to the Senate, Long paused in mid-diatribe to wave to his good friend Kingman Brewster. "I could have sunk through the floor, because from my point of view Long was the Devil incarnate, a thoroughly unprincipled man." She speculated that these men were drawn to her father, and he to them, because "they were all strong personalities with a lot of animal energy—forceful, larger-than-life."[38] Like his friends, Kingman Brewster was in many ways a dangerous man.

On the other hand, he was also a person of tremendous attractiveness and charisma. As his daughter-in-law put it, "He could charm the birds off the trees, then swallow them up."[39] Mary recalled that "my father was a great lover of life. He loved a good, sociable time. He hated New England, which he thought gloomy and solemn, and he spent much of his life fleeing it. He much preferred Washington, D.C., which was full of people and intrigue."[40]

Brewster Sr. was a strikingly handsome man, with a magnetic appeal to women. He was married five times, although the legality of several of those unions was questionable. "He needed a great deal of female support," Mary observed, "and he tried five times to find it."[41] His first remarriage, to Theo Urch, produced a daughter, Barbara. One of his later wives arrived at his funeral with two sons in tow, whose existence had been hitherto unrevealed. Kingman Jr. recalled that at his father's funeral, it was his role to keep the wives apart; they were all still fond of him.

Kingman Jr. once told an interviewer that he had been "terrified" of the father who had given him "a stepmother in every port."[42] Yet father and son shared a natural ebullience and intelligence, and apparently enjoyed each other's company. The son detested his father's racism and ultraconservatism, and so kept some distance. Like both his parents, Kingman Jr. had a certain New England reserve. While he was not secretive, it was always difficult to get him to talk about himself. He was a deeply emotional man, but never subject to the darker passions that led his father to hate on a grand scale. When something angered him, he was quick to express his feelings, but then they subsided. He did not simmer with suppressed rage or harbor lingering resentments.

Brewster's later political sensibility was undoubtedly influenced by his parents. Yet, since he wrote so little about them, any biographer who tries to deduce psychological cause from political effect is skating on thin ice. But Brewster's remarks are suggestive. He felt that his upbringing necessitated "an appreciation of contrasting extremes. . . . A real fondness for people who disagreed with each other so violently made me eager to find a ground which left room for appreciation of contrasting viewpoints."[43] Although Brewster understood that many conflicts were not subject to compromise, he drew an implicit analogy between the balance required to keep good relations with such different parents and the tolerance necessary if institutions or societies were to remain unified.

Unlike many moderates, he appreciated the clash of extreme viewpoints. A friend observed that Brewster "thought that the center is a product of the opposites that press on it from all sides. . . . [H]e always seemed to feel as though the moral center is tempered and shaped, given its form, by the debates that rage along its edges."[44]

In maintaining an affectionate relationship with his father, Brewster surely must have been, as he once put it, "trying not only to understand but to see the plausible points in extreme positions with which you disagree."[45] He was not infinitely tolerant of extreme viewpoints, however; he realized that unresolved conflict could lead to acrimony. The observation by his wife, Mary Louise, that "Kingman was never one to push an argument past the point of no return,"[46] perhaps explains why he was not susceptible to Manichaean ideological doctrines. His considerate reaction to the extreme positions of his father and mother formed the basis of his approach to disagreements of all kinds throughout his life.

IN 1930, when he was eleven years old, Brewster followed his cousins Richard King and Lyman Besse Burbank to the Belmont Hill School in Belmont, Massachusetts, a suburb of Cambridge. The institution had been founded seven years earlier, mainly by Harvard professors who wanted a school for their children to attend.[47] Brewster was a low "B" student. His Latin teacher later said that "he had a tremendous brain, but there was so much else he wanted to do."[48] He was a bright and quick but not particularly bookish boy, although he liked reading stories of air and sea travel, tales of adventure and courage, and histories of the Scottish kings. (In later years he would puzzle his correspondents by peppering his letters with archaic Scotticisms.) But even as a youngster, he was intrigued by issues and ideas, and found people more interesting than books. His main stimuli were extracurricular. Some of his energies went into singing and theatrics. He performed in a series of Gilbert and Sullivan musicals, climaxing with his performance as First Lord of the Admiralty in *H.M.S. Pinafore.* He also displayed a particular flair for pencil drawings, a skill he continued to exercise in later life on the margins of boring memos.

"I did all the things a future campus politician does," Brewster recalled of his years at Belmont Hill, "such as debating and working on the school paper."[49] As editor in chief of the *Compass,* he agitated against the Marine invasion of Nicaragua and in favor of a French teacher dismissed for having an affair. He felt that he "probably learned more from the curious regime of interscholastic debating than I did from anything else. We were locked into the library for twenty-four hours and on the basis of its modest resources were to emerge as oracular experts ready to do battle with opposing dilettantes from Saint Grottlesex," the major Episcopalian boarding schools such as Groton, St. Paul's, and Middlesex. "It was excellent preparation for writing speeches," Brewster remembered, "or indeed for a career in academic administration generally."[50]

Brewster never lost a debate during the three years that he was on the team. His greatest triumph came when Belmont Hill, taking the affirmative side on "whether capitalism is more conducive to war than socialism," defeated a Groton debating team that included Franklin Roosevelt Jr. and William and McGeorge Bundy.[51]

The Bundy brothers were already legends in the narrow world of the New England preparatory schools. Descendants of Boston's most important families, class leaders and brilliant students, they seemed destined for great things. McGeorge ("Mac" to his friends) was the younger by a year, and the brighter and more vivid of the two. His mild appearance—pink-cheeked, sandy-haired, with owlish-looking round glasses—contrasted with his intimidating intelligence and precision of expression. He received perfect scores on all his college board exams, and was a three-time winner of the Franklin D. Roosevelt Debating Trophy (named for the Groton old boy who was then making himself deeply unpopular with most of the school's alumni).

Mac Bundy was raised in what he described as a "cold roast Boston" family in the city's exclusive Back Bay. He grew up on Beacon Street, which Oliver Wendell Holmes called "the sunny street that holds the sifted few"; his father was a law clerk to Holmes before becoming partner at a prominent Boston firm. Young Bundy spent his summers much as Brewster did, sailing and blackberry-gathering at his family's enormous "cottage" at Manchester-on-the-Sea, on Boston's North Shore. Even as a boy, Bundy had the wolverine intensity, the briskness and tartness that marked him as an adult. Kingman and Mac became best friends, according to Bill Bundy, because "they were both slightly prickly, slightly self-righteous New Englanders."[52] They were also different in many ways. Brewster was less arrogant and acerbic, more speculative and open, while Bundy was more obviously brilliant, more combative and hard-edged. But they were both bright, curious, and wide-ranging, with strong idealistic streaks. Bundy could also be as funny and mischievous as Brewster, cracking jokes like a little string of firecrackers going off. Both liked to compete, and theirs would be a competitive friendship. Mac Bundy valued his reputation as Groton's greatest debater, and for years afterward he claimed that Brewster had beaten him in their schoolboy debate only because one of their judges was deaf.

Brewster's Belmont Hill was a more open and less traditional place than Bundy's Groton. The school was generally well suited to Brewster, whom headmaster Thomas Morse recalled as "an inherent iconoclast."[53] Brewster, in turn, praised Morse's "great appreciation for individuality, at a time when most prep schools were monuments of conformity."[54]

On Sunday evenings Brewster would go to the Ford Hall Forum in Boston (sometimes accompanied by his mother) to listen to a "parade of controversial intellects, mostly left wing."[55] From the time he was fifteen, and for the next three years, he was in the audience at "America's oldest forum of public expression" almost every week. The wooden panel that Brewster carved (a requirement for all Belmont Hill students) depicted the torch of the forum.

The mid-1930s, as Brewster emphasized, "was a great time to have your eyes opened to political, economic, and social consciousness."[56] In early 1933 the nation was at the nadir of the depression. The failure of the old order was complete, and the rise of totalitarianism abroad was underscored when a pro-Nazi speaker addressed the Ford Hall Forum. The violent protest that ensued must have provided Brewster with an early lesson in the controversies over free speech.[57] He would later recall that after Franklin D. Roosevelt's inauguration in March 1933, the American political scene was characterized by ferment and "ideological frothiness." The need for solutions to the national crisis conveyed urgency and moral fervor to the ongoing debate, and "no idea for the salvation of the world was considered too far out to deserve an audience."[58]

At the Ford Hall Forum, Brewster heard calls to pacifism from Norman Angell, exhortations to social commitment from Rabbi Stephen S. Wise, and praise for civil liberties from Felix Frankfurter and American Civil Liberties Union founder Roger Nash Baldwin. "Any ideology or ingenious idea was welcome," he observed, whether from socialists like Harold Laski and John Strachey or "the homegrown prophet of technocracy, Upton Sinclair." Brewster recalled that "optimistic utopianism" was the mood of the day. "Even sneering progressives like the La Follette brothers and Norman Thomas were basically robust and cheerful," he remembered. If there was any common theme, it was "a tremendous intellectual and moral self-confidence, a feeling that man-made problems would lend themselves to man-made solutions."

The Ford Hall Forum experience undoubtedly contributed to Brewster's nascent iconoclasm, but it also may have strengthened his "congenital optimism" and sense of political possibility. Although Brewster had mixed feelings about Roosevelt and the New Deal, he vividly remembered crowding into the balcony of the old Ford Hall in 1935 to hear the president speak.

"Even then I took great delight in [FDR's] confident gusto," he recalled. "In the retrospect of history I give him and his great wife even more credit for the sense we all felt, that if you had a really good idea, it stood a chance."[59]

NOT ALL THE political figures who influenced Brewster remained simply figures on a distant podium. During his political awakening, he was also able to see national movers and shakers at first hand on his visits to his father, who often took Kingman and his sister to congressional hearings and diplomatic parties. Brewster found Washington a "great whirl of influence peddling. The town seemed to consist of everyone trying to get something from everyone else. I found I didn't like that."[60]

He much preferred the scene at his mother's house in Cambridge, where, as Mary recalled, he was fearless in conversation with adult guests.[61] Many of the visitors were acquaintances through the Barn House summer colony on Martha's Vineyard, which had been founded in 1919 by Florence Besse's sister Gertrude and her husband, Stanley King. Members and guests at the Chilmark summer retreat included journalists Walter Lippmann and Max Eastman, liberal activists Roger Baldwin and Evelyn Preston Baldwin, legal and political thinkers such as Felix Frankfurter and Graham Wallas, the prominent feminist and judge Dorothy Kenyon, and other well-known artists, intellectuals, and political figures.[62] Brewster encountered this provocative crowd throughout his youth. Baldwin was one "whose spell I came under early on."[63]

In his junior year at Belmont Hill, at his family's suggestion, Brewster was tutored by a Harvard student, so that he could skip his senior year and take the 1936–37 academic year off before entering college. He decided to volunteer for George W. Norris's campaign for reelection as senator from Nebraska. Brewster wrote a letter to the senator offering his services (but neglecting to mention his age), and after his offer was accepted, he took a "long and lonely" train ride to Lincoln, Nebraska. "I arrived there," he remembered, "very much alone, bought a copy of the *Lincoln Star,* and read in it, in an article about Norris's campaign, 'Kingman Brewster, prominent Massachusetts Republican, will also speak on the Senator's behalf.' I got a room at the Cornhusker Hotel and went down to the Senator's office. His secretary was a nice old lady. A look of amazement crossed her face when she saw me. I was seventeen and was having trouble with my complexion. The shock and surprise percolated on and up in the organization."[64] Brewster was set to work licking stamps.

What led a "well protected seventeen year old New Englander," as he put it, to campaign for a seventy-five-year-old Nebraskan senator and former schoolteacher, born of impoverished and illiterate farmers?[65] A possible explanation is that Brewster, who was already inclined toward anti-interventionism, was inspired by Norris's antiwar stand in 1917. Norris was one of six senators who voted against a declaration of war, which he believed to have been motivated by financial and commercial interests. As a result, he had become the target of hysterical vilification from press, public, and government officials. By the mid-1930s, Norris's stand had come to seem heroic and prophetic to those who opposed United States participation in another European conflict.

Norris was also one of the most enduring icons of the Progressive movement—the first vice president of the National Progressive Republican League when it was formed in January 1911, as well as the leader of the congressional progressives after Robert La Follette's death in 1925. Throughout his forty years of continuous service in the House and Senate, Norris consistently opposed boss rule, corruption, political patronage, and the power of monopoly, inherited wealth, and vested interests. He was an outspoken advocate of political, economic, and social reform, civil rights and civil liberties, liberalized immigration, religious tolerance, farm relief, the rights of labor, and more efficient use of the country's natural resources. Although Norris spent most of his career as a political outsider, he saw many of his ideas come to fruition during the New Deal.[66]

Brewster recalled that he had first been attracted to Norris's independence, demonstrated in his 1936 broadcast from the Cleveland Republican presidential convention that nominated Alf Landon.[67] In his speech Norris charged that "the representatives of special interests" operating "behind the smoke screen at Cleveland nominated a man for President whose greatest asset is that nobody knows him and nobody knows what he stands for."[68] It is ironical that Brewster applauded Norris's charge that Landon was the puppet of bosses and special interests, considering that Kingman Brewster Sr. was a delegate at the 1936 convention and that Frederick Steiwer, the senator from Oregon who delivered the keynote address in Cleveland, became Brewster's law partner two years later.[69]

Norris had crossed party lines to endorse Roosevelt for reelection, and at a campaign stop in Omaha, the president broke tradition by endorsing Norris over the Democratic nominee. On election day Norris defeated his Republican challenger by over 35,000 votes and his Democratic opponent by over 150,000 votes, and so became the only Independent in the Congress.[70]

Brewster suggested that the most important lesson he learned from Norris stemmed from his initial misapprehension of the senator's political approach. While Norris's popular image was of grim-faced adherence to principle at all costs, he was, in fact, realistic and flexible, appreciative of the need to adjust to change, and prepared to compromise provided he could gain at least part of his goals. Brewster felt that Norris, for all his courage and independence, also "taught me that politics for good causes in a democracy requires the art and skill of compromise. . . . I learned then that idealism does not justify and will not be well served by an all-or-nothing-at-all posture."[71]

In the future, Brewster's pragmatic idealism would set him apart from starry-eyed peers and had much to do with his pursuit of a liberal rather than a radical course. He was also impressed by Norris's practical wisdom. Brewster recalled the senator's response when, on a Lincoln's Birthday in the mid-1930s, he was asked what he thought Lincoln would do if he were alive to see the depression. "The Senator replied, 'He would be just as uncertain and confused about what to do as the rest of us are.'"[72]

Brewster left Nebraska after the election and joined his family in Oxford and London, where Edward VIII's abdication threw the nation into crisis. Brewster thought it "an extraordinary event to witness," but he and his mother were perturbed by the event and by what he called the "unctuous glee of Stanley Baldwin." Both mother and son agreed with those who thought Edward should have married Wallis Simpson and retained the throne.[73] Around Christmastime, the family traveled to the Continent. Kingman, along with his mother and sister, went skiing in Saint Anton in Austria; Kingman lived with an Austrian family there that year before the Nazi takeover. Later, just when Mussolini threatened to throw a blockade across the Mediterranean, the family cruised through Greece and Italy. Kingman and his mother then traveled through Germany and France, viewing the ferment and decay of Europe at what proved to be the end of the interwar period. Later he took a cycling trip through Scandinavia with a school friend.

Brewster would never forget the "great turmoil on the Continent" during 1936–37: "Four years of National Socialism in Germany. Italy having just gone into Ethiopia. The Spanish Civil War in full spate. For someone who was just opening his eyes to political and social events, it was a fantastic time to be there."[74] Kingman's sister felt that this exposure strengthened her brother's nascent isolationism. "Munich in 1937 had the eerie, elusive quality of the Katherine Anne Porter story 'The Leaning Tower,'" she remembered. "It was the end of a whole era. It was the very last bit of the old Europe of the grand hotels, the *thés dansants,* and so on. The old order was vanishing right in front of your eyes. It already seemed to be part of the past, out of proportion, and beginning to be a bit rotten."[75]

Brewster himself recalled being horrified by the European scene "when the middle-ground was lost." He was disturbed by an incident in which he was fawned upon in a French train when the Tyrolean hat he was wearing made him look German.[76] Brewster was also exposed to totalitarianism— he heard Hitler on the radio, saw Mussolini harangue a Roman crowd, and had face-to-face contact with Fascists and Nazis. Traveling alone through Germany in 1937 and arriving in Berlin, Brewster was "taken in hand by a storm trooper deputized to be hospitable to unwary young foreign tourists. We sat at a cafe on the Unter den Linden. I, of course, began to argue about National Socialist policy, particularly the preference for guns over butter, a current slogan. Suddenly I realized there could be no argument, not because of the censorship of fear but because of the dogmatic dictate which said '. . . it is so because the Führer wills it so.'" He found it "terrifying" to have rational exchange "totally blocked by steely-eyed, unlistening dogmatic assertion."[77]

Brewster's experiences on the Continent left him with the general impression of "the diversity and reality of national characteristics, and at the same time the essential humanity of common innocent people everywhere."[78] However, his travels also strengthened his conviction that American democracy was a unique phenomenon and his feeling that "thank God Europe's problems are its own."[79] As a result, Brewster began to cultivate the isolationism that would lead him to help found the America First Committee while he was an undergraduate at Yale College.

FOR BREWSTER AND his peers, the college admissions process was a simple matter. If you were from the right background and schools, it was largely a matter of choice. For the most part, students selected colleges rather than the other way around. Twenty-four of Brewster's twenty-six classmates at the Belmont Hill School enrolled at Harvard. Belmont Hill's assistant headmaster Charles Jenney recalled that "everybody got into Harvard. . . . No interviews, no 'one in five' competition. The only ones that didn't go to Harvard were a few rebels like . . . Brewster, '36, who actually preferred Yale."[80]

Brewster chose Yale because of its democratic ethos and because Harvard was too close to home.[81] Kingman Sr. did not put any pressure on his son to go to Amherst, where Uncle Stanley King was president. Amherst was no longer just a school for the sons of the western Massachusetts gentry, but it was still too small and provincial a stage for young Kingman's ambitions.

Although none of his schoolmates went to Yale, his Martha's Vineyard connections ensured that Brewster would not arrive at the university friendless and alone. He had discussed his decision to enroll with his Vineyard neighbor Dean Acheson, a voluble, mustachioed lawyer who was a member of the Yale Corporation, the university's governing body. At that point Acheson had served briefly as undersecretary of the Treasury; later he would become secretary of state under Truman and a key figure in what, after World War II, would be called the establishment. It was the first of many times that Brewster would turn to Acheson for counsel. Before his freshman year, Brewster asked for advice on courses and teachers from another Vineyard neighbor, Acheson's friend A. Whitney Griswold, who was then a junior history professor at Yale. The gaunt, red-haired, fierce, and funny Whit, as he was universally known, would become one of Brewster's most important mentors. Brewster's fellow students included family members (his step-cousin Arthur Ballantine Jr. was enrolled at the Yale Law School), acquaintances from the prep school circuit, family friends, Martha's Vineyard neighbors, and Cape Cod sailors. Brewster arranged that his freshman-year roommate would be an Andover graduate, Jack Ware, who was part of his Vineyard Haven sailing group.[82]

On Martha's Vineyard, Brewster also talked about Yale with Cyrus Vance, a lanky, soft-spoken young man who had just finished his sophomore year there. Cy Vance had been senior prefect at the Kent School, an earnest Episcopalian boarding school, where he played football and ice hockey and rowed on the crew team that earned a berth in the Henley Regatta. The coach praised him as "a perfect sport and a gentleman," a label that followed him for the rest of his life. Vance at age twenty looked like a poster image of Young Christian Manhood: athletic, even-featured, refined, serious. He had been born in West Virginia, but his connections to the state were more sentimental than significant. Vance was a product of the Northeast. His mother was from a prominent clan in Philadelphia's Main Line, and his family had moved to Bronxville, New York, when he was an infant. At Yale, Vance was a quiet but effective leader: a true blue but not stuffy or a prig, one of the best-recognized and most popular students in the college. He was a good person for an entering freshman to know.

While most of Brewster's Boston friends were headed to Harvard, he continued to run into them at coming-out parties for the city's upper-class debutantes. Mac Bundy was often at these parties, and so too was Elliot Lee Richardson, another young Boston Brahmin. Brewster had recently been tutored in the art of dancing and other social graces by his sister and her friends at Smith, so he was usually out on the dance floor.

By contrast, "Mac and I spent quite a lot of time on the sidelines at the coming-out parties," Richardson remembered, "arguing about something or other." Richardson was dark-haired and intense, characterized even then by an uneasy mixture of spirited idealism and starchy Victorian propriety. He had a reputation (in upper-crust northeastern circles, at any rate) as Mac Bundy's only rival as the brightest boy of their generation. At Milton Academy he was at the top of his class, a student council leader, a varsity athlete in football, wrestling, and track, and a star actor to boot. His father had been chief of surgery at Massachusetts General Hospital and a professor of surgery at the Harvard Medical School, and he had grown up in the Back Bay, not far from the Bundys. The Richardsons and Bundys had long been friends, and Elliot sometimes dated Laurie Bundy, Mac's smart and attractive younger sister, who was "matchless among the young women I knew in those days." Richardson occasionally took time off from sailing at his family's house on Cape Cod to visit the Bundys at their summer place on the North Shore.

In the summer of 1937, Richardson had graduated from Milton and was about to enter Harvard. Mac Bundy had finished his freshman year at Yale, where he had the highest grades in his class. Mac "was already quite a well-known character even at age eighteen," Richardson recalled. "Everybody knew that Mac not only had made the highest scores on the College Boards, he had written a critique of the College Board examinations in his essay." Bundy had a preternaturally adult self-assurance, as well as a fully developed worldview and even a sense of his own destiny. Richardson said that his friend's views in his teenage years "were much the same as they were later on when he became a junior fellow [at Harvard] and worked on Plato's *Republic*. Mac saw himself as one of the guardians, the chosen elite."[83]

THE FACTORS THAT helped make Brewster and his circle guardians of equal opportunity came from a combination of privilege and of reaction against the culture that bestowed it upon them. In later years, it would puzzle observers that these thoroughly WASPish men were so ambivalent about the class that produced them. But elements of their contradictory feelings were evident even when they were young.

Certainly Brewster, Bundy, Richardson, and Vance benefited from the advantages they inherited. They came from the Northeast, the dominant part of the country, and from its leading social class. All were wealthy white Anglo-Saxon Protestants with reversible names who could trace their ancestry back to colonial times. They thought of themselves as upper middle class rather than as truly rich, but they enjoyed every material comfort and grew up with sailing and summer houses, Irish cooks and servants, Harvard and Yale tutors. Most of their parents had graduated from college, an unusual distinction given that only about two percent of twenty-three-year-olds held bachelor's degrees in the years between 1910 and 1920. (Brewster fell into a statistically infinitesimal category as the child of two Phi Beta Kappa graduates.)

By birth if not by choice, these young men were members of what Richardson called "one of the smaller minority groups making up our multicultural society," although few of their peers would have regarded themselves in quite that way.[84] Nonetheless, it was also the most powerful minority group in the United States, and bright and ambitious boys of this class had an open path to further advantages and the possibility of power. Even at a young age, Brewster and his friends were forming a widening net of associations that would be important to them later on. Their peers looked to them as the natural leaders of their generation, while influential elders cultivated them and kept track of their progress. Although they were undeniably able, they also benefited from a limited playing field. In many areas of American life, the pool of competition for power and rank included only a tiny fraction of the population, even in activities such as sports. Brewster's sailing victories, for example, were achieved at a time when competitive sailing was limited to a small fraternity of yachtsmen on the East Coast.

On one level, the boys' summer places in and around Cape Cod were merely the locales where they would sail, swim, and play ball games with other children. On another, these summer resorts were links in the establishment chain, which traced back to the movement toward social exclusivity and homogeneity that developed in upper-class circles after the Civil War.[85] So too were the New England preparatory schools they attended, particularly the exclusive "St. Grottlesex" boarding schools. While their social position gave them advantages and preparation for leadership, it also handicapped them by isolating them from the mass of the society in which they would be leaders. They lived in a sort of upper-class bubble that brought them into contact almost exclusively with other children of similar social standing. None spent so much as a day in public school. Even before attending the New England boarding schools, they went to private elementary schools near their homes—with the exception of Vance, who attended the Institut Sillig in Vevey, Switzerland, before going on to the Kent School in Connecticut.

Their privileged circumstances were not evident to them while they were growing up; few teenagers spend much time analyzing their place in America's class structure. If he thought back on it, though, Brewster would have realized that few depression-era American boys could take a months-long tour through Europe in 1936–37, as he did. Some measure of his relative comfort was obvious to McGeorge Bundy when his family lived in Washington, D.C., in 1931 and 1932, and poor people begged for food at their back door.[86] But gradually, unlike previous generations of WASP elites who accepted and upheld their privileges, Brewster and his circle became uneasy with their class. Part of the reason was the times they were born into. In 1919, when Brewster was born, towns and cities were staging victory parades for the newly returned veterans from the American Expeditionary Force. Thus he and the others grew up at a distinctly modern juncture: the United States had been reshaped by its participation in an overseas war. Although the country retreated from internationalism after the war, even nascent isolationists like Brewster would come to believe that America's new role carried responsibilities that were incompatible with prevailing social arrangements. The depression had also made many of the older generation's preoccupations seem irrelevant at best.

Subtle differences in origin, lineage, and wealth that would have been important to previous generations of New Englanders came to mean little to Brewster and his friends, who tended to dislike those who valued such distinctions overmuch. Brewster was a *Mayflower* descendant, but he could do a biting imitation of Beacon Hill blue bloods who looked down their noses at the provincial city of Springfield, where he spent his early years. Bundy descended, through his mother's side, from the exalted Lowell and Putnam clans, but his father had grown up in Grand Rapids, Michigan. It didn't matter that the Bundys had arrived in New England in the seventeenth century. In Boston society, "Grand Rapids was cheap furniture," as McGeorge's mother put it, and Mac grew up resenting the snubs to which his father had once been subjected.[87] Richardson came from the Lee clan of Brahmins through his mother's side, but he liked to point out that his Richardson ancestors had been farmers, and made much of his few (and very distant) Irish ancestral connections. "Both Kingman and I had an abundance of ancestors," Bundy later observed, "and neither of us thought it was very important."[88] Affecting a disdain for genealogical concerns was a way for these young men to turn the tables on the more pompous members of their class.

HOWEVER LIGHTLY THEY wore their family heritages, it was hard for Brewster and his friends to escape them, not least because they were saddled with first names commemorating ancestors who had married into the family generations before. Some commentators later speculated that the burden of their off-putting names (Kingman, McGeorge, and so forth) stimulated these men to achievement, but as boys their names simply made them unhappy. After a teacher called him "Kingston Brewer," Brewster decided that he wanted to be called "John." His family made a diligent effort to do so for about a year, then relapsed into calling him King. Vance also took refuge from his given name when he was a child, preferring "Bob," while Bundy liked his proletarian-sounding nickname, "Mac." (Bundy's friend and future brother-in-law, Gaspard d'Andelot Belin, avoided the awful weight of his given name by adopting the nickname "Don.") It is possible that their not-regular-guy names contributed to their shyness as children. Bundy's mother once dropped Mac off at another child's house for a birthday party, and returned hours later to find him still standing on the doorstep, because his shyness prevented him from knocking on the door.[89] Indeed, Brewster's timidity, which made it difficult for him to look other people in the eye, was (like Bundy's shyness) often interpreted as arrogance.

The boys' alienation from their elders' sense of entitlement and class consciousness was reinforced by the predominant influence of their mothers. Sometimes the fathers were absent—Brewster rarely saw his father in the years after his parents' divorce, and Vance's father died while Cyrus was a boy. More often the fathers were preoccupied with work and emotionally distant from their children, while the mothers were strong, opinionated women who were interested in molding their sons. In Richardson's case, his mother had died in childbirth when he was two, while his father was disabled by a stroke when he was eleven. The boy was raised by his governess, a strict Yankee social worker named Marguerite Browne. "She was something else," he remembered. "She was a toughie, a strong woman, you'd better believe."[90] In later years, Richardson would tell friends that many of his values were a projection of his governess's indomitable will.[91] Vance's mother was another grande dame, deeply involved in civic and religious activities, years ahead of her time in outspoken support of women's and civil rights.[92] "She inspired people to serve their communities," a family member recalled, "and she inspired her son by example."[93]

From their mothers the sons acquired a lifelong interest in art, music, and theater, to which their fathers—even when available—were often indifferent. Political idealism was a torch passed from the mothers rather than the fathers—although it was a political idealism that harkened back to pious Puritanism rather than to modern political creeds. "Mother's sense of self-righteousness was very deep," said one of McGeorge Bundy's sisters, "and so's Mac's. Mother always conveyed to us her profound belief in the clear difference between right and wrong. . . . It's an outlook that descends directly from the Puritans and we all have it. But Mac has it more than most."[94] Bundy and his mother both found many of the wealthy society people in their orbit to be boring and narrow-minded.[95]

It was not that their mothers raised them to be rebels—quite the contrary. They were raised to be polite, obedient, well-mannered, patriotic. Rather, the fact that these young men were more strongly influenced by their mothers led them in various ways to break free of the patterns laid down by their fathers. All of them would go on to careers that were different from their fathers', sometimes against the older men's wishes. Richardson felt that as the son, grandson, and great-grandson of doctors, medicine "seemed too much like a book I had read before. I wanted something more exciting."[96] As the son and grandson of lawyers, Bundy had a similar reaction. More generally, their mothers' influence led them to question the status quo and the masculine world of inherited tradition.

For example, the fact that they were not preoccupied with fine distinctions between old money and new, or degrees and gradations of ancestry, helped set them apart from many men of their fathers' generation. Kingman Brewster Sr. had been an exemplar of the old concern with blood, with his memberships in the Society of Mayflower Descendants and Sons of the Revolution and his gloomy eugenicist ruminations on "the rising tide of color." His son never invoked his background as a claim of superiority, and indeed he and his peers went out of their way to shed the blatant prejudices of their fathers' generation. As Bundy put it, in his mature years he would leave the room if someone said the sort of things about Jews that he had heard routinely around the family dinner table when he was growing up.[97] Richardson remembered that his de facto mother, Marguerite Browne, "was not part of the Social Register at all. . . . She had contempt for snobbery. And even though she was a person of modest education, no pretensions, no social standing, and really no friendships of her own, there was no proud member of Boston society who was not slightly afraid of her—because she just couldn't stand crap." Richardson credited her with ensuring that "I never had the slightest inclination to try to preserve the privileges of the Brahmin caste."[98]

To some extent the group's nontraditional attitudes were also fostered by their preparatory schools. For many reasons, this may seem surprising. Most of these academies were modeled on the so-called public schools of England. Like Eton and Harrow, the schools served as training grounds for a national leadership class. They were so Anglophilic that students in the "forms" often wrote using British rather than American spelling (as Brewster continued to do in later years). Their mission was largely to shape the character of their young charges. They drilled their values into the students through sermons, manly sports, cold baths, and teachers of high moral character. As Brewster's friend Paul Moore put it, the private schools "instilled faith in a god who looked favorably on gentlemen and demanded no shift in social values from the status quo. This god did demand courage, loyalty, and patriotism. . . . This religion had a touch of Calvinism to it, a tendency to believe that worldly success and position were blessings given to those who deserved them."[99]

But perhaps most significant, the schools put a strong emphasis on *noblesse oblige.* Those blessed with privilege, education, and stature incurred an obligation to give service and leadership to the community, and to look after the least fortunate. However, students like Brewster and Bundy who took seriously the *oblige* of *noblesse* later came to feel, with perfect consistency, that the highest responsibility might be to unsettle the status quo rather than preserve it. While Bundy, for example, never rebelled openly against the Groton ethos, he emerged as an intellectual, a questioning patriot, and a religious skeptic. Four years after his graduation, he wrote that "we are taught at an early age to salute the flag, to be patriotic, and to believe a lot of lies. It is therefore not surprising that when our eyes are opened, we react rather strongly against the innocent credulity of our childhood."[100]

ANOTHER TRADITION THAT exerted a considerable alternative influence during the formative years of these young men was progressivism, the reformist movement that had flourished in the early years of the century. Many of the themes of the Progressive Era—the spirit of antimonopoly, the emphasis on the responsibility of the individual to society (and vice versa), the belief in the value of trained expertise—were closer to their hearts than the concerns of the New Deal. Particularly important was the anticorruption, good-government variety of progressivism that was strong in Massachusetts. The historian Richard Hofstadter, who traced this tradition back to the Mugwump movement that existed in upper-class northeastern WASP circles in the late nineteenth century, noted that adherents "flourished . . . most conspicuously around Boston, a center of seasoned wealth and seasoned conscience."[101]

At the turn of the twentieth century, upper-class Boston progressives had wrestled with the populist leader James Michael Curley; their descendants were wrestling with him still in the 1930s and beyond. The notoriously corrupt Curley, tribune of Irish-American resentment against the Brahmin elite, was four-time Boston mayor and governor of Massachusetts from 1935 to 1937. Richardson's uncle Henry Lee Shattuck, who struggled against Curley across five decades, put up $35,000 of his own money for the private investigation that led to the roguish politician's imprisonment for fraud.[102] Curley was a major negative example for the young patrician scions who were in preparatory school in those years; Brewster could do an excellent Curley imitation. The bad government of Curley and his cohorts helped keep the good-government movement strong as Mugwumpism broadened into progressivism in the early twentieth century. Richardson remembered that "the tradition that I was conscious of was progressive in the Bull Moose sense, and reform-oriented in the muckraker sense."[103] Brewster, Bundy, and Richardson were all identifiably in this line of upper-crust Yankee reformers.

Each of the boys in Brewster's circle also had as a mentor a close family friend who belonged to the older generation of progressives. In Brewster's case he was ACLU founder Roger Baldwin; for Bundy, the eminent public servant Henry Stimson; for Vance, his guardian, the well-known lawyer and politician John W. Davis; and for Richardson, Henry Shattuck, longtime treasurer of Harvard and a prominent Boston politician and philanthropist. These men impressed upon their protégés different angles of the progressive tradition. More important, they were role models and inspirations for Brewster and his peers, and provided them with entree into the networks of individuals who would shape the times.

Richardson's mentor Shattuck, for example, was a progressive Republican (and a cousin of Theodore Roosevelt's first wife, Alice Lee). Known for his absolute integrity, he was a leader of the good-government forces in

Boston.[104] Unlike many of the "goo-goos," however, he was not prejudiced against the Irish, and became friends with many of his Irish-American colleagues. While he was a shy and somewhat chilly man, "he had no side," Richardson remembered. "You don't hear that term any more, but it conveyed a disinclination to distinguish among people on the basis of background, rank, or wealth."[105] Shattuck helped his nephew become a progressive Republican politician and paragon of rectitude, who could attain public office in part because he was not hampered by Brahmin prejudices. "I simply patterned myself on him," Richardson recalled.[106] In later years, Richardson would write to his uncle of his gratitude for "the constant guidance, affection, and support you have always given me. You also give me, by precept and by example, much to live up to, and for all this the only return I can make is to do my best. That I will do."[107]

Henry Stimson, on the other hand, gave McGeorge Bundy a vision of a patrician public servant operating behind the scenes. Scion of one of New York's ruling families, Stimson was a Yale College and Harvard law graduate, and a law partner of Brewster's uncle by marriage, Arthur Ballantine. Secretary of war under William Howard Taft and secretary of state under Herbert Hoover, Stimson was, as the journalist David Halberstam emphasized, a living link to the tradition of Teddy Roosevelt: "an aristocracy come to power, convinced of its own disinterested quality, believing itself above both petty partisan interest and material greed."[108] He had been an intimate friend of the Bundy family since McGeorge's father became his assistant secretary of state in 1931. Mac and his brother William were raised to look upon America's responsibilities in the world from an internationalist, Stimsonian perspective. After World War II, Mac would serve as Stimson's amanuensis in coauthoring his autobiography. Stimson personified establishment ideals of bipartisanship, pragmatism, sound judgment, trustworthiness, and the mature wisdom that his disciple John McCloy called gravitas. His example of dedicated, disinterested public service was a model for many people, Brewster and Richardson included, but his ideas also had an impact. Calling himself a "progressive conservative," he advocated Bull Moose policies of enlightened reform at home and interventionism in the service of enlightened reform abroad. Stimson's influence helped make Bundy a dedicated proponent of preparedness and intervention in the late 1930s and early 1940s and had much to with his later decisions on American involvement in Vietnam.

Vance was mentored by his guardian, "Uncle" John W. Davis (actually an older cousin), a famous lawyer and politician who stood in loco parentis to him after his father died. Davis began his career as a member of Congress from West Virginia (Vance's father was his first campaign manager), then served as solicitor general and ambassador to Britain under Woodrow Wilson. He ran for president as the Democratic nominee in 1924, with Franklin D. Roosevelt as his running mate, losing to Calvin Coolidge. Head of the prominent Wall Street firm Davis, Polk and Wardwell and counsel to J. P. Morgan, Davis argued more cases before the Supreme Court than any lawyer since Daniel Webster. As president of the American Bar Association, the English-Speaking Union, and the Council on Foreign Relations, a member of nine gentleman's clubs, and an intimate of the most prominent men in New York and Washington, Davis could fairly have been considered the chairman of the establishment, if the term had existed then. He gave his younger cousin connections and a window into power, and Vance imitated Davis's elegance and quiet authority. Some of Vance's happiest times as a boy were spent roaming Davis's extensive library at his Locust Valley, Long Island, estate and being tutored by him in law and politics.[109] Vance inherited his mentor's Democratic affiliation, but of a moderate, progressive variety that easily coexisted with the liberal Republicanism of many of his friends.

Roger Baldwin's influence on Brewster was important but more difficult to delineate, as Baldwin was hard to classify. Dwight Macdonald wrote that "Baldwin has been, successively or even at times simultaneously, a Boston conservative, a liberalistic social worker, a philosophical anarchist, a pacifist, a Soviet sympathizer, a semi-demi-hemi-Marxist, a conservative liberal, and a liberal conservative."[110] Yet he could perhaps be most accurately described as a pragmatic reformer. Baldwin was born in 1885 in Boston, the son of two *Mayflower* descendants. His grandfather William H. Baldwin was a Unitarian, an abolitionist, and a wealthy merchant whose circle of friends included Longfellow, Thoreau, Emerson, Oliver Wendell Holmes, and Phillips Brooks. As Macdonald observed, Baldwin "was born into the great New England tradition which blended culture, individualism, and social reform," a tradition that was still a palpable presence at Harvard when Baldwin was an undergraduate there in the early years of the twentieth century.[111]

In the spring of 1917, Baldwin was invited to take over the American Union Against Militarism, an organization established two years earlier to help keep the United States out of the European war. With the eruption of civil liberties violations that followed the American declaration of war, the AUAM established a subsidiary organization that Baldwin, Norman Thomas (then a Presbyterian minister), and a Quaker lawyer subsequently developed into the American Civil Liberties Union, with Baldwin as director. The ACLU soon "became the principal and often the only defender of wartime civil liberties."[112] The organization defended political dissent during the Red Scare of 1919–21, academic freedom in the famous Scopes trial of 1925, and a myriad of unpopular causes in the following years.

Like most of Brewster's heroes, Baldwin was a courageous, charismatic, independent reformer. And while Baldwin flirted with radical politics, he was operationally conservative. "Power and success have always attracted him," wrote Macdonald. "An operator by instinct, he shies away from reflection, moral or intellectual, and seeks out the levers of power—and those who control them. . . . His viewpoint is pragmatic—not so much 'Is it right?' as 'Will it work?'"[113] Baldwin deviated from his upper-class origins to espouse the cause of the less fortunate, yet never renounced his own background. He was not truly egalitarian, nor was civil liberties a radical new cause, based as it was on the Bill of Rights and ideals grounded in American (especially New England) history. Brewster emphasized these points to a Yale audience in 1969 when the university presented Baldwin with an honorary degree. "In your life," Brewster told his old mentor, "Tom Paine and Henry Thoreau have lived again."[114]

Perhaps Baldwin's most important lessons for Brewster were, first, the belief that society was strengthened rather than weakened by the troublesome agitator, although Baldwin stressed that activism was gradual and required patience. Second, Baldwin argued that change—even far-reaching change—could be achieved within the system, even if some elements of the system needed reform. Despite his radical ideas, Baldwin said, "I always *acted* like a liberal," conducting his fights through the courts and the legal process.[115]

Baldwin had raged at his Harvard classmates in the 1930s. "They were so smug," he remembered. "I was mad at those upper-class boys who said to me whenever I got together with them at a class reunion, 'We don't want to change things; we like it the way it is.'"[116] For many of Brewster's generation, the depression made such an attitude untenable: the established order seemed destined for the dustbin of history. But outside of the Roosevelt family, much of Brewster Sr.'s generation seemed paralyzed in the 1930s. "Many of the men I know today are only feeble reflections of my father and his friends," mused the Brahmin protagonist of John P. Marquand's 1937 bestseller, *The Late George Apley.* "Most of us have obeyed the older generation so implicitly that now they are gone there is nothing left but to continue in the pattern they have laid down for us."[117] Kingman Sr.'s paranoid racism, extreme anticommunism, and unbridled hatred of Franklin Roosevelt reflected an entire class's inability to cope with drastic change.

Some members of Kingman Jr.'s generation adopted the reactionary outlook of their fathers. Others turned against their class and toward communism and other radical philosophies. But Brewster and his cohorts in the liberal establishment would seek to change in order to preserve, in FDR's well-known formulation. Brewster would bring a highly critical spirit to this mission of social reform, however, which would first become apparent during his college years at Yale.

2

BRIGHT COLLEGE YEARS

O N THE evening of September 29, 1937, Kingman Brewster and the other incoming freshmen in the Yale College Class of 1941 joined with the upperclassmen for the traditional freshman parade. Led by torchbearers, varsity athletes in white turtleneck sweaters, and a band playing Yale fight songs, the mass of students undulated slowly and serpentlike across the Old Campus. They passed Connecticut Hall, an ancient ivy-covered building that was once the dormitory of Revolutionary War spy Nathan Hale, Class of 1773, whose statue stood outside. They crossed under the shadow of Harkness Tower, a massive Gothic spire that looked medieval but had been built with Rockefeller oil money only two decades earlier. They poured through the university's war memorial, inscribed with the names of Yale men killed in American wars—including the 227 who fell in the Great War less than twenty years before. Finally, the exuberant procession convened in the Woolsey Hall auditorium, where, according to custom, they were addressed by the most prominent members of the senior class. Football captain (and Heisman Trophy winner) Clint Frank pitched athletics. *Yale Daily News* chairman R. Sargent Shriver Jr. exhorted them to extracurricular activity. The freshmen sang the college anthem "Bright College Years," with its rousing last line, "For God, for country, and for Yale." They did not sing it ironically.

The freshmen also welcomed incoming president Charles Seymour, who had been elected in the spring of 1937. "Mr. Seymour," sophomore McGeorge Bundy commented acerbically in the campus newspaper, "is a Yale man born of Yale men and positively soused in Yale traditions."[1] The university's deeply conservative fifteenth president was a descendant of other Yale presidents and a member of the Skull and Bones secret society. With his bland, regular features, silver hair, and clipped mustache, he looked like an advertising executive's ideal of a college president. In his address, Seymour declared his responsibility to be "the preservation at Yale of spiritual values that have come down from long generations of Yale men." It was the existence of "certain intangibles, peculiar to Yale," he said, that made the place "distinctive, different from other universities. . . . They defy definition. The magic of the spirit of Elihu works in wondrous ways and cannot be explained in rational terms."[2]

Kingman Brewster and most of the other freshmen who wildly applauded had already been indoctrinated in the Yale spirit by Owen Johnson's great college novel, *Stover at Yale.* Published in 1911, the novel cemented Yale's all-American reputation as "a college where you stand on your own feet, all square to the wind," as one character puts it. In that era it was a school whose low tuition, devoted teachers, and legendary football teams drew boys from all parts of the country and all walks of life.[3] Eastern swells had no guarantee of success, and poor midwesterners might prosper. Indeed, one of the reasons that Brewster was among the entering class that night, according to his sister, was that "the *Stover at Yale* image may have appealed to him."[4] Near the start of the novel, Johnson's hero, Dink Stover, who struggled up from a "ridiculous beginning," pauses at the entrance to the Old Campus on his first night as a freshman. As he stands underneath the echoing arch of Phelps Gate, he looks forward to "four glorious years, good times, good fellows and a free and open fight to be among the leaders and leave a name on the roll of fame."[5] Brewster looked forward to a similar prospect.

Stover came to Yale because, he says in the novel, "It's the one place where money makes no difference, where you stand for what you are."[6] F. Scott Fitzgerald poetically compared the more aristocratic Princeton to a lazy spring day, whereas Yale was "November, crisp and energetic."[7] Unlike Harvard and Princeton, where blood and wealth were the main determinants of social success—and unlike many other universities, where success depended on campus politics—Yale provided students with the opportunity to rise to prominence by "doing something for Yale," through leadership in campus organizations and activities. Those successful would be rewarded with a tap, at the end of junior year, from one of the secret senior societies such as Skull and Bones, Scroll and Key, and Wolf's Head, each with its forbidding windowless clubhouse, or "tomb." Yale was a place that appealed to America's Horatio Alger mythology, the idea that anyone might make it to the top. And the campus mythology also strongly suggested that since Yale reflected America more than any other school, those who became leaders at Yale would someday lead the nation.

Of course, many things had changed at Yale since the early 1900s. There were 859 young men in Brewster's class, as compared to fewer than 300 in Seymour's entering Class of 1908. Although Seymour waxed nostalgic, in his Woolsey Hall address, about having been tortured by sophomores who dropped hot pennies down his shirt, the rivalries between classes were largely a thing of the past. By 1937, Phelps Gate, where Stover stops on his first night to drink in the scene, was still the entrance to the campus, but the old lantern-lit dormitories of "Brick Row" that he looks out on had been pulled down. Only the venerable Connecticut Hall, built in 1753, survived. Most upperclassmen now lived in the nine new Oxbridge-inspired residential colleges, intimate Gothic and Georgian quadrangles that turned their backs on the shabby industrial city of New Haven. Seymour's predecessor, James Rowland Angell, had transformed the institution into a full-fledged university in the 1920s and 1930s, adding many buildings, increasing the faculty, and expanding the law, medical, graduate, and divinity schools. For the undergraduates, however, Yale College was still the center of life and loyalty.

At the turn of the century, Yale had also been a comparatively plain and unostentatious place, where undergraduates lived in spare buildings like Connecticut Hall and the main source of entertainment was lingering to sing and smoke on the old Fence. When the Class of 1941 arrived in New Haven, however, its character was distinctly more monied and aristocratic: "We knew we were the elite of the country," as one of Brewster's classmates put it.[8]

Circumstantial evidence to support this proposition could be found in any issue of the Yale campus newspaper, which, throughout the depression, carried ads for velvet-collared Chesterfield coats, new Packard automobiles, New York custom tailors, and holiday vacations on the slopes of Sun Valley and the beaches of Cuba. Every Friday the paper carried a Metropolitan Weekend feature listing the entertainment at the big Manhattan hotels and clubs like the Stork and "21." Brewster realized that these luxuries were far from typical during the depression, when undergraduates walked past grown men selling apples in the New Haven streets. He often cited the statistic that the average Yale student would spend more in nine months than two-thirds of America's families would earn in a year.[9]

Even Yale's architecture, a blend of older brick buildings and lavish new Gothic and Georgian castles, was testament to the university's increasingly elevated place in the social structure. The funds to put up the more recent buildings had come from the Rockefeller fortune and other pools of money that trickled down from Gilded Age industrial wealth. Visually, Yale was a blend of what philosopher George Santayana called "polite America"—the traditional Eastern Seaboard aristocracy—and the "crude but vital America" of self-made magnates.[10] The new urbanized, industrial elite looked to the old, prestigious colleges as a way to announce that they and their sons had arrived and to distinguish themselves socially from the waves of immigrants flooding into the cities.[11] By accepting the "crude but vital America" into Yale, the college helped forge the high-status traditional authority of New England and the upstart industrial wealth of New York into a national establishment.

By the late 1930s, Yale's position in the social firmament was secure. "Yale students, as a whole, are rich," one undergraduate commented. "Their families are rich and represent the economic royalists of America." He went on to point out that three-quarters of Yale's students had attended preparatory schools, where a year's tuition exceeded the country's average annual family income.[12] A disproportionate number came from a very few schools. More than ten percent of the class came from the Phillips Academy at Andover; Hotchkiss School graduates accounted for another five percent. One-quarter of the class came from five prep schools (Andover, Hotchkiss, Exeter, Taft, and Choate)—about the same number as all of Yale's high school students combined. Most students came from states from which Yale traditionally had drawn: Connecticut, New York, Massachusetts, New Jersey, Pennsylvania, and Ohio. Yale admitted only thirty-two high school students from the rest of the country. The class contained not a single African-American, and the only members who might be considered remotely ethnic were one Filipino and two Armenians. The class had perhaps a ten percent Jewish enrollment and a five percent Catholic enrollment, but many of the Jewish and Catholic students were poor, local high school graduates who lived at home and played a marginal role in the college.

In short, Yale's perception of itself as a truly national, democratic institution rested on shaky grounds. To what extent could Yale claim to be tapping the talent of Minnesota, for example, if it admitted mainly the scions of prominent Minneapolis–Saint Paul families who attended eastern boarding schools? To what extent could it claim to be producing leaders for all the nation if its graduates were almost entirely well-to-do WASP males?

Further, the university was not becoming more democratic or more representative over time. A comparison of the Class of 1941 with the Class of 1916 confirms that the college was, rather, becoming more elite. In the intervening years, the percentage of high school students at Yale dwindled, as did the numbers of foreign-born students and non-WASP Americans. The Class of '16, for example, had included five African-Americans, three Chinese, two Armenians, two Turks, a Brazilian, and a German (who left Yale midway through sophomore year to fight for the Fatherland).

It is also likely that there were fewer students from poor or working-class backgrounds in the Class of '41 than there had been twenty-five years earlier. Many students in the Class of 1916 were the sons of farmers, carpenters, cabinetmakers, sheet-metal workers, master mechanics, pattern makers, blacksmiths, and foremen from such Connecticut firms as the Singer Manufacturing Company in Bridgeport, the Malleable Iron Fittings Company in Branford, the Birmingham Iron Foundry in Derby, and the Winchester Repeating Arms Company in New Haven. Only a quarter of the fathers of students in the Class of 1916 yearbook had been to college, compared with almost three-quarters of the fathers of students in the Class of 1941. (One-fourth of the '41 students had fathers who had also attended graduate and professional schools, and about one-sixth had mothers who attended college, as against less than one percent in the Class of 1916.)

Most strikingly, the percentage of students whose fathers had attended Yale College had soared. Over thirty percent of the Class of 1941 were following in their fathers' footsteps, almost treble the percentage of only twenty-five years before. When the number of Yale grandfathers, uncles, and older brothers is taken into account, over half the Class of 1941 had a male relative who preceded them as undergraduates. Almost a third of the Class of '41 came with a "Jr." or a number after their names, proclaiming each scion the second, third, fourth, or fifth of his line. An aura of inherited privilege hovered more heavily over Yale in the late 1930s and early 1940s than it had perhaps since the Revolution. The Yale that greeted Kingman Brewster was not the free and open place that Dink Stover would have recognized.

What had brought about the move toward greater privilege in general, and more legacies in particular? One element was certainly the depression, which made it more difficult for less-than-wealthy parents to afford to send their sons to private colleges such as Yale. Another, more specific explanation was the decline of the Sheffield Scientific School, a separate, scientifically oriented division within Yale College. ("Sheff" had attracted poor boys with its easier entrance requirements, low fees, practical curriculum, and three-year Ph.B. degree.) Most important, however, was the administration's decision in the 1920s to limit the number of students in each class, the secret aim of which was to restrict the number of Jewish undergraduates.

Yale's decision came a year after Harvard announced that it would curb the number of Jews in order to preserve the "traditional character" of the college. After Harvard's policy unleashed a storm of negative publicity, Yale was forced to deny that its restrictions were explicitly designed to be prejudicial—although many outside the university wondered why it continued to ask for every applicant's mother's maiden name. In truth, the admissions committee relied on a straightforward Jewish quota system similar to those imposed during the 1920s by Columbia, Princeton, Dartmouth, New York University, and virtually every other private eastern college. These policies reflected the turn toward nativism and anti-Semitism, which spread throughout the United States in the early twentieth century as millions of Jews and other immigrants from eastern and southern Europe concentrated in the cities. Yale's policy favoring the admission of the sons of its graduates was, in its way, a counterpart to the immigration restrictions of the 1920s, which institutionalized a national preference for immigrants of Anglo-Saxon and northern European stock.

Anti-Semitic policies adopted at Yale and elsewhere underscored the fact that the purpose of the eastern colleges was not merely to provide education, or to produce leaders, but to preserve the culture of the WASP upper class. In this view, Yale was a repository of the values and standards of the establishment—"an ancestral vault in which ancient ideals were kept safe from rot and rust," as one observer put it—and a link in the cycle through which that establishment reproduced itself.[13] Through its admissions decisions, Yale had, in effect, put culture ahead of merit.

Judge Learned Hand, who later became a hero to Brewster and a mentor to Elliot Richardson, was a critic of Harvard's Jewish quota. He wrote that "a college may gather together men of a common tradition, or it may put its faith in learning."[14] There was no doubt about which side of that question Yale came down on. By the time Brewster arrived on campus, the college's recruiters visited only the few schools and cities that historically had sent many students to New Haven. Yale's historian wrote that "as the University did not feel it should proselyte for students, the Admissions officers made it a policy to go only where invited and to speak only with those students in each school who had already expressed an interest in coming to Yale."[15]

At the same time, Harvard was moving in a different direction. While Yale grew increasingly homogeneous, Harvard's president, James Bryant Conant, inaugurated in 1933, was attempting to throw off discriminatory policies by creating the Harvard National Scholarships to attract the best students particularly from regions such as the Midwest and the South, where Harvard's draw historically had been weak. Assistant Dean Henry Chauncey began a search for gifted students with deficient preparation or insufficient means, students who might not have been able to attend any college at all, let alone Harvard.[16] The Harvard National Scholarships covered full financial need, obviating the "badge of poverty" jobs, like table-waiting, that scholarship students had traditionally held. The winners excelled, both within and outside the classroom. Their numbers included future eminences such as James Tobin, the Nobel Prize–winning economist, and Caspar Weinberger, secretary of defense under Ronald Reagan.[17] Ultimately this effort enabled Harvard to become a truly national university, as opposed to the culture-bound New England institution it had been for three hundred years. Conant also attempted to lure internationally known, interdisciplinary scholars to Cambridge, while Yale continued to draw most of its faculty from the ranks of its own graduates. This practice led *Time* magazine to observe that "Yale is a dynasty, perhaps the most inbred of all the ivy-league colleges."[18]

Many observers worried about the effect of discriminatory college admissions on the life of the nation. William Benton, co-creator (with fellow Yale graduate Chester Bowles) of the advertising agency Benton & Bowles, argued that admissions discrimination at "our great eastern colleges or universities" had the curious effect of transferring entrepreneurial aspirations to despised outsiders. While the college graduates went off to large banks, law firms, or industry, "The people who are starting businesses in America today are the Argentines, the Portuguese and the Greeks, the Irish, the Italians, the Armenians and the Poles. Why? One reason is that they are compelled to. The big, established business and financial houses discriminate against them because they talk with an accent or rub the salad bowl with garlic."[19]

In the 1930s few Americans believed that an inevitable movement toward greater social mobility was taking place. Any such efforts would depend on how leaders and institutions sided in the struggle between merit and culture. The battle lines were not clearly drawn, however, even within individual institutions. It was difficult for Yale undergraduates like Kingman Brewster to see the problem clearly, let alone make a thoroughgoing structural critique. They were products of the WASP culture that Yale celebrated, both inside the classroom and beyond, and there was much in the culture that they found valuable. Still, even as they enjoyed Yale, there was something about the university that troubled them.

*　　*　　*

WHEN HE ARRIVED in New Haven, Brewster settled into his room in Durfee Hall, one of the Victorian Gothic dormitories that looked out over the elm trees and flagstone paths crossing the grass of the Old Campus. A week after the freshman parade, Brewster watched still another parade cross the campus, this time for Seymour's inauguration as president. The governor of Connecticut, Wilbur Cross, walked with Seymour behind the emblematic silver mace and presided over the ceremonies. A flinty Connecticut Yankee, Cross had once been dean of the Yale Graduate School. The opening prayer was delivered by Henry Sloane Coffin, whose nephew, William Sloane Coffin Jr., would deliver the opening prayer at Brewster's inauguration twenty-seven years later.

Brewster's freshman ambitions, of course, were directed more toward making friends than becoming Yale president. There were only two other graduates from Belmont Hill at Yale when Brewster arrived (as compared with more than three hundred from a prominent feeder school like Andover), so Brewster's social network was relatively small. He met students at the Commons, the cavernous hall where all freshmen took meals and commiserated over the food. He was a member of the Yale Political Union (a debating society modeled after the Oxford Union), set up several years earlier by his Vineyard Haven neighbor, history professor Whitney Griswold, and a small group of students and other faculty.[20] Brewster described the group as an ideal setting for "a lot of scrappy undergraduates who enjoy[ed] the formality of public argument with each other."[21] He was also a member of the University Debating Association, and won the Freshman Debating Prize in the spring of 1938. A good deal of time during his first year was devoted to going out on the town, a foolproof way of getting acquainted.

One of the first people Brewster sought out was his sometime debating opponent McGeorge Bundy, the top student in the sophomore class, whom many freshmen already knew by reputation as the brightest boy to enter Yale since Jonathan Edwards in the Class of 1712. Brewster also made friends with Mac's brother Bill, whose grades were almost as high and who had become one of the big men in the junior class by skating, debating, writing, and fraternizing his way to undergraduate glory. Mac Bundy and Brewster became extremely close at Yale, even "across the class line," as Bundy remembered, "which was still a line in those days, but not a thick one."[22]

Although he was not as conspicuously brilliant a scholar-activist as the Bundy brothers, Brewster fit his own characterization of "Bill and Mac as examples . . . of people who did not have to make a choice as to whether they would be scholars or activists, but could find themselves honored in both camps, and in fact more honored in each camp because they had a foot in the other."[23] Academically, Brewster performed well if unevenly. His mother awarded him a car for staying on the dean's list, but this academic recognition was not much of an honor at a time when the list included almost half the student body.[24]

Brewster described himself, as a young man, as "about six feet tall, good health but no athlete. Am somewhat lazy and given to procrastination when I am not fired with a cause or given a definite responsibility, in which case I am not a bad worker. I like responsibility. I like people, especially in relation to their ideas. Am slightly self-conscious and solemn, though the latter is more apparent than real."[25] Brewster's classmates thought him an impressive figure: tall, well dressed, with wavy dark hair, "handsome but not flashily good-looking."[26] "More mature"[27] than many of his peers (partly the result, perhaps, of his year off between school and college), Brewster struck them as "a very serious-minded young man who from the beginning had definite thoughts in mind about his career."[28] And yet he was not at all dry or pompous. He loved parties, and would exclaim before a dance, "Let's shave only one cheek tonight—the cheek-to-cheek side."[29] He liked to argue and tease, winning over his opponents with a sort of rumpled charm. One roommate jokingly praised his "disorderly chaotic habits" and "delight in argument and strife."[30]

Friends spoke of his exuberance, humor, and wry sense of self-deprecation. They were also impressed by his intelligence. "He had a hell of a brain," one recalled. "He was always up there in the stratosphere with guys like Mac Bundy and the deeper thinkers.[31] Many faculty members, too, were taken by Brewster's brilliance, particularly Whit Griswold, who thought him perhaps the brightest undergraduate he had taught.[32] Brewster impressed several other younger faculty members, including Richard Bissell Jr., Max Millikan, and August Heckscher, all of whom were Yale graduates themselves.

Heckscher, former chairman of the campus newspaper, encouraged Brewster to join. Brewster needed little coaxing, given his interest in politics and journalism and the fact that the newspaper was among the campus's most powerful organizations. Sargent Shriver had told the freshmen at Woolsey Hall that "the *News* ran the University," as one of Brewster's classmates put it, and if students wanted to get behind the scenes, they had better try out for it.[33] The *News* was housed in a palatial Gothic structure at the end of Fraternity Row, a gift of Henry Luce, Class of '24 and the co-founder of *Time* magazine. In the second semester of his freshman year, Brewster entered the bowels of the building to take part in the grueling eight-week competition for the editorship positions on the "O.C.D.," as insiders called it (for "Oldest College Daily"). "Heelers" spent sixty or more hours a week—essentially all their nonclassroom waking hours—writing copy, selling ads, proofreading, running errands for the editors, and trekking to and from the printers, hours after midnight.

In the week that Brewster began the heel, the paper carried its first column by McGeorge Bundy. Mac had refused to heel the *News,* "out of some sort of feeling of intellectual snobbery, I guess."[34] But because of his ability, charm, and connections—Bill was vice chairman—he was allowed to write for the paper anyway. In the column Bundy impishly referred to his special status by describing himself as "a parasite upon the body journalistic." He advised freshmen that "those of you who wish to build for yourselves a campus career can do no better than to start with the *News.* You will meet the right people and get the opportunity, at least, to make your mark." But, he warned, "you may also lose your soul"—by which he meant that the heelers, like other Yale men lured by extracurriculars, might forget that college was for getting an education.[35]

Brewster was not deterred, and he did not abandon his studies or restrict himself to the *News.* Yale's social life never stopped, and he gladly took part. On football Saturdays, most undergraduates rode out to the Yale Bowl in old-fashioned yellow streetcars that ran along Chapel Street, pitching pennies to local children who ran alongside the cars. Spring brought prom and Derby Day, an invasion of a nearby town where crew races were held on the river. Fraternities held frequent parties. Upperclassmen ventured to women's colleges—although freshmen, forbidden to keep cars, more often sought women close to home. Some hit New Haven dives like the Knickerbocker to pick up prostitutes and get in fights with townies. Most students' entertainment was more innocent. There were four first-run movie theaters in town, and Broadway-bound plays had their openings (and sometimes closings) at the Schubert Theater.

Brewster entered college only three and a half years after the end of Prohibition. Although the raccoon coat craze of the 1920s had faded, the frantic alcohol consumption of that era had not. Elliot Richardson, while a Harvard undergraduate, had an encounter with what he called "a rum punch that concealed its potency until too late," ran over a traffic island,

and lost his license for a year.[36] In his freshman year Brewster met his classmate Paul Moore Jr. at a party where they both drank too many Cuba Libres. "The political significance of the name completely escaped us," Moore remembered.[37]

Moore came from an Old Blue family, who considered their most valuable possession to be the 1769 Yale degree of one of their ancestors. He knew plenty of Yale people through family connections; his father had been one of Charles Seymour's classmates, and he was friends with many undergraduates from his childhood summers on Massachusetts's North Shore. Moore and McGeorge Bundy went to the same day camp on the North Shore, "and since we both despised baseball, we were sent to the outfield, where we would crack jokes and hope that no one would hit the ball our way."[38] Unlike Bundy and Brewster, Moore was truly wealthy; his grandfather had helped to found several prominent companies, including the National Biscuit Company, the American Can Company, Banker's Trust, and the Lackawanna Railroad. His family owned lavish homes in New Jersey and Palm Beach. He grew up without having to think about the depression or questions of wealth and poverty. Some indication of the kind of man he would become, however, occurred on a rare encounter with poverty. Riding in his grandmother's custom-built Rolls-Royce past disheveled men on a Hoboken breadline, Moore threw himself to the limousine's carpeted floor to hide in shame.[39]

Coming to New Haven from the St. Paul's School, Moore fell in easily with a sociable, preppy crowd. He was tapped for the Haunt Club, an organization whose sole purpose was to throw all-day drinking bashes in the countryside twice a year. He recalled that "the criterion by which one was elected to this elite group was quite simple: you had to be able to drink a lot."[40] Driving back from the club's fall gathering, still sloshing with milk punch and champagne, Moore and some friends were arrested after stealing a parking sign. They spent the night in jail, singing Christmas carols to the inmates, until they were bailed out by their clothier, a stout man named J. Press.

His money, background, and sociability eased Moore into the Fence Club, the most exclusive of Yale's fraternities and watering hole for most of the "hearty" prep school set. But he knew that the merely social student would not gain a reputation; he also had to "do something" for the university. So Moore tried out for the prestigious position of football manager, a job that involved picking up sweaty clothes and soiled towels for the players. Students competed to do this dirty work only because the football manager invariably received a secret society tap. Moore had better luck on the crew team, where his height and skinniness counted. He spent the fall rowing through the murky New Haven harbor, the winter laboring in the smelly gymnasium, and the spring evading ice floes in the Housatonic River, to the accompaniment of profane abuse from the crew coach. As he suffered through the spartan training regimen, Moore (who was already interested in theology) sensed a connection between Yale's strenuous success ethic and the harsh doctrines of the college's Puritan founders. Moore preferred the Anglo-Catholicism of Christ Church, where students and faculty reveled in the incense and Gregorian chants of High Mass and took inspiration from the Church of England priests who ministered to the London dockland slums.[41]

Cyrus Vance, one of the big men in the Class of 1939, preceded Moore in the Haunt Club and was a member of the Mohicans, another drinking club disbanded after one too many episodes involving excessive consumption of firewater. By the time Vance was in college, his mother had moved back to Clarksburg, and Vance would return to West Virginia on holidays. To the Yale students of that era, this made Vance positively exotic; most had traveled to Europe many times over, but few if any had been to West Virginia. He was a cheerleader (an indication of his popularity), a Fence Club initiate, and defenseman on the varsity ice hockey team. On the ice his gangly appearance and sprawling limbs earned him the nickname Spider. Bill Bundy, who was goalie for the team, remembered that Vance was "not a gifted hockey player, but he worked hard and became a first-stringer."[42] While playing hockey, Vance incurred the back injury that would plague him for much of his career. Unusually for one of the hearty set, he had a deep interest in politics and international affairs that traced back to the influence of his "uncle" John W. Davis. His affinity for politics led to friendships with many of the *News* editors in his class, including Bill Bundy (another rare undergraduate Democrat), William Scranton, Don Belin, Thaddeus (Ted) Beal, and Stanley Resor. Like Paul Moore, Vance had a strong religious and idealistic side. During his college summers he volunteered, with several other Yale students, at the Grenfell mission in Labrador, a muscular Christian outfit that operated schools, clinics, and craft centers for impoverished residents of the Northwest River region. He seriously considered becoming an Episcopalian priest, but decided, in the end, that he could be of greater service by studying law.[43]

*   *   *

AT THE START of his sophomore year, Brewster joined the newest residential college, Timothy Dwight (usually called "T.D."), when it opened in the fall of 1938. For those who could afford to live on campus, life within the colleges was gracious and even luxurious. Overcrowding was nonexistent. Two students shared a suite that, in the fullness of time, would house four or more. Maids kept the rooms in order and made the beds. The residential college dining halls featured white linen tablecloths, silverware and china bearing the colleges' insignia, fresh flowers in place settings, printed menus, and waitress service, all of which created an atmosphere that one observer called "midway between that of an Oxford hall and an American club."[44] Each college had its own library, common rooms, game rooms, squash courts, and a variety of activity centers employed as darkrooms, exercise rooms, small theaters, printing or woodworking shops, music rooms, and so on. The college populations were small enough for students to get to know each other, and for the handful of faculty fellows to form social and intellectual bonds of their own.

Never again would the life of the residential colleges be conducted in quite the same style as it was before World War II. In December of his sophomore year, for example, Brewster and the other students joined Timothy Dwight master James Grafton Rogers, the fellows, and their families for the college's first Christmas dinner. With the college bells ringing outside, the formally dressed Prexies (as T.D. students were called) filed into the dining hall and took their places at an eighty-foot-long table decorated in holiday style. The faux-Gothic hall, with its exposed beams, wrought-iron detailing, and plastered walls, was illuminated by hundreds of candles and a yule log blazing in a great fireplace. A fanfare rang through the hall and a trumpeter dressed in a beefeater's uniform appeared. He marched around the table, trailed by an attendant in medieval costume who carried a large set of keys. Next came a dozen followers, also in medieval attire, each carrying an armful of wine bottles. After the wine was poured, toasts were made, and the waitresses entered in procession, dressed in red and green with hairpieces made of holly. The first carried a silver tray upon which sat a whole suckling pig with an apple in its mouth; others held aloft trays bearing ham, turkey, and a plum pudding alight with flaming brandy. After dinner, Santa Claus entered the hall to musical accompaniment and distributed presents. Rogers wished the college members a merry Christmas, and the festivities ended with everyone singing the school's anthem, "Bright College Years."[45]

The elegance and élan of such events augmented the sense of kinship existing among the members, some of whom, after all, had known each other most of their lives. The concept of the "Yale family" was not mere rhetoric—not, at any rate, for those who were at the center rather than the margins of college life. Before the war, undergraduates were sure that the friendships between students, and even between students and many faculty members, were made possible by their shared backgrounds and understanding. Brad Westerfield, who grew up around Yale in the 1930s and was a student and professor there after the war, recalled the university as "a deeply close-knit community. It was almost like a club. In retrospect, one understands only the vices of such a state of mind. But at the time, one understood only the virtues of it."[46]

Brewster had much to celebrate at the T.D. Christmas party, for he had just been elected chairman of the *News,* although (in keeping with tradition) his first issue would not appear until January of his junior year. In the absence of student government, the *News* chairman was the closest equivalent of a student body president, and the paper's editorials would provide a platform from which Brewster could broadcast his views across the campus and beyond. His stint at the *News* also gave him insight into the inner workings of the university. "The most important part of my college experience," he judged, was "my personal contact and give and take with members of the faculty, administration, and prominent visitors. It was the *News* Chairmanship, not any special personal attributes, which gave me this entree."[47] The *News* in those days was a for-profit enterprise, and Brewster could look forward to a payoff of nearly $2,000 by the end of his term—at that time, more than the price of a new car. That, too, was worth celebrating.

By the middle of sophomore year, the leaders of the Class of 1941 had started to emerge. Over the next year Brewster would be invited to join the committees that advised the dean, planned the junior prom, and determined which students would get campus jobs. He would follow McGeorge Bundy into the Elizabethan Club, a cozy enclave where professors and students met over tea to make witticisms and discuss literature and philosophy. He also joined Bundy in the Zeta Psi fraternity—"we thought it was not wholly uncivilized," Bundy observed—and the Pundits (Hindi for "wise men"), a group hand-selected by the venerable English professor William Lyon Phelps.[48] Brewster acquired a new roommate, the *News* vice chairman William Jackson, whose father, Robert, was Franklin Roosevelt's attorney general and would soon become a Supreme Court justice. Their classmates nicknamed Brewster and Jackson "the senators."

Just as the nation was dominated by an elite of which Yale was a part, the college itself was dominated by a smaller elite, circles within circles. As

McGeorge Bundy put it, "we do have at Yale a remarkable concentration of extracurricular activities in the hands of a very few men."[49] Most of the undergraduates were not viewed as leaders and were not treated as such. The lion's share not only of student honors but of the faculty's and administration's attention and rewards went to the chosen few such as Brewster and his circle. Brewster's classmate DeLaney Kiphuth recalled that "when I was an undergraduate, I think it was really true that [Yale] judged itself by how well it did for the outstanding undergraduates, for those who had a great deal of ability and a great deal of future promise," although he thought that this orientation was not "intentional or thought out."[50] The sifting extended even to housing arrangements, as richer students paid more for better rooms while almost a sixth of the undergraduate body commuted from home and were essentially invisible in the Yale scheme of things.[51]

The harsh, winnowing aspect of the system was camouflaged by comfortable rhetoric about the importance of solidarity, along the lines of "the main fibre of Yale is not the ruling few but the unknown many."[52] A more straightforward editorial in the News in later years warned freshmen that "by having a purpose you will not become part of that characteristic segment of each class once aptly described as 'the faceless 700.'"[53] The students knew quite well who the insiders were. An undergraduate recalled crossing the campus one night and noticing that a lecture hall was brightly lit up. "I stepped inside, and to my amazement found that I was listening to McGeorge Bundy, resplendent in white tie and tails, making a brilliant and winning oration in a contest I had not even known existed."[54]

Those who were treated as leaders tended to think of themselves as leaders and become leaders. Betty Friedan, editor of one of the Smith College campus magazines at the time, attended a meeting with other college editors for which Brewster was host. "There was something in the way the men like Kingman Brewster were expected to do big things in society," she recalled, "and that expectation propelled them to do it."[55]

Brewster attended college at a time when Yale and a handful of other "upper-class" colleges occupied a significant place in the public imagination. For example, Tap Day, when Yale's secret societies chose their initiates, was covered by the major New York papers. Yale's football teams were nationally ranked, its games were among the nation's premier sporting events, and home Saturdays drew crowds of up to 75,000. (During the mid-1930s, Yale produced back-to-back Heisman Trophy winners in Larry Kelley and Clint Frank.) Popular novelists like F. Scott Fitzgerald, John P. Marquand, and John O'Hara were mesmerized by the aristocratic elements of college life. *Esquire*'s fashion editor told the *Yale Daily News* in 1939 that "Yale men have a direct influence on college fashions throughout the country. That . . . is why we come around every Fall to take pictures of the boys in their rooms and around the campus."[56] Eight Yale men were also on the list of the nation's twenty-five best-dressed men in 1940.[57] The chairman of the *Yale Daily News* was a public figure well beyond the confines of New Haven, and Brewster's arrival home for spring break was a matter of sufficient interest to be reported in the social columns of the *Boston Herald*.[58]

Colleges across the country, both public and private, modeled their undergraduate folkways on the older colleges and the styles of their clientele. As the historian Ernest Earnest wrote, "To an amazing degree the pattern set by Harvard, Yale and Princeton after 1880 became that of colleges all over the country. The clubs, the social organization, the athletics—even the clothes and the slang—of 'the big three' were copied by college youth throughout the nation."[59] The older colleges provided exemplars of the concepts of "college men" and "college fashion" (terms that have lost their meaning in today's broader, fragmented undergraduate education).

Another advantage of the organizations to which Brewster belonged was the opportunity they gave students to forge connections with older, influential men. Brewster and Elliot Richardson, for example, were co-hosts of a dinner in honor of the thirtieth anniversary of the Elizabethan Club and the seventy-fifth anniversary of its Harvard counterpart, the Signet Society. The event took place in the Gothic intimacy of the Yale Law School faculty lounge. It was something of a family occasion for Brewster, bringing him together with his stepfather, Edward Ballantine, and his step-cousin John Ballantine. And it was very much a family occasion for McGeorge Bundy, uniting him with his father, both brothers, several cousins, and his great-uncle A. Lawrence Lowell, the former president of Harvard.[60]

Brewster, as head of the Elizabethan Club, and Richardson, as president of the Signet, each said a few words at the beginning of the event. Both the Signet and the Elizabethans were represented by speakers at the dinner, chosen from among their prominent graduates. The Harvard speaker, Richardson recalled, "was a craggy-faced man, whose name I didn't quite catch. He began his speech by making a few I thought rather heavy jokes, then pulled a sheaf of papers out of his pocket and began to read his speech page by page." As he read on, it became clear that the speaker was developing a case for a totalitarian society. "I thought, 'My God, where the hell did we get this guy?' I tried to slink under the table, I was so embarrassed. But then, having erected this edifice, the speaker began to take the case for totalitarianism apart, and by the time he finished, he had totally demolished it. And in the course of his speech, he had become powerfully eloquent. That was the only after-dinner speech I ever heard where people stood and cheered and stamped at the conclusion, despite the fact that the speaker read from a script and, aside from his opening ad-lib remarks, made no attempt at humor." It turned out that the speaker was Judge Learned Hand, "whom I had never heard of at that point. I later became his law clerk, and I regard him as perhaps the only really great man I ever knew."[61]

AS BREWSTER AND his circle were enjoying the privileges of Yale and were being raised up in the customary manner of student leaders, they were developing ideas that differed significantly from the traditional outlook of years past. Many of the two hundred or so big men on campus were looking skeptically on the system they dominated and the social values it embodied. Even in their college years, these men were questioning the aristocratic, self-perpetuating tendencies of their class and the priorities of their colleges.

This new seriousness was largely the product of the depression. Brewster later observed that "like the classes just before them, the students of the late Thirties were dimly aware that not even Yale men could count on coasting into a plush post-graduate normalcy. The Depression had broken the promise of self-perpetuating privilege. A 'traitor to his class' had broken its political power."[62] American capitalism's protracted failure to solve the economic crisis undermined the business values that had been such an important part of the Yale faith.

Brewster and many of his peers came to the consensus that the older generation had failed, that few of their generation could "bank on success by inheritance," and that the younger generation would have to find new solutions.[63] Yet Brewster viewed the prospect of re-creation as exhilarating. As he wrote in his first *Yale Daily News* editorial, "The world we shall live and work in is being refashioned and ours will not be a second-hand way of life." Within the university, he continued, "parts of the Yale machinery that are rusty with complacency and stiff with tradition will have to be hauled out and re-examined."[64]

Undergraduate excoriation of the powers that be has become so routine that at first glance it may seem a mistake to read too much into Brewster's youthful critique. Some of Brewster's contemporaries felt that he was temperamentally opposed to the status quo, whatever it happened to be. As football captain J. William Stack Jr. told an interviewer in later years,

"When I came to Yale, I thought everything about it was just wonderful. Kingman came down from his mother's salon in Cambridge and questioned everything."[65] Indeed, Brewster's positions were not representative of the majority of campus opinion, if such a thing could be determined. The conservatism of the average Yale undergraduate of the 1920s—manifested in what one critic called "the stiffest of collars, the shiniest of Packards, the gaudiest of house-party drunks, the dopiest of mental habits, and the most hopeful of hogwash about rugged individualism"—lingered on in the 1930s.[66] Brewster acknowledged that despite the depression, student life at Yale was "pleasantly fat and essentially untroubled."[67]

Most undergraduates had little interest in politics. Future Wisconsin senator William Proxmire, who graduated from Yale in 1938, wrote that he and his fellow students "lived in a kind of disembodied cocoon. . . . [M]ost of my classmates were wholly preoccupied with sports and girls and grades, and bull sessions about sports and girls and grades—in that order." He felt that "there was nothing in the Yale of my day, no challenge, no debate, certainly no protest to provoke any thought of what America stood for."[68] The novelist Louis Auchincloss, of the Class of 1939, conceded that a few of his classmates, including Cyrus Vance, Bill Scranton, and Bill Bundy, took national and world problems "very much to heart. But students generally were less politically conscious than they are today—certainly less so than they were in the sixties."[69]

The point, however, was that the late 1930s debate over national and world problems and the criticism of the university was well-nigh unprecedented at Yale, in that it came not from disgruntled outsiders but from campus leaders like Brewster and the Bundys. Their critiques were important because they were the elite around which the institution revolved. The opinions and actions of "the ruling few" mattered greatly at Yale because, as Brewster's roommate William Jackson emphasized, "no other institution of higher education is so completely dominated by the Big Men of the Class."[70] These men were the bellwethers, the small number who were able to change the culture of the college so much in a few years during the 1930s that traditionalists lamented the decline of "bulldogism." They dominated many of the most established Yale institutions, particularly the "Oldest College Daily," the Political Union, and the Elizabethan Club. As one undergraduate indicated, these men were not "representative of the Yale consensus, if indeed such a thing may be said to exist. But they are representative of that section of Yale opinion which is most vocal and most aggressive, which is conceived around the dinner tables of Zeta Psi and sundry other places, nourished in the smoke-filled rooms of certain entries in Davenport and T.D., resonantly matured in the sanctuary of the Political Union, and finally bursts forth in all its radiant maturity in the O.C.D."[71]

There was, in fact, a division between the broad mass of undergraduate opinion, which was conservative, and the outlook of student leaders, which was liberal. The "big men" opposed both the political and the social conservatism of Yale. Starting with Brewster's distant cousin Jonathan Brewster Bingham in 1935–36, the chairmen of the *Yale Daily News* gave editorial approval to the New Deal, even though three-quarters of the undergraduates voted for Republicans in the presidential elections of 1936 and 1940. The leaders criticized the business orientation of the Republican Party, which McGeorge Bundy noted "has never been more completely alienated from labor and the lower classes than it is today."[72] They criticized the societies and fraternities and tried to downplay the extracurricular race for success (from which they had, admittedly, benefited themselves). They called for admissions reform, more serious attention to academics, a larger role for the professional schools, greater emphasis on science, and a general modernization of the university. Their undergraduate efforts were often resisted by Charles Seymour's administration but were supported by a group of Young Turk junior faculty members, including Richard Bissell, Whitney Griswold, Sherman Kent, Max Millikan, and Eugene Rostow. Brewster and Bundy found, when they reread *Stover at Yale,* that they tended to identify with Brockhurst, the novel's student reformer, rather than with the football hero. Both several times quoted Brockhurst's closing lines: "I'm not satisfied with Yale as a magnificent factory on democratic business lines; I dream of something else, something visionary, a great institution not of boys, clean, lovable and honest, but of men of brains, of courage, of leadership, a great center of thought, to stir the country and bring it back to the understanding of what man creates with his imagination, and dares with his will."[73]

Brewster and his peers pointed to the ways that Yale continued to live down to the gibe that it emphasized professionalism in its extracurriculars and amateurism in its academics. They criticized "the utter boredom and waste of sitting through a course without meaning,"[74] tests that called for regurgitation rather than assimilation, and the "guts, tutoring schools, [and] ghost writers" to which many students resorted.[75] McGeorge Bundy characterized most of his studies as "a terrible waste of time."[76] Similar problems prevailed on other campuses, and many of the brightest students were among the most dissatisfied.[77] Elliot Richardson remembered that "I did not think much of Harvard education in those days before the Second World War. In most cases it wasn't worth going to class."[78]

In his sophomore year, Bundy led a rebellion against Yale's introductory economics course. He blasted its "shocking" overemphasis of the "stultifying" ten-minute quiz, absence of small-group discussion, employment of instructors "utterly without experience," and sole reliance on a conservative textbook edited by three professors in the department. Such topics as labor, government regulation, and banking, he observed, were controversial subjects, "and as long as the Economics Department takes an *ex cathedra* attitude on these questions, so long is it stifling the study of economics at Yale."[79] Bundy and several of his allies on the *News* circulated a petition calling for reform and presented it to the college dean. The whole protest was polite, even decorous. Bundy hastened to assure the dean that he was far more preoccupied with his family and his examinations than with "my puerile efforts at reform."[80] Still, his dissatisfaction with Yale's intellectual standards was hard to ignore. Bundy's revolt made him an ally of the equally critical Bissell, an assistant professor of economics who taught Brewster as well as Bundy, and who appalled the conservative department with heretical Keynesian approaches and techniques. But Bissell's seminar was an exception to the generally uninspiring course offerings.

Beyond the academic critique, it bothered many of the influential undergraduates that Yale and other elite universities had become "so identified with the moneyed classes that they have lost contact with the wants and ideas . . . [of] the great masses of our people."[81] These students did not hesitate to identify Yale with the corporate class, and to conclude that Yale, like capitalism, needed reform and rehabilitation. As Brewster wrote in November 1940, after Roosevelt had swept to a third term, "We are in large degree essentially products of the business class." Yale students were "among those who met defeat at the hand of a great majority yesterday."[82]

IN THE POLITICAL Union, Brewster and his peers identified with the dominant faction, the Liberal Party, which tended to position itself between the Conservative Party and the Labor (or Radical) Party. Their liberalism was pragmatic and nonideological rather than emotional. As McGeorge Bundy put it, "Collectively the lower classes are potentially destructive (so, of course, is any overly self-conscious class), but individually each citizen deserves a break from this great and rich nation."[83] Certainly these liberals disdained extremists of left and right, and few undergraduates advocated extreme ideological solutions to Yale's problems or the nation's. Brewster spoke for the vast majority when he declared that "we cannot share the bitterness of the sorehead or the gloomy radical."[84] He recalled later that "there was a little splinter of highly organized, regimented Marxists" at Yale during his college years, "but they were unimportant in number and certainly unimpressive in terms of communication with the rest of the community."[85] At Yale, radicals were always socially marginal—hence politically marginal as well.[86]

If Brewster worried more about the threat of fascism than of communism, perhaps it was because in his father he had all too clear an example of what American fascism might look like. "Sure, the United States will get fascism," Brewster Sr.'s friend Huey Long was supposed to have remarked. "But it will be called 'Americanism.'" Brewster was an anticommunist but not a dogmatic one, and like most of his friends he thought red-baiters were more dangerous than actual Reds. One of his first *Yale Daily News* editorials was a salute to Elliot Richardson's *Harvard Lampoon* satire of Michael A. Sullivan, a red-baiting Cambridge politician.[87] Sullivan had blustered a resolution through the City Council outlawing within city limits any printed material containing the words "Lenin" or "Leningrad." Richardson remembered that "we put out a *Harvard Lampoon* issue 'exposing' him as the underground head of all Soviet espionage activities. . . . I drew a picture of the Cambridge Lenin Library burning books under the eyes of the local cops, put Michael A. Sullivan into a photo with Lenin and Stalin, and retouched his campaign photo to 'reveal' him as Mikhail Akim Seratov. He sued us for $300,000, which was a lot of money in those days."[88]

In one representative *News* editorial, appropriately titled "Reform or Revolt?" Brewster laid out his political philosophy in detail. Although he was a Republican with mixed feelings about Roosevelt, he applauded the New Deal's "creep toward collectivism" as "good and inevitable." Brewster looked forward to "a more equitable distribution of wealth, more social insurance, more long-range, over-all planning, more cooperation and efficiency, and more government by experts." Most important of all, he thought, was "greater equality of opportunity—an equal chance for rich and poor alike." He did not believe that equality of outcome was a necessary or even desirable condition. But "if the Old Guard stifles reform," he warned, fascism would come to America: "it surely can happen here."[89]

The British journalist Godfrey Hodgson speculated that those Americans "who grew up in sheltered homes and private schools" during the depression "acquired a special compulsion to prove how tough they were" by way of compensation.[90] Perhaps it would be more accurate to say that the suffering of millions of fellow citizens forced many privileged young men like Brewster at least to ask themselves whether they might deserve the advantages they received. As Brewster wrote in another context, "I do believe that privilege always carries its burden of guilt."[91]

If Brewster and his peers had been of university age a few years earlier, at the nadir of the depression, they might have been more tempted by socialist alternatives, or some denial or evasion of their privileges. As it was, Brewster and many of his contemporaries concluded that the best way to deal with the "burden of guilt" would be to live up to the responsibilities those privileges incurred. They shared a sense that knowledge and serious academic training were becoming increasingly important and that merit rather than social class would prevail in the reconstructed world that would follow the depression and the aftermath of war. As one undergraduate put it in the fall of 1939, war overseas meant that "economic and social aristocracies will be displaced, notably in the two great so-called democracies of England and France. Castes and class distinctions will disappear. . . . The world of tomorrow, therefore, will be a world in which merit and ability will be at a greater premium than ever before."[92]

These beliefs set Brewster and his circle apart from most of their classmates and their class. Most conservatives abhorred the leading role played by bright young lawyers and academics in the New Deal. "The trouble with our country now," one GOP presidential hopeful told the *News* in 1939, "is that there are too damn many experts still in Washington gumming things up. . . . It's always been my experience that one good solid American businessman can do more actual good in twenty minutes than a pack of your high-falutin' University Professors in twenty years!"[93] The old worship of business and the hostility toward intellect were alien to the bright young students and faculty of the depression-era colleges. The social scientists Bissell and Millikan, two of Brewster's mentors, would soon depart Yale for government service, following the example of professors who served in the New Deal. Bissell and Millikan would emerge as a new breed of "action intellectuals," straddling the worlds of academia and the intelligence agencies during World War II and after.

Brewster also believed that Yale needed to open its gates to students who were equal to the greater intellectual demands required of experts and reformers. He declared that "birth, position, and wealth must be neither impediments nor advantages to the opportunity for education," as they clearly were at Yale in the late 1930s and early 1940s.[94] Another columnist, W. Liscum Borden Jr. (later an important participant in the early debate about nuclear weapons), wrote scathingly on the nation's inequality and its reflection at Yale. He noted that about ten percent of American youth attended college. "Are these the brainiest men, the ones whose ability truly merits a higher education? They are not. The ten percent who go to college roughly coincide with the ten percent whose families are wealthiest. Oh yes, we have our sops to the ideal of equal opportunity—scholarships and the like. But by and large, I venture to say, two-thirds of us here at Yale are imposing on the gentlemen who struggle so admirably to stuff *Lux et Veritas* down our throats. In our place should be those of our mental superiors whose mouths don't happen to be crammed with silver spoons."[95]

One other major deficiency of the university in that era seems much more obvious now than it did at the time: the "subliminal anti-Semitism," as Brewster put it, that permeated Yale.[96] It is far too easy to identify Jews in the Yale College Class of 1941 yearbook. Not one Jew belonged to a selective fraternity or society, and, as a rule, Jews lived by themselves or only with other Jews. Nor was this discrimination much commented on by anyone at Yale, although it certainly was at odds with Yale's professed faith in democracy and rewarding merit.

One of the few times the subject of anti-Semitism arose came in the fall of 1938 when, after Kristallnacht, some law school students attempted to raise money on campus to assist German Jewish refugees. The response, as Bill Bundy and Don Belin commented in the *News*, was that "an all too large group of students has said: 'We don't like Jews. There are too many at Yale already. Why bring more over?'" Bundy and Belin reproached their fellow undergraduates: "This is not an argument. It is an expression of intolerance and prejudice. In every way it indicates poverty of intellect and weakness of character."[97] McGeorge Bundy added that "a university is, by its very name, an institution which excludes provincialism, bigotry, and prejudice."[98] Such enlightened opinions, however, were more common among the leaders than among the undergraduate mass. It is significant that Brewster and his peers spent much of their time at Yale in extracurriculars where Jews played a prominent part, notably the *Yale Daily News* and the Yale Debating Association. As Brewster observed, "The Debate Team is one organization at Yale that takes students on proven interest and ability and not mere face value." As an organization that rewarded merit rather than breeding, however, "for the socially ambitious Yaleman, debating is not 'respectable.'"[99]

It must be said that, in the sheltered world of the prewar university, Brewster and his peers tended to see themselves as more liberal and icon-oclastic than outside observers would. Even at the high point of radical and utopian thinking in the 1930s, they were not motivated by any egalitarian political philosophy that put its faith in the common man. They believed, rather, "that the privileges of good living demand the duties of high thinking," as Brewster's roommate William Jackson put it, "that to be a gentleman requires some respect to the need for leadership."[100] Such an outlook did not translate easily into conventional liberal attitudes. McGeorge Bundy once appeared before the Political Union, "be-ribboned and be-dizened in aristocratic garb," to urge the founding of a Tory Radical Party "to lead the people ('a great beast, sir') further to the left along conservative lines."[101] It was all in good fun, but even when he was serious, Bundy's ideas carried more than a whiff of High Tory paternalism.

According to Elliot Richardson, "many of us in college were to varying degrees leftish."[102] He devoted long hours to volunteer work in Boston settlement houses, and rejected the Harvard final clubs in protest against their exclusivity. Richardson liked to say that his principal activity at Harvard was drawing cartoons for the *Lampoon* humor magazine, although he was also an impressive middleweight boxer, wrestler, photographer, and watercolorist, as well as an honors student. For many of Richardson's contemporaries, however, his wealth—he already had an income of over $100,000 a year—complicated his idealism. A classmate recalled an expedition Richardson and friends once made to Vassar: "I can still see Elliot standing in a bar in Poughkeepsie with a large glass of brandy in his hand, a great big tumbler, and we were all asking him for some. I said, 'Elliot, surely you believe in sharing the wealth.' Elliot replied: 'I believe in a system in which everybody will have as much as I have,' and drank the brandy down."[103]

For Brewster and his peers, "leadership meant fitness for the competitive race in church, civil state, or the pursuit of property," he remembered. "Inherited assumptions and values were generally accepted, more in need of refinement than serious question."[104] Mac Bundy spoke for the group when he said that "it is one of the cardinal rules of reform that it is best accomplished from inside, and it is one of the vital principles of social action that a defective institution should wherever possible be transmuted rather than destroyed—for it is only in this way that the strength of tradition and stability of continuity may be maintained."[105] The journalist Roger Starr, who was a student (and an outsider) at Yale in the late 1930s, observed that "Yale's leading undergraduates in those pre-war days accepted the stately value system that had been ordained for them, a courtly world of tweed and button-down shirts." Their values included "loyalty to one's own kind combined with good manners for all, charity for the *genuinely* hurt (and how hard they were to find), combined with a gently deprecating humor for oneself, and a wary coolness toward enthusiasts."[106]

While Brewster and his circle were more influenced by their background than they realized, they were not constrained from struggling against it. In the eyes of these establishment liberals, their opponents were not the handful of insignificant political extremists but, rather, those whom Brewster later castigated as "the legions of apathy," members of an upper-class culture characterized by the white shoe, the fraternity, the gentleman's "C," and a disdain for the rest of the world. Their apathy was encouraged by the fact that the goal for many of Brewster's classmates was "adjustment" to "the gentleman's club of inherited privilege"—an attitude that too often resulted in "a callous insensitivity to the inequities of the world." These young men were "well mannered, with their hair cut, their coats and ties, and on the whole personally decent and considerate." Nonetheless, Brewster concluded, "they do bear a heavy burden of responsibility for their indifference to everything outside their own circle. Too many of us were slow at best, reluctant at worst, to recognize the truth of the Rooseveltian aphorism that 'we must reform if we would conserve.'"[107] In the 1930s, the lines were already being drawn for the intraclass battle between the liberal establishment and their opponents—between those who wanted to bring outsiders into the inner circles and those who believed that the existing social system depended on continued preference for blood over achievement.

BREWSTER'S MAJOR SOCIAL statement as an undergraduate came in the spring of his junior year, when the secret society Tap Day approached. Tap Day was a major event in many undergraduates' lives. For a boy from "a commonplace family in a commonplace town," as one commentator observed, acceptance by these clubs could provide entree into the national establishment. Such a youngster "might hope to pass by his own native abilities into the brave, translunary world of great cities and the gilded corridors of their privileged sets." Once in the right college group, he would be taken care of. "From henceforth he would be not Jones of Columbus, but

Jones of 'Bones' or some other tight-ringed fraternity. . . . If there was a good job in a brokerage firm he would get it, because of his connections. If there was a right club where he was going, he could join it."[108]

Brewster had criticized the secret societies, but by 1940 such opposition was no longer a novelty. There existed a long tradition of prominent men challenging the system and then accepting its rewards. McGeorge Bundy commented that both Tap Day and the societies' "Black Magic" had been "openly and justly mocked," and William Jackson had declared that "I believe that the present influence of Senior Societies is not to the best interests of Yale."[109] Nonetheless, when Skull and Bones came to tap them, both accepted—in Bundy's case, because his mother traveled to New Haven to pressure him to do so.

Brewster did not mind that the system was undemocratic—"any selective system of reward is bound to be"—and he did not care, as Bundy did, that the societies' judgment often was fallible. He objected to the judging itself, and the secrecy that clouded it. "Since the Societies stand before the public on legend instead of fact, they are regarded with appalling awe instead of rational respect. . . . From the point of view of what it does to an otherwise civilized community this secrecy is an indefensible weakness." He added that "after all the day of judgment is still a matter for the Gods and not ninety Yale men."[110]

On Tap Day, Brewster did not appear in the Branford College courtyard for the ceremony in which the neophytes were selected. Instead, Harold ("Doc") Howe II, a member of the 1940 Skull and Bones delegation, sought out Brewster in the *News* chairman's office. Although various legends later arose about Bonesmen breaking down the door, or Brewster rejecting the tap while seated on the john, the reality was more prosaic. Howe offered the tap, and Brewster refused.[111]

According to William Jackson, Brewster believed that a secret society membership would be a political liability in the approaching democratic age. Brewster sometimes tried to brush the matter off with the comment that he was going out with Jackson's sister at Smith and didn't want to give up his weekend nights to sit around in a society tomb. But he also recalled that although the pyramid of which Skull and Bones was the apex "did not exclude the rebel nor guarantee the legacy . . . the fact that it was a pyramid by itself seemed 'undemocratic' in the sense that it was by definition more and more exclusive as you scrambled to its top. Even if the rewards were just and fair and noble, rewards they were and they coerced conformity."[112]

Brewster's rejection of the secret societies, a statement in favor of a more open social order at Yale and beyond, was resented or applauded by others, depending on how they felt about the existing arrangements.

AS UNDERGRADUATES, OF course, Brewster and his peers exercised major influence on their student culture rather than on the country as a whole, but their progressive views attracted wide attention in the spring of 1940. With the fall of France imminent, Brewster helped found the America First Committee (AFC), which became the most prominent organization in the struggle to keep America out of the European war. As the AFC developed into a national movement, millions of Americans were caught up in the "great debate" between the interventionists and the isolationists (or anti-interventionists, as they usually preferred to call themselves). Brewster became "one of the most controversial undergraduates of his day."[113]

The AFC has usually been viewed as an outgrowth of "conservative, Midwestern, agrarian isolationism."[114] Indeed, some historians have continued to make "America First" synonymous with Jew-baiting, racism, and homegrown American fascism.[115] Yet an examination of its founding at Yale provides a very different picture of the organization. The AFC was a student movement before it was a national one, and it was conceived out of the flow of liberal ideas that were in play on campuses like Yale in the 1930s. The young men who started the AFC did not fit the received image. Like Brewster, most came from reasonably privileged backgrounds, with few from the agrarian heartland. Of course, not everyone who became associated with the liberal establishment was anti-interventionist. McGeorge Bundy, after all, was perhaps the best-known young interventionist, despite his friend Brewster's opposition. But Brewster and his allies, who sought to keep abreast of the most advanced ideas of their day, were attracted to the anti-interventionist cause as moderate progressives who saw intervention as a defective, conservative strategy of the generation in power.

The AFC was certainly not the first student organization to push for America to stay out of the conflict brewing in Europe. Students in a variety of left-wing political and Christian pacifist groups sponsored antiwar activities throughout the 1930s. Political organizations active against intervention at Yale and other campuses included the Socialist Party and its youth wing (the Young People's Socialist League), the Young Communist League, the Communist-led National Student League, the Youth Committee

Against War, the American Youth Congress, and the American Student Union. In the religious category, the Fellowship of Reconciliation and the United Christian Youth Movement were also active.[116] There was considerable overlap between political and religious antiwar positions, organizations, and individuals. Thousands of students on hundreds of campuses subscribed to the Oxford Pledge (a modified version of the British student vow not to fight "for King and country"), attended antiwar conferences, signed petitions for peace, and participated in the annual peace strikes that began in April 1934.

Despite this activism, however, the vast majority of students were unsympathetic to socialism, let alone totalitarianism. What little effectiveness communist-directed organizations such as the National Student League possessed was destroyed by the flip-flops their advocates resorted to in order to justify the Hitler-Stalin pact and the Soviet invasion of Finland in 1939.[117] There were a handful of Nazi sympathizers on campus. One Jewish student in the Class of 1942 remembered that his freshman counselor had hanging over his fireplace "a great, four by six foot, brightly colored German swastika flag. . . . And he didn't have it there as a joke, or to see how people reacted to it."[118] But far right activists were sparse at Yale, and Nazism was not openly defended by anyone in the Political Union or other forums of opinion. Indeed, the anti-interventionists were unsparing in their criticism of Nazism, and Brewster was particularly sensitive to charges that the movement was sympathetic to Hitler. "We of the young generation are deeply aware of the horrors of National Socialism," he said in 1941. "We hate it. Hate it perhaps more than others for what it has done to the hopes of men our own age. But we feel . . . that nazi-ism can only be defeated by making democracy work as an alternative."[119]

Christian pacifism aroused considerable sympathy, and some of Yale's pacifists were among the first to be imprisoned for draft resistance in 1941. But whatever polling method was used, only a handful of Yale students claimed they would not fight in any war.[120] Charles Seymour observed that the group of conscientious objectors was small and without significant influence.[121] Paul Moore remembered that "the only conscientious objectors I knew were pale, pimply-faced youths who hung around Dwight Hall, the Christian center at Yale."[122]

Religious, left-wing, and right-wing activists were marginal at most of the nation's other campuses as well. Yet by the time fighting broke out in Europe, every poll of student opinion revealed a preponderance of opposition to

United States participation. If student isolationism did not proceed from religious pacifism or left-wing or right-wing inspiration, then where did it come from?

BREWSTER AND HIS peers were born during or just after the First World War, and disillusionment with the war cast a long shadow over their formative years. Few believed there had been any good reason for the war's sacrifices. Youthful skeptics felt that the previous generation was, as Bill Jackson wrote, "duped in 1917, not only by Allied propaganda, but more tragically by its own delusions of grandeur. They won the war but lost the peace: for the calm appraisal of later years revealed the Holy Crusade in all its nakedness as a subterfuge for pulling imperialistic chestnuts out of the fire."[123] The Second World War was seen in the same light. "Have we any reason at all to believe that the present war differs from the last?"[124] the *News* asked.

Students put forward many other reasons why the United States should stay out of this war. Brewster was confident that "the Americas cannot be successfully invaded from across the ocean."[125] Other students brooded over the suppression of civil liberties that war would entail, and the certainty that depression would follow. As one Cassandra warned, "The Class of '50 will never be employed."[126] Some denied that Britain and France were actually democracies or had any fraternal claim on the United States. To these young people, it was America's responsibility to keep the flame of democracy alive by remaining aloof, "the last, best hope of mankind." Many were frankly concerned about war's threat to their own lives. They saw themselves as but one step from the front lines, even more at risk than their non-student peers: "The draft always begins with students. The universities suffer first and worst."[127] And not least, as Brewster remembered, "we were furious at what seemed to be the false advertising, the dishonest huckstering of President Roosevelt's promise that we could enable the allies to win by providing aid 'short of war.' . . . [W]e also felt that Rooseveltian guile was depriving the people of a square confrontation of the issue of peace or war."[128]

Similar, essentially nonideological arguments for anti-intervention predominated at other campuses during the years 1939–41. Elliot Richardson remembered that "my anti-interventionism was influenced by the same kinds of considerations that Brewster had articulated . . . in terms of the cost to American values and quality of life that would flow from a total military effort dominating all activities in society."[129]

In the spring of 1940, every Yale student of draft age knew, as Brewster put it, that "whether or not America were to become an active participant in the conflict . . . war would be a determinant of his personal future."[130] But the fall of France changed many undergraduate minds about the intervention question. McGeorge Bundy, for one, while he had consistently opposed Hitler, had not always been an ardent interventionist. Even after Munich, Bundy had declared that he was "in favor of preparation for keeping out of war and for facing the economic strains that war will bring. The United States in a very important sense is the Shangrilla [*sic*] of a harassed civilization, and we must keep it safe. We shall not do so by giving a free hand to a President who was conditioned early in life by a love of tin soldiers and toy dreadnoughts."[131]

Bundy's attitude transformed when it became apparent that France could no longer hold out against Germany. Bundy wrote later that he graduated "in the month that marks the beginning of modern American life. The fall of France in June 1940 marked the end of the age in which it could reasonably be hoped that the American future lay apart from the world's great struggles. . . . To Americans, in retrospect, the pains of that month must now appear as the birth pangs of enduring worldwide responsibility."[132]

At the same time, the fall of France galvanized undergraduates who did not agree that the United States must now join the fray and exercise power on a global scale. The AFC began during the days after France's defeat, when "a handful of Yale college undergraduates and law students gathered almost nightly"[133] to discuss ways to combat the rising pressure for aid to Britain and the interventionist activities of Roosevelt and the Committee to Defend America by Aiding the Allies (CDAAA), led by the Kansas newspaper editor William Allen White. A group around Brewster had already been meeting regularly at night at a New Haven drugstore to talk about the global situation.[134] Brewster and his friends were convinced that Roosevelt and the CDAAA were leading the country into war whether most Americans wanted it or not.[135]

Under the leadership of law student Robert Douglas Stuart Jr., a Princeton graduate who eventually became head of the national America First organization, the group circulated a petition calling for hemispheric defense and nonintervention. Members opposed "any increase in supplies to England beyond the limitations of cash and carry," as well as military intervention, "even if England is on the verge of defeat."[136] The group drew up its petition while another noninterventionist petition was already in motion at Yale, calling for Roosevelt to "grant no credits, give no supplies, and send no men." It was signed by nearly half the undergraduates in Yale College.[137] Similar petition campaigns were launched at other colleges, with similar results.[138]

While Stuart was the administrative head and prime mover of the organization, Brewster was what Stuart called "the idea man"[139] and another supporter called "our super-diplomat."[140] Brewster strategized with the aviator Charles A. Lindbergh, the nation's best-known isolationist. He persuaded the revisionist historian Charles Beard to write a manifesto, labored over a mimeograph machine, wrote letters, and came up with lists of prominent supporters who could be persuaded to join the still-unnamed organization's national committee. Stuart and Brewster lobbied these potential supporters in New York, buttonholed sympathetic isolationist senators like Robert Taft, Burton K. Wheeler, and Hendrik Shipstead in Washington, and pushed the anti-interventionist line at the Republican convention in Philadelphia and the Democratic convention in Cleveland. They began calling the organization "The Emergency Committee to Defend America First," but at the suggestion of Brewster's step-cousin Arthur Ballantine Jr., among others, the name was shortened to the America First Committee.[141] In the fall of 1940, Stuart directed the national office in Chicago, while Brewster became chairman of the AFC's first chapter.

Brewster warned Stuart not to overload the organization's national office with conservatives. "The National Committee should be substantial and prominent, but not stuffy or corporate," he wrote. "You need laborites and progressives. It would be awful if the Committee turned out to be the instrument of one class."[142] The AFC National Committee eventually included progressives such as Chester Bowles, John T. Flynn, and Robert M. La Follette Jr., and enlisted the support of people of such opposed views as John L. Lewis and Herbert Hoover. Lindbergh biographer A. Scott Berg noted that "while many of the other antiwar organizations had distinctly reactionary—often anti-Semitic—taints to them, America First seemed to attract men and women of all ages, political persuasions, and religions— including a number of influential Jews."[143] Brewster saw the antiwar cause as transcending politics; indeed, he wrote that part of the Yale group's strength as a student movement was the hope "that our age and our lack of past or present political affiliations will give us a unique opportunity to enlist the public support of public men who see eye to eye on this one issue regardless of their differences on other matters."

Brewster took care to ensure that the noninterventionist movement on campus was not led by social outcasts or malcontents but by "students who had attained relative respect and prominence during their undergraduate years,"[144] as he put it. The founding members of the AFC and its closely related committee, College Men for Defense First, included many of the East Coast universities' brightest and best, from valedictorians to football all-Americans to campus newspaper editors.[145] While the activists on either side of the interventionist question constituted a small fraction of the student body—Brewster recalled that "relatively few were actively and articulately concerned with such matters"—many of these men later achieved national reputations.[146] They included Brewster himself; Congressman Jonathan Brewster Bingham; Sargent Shriver, the first director of the Peace Corps; Supreme Court Justice Potter Stewart; and President Gerald Ford. Closely allied were some of the brightest lights in the faculty, including several of Brewster's advisors and friends such as Griswold, Millikan, and Bissell.

Brewster emphasized again and again that his group represented mainstream campus opinion, that its views were "in agreement with the great majority of Americans of all ages"[147] and that despite its antiwar and mildly antiauthoritarian stance, its members were patriotic and respectful of government and of democratic outcomes. He characterized his generation as skeptical but not cynical. "We are willing, we are eager to give our lives and our deaths if need be, in the service of the nation," he declared. "But we do insist that those lives or those deaths not be wasted."[148] Brewster also campaigned to win mainstream, normally apolitical undergraduates to his side, and to centralize antiwar opinion in a moderate, bipartisan organization focused on the single cause of keeping out of war.

Brewster's class history joked that "there was actually a week when King Brewster made no speech, did not get near a mike, and even gave up his daily press conferences."[149] He speechified at Yale and other campuses, and wrote anti-interventionist editorials in the *Yale Daily News* that attracted national attention and were reprinted in the *Congressional Record*. Brewster and the president of the *Harvard Crimson* coauthored an antiwar article in the *Atlantic Monthly*. He took part in a radio debate heard by tens of thousands of listeners on NBC's *America's Town Meeting of the Air*. He also testified against the Lend-Lease Act before the Senate Committee on Foreign Relations, where he displayed a chess player's ability to steer clear of the leading questions of unfriendly senators several moves in advance.

The AFC suited Brewster's temperament because the practical needs of the organization required moderation and pragmatism but also allowed some vent to his independent and rebellious side. He took to heart "the wise but sad warning of my college roommate's father when I asked him about political life." Attorney General Robert Jackson told Brewster, "The trouble with politics is that you have to pretend that you are one hundred percent for things you are really only fifty-one percent for."[150]

At the same time, Brewster's opposition to some powerful older figures (who shared much of his background) carried overtones of iconoclasm. In one of his anti-interventionist speeches, Brewster displayed a muckraker's zest in hammering away at government bureaucracy ("inefficiency, waste, full of people who are in there to get what they can"), Congress ("cheap politicians, brainless windbags, bent on self-perpetuation at best, as common tools of blocs and interests"), business ("making mints out of every contract, getting by with what they can and getting the most out of it"), and labor ("holding out for its slice of the melon, hell bent to build and stock its own fortress as against the nation"). The idealistic expectations of youth, he warned, were "not contingent upon their fulfillment by others, they are *absolute.*" As many a student orator would do in the 1960s, Brewster concluded—presumably at top volume—"WE SHALL NOT ONLY EXPECT, WE SHALL *DEMAND* THESE THINGS."[151] For Brewster, as one of his friends observed, such early experiences as America First were "part of what made him sometimes take a somewhat—rebellious isn't quite the word—challenging role. He didn't mind twisting the tail of the established order every now and then. When he had a good idea, the fact that it upset some people who were committed to a traditional way of looking at something didn't really trouble him too much."[152]

Charles Lindbergh's wife, Anne Morrow Lindbergh, recorded her impressions of Brewster during these years: "Kingman Brewster, a senior at Yale, comes down to see us. . . . He is sensitive, very intelligent, with a precise, searching mind. I feel on my toes keeping up with it. He asks C. about the war and the after-the-war conditions. In our own country and abroad. He is worried (as I am) about the reaction which may take place here against the present party in power and against the Jews. He wishes we could do something to avert that bitterness and reaction—now. To plan for the future—for some kind of rapprochement of the opposing parties—with a constructive plan of reform for the United States. I like him—*how* I like him—his sensitivity, his earnestness, his intellectual integrity (hard as steel), and something soft, too, within, a gentleness, beside his hard thought. I think he gets from C. a kind of vigorous faith that grows outside academic life and is strengthened by it."[153]

Brewster arranged for Lindbergh to give a highly publicized address at Yale in October 1940. When Lindbergh arrived in New Haven, he had dinner with Brewster and a small group of faculty at Whit Griswold's house. At Woolsey Hall, which was packed beyond capacity, Brewster presided and made some brief prefatory remarks, after which his teacher Richard Bissell formally introduced the famous aviator. Lindbergh's speech, his fullest exposition of his views to that point, was raptly received by the nearly three thousand people in attendance.[154] It was almost a year before Lindbergh would deliver the talk in Des Moines, Iowa, that, in passing, indicted Jews as one of the main interventionist forces in America, a comment that would forever stain the aviator's reputation.

Brewster's attraction to Colonel Lindbergh in the early months of the anti-interventionist movement is not difficult to interpret. Brewster had been a self-professed "bug on flying" since he was a boy, and Lindbergh had been his childhood idol. Lindbergh's father, an insurgent Republican progressive who served as member of Congress from Minnesota, had been traduced and threatened along with George Norris when he opposed American participation in the First World War. And, like Brewster's mentor Roger Baldwin, Lindbergh was the sort of larger-than-life independent, who could not be bought or intimidated, that Brewster was drawn to during his youth.

ANTI-INTERVENTIONIST STUDENT activism at Yale and other campuses touched a national nerve as no previous antiwar demonstrations had, because the question of intervention became more immediate and less abstract as the Continent fell to Hitler's control, because students emerged as the cutting edge of noninterventionist opinion, and because the leaders were coming from schools where anti-interventionism was least expected.

The vast majority of the Yale anti-interventionists hailed from upper-crust families on the East Coast and a few northern urban centers, where ties of blood, money, history, and heritage produced the strongest interventionist opinions in the country. Brewster assured the United States Senate that Yale students were "of English descent, have traveled in England, have studied English literature, and all hold the common English tongue and traditions."[155] Indeed, Brewster's cousin by marriage Edward R. Murrow was riveting the nation with his broadcasts from the London Blitz.[156] Yale's traditional Anglophilia permeated the curriculum, and its military tradition was manifest in its war memorials and the presence on campus of one of the earliest ROTC units in the nation.

Yale's president, Charles Seymour, observed that "it is certain that the prevailing attitude of students in our universities has been definitely opposed to any intervention in the European war and to any measures that might tend to bring us into the war. It differs in marked fashion from . . . 1916 and 1917, when there was much enthusiasm for entrance into the war, practically no objection to it and an almost universal desire . . . to get overseas and to fight."[157] Seymour was, in fact, a member of the national committee of the CDAAA, and, like the presidents of Harvard and Columbia, he was not shy about using the bully pulpit of his presidency to speak out for the interventionist side, at Yale and before national audiences. Seymour wrote to an alumnus that he hoped that the America First position did not represent the thought of Yale undergraduates as a whole: "if it did, it would mark, I am sure, a great gulf between the younger generation and the alumni body."[158]

Because many of the students in the late 1930s and early 1940s had fathers who fought in World War I, the isolationist movement set many sons against their fathers' examples. Young and old commentators agreed that the younger generation had been decisively shaped by the experiences of the previous world war and its aftermath. As Brewster coolly observed of the older generation, "They studied and worshipped a European culture, we are introduced and educated to a new concept of indigenous American culture. They saw Britain ascend to unchallenged world power, we saw only a [declining] Britain which misused the ideals of 1919. . . . They knew the thrill and glory of the crest of a world crusade 22 years ago, we knew only the depravity and destitution of war's undertow. Small wonder that these different experiences should lead to different conclusions."[159] Brewster commented years later that "the assumptions, values and goals of our fathers' time were up for rejustification. For many they did not quite satisfy."[160]

The First World War and the depression provided the death blow to what the literary critic Paul Fussell called "the static world, where the values appeared stable and where the meanings of abstractions seemed permanent and reliable," where "everyone knew what Glory was, and what Honor meant."[161] Into the void rushed the ideas associated with modernism, in the form of revisionist histories of the war, the literary experimentation of authors like Joyce, Hemingway, and Pound, and intellectual movements in a range of fields of thought.[162]

At Yale the impact of these new movements was felt in the classroom and outside it, but particularly in the study of international relations and law. Brewster was a student in Nicholas Spykman's popular lecture course on international relations, which emphasized realpolitik and the balance of power. And Yale Law School was the leading source of legal realism, which demolished conservative ideas of natural law and rigid precedent. Led by brilliant scholars such as Thurman Arnold, realism presented a view of law as determined by social context and competing interests and shaped by the manipulation of symbols.[163] Realism was attractive to progressively minded individuals in the 1930s because, as the legal scholar Morton Horwitz noted, it was "a continuation of the reformist agenda of early-twentieth-century Progressivism."[164] Brewster's critique of the Yale system was influenced by the intellectual current flowing from the law school, as evident in his editorial comment that "like the law, Campus 'merit' is what the judges say it is."[165]

Thus it is no accident that many of the founders of the AFC were students at the law school that was most closely identified with legal realism. Cyrus Vance graduated from Yale in 1939 and, with his classmate William Scranton, went on to the law school. Both were in the Corby Court eating club there, at a time when it included Sargent Shriver, Gerald Ford, and future Supreme Court justices Potter Stewart and Byron White. Scranton recalled that the group "used to have lunch there every day. And inevitably, because the war had already begun, the entire conversation was devoted to the international situation. . . . [M]ost of the very bright people were America Firsters."[166]

The young anti-interventionist students were convinced that they were smarter and more sophisticated than the members of their fathers' generation had been. They laughed at the clumsy superpatriotism of the American Legion; one student sneered that "almost any freshman can run intellectual circles around our average ex-doughboy pal."[167] They congratulated themselves on being more serious about their studies than their predecessors. These young progressives saw themselves as more realistic, more enlightened in their treatment of pacifists and dissenters, less vulnerable to propaganda, less sentimental and moralistic, and less innocent. However, the new ideas they absorbed were primarily negative, debunking theories. Undergraduates no longer believed in the moral and idealistic certainties that had motivated American participation in the First World War but were often at a loss when asked to describe what they did believe in. Such lack of response was not a tenable position for young men who saw themselves as builders of a better future.

And yet the prewar generation was skeptical but not cynical, to use Brewster's favorite formulation. Most of these young people conceded that the American system was flawed, but they refused to accept that it could not be repaired and renovated. "We cannot devote our minds exclusively to the past," Brewster chided the back-to-the-classics educator Robert Maynard Hutchins, "but must take cognizance as well of modern thought and contemporary trends. For we are interested not only in where the race has been but more especially whither it is heading. And we will not bury ourselves entirely in the best that has been thought and written in the past, for we have faith that the best in human thought has yet to be written."[168]

The interventionist commentator who best understood the intellectual complexities of student anti-interventionism was McGeorge Bundy, who wrote a celebrated essay on the beliefs of his Yale classmates in the 1940 interventionist anthology *Zero Hour: A Summons to Be Free.* "Back of our disillusionment with war," he wrote, "back of our fear of propaganda, is a deep-seated uncertainty about all ideals and every absolute. . . . [F]ighting faith is not prevalent among contemporary college men. About the things for which we are willing to die, we are confused and bewildered; we have played with many ideals, but we have generally given our devotion to none."[169] Furthermore, "the basic lack of faith of the average undergraduate expresses itself in a great variety of specific opinions, almost all of which lend support to the isolationist position."[170] For this, Bundy put the blame squarely on the college's faculties, who had "succeeded, often unintentionally, in making a case against the idealism and faith without which no settled way of life can be maintained."[171]

IN LATER YEARS Brewster marveled that "in contrast to the hysteria and acrimony of the national debate" over intervention, "at Yale differences were almost never warped into personal distrust. Looking back at the issues at stake, remembering how wrong each side thought the other was, this seems to me remarkable."[172] Arthur Schlesinger Jr., who was at Harvard at the time, later reflected that of all the intense national quarrels that took place in his lifetime, including the storms over McCarthyism in the 1950s and Vietnam in the 1960s, "none so tore apart families and friendships" as the great debate of 1940–41.[173] *Time* magazine called the AFC a collection of "Jew-haters, Roosevelt-haters, England-haters, Coughlinites, politicians, demagogues"; interventionist groups labeled it "a Nazi transmission belt" and "the first fascist party in this nation's history." Interior Secretary Harold Ickes determined the AFC to be a group of "anti-democrats, appeasers, labor baiters, and anti-Semites," while other government officials, including President Roosevelt, questioned the patriotism of AFC members and charged them with outright treason. (Brewster later said that he could never forgive Roosevelt for his treatment of Charles Lindbergh.[174]) These charges "helped create a climate of opinion in which dissent became suspect," according to the historian Justus Doenecke.[175] As Brewster wrote in 1941, "I think the day will come when Yale will be proud to have presented and acclaimed [Lindbergh] when the rest of the seaboard was on fire with hysteria."[176]

Why, then, did civility prevail at Yale even at the height of the debate over interventionism? The pronounced similarity among the undergraduates in matters of background, class, manners, and schooling had much to do with the maintenance of decorum, as well as traditions of gentility and rhetoric about "the Yale family." In part, Brewster's recollections may have reflected his personal philosophy, as he later expressed it, "of trying not only to understand but to see the plausible points in extreme positions with which you disagree."[177] He recalled "one wonderful evening at the offices of Farrar and Straus" when the interventionist publishers, along with the journalist Walter Millis and the poet Stephen Vincent Benét, "flattered me by trying to find out how such an 'otherwise amiable and sensible young man' could be so wrong about the war. I remember vividly insisting that it was all right to call Lindbergh a fool, but not acceptable to conclude that he was a knave if you believed in the presumption of innocence. We parted friends."[178]

An even more important reason, Brewster thought, for the "relative sanity" of the debate at Yale was the fact that "most undergraduate isolationists and interventionists alike were members of a generation which had to be shown and convinced, not just told or herded."[179] Brewster cited with great approval one of McGeorge Bundy's statements on undergraduate war opinion: "A man who has the propaganda bug," Bundy wrote, "will not listen to any arguments at all until you can convince him of your good faith and of his obligation at least to listen to you. A man without faith cannot be told straight out that it is worth while to make sacrifices for this, that or the other ideal; he must first be convinced that idealism exists as something more than a term of reproach."[180] The fact that Bundy's conclusions were completely opposed to Brewster's did not impair their friendship or prevent either man from appreciating the other's arguments.

The gentlemanly, intellectual aspects of the student movement at Yale were rather quickly submerged when the AFC went national. The image of the AFC that has led subsequent observers to label it a Nazi organization dates from the period when it had become a far more populist movement— quite unlike the interventionist movement, which retained its elite leadership throughout.[181] One wonders whether this illustration of the potential dangers of populism may have been one of the lessons that future policy makers learned from the battle over interventionism.

BOTH BREWSTER AND Bundy understood that the high-blown Victorian romanticism about war was dead. Much of what Americans had believed about themselves before the depression was also beyond recovery. What, then, was left to believe in? The issue preoccupied the more philosophical students in both the isolationist and the interventionist camps.

Brewster decided to address his senior thesis to the question. It was a task he kept at throughout his work with America First; as he wrote to Stuart in the summer of his junior year, "I'm getting panicky about my Senior thesis which is supposed to be first drafted by the time college opens. I even gave up the Nantucket Regatta, so you can see that all is not horseplay."[182] Brewster was as troubled as Bundy that America lacked a faith worth fighting for. He poured his worries and his search for inspiration into his essay on the English neo-Idealist philosopher Bernard Bosanquet (1848–1927). "The crying need with which I am concerned here," he wrote, "is the need for a *rationale* on which to organize," some purpose for individuals and society, and "some end for the state other than power *per se*."[183] This was all the more important in "such times as these, when the bottom seems to have fallen out of society, when we seem to be waiting for a new world to be born."[184]

Brewster did not come up with any grand synthesis, but he did expend a great deal of effort in thinking about freedom, opportunity, and community, concepts that he would continue to puzzle over throughout his career. Bosanquet's attempts to find a middle path between liberty and community, the individual and society, moral absolutism and philosophical uncertainty prefigured similar efforts of thinkers after World War II. In later years, Brewster recalled that he arrived at his definition of freedom "as a

Yale undergraduate when I wrote a senior thesis on the political philosophy of an obscure British philosopher, Bernard Bosanquet. I remember his suggesting that freedom was the product of capacity times opportunity. It means simply that you are not free to play the piano, even though you have one, if you don't know how to play it. It also means that even if you know how to play the piano, you are not free to play it if you don't have one."[185]

By the latter half of his senior year, Brewster was no longer a member of the AFC. He officially resigned from the committee in the spring of 1941, after the passage of the Lend-Lease Act. "I still believe it outrageous to commit this country to the outcome of the war abroad and wish to limit that commitment as much as possible," he wrote to Stuart, but "the question from now on is not one of principle it is one of military strategy and administrative policy." Since Lend-Lease had become law, "there seems to me no room for an avowed pressure group huing [*sic*] a dogmatic line. Whether we like it or not America has decided what its ends are, and the question of means is no longer a legislative matter. A national pressure group therefore is not aiming to determine policy, it is seeking to obstruct it. I cannot be a part of that effort."[186]

The bombing of Pearl Harbor did not settle the great debate so much as make it moot. The underlying question of the America First movement had been whether the president could commit an unwilling nation to foreign wars if the United States was not attacked. In the wake of Pearl Harbor, virtually all of Yale's former America Firsters enlisted en masse and fought with bravery and distinction, which helped to obscure what the debate before Pearl Harbor was all about. The country forgot about dissent among mainstream students at elite universities like Yale in the 1940s. The rise of activism and dissent in the universities in the 1960s, following as it did the era of the "silent generation," was seen as a strange phenomenon. In a longer historical view, however, student dissent in the 1960s looked more like a return to form. The shopworn, invidious comparison between the patriotic Ivy Leaguers who served in World War II and the shirkers of the Vietnam era overlooks the widespread resistance of undergraduates—especially the more privileged, progressive undergraduates—to entry into the Second World War and the outrage their dissent provoked.[187]

The issues posed by the intervention question presented Brewster with a set of moral conundrums that he puzzled over for much of the rest of his career. On the one hand, the young activists in the AFC were more in tune with national popular opinion than were the older members of the Anglophile elite. Until Pearl Harbor, some seventy to eighty percent of

Americans opposed participation in World War II. The distance of the elite from the people was evident in the out-of-touch pronouncements of Harvard's William Yandell Elliot, who declared that he had found the battlefields of the Great War to be not much worse than the traffic in Harvard Square.[188] And yet in the cold light of moral analysis that followed the war and revelations of the Holocaust, the elite had been right and the young AFC progressives wrong. No one with any moral decency could any longer write, as one *Yale Daily News* editor did in 1939, that "in the present war, as in all wars, there is no preponderance of good and bad on either side."[189] How did the chastening experience of having been on the wrong side of a defining moral issue affect Brewster? Did it help correct his youthful tendencies to arrogance and pretension? Probably Brewster himself would not have been able to say for sure. Still, the adult Brewster's ironic view of himself may well have been born of early knowledge of his own fallibility.

Even weighty thoughts of impending war did not make for undergraduate doom and gloom. Toward the end of senior year, after Brewster had concluded his highly successful *News* chairmanship, he went to celebrate at Mory's, the famed Yale tavern. Returning to his room from the evening's revelry, he lit a cigarette, passed out, and woke to find the living room couch on fire. He threw open the windows of the suite, stepped out onto the balcony, and began to mimic a speech by Mussolini, haranguing the crowd in the courtyard below as the flames leaped behind him. Cooler heads called the fire department, which extinguished the blaze, but the room was badly damaged by smoke. Nonetheless, the only outcome for Brewster was that he and Jackson had to move to a new suite, and Brewster briefly acquired the nickname Fireball.[190] At graduation, Brewster graduated cum laude and was awarded the prize for the best senior essay in history. In a semiserious poll of his class, Brewster was judged to have "done the most for Yale."[191]

In an address to the alumni in his senior year, Brewster declared: "The hotter and more intolerant the atmosphere becomes, the more certainly must the universities serve truth and the free conflict of ideas, no matter how uncomfortable that may be. While preserving the culture of the past which makes men civilized, Yale must provide greater ground for the cultivation of new political, social and economic thought and techniques."[192] By June 1941, when he delivered the Class Oration at the Class Day ceremonies, Brewster was resigned to the inevitability of American (and his own) participation in the war, yet he called upon his classmates "to be at peace with the universe though at war with the world."[193] The men of

Brewster's circle emerged from college with what Bill Bundy called "our profound conviction that educated men should be the practical, intellectual, and spiritual leaders of a democratic state."[194] The war and the postwar years would allow Brewster and his peers to put some of their leadership ideals into action.

3

THE LEADERS OF
THE GI GENERATION IN WAR
AND PEACE

THE EXPERIENCES of World War II and the changes that accompanied it transformed the members of the liberal establishment, at the same time that it altered the institutions and the society of which they were a part. Willingly or unwillingly, they went to war and returned as heroes, junior officers with new ideas about the world and their part in it.

Kingman Brewster intended to study law at Harvard after graduation, but the likelihood of war led him to defer entrance. Instead Brewster spent the summer of 1941 as a participant in the inaugural session of the Association of Committees for Inter-American Placement. The ACIP was intended to train young college graduates to be well-informed and culturally sensitive representatives in Central and South America. It grew out of an understanding of the greater importance of South America as war severed normal relations between the United States and Europe, as well as of the interest of both pro- and anti-interventionists in strengthening Western Hemisphere ties and countering Nazi and Fascist activities south of the border.

Williams College provided the facilities for the program, and Jacob Javits (later a prominent liberal Republican senator from New York) provided funding.[1] Brewster knew little about Central or South America and did not speak Spanish or Portuguese, but as *Yale Daily News* chairman he had campaigned for a department of South American studies. Such a department, he editorialized, would broaden the curriculum, emphasize the needs of hemispheric defense, counter Nazi influence, enlighten Yanquís about the southern continent's cultural and political importance, and stimulate Yale men to seek their careers in South America.[2] Perhaps he was also influenced by his friend McGeorge Bundy, who spent the year after graduation traveling through Latin America. Bundy, too, had expected to go to Harvard Law School after study in England. He went south instead "because you couldn't go to Europe in the year 1940–41; the *Wanderjahr* or the fellowship to Oxbridge were not options."[3] Bundy served as a cultural ambassador of sorts, a volunteer for a State Department project to promote a positive image of the Colossus of the North by distributing books on American culture and literature through the United States embassies.[4]

Brewster was one of seventeen students from across the country selected for the first ACIP session, at Williamstown, Massachusetts, beginning in June 1941. For six weeks the students were housed, along with their instructors, in the Delta Phi fraternity house, receiving an intensive, all-expenses-paid course in the languages, history, culture, politics, economy, and geography of Latin America. Business executives, government officials, economists, editors, artists, and musicians from the other American republics also conducted seminars and discussions to give the group a well-rounded understanding of South America.[5] The students attended classes all day, heard lectures and occasional concerts at night, and took their meals with their instructors. After the session concluded, Brewster shared an apartment in Washington with another ACIP alumnus, Nebraska native Frank Norall, and several other participants in the program stayed in their guest room. The bombing of Pearl Harbor interrupted planning for ACIP's second summer, and the first session turned out to be the last.

In a personal statement prepared midway through the ACIP session, Brewster described himself as "personally conservative, intellectually independent." He wrote that the European war, "combined with the inevitable come down which faces a campus 'big shot' upon leaving his little collegiate empire," had unsettled his basic assumptions and aspirations. Amid the uncertainty, however, he clung to his core principles: a respect for reason, intellectual honesty, "freedom to fulfill the best in you," and respect for "the value of human beings simply because they are human beings, quite above their usefulness or wealth." He was interested in public affairs "because it is here, I feel, that the fate of these principles will be decided. To me this does not mean 'going into politics.' At this stage of the game my career intention is in the field of opinion, anywhere from teaching to radio work. I definitely do not want to be a pedagogue."[6]

Later that summer, Brewster started his first job, working in Washington for the Office of the Coordinator of Inter-American Affairs under Nelson Rockefeller. Like the ACIP, the CIAA existed to foster understanding between North and South America and to combat German and Italian influence in the Western Hemisphere. The CIAA oversaw all aspects of United States–Latin American relations, including cultural exchange, financial and technical assistance, trade negotiations, health, education, and communications.[7] The year before, Brewster had editorialized that "so complete is the general blackout on knowledge of Latin affairs that Nelson Rockefeller, whose chief qualifications consist merely in his experience with Venezuelan oil wells, is the only outstanding authority the State Department could locate to coordinate our relations with South America. No wonder the 'Good Neighbor' policy frequently stalls and breaks down."[8] Perhaps Brewster's experience at the CIAA improved his opinion of Rockefeller, although he had little contact with him or other high-level CIAA officials such as Paul Nitze and John Hay Whitney.[9] Brewster's immediate superior was Carl Spaeth, who had graduated from Dartmouth a year before Rockefeller and had taught at the Yale Law School when Brewster was an undergraduate.

Frank Norall, who also went to work at the CIAA, recalled that Brewster's father once came to visit their "very grungy, shabby bachelor's apartment" and was "appalled." One can only imagine the reaction of Brewster Sr. if he had found out that one of his son's roommates was a card-carrying Bolivian Communist named Jose Antonio Arce, another participant in the ACIP session and a fellow CIAA employee. Arce's Communist affiliation was hardly a secret; he "wore it on both sleeves," according to Norall.[10] Arce would spend late nights in the kitchen with a mimeograph machine, cranking out manifestos in Spanish urging the Latin American proletariat to rebel. Brewster and his friends were less than alarmed by these activities. Arce was charming, eccentric, and "slightly crazy," with a knack for getting into scrapes; Brewster liked to imitate his broken English and excited gesticulations.[11] He thought Arce's presence on Rockefeller's payroll was more an amusing contradiction than a subversive threat. Brewster and his friends believed that the revolutionary potential of Arce's leaflets and his radio broadcasts in the Quechuan language was nonexistent.

While Brewster focused his attention on Latin America, the impending war with Germany escalated. By the fall of 1941, the United States had established a military presence in Iceland, American destroyers were escorting British convoys across the Atlantic, and, after German submarines attacked U.S. destroyers in October, Congress dismantled the last of the 1930s neutrality legislation.

In October, when Brewster returned to New Haven for the Yale–Dartmouth weekend, however, the autumn round of classes and extracurricular activities seemed to be continuing at its usual pace. On Sunday after the football game, Brewster met a Vassar junior, Mary Louise Phillips, over milk punch in the Zeta Psi fraternity house. His wife-to-be was an attractive, intelligent, artistic young woman whose sense of the world was an exact fit for his own. In later years, Brewster confided to a friend that "you cannot put the thinnest tissue paper between Mary Louise's views and mine."[12] He detached her from the Yale student she was then dating, and soon he was making regular visits to see her in Poughkeepsie. Phillips had grown up in Providence, Rhode Island, and graduated from Miss Wheeler's School in 1939. Her family was reasonably affluent and respectable in Providence society. Her father, Eugene James Phillips, a Yale College and Yale Law School graduate, had been an attorney for the New York, New Haven and Hartford Railroad for many years before joining a prominent Providence law firm in 1935.[13]

McGeorge Bundy came to visit Brewster in Washington, where his father had been working since the spring as special assistant to secretary of war Henry Stimson, to whom Harvey Bundy had also been an assistant when Stimson was secretary of state under Hoover. Stimson, the establishment's grand old man of public service, by then in his seventies, had been called back into office by Roosevelt as the ultimate symbol of bipartisanship. By this time Mac Bundy had decided not to go to Harvard Law School and had rejected an editor's position at the *Atlantic Monthly*. Instead he joined Harvard's Society of Fellows, a special program founded by his great-uncle A. Lawrence Lowell in imitation of Oxford's All Souls College. The fellowship selected between six and eight talented men each year for three-year terms and provided them with a stipend and room and board in Lowell House. As in the British university system, the program allowed a few highly talented people—the sort who would graduate from Oxford or Cambridge with undergraduate "First" degrees—to bypass what William James called "the Ph.D. octopus" and proceed straight to academic positions, without further credentials or departmental supervision. The senior fellow who had interviewed Bundy was Elliot Richardson's uncle Henry Shattuck, an old family friend. Bundy was selected as a junior fellow and took his place at the society's Monday night dinners, where the brightest lights of Cambridge held forth in oak-paneled splendor, and sherry was served on the very breakfast table over which Oliver Wendell Holmes had been self-proclaimed autocrat.[14]

Shattuck had been interested to hear Bundy say that he wished to study not only Plato but also "the theory and practice of politics," and in the fall of 1941 he recruited Bundy to run to succeed him in his seat on the Boston City Council. Shattuck had previously groomed Christian Herter (later secretary of state under Eisenhower) for politics, and the Back Bay district in which Bundy campaigned was considered to be safe Republican territory. Bundy did little door-to-door campaigning, refused to buy ads in a local newsletter, and lost by ninety-two votes to a Democrat who came from the "wrong" side of Beacon Hill. Years later, he wrote that "I did not run hard enough or well enough to deserve to win, and . . . from this experience I drew the conclusion—right or wrong—that I was not cut out to be a political campaigner."[15] Elliot Richardson recalled that "Mac didn't do a damned thing in his campaign, and lost. Uncle Henry was disgusted with him; he felt let down by Mac's failure to run harder. I think Mac thought he was so superior that people would be tickled to pieces that he had deigned to run at all."[16]

PAUL MOORE HAD graduated from Yale with Brewster in June 1941. At the Yale–Harvard boat races that were part of the celebrations, he and his friends were described by a gossip columnist as "the golden youth of American society, rich boys, who threw beer cans at the townspeople." Moore spent the rest of the summer partying at his family's camp in the Adirondacks and summer mansion on the North Shore. While still in college, Moore and his friend George Mead—another one of the class's big men, the football team manager and a close friend of Jack Kennedy—had enlisted in the Marines. In November, after buying their boots at Abercrombie and Fitch and with golf clubs in tow, they arrived at Quantico for the Marines' officer training corps. A month later, Moore went home for his first weekend leave, and on Sunday afternoon, December 7, he was sitting in the living room of his parents' home in New Jersey, drinking martinis. The family's English butler appeared in the doorway and said to Moore's mother, "Excuse me, madam, but I thought you should know that the Japanese have just bombed Pearl Harbor."[17]

While the Japanese attack was still in progress, an operative for British and American intelligence drew up a list of Americans who were suspected recipients of Nazi funds. One of those names was Kingman Brewster Jr., identified as a leader of the America First Committee.[18] The charge was baseless, as Brewster had always opposed the Nazis, was no longer even a member of the AFC, and enlisted promptly after the assault on Pearl Harbor. But the episode underscored just how much the America Firsters' opponents questioned their patriotism. Virtually all of Yale's America Firsters enlisted after December 7, although some of the school's pacifists (including David Dellinger) would spend the war in jail for their beliefs.

Once he had decided that war was inevitable, Brewster spent a good deal of time talking with his friends about what would be the best conditions under which to serve. He preferred to be an aviator, because of his long-standing love of flying, and, as his Yale classmate Wallace Campbell put it, "we didn't want to be slogging around in the mud; we would rather be glamorous guys wearing wings." Brewster and Campbell also agreed that it would be best to end up in a branch of service where death would come "all at once and completely, rather than something that more likely was going to be painful and gruesome."[19]

To be near Mary Louise at Vassar, Brewster declared a fictitious residence in Scarsdale, New York, thus shifting from the first to the third Naval District. He was told that it would be months before he was called up, but since he was impatient to get into flight training, he asked whether he could join the Yale Naval Unit Number Three, which was soon to be inducted. He was put on the unit's list as a substitute in case any of its members dropped out before induction, and one did. "Thanks to this anonymous benefactor," Brewster was pleased to recall, "I happily avoided the pre-flight and pre-pre-flight training which were to afflict later classes and which I probably would not have survived."[20]

The second and third Yale aviation units of World War II echoed the original Yale Flying Unit, formed before World War I, largely at the initiative of undergraduates F. Trubee Davison and Robert Lovett (who would become secretary of defense). The first Yale unit was a cavalier outfit of young, upper-class interventionists. Lavishly financed by Davison's investment banker father, the group was dubbed "the millionaires' unit," much as the Plattsburgh military training encampment for well-heeled young preparedness advocates was "the millionaires' camp."[21] The second and third Yale units were not cast in the same romantic upper-class mold. They were merely recruiting devices to attract Yale students to Naval Aviation before Pearl Harbor made incentives to enlist unnecessary.

In February 1942, the members of Yale Naval Unit Number Three reported for basic training at Floyd Bennett Field in Brooklyn, then still a commercial airport. The Yale unit consisted of ten men, including Brewster and one other recent graduate, a law student, and seven undergraduates who interrupted their education to go to war.[22] Unlike the original Yale unit, it consisted of men from varied backgrounds, including two Jews. The ten students were outnumbered by the forty men from Fordham University who constituted the rest of their company, which made the Yale affiliation of minor importance. The cadets in the company wore identical uniforms and khaki coverall flight suits, slept in bunk beds in one large dormitory room, took courses in navigation, aerodynamics, and flight mechanics, and received rudimentary flight training in N3N Steerman biplanes. Most of the group had no previous flight instruction.

Brewster, playing his cards close to the chest, did not reveal to his instructors or fellow trainees that he already had a pilot's license. The other members of the Yale unit thought him an affable, good-humored person, who was not earthy enough to be considered "one of the boys" but was respected as a leader and as "an intense and dedicated student."[23] The cadets held him in high esteem and looked out for him to the point of standing up against their NCOs on one occasion when Brewster was falsely accused of cheating (because his scores were so high).[24]

After six weeks at Floyd Bennett, the Yale unit was sent to the Naval Air Station at Jacksonville, Florida, for advanced flight training. The cadets flew SNJs, more powerful planes than the N3Ns, and practiced navigation, gunnery skills, and aerobatics, supplemented by ground instruction and punctuated by occasional trips to the Inlet, a bar and restaurant at nearby Ponte Vedra. In September 1942, Brewster wrote to Whit Griswold that despite the "intellectual vacuum" and the length and heat of the Florida military day, "I am glad as hell to be where I am [for] I still love the flying and am pleased with my ability to get through it."[25] When the cadets were given the opportunity to specialize in one line of military aviation, Brewster opted to do his operational training in antisubmarine bombers on the multi-engine PBYs. There was considerable demand for antisub bombers at the time, since German U-boats were then wreaking havoc on Allied shipping in the Atlantic and had even landed at several points along the East Coast, including Ponte Vedra.[26]

Shortly after Brewster received his ensign's commission, he and Mary Louise Phillips were married in a Jacksonville hotel room by a Navy chaplain in a nondenominational service on November 30, 1942. Both of Brewster's parents (and Mary Louise's) were in attendance, and the rest of the party was composed of Navy friends. "I can think of no one," Brewster wrote to Whit and Mary Griswold afterward, "whose matrimonial state gave me more strength than did you two for that trembling waddle to the altar. . . . I'm an obnoxiously happy man."[27]

The Brewsters' marriage was traditional in that Mary Louise's first priority was and would continue to be her husband, and she was dedicated to him and his career. (McGeorge Bundy would speculate that his mother and other women of her generation gave the balance of their attention to their children, "while our own wives have weighed the scales toward us; so we have won both ways."[28]) She left Vassar during her senior year and followed Kingman to the various naval air bases where he was posted. Theirs was to be an extraordinarily close and supportive union. Their friend John Blum recalled seeing Kingman and Mary Louise, arms around each other's waists, on a bluff looking over the ocean one night after a party on Martha's Vineyard: "Observing them from ten paces back, you simply knew that this was a couple involved in an incomparable marriage. You just felt the wonder of these two in that moment in the moonlight overlooking the Atlantic."[29]

As an antisubmarine patrol bomber in Flight Squadron VPB-129, Brewster was hardly in the most combat-intensive branch of the military. During his service on the East Coast and in Brazil, he never actually saw an enemy submarine. As he wrote to Whit Griswold from North Carolina in 1944, "The Navy function which we perform is too little and much too late. Time was when the Nazis roamed off Hatteras at will, but we have only a memory to hold down as we boldly sail forth over the untroubled waters of the Western Atlantic in our 'medium bombers.' Better called tedium bombers."[30]

Frustrated at not seeing more action, Brewster trained to transfer to carrier-based night-flying bombers, one of the most hazardous forms of military aviation. Flying an airplane in wartime in any capacity was an inherently dangerous activity. Brewster later made a jocular confession to a member of his flight squadron that he was "the same Kingman Brewster who damned near left you stuck in the sand by a late pull-up on a Maine coast rocket range; who damned near croaked when the down wing engine sputtered while banking over Brunswick."[31] Four of the ten members of the Yale Naval Unit Number Three died in plane crashes, none of them in combat.[32]

Brewster recalled that his experience in the Navy air corps "was for me as for almost everyone an exposure to types, and styles, and values and beliefs of all kinds, mostly in contrast to my sheltered own."[33] Until they went to war in their early twenties, Brewster and his peers had spent their lives in the distinctive milieu of the northeastern upper class. While the experiences of the depression, the New Deal, and conflict in Europe had motivated Brewster and other young, well-placed progressives to call for change in the American social structure, they were nonetheless a homogeneous, even insulated group. Still, while they were similar to the generation of Yale students who fought in World War I, their military service typically brought them into greater contact with different socioeconomic and ethnic groups than their predecessors (in the original Yale Flying Unit, for example) had experienced.[34]

World War II was what sociologist E. Digby Baltzell called "the most leveling and homogenizing war in our history."[35] The imperative of victory set a higher value on intelligence and ability than on family background. The need for national unity and full participation in the war effort stirred egalitarian sentiments. During the war Brewster developed a concrete rather than abstract appreciation of what it meant to depend on men from varied backgrounds. Serving alongside men from different walks of life made him realize that in the crunch, "guts and generosity and cheerfulness" mattered more than "refinement of intellect" or "competitive aggressiveness" or other qualities cultivated at places like Yale.[36] His friend Doc Howe, who was captain of a minesweeper, learned that "leadership works best and your crew will perform better if everyone knows why they're being asked to do things and not when they're told, 'Just do it. Don't ask questions. I'm the boss.'"[37] Brewster also became convinced that his class had to emerge from its self-absorption. While still in service, he gave a speech on the sense of "mutual reliance" that grew out of the war: "there has been nothing in our experience to make us believe that reliability is the monopoly of any one group or class or race. . . . There is no solution for one apart from the destiny of all. We may want to go our own way in peace alone, in the company of our own choosing, but we are in the company of all America."[38]

PAUL MOORE WAS among the first Marines to reach the South Pacific, in 1942. He led a platoon in horrific fighting on Guadalcanal, at the Battle of Bloody Ridge and other engagements, before he was shot through the chest in November. The bullet missed his spine by two inches, and he survived because his heart was on the "in beat" when the bullet hit. Awarded the Navy Cross, Silver Star, and Purple Heart, he returned to Guam as a company commander. Moore did not romanticize his military service. The war for him "was mostly boredom in faraway places," and some of his most vivid memories were of "the humiliation of corporate living, corporate eating, corporate crapping, [and] being screamed at by sergeants." For many young people, part of the experience was also "getting married to a virtual stranger in a hurry," although Moore had gotten to know his wartime bride, Jenny McKean, during a summer on the North Shore.[39] Still, for Moore as for Brewster, "the war was the most formative experience of my adult life. Finally I broke out of the sheltered world of privilege and met men from other places, men with other ways of thinking, speaking, and acting."[40]

For Richardson, who was more aware of America's class structure than most of his peers, war service was a sort of expiation of class guilt. In the summer of 1941, after graduating from Harvard, he took the most grueling working-class job he could find, welding steel spools and socket wrenches for twelve hours on end. At night he drew cartoons for the newspaper of a CIO union of shipbuilders. In the fall he enrolled in Harvard Law School. "I tried to get into all manner of military activities after Pearl Harbor was bombed," he recalled, "but my eyes kept defeating me, which is how I finished my first year of law school." He was rejected for service in the Office of Strategic Services (the precursor of the CIA) and on Harry Truman's investigating staff: "I suspect that my left-leaning views were held against me."

Finally Richardson memorized the eye chart and became commander of a platoon of stretcher bearers in the Twelfth Infantry Regiment of the Army's Fourth Infantry Division. "I'm probably one of the few people you'll run into who liked being in combat," he said, in large part because it freed him from his sheltered upbringing. "I do not like being thought of as this aristocratic Boston Brahmin, regardless of my background. That attitude was greatly reinforced by my going through basic training and being a platoon leader." No one was likely to mistake Richardson for a regular grunt; his constant companion on the battlefields was *The Mind and Faith of Justice Holmes.* Nonetheless, he and the men in his platoon, who "came from a great variety of backgrounds, circumstances and levels of education," became "very close. I didn't think I was any better than they were." When his platoon prepared to take part in the Normandy invasion at Utah Beach on June 6, 1944, "I thought I was going to get killed or at least badly wounded, and became quite reconciled to the idea, partly because I thought, 'Well, if these guys can get killed, I can get killed.'"[41]

Richardson was twice wounded in the Normandy landing and earned a Bronze Star and a Purple Heart with Oak Leaf cluster for crossing a minefield to rescue a soldier. Following D-day, Richardson's regiment endured seventy days of near-constant fighting. He was the first American soldier to reenter Cherbourg, and in the course of holding off three Panzer divisions, his regiment suffered a casualty rate of almost two hundred percent. As a result, it was chosen to be the first American unit to liberate Paris. On August 25, 1944, Richardson and his men entered the city from the south, their route thronged with the cheering French, who threw flowers in their path and cried, "Les Americains, les Americains!" In a photo taken that day in the Bois de Vincennes, Richardson sits on the hood of a jeep, a carnation in his collar and a small fox terrier on his lap, in front of a crowd of joyful Parisians. "By the end of that day," he remembered, "for the first and only time in my life, my face ached from smiling."[42] He was preparing to go to Japan when the atom bomb was dropped. "I must have been just about the only one in the division who was deep-down disappointed that we weren't going to be in the second invasion."[43]

While Richardson hit the beach on D-day, McGeorge Bundy was watching the landing from a heavy cruiser twelve miles offshore, along with the command staff of the operation. Bundy, too, had struggled with his draft board over his poor eyesight. For a time he worked with his brother Bill in the Office of Facts and Figures in Washington, with Bundy family friend Archibald MacLeish, but Mac eventually gained admission to the armed forces as Richardson had, by memorizing the eye chart. In the spring of 1943, Bundy became an aide to Rear Admiral Alan Kirk, another old family friend. His main responsibility was to decipher German intercepts received through the Allied's Ultra cryptographic operation at Bletchley, England, where Bill Bundy was the commander of a contingent of code breakers. Mac joined Kirk for the invasion of Sicily and then to England for the planning of Operation Overlord. On June 6, 1944, he watched with Kirk, General Omar Bradley, and other top brass as the hundreds of amphibious ships struggled toward the Normandy shore.

Bundy was not vain about his wartime role. He wrote to one of his fellow officers that "a part of the operation, we surely were, and we have a right to be proud of it, but in larger terms . . . you cannot but admit that the war belongs to Ernie Pyle's men more than ours."[44] He recalled that "I always was jealous of those of my friends whose physical condition had given them that kind of active role. [Brewster] may have thought, 'There's Bundy in London or in Paris, watching the political side of the war and I'm not.' While I would have felt the other way around. We never talked about it."[45] Bundy's role offered him less of the democratic experience of mingling with men from different backgrounds. On the other hand, he was in a position to see that the war was won not only by soldiers' sacrifices but by trained intelligence, scientific expertise, technology, and massive federal intervention. These developments would have a huge impact on American life and would shape the destinies of Bundy and Brewster and the institutional communities to which they belonged, particularly the universities.

Before the war, for example, Bundy had met the economist Edward Mason at Harvard through the Society of Fellows. Mason had taken part in the New Deal as a consultant for the Labor Department, and followed his Harvard colleague William Langer to the division of research and analysis of the OSS, where he became chief economist. He went to London to form the Enemy Objective Unit of the combined Allied Air Forces, informally known as the Jockey Committee. The group's economic analyses of German industrial production determined target selection for the Eighth Air Force bombing raids. Mason recruited a group of bright young men to assist him in this task, including recent college graduate Carl Kaysen, who crossed paths with Bundy in London and later would serve as his assistant in the White House. "It was a dedicated and passionate group," Kaysen remembered. "We were kids, captains and majors, telling the whole world what to do."[46] The war-born excitement and the application of intellect in confronting the nation's problems would influence a generation of academics and policy makers.

BREWSTER FOUND IT difficult to talk directly about his war experiences, as his emotional reticence got in the way. When a cousin returned to the States after two years in a German prison camp, Brewster wrote him a letter in which he vaguely apologized for not having written sooner, made no mention of his cousin's ordeal, and then launched into a numbingly detailed exposition of American politics. Nonetheless, he knew that personal loss was one of the common ties that bound the war's survivors. He later commented that everyone in his generation shared the feeling of "bottomless emptiness upon hearing that someone he cared terribly for was no longer alive."[47] Twenty-eight of his Yale classmates died in military service, including his friend (and Paul Moore's fellow Marine officer) George Mead Jr.

The obvious question, as Brewster saw it, was what the survivors could do to justify their comrades' sacrifice. The returning servicemen, he wrote to his cousin, would represent the greatest common-denominator group in the country. "Their experience, their hopes, and finally their demands will undoubtedly shape the collective fortune of the country."[48] And they had the opportunity to create a new global order. Brewster declared that "this generation does not inherit the world of its fathers, it inherits a world made by its own fighting and building. . . . The responsibility for the future is ours. . . . Wanted or not, for this generation of Americans a coincidence of time and circumstances makes their best years fall in the zenith of American power and potential."[49]

FOR BREWSTER AND many of his peers, the path toward public service would lead through the universities. Brewster took up his war-deferred studies at the Harvard Law School, as did Elliot Richardson and William Bundy, while McGeorge Bundy returned to the Harvard Society of Fellows. Harvard had been changed considerably by the war. Through the Society of Fellows, Mac Bundy had met Harvard president James Conant, who together with MIT vice president Vannevar Bush was largely responsible for restructuring the universities' relationship to the government. Through the Office of Scientific Research and Development, Conant and Bush had organized wartime scientific effort, coordinating the research subcontracted to universities with production at large corporations like General Electric and Du Pont. The two largest OSRD initiatives were the Radiation Laboratory at MIT and the Manhattan Project, which resulted in radar and the atomic bomb. (Harvey Bundy, McGeorge's father, was Henry Stimson's personal representative to the OSRD and thus one of the government officials best informed about the atomic bomb.) At war's end, Conant helped create the network of government agencies that channeled vast funds to the leading universities to support research—predominantly in projects with obvious defense applications, but in the social sciences as well.

In his wartime letters to Whit Griswold, Brewster had expressed an interest in teaching, although he worried that "so damned much of the time of life will be passed by the time I would get a PhD after emerging from the war that I would be pretty well along even at the start of a teaching career." He asked Griswold whether the postwar universities would find room for "teachers from experience and technique rather than the book," a question he would pose again as Yale president.[50] Brewster later asked Griswold about the possibility of working part-time in Yale's programs of education and readjustment for former servicemen, while "pursu[ing] my own academic interests in the field of public affairs." Such a position, he thought, would allow him to crystallize "my interests in either teaching, journalism, or opinionating."[51]

Brewster's former CIAA boss, Carl Spaeth, urged him to go to a major law school, telling him, "You'll find yourself in the company of people who play a significant role in things."[52] Brewster would observe that he had gone to law school "for defensive reasons. I knew I was interested in public affairs. I thought I might be a politician or a journalist, but I felt that whatever I did, I would be at a disadvantage if I didn't know what the lawyers were talking about."[53] In hindsight, Brewster felt that his ability to approach law school with this sort of freedom rose from his privileged background: "Above a self-respecting minimum, how I did in school didn't really prejudice my chances of getting into college. What I did in college didn't really affect my chances of getting into graduate school. . . . Four years of flying for the Navy was safe in career terms if in no other terms, for the simple reason that there was nothing else to do which would be any closer to where I might want eventually to end up. So, on to law school, not to become a lawyer but because it seemed like the best way of scraping the rust off the intellectual wheels and to move forward without burning any bridges. So I arrived at the ripe age of thirty still uncommitted, as the saying would now go, career-wise. At at least four different junctures I had the illusion of being able to choose what to do next without having to choose what I would be when I grew up."[54]

William Sloane Coffin Jr., who returned to Yale after war service, observed that "the war was in a way a sort of *Wanderjahr*. It was an opportunity to collect your thoughts, to figure out what you really thought and felt and believed. The war played that sort of role for many of us. Many people changed their ways, and a lot of people decided that they didn't want to do what they had been expected to do before the war."[55]

Paul Moore, for example, was destined for work in the family businesses after graduation. When his brother had graduated from Yale before the war, their father bought a nearby dish-towel manufacturing plant so that his offspring could have the grim but instructive experience of working their way up from the factory floor before going on to Banker's Trust. Moore's near-death in the war, however, strengthened his conviction that he wanted a more meaningful existence. He decided to become an Episcopalian priest. Such was his undergraduate socialite reputation that when he returned to Yale in 1946 for his fifth-year reunion, his classmates were shocked to hear that he planned to study for the ministry. One classmate put his hand on Moore's shoulder and said with great sympathy, "Gee, Paul, I didn't know you had that hard a time in the war."[56] But since the war, Moore once said, "I have felt like I've been living on borrowed time, and perhaps owe the world a little extra."[57] His father, who was adamantly opposed to his becoming a priest, suggested that he take up the ministry as a hobby after he had established himself in a real career. But the war had given Moore the resolution he needed to stand up to his father, and he enrolled at General Theological Seminary, in New York City, after taking graduate courses in history at Columbia University.

John Lindsay had also been deeply affected by the war. Entering Yale with the Class of 1944, he had been in the audience in the fall of 1940 when Kingman Brewster and the other big men in the senior class bestrode the Woolsey Hall stage to tell the freshmen the facts of Yale life. As president of his class at the St. Paul's School, Lindsay came to college with a reputation and wide range of firmly established friendships; he had been supervised by Paul Moore and his friends at prep school and he followed Moore as a counselor at the school's summer camp for underprivileged boys. Lindsay was a social success at Yale; he had what one of his roommates called "a great attraction for a considerable portion of the feminine population of the Eastern seaboard."[58] He ascended to BMOC status through extracurricular associations like the Political Union, the Elizabethan Club, the crew team, the Fence Club, and Scroll and Key, but his undergraduate existence was cut short midway through his sophomore year on December 7, 1941. He accelerated his studies to graduate a year early. (Like Brewster, his most important intellectual experience at college was writing his senior history essay, on Oliver Cromwell.) Lindsay entered the Navy in May 1943, serving as a destroyer gunnery officer in the Mediterranean and Pacific theaters.

"The war had a lot to do with my eventual decision to go into public service," Lindsay recalled. "I lost a barrel of friends. One of my roommates was killed, and one of my closest friends was among the initial casualties at Guadalcanal. Twenty percent of my class at St. Paul's was wiped out. I felt something had to be done to make sure it wouldn't happen again."[59] After his discharge, in May 1946, he enrolled at Yale Law School to prepare himself for public service.

The universities to which Brewster and his friends returned as graduate students were crammed with returning servicemen. The war had affected veterans' perceptions of themselves and their path in American life. Military training and combat overseas lessened the nation's insularity and helped assimilate individuals who had been isolated from the mainstream because of poverty or ethnicity. Exposure to a broader world led many GIs to reconsider the importance of education and emboldened them to seek avenues of upward mobility. Participation in the shared sacrifices of war provided veterans with the opportunity to meet their increased expectations. The 1944 Serviceman's Readjustment Act, better known as the GI Bill of Rights, offered every demobilized member of the armed services free or subsidized education at the undergraduate, graduate, or professional level, and some 2.2 million veterans (nearly all men) went to colleges and universities under the program.[60] The GI Bill allowed many men to attend college who would not have done so before the war, and many who were not part of the traditional constituencies of the elite universities suddenly wanted in.[61] With tuition paid by the government, as *Time* magazine asked in 1946, "why go to Podunk College when the Government will send you to Yale?"[62]

The elite universities did not want to open their gates to this tide. Many of the applicants were older, from nonnative stock, educated in high schools rather than prep schools, and more likely to be married and have children. Harvard's president, James Conant, worried that the GI Bill did not "distinguish between those who can profit most by advanced education and those who cannot," while Robert Maynard Hutchins, at the University of Chicago, predicted that "colleges and universities will find themselves converted into educational hobo jungles."[63] But it would have been indecent and un-American to refuse admission to the nation's returning heroes because of their race, religion, or class background, particularly after a war against Hitler's "master race."

Revisionist historians are correct to point out that the wartime spirit of democratic, national unity was largely a myth and that racism and anti-Semitism persisted during and after the war.[64] But there was, at least, a wave of egalitarian sentiment, which conditioned what the public expected of American institutions. Revulsion over the Holocaust made it impossible for elite universities to justify an explicit policy of anti-Semitism, even to themselves. And so postwar Harvard admitted transfer student Henry Kissinger, for example, from the City College of New York, where he had planned to study accounting. At Harvard, he would mingle with *Mayflower* descendants such as Kingman Brewster and Brahmins like McGeorge Bundy.

The influx of veterans shattered enrollment records and democratized the social tone, especially at the more traditional schools. Students doubled up in dorm rooms, took up abode in the gym and other improvised housing, or moved into Quonset and Nissen huts. The veterans had little time for the rituals and extracurricular activities that had once defined the college experience. Men who had stormed Japanese machine gun-nests could not be compelled to wear freshman beanies or participate in demeaning fraternity shenanigans.[65] The veterans also had little patience for the customary genteel prejudices. Barriers at Yale toppled as Jews, Catholics, and blacks won campus offices and social honors, most dramatically so in 1949 when Skull and Bones tapped both a Jew and an African-American.[66]

Returning servicemembers were noted for the seriousness, motivation, and maturity with which they approached their studies, earning higher grades than nonveterans and failing less often. *Newsweek* reported in 1946 that not one of Columbia's 7,826 veterans "was in serious scholastic difficulty at the last marking period."[67] This was a significant statistic, given that up to a third of the classes at Ivy League institutions had left college for academic reasons during the 1930s, while the rate was even higher at the state universities.[68] Many professors thought then (and still think today) that the veterans were the best group of students ever assembled on campus. One professor in the Yale English Department recalled that he and his colleagues were excited to find that the more mature veterans, many of whom were married and had encountered battle, triumph, and loss, "were suddenly people who understood what the great writers were saying. For the first time they had enough experience so that they instantly understood what we were trying to communicate."[69]

PAUL MOORE OBSERVED that many members of his generation shared "a continuing concern for the world we thought we once had saved in World War II."[70] Brewster and his peers were too junior to play a major role in creating the international institutions, from the IMF to the UN, that would provide a structure for much of the postwar world. Even so, several of Brewster's friends assisted delegates at the conferences that created the United Nations, and his roommate William Jackson participated in the Nuremberg trials as an assistant to his father, who was chief prosecutor. Jackson wrote to Brewster that the trials were "an opportunity to do something concrete for world peace by putting teeth in international law, and by making it unhealthy to launch aggressive warfare."[71]

In addition to sharing the belief that the United States should help create a better world order, Brewster and his friends felt an eager anticipation that they would soon be leading the effort. As McGeorge Bundy wrote to one of his Skull and Bones friends, "I begin to think, in a fuzzy and indefinite way, that I know how I want to spend my life. . . . I want to make the world my oyster—in this sense—that no grasp of politics today is valid if it does not comprehend the whole world, and in the next forty odd years there will be no peace nor order that is not built along that strange new path. I'd like to find out what this Interdependence they all talk about really means—what it entails, what its parts are and how they can be geared."[72]

Bundy was not alone in this desire. Many veterans joined groups that advocated progressive, idealistic national and international policies. Brewster took a leading role in two of the most important world government organizations of the time, the American Veterans Committee and the United World Federalists. His shift from isolationism before the war to world federalism was a dramatic reversal, although he had always held strong international interests and concerns.

In October 1945, Brewster attended a conference in Dublin, New Hampshire, to discuss the problems posed by the atomic bomb as well as the possibilities of peace and world organization. Principal sponsors were Supreme Court justice Owen Roberts and Grenville Clark, a prominent New York lawyer who had a summer home in Dublin. Clark, a liberal Republican in the Bull Moose tradition, was another of Brewster's older mentors. An intimate of Theodore Roosevelt, he was an old-stock Yankee, heir to a banking and railroad fortune, and a member of the Harvard Corporation, along with Elliot Richardson's uncle Henry Shattuck. A law partner of Elihu Root, secretary of state under Roosevelt, and of Brewster's step-uncle Arthur Ballantine, Clark was a familiar figure at Kingman's boyhood home in Cambridge.[73] Brewster fondly recalled Clark's "chin to rival Leverett Saltonstall and eyebrows to compete with Learned Hand," and admired his wisdom and tenacity, the puckish humor behind his formidable facade, his pragmatism in the pursuit of lofty goals, and his "capacity for moral outrage and high idealism."[74]

Richardson, another of Clark's protégés, often visited his rambling, book-filled redbrick farmhouse in Dublin, which had been in the family for a hundred and fifty years. There, Richardson noticed a photo of Clark's father, a Victorian patriarch with muttonchop whiskers and a heavy gold watch chain. He remembered that "the elder Clark's face and bearing betrayed no doubt whatever as to the importance of the role he occupied or the ultimate validity of the social order of which he was such an impressive symbol."[75] Grenville Clark, who possessed his father's authority but not his complacency, used his formidable wealth and connections in an effort to improve the world. His friend Felix Frankfurter wrote that Clark was "that rare thing in America, a man of independence, financially and politically, who devotes himself as hard to public affairs as a private citizen as he would if he were in public office."[76]

Clark had helped America prepare for the First World War by persuading Roosevelt to support the Plattsburg Camp, and for the Second by crafting the Selective Service Act and persuading Franklin Roosevelt to appoint Henry Stimson as secretary of war. During the later war, Clark served with McGeorge Bundy's father as an aide to Stimson; he resigned after the Normandy landing, telling the secretary of war that he would devote the rest of his life to peace. Clark liked to say that Stimson then ordered him, "Go home and prevent World War III!"[77]

The conference in Dublin included politicians, scientists, lawyers, financiers, philanthropists, and writers.[78] Among them were Thomas K. Finletter, a future secretary of the Air Force with a hard-nosed belief in the country's air and atomic superiority, and Harvard law professor Louis B. Sohn, with whom Clark would write his famous blueprint for a world constitution, *World Peace through World Law.* Also in attendance were young activists including Brewster, Cord Meyer Jr. (a friend of Brewster's from the Yale Class of 1943), *Saturday Review* editor Norman Cousins, and future senator Alan Cranston. Cousins wrote that Clark had "sprinkled in with the salt a little bit of the pepper of youth, the younger people felt to be among the future leaders of the country." Cousins remembered that John F. Kennedy, still a lieutenant on active duty, came up for a few hours one afternoon.[79]

The younger men were invited largely because they were known for their writing. Cousins's impassioned editorials in the *Saturday Review* had already attracted a select readership, and Alan Cranston had written a much-praised book, *The Killing of the Peace,* about the Senate's battle over the League of Nations. Meyer had come to Yale from St. Paul's School, in the class ahead of Lindsay, and followed the familiar trajectory of other bright, well-connected boys, joining the Elizabethan Club, the Fence Club, and Scroll and Key, and graduating near the head of his class. He was also a talented writer for the college literary magazine. After graduating a year early, he joined the Marines and was grievously wounded in the attack on Guam, in which a grenade blew away half his face and destroyed his left eye. His twin brother, whom a classmate described as "one of the handsomest men who ever walked," was killed in action in Okinawa.[80]

Meyer returned to the States and studied briefly at Yale Law School before transferring to the Harvard Graduate School to take courses in government. In November 1944 he was an usher at Paul Moore's wedding. After serving as an assistant to delegate Harold Stassen at the San Francisco conference at which the United Nations Organization was formalized, he wrote a widely read account of the meeting for the *Atlantic Monthly.*

Brewster later said that "Dublin in the Fall of 1945 was an inspiringly exciting experience. . . . The air was tingling with insistent hope that the awe-full power which had been released might be used to establish a world-wide authority capable of protecting the sovereignty of people everywhere."[81] The conference's declaration, published in its entirety in the *New York Times,* warned of the damaging effects a nuclear arms race would have on traditional American freedoms. Meyer left Dublin "with the conviction that World War III was inevitable, if the U.N. was not substantially strengthened."[82] The Dublin declaration attacked the inadequacy of the UN charter and called for its replacement by "a World Federal Government with limited but definite and adequate powers to prevent war, including power to control the atomic bomb and other major weapons and to maintain world inspection and police forces."[83] Brewster later explained in the *New York Times* that "the great majority of those desiring world government" sought to accomplish their aims by amending and strengthening the existing UN organization rather than rejecting it altogether.[84]

Another young participant at Dublin was Charles G. Bolté, the national chairman of the American Veterans Committee. After graduating from Dartmouth in 1941, Bolté had volunteered with the British King's Royal Rifle Corps and lost a leg at El Alamein. He became one of the early leaders of the AVC, which had been formed by Gilbert Harrison (later editor in chief of *The New Republic*) and four other servicemen in 1943 as a correspondence circle among friends worried about their future in the postwar world.[85]

The AVC, formed exclusively for veterans of World War II, sought to distinguish itself from the American Legion and older veterans groups, not only by avoiding funny hats and ceremonial hocus-pocus but by putting veterans on the side of "a more democratic and prosperous America and a more stable world." The group was open to World War II veterans regardless of race, ethnicity, creed, or gender. Its motto was "Citizens First, Veterans Second."[86] Its 1945 "Statement of Intentions" and subsequent pronouncements called for housing assistance, increased educational allowances under the GI Bill, active involvement of veterans in elections, and a job for every veteran.[87] The AVC opposed racial discrimination in all forms, calling for civil rights and civil liberties reflecting "the kind of America in the kind of world we fought for," and a supranational world government "strong enough to prevent our having new veterans from a new war."[88]

In his first year at Harvard, Brewster formed an AVC chapter with his law school classmate Endicott ("Chub") Peabody, a descendant of a governor of the Massachusetts Bay Colony and a grandson of the Reverend Endicott Peabody, the founder and for fifty-six years the headmaster of Groton School. A former football all-American, he had been a year behind McGeorge Bundy at Groton and a classmate of Richardson's at Harvard.[89]

The AVC chapter, which Brewster chaired, originally consisted only of Harvard and MIT students, but ultimately opened itself to all Cambridge residents. The chapter's officers included, besides Brewster and Peabody, Cord Meyer (who followed McGeorge Bundy into the Harvard Society of Fellows) and Deborah Solbert (the wife of Brewster's Yale and Harvard law classmate Peter Solbert).[90] Nationally, AVC members included Bill Mauldin, Ronald Reagan, Franklin D. Roosevelt Jr., Harold Stassen, John Hay Whitney, and William Sloane Coffin Jr., who was head of Yale's chapter.[91]

Although the AVC numbered tens of thousands of members at its zenith, it was not able to expand much beyond its base of "East Coast college intellectuals" and upper-class progressives.[92] John Blum remembered that he "found the atmosphere a little too muscular-Christian for my taste."[93] Much of the group's successes came through legal rather than popular action. For example, Chub Peabody was instrumental in persuading the Massachusetts legislature to prohibit racial discrimination in the state National Guard.[94] The crush of law school work forced Brewster to step down from the Cambridge chapter chairmanship at the mid-February 1946 elections, although he continued to play a role in the group and remained in close contact with Bolté and Harrison.[95]

BREWSTER WAS ALSO active in the cause of world federalism and its principal organization, the United World Federalists. Many groups advocating world government had cropped up after the war, including the Student League for World Government, organized at Yale in December 1945,[96] and the Student Federalists, started by Harris Wofford Jr. (later an aide to Chester Bowles and John F. Kennedy and a Pennsylvania senator) at the tender age of fifteen.[97] Representatives from five federalist organizations met in Asheville, North Carolina, in April 1947 and amalgamated to form the United World Federalists (UWF), with Cord Meyer its first president.[98] Other leading members included UWF vice presidents Clark and Finletter, former America Firster Chester Bowles, New York publisher Cass Canfield, Cousins, Albert Einstein, and Cranston, who succeeded Meyer as president.

At its peak, in the late 1940s, the UWF was the largest of the world federalist organizations, with over 50,000 dues-paying members. The group induced seventeen state legislatures to urge Congress to plan for world government, and in June 1949 convinced ninety-one members of Congress from both parties to sponsor a House resolution that "it should be a fundamental objective of the U.S. to support and strengthen the U.N. and to seek its development into a world federation open to all nations with defined and limited powers adequate to preserve peace and prevent aggression through the enactment, interpretation and enforcement of world law."[99] One historian noted that although world federalists were "not very powerful numerically," they were "a part of that elite opinion . . . which deserves to be regarded as of more importance than mere numbers suggest."[100]

The leaders of both the AVC and UWF were determinedly nonideological, pragmatic idealists. Brewster hastened to inform the *New York Times* that world federalists like him were not "motivated by any superior idealism" but rather were compelled by a conviction that international control of nuclear weapons was "a necessity on the realistic level of survival itself."[101] Their pragmatism led them to oppose pacifists, whom the progressives tended to regard as well-meaning but ineffectual dreamers (just as Brewster's America Firsters had opposed pacifists in the late 1930s). However responsible the world government activists were, though, their moment soon passed. The most ambitious official proposal for international control of atomic weapons and energy, the Acheson-Lilienthal plan (1946), never became policy. Congress then passed the Atomic Energy Act, which forbade the sharing of atomic "secrets," and by 1949 the superpowers were engaged in a nuclear arms race.[102]

The Soviets, bitterly attacking world federalism, instructed their adherents in the United States to infiltrate and take over the AVC. McGeorge Bundy joined the Cambridge AVC chapter "in order to help Meyer retain control over the organization" by battling the Communists, who concealed their allegiances and their agendas.[103] The Bolté–Harrison faction finally succeeded in barring Communists from AVC membership at the organization's third convention, in 1948, but the AVC was damaged by its internecine battles against unscrupulous Communists acting on direct orders from Moscow.[104] The tension helped transform many world federalist leaders into dedicated anti-Communists: Cord Meyer shocked many of his liberal hero-worshipers by joining the CIA in 1951.

Nonetheless, the AVC and UWF were viciously red-baited by conservative and "patriotic" groups. Many whom Joseph McCarthy derided as "one-worlders" made attractive targets because of their internationalism, progressivism, elite backgrounds, and ties to the establishment.[105] At the height of McCarthyism, *Newsweek* reported that "loyalty investigators are now asking would-be government employees if they ever were members of the United World Federalists."[106] Meyer, whose CIA career was nearly destroyed by McCarthy, lamented that "any proposal for the radical reform of society, no matter how well intentioned, brings down on the reformer's head a heavy weight of emotional hatred and personal invective."[107] It was a truism that establishment world savers like Brewster would have cause to reflect upon throughout their careers.

Brewster's involvement with large causes like the AVC and UWF fit well with his law school studies, which he would ultimately describe as the "most important influence in my life."[108] Brewster and his peers found the legal curriculum challenging, and they were fascinated by the Socratic method in classes where professors interrogated students with the zeal of Torquemada. As Brewster's classmate Roger Fisher observed, after the intellectual tedium of the military, being able to apply one's mind to human issues was refreshing. "Being shot at by a professor was better than being shot at by the Japanese."[109] Brewster studied and argued day and night, "giving and taking more under pressure than ever before or since."[110] Richardson felt that "the worst class I had in the law school was better than the best I had in [Harvard] College."[111]

Benjamin Kaplan, who arrived on the Harvard law faculty in 1947, recalled lively sessions with students and young instructors at dinners at the Brewsters' home, where an "amazing collection" of about a dozen young people alternated between propositions and defenses. On one such occasion the group discussed the possibility that an A-bomb could soon be constructed in a bathtub and detonated from three thousand miles away. How would the law deal with the proliferation of nuclear technology? The scene, Kaplan remembered, was "electric and brilliant. . . . I had never seen anything like it."[112] Hugh Calkins, a classmate of Brewster's who sometimes attended the dinners, was equally dazzled. He felt that "the group which emerged from the universities and law schools, especially the prestige ones, in the postwar period . . . had more confidence and self-conscious public spirit than any other group of young people in American history. . . . [O]ne has to go back to the 1770s to find similar people."[113]

Brewster excelled academically, served as treasurer and note editor of the *Harvard Law Review,* and graduated magna cum laude. Thomas Reed Powell was so impressed by Brewster's and Richardson's constitutional law exams that he saved them to show to subsequent generations of students.

Richardson, president of the *Review,* remembered Brewster as "a congenial member of the board, and obviously a very bright guy. He had a piquant, wry sense of humor, which would sometimes accompany his rather elaborate, even ponderous sentences. But he often wore sort of a mischievous expression as he navigated through his convoluted clauses and subclauses. You could see he was doing it for the fun of it, and was amused with himself in the process."[114] Richardson shared Brewster's quasi-religious veneration for the law, the professors who taught it, and the premises of their teaching: "justice as fairness, the law's regard for human dignity, and the primacy of the public interest."[115] Brewster also agreed with Richardson's dictum that "a *Harvard Law Review* man can do any job," although non-Harvard people often thought that the statement revealed a certain parochialism.

Brewster and Richardson sometimes met for lunch at the Signet Society, where they became involved in planning for the Salzburg Seminar in American Studies, an extraordinary venture begun by Harvard students and faculty in 1947. The seminar, held in a run-down eighteenth-century archbishop's palace in what was still war-divided Austria, joined students from different European countries with professors for lectures and discussions on American civilization. The goal was to strengthen the foreigners' faith in the democratic reconstruction of Europe and, as Richardson put it, convey "a better understanding of the United States itself—government, politics, economics, literature, and so on—on the basis that, given the role of the United States in the postwar world, they ought to know more about us."[116]

BREWSTER'S THINKING ABOUT national and even international problems reflected the legal process school of jurisprudence, a Harvard creation that dominated legal education in the 1950s. The process school could fairly be called Brewster's major intellectual influence. In simple terms, the legal process thinkers tried to hold a middle ground between conservative adherence to precedent and "legal realism," which claimed that law was essentially whatever the courts would do. They were moderates who stressed the importance of arriving at decisions through clearly delineated procedures, based on objective principles. Conceding that the principles were ideals, they argued that the essence of the American system was the search for objectivity through unbiased processes. The process thinkers generally held that any decision was fine as long as the process leading to it was fair. One of Brewster's professors joked that the essence of his philosophy was summed up by the Fats Waller song "It Ain't Whatcha Do, It's the Way Thatcha Do It."[117]

The process theorists offered an equally hopeful vision of cooperation between responsible citizens and responsible leaders, threading a pathway between populism and elitism. The process school radiated optimism about government and democracy that came from public service and victory in World War II. Brewster commented that the members of his generation "had unlimited confidence in the capacity of organized power. No specific objective seemed unattainable if sufficient resources were mobilized to achieve it."[118] This belief reflected the unprecedented American postwar prosperity that gave hope that the pie would always expand, that politics as a zero-sum game was a thing of the past.

The legal process school had much in common with other attempts to forge an American consensus in the late 1940s and early 1950s.[119] Its thinkers shared many contemporary intellectuals' aversion to social conflict, a view that was only reinforced in the early 1950s when Senator McCarthy attacked civil liberties in the name of anti-Communism. In essence, the process school opposed extremism of any kind, viewing moral absolutism and inflexible ideology as reminiscent of the harsh debates of the 1930s, perhaps even of the totalitarianism of that era. McGeorge Bundy often cited his friend Isaiah Berlin, a prominent British philosopher, to emphasize the message that absolute certainty was the hallmark of totalitarianism.[120] Brewster and his peers agreed that dogmatism was an irrational, unrealistic way to approach the complex problems of the modern world.

The process school became, as well, an intellectual touchstone for many of Brewster's contemporaries. Even McGeorge Bundy, who did not go to law school, absorbed the process philosophy of his friends. Bundy once told a reporter that "I believe in Heraclitus," a highbrow way of saying that he believed in change and the impossibility of stepping into the same river twice. The reporter noted that Heraclitus was the philosopher of process and that "Bundy, in the deepest sense, is an organizer of process."[121]

After graduating from Harvard Law School in 1946, Richardson clerked for Learned Hand, the senior judge of the powerful Second Circuit Court of Appeals, in New York City, whom Richardson had first heard speak at the Yale–Harvard literary dinner he cosponsored with Brewster. Although Hand, a wise and formidable blue blood with an enormous head, bushy eyebrows, and forbidding visage, turned seventy-five in 1946, he walked four miles to work each morning from his brownstone on the Upper East

Side.[122] He had a deep, even poetic love of the law and used to say to Richardson, gesturing toward the shelves of law reports that flanked his desk, "These books are what separate us from the cave and the club."[123] Oddly, though, Hand would warn Richardson to "beware the man of principle!" By this he meant not that one ought to be unprincipled but that it was better to trust a neutral process than precast ideologies. Richardson later wrote a book on process, in which he declared that "liberty, democracy, the protection of individual rights, citizen participation—all these are matters of process. They are what the Declaration of Independence is about. They are what the revolution was fought over. They are the central concern of the Constitution and the Bill of Rights. This is what we mean by a 'government of laws and not men.'"[124]

The next year, Richardson took a Supreme Court clerkship under Felix Frankfurter. A Viennese immigrant, former Harvard law professor, New Dealer, and protégé of Learned Hand, Frankfurter was short, sharp-witted, and excitable, with a clear affinity for law and argument. Richardson remembered that once when Frankfurter was waiting for him to finish a draft opinion, the judge began to bounce with impatience and yelled, "This is a war we're fighting! Don't you understand? A war!"[125] A childless man, he was affectionately paternal with bright, talented youngsters like Richardson, Brewster, and Bundy and spurred them on to public service as he had Dean Acheson a generation before. "A continuous supply of the best type of young men," he believed, "would furnish constant renewal of energy in public administration."[126]

The most important insights that Brewster took away from his legal training dealt with the notion of good leadership. One of his favorite quotations was Hand's dictum that "the spirit of liberty is the spirit which is not too sure that it is right." He was convinced that his "baptism in the law" was a useful corrective to his tendency to see all sides of an issue. "At the end of the day," he wrote, responsibility and the law's action imperative demand that "a decision has to be made."[127] Although Brewster knew that leadership requires decision making, he was keenly aware that the decisions he made might be wrong. Perhaps this concern stemmed from his having found himself on the wrong side during the isolationist–interventionist debate. Brewster's solution to this dilemma was to trust in a neutral process that was larger and more objective than any individual decision maker. "It was at law school," he recalled, "that I became aware of the importance of minimizing resentments—particularly those resentments which stem from having your fate decided by fallible men." The whole legal system and its often tedious procedural rules were "designed to convince the loser that he had been fairly and seriously dealt with, had an opportunity to present his version of the matter, and could appeal the verdict if it seemed unfairly arrived at."[128]

The quality of the decision makers was equally important, Brewster believed. No legal process could assure decency if there was not also "an abiding sense of fairness, an ultimate integrity in the judicial chambers, in the legislative halls, and in executive offices."[129] It was also essential that the leaders and the led share a respect for reason. Manners and civility were important, "but in matters of substance where interests and judgment are in fundamental confrontation, it is respect for reason which prevents disagreement from festering into distrust, and prevents distrust from exploding into conflict."[130]

The process school advocated anything but mechanical devotion to form and procedure. The legal process would be sensible and flexible because those who applied it were too. The idea of process was in a sense the credo and self-justification of the liberal establishment. It was not separable from the ideals of wise leadership, balance, and proportion that were embodied in their heroes and that they tried to live up to. Modern legal scholarship has paid far less attention to the legal process school than to legal realism, and with reason; process theory was more ambiguous and less philosophically deep; it rested upon assumptions about consensus that began to unravel as early as the 1950s. But process theory is an excellent guide to the attitudes of decision makers in the years after World War II.

One of the sharpest critics of the legal process school in later years was Brewster's stepnephew Duncan Kennedy, who felt that it was "Kingman all over, the idea that there's an intermediate way. . . . Everything is ambivalent. On the one hand, rules and structures are incredibly important, and you've got to understand them and be loyal to them. On the other hand, if you take them too seriously, you really run off the rails." He emphasized that the attitude of the process thinkers "was progressive and pragmatic, with an underlying idea: you can be loyal to the structure if you get the structure right. If you get the structure right, then you owe it to the structure to perform your role and not interfere with someone else's role." This was not mere conservatism, however, since "everything is open to negotiation and change, and you shouldn't be rigid about it."

A wise and liberal establishment, in other words, would welcome criticism and change. This was a congenial formulation for men like Brewster and Bundy, with their temperamental need to be both loyal and rebellious, with one foot inside the system and one foot out. A further reason why

Brewster and his peers believed in the fairness and workability of the system, according to Kennedy, was that they personally knew and respected the other members of the establishment: "the basic parameter was the idea that everyone is more or less in good faith. How do you know? You know because you know them. You know the system's architecture, taken as a whole, is good, because you've studied it and thought about it. 'We are the system, and we've studied it.' The institutional competence idea validated existing understandings as sensible and philosophically sophisticated."[131]

Harvard's faculty during this period tended to divide into two camps, the intellectuals and the operators, and Brewster (like McGeorge Bundy) undoubtedly belonged to the latter group.[132] Brewster thought the mixture was part of what made Harvard great, and joked that "a university law school must offer exercise for the operator just as it must offer cloisters for the monk."[133] His mentor was Milton Katz, a consummate academic empire builder, for whom theoretical consistency was less important than networking, influence, and practical results. But the distinction between theorists and operators can be overdrawn, for a concern for process "infused practically all teaching at Harvard in that period," as Kaplan recalled; it was the common language of instruction and means of communication between specialists in different fields of law.[134] Kennedy also concluded that "the people who have the ethos aren't appropriately categorized as either pragmatists or moralists. If you try to play them off of that supposed dichotomy, or to deal with them as one or the other, you just get fucked every time. It turns out that the hard-headed deal gets retracted for reasons of principle which are just moralistic reasons, and what seems like an obvious moral principle gets sold down the river because 'Only a fool would think that would work!'"[135]

Katz had graduated from Harvard College in 1928 and from the law school three years later. Most of the 1930s he spent working for the government in various capacities. He returned to Harvard in 1939 as a lecturer and was soon promoted to professor, but went on leave of absence in 1941 for war service with several agencies, including the OSS. After the war, he played a major role in shaping the Ford Foundation. Brewster admired Katz for having been "in on the ground floor, the creative aspect" of "contributions of significant and truly innovative social architecture."[136]

Katz, along with colleagues like Richard Bissell and Ed Mason, helped create a tight network spanning the major East and West Coast universities, the largest foundations (Ford, Rockefeller, and Carnegie), and the federal government. The historian Donald Blackmer observed that the network was made up of "people with similar backgrounds and shared perspectives on international affairs who often joined forces to get things done—opening doors, recommending job applicants, making grants, serving on advisory boards, organizing conferences."[137] Over time, this network would draw in older members of the foreign policy community, such as Robert Lovett, Dean Acheson, and John McCloy, to give the establishment a more academic cast.

ON JUNE 5, 1947, about a year and a half after he rejoined the law school faculty, Katz sat in Harvard Yard listening to George Marshall deliver his commencement oration on the need to help Europe's economic and political systems recover from the war. "Nice speech," he thought, and went on his way.[138] By the following year, he had been named general counsel in the European headquarters of the Economic Cooperation Administration, commonly known as the Marshall Plan. Between 1948 and 1952, the United States spent $13.34 billion—a stupendous sum—to rebuild Western Europe and integrate it into what turned into a United States–led anti-Soviet alliance.[139] Katz took with him two assistants, Brewster and Roger Fisher.

Brewster and Fisher shared an office in the ECA's Paris headquarters in the Hotel Talleyrand, one of the city's grandest mansions. From their third-floor window they had a glorious view of the Place de la Concorde, with its obelisk where once the guillotine stood and the Seine curving behind. Because heating oil was short, a servant would bring in wood every winter morning and light a fire in the marble fireplace, adding to the eighteenth-century ambience.

The offices of Katz and of ECA special representative Averell Harriman were also in the building. Katz recalled that "Brewster was like an aide in the White House. He saw all the papers on my desk, and gained experience by doing research on financial and legal matters."[140] Between them, Brewster and Fisher read all the cables that came and went between the headquarters and ECA operations in seventeen countries; as a result, they were among the best-informed people in the Economic Cooperation Administration.

The young aides worked assiduously at their duties, usually staying at their desks until 8 or 9 P.M. and working Saturdays as well. Harriman, a Yale graduate and wealthy business executive who had become a special envoy and roving statesman under Franklin Roosevelt, was their role model. Fisher remembered that "the Crocodile" (as McGeorge Bundy nicknamed him) worked late into the night and that he "couldn't care less about credit.

Just doing it was what counted for him. In fact, Harriman didn't give people as much positive feedback as they deserved, because he just didn't feel a need for it."[141] In the Marshall Plan office, Katz noted, Brewster "was a lively, flexible, intelligent fellow—a broad-gauge man who easily learned to cross the lines of all our legal, political, social, military and economic problems." Fisher commented that "I was constantly struck when we worked together in Paris that Kingman would see the more profound issues involved in any question. He always worked toward a deeper generalization and had an almost philosophical vision and understanding of our problems."[142]

The Marshall Plan demonstrated process-oriented thinking in action. Brewster, Fisher, and Katz were not planners: "We were more process people," Fisher emphasized. They were watchmen on the walls rather than policemen on the ground, laying out a framework for the Europeans and "stimulat[ing] them to do better" rather than coming up with all the solutions. Their work "was process: how do you make this happen? How do you get this working?" The Marshall Plan had to be about process, in Fisher's recollection, because the American involvement would last only a few years and because the administrators had no specialized knowledge of the hundreds of areas targeted for technical assistance. It was their job to locate the specialists and to find a way to share expertise and implement it: "We were constantly plotting how to get something done, and who should do it."

Their task was not merely to enable problems to be tackled but to seek a basis for European collaboration. Brewster in particular was helping to lay the groundwork for a European economic and political union, Fisher remembered. He "was constantly questioning the way that something was going on, and searching for a bigger, more profound way of looking at it. He would try to line up incentives so that the people would work in the right direction. He knew the importance of making the system work, of trying to get the business community and the government to work together so that they operated constructively. Those were views of his that were formed, and continued, with the process." In short, the young Americans were "dealing with difficult issues of how to organize the world and make it work better."[143]

Organizing the world is not the same as trying to control it, but Fisher's comments make clear that the process approach was hardly about means without ends. The historian Michael Hogan labels the vision Fisher attributes to Brewster as a "corporatist" attempt "to remake Europe in the likeness of the United States." The reconstituted European political economy would feature capitalism with free trade and free markets, as well as close cooperation between labor, management, and government.[144] This was not a generically American approach so much as the worldview of the American liberal elite, and indeed Hogan traces the roots of the Marshall Plan to the ideas of early-twentieth-century writers like Herbert Croly and Walter Lippmann, progressive politicians like Theodore Roosevelt and Woodrow Wilson, and Herbert Hoover's associationalism.[145]

The Marshall Plan was neither the covert imperialism charged by New Left historians[146] nor the act of selfless generosity it was sometimes claimed at the time to be. It was a hardheaded yet progressive response, in line with the process school's prescriptions for enlightened leadership, that brought together government, university talent, and support from the Ford Foundation. Not surprisingly, among individuals affiliated with the Marshall Plan one finds several of the older establishment leaders whom Brewster admired, including Harriman, Stimson, Acheson, Lovett, and Marshall himself. There were, too, more junior "Wise Men" cut from much the same cloth, such as George Ball and Paul Nitze. Brewster dealt directly with several of his former teachers at Yale who held important positions in the ECA, notably Richard Bissell and Max Millikan. McGeorge Bundy worked with Bissell in Washington and later was part of the 1949 Council on Foreign Relations study group on the Marshall Plan that brought him into contact with more of the "Wise Men," including Allen Dulles, Dwight Eisenhower (then president of Columbia University), George Kennan, and David Lilienthal. John McNaughton, who had been on the *Harvard Law Review* with Brewster and would soon be a faculty colleague at the law school, succeeded Brewster in the Paris office. Other young men connected with the Marshall Plan were Alexander Bickel (another *Harvard Law Review* colleague) and Michael Forrestal (son of Defense Secretary James Forrestal and later an aide to McGeorge Bundy).

The task of organizing a new world was heady work for men still in their twenties. The writer Evan Thomas has put a sinister cast on the ECA, commenting that, with its secrecy and autonomy, it "was exactly the model for the CIA—a small, elite group, privately manipulating the world with American funds and power."[147] Those directly involved in the Marshall Plan, however, felt keenly the eagerness and enthusiasm that led them to put in six-day weeks and the thrill of working with seasoned leaders like Harriman. They reveled in the idealism and fulfillment of public service, the sense of purpose and commitment in resisting the totalitarian threat from the Communist bloc, and the gratification of seeing international cooperation and the reconstruction of Western Europe take place.

Brewster took "pride in the glory of ingenious, practical compromise,"[148] but also found pleasure in the work. The Americans who served in the Office of the Special Representative lived in high Parisian style, enjoying the benefits of hard currency, travel, priority at gasoline pumps, and European gratitude.[149] Brewster and his young family lived in a small house outside Paris in Le Vesinet, with a stream running through the back garden. His dollars went far enough to hire the services of a cook, a nanny, and a laundress. Whereas his French was adequate, Mary Louise's was excellent, and she enrolled in cooking classes at the Cordon Bleu, along with Julia Child.[150] Brewster spent many late nights after work at the Lapin Agile and other cabarets and bistros, still arguing over problems the ECA dealt with and searching for solutions. It was one of the happiest times of his life. Ultimately the Marshall Plan experience "was very challenging work, and it was exciting," Fisher recalled. "The world was our oyster. We could take on any problem that we thought needed attention and figure out what could be done."[151]

Brewster was looking forward to another year in Paris when the Massachusetts Institute of Technology asked him whether he would take the instructorship in economics that he had been offered in 1948 but had deferred for a year.[152] He walked into Katz's office, hoping and expecting that his mentor would advise him to reject the offer and stay on with the ECA. Katz told him to take the job. Brewster's face fell, the older man remembered, "almost as though I had slapped him."[153] Katz felt that his protégé had "a very endearing characteristic but [one] which could hurt him, and that was a tendency to attach himself to senior people whom he particularly liked. . . . I hated to lose him as much as he hated to leave. But I thought, for his own sake, it was terribly important that he develop his own career path."[154]

BREWSTER RETURNED TO the United States in the fall of 1949 as a research associate in the Department of Economics and Social Science at MIT. He described himself as Millikan's "very junior partner when we first came to M.I.T.—working with Rupert MacLaurin on low cost housing."[155] (Brewster was not employing the royal "we"; Millikan had also just arrived at MIT from Yale and the ECA.) He was pleased to be working alongside his teachers and Marshall Plan colleagues Millikan and Bissell and proud to play a part in the effort to solve the nation's housing shortage. But his work did not portend any particular career direction, and Mary Louise hated the absence of faculty community at MIT and the gardenless house in which the family lived.[156] Both of them were ecstatic when Brewster was offered an assistant professorship at Harvard Law School in 1950. "I had great reverence for Harvard Law School," he remembered, "because of the impact of its teachers and graduates on national affairs. My only fear was that I wasn't good enough." He confessed this worry to his longtime advisor and family friend Felix Frankfurter (who played a similarly avuncular role in counseling Richardson and McGeorge Bundy). Frankfurter replied that when he was in Brewster's position thirty years earlier, he said the same thing to Justice Louis Brandeis. "That's for them to decide," Brandeis replied.[157]

Brewster also considered running for political office. But big-city politics, he thought, were "too impersonal."[158] When he was stationed in Brunswick, Maine, during the war, he had envisioned moving to that small college town, hanging out a shingle, and running for office. (He may have been pondering the example of a distant relative, Maine senator Ralph Owen Brewster.[159]) Whereas the previous generation of establishment leaders had looked askance at Harriman's direct involvement in politics, the men of Brewster's generation were more likely to agree with Chub Peabody that "everyone has a duty to participate in public affairs,"[160] including running for office. Richardson criticized "the indifference of the most comfortable, best-established groups in the community" who "turn[ed] their backs on the messy business of party politics."[161] In Richardson's criticism of his class there was a definite echo of Theodore Roosevelt's castigation of "the refined gentlemen who shook their heads over political corruption and discussed it in drawing rooms, but were wholly unable to grapple with real men in real life."[162] However, the common man (or woman) was not necessarily eager to vote for such uncommon men, as McGeorge Bundy's failed 1941 run for a safe seat on the Boston City Council showed.

Richardson, who had listed "politics" as his intended vocation in his Harvard classbook, commented that "when I got back to Massachusetts in 1949, the Democratic Party was flawed by the kinds of characteristics that us progressive, reform-minded, anti-corruption types didn't like."[163] Ethnic political machines and their hold over Democrats in most East Coast cities helped incline WASP liberals toward the Republicans. In the fall of 1948, Bundy played a key part in the presidential campaign of the moderate Republican candidate Thomas Dewey. Bundy, together with Christian Herter, New York financier Douglas Dillon, and Wall Street lawyers Allen and John Foster Dulles, "served in effect as Dewey's state department [and] central intelligence agency."[164] Kaysen remembered that Bundy came to the Harvard Society of Fellows' Monday night dinner, just before the election, "explaining who would get what cabinet post, in perfect confidence of Republican victory which was shared by all the people who worked for Dewey and by a lot of the political pundits at the time. . . . He was able to laugh at himself on Tuesday, after the election results came in."[165]

John Lindsay was also active in Republican politics. He graduated from Yale Law School in 1948, at the same time that Brewster received his LL.B. from Harvard, and the next year joined the white-shoe New York law firm Webster, Sheffield & Chrystie. His mentor there, Bethuel M. Webster, was also a mentor to Brewster in the 1950s and later served as one of McGeorge Bundy's trustees on the Ford Foundation. Lindsay, who became a superb trial lawyer, was complimented on his presentation of a case before the Supreme Court by the noted talent spotter Felix Frankfurter. He led the liberal wing of the New York Young Republicans and was one of the eleven founders of the Youth for Eisenhower movement. After Eisenhower's 1952 election victory, Lindsay went to Washington as assistant to Attorney General Herbert Brownell, a contact from Yale Law School. He returned to New York in early 1957, and the next year ran for the seat in the Seventeenth Congressional District. After overcoming the candidate supported by the regular Republican organization in the primary, Lindsay defeated the Democratic-Liberal nominee in the November election.

BREWSTER CAMPAIGNED ACTIVELY for Eisenhower in 1952 and 1956, along with Richardson, Bundy, and Lindsay. He wrote that "I count myself a conservative—if by that is meant more confidence in a dispersion of initiative and competition among free men rather than planning, programming, and direct regulation. Maybe I got that way as a professor of antitrust law!"[166] But Chub Peabody believed that by enlisting with the Republicans, progressives were shirking the real battle. As a "brahmin Democrat," he believed that his greatest contribution to Massachusetts politics was "breaking up the racial and religious holds of the parties and making them truly parties of reform."[167] His concurrence with this view was undoubtedly part of the reason that Brewster, although a liberal Republican and an Eisenhower supporter, masterminded Peabody's campaigns for various state offices in the 1950s and wrote that Peabody was "the best bet among my generation to make the kind of breakthrough that might upgrade Massachusetts politics."[168]

Brewster abandoned his plan to pursue a political career in Maine after he visited the state on a dreary March day and "just said the hell with it."[169] While he was frequently mentioned as a candidate for public office, he never did run. His friend William Scranton, the Pennsylvania governor, felt that "those of us who are practical politicians would tell you that running a person of his sort is a very difficult thing to do." The problem was partly Brewster's patrician background (which Scranton shared) but mostly his intellectualism, idealism, and independence.[170] Brewster agreed that the major factor in steering him away from politics was a "fear of dependency on political issues, success at any price."[171]

In any case, Brewster believed that the Harvard Law School could "devis[e] public arrangements for world development comparable to its contribution to the nation in the past."[172] He became a full professor in 1953. Besides teaching, he worked alongside Milton Katz once again, helping to lay the groundwork for the Center for International Legal Studies that was Katz's brainchild. Moreover, Brewster served as a consultant, in his first two years, to various government agencies. He had other options as well: while he was an assistant professor, he was offered a full professorship at the University of Chicago Law School[173] and a position on Chester Bowles's ambassadorial staff in India.[174]

As professor, Brewster concentrated on government regulation of business and the legal problems of international investment. His work fit in well with the program being developed by the Center for International Legal Studies, Millikan's Center for International Studies at MIT, and Harvard's Center for International Affairs. Brewster's research also brought him into contact with the Littauer School of Public Affairs and under the influence of its longtime dean, Edward Mason, another of Harvard's great empire builders. The journalist T. H. White described Mason as "a large, burly man, his balding head a Daniel Webster dome, his high cheekbones and Roman nose giving him a senatorial visage."[175] Like Katz, Mason moved easily between government and academia; among his other jobs he had been a member of the President's Committee on the Marshall Plan.

Mason was particularly skilled at selecting promising young men, placing them, and "guid[ing] them over the years on the zigzag escalation back and forth between campus, foundation and government to leadership."[176] His student M. Joseph Peck recalled that Mason was "very taken by Brewster. Antitrust policy, Brewster's teaching field, was central to Mason's field of industrial organization. I remember Mason saying to me very early on, 'Brewster will make his mark.'"[177] Mason confirmed Brewster's belief that those trained in the social sciences would make excellent "action intellectuals" (the term was T. H. White's), who could have an impact on public life as well as within the academy. Brewster's view of the role of social scientists was similar to Mason's: "We'll always have social problems, but they can be studied, and if we understand the problems better, we can send our action intellectuals in there to work on them."[178]

Brewster later spoke of his time at the Harvard Law School as "ten fabulous ulcerating years,"[179] and certainly he took his teaching and research seriously. John Blum remembered that Brewster "suffered the terrors of the damned" in teaching and that "he was so tense he had bleeding hemorrhoids. He had to sit in a pail of ice the night before he taught."[180] One of his students, George Zeidenstein, was acutely aware of the cultural gap between Brewster's background and his own Ukrainian Jewish origins. "Kingman Brewster struck me as the WASPiest of the WASPs when he'd walk into class, dressed as he did in a tight-collared shirt and elegant tweed jacket that had all the buttons buttoned, and so on. Brewster was almost from another planet so far as I was concerned. But he was a very good teacher."[181] His popularity among students led to the formation of a Brewster Club, and he developed close, continuing friendships with several students, including Joseph Califano (later an assistant to President Lyndon Johnson) and Derek Bok. He was considered to be a good teacher but a hard grader, and his friendship with Bok did not prevent him from giving the future Harvard president his second-worst grade in law school.[182] Thomas Eagleton, senator from Missouri and the abortive Democratic vice presidential nominee in 1972, reminisced that "since I was interested in snap courses with a possibility of high marks, I avoided Brewster like the plague."[183] While Brewster was not considered to be the law school's brightest young star in scholarship, one of the earliest writers in international antitrust believed that Brewster's "research techniques are models for all writers in the law" and that his major work on the subject, *Antitrust and American Business Abroad,* was a classic.[184]

Brewster had a major impact in the faculty and administrative councils of the law school and the university beyond. He circulated widely among the faculty, and was an associate fellow of Lowell House. He served as an active member of a faculty committee on overhauling legal education and on other university-wide committees. Brewster's interests and social connections extended outside the university. He rubbed shoulders with Richardson, Cord Meyer, and John F. Kennedy in the Tavern Club, an upper-class Back Bay watering hole and amateur theatrical association. He discussed foreign policy with the Bundys in the Council on Foreign Relations and talked about scholarship with Richardson at the American Academy of Arts and Sciences. He was chairman of the board of trustees at the Buckingham School (his first position in academic administration), an active participant in the Cambridge Civic Association, and commodore of the Vineyard Haven Yacht Club. The Brewsters' home on Craigie Street was the scene of much socializing (particularly in the years when the Yale–Harvard football game was in Cambridge) and the rough-and-tumble of Constance, Kingman III, Deborah, Alden, and Riley, their five children—a reflection, perhaps, of the optimism of the era. Many of the Brewsters' friends also had large families—the McGeorge Bundys and the Lindsays had four children, the Vances had five. None, however, approached the tally of Paul Moore and his wife, who had nine.

MCGEORGE BUNDY HAD returned to Cambridge after the war, still a member of the Society of Fellows, but he soon relocated. "I am on safari down here in the wilderness of Long Island," he wrote to Mary Louise Brewster in July 1946, "working with Mr. Henry Stimson on a book about his life and doings."[185] He returned sporadically to Cambridge and continued to exchange letters with Brewster, usually to argue about a new book or a new idea, while Brewster was a student at Harvard Law School.

On Active Service in Peace and War, the work that resulted from Bundy's collaboration with the former secretary of state and secretary of war, was a combination of Bundy's narrative and diary entries from the influential public servant whose career spanned the era between Theodore and Franklin Roosevelt. It became a sacred tome of the foreign policy establishment for its advocacy of enlightened internationalism and its idealistic call for citizens of intelligence and talent to serve the public interest.

Stimson was a hero to Bundy and his friends because of his devotion to bipartisan public service and his wide accomplishments, but also because his experiences had given him a pragmatic, action-oriented, basically hopeful wisdom. Brewster often quoted Stimson's ringing charge to younger generations: "Let them learn from our adventures what they can. Let them charge us with our failures and do better in their turn. But let them not turn aside from what they have to do, nor think that criticism excuses inaction. Let them have hope, and virtue, and let them believe in mankind and its future, for there is good as well as evil, and the man who tries to work for the good, believing in its eventual victory, while he may suffer setback and even disaster, will never know defeat. The only deadly sin I know is cynicism."[186]

Stimson's example influenced two generations of American policy makers. During the Cuban missile crisis, former Secretary of Defense Robert Lovett noticed Stimson's photo on Bundy's desk and said to him, "Mac, I think the best service we can perform for the President is to try to approach this as Colonel Stimson would."[187] Bundy had no intention of imitating every aspect of Stimson's life; he had no wish to enter a sound profession like banking or corporate law and did not at all share Stimson's Rooseveltian love of the great outdoors. His Yale classmate Doc Howe visited Bundy and Stimson while they were working on the book. "After dinner," Howe remembered, "Secretary Stimson regaled us with tales of wild animal hunting in the Rocky Mountains. Mac was bored, and to prove it he went to sleep and snored while the Secretary was talking."[188] Arthur Schlesinger Jr., who knew Bundy through the Harvard Society of Fellows, recalled that "Mac wasn't much like Stimson personally. . . . Mac loved dancing, he liked pretty girls, and he was great fun."[189]

However, Bundy hoped to exercise a similar sort of national responsibility, and Stimson's sense of duty, wisdom, and integrity would remain his creed when he entered government. Stimson's memory also affected Bundy's conception of his duty as a presidential advisor, or even an ex-advisor. At a 1968 Harvard debate over Vietnam, Bundy told the audience that he had "worked as an assistant to a great cabinet officer who worked for seven presidents in different ways, and who made it his binding rule to engage in no criticism of any of the seven while that man was still in active public life. That is my position too."[190] This self-denying ordinance meant that the ex-advisor who sought to take part in public debate could not be wholly candid, a condition that was problematic in the late 1940s and would become more so as time went on.

The Bundy–Stimson book also minimized Stimson's role, as secretary of war, in sending over 100,000 Japanese-Americans to detention camps in the early years of World War II. The memoir proffered various excuses: the decision was approved by the Supreme Court; anticipated Japanese raids on the West Coast might have received help from individuals of Japanese origin; internment would shield Japanese-Americans from lynchings; it was for their own good to be resettled in more widely dispersed communities after the war; and so forth. Bundy and Stimson, acknowledging that "to loyal citizens this forced evacuation was a personal injustice," hastened to add that "Stimson fully appreciated their feelings."[191] It was hardly an adequate apology for one of the federal government's most egregiously unconstitutional and inhumane actions of the twentieth century. Years later, Bundy rounded on one of his colleagues who was criticizing the internment of Japanese-Americans, calling the surprised younger man "a bleeding-heart liberal."[192] Stimson's decision was indefensible and Bundy knew it, but his loyalty to his mentor prevented him from admitting the magnitude of Stimson's error, which included the secretary's unwillingness to make public amends for it.

BUNDY RETURNED TO Cambridge in the fall of 1949 as a lecturer in the government department. His first course, Government 180: The U.S. in World Affairs, was immensely popular, with standing-room crowds for the lecture in which he recounted the West's sellout of Czechoslovakia at Munich. Not long after the semester began, Bundy went on a blind date with Mary Lothrop, a pretty, thoughtful, socially conscious young woman who had graduated from Radcliffe in 1946 and returned to become the college's associate director of admissions. She came from a Boston Brahmin family, grew up on Beacon Street not far from the Bundys, and had been a childhood playmate of Mac's younger sister, Laurie. They went to a small dinner party in Cambridge given by Grenville Clark's daughter, and Mac was smitten. He proposed after just one more date—confounding friends who thought of him as a pure rationalist—and they married in June 1950.

For a while the Bundys lived in one of the Harvard houses, then moved to a home around the corner from the Brewsters, next door to John McNaughton and near Milton Katz and other professor friends. The men would walk to work at Harvard, the wives raised the children and ran the households, and they frequently met for spirited dinner parties. Bundy and Brewster "became tremendously close family friends when we were in Cambridge," Bundy recalled, "because we both had children, and we lived a block apart, and we dined back and forth."[193] The two men and their wives "visited back and forth at the Vineyard" and went on vacations together to the Mill Reef Club at Antigua, where they drank and talked politics with Dean Acheson and Archibald MacLeish. Often some of the Brewsters' friends would come over to his house on Sundays to quaff martinis and go through the barrels of oysters that Kingman's mother sent from the Vineyard.[194] It was a period that many of Brewster's friends looked back on with considerable nostalgia. "You know, one gilds it," Bundy remembered. "But once you were over the bridge and were a permanent member of the Harvard faculty in the 1950s, all you had to do was your best. You didn't have to worry about anybody else."[195]

One of the regular social events for Brewster's crowd was the Cambridge Dinner Dance series at the Commodore Hotel. Most of the participants were Brewster's friends from college, including the Bundys, Don Belin (who married a Bundy sister), Ted Beal (who married a Bundy cousin), Chub and Toni Peabody, and Elliot Richardson. Richardson, who had dated another Bundy sister in his college years, had been on the verge of asking out Mary Lothrop when he heard that Mac Bundy had proposed to her. Richardson had no hard feelings; he toasted the couple at their wedding, alongside Brewster. Not long afterward he met another Radcliffe student, a tall, hazel-eyed brunette named Anne Hazard, who had grown up with Mary Louise Phillips in Providence. They met at a dance where Richardson made a pest of himself by constantly cutting in, although she didn't mind because he was such a good dancer. They became engaged and married when she graduated from college.[196]

After clerking for Hand and Frankfurter, Richardson was unsure of his goals. Frankfurter advised him not to have any, since young men who were too focused on specific career ambitions became calculating, indifferent to the satisfactions of what they were doing, and usually ended up disappointed. In 1949, Richardson was offered a position as special assistant to the new secretary of state, Dean Acheson. "I greatly admired Acheson and I felt torn between this tempting offer and the aim of learning the lawyer's trade," he remembered. "The idea of being in the State Department was exciting. On the other hand, I always had in the back of my mind going into politics. If I stayed in Washington, I might end up a government hack." Richardson asked his former professor Archibald Cox for advice. Cox, who had also clerked for Hand, replied, "Well, Elliot, I always thought it was important to come from somewhere."[197] As Katz had counseled Brewster, Cox advised Richardson to develop practical expertise and independent experience rather than continue to attach himself to eminent older men.

By the early 1950s, Richardson was working at the old-line Boston law firm of Ropes, Gray. He continued to play a role in academic legal debates and published a much-noted *Harvard Law Review* article on civil liberties; Brewster and Bundy had helped with early drafts.[198] He also taught briefly alongside Brewster at the law school and turned down an opportunity to take Katz's place as the school's specialist in administrative law when Katz left for the Marshall Plan.[199] Soon he became active in local and state politics, and held positions of responsibility at Harvard and the Massachusetts

General Hospital (which he called "the home of my ancestors").[200] In a story Richardson liked to tell, Judge Augustus Hand (cousin of Learned), meeting him in Boston, sized him up as a potential Harvard trustee: "You're the kind of enlightened young man they need. And besides, you're just enough of a stuffed shirt."[201] Once in the early 1950s, Richardson was on a Boston-to-Washington train and discovered that he had forgotten his wallet, one of his bad habits. The conductor agreed to take a personal check if Richardson could establish his identity. Richardson led the conductor through the car until they found someone reading that week's issue of *Life*. Richardson showed the conductor his picture in a feature entitled "Hope for the Future," profiling the nation's fourteen most outstanding young people. The conductor took the check.[202]

Although Richardson struck many people as epitomizing the cool, aristocratic, reserved, and self-assured Boston Brahmin, his friends knew him as a warm, dryly witty man. He retained some of the archaic habits of his forebears, such as walking around the border of his Brookline property every morning, rain or shine, like some medieval lord beating the boundaries of his estate. But he radiated an energy unusual in Brahmins, which he channeled into his work and his recreations: kicking out his heels while dancing the athletically demanding *kazatsky* at parties, painting stylish watercolors at the family compound on Cape Cod, canoeing through the Canadian wilderness with Anne, bonefishing off the Bahamas.

In 1953, Richardson took a leave of absence from his law office to become an aide to Massachusetts senator Leverett Saltonstall, another liberal Republican mentor. Saltonstall, a craggy-faced descendant of nine Massachusetts governors, was once asked what he believed in most. "Well, it might sound more impressive if I said something like 'democracy' or 'the country,'" he replied, "but let's not be pretentious   what I believe in most is Harvard and my family."[203] And yet Saltonstall was a hugely popular politician, a favorite of the South Boston Irish as well as Back Bay Brahmins. "Salty is aptly regarded as the conscience of the United States Senate," Richardson observed, "and his voice has been an eloquent one, at all times calling for service above self."[204] Brewster, too, had been an admirer of Saltonstall since sharing a podium with the senator in 1940 before the Yale Club of Boston, and was friends with the senator's son, another member of the Cambridge Dinner Dance circle.

Brewster was a favorite at such gatherings because he was graceful, witty, and intelligent, with a high tolerance and good head for alcohol. He was a generous host, a splendid dancer, a skillful mimic, and the life of every party. Blum remembered when, after one of the dinner dances, a group was gathered in a friend's basement at one in the morning, and Brewster decided that they would put on a rendition of *My Fair Lady,* which had just opened in New York. One woman with a good voice sang the part of Eliza Doolittle, and everyone else was assigned parts. "But in the end, Kingman sang all the other parts—in his cups, but with gusto, never missing a beat. The sheer energy and exuberance that went into it were memorable."[205]

Another of Brewster's and his friends' associations in Cambridge was what Bundy referred to as a "self-important little dining club," the Friday Evening Club.[206] The group had its origins in Project Troy, a joint university–government collaboration that began in 1950 when the State Department asked MIT to help overcome the Soviets' jamming of the Voice of America broadcasts into Russia. The university widened the scope of the inquiry and brought together an eclectic mix of scientists, technicians, social scientists, philosophers, poets, and practitioners of international relations, such as George Kennan, to conduct the study.[207]

One of the participants, the MIT historian Elting Morison, later wrote that the project "didn't change the course of history—or even of State Department policy, but it gave the people who worked together in it the best possible liberal education for the world they were living in."[208] The success of the effort led to the creation of the Center for International Studies at MIT, one of the first such postwar institutes and a model for the many to come. Because the CIS was headed by Millikan, Brewster's teacher, friend, and collaborator, Brewster naturally played a consultative role. Bundy also helped start the institute, which actually drew more heavily on Harvard rather than on MIT faculty. The center was one of the few facilities in Cambridge that had sufficient security (including a vault and guard) to host meetings on classified matters, and so Bundy would often come there to discuss control of nuclear weapons with a small group that included Kennan and Robert Oppenheimer. The CIS also provided a haven for Bissell between his CIA engagements; except for its initial grant from the Ford Foundation, it was almost entirely supported with CIA funds, although this arrangement would not become public knowledge until the 1960s. The institute worked hand in glove with the government to supply intellectual undergirding for Cold War strategy and forge a Cold War consensus.[209]

The Friday Evening Club began in 1951 when Morison and Julius ("Jay") Stratton, the provost of MIT and another Troy participant, were walking through the university's back parking lot. Stratton, who had a Ph.D. from the Swiss Institute of Technology in Zurich, squinted up at the bleak, forbidding bulk of MIT's main building and said, "The spirit of Zwingli broods over this place. We ought to change it."[210] (Huldrych Zwingli was an excessively puritanical Swiss Protestant reformer, and MIT was then a place of grinding intellectual endeavor narrowly directed at science and technology.) Morison and Stratton reconvened several of the Troy participants and invited a few new members, with the aim of re-creating the interdisciplinary, collaborative atmosphere of Project Troy.

The group met on the first Friday evening of the month in a gentleman's club, usually the Saint Botolph in Back Bay. The club's name derived from an ancient Boston tradition of naming evening clubs for a day of the week. (Richardson belonged to the century-old Thursday Evening Club.) The original members included seven from the Harvard faculty—Brewster, Bundy, psychologist Jerome Bruner, art historian Myron Gilmore, sociologist George Homans, physicist Edward Purcell, and Byzantine historian Robert Wolff; five faculty members from MIT—Morison and Stratton, Millikan, engineer William Hawthorne, and physicist Victor Weisskopf; and also the Polaroid inventor and industrialist Edwin ("Din") Land. In the first year of its existence, the club admitted Wassily Leontief, a Harvard economist; no other members were admitted thereafter.

Bruner joked that, in this respect, the club was like the Junta in Max Beerbohm's *Zuleika Dobson,* "which met regularly to consider new members, only to blackball any that were proposed."[211] The group met every month for fifteen years until it foundered on the rock of Vietnam, and more specifically on the issue of Bundy's role in the war. It was an astonishing collection of men, all activists and intellectuals, who went on to national and international prominence. All were intellectually adventurous although outwardly conventional, perhaps because, as Din Land put it, "if you intend to be a revolutionary in one domain of life, you must be a conformist in others."[212] Or as Brewster's mentor Roger Baldwin had written to him, "After all it is the *sound* who run the world on all fronts, but those out in front of progress conceal beneath their soundness what you've got—a bit of Puritan heresy."[213]

The Friday Evening Club meetings had no agenda or set topic, and no minutes were kept. The members dined and drank well, and reveled in each other's company. Weisskopf recalled that "sometimes, particularly interesting visitors to Cambridge were asked to speak to the club"—Lippmann, Oppenheimer, Alfred Kazin, and several others—"but on the whole, the topics developed informally out of our freewheeling conversations."[214] And yet the lodestone to which the talk returned, as one might expect in a

Harvard–MIT group, was the role of science in the modern world. "Science was often discussed, never in a pedagogic or didactic spirit," Bruner recalled. Weisskopf, who had been a theoretical physicist with the Manhattan Project, and the Nobel Prize–winning experimental physicist Purcell "particularly welcomed the chance to put their dilemmas and quandaries in the form of comprehensible metaphors."[215] However enlightening the meetings were for the members, many faculty and administrators at Harvard and MIT considered the club to be the ruling cabal of both universities, and regarded it with envy and suspicion.

KINGMAN BREWSTER'S EXPERIENCE at Harvard Law School not only affected his outlook and gave direction to his career; it also exposed him to the leading meritocratic institution within America's leading meritocratic university. And yet Harvard's meritocracy was a recent development. When Brewster's father received his LL.B. there, in 1911, Harvard was by consensus America's premier law school, yet competition for admissions was not intense. The law school began requiring a college transcript only in 1926, and not until the next year did applicants have to graduate from colleges "of approved standing." After 1927, all graduates in the upper three-quarters of their class were accepted.[216]

And yet the decision to impose admissions standards of any kind was important. Harvard was gambling on what the nation's leadership would look like in the future. War-born rising expectations meant that non-WASPs would no longer regard gateways into the professions, like Harvard Law School, from a deferential distance. The children of immigrants were becoming assimilated into American society and adopting its ideals of success. The selective institutions would soon experience a significant imbalance in the ratio of applicants to places, and would have to winnow the wheat from the chaff along increasingly meritocratic lines. As the economist Joe Peck pointed out, Harvard's "sense of meritocracy and fair competition was very important, because there was a lot of anti-Semitism and racism in the legal world in the 1950s."[217] Davis Polk & Wardwell, the law firm headed by Vance's guardian John W. Davis, did not admit a Jew to partnership until 1961.[218] As late as 1964, a sociological study of Wall Street law firms concluded that they wanted attorneys who were "Nordic, have pleasing personalities, are graduates of the 'right' school, [and] have the right social background."[219] Peck observed that the meritocratic attitude of Harvard and universities like it "gradually transformed the Wall Street law firms from white-shoe outfits to places that were open to talent even if it came from nontraditional backgrounds."[220]

In the 1950s the old-boy network still appeared to be alive and well, and even an institution like Harvard Law School did not judge merit by grades and test scores alone, but also through subjective assessments of quality, character, and ability. It was what Katz referred to as "Kingman's own distinctive blend of high endeavor, proportion, and laughter," not just grades or test scores, that led the new general counsel to the Marshall Plan to pick Brewster as one of his two assistants, out of hundreds of applicants for the assignments.[221] The same personal connection enabled Katz to have Brewster hired as an assistant professor at Harvard Law School in 1950, and indeed when Brewster was named full professor he had written only a single article. His stepnephew Duncan Kennedy observed that the law school during the 1950s had "no elaborate formal appointments process at all. You just got hired through the old-boy network."[222]

At about the same time that Brewster was named assistant professor, McGeorge Bundy was advanced to tenure in the Government Department even though he lacked a Ph.D. and had never taken any graduate or undergraduate courses in government. As David Halberstam told the story, President Conant endorsed the recommendation with a sigh, adding, "All I can say is that it couldn't have happened in Chemistry."[223]

Brewster's ascent followed the establishment pattern. But he broke with it in two important respects: he had no truck with the prejudices that had limited the pool of talent, and he moved in a world where power came from trained intelligence allied to government, rather than from corporate wealth. The postwar years inaugurated the period in which Harvard finally hired Jews in large numbers to the faculty,[224] a development Brewster welcomed. It was a hallmark of the men of the liberal establishment that they had emancipated themselves from the prejudices of their parents' generation. Brewster's mentors and friends at Harvard were people who came from many backgrounds but shared both great talent and a desire to put it to use in the service of the public—White's action intellectuals.[225] As prejudices receded after the war, the promise glimmered that Harvard could bring together able people from all backgrounds. Their ability and expertise could then be put to use in the nation's service. For Brewster and many of his establishment peers, it was an exhilarating prospect.

Kaysen's career captured the sense of change. Kaysen had been the top undergraduate in economics in his class at the University of Pennsylvania before the war. But his advisor informed him that he had arranged that Kaysen not have a fellowship or be admitted to graduate programs to which he had applied. Kaysen recalled that the advisor thought "he was doing me a favor by telling me this because, since I was Jewish, I could not get an academic job." After the war Kaysen became an assistant professor at Harvard, one of the first Jews to be hired by the Economics Department.

At Harvard he became friends with Brewster and McGeorge Bundy. On New Year's Eve 1948, Kaysen and his wife, together with John and Mary Kelleher, another young faculty couple, attended a party at Bundy's parents' home in Boston. Kaysen said that "it struck me then and strikes me still that Mac had invited an Irish Catholic couple and a Jewish couple to his parents' home. I was from a petit bourgeois background, John was actually from a working class background, and the gap between Groton (where Mac had gone to school) and Overbrook High School (where I had gone) was fairly wide. Mac's mother's maiden name was Katharine Lawrence Putnam, and she was from a circle so elevated that when she married Harvey Bundy from Grand Rapids, Michigan, she was dropped from the Boston social register for several years. And yet, here we all were. In a sense, it was Harvard—postwar, meritocratic Harvard—which had made it all possible."[226]

JAMES CONANT ANNOUNCED in early 1953 that he would leave the Harvard presidency to become high commissioner to the Federal Republic of Germany. "It seemed ten steps down," McGeorge Bundy commented, "for the president of Harvard to merely run Germany."[227] Bundy was on the short list of possibilities to succeed Conant, and his candidacy was promoted by influential Harvard trustees such as Charles Wyzanski, Walter Lippmann, and Learned Hand, who declared Bundy "the brightest man in America."[228] Bundy tried to deflect such talk by pointing out that he could never become president because the senior fellow of the Harvard Corporation, Charles Coolidge, had held him on his knee as a baby and still tended to think of him that way.[229]

Felix Frankfurter also had a high opinion of Bundy, and had once offered him a Supreme Court clerkship despite his lack of a law degree. Frankfurter's candidate for the Harvard presidency, however, was Elliot Richardson, who was only thirty-three years old at the time. Richardson had impressed Frankfurter with his insistence on taking an hour each morning during his Supreme Court clerkship to read Shakespeare.[230] Brewster also had his supporters, as did several other Harvard faculty members. The Corporation, however, chose Nathan Marsh Pusey, the forty-six-year-old president of

Lawrence College in Wisconsin. (When the appointment was announced, one Harvard professor quipped, "Sic transit gloria Bundy.") Pusey seemed to his detractors to have the smooth and untroubled appearance of the back of a spoon. His qualifications were largely that he was a pious Christian, had raised a lot of money for Lawrence College, and had stood up to Joseph McCarthy in his home state. The latter was important because Harvard was headed toward a long-anticipated confrontation with the red-baiting Wisconsin senator, a confrontation that had been brewing since the early 1950s.

One of the first McCarthyist salvos against the establishment universities came not from McCarthy but from William F. Buckley Jr.'s 1951 tract *God and Man at Yale,* in which the 1950 graduate charged that his once-conservative alma mater had become a hotbed of atheism and socialism. Buckley declared that academic freedom should, in effect, be abolished, that the alumni should govern the university directly and remove any faculty member whose teachings failed to exhibit proper allegiance to Christianity and capitalism. McGeorge Bundy denounced Buckley in the November 1951 *Atlantic Monthly.* The magazine's editors afforded Buckley a response in the next issue, followed by a rejoinder from Bundy. Considering that Buckley popularized the term "establishment" in this country and that this was his first serious clash with the establishment personified by Bundy, their exchange carried more significance than the usual literary fracas.

For all that Buckley would later seem, to many Americans, to be the epitome of the upper-crust WASP gentleman, his background was very much that of an outsider compared to someone like Bundy. He was Irish and Catholic, the grandson of an impoverished immigrant turned Texas sheriff and sheep farmer and the son of a self-made Texas oilman. His parents were southerners, and he spent his winters in South Carolina, where Strom Thurmond, a rising segregationist politician, was a family friend. Buckley's background helped make him a tribune of a hard-right conservatism that resented the East and its liberal Protestant establishment.

Bundy's mordant criticism of Buckley's book was less memorable than his characterization of the author as "a twisted and ignorant young man."[231] The review exemplified Bundy's overkill style of debating, which consisted of establishing his objectivity by conceding a smidgen of truth to an opposing argument ("In attacking Mr. Buckley's book, I do not wish to say, or seem to say, that Yale is perfect"), then lobbing round after round onto the charred and smoking remains of his opponent. It was a technique that aimed to punish rather than to convince. Bundy's review was motivated by unfeigned anger; his wife remembered him staying up late into the night tapping furiously at the typewriter.

Bundy was prone to respond angrily to people, like Buckley, whom he considered irresponsible or who criticized the individuals or institutions they properly owed loyalty to. Buckley's response over the course of the years was to ask, in effect, why the establishment should be allowed to determine the definitions of "responsibility" and "loyalty." Why should challenges to political moderation, and indeed the establishment itself, automatically be dismissed as extremism? Why should all "loyal" and "sensible" individuals defer to the authorities merely because they were declared to be the authorities? Buckley's challenge to the establishment was destined to be taken up and reamplified not only on the right but, in the 1960s, on the left as well. Indeed, Buckley's castigation of Bundy and his peers as "haughty totalitarians who refuse to permit the American people to supervise their own destiny" prefigured the antielitist language as well as the sentiment of the New Left.[232]

The Bundy–Buckley exchange was not, as one might expect, a battle between liberal and conservative, but rather an engagement in a longer war over what the label "conservative" should mean. Along with a few other Ivy Leaguers like August Heckscher and Peter Viereck, Bundy was a leader in a now-forgotten postwar movement called the new conservatism, whose adherents tried to distance the GOP from the racist, reactionary, isolationist, and materialistic Old Right. They respected the force and cohesion of tradition but proclaimed that government needed to provide for the welfare of all its people by building on the accomplishments of the New Deal. They called for the United States to accept the mantle of international responsibility, and upheld civil rights and civil liberties for all as essential components of the American creed. They opposed hard rightists like Buckley at the intellectual level, while liberal Republicans like Lindsay and Richardson opposed them at the political level.

"What the western world needs is an exciting, inspiring—yes, thrilling program to answer communism," the new-conservative Viereck wrote in a critique of *God and Man at Yale*. "Adam Smith, be he right or wrong, is hardly such a program! Nor, on the other hand, is statism and socialism. I find exciting what the Roman Catholic parties, in France and Italy, are working out . . . a mixed economy in which the Christian virtues of humaneness and compassion . . . modify capitalism."[233] Bundy's liberal conservatism was not far from the conservative liberalism of "vital centrists" like Schlesinger and the anti-Communist liberal organization Americans for

Democratic Action, formed in 1947. The new conservatives were as opposed to rightists like Buckley taking over the term "conservative" as ADA'ers were to socialists appropriating the term "liberal." As Buckley wrote to Viereck, "If I represent the 'new conservatism,' why then you all of the Vital Center have got two battles on your hands."[234]

What truly separated new conservatives like Bundy from new rightists like Buckley was their attitude toward McCarthyism. Bundy observed that *God and Man at Yale* was "clearly an attempt to start an assault on the freedom of one of America's greatest and most conservative universities. In this sense it is in some degree a sign of the times."[235] Buckley's book was not actually a classic example of red-baiting. Although he didn't accuse anyone of being a Communist, the tenor of the book was that of a McCarthyist exposé. Buckley would go on to author a defense of McCarthyism; he was also an occasional speechwriter for and close associate of the senator whom establishment figures dubbed "the mad Irishman." Bundy's review was hotter because he wrote it just after having completed an annotated collection of public statements by his brother's father-in-law, Dean Acheson, who was perhaps McCarthy's favorite target. (Acheson's son-in-law William Bundy would later narrowly avoid losing his job with the CIA after coming under McCarthy's attack; so, too, would Charles Bohlen, Cord Meyer, and other friends. Bill Bundy, writing to Elliot Richardson while counterattacking McCarthy, emphasized that he was fighting "the power of evil."[236])

Establishment conservatives like McGeorge Bundy detested McCarthy for all the usual reasons—his abuse of civil liberties, his cynical manipulation of the media and the public, his sinister belief that the means justified the end, and so forth. Bundy thought that McCarthy actually discredited the anti-Communist cause: "By making charges so wild and loose that they failed in the end to command respect, by making a wild anticommunism an object of legitimate scorn, Senator McCarthy gravely impeded the continuing and accurate understanding of the reality of communism."[237] But McCarthy also represented a populist, nativist, almost anarchistic challenge to the establishment. To men like Bundy, McCarthyism was a personal assault. He believed that McCarthy's animus was not so much against Communism as against the American order, which included the Constitution, the courts, the most decorated and paternal generals, the Episcopal Church and Harvard ("the leaders of our most deeply established religion and precisely the *most* ancient of our universities," as Viereck put it), and "the oldest, most rooted, and most deeply educated patrician families."[238]

As Bundy's review of Buckley revealed, this sort of establishment criticism of McCarthyism could come across as upper-class contempt for upstart yahoos. "The greatest snobs I have ever encountered," one right-winger wrote to Buckley in the 1950s, "were Liberals—do you not find it so? There was a fellow, Viereck, I think was his name, who seemed to be peddling the theory that the Porcellian crowd and the ADA'ers had the true light, while opponents of Liberalism were muckers from the Middle West and Texas, secretly seething because they would never make the social grade. . . . [Liberals] were always telling you about Roosevelt's respectable and substantial forebears, and it was pure headwaiter, society-editor snobbism."[239]

The bitterness that colored Buckley's response to Bundy, and that extended over much of what became the new right, came from the feeling that the establishment did not treat its challengers as equals but rather as a rabble of pitchfork-wielding peasants massing outside the castle walls. Such sentiments were understandable. According to Buckley's father, when his son challenged Bundy to formally debate *God and Man at Yale*, "Bundy stated that he would not engage in the debate because it was an 'inferior book' written by an 'inferior character.'"[240]

Bundy delivered stings beyond the "inferior character" accusation. He was one of the few reviewers who charged that Buckley had concealed his identity as an "ardent Roman Catholic" and that this invalidated much of his book. "In view of Yale's Protestant history," Bundy wrote, "it seems strange for any Roman Catholic to undertake to define the Yale religious tradition."[241] Arguably, Buckley's book represented the Catholic conception of education as sublime and infinite recapitulation rather than as a process of growth and change. But such attacks as Bundy's gave Buckley and his supporters an opportunity to denounce the anti-Catholicism of the WASP establishment.

McCarthyism drew strength and opposition from all segments of society, but the lower-middle-class conservatives who supported the senator constituted the segment of society for which Bundy and many of his friends had the least understanding and sympathy. As a *Yale Daily News* columnist, Bundy had flayed the American Legion as "composed largely of the same class of people as those who brought Hitler to power—the penny-proud, ignorant petit bourgeois folk who detest the left-wing labor movement, fearing to see their prized (and largely imagined) 'social superiority' vanish in something vague called communism."[242]

In practical terms, Bundy's critique of *God and Man at Yale* helped him become dean of the Faculty of Arts and Sciences at Harvard in 1953. "I'd read William F. Buckley's *God and Man at Yale*. . . . it made me sick to my stomach," recalled Pusey, Harvard's new president. "And then I'd found an article by Mac Bundy in the *Atlantic Monthly* attacking Buckley. So I pointed to Bundy's name on the list and told [the secretary], 'He's the first fellow I want to see.'"[243] None of the other candidates were even interviewed. Bundy became dean of Harvard at the precocious age of thirty-four. Kingman Brewster offered congratulations by sending his friend a spray of funeral lilies, to symbolize his death as a scholar and rebirth as an administrator. (Bundy reciprocated the gesture when Brewster left law teaching to become provost of Yale in 1960.)

BUNDY WAS A triumphantly successful dean. Professors later recalled that his "natural assurance, crisp style, mastery of precise language, impatience with fools, and extensive curiosity allowed him to be both an imperious and an extremely popular leader of the faculty; at faculty meetings, he was something of a tamer lionized by his dazzled lions."[244] When Pusey turned out to be a colorless and unassertive administrator, Bundy became, in effect, the intellectual leader of the university. He built upon Conant's strategy of transforming Harvard from an institution serving the northeastern upper class into a national and even international university based on merit. While Harvard College accepted sixty-three percent of all applicants in 1952, by 1960 that figure had dropped to thirty percent.[245]

Bundy helped change what the sociologist David Riesman called the prewar Harvard "of careless preppies, marginal strivers and green bag commuters" into a genuinely academic culture.[246] During Bundy's seven years in the deanship, the university boosted faculty salaries (particularly in the junior ranks), added new chairs, set up new centers, built laboratories and arts facilities, and expanded financial aid. He eliminated some gentlemanly relics such as the tradition of paying the faculty quarterly rather than monthly. Some faculty members resented Bundy's ascent to the deanship without having to undergo the purgatory of graduate training, but others perceived that his freedom from the academic's *déformation professionelle* could be a virtue. A broad-minded man with deep and varied interests, he was an effective critic of academic specialization and disciplinary barriers. The point of a university, he thought, ought to be "the rediscovery of the high purpose of man as a living, loving, thinking, and acting moral entity," a mission that transcended the blinkered vision of disciplinarians.[247]

Bundy could sometimes impose sparkling appointments on a resistant faculty, as in the cases of the psychologist Erik Erikson (who lacked a

Ph.D.) and Riesman (who was considered a popularizer). Bundy's open, anti-bureaucratic style made him popular with professors and students alike. And for all the chilliness of intellect that occasionally radiated through his ice-blue eyes, Bundy could be a social animal, full of wit and charm and fun. Beneath his steely exterior he had reservoirs of emotion that only his family and intimate friends ever saw. It would have surprised people who saw him as coldly analytical to learn that he cried at movies and that he spent an hour each day dictating the complete works of Jane Austen for his mother when her eyes were failing.

Although he was an elegant writer and speaker, Bundy was curiously ill at ease with humanists on the faculty, generally preferring the company of scientists and social scientists. Some faculty members could never get away from the idea of Bundy as a Boston Brahmin. Kissinger, whose career Bundy greatly assisted, wrote that the dean "tended to treat me with the combination of politeness and subconscious condescension that upper-class Bostonians reserve for people of, by New England standards, exotic backgrounds and excessively intense personal style."[248]

If Kissinger meant to insinuate that Bundy was anti-Semitic, there is ample testimony to disprove this. "The only time we ever thought about Jew or non-Jew," Bundy remembered, "was when we would arrange a dinner for the ten people we most wanted to see. We had to remind ourselves after we'd made the list that there ought to be someone there who was not Jewish, so that no one in the dinner party would think, 'The Bundys are having their Jewish friends this time.'"[249] Bundy admired his Jewish friends' energy and intelligence, and appreciated that their presence helped puncture Harvard's starchy exclusivity.

Many Jews, in turn, liked Bundy's intellect, drive, and love of argument. They also recognized that his emphasis on merit had helped get them to Harvard. David Halberstam, who was an undergraduate when Bundy was dean, recalled him as a sort of necessary transitional figure. "He not only was smarter than most WASPs, but in a world that was then becoming a meritocracy, where the young and upcoming instructors had names like Kissinger and Brzezinski, he had this blue-blood background." The advantage meant that, like Brewster at Yale in the 1960s, "Mac could speak for both the old Harvard and the new Harvard. There was a struggle going on between these two worlds, and here was this enormously facile, quick, almost glib figure who could move in both worlds."[250]

Brewster undoubtedly picked up useful insights into academic leadership by observing his friend, and Bundy relied on Brewster as a sort of consigliere during his major political crises as dean. The first involved McCarthy's continuing threat to Harvard, a confrontation in which three faculty members were accused of Communist leanings. They had taken the Fifth Amendment rather than incriminate themselves or name their former associates before congressional inquiries.

The presence of Communists on the faculty presented a dilemma to civil libertarians like Brewster. He and Bundy worked together to come up with ideas about how the university should respond. Even before he became dean, Bundy had written to the provost that Harvard should not knowingly hire a Communist professor but that professors taking the Fifth Amendment at congressional investigations need not be fired if they were candid with the university authorities. Later in the fall of 1953, Brewster typed out a policy statement that Bundy then edited. It declared that the accused faculty had "misused the privilege afforded by the Fifth Amendment. Further, we firmly believe that they have acted irresponsibly toward their government and in a manner which has caused great trouble for their university. We believe, however, that errors of law, including misuse of the Fifth Amendment are matter[s] which in the first instance are the concern of Congress and ultimately for the courts, not for the governing board of the university. Errors of political judgment, even political irresponsibility . . . are not matters on which we can base dismissal."

Brewster went on to say that "we do believe that the covert or self concealed Communist should be dismissed. This is not so much because of his ideology as because he is trying to mislead others on a matter which he knows to be of legitimate concern to them."[251] The question of whether the faculty members should be retained, then, hinged on their candor and credibility.

The assertion was not exactly a pie in the face of McCarthyism, but Harvard refused to dismiss any faculty members who came under fire. It seemed a brave stand at a time when McCarthy's attacks on the university appeared to draw a bright line between the liberal establishment and a dangerous, anti-intellectual populism.[252] McCarthyism was a force that even the most courageous easterners could not challenge.

When Senator Saltonstall ran for reelection in 1954, his criticism of McCarthy was limited to condemnation of his methods. Brewster wrote Richardson to urge that his liberal Republican boss do more. Richardson was a longtime foe of McCarthyism; in 1950 he had written to Senator Henry Cabot Lodge decrying McCarthy's "shameful" and "sordid sideshow."[253] In early 1954, however, Saltonstall's electoral chances depended on his cooperation with the state's junior senator, John F. Kennedy, who (together with much of his Boston Irish constituency) supported McCarthy's red-baiting and whose younger brother Bobby had been McCarthy's assistant. (When Brewster's cousin by marriage Edward Murrow addressed a Boston dinner not long after his scathing anti-McCarthy television documentary had aired, Senator Kennedy pointedly walked out.) Richardson wrote back to Brewster with some agitation that "I too would be greatly excited if at least one of the senatorial candidates in Massachusetts—or anywhere else . . . would take a more forthright position. But let me ask you this: Would you do so yourself as candidate for Senator? Do you seriously think that if you were in my position you would urge Senator Saltonstall to do so?"[254]

In May 1954, Brewster, as head of the Harvard chapter of the American Association of University Professors, organized a ceremony in Sanders Theater to honor Harvard's administrators for standing up to McCarthy. The poet Archibald MacLeish and the historian Samuel Eliot Morison denounced McCarthy and his committee for attempting to "place thought in prison and universities in chains."[255]

Later critics would argue that men such as Bundy and Brewster partook of the general McCarthyist mentality when they called dissidence "political irresponsibility," stated that covert Communists should be dismissed, and pressed former Communists not to hide behind the Fifth Amendment. In the 1970s, several former Harvard junior faculty members asserted that Bundy had pushed them to cooperate with government investigators. Others claimed that they had been denied promotion, or were not hired, on political rather than academic grounds—charges Bundy denied and that would appear difficult to prove or disprove in the absence of documentation.

Undoubtedly Bundy and the rest of the establishment accepted certain Cold War assumptions without questioning. Their latter-day critics, however, tend to be in the grip of their own certainties, blaming McCarthyism on liberals more than on McCarthy himself and overlooking evidence from ex-Soviet archives that, in fact, there were Communist moles in the United States government and that the American branch of the Communist Party prostrated itself before Stalinism.

HARVARD'S OTHER MAJOR political crisis of the decade was the 1958 Memorial Church incident. It began when Pusey declared that the Harvard Yard church "had always been a Christian institution" and therefore could not be used for non-Christian weddings or funerals. The pious president's policy seemed to be aimed particularly against Jews; rumor had it that Pusey thought the wedding ritual of breaking a glass underfoot would tear the church's carpet. Bundy was mortified. But he could not enter the debate directly, since, in his words, "the dean of the Faculty wasn't about to squabble with the president."[256]

Brewster again dragged out his typewriter and, with the approval of Bundy and law school dean Erwin Griswold, constructed a face-saving statement for the president. It said, in part, that "truth is a search which is never wholly successful," although Brewster granted that most people held "convictions that some paths are better than others."[257] Pusey cannot have been pleased by this view of religion as a sort of legal process, but in the end he backed down and the controversy subsided.

Pusey's conception of Harvard as a Christian university would have been shared by most people associated with the institution throughout its existence. His Memorial Church edict was, in a sense, a protest against a falling away from tradition, not unlike Buckley's characterization of Yale. But the reaction brought home the reality that Harvard was no longer the property of the New England upper class; it had become a national institution. Harvard's widened responsibilities meant that it had to abandon some of its traditions. Although men like Brewster and Bundy wore religion lightly if at all—Bundy liked to say that he was "an unconvinced Episcopalian"—their disagreement with Pusey was not a reaction against religion per se. It was, rather, the result of their broader conception of the role of establishment institutions and establishment leaders.

The end of the 1950s was marked by a pronounced restlessness among the nation's thinkers and doers—a product both of impatience with Eisenhower's cautious approach to change and of the energies of young men in their late thirties and early forties who wanted to make their mark. Men like Brewster and Bundy had a genuine wish to be of service to the nation, a desire that was a complicated mixture of Stimsonian idealism, personal ambition, and what Bill Bundy had called in his 1939 Yale class oration a conviction that "if we are to consider ourselves as a group and a class of special significance, we must get right down to earth and perform special services, for it is only on that basis that the idea of class can be tolerated in a democracy."[258] As the 1960s dawned, the older generation seemed finally to be passing the torch; the brightest spirits of the liberal establishment would, at last, have the chance to create the world they had talked about since the war.

4

NEW FRONTIERS

IN THE fall of 1959, Brewster and his longtime friend, Yale's president Whit Griswold, were sailing in Griswold's catboat off Martha's Vineyard. Brewster and his former teacher liked to meet on autumn weekends, when the dunes were touched with color and the air filled with migrating birds, and meander through the waters that each had sailed for decades, drinking beer and talking about higher education. Their conversation consisted partly of serious discussion of the problems facing American universities, partly of Brewster teasing the president about Yale's shortcomings, especially in relation to Harvard. This time Griswold shot back: "Well, why don't you come to Yale and do something about it?"[1] Shortly thereafter, it was announced that Brewster would leave his Harvard law professorship to become Yale's Provost-Designate on Leave of Absence for the 1960–61 academic year.

Brewster was not Griswold's first choice as provost. The other top candidates were also Yale graduates who went on to become Harvard professors: the physicist and engineer Harvey Brooks and the classicist Zeph Stewart.[2] The Yale-to-Harvard trajectory of all the candidates was significant: Griswold clearly was looking to Yale's best and brightest for help in emulating Harvard's more intellectual orientation. Stewart recalled that Griswold had been "very disappointed" with what he had found of Yale's alumni around the country: "As he would go from city to city, the Yale graduates would be the heads of the local Red Cross, the community chest, various do-good campaigns . . . but the Harvard people would be the heads of the symphony orchestras, the museums, and the intellectual things. And he thought that was the difference between Harvard and Yale that he would like to work on changing."[3]

It was important for Griswold that his provost have had exposure to the Harvard model and bring some Cantabridgian influence to New Haven. As Stewart put it, "He would have felt that if people were good enough to be well thought of at Harvard, that would be kind of a cachet at Yale."[4] Moreover, the choice needed to be a man who was not only bright and able but who was personally known to Griswold and his circle and came from the same privileged culture. Stewart and Brewster especially fit the bill. Stewart was in the Class of 1943 at Yale. He had been president of Phi Beta Kappa, wrote editorials for the *Yale Daily News,* was tapped for Skull and Bones, and worked with Brewster in the America First movement. After the war, he was taken into Harvard's elite Society of Fellows along with McGeorge Bundy, and like Brewster held a government job in Paris. His older brother Potter was a Supreme Court justice.

But Brewster's connections with Griswold were more extensive than the other candidates'. The relationship between the two dated back to Brewster's early years on Martha's Vineyard. Both families had homes in Vineyard Haven, and, in season, the two would meet on the water or over drinks. On these occasions, Brewster "would needle the new president about various Yale misfortunes—lost football games or professors snatched by other colleges."[5] Griswold appreciated this adult impudence.

Griswold's first preference for a provost was a humanist academic, however, and in November 1958 he offered Stewart the position. Brewster and McGeorge Bundy urged him to accept, but after mulling it over for nearly a year, Stewart decided that the job had limited possibilities and would not allow him to carry out much educational reform. Nor did he see the job as a springboard to greater responsibilities. "One of the things that Whit held out to me," he recalled, "was that he said, 'When I stop being president, the person who is provost would be very much in line for the presidency.' . . . 'Well,' I thought to myself, 'that is great, but Whit is going to be president for twenty years more.'"[6]

Griswold had asked the history professor John Blum to appraise Stewart and Brewster as candidates. Blum, who knew both men well, expressed a clear preference for Brewster: "I thought Kingman had more style—administrative style, flair, personal style—than Zeph . . . And I thought Kingman had a more educated sense of the world, both of the academy and the academy in the larger environment."[7] Blum's evaluation may have confirmed Griswold's decision to offer the post to his second choice.

Griswold selected Brewster not because he thought he would be a modernizer but because, as Bundy put it, he saw in his protégé "character and quick intelligence and human sympathy and an ease of communication . . . and Kingman's lively sense of what a university is about."[8]

When Brewster asked his friend Bundy whether he ought to take the job, he received a hearty approval. "It was what Kingman wanted to do, and it set him free to do the kind of thing that interested him vastly more than being a professor of law." Brewster was suited to be the president's top assistant, Bundy thought, because "Kingman had character. Whit was an uncommonly honest man, and so was Kingman, and they could be absolutely sure that there would be no cloud on the clarity and the closeness and the ease of their conversation." Bundy also saw that "both believed that one of the most important things about important things is that they should also be fun. And they understood that about each other, and had an absolutely marvelous time."[9]

As Brewster later observed, his major reason for taking the job was the opportunity to work with his "friend and hero" A. Whitney Griswold.[10] Yet his was not an uncritical loyalty. Brewster saw "great unfulfilled potential" in Yale and in Griswold himself. Yale was "a little dull and parochial," Brewster thought, although "Whit was struggling mightily to break out of it."[11] Unlike Stewart, he perceived his role as provost to be a catalyst, managing what Stewart called "the material side of the university" in a way that would have direct educational impact. The job also offered Brewster what he called "a riskless chance to find out whether I liked academic administration and was any good at it. I told Whit that I would not want to stay in the job more than ten years at the most; and that he shouldn't feel poorly dealt with if I decided I didn't like it. Conversely, he should be quick to tell me if he thought I was no good at it."[12]

The provostship allowed Brewster a graceful exit from the Harvard Law School, where he had become restless as a professor. It was clear that he had been searching for a way to apply his talents and ideas more directly.[13] At the Friday Evening Club send-off for Brewster, Bundy rhymed a tribute to "Kingman Brewster, Junior Provost / Sing-and-swimster, friend in foremost," and poked gentle fun at his friend the "Flyer, Drinker, Clever Sailor / Higher-thinker, ever Yaler."[14]

The timing of Brewster's selection as provost meant that he took himself out of the running for a political appointment in whatever administration would succeed Eisenhower's. That prospect had begun to preoccupy many leading members of the Harvard community as the 1960 presidential contest reached its climax. Kennedy had not impressed Brewster or many of his friends over the years. The Kennedys, as the historian Alonzo Hamby noted, were "wealthy but hardly members of the patrician world in the mode of the Roosevelts or the Tafts." They were "on the fringes of an establishment of which they were not quite a part but from which they were not alienated."[15] Richardson had lived in the same entryway as John Kennedy at Harvard, where Kennedy had been a playboy and a "C" student, and remembered him as "a mousy guy whom nobody noticed much."[16] Brewster's Nantucket sailing rival Alfred Chandler "remember[ed] thinking as I watched the 1960 Democratic convention on TV, 'How can Jack Kennedy be President?'"[17]

Politically, Brewster and Richardson and their reform-minded friends were wary of Kennedy, because he had supported McCarthy in the 1950s and his father had bankrolled James Curley and other crooked pols in Massachusetts' Irish political machine. Brewster blamed the Kennedys for not cleaning up "the worst political sinkhole in the United States north of Mississippi."[18] That Jack Kennedy did not meet Brewster's rather rigid moral and personal standards had been evident since their sailing days in the 1930s. Jack and his older brother, Joe Jr., came to Martha's Vineyard to compete in the Edgartown Regatta and spent the night in jail following a bout of drinking, destructiveness, and rowdiness.[19] Kennedy's out-of-control philandering offended men like Brewster, Bundy, and Richardson, who by all accounts were virgins until marriage and never cheated on their wives.

Brewster's—and Bundy's—preferred candidate was the liberal Republican Nelson Rockefeller. Nixon's nomination as the GOP candidate put both men in a bind. Brewster had "no particular respect or affection for Nixon," as he wrote to his friend Peter Solbert, because of his red-baiting activities in the 1940s and 1950s.[20] Bundy concurred that "Nixon had been a real four-letter word to me ever since his Senate race against Helen Gahagan Douglas.[21] Bundy, who had been casually friendly with Kennedy since the two attended grade school in Boston, developed a political relationship with him in the late 1950s through Democratic friends like Schlesinger. Meeting with Bundy in a private room at Locke-Ober's, a Boston restaurant thick with old Harvard associations, Kennedy was impressed by the dean's intelligence and willingness to criticize members of his own Republican Party.[22]

Brewster began to hear positive reports of Kennedy from Bundy and from his Yale classmate Charles Spalding, who was part of Kennedy's inner circle. Brewster would have voted for Kennedy in the election, somewhat reluctantly, had he met the residency requirements in Connecticut when he moved to New Haven in the fall of 1960. Other friends were more enthusiastic when Kennedy won his narrow victory. Paul Moore had known Kennedy socially in Palm Beach, where both their families wintered, and Kennedy had come to dinner at the Moores' on occasion. The two also had many friends in common, including Spalding and the late George Mead Jr., whose grave Kennedy had visited on Guadalcanal during World War II.[23] Moreover, both had been wounded in the war, and Moore felt, with Kennedy's election, that "we had paid our dues, we had done our apprenticeship in our respective vocations. Now the time had come for our generation to lead."[24] As they moved into positions of power, Brewster and his contemporaries were acutely conscious of the weight of their responsibilities. Generally, these men entering their early forties were in a more serious mood than the star-struck younger people drawn to the New Frontier. Still, it was an optimistic time for the liberal establishment as well.

After his election, Kennedy offered Bundy several posts. According to his son, Bundy was actually keen to become head of the Department of Health, Education, and Welfare, a position that went to another Republican, John W. Gardner.[25] But, as it happened, all the president-elect's offers to Bundy were in the area of foreign policy. When the president-elect suggested Bundy become undersecretary of state for administrative affairs, Bundy consulted Brewster and several others before turning down the offer. Finally Kennedy proposed that Bundy become a special assistant to the president for national security affairs.

CYRUS VANCE ALSO secured political appointment through Kennedy's victory. After graduating from Yale Law School and serving in the Pacific during the war, Vance had worked for a year as assistant to George Mead, the president of the Mead Paper Company, whose son Vance had known through the Scroll and Key society at Yale. After passing the New York bar in 1947, Vance had risen through the ranks at the Wall Street law firm Simpson, Thacher & Bartlett, which would serve as his home base for the rest of his life. Specializing in civil litigation, he became known for his efficiency, precision, sound judgment, and stamina for hard work.

Vance joined the Council on Foreign Relations, the favored debating society of the policy elite, in 1957. Later that year the Soviets launched *Sputnik,* the first artificial satellite. The event badly shook American complacency over the state of national scientific and technological capabilities. The Senate majority leader, Lyndon Johnson, tapped Vance and his law partner Edwin Weisl (a longtime associate of Johnson's) to be counsel to a preparedness investigation committee. Vance thought that "a useful service could be rendered for the country" by having nonpartisan hearings to decide whether a military or civil agency should direct America's entry into the space race.[26] Vance and Weisl knew nothing about astronautics but were confident that as trial lawyers they could handle any case, whatever the subject.

The next year Vance helped draft the act establishing the National Aeronautics and Space Administration (NASA). His performance on the preparedness committee led to service as counsel for other defense-related Senate subcommittees over the next years. Vance had developed a deliberately nonflamboyant persona. One person who took part in the 1957 hearings recalled that "Vance was around for two weeks before many of us realized that he was there."[27] Those who did notice Vance—Johnson among them—were impressed with his effort, skills at negotiation, and detailed understanding of the defense establishment. Vance and Weisl also assisted Johnson at the 1960 Democratic convention, in Los Angeles. When Johnson was elected vice president, on the Kennedy ticket, he recommended Vance to the new defense secretary, Robert McNamara. On Christmas Eve 1960, Deputy Secretary of Defense Roswell Gilpatric, an older friend and fellow Yale graduate, offered Vance the position of general counsel. Vance accepted and was sworn in by Kennedy in January 1961, at a ceremony at which Vance's mother was in the audience.[28]

Vance would become perhaps the highest-achieving, lowest-profile government official of the 1960s. As general counsel, and later as secretary of the Army and deputy secretary of defense, he remained almost completely unknown to the general public. Within establishment circles, however, he became something of a legend. His precision of thought, attention to detail, and lack of appetite for self-promotion made him invaluable to McNamara, for whom he acted as a virtual alter ego. McNamara, in turn, became Vance's major influence in government. "When Vance first came to Washington," one associate said, "he was essentially the man in the Brooks Brothers suit, a conservative member of the Eastern Establishment. McNamara broadened his horizons, broadened his perspective and philosophy. Both men have gained considerably from their friendship."[29]

An able spotter of talent, Vance helped McNamara recruit many of the key staff members who revolutionized Pentagon operations. Vance brought Joseph Califano Jr.—later Johnson's powerful presidential assistant—into government when Califano was, in his recollection, "just a young lawyer from Brooklyn without any special contacts."[30] Background meant nothing to Vance, intelligence and competence everything. He established an open-door policy and shook up the military with his disregard for stars and braid, cutting through protocol to quiz bright junior officers with firsthand operating experience. His legal talent stood him in good stead; one official grilled by Vance felt that "I had been sucked completely dry of anything I had ever learned since grammar school."[31] Vance's capacity for work was also notorious. He typically arrived at the office at 7 in the morning and left between 9:30 and 11 at night, six days a week and two Sundays a month. His schedule left little time for social engagements, although he was obliged to attend occasional black-tie events such as the White House Correspondents dinner, the Gridiron Club dinner, and the Wallow of the Military Order of the Crabao. While he didn't see much of his children, he tried to set aside time to take them to Redskins games and to attend fathers' nights at their schools.

Few of Vance's coworkers at the Pentagon got to know him well. His low profile stemmed, in part, from his extreme shyness, a quality he shared with his friends Brewster and Bundy. "Vance was not a guy with whom you had personal conversations," Califano observed. Although Califano worked alongside Vance nearly every day for several years, he said, "I don't even need one hand to count the number of personal conversations we had. . . . I don't want to give the impression that he was cold, or chilly to work for. He was terrific to work for. He had a good sense of humor, he wasn't overbearing, and he was very modest. But he was very focused on work."[32]

Vance's embodiment of the highest establishment ideals of character earned him respect and acclaim in his circle even while it made him bad copy for journalists. He made no enemies, incurred no criticism, and won unanimous, monotonously hyperbolic praise from all quarters. Integrity, honesty, balance, fairness, modesty, warmth, level-headedness—all who knew Vance chose the same gentlemanly, respectable, slightly gray qualities to characterize him. His only vice, as far as could be determined, was a weakness for smoked Irish salmon flown in from Shannon duty-free. He had no need to throw his weight around or stand on his authority; once when copies of 150 Pentagon speeches were needed within twenty-four hours for a congressional committee, he spent the night on the copying machine alongside the secretaries.[33] "Cy's great advantage," one of his Yale classmates noted, "is that he has never hungered for fame or recognition, just solid achievement. Because of that he is more secure than most men."[34] Vance seemed completely fulfilled by public service. He told graduating students at his old prep school that "I can say from my own brief experience in government service that I have never experienced greater satisfaction and happiness. It is an inspiration and a privilege to be associated with a host of dedicated men who are devoting their lives to the defense of our country."[35]

In taking on his government assignments, Vance believed that he was living up to what was expected of him. "A lot of us were raised in families where we were taught that we were very fortunate, that we were going to have a good education," he recalled. As a result, he felt "that we had the responsibility to return to the community some of the blessings we had, and that there was an obligation to participate in government service at the local, state and national level." Vance's view, "in a nutshell," the *New York Times* later commented, "was the unself-conscious voice of the establishment."[36]

For Richardson, who also believed deeply in the obligation of service, the Kennedy victory meant that he had to find a new job. After serving as assistant to Senator Saltonstall in 1953–54, Richardson had returned to Ropes & Gray. For Richardson as for Vance, the law firm would be stable territory between stints of government service, although he believed that the legal calling didn't match "the satisfaction of doing a good job for the public."[37] While in private practice, Richardson remained active in Republican politics; he served for a while as acting counsel to Massachusetts governor Christian Herter, another political protégé of Richardson's uncle Henry Shattuck. In 1956 he wrote the speech, nominating Vice President Richard Nixon for a second term, that Herter delivered at the GOP convention. Later that year, Richardson was asked to become Eisenhower's speechwriter. He politely refused, since he was already committed to writing speeches for Herter's lieutenant governor, Sumner Whittier, and thought it would have been dishonorable to break his commitment.[38] In 1957, Eisenhower appointed Richardson assistant secretary in the Department of Health, Education, and Welfare. "Many of us who joined President Eisenhower's administration at the beginning of his second term," Richardson remembered, "came to Washington in high hopes of helping to build a new political consensus."[39]

Richardson looked forward to the prospect of helping construct "modern Republicanism," a hard-to-define philosophy that accepted an expanded role for government and the social safety net but tempered New Deal welfarism with business-friendly policies and fiscal prudence. It would be, he wrote, "an exciting new blend of conservatism and compassion"—a phrase later hijacked by considerably less modern Republicans. "Our philosophy began and, some people thought, ended with an utterance by Abraham Lincoln which we quoted at every opportunity: 'The purpose of government is to do for people what they cannot do at all or do so well for themselves.'"[40]

According to Richardson, he entered public service because "I have some of the reform-mindedness, the desire to fix things that seem wrong, that's characteristic of New Englanders."[41] His work at HEW had involved drafting legislation for unemployment relief, public health, juvenile delinquency, medical education and research, and a host of other social issues. Occasionally he sat in on Eisenhower's cabinet meetings and served as acting secretary of HEW in 1958. The *Sputnik* launch that brought Vance to preparedness hearings in Washington led Richardson to draft his most important and controversial initiative, the National Defense Education Act. The measure provided federal aid to schools and universities, breaking the tradition of exclusive state and local funding for education. Partly for that reason it was billed as a Cold War defense measure, to which Congress attached a loyalty oath. The oath had caused problems for McGeorge Bundy at Harvard. Dean Bundy tried to persuade the faculty that Harvard would play no direct role in the oath taking but would merely return the oaths the students had signed (or not) to Washington. "We're simply licking the stamps," he said. To which the Italian scholar Renato Poggioli retorted, in heavily accented English, "Mr. Dean, I have spent much of my life in Fascista Italy. And in Fascista Italy, you learna one thing. First you licka the stamps. Then you licka something else."[42] Harvard and Yale had rejected the NDEA grants. But the measure was still, Richardson thought, "greatly in the national interest."[43] It was the first funding bill for elementary and secondary education to pass Congress in some fifty years, and many observers felt that Richardson had executed its passage "almost single-handedly."[44]

In 1959, Eisenhower named Richardson United States attorney for the District of Massachusetts. "We will miss you in Washington," his friend John Lindsay wrote, "but I trust it will not be long before you are back."[45] Lindsay told other friends that Richardson was "the kind of public servant and Republican that warms my heart and gives me hope for the future."[46] John Kennedy's aide Theodore Sorensen joked at Richardson's farewell: "Avaunt all ye Hoffas and hoodlums / Gather ye hot goods while you may / For your syndicates and empires are crumbling / Old Elliot's to be the D.A."[47] Returning to Boston as a criminal-law enforcer, Richardson proved to be a relentless, incorruptible Mr. Clean. His Puritan uprightness harkened back to Governor John Winthrop's stern admonition: "We must always consider that we shall be as a city upon a hill—the eyes of all people are upon us." In the poisoned swamp of Massachusetts politics, Richardson found ample opportunity to demonstrate his unyielding New England integrity. Every tax evader charged by his office was convicted and jailed, although his prosecution of Bernard Goldfine, a textile manufacturer who had made gifts to the White House aide Sherman Adams, proved a major embarrassment to the Eisenhower administration.

As a U.S. attorney, Richardson once again was following in the footsteps of Henry Stimson. This fact was impressed on him by his former boss Felix Frankfurter, who, in his turn, had been an assistant U.S. attorney under Stimson. Frankfurter remembered that as a U.S. attorney, Stimson had been so scrupulous about fairness that he would require his assistants to accompany government agents on raids to make sure that they kept within the limits of the search warrant. "So indelibly, indeed, did Frankfurter's teaching transmit to me the standards of his former chief," Richardson wrote, "that when I became a US attorney myself in 1959, I thought of Stimson as the invisible watchdog of my own prosecutorial behavior."[48]

Calling on the resources of federal investigative agencies and Harvard professors, Richardson was the first U.S. attorney to systematically analyze organized crime in his district. His pursuit of crooked officials paralleled Shattuck's earlier good-government efforts against grafting Boston pols like his archenemy William F. Callahan. Indeed, Callahan later became Richardson's archenemy as well, "and almost did me in."[49] Richardson also made use of the bully pulpit afforded by his position to inveigh against corruption, which he saw as a reflection of "the ego-centered, self-indulgent, conscienceless amorality of a fast-buck, expense-account society." The state's slide toward mediocrity and decay could be arrested only by "intelligent long-range planning, by the effective use of experts, and by responsible officeholders who understand the need for both."[50]

Although Richardson's stern admonitions often made him come across as wooden in writing and speeches, those close to him saw the exuberance and zest he brought to public service. "I'm a short-loop feedback type," he once said. "I liked combat. I liked prosecuting people. I loved sending crooks to jail. I liked politics and bureaucratic infighting and pushing legislation on the Hill." His time as U.S. attorney for Massachusetts, however, came to an end after the 1960 presidential election, when the new attorney general, Robert Kennedy, "threw me out in the winter of 1961."[51] Kennedy demanded his resignation with unseemly haste.

Richardson was convinced that the president's brother had acted to prevent a grand jury indictment of Callahan and other Democrats caught with their fingers in the till of the Massachusetts Turnpike Authority. When he met with Kennedy the day after his termination, he mentioned that his abrupt departure had stirred a good deal of speculation in Massachusetts. "I don't give a shit what they think in Massachusetts," the attorney general replied harshly, fixing Richardson with a hard stare.[52] Their confrontation resounded with the echoes of battles between Boston's Brahmins and Irish. Richardson recalled later that "Bobby Kennedy was the one guy I ever came up against in my political life who struck me as a grade-A prick."[53]

Returning to Ropes & Gray to plot his next political move, Richardson included Brewster in his proposal to Nixon that the defeated Republicans establish "a thoughtful, high-level journal of opinion" that could "serve as a forum for responsible criticism, constructive alternatives to administrative proposals, new ideas, and the gradual articulation of a positive and dynamic Republican philosophy."[54] In 1961, he informed a friend that "I am planning to run for Attorney General of Massachusetts and will, in all likelihood, have competition for the nomination from an attractive and articulate young Negro named Edward W. Brooke."[55] Richardson lost narrowly to Brooke (who later became a senator and close friend) in the 1962 Republican primary. "I was disturbed, sunk and saddened by the result at the convention in re yourself," Richardson's friend John Lindsay wrote to him. "You deserved [the nomination] . . . you are what this Republican Party badly needs."[56]

LIKE RICHARDSON, LINDSAY was a patrician exemplar of integrity and independence in political action. He, too, believed that public service was the highest calling and found the mere acquisition of wealth to be unsatisfying. One friend said later that Lindsay and his wife, Mary, "could so easily have turned into bloodless Long Island types like everybody else they knew," but Lindsay chose a less lucrative but more rewarding path.[57] "By the time I finished Yale," he commented, "I had had all the 'advantages,' and what the hell was all that money for if I didn't do more with my education than just make a good living?"

After winning his first election as member of Congress representing New York's Silk Stocking district, Lindsay became one of the leading standard-bearers of liberal Republicanism. To the extent that liberal Republicanism survives today, it lingers on as a bland, beige-suit-wearing, difference-splitting centrism. Lindsay, however, was a model of principled and courageous independence. As congressman, he was a maverick hero along the lines of Brewster's boyhood idol George Norris. Lobbyists were alarmed to discover that Lindsay was absolutely incorruptible and unbuyable, a man who would return the gifts that other congressmen accepted as perquisites of the job, and was equally unbending toward labor and business lobbyists.

Republican elders also found out, to their dismay, that Lindsay was impervious to party discipline and unyielding in his idealism. His ideas were not radical in and of themselves. He believed in the professed Republican tenets of individual rights and liberties, he distrusted highly centralized government power, and he echoed Eisenhower's warnings about the military-industrial complex. What made Lindsay an independent, however, was that he retained his boyish, prep school idealism and pursued it consistently. Nineteen days after he was seated in Congress, he broke the unwritten rule that freshmen do not publicly challenge the presumptions of their elders. Unable to sit still while one senior Republican troglodyte accused the Supreme Court under Chief Justice Earl Warren of "brazenly" substituting "Socialist doctrines" for Americanism, Lindsay emotionally declared that "I will defend as long as I have voice in my body the jurisdiction of the Supreme Court in every area involving the personal rights and liberties of our people, including the area of internal security. . . . In my view, historians will write that this Supreme Court is one of the great courts of our country."

Lindsay went on to infuriate Republican regulars through his support of the United Nations, public school integration, and an increase in the minimum wage, as well as his opposition to nuclear testing, the House Un-American Activities Committee, and a constitutional amendment to permit prayer in the public schools. He earned the censure of the New York Young Republican Club by casting one of the deciding votes to enlarge the Rules Committee, through which Republicans and southern Democrats had long strangled civil rights reform. By casting the lone vote against a bill allowing the postmaster general to impound allegedly obscene material if doing so was in the "public interest," he showed up his colleagues as cowards. Other congressmen privately agreed that the bill was blatantly unconstitutional, but no one else had dared to challenge it.[58]

While Lindsay was open to compromise under certain circumstances and always gave an issue an open hearing, his integrity and fidelity to matters of principle threatened the accepted, everyday inadequacies of Congress, its logrolling and petty corruption. Lindsay defended the national interest as he saw it, even at the cost of his party, his constituents, or his own future;

he knew full well that his defiance would cost him the Foreign Affairs Committee appointment he badly wanted. He would never stoop to conquer to advance his career, as, for example, the Yale graduate and budding politician George H. W. Bush did by cultivating right-wing votes in Texas. Although Lindsay had met his wife-to-be at the wedding of Bush's sister, Mary Lindsay blasted George's betrayal of the liberal Republican tradition in his pursuit of political gain: "Well, you can bet *my* husband wouldn't have done it."[59]

Once while crossing the Capitol rotunda with a reporter, Lindsay pointed to a group of tourists standing reverently in the echoing stillness of the Statuary Hall. "Look at them," he said. "Look at the expressions on their faces. They're really moved. When I walk by here, I always wish Congress were a better place than it is. The trouble is we have to make up these deliberative bodies with human beings, and the members don't always stand up to the white marble."[60] In a way it was that desire that lay at the bottom of the establishment ethos: not just to emulate wise mentors like Henry Stimson and John McCloy but to measure up to the tradition of morality, probity, intelligence, honor, and farsighted statesmanship set by the Founding Fathers. But what would that mean in the context of the early 1960s?

THE FIRST ORDER of business for these would-be leaders was to come to grips with the contours and requirements of their positions. In some respects, Brewster's situation when he came to Yale as provost-designate in 1960 was highly tentative. He had no real background in university administration and lacked a Ph.D., the passport to intellectual respectability as far as many faculty members were concerned. His legal rather than humanistic background aroused fears that he would cater to research and the professional schools at the expense of teaching, the liberal arts, and the undergraduate college.

There was also the fact that Brewster came from outside; unlike most of the university's administrators at that time, he had begun his professional career at another institution and so did not have an intimate, in-depth knowledge of Yale. Suspicion of Harvard remained in some quarters, notably in the law school and among the college faculty, particularly those who were Yale College graduates. Brewster brought with him a sound if not stellar reputation from Harvard. Yet the Yale Law School faculty grumbled at giving him tenure on his appointment, not only because he had been at the rival institution but because, one law professor said bluntly, "we had the impression of Brewster as a straight-shooting mediocrity."[61] Yale at that time was also administratively underdeveloped. The provost commanded little power, resources, or influence, and the office dealt mainly with buildings-and-grounds issues. In short, Brewster needed a strategy that would allow him to overcome his weak position, redefine his office, and give Yale a modern managerial structure that would enable it to play a larger role in the national life.

The key to Brewster's approach lay in the support of the president—Alfred Whitney Griswold—who resisted easy definition, academically, politically, or socially. Brewster remembered that "the most extraordinary fact about the man was his vividness,"[62] and it is surprising that, nearly half a century after Griswold's death, many people can clearly recall the sound of his voice and the force of his personality. Stories about his sardonic humor abounded. Once as he and his wife were driving across a bridge into Manhattan to attend a concert, he suddenly turned to her and said, "You know, I wish we had our piano here with us." His wife looked at him askance and asked why. "Because our concert tickets are on top of the piano," he replied. He had sparkle, fierceness, and influential friends; he was one of Acheson's handful of intimates.[63] And yet few people could claim to have known him well.

Griswold was perhaps the most ivory tower president of Yale in the twentieth century, and in many ways the university turned toward conservatism in the decade after his inauguration, in 1950. Yet he undoubtedly thought of himself as a progressive. One of a handful of Democrats on the Yale faculty in the 1930s, he was, according to his wife, "drummed out of the regiment" in family circles for his pro–New Deal views.[64]

As a graduate student, Griswold had pioneered in the new academic field of history, the arts, and letters (in which Brewster majored as an undergraduate) and produced the first doctoral dissertation in American studies in the country.[65] His scholarly model was the noted progressive-isolationist Charles Beard, who wrote of Griswold that "there is no student of his generation for whose talents and labors I have a higher regard."[66] As a Young Turk dissident faculty reformer, Griswold was one of the most vocal critics of president Charles Seymour, whom he impertinently described as "descended from a long line of bronze statues."[67] Griswold was named to the Yale presidency because the Corporation thought a young, idealistic insider was best suited to rouse the university from the sluggishness and anomie into which it had sunk during the Seymour presidency.

And yet for all his academic idealism and progressive political views,

Griswold was quite conservative culturally and to some extent socially. After Brewster had rejected Skull and Bones and the other secret societies on Tap Day in 1940, he bicycled to Griswold's house, no doubt expecting that his mentor would be pleased by his youthful independence and iconoclasm. Instead, Brewster learned that Griswold was downtown helping the Wolf's Head delegation tap Paul Moore and several other of Brewster's classmates. To a greater extent than many realized, Griswold's views had been formed in predepression Yale and the WASP upper class of the interwar years.[68]

Griswold admired Harvard's James Conant, but more for Conant's devotion to scholarship and improvement of the faculty than for his efforts in the sciences, his commitment to meritocracy, or his administrative expertise. Griswold's educational philosophy was much closer to that of Robert Maynard Hutchins, the antimodernist, reforming president of the University of Chicago. Griswold shared Hutchins's fear that the exigencies of World War II would overwhelm the humanistic orientation of universities such as Yale and Chicago. In the fall of 1942, Hutchins warned Griswold that "by the end of this academic year all the universities will have become technological institutes and there will be no centers of intelligence left."[69]

An antipathy to technology and institutes would characterize Griswold's presidency and point to his position as a conservative reformer. He was not a traditionalist. He tried to free Yale education from what he called the "false myth of Yale—the Yale of casual but big-time activity." Even before becoming president, he campaigned with allies on the Corporation and in the faculty to emphasize learning over the extracurricular activities for which Yale was better known and which Griswold often deprecated as "that Dink Stover crap" and "Bonesy bullshit."[70] He despised the sleepy amateurism that epitomized Yale's old-boy administration and clubby faculty hiring practices. Envious of the academic culture and respect for scholarship that characterized Harvard after World War II, he frankly sought to emulate Harvard.[71] Even the most acerbic critics of Griswold, such as the historian Roger Geiger, conceded that he brought "a fierce regard for academic excellence" to the presidency.[72] While Griswold was hostile to the old-guard traditionalists, however, he was equally hostile to modernization.

The institution that Griswold inherited on his election in 1950 had been poorly served by the depression, World War II, and Charles Seymour. It was beset by serious financial problems, administrative paralysis, and academic weakness outside the humanities. As the tide of veterans receded, an unconscious conspiracy was played out by many administrators, faculty members, and students to reorient the institution to the half-remembered, half-imagined concept of a school for the elite.

This conservatism represented a counteroffensive of tradition against modernization. An apt symbol of the counterreaction was the faculty's decision, in 1952, to impose a coat-and-tie rule on undergraduates. Such a dress code had never been required before but was deemed necessary to combat the "disorderliness" and "sloppiness" of the "ill-bred," nontraditional students who had appeared on campus during the veteran years.[73] An equally apt symbol was the continuing informal limitation on Jewish admissions, which hovered around the ten percent level throughout the 1950s.[74]

If Griswold did not willingly inaugurate the new turn toward conservatism, he abetted it by setting his standard against the most crucial aspect of modernization—meritocratic selection in university admissions. He had little interest in the effects of higher education on class and mobility and disdained any notion of universities as stepping-stones to the professions. The purpose of a college education, in his view, was to strengthen one's powers of thought and instill a knowledge and appreciation of civilized values.

The prewar university, Griswold felt, had been infused with a powerful ethos of community, solidarity, and unquestioned purpose. He aimed to reform the institution to emphasize what he called "the mature, intellectual purposes and activities of the University."[75] During the 1950s he introduced a spirit of academic reform that helped change Yale, sometimes in ways he had not anticipated or intended. Yet Griswold himself remained something of an academic isolationist at heart. Through most of the decade, Yale kept at arm's length from federal support, at a time when such aid was increasingly generous.

At his best, Griswold tried to balance tradition and meritocracy, uniformity and diversity, inbreeding and talent searching, teaching and research, college and university values. He was not opposed to ideals of meritocracy per se. He contributed to opening Yale to previously excluded groups, but essentially in response to others' initiatives. Within the university a feeling lingered that Yale was an institution that educated men who would hold property and power in a society that deferred to upper-class standards and leadership.

Ultimately Griswold's positions undermined his overarching goal of academic excellence and were modified or reversed in the years after 1960 when Kingman Brewster came to Yale as provost. Brewster's outside perspective was needed at a time when, as Griswold stressed, private universities were facing unprecedented competition from public universities, and institutions of higher education could no longer rest on regional reputations.

The emphasis that Brewster placed on the professional schools was long overdue. He had well-developed ideas of process that he itched to apply to the problems of management. (Friends in Cambridge recalled him saying on many occasions, "I want to run something."[76]) He had some familiarity with academic administration through extensive contact with Harvard administrators like Bundy, and exposure to the problems of modernizing universities through his participation in the 1958–59 Ford Foundation Seminar on the Financing of Higher Education.

Bundy felt that Brewster "used to take the position that all administrators are the enemy."[77] Perhaps it is more accurate to say that Brewster objected to the tendencies of many administrators to settle into comfortable, uncontroversial routines. As he wrote to Griswold in 1943, "Now that you have become an 'administrator' *don't stop thinking—please.* . . . I hope you share my opinion that an administrator . . . is not worth his salt . . . unless he is willing—even eager—to scrap now and then."[78] As provost and president, Brewster would live up to his own youthful charge.

In the 1960–61 academic year, Brewster had no formal responsibilities and was free, in effect, to reinvent the provostship from the ground up. He did not work closely with the regular provost, Norman ("Steve") Buck, who had been allowed to stay for a year beyond retirement age to familiarize Brewster with the office. Buck, who referred to Brewster as "the boy," did not sympathize with the younger man's modernizing view of administration. Even so, no major flare-ups occurred between them, and Brewster became Yale's full-fledged provost in July 1961.[79]

Brewster's aim, during his early years, was to learn as much as he could about Yale and get to know people. He burrowed through the budget (such as it was), thinking about ways to rationalize it and introduce long-term planning into the university's calculations. He sat in on classes. He joined undergraduates in the dining hall, both to listen to their concerns and to check on the quality of the food. He was in communication with scholars and administrators around the country, to get an external reading on the institution's strengths and shortcomings. He talked with deans, department heads, college masters, and faculty, finding out what was happening within the disciplines, who was well regarded, and whom he could trust. He hired bright young assistants, including David B. H. Martin, who had been one of Richardson's closest aides at HEW.[80] And he spent countless hours in conversation with Griswold.

Because he was a gregarious man and a quick study, able to digest an enormous amount of information through conversation, Brewster had little difficulty learning his way around the institution. He had excellent taste in people, and possessed personal qualities that inspired fierce loyalty in the people he led. Corporation member Harold Howe remembered that "he had a kind of élan about him that was very powerful. He picked people up and carried them along with both logic and enthusiasm."[81] Another observer commented that Brewster had "a born patrician's air of authority."[82] Further, he was already plugged into a network of scholars (many of them from the Cambridge academic community) that he could call upon for advice and rumors from the academic grapevine.

As provost, Brewster was widely credited with inspiriting the place with a tangible feeling of revival, to the extent that people began talking of a "New Yale." A young and energetic corps of administrators came to the fore, all of whom had considerable experience outside the embrace of Yale.

The new dean of the graduate school, John Perry Miller, who had received his undergraduate and graduate training at Harvard, was a protégé of Brewster's mentor Edward Mason. Miller had won his administrative spurs at Yale by helping wrest control of the Economics Department from its conservative elders and had significantly enhanced its size and reputation. (His efforts were greatly assisted by the funds and attention that came to the department after Buckley attacked it in God and Man at Yale; "we owe Bill Buckley a great deal," Miller concluded.[83])

Georges May, the new dean of the college, represented an even further departure from the Old Blue stereotype. A Frenchman born of a Jewish mother and an agnostic father, he had not even come to the United States until he was twenty-one. He fought with the French and American armies during the war and served in the Office of Strategic Services. Brewster, who pushed for May's appointment, described him as "a civilized, urbane, tough, compassionate man with a great sense of humor and no self-seriousness."[84]

Each of these men was a strong leader within his bailiwick, and they worked well together. Brewster revamped and invigorated key aspects of university life, including faculty hiring, departmental organization, administrative management and planning, and government relations. He spearheaded Griswold's reforms of the School of Engineering and the freshman year administration, measures that Griswold called "two of the most constructive accomplishments during my tour of duty as President."[85]

THE BREWSTER FAMILY was "housed in conspicuous institutional luxury," as Kingman put it, in a mansion at 55 Hillhouse Avenue, a few doors up from the president's home at 43 Hillhouse.[86] The boxy old house was painted a peculiar shade of brownish purple—hence its nicknames the Purple Orchid and the Purple Cow. The house previously had been used as storage space by the nearby Peabody Museum of Natural History, and when the Brewsters first moved in, they discovered that there was a fifteen-foot python loose in the basement. That particular problem was soon solved and the house refurbished. It included a ballroom, a solarium, and a kitchen built to Mary Louise's specifications.

The provostial residence quickly became a campus social center in a way that the president's house under Griswold never was. It was an immense asset for Brewster in getting to know the university territory and its key figures and in developing a sense of institutional community. His establishment background helped win over people like the multimillionaire Corporation member John Hay ("Jock") Whitney, who was charmed by the Brewsters' "fancy hospitality": "It was like a weekend in a stately home, pre-war—all scented and all the right books and everything. Plus fun at breakfast which is the difference."[87] Georges May recalled that when the Brewsters lived at 55 Hillhouse, "there continually seemed to be in those days a gathering of people in the front parlor vigorously discussing with [Brewster] some important matter. His style of decision-making already consisted in convening—or, as he likes to say, 'impaneling'—small ad-hoc groups of faculty members for free-wheeling discussions."[88]

From the start, Brewster's style revolved around conversation rather than solitary contemplation. "I get more stimulation by talking to people," he said on several occasions, "than by retreating to the library—it's out of the hurly-burly that I get my ideas."[89] (In this regard he was much like Richardson, who confessed that "I'm not very well read. . . . I like to get information directly from people."[90]) The mix of informative visitors at Brewster's house sometimes included students. He met frequently with editors of the *Yale Daily News,* and student singers from groups like the Whiffenpoofs and the Yale Russian Chorus came over for Halloween and other occasions. He also spiced the gatherings with friends such as Bundy and Richardson, who, like Brewster himself, were comfortable at the intersections of the worlds of power and ideas. In late 1960, Brewster was brought into the Century Association, a gentleman's club described to him as "one of the oldest in New York, [which] draws its members principally from the arts and professions, with a healthy smattering of men in public life, and a few businessmen to keep its atmosphere from becoming too ethereal."[91] That was an apt encapsulation of Brewster's world. The Century counted among its members

Cyrus Vance, John Lindsay, Paul Moore, the Bundy brothers, and many other friends.

Another such convergence of forces lay in Washington, where Brewster traveled sometimes to see his friend McGeorge Bundy, who exemplified what Sorensen called Kennedy's "ministry of talent." The new president was determined to make his administrative appointments on wholly meritocratic lines, on the basis of "superior ability" alone. He rejected factionalism, regional considerations, interest groups, voting blocs, campaign contributors, or political benefits. Kennedy "did not pretend or attempt to achieve an average cross-section of the country—he wanted the best."[92] He relied on the advice of the northeastern legal and financial community: "that arsenal of talent," as Schlesinger called it, that was "the heart of the American Establishment."[93] The glittering array of experts selected by the president carried with them, in the words of David Halberstam, "an exciting sense of American elitism, a sense that the best men had been summoned forth from the country."[94]

They came from the nation's finest universities, its major corporations and foundations, the boards and executive suites of the most prestigious law firms and financial institutions. Kennedy's appointments included Republicans as well as Democrats, more Jews in the cabinet than ever before, more Ivy League graduates, professors, and administrators, and even fifteen Rhodes scholars. Within the New Frontier were a large number of Bundy's friends and college contemporaries—Vance, Schlesinger, Sargent Shriver, Nicholas Katzenbach, and Mac's brother Bill, who became deputy assistant secretary of defense for international affairs. Despite Sorensen's boast that the president would not "name a woman or a Negro to the cabinet merely for the sake of show,"[95] Carl Brauer noted that "Kennedy chose a dramatically large number of Negroes for high-level appointment," many of whom dealt with matters unconnected with race. They "took pride in their conviction that race had been irrelevant to their being hired."[96] But true to Sorensen's claim, Kennedy's assemblage of "the best and the brightest" included only a handful of women, few of whom occupied positions of any real power or visibility. Even Eisenhower had appointed more women to top posts, because he had relied more on traditional appointments procedures, which, according to the historian Cynthia Harrison, "had been sensitive to the political utility of women party members."[97]

Mac Bundy was at the nexus where the establishment met the intellectual community. The job at the National Security Council required long days and weekend work, but Bundy was a prized guest at Washington salons and parties. Socially, he fell naturally into a gregarious Georgetown circle that brought together journalists, intellectuals, policy makers, and people who were all those at once. He was friends with Joseph and Stewart Alsop, fellow Grotonians who were perhaps the most influential columnists of their time. When he had a chance, he visited with his old mentors Lippmann and Frankfurter. His onetime economics professor Richard Bissell was now the number two man in the CIA, and a sometime tennis partner as well. Bundy got along well with the young as well as the old. Vance's daughter Amy remembered that she and her siblings liked Bundy "because he was interested in us. He wanted to hear your views and what you had to say, and that was not true of all my parents' friends."[98] Much of Bundy's socialization was a continuation of his work, but he was far from being a wonk. One onlooker commented on his "fine taste for malice and a somewhat forced, giddy gaiety, most noticeable in uproarious tête-à-têtes with Washington's most elegant hostesses."[99]

From the beginning, Kennedy relied most on Bundy's foreign policy judgment. "They think alike," an NSC staff member explained. "Bundy knows the President's mind. . . . The President's intensity is perfectly complemented by Bundy's ability to move things."[100] And move them he did: he was able to fulfill this role because he had, in effect, invented it. The National Security Council that he directed, a postwar creation, had not been a powerful entity under Eisenhower. But with Kennedy's approval, Bundy shrunk the council and made it a more flexible organization, primed to produce concise action plans rather than turgid policy briefs. While recruiting an energetic, focused young staff that included former Cambridge associates like Carl Kaysen and Walt Rostow, he took on the responsibility of passing the daily flow of national security information to Kennedy and of structuring the briefings so as to facilitate the president's decision making. To gather the information and coordinate government policy, Bundy cut across the bureaucracy to deal directly with State, Defense, the CIA, and other departments or outfits as he saw fit. Bundy, like Brewster in the Yale provostship, had seen a bureaucratic opportunity and seized it.

Bundy's role as the president's advisor and his mastery of bureaucratic paper flow meant that he, in effect, controlled the agenda of cabinet meetings, and even the members' access to the president. It was a role ripe with opportunities for manipulation, but virtually everyone agreed that Bundy played fair. Schlesinger commented that Bundy "knew everybody, feared nobody, respected the President's power of decision, [and] stated each side of an argument better than the protagonists."[101] He was directly involved in every major foreign policy decision from 1961 until he left office in February 1966. Much of his power came at the expense of Dean Rusk, the colorless secretary of state whom Bundy displaced rather as he had Pusey at Harvard. Bundy preferred the company and intellect of secretary of defense McNamara, the Ford Motor Company president who had been on the Harvard Business School faculty during Bundy's deanship.

Many of the skills that had made Bundy an effective dean at Harvard helped him in government. He was a generalist among specialists, able to listen to opposing experts and make an informed decision between them. A master of institutional processes, he knew what made groups work and how to manage them. Bundy "liked institutions," his son remembered. "He was a shy person, in the sense that intimacy was difficult for him, but not a loner. He liked the intermediate level of sociability involved in working with other people."[102] He did not believe in rigid organizational structures, and he trusted the members of his staff to do what they thought needed doing.

"It was tremendously exciting to work with Mac," his assistant Carl Kaysen remembered. "The staff was small, very intense, very collegial. We worked like mad, and we were in a state of perpetual excitement. It was a lot of fun. . . . You felt that you were at the center of the world, that you had your hands on everything."[103] Bundy could be a tough boss, and all his staff had what one called the "irritating, humiliating experience" of having him redictate their memos for the president, making them sharper and clearer.[104] And yet he always listened, and could change his mind.

Bundy's relationship with Kennedy did not get off to a positive start. The president initially neglected foreign affairs, and thought meetings of the National Security Council unnecessary. Then came the Bay of Pigs. On April 15, 1961, eight B-26s flown by U.S.-trained Cuban exiles bombed Castro's airfields. The next day the president launched the invasion force that he hoped would topple Castro, but he rejected further bombing raids or U.S. air cover, without which the mission had no chance of success. Within two days of the landing, all but a handful of the brigade had been captured or killed, and the government's claim that it was not involved had been exposed as a lie. It was a complete fiasco.

The operation, inherited from the Eisenhower administration, was a textbook example of poor planning and worse communications. The failure belonged to the CIA's Bissell, Bundy's old friend and professor who had planned the operation, and to Kennedy, who had blithely accepted the rosy projections of the CIA and Joint Chiefs. Bissell's career was over—a tragic end, Brewster and many of his friends thought, for the man once considered likely to become the top economist of his generation. His example showed some of the dangers of floating between the worlds of academia and government. Further, the Bay of Pigs debacle, as journalist Evan Thomas wrote, "marked a deep loss in the confidence, in the certainty and optimism, of the Georgetown crowd."[105]

But Bundy was also to blame, for not asking the hard questions and for failing to be the interface between Bissell and Kennedy. He was too trusting of his old professor, and too "awed by the Presidency," to argue against the plan that Kennedy approved.[106] In the wake of the disaster, Bundy submitted his resignation, but Kennedy did not accept it. Indeed, he relocated Bundy from the Old Executive Office Building to the West Wing of the White House, with instructions to analyze what was wrong with their working relationship and to fix it if he could. "We do have a problem of management," Bundy wrote to Kennedy. "Centrally it is a problem of your use of time. . . . We can't get you to sit still." Bundy urged Kennedy to keep the National Security Council on a regular schedule, to give more sustained attention to foreign policy, and to listen to what his national security apparatus was telling him rather than simply reacting to leaks in the press. For his part, Bundy would make whatever changes were necessary to give the president confidence that his staff had oversight of all government operations in the national security area. He would ensure that "there is no major problem of policy that is not out where you can see it, and give a proper stimulus to those who should be attacking it."[107] The two men staked each other to higher expectations, and they worked better together after that.

Ultimately a great friendship developed, although Bundy was uneasy about Kennedy's sexual recklessness and was never "one of the boys" to the president's Boston Irish contingent. Kennedy depended on Bundy, and respected him without feeling threatened by him. Bundy had what Schlesinger called "the indestructible personal vitality Kennedy enjoyed so much." It used to madden Schlesinger (who served as a special assistant to Kennedy) when Bundy, who worked as late as or later than everyone else, would come bounding into the office after an hour of tennis before breakfast, "pink-faced and merry, emitting a rapid fire of bulletins, instructions, questions and jokes."[108] Other members of the staff remembered Bundy's emphasis on respect for the president and the presidency. Considering that Kennedy had been scorned by upper-class journalists like Lucius Beebe as "a rich mick from the Boston lace curtain district" who lacked "gentility, good breeding and manners," it probably was important to the president that he was esteemed by such an impeccable WASP.[109]

Bundy's loyalty and admiration for Kennedy, in turn, was a way of announcing to the nation that the old Brahmin habit of looking down on the Irish was a thing of the past. His Republicanism came in handy as the president tried to build bipartisan support for his foreign policy. As part of Kennedy's inner circle, Bundy defined the cool, forceful pragmatism the president wanted his administration to project.

Newsweek noted that Bundy had two boxes on his desk, one labeled "For the President," the other "Cuba." Fallout from the Bay of Pigs intensified Cold War tensions and led to United States–Soviet confrontations over Berlin and Laos, and to Kennedy's decision to send the first military advisors to South Vietnam. The next year, the two superpowers teetered on nuclear catastrophe during the Cuban missile crisis. On the evening of October 15, 1962, Bundy was hosting a dinner party for his diplomat friend Charles ("Chip") Bohlen when he was interrupted by a call from a CIA director who told him that U-2 spy plane photos had detected Soviet medium-range missiles in Cuba. Bundy chose not to call the president with this dire news but, rather, returned coolly to his guests. He decided it was better to let Kennedy have a decent night's sleep before dealing with the crisis, and worried that a panicky midnight meeting of top advisors would attract the attention of the press. The public did not learn of the situation until Kennedy's televised speech on the evening of October 22.

As Bundy later dryly remarked, "Forests have been felled to print the reflections and conclusions of participants, observers, and scholars" about the crisis. Several aspects of the event are worth pointing out. When Bundy convened the Executive Committee (or Ex Comm) to deal with the emergency, he and the president brought in key members of the older generation of Wise Men for advice and consultation. Bundy friends and mentors like Bohlen, Acheson, Robert Lovett, John McCloy, and Averell Harriman were involved in various ways. In his account of the thirteen days, in his book *Danger and Survival,* Bundy paid particular tribute to the role played by Lovett, the former secretary of defense under Truman. On taking office, Kennedy had offered Lovett his choice of State, Defense, or Treasury, but he had rejected all, claiming ill health.

Bundy noted that "the president and Lovett were much alike; both had charm and wit, both knew that 'life is unfair,' and each understood and enjoyed the unusual grace of the other." Lovett advocated the restrained step of a naval quarantine of Cuba rather than an air strike to remove the missiles. Bundy also observed that his fellow Skull and Bones member was "a match in record and reputation to any advocate of a more drastic course." It seems likely that Lovett would have influenced Bundy more than any other figure, even Acheson, an ardent advocate of air strikes.[110]

It was difficult, however, for many participants to tell exactly where Bundy stood. On the first day of the crisis, Bundy and McNamara initially suggested a naval blockade around the island. When Bundy later discussed the crisis with his wife, she hoped the Ex Comm would choose the least violent course available. And so Bundy recommended to the group that the United States do nothing, that it reconsider the possibility of offering a diplomatic response. This advice was roundly rejected—"Everyone jumped down my throat," he recalled.[111] Later in the week, with a consensus forming around the blockade option, Bundy reopened the option of an air strike on the missiles, siding with the Joint Chiefs. Many committee members grew annoyed with this apparent vacillation. Robert Kennedy wrote at the time that Bundy "did some strange flip-flops. First he was for a strike, then a blockade, then for doing nothing because it would upset the situation in Berlin, and then, finally, he led the group which was in favor of a strike— and a strike without prior notification, along the lines of Pearl Harbor."[112]

Bundy later said that in arguing for the air strike, he had been following the president's orders to play devil's advocate. In March 1964, he recorded in a memo that "President Kennedy gave up the notion of a limited air strike against the Soviet missiles in Cuba only . . . very late in the game, and after specifically instructing me . . . to keep that option open as best I could."[113] Bundy did not see himself as an exponent of any particular position. "The single most important lesson of our experience with crises," Bundy believed, "was that the president was ill served if all reasonable options were not carefully explored." His institutional role, as he conceived it, was to pose questions rather than answer them—to clarify and frame the issues succinctly, without prejudicing the outcome, so that the president could make the best decisions. It was the process philosophy of Harvard, put to the ultimate test. Bundy's assistant Kaysen, who saw him on each of the thirteen days, observed "that what appeared to Robert Kennedy to be Bundy's waffling in the Cuban missile crisis was what Bundy would have seen as his organizing the process through which views on all sides could be heard."[114]

The journalist Meg Greenfield commented that the Ex Comm "has been the mind's-eye model of power in Washington" ever since: "the tense meeting of an anxious, grim, omnipotent few in a hidden room somewhere, making life-or-death decisions."[115] Given that the toughest decisions were made by the president with Bundy and McNamara and a handful of men closest to him, the crisis reinforced Kennedy's preference for an elite model of decision making. Conspicuously absent from what Kennedy called "the 'inner club'" were the military leaders, who alarmed the president with what seemed their dangerous, irresponsible readiness to use force and risk nuclear war. The civilian leadership's view of the blockade as a form of communication with the Soviet leaders contrasted sharply with the Joint Chiefs' view of the response as a strictly military exercise; the disparity of perspectives foreshadowed similar civilian–military misunderstandings that would plague American intervention in Vietnam.

One of the consequences of the missile crisis was a deescalation in Cold War tensions. At the same time, the episode was seen to tilt the Cold War balance in favor of the United States, and burnished the reputation of the president and his advisors as tough-minded yet moderate leaders. The Kennedy administration's new position of strength vis-à-vis the Soviets allowed the president, at Bundy's urging, to deliver his June 10, 1963, "peace speech" at American University. In it, Kennedy called on Americans to reexamine their attitudes toward the Soviet Union, and proposed a moratorium on atomic testing.

THE TEST BAN, a major goal of advocates of nuclear arms control, became the first full-fledged issue of the national student and youth movement that developed in the early 1960s. Bundy had had an early encounter with the movement when the Cambridge group Tocsin sponsored an antinuclear march on Washington in February 1962. Kennedy, demonstrating an understanding of the power of co-option, sent a White House butler out into the snow with a huge urn of hot coffee for the protesters. While the students debated whether drinking the coffee amounted to selling out, march leaders, including Todd Gitlin and Peter Goldmark, met with Bundy and other officials in the White House basement. Although Bundy scored points for accessibility, Gitlin (who later became president of Students for a Democratic Society) complained that the meeting "felt to me at the time like a dialogue of the moral with the deaf."[116]

Bundy privately shared many of the group's reservations about civil defense and supported a test ban treaty. Perhaps reacting against the moralism of the protesters, however, he pointed to conservative opposition and the difficulty of inspecting Soviet nuclear sites, and invoked the tired maxim that "politics is the art of the possible." Goldmark, who later served as an aide to John Lindsay, remembered that "Bundy was a smart man—and he was listening very closely, as his comments during the meeting showed." Still, Goldmark would have appreciated some acknowledgment that Tocsin's goals were in fact plausible, since "nearly everything we recommended, which was denounced by Bundy in the meeting as 'impractical' and by opponents as traitorous, came to pass in the next few years," including the test ban treaty.[117]

When Harriman negotiated the signing of the Limited Test Ban Treaty in Moscow in July 1963, most liberals hailed it as an important step toward peace and further evidence of the Kennedy administration's statesmanship. For many of the young antinuclear activists, however, it was too little, too late. Gitlin, for one, felt that the obstacles to progress were not the conservatives who Bundy struggled against but establishment types like Bundy himself, representatives of what Gitlin later identified as managerial liberalism. Meeting with Brewster's friend Adam Yarmolinsky, an assistant to McNamara, Gitlin had an epiphany: "Men such as this were not going to be persuaded to be sensible. They were grotesque, these clever and confident men, they were unbudgeable, their language was evasion, their rationality unreasonable, and therefore they were going to have to be dislodged."[118]

When Gitlin wrote to Whitney Griswold, in 1962, asking his support for the antinuclear movement, the Yale president scribbled on Gitlin's letter: "let time take care of this."[119] But the student movement, and changing attitudes and outlooks, gathered greater momentum with each passing year. So, too, did the movement for black civil rights, which entered a new phase in January 1960 when black students began nonviolent sit-ins at segregated Woolworth's lunch counters in the South.

Bundy initially was tone-deaf to the moral urgency of the civil rights movement. Like many men in his circle, he was personally unprejudiced, although he also knew few, if any, black people. At the same time, it was a political fact of life that segregationists controlled Congress and that Kennedy owed his election to them. Civil rights, therefore, was not a high priority for the administration. When Bundy came to Washington, he joined the Metropolitan Club, even though Attorney General Robert Kennedy and Bundy's own brother had resigned after it became clear that blacks would not be admitted even as guests. "This is a question each man must decide for himself," Bundy told reporters. "I have no quarrel with those who reached a decision to resign."[120] Nor did Bundy closely follow the growing number of media stories about the civil rights movement, absorbed as he was in the pressures of foreign policy.

Still, "even the most preoccupied of Americans could tell," he later said, "that history was being made year after year in the struggle for civil rights in the United States." To work in the White House in those years was to experience "the tempered grandeur of the march on Washington—and to understand the inner serenity and sense of fulfillment which came to two Presidents in succession as they grasped the nettle of decision and found the country with them. These dramatic events belong to our history and thus to all of us, however small our own part may have been."[121] Gradually Bundy came to accept that a private, personal matter—such as belonging to a racially exclusive club—could have political and even ethical implications. The president's "persistent and not always gentle needling" finally persuaded him to resign in protest from the Metropolitan in the fall of 1963, although he regretted that he never had the chance to tell Kennedy about his decision.[122]

CYRUS VANCE, TOO, was surprised to find the civil rights movement forcing its way to his attention. Like Bundy, he had initially been preoccupied with the traditional concerns of foreign policy, especially the Cold War. His first significant assignment for the Defense Department was to negotiate the release of the Cubans taken prisoner in the failed invasion at the Bay of Pigs. After his appointment as secretary of the Army in late 1962, he became the Defense Department's executive agent for the Interdepartmental Coordinating Committee on Cuban Affairs, created by Bundy to manage all aspects of the government's policy toward Cuba.[123] Here Vance and his deputies, soon-to-be presidential assistant Joseph Califano Jr. and future secretary of state Alexander Haig, debated proposals to isolate or overthrow Castro, which ranged from mild to wild and few of which ever came to fruition.

According to Califano, however, "the Army had a lot more involvement with civil rights than you might have expected."[124] Early on in the Kennedy administration, Vance worked with McNamara on a plan to eliminate discriminatory treatment in the armed forces, but as McNamara later observed, "then, in effect, we forgot the matter, assuming that the instructions would be carried out."[125] There seemed no urgent need to act against discrimination. Vance and other white officials were not awakened to the necessity of active engagement until disturbances over integration turned violent and the National Guard had to be called out.

Complacency over the difficulties of desegregation led to Vance's worst career blunder, in September 1962, when a mob in Oxford, Mississippi,

attempted to prevent James Meredith's registration as the first black student at the University of Mississippi. Because Governor Ross Barnett had
defied a court order that Meredith be allowed to enroll, the young man was
accompanied by three hundred federal marshals under the direction of
Assistant Attorney General Nicholas Katzenbach (Vance's fellow Yale Law
School graduate). As the mob grew to over two thousand, state police officers were withdrawn, and the marshals came under gunfire, Katzenbach
asked that the Army be sent in.

"We didn't know much at that point about handling domestic racial
violence," Califano recalled. "We made a terrible miscalculation."[126] Drastically underestimating how long it would take for troops to arrive from
Memphis, Vance repeatedly assured the president that they would soon
reach Oxford by helicopter—when in fact they had just begun forming
up. As the hours went by and casualties mounted, the president had
"the worst and harshest conversations with Cy Vance and with the General [Creighton Abrams in Memphis] that I think I've ever heard him [con-
duct]," Robert Kennedy said later.[127] Vance compounded his error by
allowing a military official to prohibit black troops from stopping white
motorists at roadblocks—"Cy let him resegregate the Army," Katzenbach
observed. "[That was] the only really dumb decision I ever remember
Cy making."[128]

While, even after Mississippi, Vance and his peers were slow to appreciate the compelling moral aspect of the civil rights movement, the episode
provided a practical lesson in the necessity of taking the issue seriously.
(Vance, of all people, should have realized its urgency, since he had seen
how the reputation of his mentor, John W. Davis, plummeted after Davis
opposed Thurgood Marshall before the Supreme Court in the 1954 *Brown
vs. Board of Education* case.) The Army was called on again in 1963 to deal
with civil rights activities. "We did [the integration of the University of]
Alabama right and we did the March on Washington right," Califano
believed, "because we had learned. We did all kinds of meticulous planning
then, and those efforts really paid off."[129]

PAUL MOORE, WHO was elected the Episcopal suffragan bishop of Washington in the fall of 1963, needed no such period of adjustment to the civil
rights movement. Moore had graduated from the General Theological Seminary in New York in 1950. As a student there, he encountered Reinhold
Niebuhr, whose pragmatic emphasis on evil in human society made him

what Bundy called "our favorite moral philosopher."[130] Moore felt that Niebuhr's participation in political matters, through his engagement in organizations like Americans for Democratic Action, "gave stature to the Church as a critical, prophetic force in the debate of national and international issues. I was delighted that a theologian was being consulted by congressmen, the President, and the Secretary of State."[131] Although he thought Niebuhr overly influenced by realpolitik, Moore would ever after be unimpressed by the argument that the church ought not to stray into politics for fear of losing its special place in society.

At the seminary Moore's heroes were priests who had sought out the working class, like the Anglo-Catholics in London's dockside slums and the French worker-priests who lived and labored alongside the industrial proletariat. The church, he believed, "should be set in the midst of the world and not a quiet place apart."[132] It occurred to Moore that blacks in the United States might be the equivalent of the European working class, a conviction strengthened by his exposure to the struggles of tenement dwellers on the West Side of Manhattan. Moore and some of his fellow seminarians forcefully argued that the church ought not to follow its affluent parishioners who were fleeing the city for the suburbs. Instead, it should seek to help the poverty-stricken minorities who had moved into the neglected parishes abandoned by white flight.

Moore was well aware that the Episcopal Church's reputation was as an upper-class organization. Most society weddings took place in Episcopal churches, the elite St. Grottlesex preparatory schools were Episcopalian, and the congregations would expand substantially in the 1950s—not least because membership was a smart move for upwardly mobile families. At some rarely acknowledged level, the church was an establishment institution, many of whose adherents looked on its mission as partly to uphold a particular WASP culture, just as Yale's mission was usually thought of in cultural as well as educational terms.

Their religion's cultural-preserving role gained no sympathy from Moore and his colleagues. "We did not resent our Church's ministry to the rich, but we felt strongly that [it] should and could reach out to poor people as well." They thought the church needed to be shaken up and modernized, to conceive a new notion of its relation to all people in society. Their idea was to "identify with the people whom we served, live in the same neighborhood, and share, as much as possible, their hardships and suffering."[133]

With two associates, Moore wrote to Episcopal bishops asking for a ministry in a downtown slum area, and in 1949 they were given Grace Church in Jersey City. Moore and his wife took down the KEEP OUT sign from the gate, removed a dead dog from the front yard, and welcomed black and white alike to the church. The Moores furnished the rectory with second-hand furniture from Goodwill, kept its door open at all times, and made the kitchen table a community center. The thirty-year-old priest's efforts to better the lives of his parishioners, from improving playgrounds to desegregating public housing, brought him up against Mayor Frank Hague's political machine. Moore, as intolerant of urban corruption as Richardson, became a social activist by necessity. "In Jersey City if we wanted anything to happen," he said, "we either had to have a picket line or street-corner meetings with PA systems screaming and yelling about public housing."[134]

Firsthand exposure to injustice against African-Americans led Moore to make a sizable donation to the NAACP Legal Defense Fund. In 1951 he joined a legal team, headed by Thurgood Marshall, that went to Groveland, Florida, to seek a change in venue in the trial of three black boys accused of raping a white woman. The local sheriff shot the boys dead on the way to the courthouse. "I could not begin to deal with it," Moore recalled. "This was the United States of America. This was the country I fought for because I believed in our democracy, our freedom. And here we were in a place that felt like a police state. This was a turning point in my life. Never again would I trust the American system when it came to dealing with African Americans."[135]

Moore returned to Jersey City to preach the gospel of social action, "a gospel spelled out in civil rights, integration, and improved housing, in meeting the needs of poor people by empowering them to change the system that oppressed them."[136] After Moore had been eight years with Grace Church, its Sunday congregation had grown from twelve worshipers to over three hundred, and reached more than a thousand people through the ministry's "open rectory."

In 1957, Moore became dean of Christ Church Cathedral in Indianapolis, an assignment he found considerably less fulfilling. In hindsight he thought that he and his wife were guilty of "a reverse snobbism against what we felt were the bourgeois values of Indianapolis."[137] (On this score he saw eye to eye with his friend and classmate Kingman Brewster, who jocularly wrote that "although I do not come from a family of missionaries, I can see the manifest public benefit in spreading Eastern culture and civilization to the Mid-West heathen."[138])

Moore's parishioners, mainly prosperous white Hoosiers, were discomfited "because I used to preach about race once in a while ... very mildly."[139] Fortunately he had the firm support of the cathedral's senior warden, Eli Lilly, the city's richest man, when the junior wardens rebelled against Moore's baptizing several black children at the traditionally all-white eleven o'clock mass. The dissidents, he wrote, did not understand his aim "of using the institution to reform society even at its own expense." One of the wardens "said to me, 'Father, you are good with poor people, you are at home with rich people, but you don't give a damn for the likes of us middle-class folks.' He was partly right," Moore reflected.[140] Donations from the rank and file dropped during his deanship, but the difference was more than made up for by a million-dollar grant from Eli Lilly.[141] Moore could afford mutiny in the ranks as long as he retained support at the top.

Back at Moore's alma mater, campus interest in civil rights increased gradually during the early 1960s. While relatively few Yale students played a direct role in civil rights activities, many others eventually came to share a broad, vicarious sense of participation in the movement. As in the late 1930s and early 1940s, the success of a movement at Yale depended less on numbers than on the prestige of its leaders. In 1960, when a handful of undergraduate civil rights activists picketed the New Haven Woolworth's in sympathy with the sit-in strikes in the South, the *Yale Daily News* editorialized that "there is nothing that sets Southern public opinion more against integration than political activists from the North. This may grate against the idealistic grain of Yale's self-styled martyrs, but it is merely plain truth."[142] Three years later, *News* chairman Joseph Lieberman led a delegation of students south to campaign for the Mississippi Freedom Ballot.[143] Undergraduate Peter Countryman founded the Northern Student Movement at Yale to push for integration in the North as well as in the South.[144]

Yale's chaplain, William Sloane Coffin Jr., also played an important role in changing the political climate at the university. In many ways, Coffin came from the same establishment tradition that had shaped Brewster and his peers. He was from a wealthy New York family, owners of the furniture company W & J Sloane; his cousin Grace "Gay" Sloane married Cyrus Vance. The family had a summer home in Oyster Bay, Long Island, as well as a penthouse apartment in the Upper East Side, and Coffin spent his early years surrounded by governesses, tutors, and chauffeurs. He prepped at the Buckley School, Deerfield Academy, and Phillips Andover. He came from a deep Yale tradition; his uncle Henry Sloane Coffin served on the Yale Corporation for twenty-three years. He enrolled at Yale before the war, and served with distinction in the Army. Returning to Yale, he headed the American Veterans Committee chapter in New Haven while Kingman Brewster led the AVC chapter in Cambridge. He was tapped for Skull and Bones, followed Brewster and the Bundys as class orator, and was identified by more than a few talent spotters as a potential president of the university.

Coffin had begun his undergraduate studies as a political science major but realized that he had seen too many atrocities during the war for his "boyhood idealism" to survive.[145] After graduation he enrolled at the Union Theological Seminary, in New York, studying with Reinhold Niebuhr and other teachers. When the Korean War broke out, he joined the CIA, which he identified as a generally liberal organization. He remembered that the officers who interviewed him "believed that communism was essentially a parasite feeding on various diseases in the body politic caused by right-wing neglect; in the long run the answer to communism was probably some form of socialism."[146] He spent the next three years sending clandestine agents into the Soviet Union, leaving the agency in 1953 to study at the Yale Divinity School. He married the pianist Arthur Rubinstein's daughter and became chaplain of Andover in 1956, Williams College in 1957, and Yale in 1958.

Despite his establishment pedigree, there were aspects of Coffin's experiences and makeup that set him apart from Brewster's circle. His father died when he was nine, and his mother relocated the family to Carmel, California, and sent the children to public schools. Coffin felt that the education gave him an early lesson in democracy and that life outside the East Coast upper class broadened his outlook. A standout athlete, he also became an accomplished musician and trained as a pianist in Paris and Geneva before the war. Although he was at home in intellectual debate, he also craved physical excitement and danger, reveling in nighttime parachuting during his CIA years, skiing and motorcycling over the Alps. To him the men of the establishment could seem bloodless, morally cautious, and excessively tied to the status quo; their lives lacked romance, passion, and commitment. And yet the part of Coffin that he called "my dutiful WASP self" not only kept him from going to the extremes to which he was drawn but actually led him into service at establishment institutions like Yale.[147]

As Yale chaplain, Coffin combined theological insight with a dedication to living, as well as preaching, the uncomfortable Gospel. Somewhat like John Kennedy, he made activism seem glamorous. He inspired students to change the realities that undergraduates had taken for granted in the 1950s. He pointed the way through his weekly sermons in Battell Chapel, through his leadership of Operations Crossroads Africa (a precursor of the Peace

Corps), and through direct involvement in the civil rights movement. Later he recalled that "I felt very strongly that Yale, as a place of obvious privilege, had a kind of special responsibility."[148]

The chaplain took part in numerous civil rights protests, starting in 1961 when he led a group of northern white ministers on the Freedom Rides, confronting the often-violent mobs that gathered as the group integrated bus stations in Georgia, Alabama, and Mississippi. Each of his actions was followed by a soon-predictable rash of outraged alumni demanding Coffin's resignation, canceling their donations to the university, and removing Yale from their wills. Although Coffin's activities in later years cost Brewster both controversy and lost donations, he never ceased to support the chaplain's right to follow the claims of conscience.

FOR BREWSTER, CIVIL rights had been a concern related, but secondary, to his interest in civil liberties. As provost in the early 1960s, he moved slowly toward a more active role in promoting racial equality. In the fall of 1962, John Kennedy summoned Brewster to Washington along with Harvard's Pusey, Notre Dame's Theodore Hesburgh, and a few other presidents of the nation's most prestigious universities, to talk about civil rights. Kennedy implored the group to increase the number of minorities in their ranks. As Brewster recalled the scene, according to Yale's then-dean of admissions Arthur Howe, Kennedy told the group, "I want you to make a difference. . . . Until you do, who will?"[149] The provost's main concern in the 1962–63 academic year, however, was the failing health of Whit Griswold.

Yale's president was diagnosed with virulent colon cancer in the fall of 1960, shortly after Brewster arrived on campus. Brewster recalled that his mentor suffered through a "dreadful" operation the following January but emerged "triumphant and buoyant" in the spring, and was healthy through the "wonderful" 1961–62 academic year.[150] After his first operation, Griswold spent long periods recuperating in Hobe Sound, Florida, and increasingly delegated responsibility to Brewster and the newly appointed graduate school dean, John Perry Miller.

The unexpected tragedy of Griswold's illness forced Brewster to take on more duties earlier than anticipated. The last months of Griswold's illness were an ordeal for Brewster; not only did he have to shoulder most of the presidential as well as provostial responsibilities, but he had to boost Griswold's morale, "keep the Corporation from panic," and get on with "the job of keeping Yale not only afloat but on Whit's course."[151]

Griswold died on April 19, 1963, at age fifty-six. His funeral took place on a soft, perfect spring day. "The undergraduate reaction," one student recorded, "was solemn, respectfully sorrowful, and distinctly unemotional; the President, we all dimly perceived, had been a great man but one whose brutally demanding office had kept him from any close contact with the undergraduate body."[152] Those who had known Griswold better, who had seen him in the moments when he let slip the stiff, formal exterior he often felt obliged to present to the public, were overwhelmed. He had faced the end with courage and even good humor, calling his catheter "my Oak Street Connector," after a controversial highway extension then under debate. John Blum remembered that the president "was genuinely, deeply mourned." He recalled seeing Barnaby Keeney, the president of Brown, standing by himself and weeping outside the funeral service in Battell Chapel.[153] Several of the pallbearers who carried Griswold's casket out of Battell were also in tears. A photograph of the procession shows Dean Acheson at the head of the honor guard and Brewster at the rear, both their faces masks of grief.[154] In his memoirs Acheson wrote that during the years of Griswold's presidency, "I worked with him closely and loved him. On the afternoon he died I sat beside his bedside and, when talk tired him, held his hand."[155] Brewster, for whom Griswold was not only a friend but akin to a father, was devastated.

Griswold's friends lamented that he could have accomplished so much more, if only he'd had time—and yet Griswold had been head of Yale for thirteen years. The impression lingers because the three years of Brewster's provostship were the most eventful and productive of Griswold's presidency. The rapid pace of change during Griswold's last years was stimulated in part by the energies of the younger administrators around Brewster and in part by Griswold's desire to move as swiftly as he could in the time remaining to him.

Several of the changes implemented in Griswold's last years would bear fruit only during Brewster's presidency. One was the Report of the Committee on the Freshman Year, which advocated a thorough overhaul of undergraduate admissions. The committee, which recommended that the faculty become more actively involved in the admissions process and that Yale should eventually "concern itself with the education of women at the undergraduate stage,"[156] also believed that better students would be attracted to a more intellectually oriented Yale, through increased academic guidance, a more flexible curriculum, and innovations to allow each student to have "a creative experience." Ultimately, the members felt that "more of the graduates of Yale College . . . must become professional scholars and teachers."[157] At the faculty meeting at which the report was approved, Griswold struck many as a man well aware that he was cashing in his chips.[158] The Freshman Year report was the next best thing to a blueprint for the early Brewster presidency. All of its recommendations ultimately were implemented.

A final innovation, not approved by the Corporation until two months after Griswold's death, committed Yale to meet the financial needs of any admitted student.[159] Yale appears to have been the first university in the country to adopt such a policy, although Harvard soon followed. While a true policy of need-blind admissions was not fully implemented until 1966, the increased scholarship commitment would help make Yale accessible to all social classes. At the end of the 1962–63 academic year, the campus newspaper noted that "during the past year a quiet revolution led by president Griswold has acquired enormous momentum within the University," extending from revised admissions standards to tightened academic requirements to a deemphasis on extracurricular activities. "Clearly," the editorial concluded, "we are witnessing the birth of a new institution."[160]

Griswold's commitment to modernization in his later years resulted in his falling out with the two senior members of the Corporation, Wilmarth ("Lefty") Lewis and Edwin ("Ted") Blair. Lewis and Blair had been Griswold's original sponsors for the presidency; they backed him enthusiastically during the 1950s when he was a reformer battling the traditionalism of the old guard. Once Griswold moved away from reformism toward modernization, after 1960, Blair and Lewis turned against him. For the same reason, they did their best to prevent Brewster from becoming president.

Brewster, who quickly became the leading candidate to succeed Griswold, had tremendous support from the faculty, the younger members of the Corporation, and the undergraduates. *Yale Daily News* managing editor David Gergen attested that "we campaigned for Brewster" through editorials and petitions of support,[161] and in June the *News* declared that "during this interim period we have been extremely impressed by the accomplishments of Provost Brewster. Never before in the recent history of Yale has a provost so quickly commanded the respect of the community, both faculty members and students. His most arresting characteristic has been the development of an articulate and far-sighted philosophy for the future of Yale."[162]

Blair and Lewis disliked both Brewster's vision of modernization and the force with which he expressed it and moved to implement it. In the weeks and months after Griswold's death, when he was discharging the duties of the president, Brewster did not hesitate to make major decisions. He told a student reporter that "it is important that we maintain the momentum of the university, so I am encouraging people to bring forward their problems or proposals. We will deal with them."[163] While this initiative was applauded in some quarters, it seemed headstrong and presumptuous to the two senior fellows.

Blair's objections to Brewster were of a rather traditional nature. "Ted was the embodiment of old Yale," according to Harold ("Doc") Howe, a younger Corporation member.[164] Blair's hesitations seem to have revolved around Brewster's rejection of Skull and Bones and the other secret societies as an undergraduate, a fear that Brewster would toughen Griswold's already hard line on amateurism in athletics, and a sense that Brewster would somehow change the place Blair knew and loved.

Lewis's reservations were more complicated. He had graduated from Yale College in 1920, and, living off inherited wealth, had created an identity for himself as a debonair Farmington and Newport gentleman and a connoisseur of eighteenth-century English culture. As a fellow of the Corporation, he exhibited a strong bias toward the humanities and the university's museums, galleries, and libraries. He considered his interest in Yale to be of a higher level than most Old Blues, and complained to Griswold about alumni conclaves in which "instead of discussing high matters of University Development the boys are either playing golf or are leading the orchestra with celery branches."[165]

Lewis explained that his main reservation about Brewster was that he was not a humanist and lacked a Ph.D. To some other Corporation members, he confided that Brewster was a dangerously ambitious man, who had an overly strong conception of the presidency and was insufficiently deferential to the Senior Fellow, one Wilmarth Lewis. Certainly Brewster had not allowed Lewis to give the commencement address after Griswold's death, which the older man would have dearly loved to do. Perhaps in response, Lewis promoted a plan whereby the presidency of Yale would be replaced by an academic senate, leadership of which would rotate through the membership.[166]

Lewis was unimpressed by Brewster's new approach to planning and professional management of the university. He freely admitted that he knew nothing of finances and made fun of those who did; when the Yale treasurer warned of a deficit, Lewis jested to the Corporation that "everyone knew that manna—extra dividends, gifts—would avert the promised disaster." Even if the university was to endure "a series of fearful deficits one right after another," he hypothesized, "what would emerge after the shambles had forced pruning of dead and decayed courses and activities might, I think, be a better university."[167] It was difficult to persuade a trustee holding such a viewpoint that the university needed to modernize.

While he was provost acting as president, Brewster made a misstep that gave ammunition to his critics. On September 2, 1963, four days after the Birmingham, Alabama, church bombing that killed four black children, Brewster asked the Yale Political Union to postpone its invitation to Alabama governor George Wallace to speak on the Yale campus on September 7. He later noted that "Governor Wallace was not banned. The student group was urged to reconsider his invitation in view of the likelihood of violence so shortly after the bombing of the church in Birmingham which killed the four girls, and Governor Wallace's reported callousness in response to the event."[168] Brewster was concerned with the offense the invitation might cause the New Haven black community and the university's reputation in the national black community. The local NAACP told the Yale students that unlike a presentation by garden-variety segregationists such as Strom Thurmond or Ross Barnett, putting Wallace before the black community would be like "having Eichmann or Goering parade before a gauntlet of survivors and relatives of the Jewish victims of Dachau and Buchenwald."[169] The very physical safety of Yale was threatened. New Haven's highly active NAACP and CORE chapters promised a major demonstration on the campus to protest Wallace's visit. As luck would have it, Wallace's address would have taken place on the night before a closely fought New Haven mayoral election. Brewster feared that mayor Richard C. Lee, for whom the black vote was imperative to reelection, would not send police to the Yale campus if the planned protest turned into a riot.[170]

National reaction to the Political Union's rescinded (or postponed) invitation was vehemently negative. Brewster stood accused of siding with sensitivity to minorities over the hallowed principle of free speech. Several years later a Wallace aide gloated, "Why, Yale practically got him [Wallace] elected in the '64 Presidential primaries! He used that incident in just about every one of his speeches."[171] The episode demonstrated how and why elite institutions could not remain aloof from the struggle over civil rights.

Jonathan Fanton, an undergraduate in 1963 and later an aide to Brewster, felt that the Wallace controversy shocked Brewster into an awareness of the way in which the ghetto springing up around Yale could directly affect the university, particularly as the manufacturing jobs that had drawn large numbers of blacks to New Haven began to dry up in the early 1960s. Nonwhites became a majority of the city's population in the early 1960s. By the late 1960s, more than half of public school students (and two-thirds of elementary school students) would be black.[172] Brewster was the first Yale president to pay serious attention to the way in which the university's role as the largest corporate employer in the city affected the urban population, particularly the minority population. For this reason, Fanton believed, Brewster "probably engaged with social problems more quickly and deeply than the presidents of most institutions in the period. And clearly he saw what we now call the underclass in the making."[173]

AFTER GRISWOLD'S DEATH, the Corporation organized one committee to select candidates for the presidency and another to analyze the nature of the presidency. The latter was regarded within the Corporation as a stalling tactic on the part of Lewis and Blair, who "wanted to prevent what they would have regarded as a headlong rush to the decision, which would end up with Kingman."[174] As it happened, the committee was in the hands of Howe and Caryl Haskins, both Brewster proponents, who worked assiduously through the summer of 1963 and finished their report long before the senior fellows had anticipated.

The committee had consulted a wide range of individuals inside and outside the university. Although the respondents did not speak with a single voice, nearly all agreed that the new president should seek to make the administration more efficient and effective, build up the sciences, strengthen the graduate and professional schools, raise the scholarly distinction of the faculty, and provide its members with more attractive conditions. While most respondents paid obligatory tribute to the time-honored ideals of the liberal arts, the consensus differed sharply from the traditional approach in one crucial aspect. Yale, they felt, should become more relevant to the nation, and its president ought to be a national leader. Their conclusions were an implicit endorsement of Brewster, who was temperamentally inclined toward activism and advocacy and whose view of the wider purpose of the university was confirmed by his years in Cambridge. Already as provost, Brewster had played an important role beyond the academy, through his membership on the committee that created the National Endowment for the Arts and the National Endowment for the Humanities. In addition, he had been exposed to the problems of international higher education in the

Cold War, through his March 1961 visit to universities in the Soviet Union.[175] Even so, the Corporation went through an orderly process of winnowing a list of some 160 candidates to a handful of possibilities.

There is a persistent rumor that McGeorge Bundy, while he was national security advisor, was asked to be president of Yale and refused. David Halberstam claimed that Bundy was offered the position in 1962 and rejected it, after Kennedy, "in a rare show of emotion . . . declared that the possibility of Bundy's leaving the White House was *out of the question*."[176] Griswold, of course, was still alive in 1962. The *Washington Post* reported in April 1963 that Bundy had declined a tentative offer.[177] Even some Kennedy staff believed that it was only just before the president's assassination that Bundy decided not to become president of Yale.[178] The fact that Brewster had already been president of Yale for a month underscores the insubstantiality of this rumor.[179]

Doc Howe recalled that in the course of his investigation into the nature of the presidency, he went to Washington to talk to his classmate (and Bonesmate). Bundy told his friend that he was thinking of leaving the government, and wanted to become either head of the Ford Foundation or editor in chief of the *Washington Post*. Howe remembered that "I said, 'Well, what about Yale?' And his answer was, 'That's Kingman's.'"[180] Bundy knew that the period when the Corporation was weighing whether to make Brewster president "was awful for Kingman, because he knew he wanted it and he knew that he had to behave himself, and that was hard, because it was very long and slow."[181] Bundy no doubt felt that he himself was perfectly qualified for the job, but he had plenty of other opportunities. Surely no one else in America might have been in the position of deciding whether to remain the nation's top foreign policy maker or become the nation's leading philanthropist or opinion maker.

Certainly Bundy and Brewster had similar qualities, and the Corporation was looking to find a young establishment leader who would be attuned to the future yet sensitive to the past. In fact, the final three candidates for the Yale presidency in 1963 were the same men that Griswold had considered for the provostship in 1959: Brewster, Harvey Brooks, and Zeph Stewart. They had a shared background, longtime acquaintance with one another and with many members of the Corporation, a Yale-to-Harvard trajectory, and similar ideas about the need to modernize the university. By 1963, however, Brewster was the clear favorite, and even Lewis conceded that Brewster had "overwhelming support from the faculty and within the Corporation itself."[182] Lewis and Blair eventually ran out of plausible alternative candidates, and the younger Corporation members brought the succession issue to a head. On the evening of October 11, 1963, the Corporation met in Woodbridge Hall to decide whether Brewster should be made president. The members voted in favor 13–2, with Blair and Lewis opposed. A second vote was held, and the two senior fellows changed their votes to elect Brewster unanimously.

Lewis, as the Senior Fellow, and Blair and Howe, as the chairmen of the two committees on the presidency, were deputed to make the offer to Brewster. They got into Jock Whitney's limousine and were driven over to 55 Hillhouse Avenue, where the Brewsters were hosting a small party. The Corporation members asked to speak to Brewster alone, and offered him the presidency. Brewster's reply—"I'll think about it"—was a curious response, considering the intensity of his desire for the position, and the strain he had been under during what he called "my purgatorial year" while waiting to see whether he would be chosen.[183]

Howe remembered that "Kingman was going wild with frustration—you could tell by various seepings of smoke coming out from under the door of his mansion, so to speak."[184] Brewster had rejected the deanship of the University of Chicago Law School, among other offers, while waiting for the Corporation to make up its mind.[185] In retrospect, he was unable to account for his hesitation when the offer finally arrived. "The psychology of that past moment is impossible to retrieve," he confessed. "I'm not very good at emotional recall."[186] Perhaps it may have had to do with the irony of the offer coming from the two individuals who had struggled hardest to prevent it, and the man who had unsuccessfully attempted to tap him for Skull and Bones twenty-three years earlier. At any rate, when he was pressed for an answer, he consulted with Mary Louise, who was also hesitant—"it was a lot of responsibility, and a big thing to take on," she felt— and then accepted.[187]

"Brewster Is Elected: Long Live the King," blared the banner headline atop the next day's *Yale Daily News*. The *New York Times* commented that "Mr. Brewster's appointment, which is known to have been opposed at first by two or three corporation members, is generally considered to mean a swing toward strong and personal university leadership."[188] The *Times* later editorialized that "Mr. Brewster represents a new generation of intellectual but decisive leaders who know that tomorrow's university, while still depending on its strong individual character, must be deeply conscious of national duties."[189] Brewster received numerous congratulations from his supporters, including Acheson, who wrote that "these last few months have been a trying—and unnecessarily trying—time for you, but not wholly a wasted time. Your courage, dignity and good nature, as well as good sense, through these months have deeply impressed many of your colleagues and bound them to you in a most important way."[190] Perhaps the most enjoyable of the congratulations Brewster received was an elaborate poem from McGeorge Bundy, welcoming him to the ranks of top administrators. Mary Bundy remembered that "the poem was written on five or six wine bottles, which Mac had wrapped up in a complicated way so you had to lift up a flap to read the last two words of each stanza, which were written on the wine label. The only part I remember was the last line of the last bottle, which was: 'Bienvenue, bâtard!'"[191]

At a press conference the day after his appointment, Brewster confessed that he had accepted the presidency with "shaky and nervous hesitancy," and, when asked what his most pressing problem would be, replied, "Kingman Brewster Jr." "No more shooting from the hip," he vowed. He emphasized that he would strive to maintain Yale's standards of quality and the university's "line of credit" with alumni, private foundations, and the government. The new president said that he had "no grand design, just a grand inheritance, left by Whitney Griswold," but added, "I obviously don't want to say that nothing will ever change."[192]

Brewster's statement begged the question of what exactly Griswold's legacy was and what fidelity to it meant. "When Whit was president," one faculty member recalled in the late 1960s, "we felt real direction. Whit had a number of tenets, both educational and philosophical, both religious and secular, and we felt his hand, a moral and righteous hand, guiding us."[193] Obviously Brewster was not an educational philosopher in the Whit Griswold or Robert Maynard Hutchins mode; he joked that his educational philosophy was "Don't get caught having a Philosophy of Education."[194] Generally, Brewster believed that he "kept the faith" (to use one of his favorite expressions) in following the direction that his mentor had ordained. He defended the liberal arts, warned that the college should not be swallowed up by the pressures of graduate study and professionalization, and stressed that Yale "should emphasize the basic and theoretical as against the topical and vocational."[195] Still, Brewster's was a flexible, tolerant faith that had passed the point of needing to issue edicts and burn heretics. In some sense he regarded the question of the institution's educational ends as having been settled by Griswold, and concentrated on adapting the means to meet those goals in accordance with new circumstances and changing times.

Brewster had a strong, clear vision of what Yale should be: an institution second to none in academic quality, a close-knit community that was not an ivory tower remote from the world. He consistently pursued this vision, but left room for improvisation. The themes of academic excellence and community were links to Griswold's beliefs, and those of an older Yale. The concept of relevance to the larger society drew on Brewster's experiences at Yale and beyond, and was also an identifiable part of the university's activist traditions. It was, however, his major departure from Griswold's ideas. Driven by his ideal of the lonely scholar in a garret, Griswold felt that the faculty should focus on pure scholarship, not grapple with current issues. Brewster felt that the university had a positive obligation to share the fruits of its studies with a troubled, turbulent society desperately in need of knowledge and guidance. And because Brewster had a broader conception of the university, he placed more emphasis than Griswold had on the professional schools and their ties to the wider world of experience.

A MONTH BEFORE Brewster's elevation to the presidency, Paul Moore had experienced his own apotheosis. Moore's writings on the urban church and his participation in organizational conferences and committees made him an attractive candidate for bishop in several dioceses in the early 1960s, particularly as concern over the civil rights movement grew. His St. Paul's and Yale connections and war-hero status added to his appeal. He allowed his name to be put forward for the Pennsylvania bishopric, but was passed over. In the summer of 1963, Moore left his family's summer vacation at his Adirondacks camp to take part in the March on Washington for Jobs and Freedom. The march coincided with a political battle over the election of a suffragan bishop for Washington, and Moore spent the night before the event being looked over by the urban social action caucus. Moore and his son Paul marched with the peaceful, integrated throng, and "if I had any doubts about wanting to be a bishop in Washington, they disappeared as Paul and I paraded down Constitution Avenue and stood before the Lincoln Memorial to hear the great dream of Martin Luther King, Jr. The future was bright. We were all together."[196] In September, Moore was elected bishop.

Moore and his wife, Jenny, traveled to the capital to look for a house and schools for their children. Moore had numerous acquaintances in the city. Ben Bradlee, then Washington bureau chief for *Newsweek*, was a friend from childhood summers on the North Shore. Cyrus Vance and Mac

Bundy were college friends, as was Cord Meyer, who threw a party for the Moores on their arrival. In fact, the multitude of social connections that bound the Moores to the Washington crowd bordered on the incestuous. Bradlee had been one of Jenny Moore's first boyfriends. Moore used to dance with Bradlee's wife Antoinette (*née* Pinchot) at New York parties back in the 1930s and 1940s. Toni Bradlee's previous husband was Moore's Yale classmate Steuart Pittman, who was then working with Vance in the Pentagon (and had followed Kingman Brewster into the Economic Cooperation Administration). Toni's sister Mary, an artist and famed beauty, had married Cord Meyer. After their divorce, she became one of President Kennedy's mistresses.

Moore and his wife secured an appointment with the president, and visited him in the Oval Office on a brilliant Indian summer morning in September 1963. Kennedy and the new bishop walked out to the terrace, talked of old friends, shared war recollections, and discussed the national outlook. "As we looked out on the Washington Monument and sensed the beauty and the power of the city," Moore remembered, "it seemed that anything was possible and that we would have a hand in bringing in a time of real peace and justice to our country and the world."[197]

Two months later, on November 21, McGeorge Bundy sat in his West Wing office and typed a letter to Kingman Brewster. They had been in touch all week about the case of Frederick Barghoorn, a Yale professor detained by the Soviets on false charges of espionage. "Your phone call this morning was the brightest spot in it," he wrote, "and I should have saved this piece of stationery by telling you, in behalf of the President, that he was grateful for your telegram of November 14 about the Barghoorn affair."[198]

On the same day, Bundy wrote to his brother Bill over at Defense, referring him to a memo detailing steps the United States would take in South Vietnam "to assist the people and Government of that country to win their contest against the externally directed and supported Communist conspiracy." Three weeks earlier, Mac had sanctioned a coup against the Vietnamese ruler Ngo Dinh Diem; now he was authorizing expansion of military operations beyond the South into North Vietnamese supply lines in Laos.[199]

Later that afternoon, Kennedy left with his wife for a trip to Dallas. The next day he was dead. After the assassination, Bundy talked briefly with Lyndon Johnson while he was returning to Washington aboard *Air Force One,* and he was at Andrews Air Force Base to meet the new president on his arrival and to assist in the transition of power. The British journalist Godfrey

Hodgson noticed him standing slightly apart with an orange folder under his arm, "a wiry, fortyish man with thinning blond hair, a noticeably square jaw, and, behind light-rimmed glasses, quite unforgettably cold blue eyes."[200] Bundy, Johnson, and McNamara boarded an Army helicopter and flew to the White House lawn. En route, Johnson praised Kennedy for having "gathered around him the ablest people I've seen—not his friends, not even the best in public service, but the best anywhere." He appealed to Bundy to remain in his office: "I need you. I want you to stand with me."[201]

Despite his reputation as an unemotional man, Bundy grieved deeply for Kennedy, though in private. "Friday and Saturday I cried at home—after that not," he later wrote.[202] One Yale undergraduate remembered that when Kennedy had come to New Haven the previous year (during the Cuban missile crisis, it later emerged), the students "lined the way with jeering posters . . . we followed him to the Green and hissed and booed his speech. He had proven himself an ineffective president, a bad president, and we were showing this handsome, arrogant, ladies-man Harvard boy that we weren't falling for his act. . . . Almost exactly one year later, many of us would cry for this same man."[203] Chaplain Coffin remembered that "the ensuing sorrow gripping the country was of a refined order, quite transforming. In my recollection Americans have never been so kind to one another." From Coffin's point of view, Kennedy had been timid on civil rights, but he "was the kind of leader who helped to create a climate in which many good people were inspired to try many good things."[204]

In the end, Kennedy was a sort of transitional figure between the 1950s and 1960s, and between an older model of politics and a new liberalism. The style of leadership he brought from New England to the White House—cultured, cautiously idealistic, pragmatic, witty, ironic, elitist—made intelligence seem glamorous and was perfectly attuned to the leadership styles of Brewster, Bundy, and their peers. It was a style that, briefly, seemed destined to dominate the national political culture. In fact, the Kennedyesque pragmatic idealism would soon be pushed aside by the right, for whom it went too far, and the left, for whom it didn't go far enough. In that sense, Kennedy was the last president of the liberal establishment.

5

MODERNIZERS
ON THE MOVE

IT WAS a glorious spring day in 1964, and trumpets sounded a triumphal march. Kingman Brewster was about to be inaugurated as the seventeenth president of Yale University. The forty-four-year-old Brewster was tanned and vigorous, his short brown hair just beginning to go gray. Draped over his three-piece suit was a sumptuous, satiny blue academic robe edged with black velvet. Around his neck he wore an astonishing gold collar, its chain of filigreed links descending to a jeweled sunburst from which hung a shield surmounting crossed maces, a Latin-inscribed banner, and a riot of gilded heraldic devices. Weighty with antique splendor, the collar offered a reminder that the university over which Brewster presided was considerably older than the United States itself. But he seemed to bear the symbolism comfortably, flashing an amused grin at the cameras, enjoying his part in the play.

The inaugural procession moved slowly across the campus, as the leaders of the world's most prestigious universities and colleges, garbed in polychromatic medieval robes, hoods, and archaic scholarly headgear, marched beneath brightly colored heraldic banners waving in the breeze. Just ahead of Brewster was an official bearing a magnificent four-foot silver mace, an emblem of presidential authority, that shone and sparkled in the sunlight. In a brief ritual on the library's lawn, Brewster received the symbols of his presidential office: the original manuscript of Yale's 1701 charter, the university seal, and a set of ornate keys.

The parade moved past thousands of onlookers and into a packed auditorium. In the crowd and up on the dais were many of America's elite leaders from an older generation, including former secretary of state Dean

Acheson, *New York Herald Tribune* publisher John Hay Whitney, Pan Am founder Juan Trippe, Federal Reserve head William McChesney Martin, and poet laureate Archibald MacLeish (on hand as an official delegate from the University of the West Indies). Nearby were their protégés and successors in Brewster's circle of friends, including Massachusetts governor Endicott Peabody, New York congressman John Lindsay, and national security advisor McGeorge Bundy.

The inaugural ceremony blended ancient ritual and modern ambition. The congregation rose to sing a traditional Yale hymn that began, "O God beneath thy guiding hand / Our exiled fathers crossed the waves," and went on to extol the "Laws, freedom, truth, and faith in God" that "Came with those exiles o'er the waves." It occurred to many in the audience that the hymn was particularly appropriate, given Brewster's *Mayflower* background. But when the new president walked to the podium, he called for boldness and innovation rather than evoking past glories.

Sounding the familiar notes of excellence, community, and academic freedom, Brewster added a distinctive emphasis on the university as a key institution in modern society. He underlined the significance of universities as "a common trust of the continuity of civilization" but warned that they would have to come to terms with the revolutionary changes of the times, particularly the knowledge explosion, population growth, and "the uncanny development of automated machines and mechanized intelligence." Noting that young people "yearn to become involved in something more meaningful than inherited patterns of success," he proposed concrete ways that the universities could meet this desire, including a peace reserve training corps, a system of free exchange of scholars, and a program that would send sophomores to a non-Western country for a year, thereby "splic[ing] experience with learning, especially in exposure to contrasting cultures."

The university, Brewster emphasized, would have to stay relevant to society: "We dare not admit that in order to be true to our University tradition we must seal the windows against all relevance to the real world. Indeed, in order to keep the business of learning itself uncorrupted it may be important to open the gates of the walled city more frequently for those who would sample experience." Neither could the president restrict himself to the ivory tower, since "the world needs a credible spokesmanship for the human purposes which transcend nations."[1]

After the well-received speech, Brewster greeted his guests at the president's expansive Victorian mansion at 43 Hillhouse Avenue. Some forty or more inaugural dinners were held across town, followed by a party and dance in the soaring space of the skating rink, which for the occasion was filled with flowers and "decked out like a scene from *The Arabian Nights*," as one guest remembered it.[2] In white tie and tails, Brewster showed off his uncanny memory, welcoming the hundreds of attendees by name. It was a terrific party. In the swirling aftermath, Bundy ran into Brewster's mother and remarked on what a splendid time everyone had had, especially her son. "Yes," she replied, "but as the Scripture has it, 'His reward is with him, his work lies ahead.'"[3]

WHEN WHIT GRISWOLD had been inaugurated in 1950 amid the austerities of the Korean War, the ceremony was pared to its original colonial simplicity. The lavish scale of Brewster's ceremony provoked campus wits to joke that it was more coronation than inauguration, like Charles succeeding Cromwell. But although stylish, the style had substance. The new president used the occasion to proclaim that the university had assumed its place alongside government and business as one of the major estates of American society. A panel discussion on the relationship between the modern university and the national government, held the day before the main event, suggested the outward-looking direction of Brewster's efforts as president. Brewster's insistence on including Charles Odegaard, the dynamic president of the University of Washington, on the panel signaled a new awareness of and respect for competition from public higher education. The presence of Noël Annan, the head of King's College, Cambridge, alluded not only to Yale's Oxbridge origins but to the transatlantic community of "those who make their times significant and form opinion," in Annan's knowing phrase.[4] And the international dimension was further suggested by the participation of the heads of the University of Puerto Rico and the Fourah Bay College of Sierra Leone, and of Brewster's old teacher at the 1941 Williamstown seminar on inter-American affairs, Enrique Sanchez De Lozada (by then the Bolivian ambassador to the United States).[5]

In hindsight, many in Brewster's circle would look back to the spring of 1964 with nostalgia. The campus was green and pleasant, undergraduates still wore the unofficial uniform of coat and tie with crew cut, and the alumni were largely content. Bill Bundy, who became a trustee of the Corporation in 1961, recalled that "as it was the heyday of national bipartisan consensus, so it was the heyday of alumni consensus on the purposes of Yale. It was, I suppose, in some sense the twilight of the old establishment."[6]

*   *   *

THERE WERE MANY pleasant aspects to becoming president of Yale. When Brewster and his family moved into the president's house, he furnished it with art borrowed from the Yale gallery; Edward Hopper's *Rooms by the Sea* hung in the living room for many years. In his first year in office, Brewster received honorary degrees from Harvard, Princeton, Columbia, and other universities, which was something of a professional courtesy extended to new Ivy League presidents. Still, Princeton perceptively praised Brewster for bringing to his post "a freshness of view, a keen awareness of the needs of our time." The New York gentlemen's clubs threw open their doors to Brewster, who would transact a good deal of university business within the dark, wood-paneled enclosures of the Century, Links, Brooks, and other Manhattan enclaves. The Rockefeller Foundation offered him a month's retreat at its Italian lakeside villa for writing and reflection.

Speaking invitations also began to pour in, and newspapers and television shows increasingly sought out the Yale president. Brewster's high visibility led to his election as the sole North American representative to the fourteen-member administrative board of the International Association of Universities, which meant regular trips to IAU headquarters in Paris and globe-trotting assignments to Colombia, Japan, the Soviet Union, and other exotic locales. Brewster rubbed shoulders with other well-known, powerful men at the Bohemian Grove in California, addressing the gathering along with speakers like Wernher von Braun, Robert Kennedy, and Barry Goldwater. Richard Nixon, plotting his political comeback and seeking out Republican up-and-comers, congratulated him on his Bohemian Grove talk and invited him to get together in New York; Brewster gave a friendly but noncommittal reply.[7] Not all the attention was welcome, as cranks of all sorts also began to write, call, and sometimes stalk. Still, Brewster reveled in the job. Speaking on behalf of his fellow college presidents, he admitted his secret love of "the pomp and circumstance of outlandish haberdashery which we alone in this dryly plebian society share with shriners and drum majorettes" and pointed out that "the damndest people have to be nice to us."[8]

All the benefits would mean little to Brewster, however, if Yale could not hold its place among the first rank of universities. The school's self-review in the months before Brewster's election had shown that Yale would struggle to keep pace with the rising public universities (with their seemingly limitless resources) and that Yale's hidebound devotion to tradition posed serious obstacles to the massive changes required for the institution to accomplish its aim.

Brewster's first effort to modernize Yale began with the faculty, which he believed to be the heart of the university. His friend Mac Bundy had taught him that "no board of trustees has ever made a university great, and that where a president has done so it has been always and without exception through his faculty."[9] Brewster's principal goal was to build a faculty that was the equal of any competitors. In preceding years academic deficiencies had stemmed largely from an excessive number of faculty members with Yale degrees. Even by 1960, almost half the faculty were Yale products. The inbreeding had its virtues. Dean William Clyde DeVane praised "the old sense of cohesion and responsibility," the emphasis on teaching that had eroded at other research universities, and the feeling of shared purpose in a professorate that "had many of the characteristics of an excellent club."[10]

But a wealth of anecdotal opinion supports history professor Edmund Morgan's charge that by the late 1940s, when something on the order of two-thirds of its faculty members were homegrown, Yale was "so inbred, so dead that it was on the verge of ceasing to be a great university."[11] The habit of hiring from within meant that the standards for appointments and promotions tended to emphasize citizenship rather than scholarship, clubability rather than merit. Inheritance, wealth, background, and social standing were significant criteria at the faculty level, as well as at the level of undergraduate admissions. In many departments dark blossoms of anti-Semitism and anti-Catholicism flourished. And the pay was so poor that one almost had to be a gentleman of independent means to afford to hold a faculty position.[12]

Too many faculty members were dedicated teachers but had no reputation outside the university; the university often did not attract the best of either Yale or the outside world. In the postwar era, no university could resist externally defined standards of quality in faculty hiring (or graduate student recruitment, for that matter) without damaging its academic reputation—particularly in the social, natural, and physical sciences, where a scholar's professional standing depended on his or her ability to receive government funding. It was no coincidence that Yale's standing was weakest in the fields that played a pivotal role in university development after World War II. Brewster's teacher and friend Richard Bissell, one of the most promising economists of his generation, was lured away from Yale during the war when MIT offered him a tenured associate professorship at a higher salary and half the teaching load. Bissell wrote to Whit Griswold that there was "something irksome in the calm assumption that a man should be willing to work twice as hard for 25 percent less pay just for the privilege of being at Yale." His outlook for the university's faculty standing was highly pessimistic: "Yale simply does not have the financial resources to hold its own, nor is it sufficiently flexible (in my humble opinion) to make the best use of those it has. . . . I simply cannot believe that Yale will be a better place than M.I.T. *as a university* for as long as I can see ahead."[13]

Excellence implied an emphasis on merit that often proved incompatible with tradition. An example of this logic at work was the first official Yale historian, George Wilson Pierson. The son of the valedictorian of the Yale College Class of 1886, he began teaching at Yale after receiving his B.A. in 1926, and spent his entire adult life at the institution. Pierson was part of the Old Yale, memorialized it affectionately in his histories, and argued its virtues with earnest, angular intensity. But he was too ambitious for the university to let it rest on memories of happy golden bygone days.

As a deep-dyed Old Blue, Pierson wanted to continue the traditional hold of the exclusive preparatory schools over Yale College, yet as a faculty member he helped push Yale toward the emphasis on merit and talent that undermined prep school dominance. Although his intellectual interest was principally in Western civilization, as chairman of the History Department he helped expand the curriculum to emphasize non-Western societies. Imbued with the prejudices of his age and class, he nonetheless believed that Yale had to have the best faculty and graduate students; as a result, he recruited unprecedented numbers of Jews, blacks, and individuals from unprivileged backgrounds. And even though he would cast the lone faculty vote against coeducation and had long opposed women on Yale's faculty, Pierson succeeded in having Mary Wright made the first female full professor on the Faculty of Arts and Sciences, over the protests of some of his colleagues. As he saw it, justice and the university demanded nothing less. His vision was larger than he was, and he knew it.

OTHER DEPARTMENTS, HOWEVER, remained set in their ways. The thicket of issues obstructing Yale's attempts to modernize was especially dense in the sciences. The woeful history of twentieth-century science at the university could be traced to many sources, including the prejudice against hiring the distinguished Jewish professors who came to the United States before, during, and after World War II as refugees from the Nazis. A 1959 report criticized "promotions based on general competence, pleasant personality

and loyalty, rather than on rigidly applied objective considerations of scholarly ability. . . . We cannot state too strongly our conviction that the matter
of faculty appointments is the single most important problem in the revitalization of science at Yale."[14]

The university's scientists, in particular, had felt threatened by the tone
of the Yale conservatism of the 1950s: preppy, weighted toward the humanities, nonpragmatic, strongly opposed to specialization and vocationally oriented disciplines. They complained about the lack of scientists in the
administration, lack of support for scientists' grant-seeking efforts, discrimination against aspiring scientists in undergraduate admissions, and even
the absence of science majors in the secret societies.[15]

Clearly, Brewster had brought with him from Harvard an affinity for the
social sciences. But as provost and president, he needed no convincing that
the position of the natural sciences must also be improved. The microbiol-
ogist Edward Adelberg felt that "there is no doubt that he came to Yale with
an agenda. It was part of his mission from day one to build up the sciences
at Yale."[16] Before Brewster had been named provost-designate, he spoke
with Corporation member Acheson.[17] As Adelberg remembered, the former secretary of state asked his younger friend, "Tell me, Kingman, we
understand Yale is supposed to strengthen the sciences. Why shouldn't we
appoint a scientist as provost?" Brewster replied, "If a provost who was a
scientist came to you and told you to spend more money on the sciences,
you wouldn't listen to him. But if a lawyer told you that, you'd have to!"[18]

Brewster's witticism aside, he brought a new sympathy toward science
and technology, developed in Cambridge during his year on the MIT faculty and through his membership in the Friday Evening Club. William
Doering, who was director of the Division of Sciences at Yale from 1962 to
1965, remembered that "Kingman mentioned [the Friday Evening Club]
again and again and again as the place where he had developed his vision
of where science was supposed to go, and how it was supposed to operate."[19] The club also linked Brewster to a wide network of scientists who
could advise him where Yale ought to place its bets, intellectually speaking,
and how to achieve promotions truly based on merit.

Brewster quickly won the allegiance of members of the scientific faculty
by actions that made clear his interest in and dedication to their needs. In
the early 1960s, the Physics Department, for example, was trying to make
up for missed opportunities in nuclear physics—in part by joining a project
at the scientific facilities in Brookhaven, New York, a collaboration with
other universities and the Atomic Energy Commission to build accelerators

on a scale beyond the resources of any single institution. Yale, only a short flight from Brookhaven, across the Long Island Sound, was well placed to take part in this effort. Jack Sandweiss, one of the young faculty at Brookhaven, remembered an on-site visit from Provost Brewster. "I had never seen Griswold or the previous provost. I didn't even know who the previous provost was. . . . Nevertheless, Brewster . . . actually spent an hour with me and my colleagues, looking at and trying to understand what we were doing. I thought that was amazing."[20]

Another of Sandweiss's colleagues, D. Allan Bromley (later science advisor to President George H. W. Bush), remembered being in Washington, attempting to persuade the AEC to fund a nuclear physics laboratory at Yale. "Kingman said, 'Hang in there. I'm coming down.' That shocked the hell out of the people at the A.E.C.—first, that an Ivy League provost was sufficiently interested in something scientific (which was unusual) to actually do that, and second that when he got down here to A.E.C. headquarters— he flew down—he knew exactly what he was talking about and made a marvelous presentation about the importance of what I was trying to do. I really believe that made all the difference in terms of convincing the A.E.C."[21]

For the scientists at Yale, Brewster was a breath of fresh air. While many of them continued to kick against and complain about the dominance of the humanities, they generally began to look upon the administration as an ally rather than an oppressor.

As Bromley's anecdote suggests, Brewster held a considerably more liberal attitude toward government and foundation moneys than most other Yale administrators. Still, Brewster shared his predecessor's fierce sense of university independence and self-determination. As a member of the visiting committee for the MIT Center for International Studies, he pushed the institution to wean itself from CIA funding.[22] Once in the middle of a speech to foundation grant officers, he sang a line from Irving Berlin's "No Strings": "No strings and no connections/No ties to my affections."[23] But he also courted and cultivated the foundations and government funding agencies as never before. He lobbied for full recovery of indirect costs from government-funded research—a procedural change that greatly increased the value to the university of such contracts. Brewster testified before the House to oppose pressure to dole out research support to all universities on an equal basis. His frankly elitist warning was that "shattering and scattering the top of the pyramid of American science would be disastrous."[24]

Brewster was fortunate to have a large amount of money available to build the sciences, thanks in part to the fund-raising drive of the early

1960s. Edward Adelberg observed that Brewster "diverted resources toward the sciences on a scale not seen during the Griswold era. It would be difficult to quantify this, but the growth of the sciences during Brewster's presidency was evident. The result of the internal shift of resources, plus new federal funds, plus [philanthropy] was a quadrupling of resources for the biological sciences."[25]

The buildup did not take the form of a random shower of cash on delighted scientists, but was, rather, a deliberative intellectual exercise in planning, entailing shrewd decisions by Brewster and his advisors about the areas and individuals in which to invest. In many cases, Brewster consciously took power away from the senior members of the departments and their often outdated approaches and chipped away at the "excessive departmental autonomy which has frustrated interdisciplinary frontier work."[26] Because he had consulted with Cambridge-based scientists George Wald, Arthur Solomon, and Sidney Brenner, all of whom "saw the molecular biology revolution coming,"[27] Brewster engineered the creation of the interdisciplinary Molecular Biophysics and Biochemistry Department, over considerable opposition. Because of this, Yale was able to play a leading role in the biomedical revolution that followed.[28]

The Yale president also oversaw the creation of the Ivy League's first computer science department. He chose to place the preponderance of Yale's resources in nuclear physics, against the wishes of the Physics Department chairman; this too was a bet that, in hindsight, proved to have had the highest scholarly payoff. The physicist Charles Bockelman observed that "an instinct for the long-term view was one of Kingman's geniuses."[29] Brewster's success did not derive from a deep understanding of scientific matters but from his use of process and a visceral judgment about the capabilities of individuals on different sides of the issues.

WHEN APPOINTING ADMINISTRATORS, deans, department chairs, and other key figures, Brewster also combined process and intuition. He formed search committees for most major positions but often structured the committees in such a way that they would pick the candidate he wanted. Often his choices involved what he called "creative risk"— educated gambles that those selected would display talents of which they might themselves have been unaware. In his search for a provost in 1963, for example, he first approached Harvey Brooks and Lyman Spitzer, two scientists who had graduated from Yale a few years before him. Because, as it turned out, neither could be dislodged from his empire, Brewster selected Charles Taylor, a little-known thirty-five-year-old associate professor of English and an assistant dean in the graduate school. Although Taylor was not a scientist, he shared some qualities with the other candidates: establishment background (he was part of the family that owned the *Boston Globe*), exposure beyond Yale (he had taught at Indiana University), and proven administrative ability. Above all, as one of Brewster's associates pointed out, "Kingman saw in Charlie qualities that he thought could make Charlie explode in the provostship."[30] The scientists, in particular, were skeptical initially, and Brewster had to give Taylor the sort of one-year probationary period he himself had undergone. In the end, scientists were among the new provost's most enthusiastic supporters, because he had patience and a phenomenal learning curve and was perhaps the first Yale administrator to work sixteen-hour days on a regular basis.

The 1963 appointment of Henry ("Sam") Chauncey Jr. as special assistant to the president was another inspired example of Brewster's trust in a young, relatively untried individual. Chauncey's background resonated with Brewster, just as Taylor's had; he was a descendant of Yale College's first graduate, and his father had been James Conant's point man in establishing meritocracy at Harvard and then, as founder and head of the Educational Testing Service, throughout the nation.[31] Chauncey also had served in the Yale College dean's office since his senior year, in 1957.[32] Even so, it was a tremendous gamble for Brewster to make the twenty-eight-year-old Chauncey his alter ego, in effect, and one of the three most powerful officials at Yale. The wager not only paid off but led to a considerable extension of Brewster's administrative capacities.

Other outstanding appointments of the mid-1960s included novelist John Hersey as master of Pierson College, *New Republic* drama critic Robert Brustein as head of the drama school, psychiatrist Frederick Redlich as dean of the medical school, and twenty-nine-year-old R. Inslee Clark as dean of admissions. A few years later, Brewster would write to Mac Bundy that his "substantive changes in decanal leadership, new programs, faculty appointments and admissions policy have brought a spirit of creative questioning to an institution which had suffered from excessive like-mindedness."[33] The energies that Brewster's appointees brought to their tasks helped energize the entire university—as, for example, science benefited from the new admissions procedures put in place by Clark.

To Brewster, the question of improving faculty quality was straightforward. He often told the story of meeting Yale's longtime economics chairman,

Lloyd Reynolds, on Martha's Vineyard. Brewster remembered asking Reynolds, "'Would you take me out behind the barn some day and tell me how it is you turned one of the worst departments in the country into one of the best?' He said, 'I don't have to take you out behind the barn, it's very simple—just be willing to hire people who are brighter than you are.'"[34]

Brewster devoted less attention to the departments in which this principle was generally followed and concentrated his firepower on those in which considerations other than merit held sway. He also standardized the schedule of faculty rank and salary, which had varied considerably across (and sometimes within) departments.[35] At the same time, a new committee-based, stringent system of tenure review was established in each academic division. In the early years, graduate school dean John Perry Miller estimated, the committees rejected four to five proposed appointments a year, sometimes amid bitter controversy.[36]

The system of regular external reviews that Brewster instituted were unsentimental evaluations of Yale's weak spots by leading authorities from outside the university. When a few of the world's leading experts in a subject "were sitting around a table together," as Doering recalled, "it was surprising how helpful they were."[37] Moreover, following the model developed by Harvard's president James Conant, Brewster called on outside experts to assess the qualifications of Yale's proposed appointments in problematic areas such as physics and biology. Conant had inaugurated the ad hoc committee system to stamp out mediocrity and to nationalize and even internationalize recruitment of faculty, just as he had moved to nationalize recruitment of undergraduates.[38] Yale's departments now posed a series of searching questions to the outside experts when appointment decisions arose. One such letter, in 1964, asked: "Regardless of age, who are the most original, significant men in the field? With due regard to the differences in accomplishment arising from difference in age, how does the candidate compare with these men? Are there those among them whom the University should consider, within obvious limits of availability, for appointment to tenure position, either to associate or full professorship?"[39]

In emphasizing the recruitment of new, world-class faculty, Brewster created what the biologist Edgar Boell called "an environment in which change was expected and became possible."[40] Brewster's deputy provost for the sciences added that "I don't think he ever did it by dictate or by fiat, but my God, he was a talented arm-twister."[41] This ability and Brewster's competitive streak came in handy when he sought to tempt top scholars to come to Yale. University of California president Clark Kerr noted that Brewster had "a keen eye for able faculty members and a persuasive tongue, and the presence of several of our most valued former faculty members now here at Yale is all too eloquent testimony to this. We have viewed him as one of the most active raiders—(I had in my longhand manuscript here at one point written down, 'ruthless raiders'; I changed that to 'active')—in all of American higher education."[42] Brewster, who greatly enjoyed what he called "the safari," never hesitated to go after individuals identified as the top in their fields. Once he attempted to lure an entire team of geneticists away from the National Institutes of Health.

According to John Blum, Brewster "was a great recruiter," who "put his heart and soul into it."[43] When a prospective recruit arrived at Yale, Brewster invited the candidate and his or her spouse to dinner at the president's house, along with one or two couples from the recruiting department and some of the Brewsters' friends. While cocktails were poured, a string trio or other musical ensemble would play unobtrusively in the background—a subtle reminder of Yale's culture and elegance. Dinner would be served with the Brewsters' customary attention to details—the white damask tablecloth, candles, shining silver, fresh flowers, and wines carefully matched with the courses. After dinner, the men would separate for brandy and cigars in the front parlor, where the senior member from the recruiting department would lead the candidate through a discussion of his or her work. Brewster asked intelligent, probing questions, and typically the candidate would spend the night at the president's house, rather than in an impersonal hotel room.

The next day the candidate would have a long meeting with the provost to discuss salary and employment matters, and a short meeting with Brewster in his tiny office in Woodbridge Hall. Robert Brustein, who came to Yale as dean of the drama school, remembered that Brewster spoke "in soothing, mellow tones that made it a sensuous experience to be in his presence. Conversing with a visitor in his office, he would sit back casually in a high-backed desk chair, and, while the grandfather clock ticked a languorous accompaniment, hypnotize the auditor with his rolling dialogue. . . . [T]hat ticking clock and that sonorous voice created an atmosphere in the room that worked on one's spine like a massage."[44]

Brewster used his one-on-one interviews to persuade and to tout the university's virtues, but also to inform himself. The sociologist Kai Erikson recalled that when he came to Yale to be recruited, he was surprised to learn that his first visit was with Brewster; he had never even met the presidents of the two institutions where he had taught for the preceding seven years. Part of the reason for the meeting was that Brewster's mission was to persuade Erikson to leave a tenured position for a lower-salaried, untenured position at Yale. The president acknowledged the awkwardness of this offer but proffered smooth assurances that tenure would be forthcoming (as indeed it was). Ten minutes into the meeting, Erikson accepted the appointment. "Good," said Brewster, adding, "Now what I really wanted to talk to you about . . ." Erikson wrote later that what followed was "as focused a set of questions as I have ever heard on the discipline of sociology nationally, on the needs of the department locally, and a number of related matters." Erikson soon realized that the performance was typical of a leader who "was always trying to fill in the gaps in his already formidable knowledge, and, more to the point, always listened to what others said with unfailing interest and respect."[45]

Describing his role as that of an "intellectual investment banker," Brewster emphasized the need for flexibility in building up the faculty. "Intellectual imagination is the rarest gem," he told an alumni audience, "and we have to grab it, hold onto it, reward it."[46]

Together with provost Taylor, Brewster raised faculty salaries to near the top of the national scales. The average salary leaped from under $10,000 in 1962 to over $19,000 in 1970; a real increase of approximately two-thirds, it boosted faculty pay to levels comparable to those of other professions.[47] Brewster and Taylor lowered teaching loads, increased research support, and instituted an unprecedented policy of paid leaves of absence for research every three years. They permitted departments to overstaff faculty slots in advance of anticipated retirements if a great scholar was available. It was an expensive policy but one that allowed Yale to move rapidly in making appointments. Bromley remembered that "Kingman's attitude was, 'If this guy or this woman is the best in the world in this field, let's hire them. . . . We're not going to get this chance again.'"[48]

The increase in faculty support and funding sources, combined with the explosion of knowledge and the conscious decision to teach the new fields, produced a concomitant explosion in the size of the faculty. The ladder faculty—assistant, associate, and full professors—jumped by eighty percent between 1963 and 1969.[49] More and more departments achieved what Brewster called scholarly "critical mass"—the mere presence of so many eminent colleagues was itself a powerful lure to other academics. The quality, morale, and reputation of Yale's faculty rose continuously, nationally and even internationally, throughout the 1960s, discomfiting many of the university's academic rivals. "When I came to Yale," Brewster wrote to Mac Bundy, "I found Yale's 'Harvard Complex' suffocating and stultifying. I cannot suppress my delight in some signs of a developing 'Yale Complex' in Cambridge."[50]

SAM CHAUNCEY RECALLED that Brewster "felt that it was going to take a huge investment to get the kind of faculty and facilities that the institution needed to have to be a university—particularly in the sciences, but also across the board."[51] Contrary to some contemporary impressions, however, Brewster and his lieutenants did not simply spend money like drunken sailors on shore leave. An enormous amount of intelligent forethought went into the faculty expansion. As provost, Brewster had been the first administrator at Yale to dip a toe into serious efforts at planning. As president, he led a management revolution to overcome the obstacles and traditions that had, in past years, made it impossible to develop long-term goals.

Joseph Peck, Brewster's economist friend from Harvard days, remembered that "Yale was not well run when I first arrived; it seemed amateurish compared to Harvard. . . . The Yale administration was full of alumni from rich families, who weren't wanted in the family business, and who ended up in easy, comfortable, and moderately prestigious jobs at Yale."[52] The lore of operating the university was handed down from society brother to society brother, without much adjustment to changing times, which could result in some curious anachronisms. Roland Marsh, the university registrar until 1965, had worked in the Yale College dean's office since 1920. Chauncey, who worked for Marsh before becoming assistant to Brewster, remembered him as a man who seemed straight from the pages of Dickens. He wore a heavy, dark suit and white starched shirt every day, even in the hottest summer days in the era before air-conditioning. He sat at one of Yale's old octagonal examination tables, on which rested a blotter, a sharpened pencil, a telephone, and a key. Chauncey recalled that the telephone "was the only telephone in the office, and all the ladies—there were a series of ladies who worked for him, including Mrs. Marsh, whom he referred to as 'Mrs. Marsh'—if they wished to make a phone call, had to stand beside him and use the telephone. And the key was the key to the ladies' room, and the ladies were allowed to go once in the morning and once in the afternoon."[53]

Some found this sort of thing charming in a dusty, antiquarian way, but tradition restricted the university and its ambitions. Employees were promoted by seniority rather than by merit, and managers often were hired for reasons of background, inheritance, and even secret society membership. As a result, Yale's nonacademic support systems were underskilled, underfinanced, and ill equipped to meet the needs of a modern research university.

Brewster's academic approach required what he called "a belief and willingness to commit the institution firmly to a new course of long-range planning, major organizational changes, and the recruitment of a whole new cadre of men willing to work toward the creation of a dynamic and viable educational and financial blueprint." He concluded that "our planning, our determination of policy, our execution of programs can never again be of the order which has characterized us and our sister institutions in the past. It is clear that we can only maintain leadership as the result of the most extraordinary management at all levels and acquisitions of all kinds of a magnitude far greater than historical trends and traditions."[54]

The president and his advisors strengthened Yale's administrative capacity in much the same way that they had raised faculty quality. Brewster did not purge all of the Old Blues; he recruited and relied on men like Howard Weaver and C. Tracy Barnes, both blue-blooded but progressive ex-CIA agents. He did, however, ease out many of the timeservers and replaced them with young dynamos. He lured Howard T. Phelan (then only twenty-eight) from the management consulting firm Arthur D. Little to be director of operations and development. Phelan's introduction of computerization and systems analysis to Yale's cost accounting enabled administrators to identify the institution's costs for the first time, in the process saving the university a million dollars a year. Phelan, who told *Time* magazine that "Kingman is committed to making this a showcase of how to run a university,"[55] also oversaw an attempt to raise $388 million over a ten-year period, through expanded solicitation of potential sources and a variety of innovative devices for encouraging and leveraging gifts to the university.[56]

Twenty-nine-year-old John Embersits was induced to leave the Inland Steel Corporation to become Yale's business manager. Up until that time, Yale's employee relations had been run along threadbare paternalistic lines. The union was weak, and although Yale jobs paid less than the New Haven average, they were secure and no one had to work very hard at them. Unskilled workers were given time off instead of higher wages, and Yale's few skilled workers were retained by guaranteeing them overtime. Embersits demolished the old culture and brought in minority hiring, training programs, competitive compensation for different skill grades, and advancement by merit. These changes exacerbated tensions between unskilled labor, mostly in the dining halls, and the less numerous skilled craftsmen in the physical plant and elsewhere. Embersits's initiatives, by destabilizing the old arrangements, helped bring about a series of angry strikes starting in the late 1960s. His efforts were arguably necessary, in order to have more professional management and a higher skill bank, but the price was high, as Yale went on to have the worst labor relations of any university over the next four decades.[57]

IN ASSEMBLING A team of bright young hotshots to push through a managerial revolution, Brewster took inspiration and example from the much-ballyhooed efforts of Secretary Robert McNamara and his deputy Cyrus Vance to modernize the Department of Defense. Vance's role in the modernization process went unsung by the media, but he was McNamara's most important ally in bringing new management to the fractious military services. "Bob knew Cy would get the job done, whatever it was," Vance's deputy Joseph Califano remembered, and Vance was "instrumental in helping to bring about the enormous changes that McNamara brought to Defense and the armed forces in general. We were really changing the whole posture and makeup of the Army."[58]

As secretary of the Army, Vance overhauled its organizational structure, presided over an enormous increase in its size and expenditures, and launched it into the sky by creating the first helicopter cavalry, the Eleventh Air Assault Division. Since the Pentagon had no more idea of its expenditures than Yale did, McNamara and Vance directed the effort to computerize operations and bring in talented young social scientists from universities and think tanks—the so-called whiz kids—to analyze the costs and benefits of new weapons systems. These systems analysts pioneered the large-scale use of Program, Planning, and Budgeting Systems (PPBS), a scientific approach to management that was later implemented across the government under Lyndon Johnson.

Vance's interest in systems analysis fit well with his and McNamara's vision of a military force that was technologically advanced, efficient, and orderly. Systems analysis was another tool to empower civilians to reduce the bickering among the services by getting them to adopt rational reforms, such as the use of uniform supplies and equipment. As Vance told one military gathering, "I am particularly concerned that we conceive of our aircraft as systems. Vehicles, radios, weapons, navigation aids and fuels must be developed apace, each with the operational objective in mind, and each with total compatibility in view. Only through integrated effort can we achieve fully effective systems which make sense in terms of both cost and operational effectiveness."[59]

As Joseph Peck observed, "Brewster was impressed with systems analysis, and there was some talk of bringing in some of McNamara's whiz kids to run Yale." Brewster brought back his old professor Richard Bissell, fired from the CIA after the Bay of Pigs debacle, to consider the ways in which systems analysis, modeling, and long-range planning might be applied in a wide variety of university activities.[60] The success of McNamara and Vance in dealing with some of the same managerial and operational challenges that confronted Yale confirmed what Peck called Brewster's belief "that social scientists actually make pretty good operators, who can move back and forth between the different sectors of society."[61]

Perhaps the most important parallel between Brewster's efforts at Yale and Vance's at the Pentagon was that the aim of both was to reform their institutions to better serve the national interest. According to Alain Enthoven, perhaps the most famous of the whiz kids, the fundamental idea behind systems analysis was decision making based on the national interest, as opposed to "decision-making by compromise among various institutional and parochial interests."[62] The enemies of both efforts were conservative prejudices, tradition, and an inability to look beyond one's own narrow constituencies to the greater good.

The two attempts to modernize institutions—and in doing so, to challenge traditional cultures—created significant backlashes. McNamara's and Vance's determination to run the Defense Department in the national interest infuriated those who resisted the change, including not only military figures but also conservatives and even whole regions of the country, such as the South and the West. McNamara made enemies of the members of Congress who "saw things through the narrow parochial views of the military," as he put it. "Men such as [Strom] Thurmond and [Barry] Goldwater, for instance."[63] Many in the military objected to what they saw as the arrogance of the planners as well as the disruption of traditional arrangements. Air Force Chief of Staff Curtis LeMay felt that McNamara's mandarins were "the most egotistical people that I ever saw in my life. . . . They felt that the Harvard Business School method of solving problems would solve any problem in the world. . . . They were better than the rest of us; otherwise they wouldn't have gotten their superior education, as they saw it."[64] Vance, always the diplomat, was often dispatched to soothe the hurt feelings of politicians and military leaders discomfited by change. But he never backed away from the changes, which he, too, saw as being in the nation's best interest.

The controversies that Brewster encountered in modernizing Yale were not of the same order but had some similarities. While the greatest backlash against his reforms would come from the alumni, there was always a segment of the older, bluer, and more traditionalist faculty and administration who disliked and even hated him. The complaints of the traditionalists tended to be rooted in nostalgia, the wish to maintain a pleasant lifestyle, or distaste for the new types arriving on campus. And yet it was in some ways difficult not to sympathize with those who were pushed to the margins of an institution and the society they once dominated. They were also correct to argue that there was much of value in the culture being swept away in the shifts in faculty and administration. Brewster's old, conservative professor L. P. Curtis believed that the changes in faculty composition imperiled Yale College and its civilizing mission of teaching. He warned Brewster against "the conquest of the professionalized, grad-school mentality over that priceless amat[eur]ism of Yale College," an attitude that would make curious allies of the faculty conservatives and a rising generation of student activists.[65]

Joe Peck pointed out that the Yale president "was not unsympathetic to the Old Blues. Brewster knew them, had grown up with many of them, and he was very gracious and charming to them, as he was to everybody." But he had no desire to squander, in the interest of class protection, what he saw as Yale's potential contribution to civilization. Rather, he thought, the university would have to meet the responsibilities that the United States increasingly expected of its institutions. Peck believed that "Brewster's problem with Old Yale was that he felt too many of the Old Blues were in sinecures. They were nice people leading nice lives, but Brewster was more driven than that."

Brewster never deviated from his lifelong view that the privileged must live up to their privilege, and that establishment institutions such as Yale had to make room for talented outsiders. Peck, who came from modest circumstances in a small town in Ohio, remembered that "many of the adherents of Old Yale and Old Harvard" didn't feel comfortable with people like himself and his friend Carl Kaysen, Brewster's former colleague at Harvard. "Kaysen and I couldn't have come from more different backgrounds than Brewster, and yet Brewster was changing Yale along meritocratic lines to make a place for people like Kaysen and myself. . . . Brewster was the ideal president for the transition. In manner, dress, deportment, and demeanor, he was the Old Yale; he looked like what a Yale president should be. And yet his ideas were the New Yale."[66]

THE FIRST CRACKS in the apparent unity of outlook between Yale and its alumni appeared in June 1964, when the university became one of the first to award an honorary degree to the Reverend Martin Luther King Jr., who came to New Haven directly from jail in Saint Augustine, Florida, where he had been arrested for violating segregation laws. (Twenty members of the Yale community, including William Sloane Coffin, had earlier been arrested in Saint Augustine, along with Mrs. Malcolm Peabody, mother of Brewster's friend Chub Peabody, who was then governor of Massachusetts. Paul Moore was amused to remember that "the governor of Florida called Governor Peabody and said, 'Hey, Chub, I got your Mom in the slammer!'"[67])

The honorary degree ceremony was one of the few instances in which Yale put its institutional seal of approval on individuals (and implicitly their activities). The 1964 honorands included, besides King, Brewster's heroes Averell Harriman and Edward Mason and friends Sargent Shriver and Victor Weisskopf. In the elevated language of the occasion, Brewster told King that "as your eloquence has kindled the nation's sense of outrage, so your steadfast refusal to countenance violence in resistance to injustice has heightened our sense of national shame."[68] King dined with Brewster and the other honorands at the president's house, and met with the mostly black house staff and their children, who were groomed and starched within an inch of their lives. King later wrote to Brewster thanking him for the honor: "Such an expression of confidence and support will give me renewed courage and vigor to carry on in the struggle to make the American dream a reality."[69]

News of honorary degree recipients is kept secret until the commencement ceremony. But no sooner was King seen on the podium than alumni began writing to criticize, cancel donations, and even resign membership in their Yale classes.[70] In hindsight, it might seem surprising that honoring King would be even faintly controversial, but a large number of alumni echoed one southern newspaper's charge that Yale was violating institutional neutrality by "upholding a petty criminal as an example to American youth."[71] The twin issues involved were the movement for black equality, controversial in itself, and the tactic of nonviolent civil disobedience, which many felt fostered a disrespect for law that could lead to anarchy. As one alumnus wrote, "I see Yale's laurels to Dr. King as evidence of its support of the idea that every man is free to pick the laws he will obey."[72]

Brewster was able to draw on his experiences with pacifist classmates in the early 1940s as well as his legal background in defending King.[73] But he actually agreed that Yale was not being neutral with regard to the civil rights movement, and should not be. As he wrote to one of the justices of Mississippi's Supreme Court, Yale's "educational as well as moral obligation is to reaffirm the ideals we believe in. . . . [T]he effort to cure racial injustice must not be allowed to fester into a war between the races. Therefore it is especially important for the institutional symbols of white privilege to let it be known that they share this cause."[74] Later Brewster observed that "by all odds the [honorary degree] that has troubled alumni most is the Martin Luther King degree. . . . At the time the degree was conferred it seemed terribly important to minimize the gulf between the privileged establishment and those who had been for a hundred years of so-called 'emancipation' so largely excluded from the opportunities of the society, economy, and government." The award of the honorary degree to King was "an attempt to serve and to strengthen the hope that ours might become truly a society where the power of some people to push other people around would be progressively eliminated."[75]

Brewster opposed religious and racial discrimination mainly through personal example and behind-the-scenes negotiation. He was a stalwart defender of Chaplain Coffin's civil rights activism, and also refused to participate in social and educational functions that took place in establishments that discriminated against racial and religious minorities. For example, when he learned that the University Club of New York refused to accept blacks as members, he was instrumental in persuading the Association of American Universities to hold its meetings elsewhere. Along with Paul Moore, McGeorge Bundy, and John Lindsay, Brewster joined the Federal City Club in Washington, formed by Robert Kennedy in protest against the Metropolitan Club's refusal to admit blacks and women. (The club dissolved after the Met eliminated its discriminatory policies; Federal City members remembered the club as an interesting and far less stuffy alternative, although the food was never as good.[76]) Brewster pointedly avoided the clubhouse of the racially restrictive Pittsburgh Harvard–Yale–Princeton Club when the Yale alumni conference took place in that city, and he refused to travel to Atlanta for Yale functions during the years when the city's hotels were segregated. Brewster later claimed that these actions were "simply a matter of new sensitivities that Yale and other universities were beginning to develop."[77] Indeed, these decisions were not publicized at all for fear of upsetting conservative alumni.

THE CONSERVATIVE BACKLASH brewing up from the South and the West against liberal eastern establishment leaders like Vance and Brewster found expression in Arizona senator Barry Goldwater's 1964 presidential campaign. By the time Yale awarded King his honorary degree in mid-June, Goldwater appeared to have sewn up the GOP presidential nomination. His candidacy represented the uneasiness that many Americans felt toward modernization and expanding government, worries about unruly youth and minorities, and long-standing provincial resentment of the wealthy, urbanized East.

To eastern moderate Republicans, Goldwater looked like the epitome of political irresponsibility. They were deeply alarmed by his populism, his opposition to the 1964 Civil Rights Act, his seemingly dismissive views on the dangers of nuclear weapons, and his accommodation to extreme right-wing elements—not to mention his famous statement that the country would be better off if the Eastern Seaboard were sawed off and allowed to drift out to sea.

Brewster became involved in controversy over Goldwater when in one of his speeches he hoped that "educated men" would not "let recklessness masquerade as courage" or "accept venom as though it were eloquence."[78] The conservative writer William Buckley commented: "Dried out, that means: Vote for LBJ. . . . Evidently Brewster . . . considers [Goldwater] unfit to be President of the United States."[79] (Later Buckley would claim that Brewster had made "rather abrasive references to Goldwater as a fascist and a demagogue."[80]) Brewster retorted that he hadn't had Goldwater in mind when he made his remarks but "the man who knows Mr. Goldwater best felt that when I spoke of recklessness and venom, I spoke of Senator Goldwater. All I can say is that I merely fashioned the glove, and Mr. William F. Buckley found the hand."[81] Cyrus Vance also weighed in, publicly criticizing Goldwater's apparently cavalier attitudes about battlefield use of what the senator called "small and conventional" tactical nuclear weapons. "'Small' and 'conventional' are dangerously misleading and totally inappropriate adjectives when applied to any nuclear weapon," Vance scolded.[82]

The liberal wing of the Republican Party, seeking a sound alternative to Goldwater, pushed Pennsylvania governor William Scranton to oppose him at the GOP convention in July. Scranton's connections to Yale and Brewster's circle ran deep. He was the son and grandson of Yale men and the Yale College and law school classmate of Vance and Bill Bundy. He was also a college friend of Brewster's (whom he rather resembled, with his broad, handsome face and dark hair). His column had run in the *Yale Daily News* alongside McGeorge Bundy's. Scranton followed in Bundy's and Richardson's tracks as an aide to Christian Herter, and one of his main Republican backers, former attorney general Herbert Brownell, was also one of Lindsay's political mentors. Scranton joined Lindsay in the House of Representatives in 1960, and with Lindsay was one of only twenty-two Republicans whose votes enabled reform of the conservative-dominated Rules Committee. In 1962 he won a surprise victory to become Pennsylvania's governor, which catapulted him into consideration as a dark-horse nominee in the presidential race two years later.

Scranton described himself as "a liberal on civil rights, a conservative on fiscal policy, and an internationalist on foreign affairs."[83] Goldwater supporters, however, described him as "the Eastern Kingmakers' candidate" and "an ardent Leftwinger with a record of actions which prove his softness-on-Communism." To the right, the 1964 Civil Rights Act that Scranton strongly supported was "the most drastic piece of Socialistic police-state legislation to be advanced by the Democratic Liberal theorists."[84] The differences between Goldwater and his supporters and eastern liberals like Scranton, Henry Cabot Lodge, and Nelson Rockefeller were seen in class and ethnic as well as political terms, as one editorial made clear: "Governor Scranton, Mr. Lodge, and Governor Rockefeller are clearly Wasps, as the old moderate leadership of the party always has been. Senator Goldwater, with his mixed parentage and origins, barely qualifies. The Episcopal Church, to which all the best Wasps are said to belong, has a fine record of liberalism especially in the racial issue. It was never a party to American anti-intellectualism, which had its roots in a kind of eighteenth and nineteenth century Goldwater religious reaction."[85] At the convention in San Francisco in July, Scranton contested the nomination in an atmosphere that was notable for the hostility conservatives expressed toward the East, the media, and the establishment.

Buckley's magazine *National Review,* a prominent booster of Goldwater's candidacy, had also been among the first American journals to speak of an "establishment," or more commonly a "liberal establishment." Buckley remembered "that when I used the word 'establishment' in a speech to the National War College around 1956, most of the 'students' there did not know what it meant."[86] "Establishment" originally had a religious meaning, but nineteenth-century historians like Macaulay and Carlyle broadened the term to refer to the dominant men and institutions of the social and economic order. By the 1950s, British commentators such as the historian A. J. P. Taylor and the journalist Henry Fairlie were using the word to describe the small group of powerful men who shared personal connections and political beliefs, and who exercised power and influence outside the constitutional or political realms.[87] In 1959, the British journalist Hugh Thomas wrote that "the word 'Establishment' simply indicates the assumption of the attributes of a state church by certain powerful institutions and people."[88]

The analogy to an established state church would not apply to the United States, so when the journalist Richard Rovere popularized the term in a 1961 *American Scholar* article, he semiseriously described the establishment as "that group that gives American society its direction, that fixes major goals and that constitutes itself a ready pool of manpower for the more exacting labors of leadership. Its powers are greatest in the Executive and Judicial branches of government, in education, in organized religion and in science. It is in effective control of the new world that has been created by the philanthropic foundations."[89]

Right-wing groups reacted to the article as though the secret history of the universe had suddenly been laid bare. The voluptuously paranoid John Birch Society inveighed against "the Establishment that has been running the Roosevelt–Truman–Eisenhower–Kennedy Administration. . . . those tremendous forces which, throughout all of this one continuous administration under different names and fronts, have been striving 'so to change the economic and political structure of the United States that it can be comfortably merged with Soviet Russia in a one-world socialist government.'"[90]

Buckley knew that this sort of extreme conspiratorial vision was ridiculous. He pointed out that one "might as well say: the principal leaders of American life are all listed in Who's Who. Therefore, Who's Who is the invisible government."[91] However, although Rovere's article was a spoof, Buckley commented that Rovere "gives every indication of knowing that the idea of an Establishment is not sheer nonsense."[92] It was a reality, as GOP pollster Kevin Phillips observed, that many of the establishment strongholds that had bitterly opposed the New Deal in the previous generation—the Episcopal Church, the great metropolitan newspapers, the prestigious universities, the Supreme Court, Manhattan's Upper East Side—by the 1960s were liberal forces opposed to populist conservatism.[93]

The individuals connected with these institutions typically responded with indignation when it was charged that they represented some sort of cartel or conspiracy. The *New York Times'* Tom Wicker wrote to Buckley taking issue with "your suggestion that we are 'evolving into an official national newspaper!' I could understand it if you felt we were an official liberal journal. But the fact is, in recent years, that we have taken an unmerciful beating from the Kennedy Administration for David Halberstam's reporting on Viet Nam."[94] The shift in establishment outlook was the result not of any conspiracy but of the tendency of big, established institutions to take their cues from other established institutions that also had national scope and responsibilities. Another *Times* editor wrote to Brewster that "we're uncritically generous with the space and prominence we give to palpable nonsense, so long as the source is authoritative. If the President of the United States says it, or the president of GM, or the president of Yale, it's big news in the N.Y. Times, even if it's really no news at all."[95]

Any talk of an establishment, Buckley argued, raised the question "of whether there is, or has been, co-ordination of purpose between people who administer in the White House, teach at Harvard, write in the *New Yorker*, and preach at St. John the Divine. Of course there is co-ordination, however informal, and it is as naïve to believe there is not, as it is naïve to suppose that *only* conspiratorial action is responsible for historical events."[96] As Buckley's protégé M. Stanton Evans put it, the members of the establishment "work in concert although not necessarily by pre-arrangement. . . . [S]ince they are constantly engaged in the normal communication required to administer the affairs of a vast society—through government, civic institutions, academic duties, foundation work, the public media—they readily develop a common idiom and portfolio of tactics."[97]

AT THE 1964 Republican convention, the Goldwater delegates lacked Buckley's nuanced view of the establishment, but they responded on a gut level to his belief that he "would rather live in a society governed by the first 2000 names in the Boston phone directory than in one governed by the 200 members of the Harvard faculty."[98] They shared his sense that for too long the eastern liberal Republicans had looked down on them while the East's money, institutions, and ideas had shut them out of power. Now the convention offered a chance for payback. Heckling the media, the conservatives shouted down Rockefeller and applauded speech lines that alluded to rising black crime. They roared their approval when Goldwater taunted the liberal wing that "extremism in the defense of liberty is no vice."

Richardson was on hand as a delegate to witness the spectacle. A Scranton supporter, he was particularly upset by the GOP's turn against civil rights. As he wrote to his political mentor Leverett Saltonstall, "the Republican Party would be making an irretrievable mistake to bargain away its civil rights heritage for the sake of white Southern votes. We are not only likely, in the short run, to regret the impact of any such bargain on our position outside the South, but to suffer also in the South itself as more and more Negroes are enrolled to vote."[99] Richardson was steamrollered, along with Lindsay and the other eastern liberal delegates. The Credentials Committee denied Lindsay's motion to prohibit racial discrimination in choosing delegates, and the delegates rejected other platform motions supporting civil rights and opposing extremist groups like the John Birch Society and the Klan. Scranton was defeated by the Goldwater forces on the first ballot, 883 to 214. Alabama governor George Wallace, who had garnered surprising numbers of votes in the primaries with his attacks on pointy-headed liberals, intellectuals, elites, and government bureaucrats, withdrew his independent candidacy—because, he said approvingly, the GOP had passed a segregationist platform. As one Texas delegate leader boasted, "The South took the Mason-Dixon line and shoved it right up to Canada."[100]

Even while the convention was, in effect, upholding segregation, white college students and liberal activists were traveling south to take part in the Freedom Summer in Mississippi. The campaign, building on the program of black voter registration that had drawn Yale students to the state the previous year, mobilized blacks to vote and established "freedom schools" for black children. The campaign drew national attention when two white participants, Michael Schwerner and Andrew Goodman, and one black activist, James Chaney, disappeared; their bodies were found in late August.

Paul Moore remembered that "little by little" that summer, "I was absorbing the weight and complexity of the fight against racism. The issue became part of my life."[101] He went to Mississippi in July, taking part in a ministers' project working with civil rights groups. The clerics met with colleagues in the universities and churches, helped register blacks in the Mississippi Freedom Democratic Party (a mostly black organization that put itself forward as an unofficial replacement for the regular Democratic Party in the state), and provided some measure of protection for the civil rights workers. "I had fought for freedom in the Marines," Moore recalled, "but

I'd never *felt* freedom until I swayed back and forth to a freedom song in the basement of a Negro church that summer."[102]

Unfortunately, the Freedom Summer ended up widening the split between liberals and younger, angrier activists. In August, recent Yale graduate Joseph Lieberman, writing from the Democratic convention in Atlantic City, informed Brewster that he was "bemoaning your association with the Republican party. Otherwise, you would certainly figure in Vice-Presidential speculation."[103] But the smooth workings of the convention came unglued when President Lyndon Johnson, in a compromise deal, allowed only two of the Mississippi Freedom Democratic Party delegates to be seated, rather than unseating the regular all-white Mississippi delegation, as MFDP activists demanded. The MFDP and its supporters felt betrayed. Todd Gitlin, leader of Students for a Democratic Society, wrote that "to the New Left, Atlantic City discredited the politics of coalition—between militants and the liberal-labor establishment, between whites and blacks, between youth and elders."[104] The convention marked a division between youthful activists like Lieberman, who continued to work with mainstream politicians, civil rights groups, and liberal organizations, and the radicals, who increasingly cut themselves off from all but the most left-wing forces.

Paul Moore, who tried to serve as a mediator at the convention, had a firsthand view of the shape that untethered radical and racial anger might take. Flying back from Mississippi, he arrived in New Jersey to find that a riot had erupted in his old parish in Jersey City. Blacks threw bricks and bottles at police cars, while the police repeatedly charged the crowd, brandishing nightsticks and firing into the air, and "needlessly harassing innocent bystanders."[105] Moore attempted to calm his former parishioners in the face of what he considered police provocation, trying to direct the crowd's resentments "into political channels . . . registration and petition." He was part of a multiracial delegation that sought to persuade the mayor and the police chief to call off the cops, only to be told, "We will meet force with force." Moore felt that this kind of response turned the responsible, would-be mediators "back upon their own resources and soured them once more on the methods of working through ordinary channels."[106] The establishment, he realized, would have to make a renewed effort to ensure that people in the inner cities would not lose faith altogether in peaceful processes of change.

One other series of events that summer involving Brewster's circle of friends would have major repercussions. Early on the morning of August 2, Vance was awakened and summoned along with a few other officials to the home of Secretary of State Dean Rusk. There he was informed that the destroyer USS *Maddox* had been attacked by three North Vietnamese torpedo boats in the Gulf of Tonkin. For about an hour the officials looked at a large map of the gulf spread out on the floor, then went to the White House to brief Johnson. The discussion omitted the fact that the attack on the *Maddox,* which was engaged in highly classified electronic snooping against North Vietnam, had occurred concurrently with a covert 34-A commando raid on the North Vietnamese coast.[107] Responsibility for both missions, as well as for all major U.S. covert operations worldwide, rested with the four-person 303 Committee, chaired by Bundy, which also included Vance, U. Alexis Johnson from State, and Richard Helms from the CIA.[108]

The president, who did not seem overly upset by news of the attack— and in fact subjected his advisors to a long lecture on the difficulty of moving the new postal bill through Congress—ordered the *Maddox* to continue its patrol, augmented by the USS *Turner Joy.* "We were determined not to be provocative," Johnson wrote in his memoirs, "nor were we going to run away. We would give Hanoi the benefit of the doubt—this time—and assume the unprovoked attack had been a mistake."[109]

On the morning of August 4, Vance was at the Pentagon, on the radio with the commander of the destroyer division in Tonkin, who reported that the ships were under "continuous torpedo attack." Rusk, Bundy, and CIA head John McCone joined McNamara, Vance, and the Joint Chiefs of Staff at the Pentagon, and the group agreed to recommend that Johnson authorize a limited air strike on the torpedo boat bases.[110] Bundy and Vance, along with McNamara, Rusk, and McCone, went to the White House to lunch with Johnson. The president agreed to retaliate.

Subsequent reports from the destroyer division, however, reported that the second attack may not have taken place. McNamara convened the chiefs, and Vance got on the phone to Admiral Ulysses Sharp, seeking confirmation. Chester Cooper, one of Bundy's deputies, remembered that "the stuff that was coming into the Situation Room was absolutely incomprehensible, and there was Mac and everybody else shouting, 'Was there an attack or wasn't there an attack?' There was nothing we had available which could give us enough information to say yes or no."[111] In the end, McNamara assured Johnson that there had been a second attack.

Johnson inevitably viewed the Gulf of Tonkin incidents in the context of the presidential campaign; he was concerned that Goldwater not be able to use them against the White House. At the same time, the president wanted congressional backing for the administration's actions in Indochina, if only to ensure that American operations there would not become an issue to interfere with the passage of Great Society legislation. Early on the morning of August 4, as Bundy remembered it, Johnson told him to prepare a resolution for Congress authorizing the president to take whatever steps might be deemed necessary to prevent further aggression from the North Vietnamese. "I said something like, 'Mr. President, that seems too fast to me.' He said, 'I didn't ask you that question.' . . . [T]he two attacks together gave him the perfect opportunity for something which he had perceived as desirable for a long time."[112] The result was the Tonkin Gulf resolution, a near-unanimous, open-ended congressional authorization of the use of force to prevent further aggression in the area. While the United States presence in Vietnam did not increase substantially during 1964—the number of military advisors increased only from 17,000 at the end of 1963 to 23,000 at the end of 1964—the groundwork was laid for the enormous escalation that would begin the next year.

IN THE FALL of 1964, however, the conflict in Vietnam was not yet a contentious issue for most Americans. Lyndon Johnson won a landslide victory in November after a campaign in which he posed as the peace candidate. Promising that "American boys" would not be sent "to do the fighting for Asian boys," he painted his Republican opponent as a warmonger eager to drop nuclear bombs on Vietnam.[113] The Democrats' overwhelming victory in the 1964 elections made it appear that the future would belong to liberalism. Conservatism as a principle seemed to be thoroughly repudiated, even within the Republican Party. In the short term, as the political fortunes of liberal Republicans like Richardson and Lindsay increased, so did their political ambitions.

Richardson had been narrowly defeated in the 1962 Republican primary for Massachusetts attorney general. "I went to a lot of trouble to make sure that my primary campaign was gentlemanly," he remarked later. "I didn't want to leave any scars if I lost, which I thought I probably would." In 1964, John Volpe was trying to regain the Massachusetts governorship he had lost to Richardson's Harvard classmate, a Democrat, Chub Peabody two years before, and the Republicans took it for granted that the election would be a rematch against Peabody. "Volpe accordingly wanted to balance the ticket with a Yankee, and he asked me to run for Lieutenant Governor. This gave me some bargaining power." The lieutenant governor's office in Massachusetts has few duties, and it would have been inconsistent with his activist nature for Richardson to be content with a political sinecure. He got Volpe to agree that if they were elected, Richardson would take on responsibility for coordinating all of the state's health, education, and welfare programs; he believed that leadership and the application of trained intelligence could solve even the most intractable problems posed by poverty, race, and urban decay.

Richardson's Democratic enemies from his years as Massachusetts attorney general had lain in wait for revenge, and when the campaign began, flyers describing his erratic driving record appeared in downtown Boston. Richardson believed his nemesis, William F. Callahan, was responsible; indeed, when Callahan's office safe was opened after his death, it was found to contain one copy of the 1948 Massachusetts highway master plan and fifty copies of the anti-Richardson flyer. Richardson had only once been found guilty of drunk driving, as a Harvard undergraduate, but had accumulated ten arrests over twenty-five years, mostly for speeding and other traffic violations. Getting behind the wheel could bring out his taste for aggression and risk taking, seemingly at odds with his usual deliberateness and restraint.

The same desire to beat the odds lay behind Richardson's plunge into the hurly-burly of politics, despite the fact that he was far from a natural campaigner. His upper-class demeanor was a liability, and he tended to come across as starchy and overintellectual in public appearances. He believed that a Yankee Republican like himself, however, could win in Irish, Democratic Massachusetts by "more organization, harder work, and more money."[114] He sunk a quarter of a million dollars of his own money into his political campaigns, shook a quarter of a million hands, and energized and attracted large numbers of bright young people to his organization.

It turned out that Peabody was beaten in the primary, and the Democrats were fractured. The Volpe–Richardson ticket ran almost a million votes ahead of Goldwater in the election—in liberal Massachusetts, Nelson Rockefeller actually beat Goldwater on a write-in vote—and Richardson squeaked into office.

Like Lindsay, Richardson combined incorruptible integrity with a genuine desire to be a public servant. He thought of himself as a man for the people, if not necessarily of them. He truly loved the experience of taking to the hustings and meeting the electorate. On the last day of the campaign, he traveled around the state to thank his supporters in each county. Flying into Worcester on a raw day and pulling up in front of a crowd of friends and supporters, Richardson had an epiphany: "I suddenly realized that even after all that handshaking, nonetheless every new person I met struck me as different from all the others. There flashed into my mind the dedication of one of my favorite books, *McSorley's Wonderful Saloon* by Joseph Mitchell: 'This book is dedicated to the people who are sometimes called "the little people." Well, I want you to know they are just as big as you are, whoever you are.'"[115]

Lindsay had refused to support Goldwater in the election, since he found the Arizonan so much at odds with the progressive tradition he saw as the Republicans' heritage. "It seemed to me that it was important that this was the party of the individual," Lindsay said after the election. "It's the party of Lincoln, of civil rights, the protection of the person and his liberties against the majority, even against big business or the federal bureaucracy."[116] In the apparent national repudiation of conservatism that followed Goldwater's defeat, it seemed likely that Lindsay would lead a liberal, revitalized, pro–civil rights Republican Party against the Democrats in the next presidential election. Lyndon Johnson and Bobby Kennedy were said to have exchanged rueful speculation as to which of them would have to face Lindsay in 1968.

One of the apparent losers in the Goldwater debacle was George Herbert Walker Bush, who abandoned his liberal Republican principles to play to the right and was defeated by Ralph Yarborough in the Texas senatorial race. Bush's loss seemed to confirm Richardson's prediction that the Republican Party would suffer from its opposition to civil rights. As the *New York Times* editorialized, "The large Negro vote for Senator Ralph W. Yarborough, Democrat, of Texas was conclusive. . . . Some 260,000 Negroes went to the polls and more than 95% of them, about 247,000, voted the Democratic ticket. In 1960 only about 105,000 Negroes voted." Bush's oldest son, George W., then in his first semester at Yale, encountered William Sloane Coffin on the Old Campus shortly after the election. "The better man won," Coffin allegedly told him, although the chaplain later thought it unlikely that he would have made such a harsh statement to an incoming freshman.[117]

In the longer view of hindsight, however, the Republican convention that chose Goldwater had highlighted the political, economic, and cultural divergence between the East and the rest of the country. The convention also marked the end of the liberal Republicans' leadership within the party; it was also notable as an indication that the power of the East had declined in other ways as well. The journalist Murray Kempton observed that the convention was "historic because it is the emancipation of the serfs. . . . The serfs have seized the estate of their masters."[118] In the years between the U.S. entrance into World War II and the mid-1960s, the population of the South and West almost doubled, while that of the North shrank; at the same time, the Northeast lost its predominance in manufacturing, banking, and other key sectors.[119] As northern industries deteriorated (like the railroads) or relocated to the South (like textiles), many of the region's large cities decayed. The newly rich who made big money in southern and western agribusiness, oil and gas extraction, and defense industries developed a raw, aggressive style of conservatism that was worlds removed from the socially conscious and temperate style of northeastern liberal Republicanism. The divide would widen as the civil rights movement, the student movement, and the antiwar movement polarized the country, but the divisions were already visible in 1964.

TWO WEEKS AFTER the election, Kingman Brewster landed on the cover of *Newsweek*. The lead article assessed the question of whether the eastern universities, and in particular the eight ancient establishments that made up the Ivy League—Harvard, Yale, Princeton, Columbia, Cornell, Dartmouth, Brown, and Pennsylvania—remained the nation's finest. The verdict was a qualified yes, despite the millions of college-age baby boomers and billions of tax dollars pouring into high-quality public and private universities in other parts of the country. The magazine's editors, impressed with Brewster's managerial revolution, used him to spotlight growth and change at ivy-covered eastern campuses. Although the president of Harvard traditionally had been the natural leader among American educators, and the Yale president had been in office for little more than a year, *Newsweek* declared that "in Yale's Kingman Brewster, the Ivy League may have found its most eloquent spokesman." He presented an interesting paradox: a man who spoke with "aristocratic poise" and looked "like a button-down Cary Grant," but who was an innovative leader with a common touch. The article observed that even Brewster's aides doubted whether he could "break through Yale's encrusted traditions" to set new ideas in motion, but concluded that "Kingman Brewster has bucked tradition before, and besides, he plays to win."[120]

Newsweek was fascinated by the spectacle of such an establishment leader taking on the forces of WASP tradition. The week before the Brewster piece, the magazine had published an article on the sociologist who, as it happened, popularized the acronym WASP and was the foremost scholar of the establishment. In his monograph *The Protestant Establishment,* the University of

Pennsylvania sociologist E. Digby Baltzell recognized that it was too complex an entity to fit into traditional political categories and that it was only one power grouping among many in the United States. He also pointed out that a society need not have an establishment at all. A society might have a national upper class, and there would always be people in positions of power, but there wouldn't necessarily be overlap between the two groups. Baltzell believed that American society needed an establishment, both because a sprawling, multicultural democracy required a source of authority and because a public service ethos operated as a check on elites who otherwise might destroy the republic through greed and lust for power. But he worried that the establishment was undermining itself and in danger of becoming a caste by refusing to "assimilate new men of talent and power regardless of ethnic or racial origins."[121] What Baltzell wanted, in other words, was a liberal establishment—liberal not so much in political affiliation as in devotion to civil rights, civil liberties, equal opportunity, and social mobility.

BALTZELL COULD HAVE made an interesting sociological study of the Yale Corporation, the university's governing body. The Corporation comprised ten self-perpetuating successor trustees (successors to the original ten Protestant ministers who had founded Yale), six elected alumni fellows, and ex officio Kingman Brewster (as president of the university) and the governor and lieutenant governor of Connecticut (who rarely attended). The group met for a weekend each month during the academic year, usually around the huge oval mahogany table in Woodbridge Hall, the university's administrative headquarters, but occasionally in New York.

The Corporation at that time included a number of important national figures. Several were well known in the business community, including William McChesney Martin (head of the Federal Reserve), Juan Trippe (the founder of Pan Am), and J. Richardson Dilworth (financial manager for the Rockefellers). Lindsay joined in the summer of 1964, and Moore at the end of the year. Brewster observed that the Corporation included the executive branch represented by William Bundy, the legislative branch represented by Lindsay, the financial establishment represented by Martin, "and now it's all topped off by the ecclesiastical elegance of the Suffragan Bishop, my classmate Paul Moore. With that many Washingtonians on the Corporation, why should we worry about interference from Washington?"[122]

Three other trustees on whom Brewster relied heavily were his contemporary Harold ("Doc") Howe and the two most generous benefactors of Yale on the Corporation, John Hay Whitney, owner of the *New York Herald Tribune*, and J. Irwin Miller, owner of Cummins Engine Company.

Howe was the brother of Yale admissions head Arthur Howe Jr. and grandson of the founder of the Hampton Institute, one of the nation's oldest and most prestigious historically black colleges. The Howe brothers spent several formative years in the nearly all-black environment of Hampton during the decade that their father was president of the institute. While both brothers acquired an interest in education and civil rights, Doc recalled that "I didn't think the private schools mattered that much. The real issue with education in the United States was with the public schools. . . . Artie didn't really approve of my activities. He stuck with the elite."[123] Doc Howe was not opposed to tradition. He joined Skull and Bones at Yale and got married in the same chapel, on an island in Squam Lake, where his parents had married. (The Howes owned a two-mile stretch of shoreline on the lake.) He did oppose traditionalism, which was rather a different thing. After serving as teacher, high school principal, and school superintendent, in 1964 he became director of the Learning Institute of North Carolina, working with Terry Sanford (arguably the South's most progressive governor) to reform and integrate the state's public schools. Howe was in Skull and Bones with McGeorge Bundy and was one of his closest friends; Bundy's sons called him "Uncle Doc." Howe would be the man both Bundy and Brewster turned to for guidance when attempting to navigate the treacherous waters of race and education.

Whitney was among the closest American approximations of the British aristocracy. "Jock" was descended from a glittering array of industrial barons and statesmen; his mother's father was Secretary of State John Hay. He was president of his class at Groton, then followed in his father's and grandfather's path to Yale, from which he graduated in 1926. Whitney once mused that he couldn't think of any material object he had wanted and been unable to afford, and he indulged in many of the pastimes of the absurdly rich, including polo, fox hunting, and collecting (race horses, artworks, and starlets). He had more depth than most members of his class, however, and felt that his affluence imposed an obligation of public service. From 1940 to 1942, he worked alongside his friend Nelson Rockefeller at the Office of the Coordinator of Inter-American Affairs and served as colonel in the war, during which he was captured by the Nazis in southern France and barely escaped alive. He bankrolled a number of successful plays and movies (including *Gone with the Wind*) and founded one of the nation's first venture-capital firms. His support of Eisenhower resulted in his appointment as ambassador to the Court of Saint James's.

Whitney backed a number of liberal Republican candidates, including Lindsay and Scranton. He furthered their political line through his support of the Ripon Society, an organization of young liberal Republican professionals founded in 1962 as a counterpart to Americans for Democratic Action, and his ownership of the money-losing *New York Herald Tribune*, virtually the mouthpiece of liberal Republicanism. In the 1964 presidential race, however, the newspaper endorsed Johnson over Goldwater, supporting a Democrat for the first time in its history. Whitney lamented that the nation was "dealing with the temporary, we hope, disintegration of a great party."[124]

Miller was more directly involved in support for equal opportunities and civil rights. *Esquire* magazine once put Miller's picture on the cover above the headline "This man ought to be the next President of the United States." Miller was born in Columbus, Indiana, where his family had been prominent since the 1820s. After serving in the war, he became president and CEO of one of his family's businesses, Cummins Engine. Under his leadership it grew to control half the market in diesel engines for trucks, and by the mid-1960s had become the nation's largest family business. Like Jock Whitney, Miller had an innovative venture-capital firm and a philanthropic foundation. Furthermore, he was trustee on a number of boards, including Yale and the Ford Foundation; in 1960 he had become the first lay president of the National Council of Churches of Christ, representing thirty-nine million members from thirty-four Protestant denominations.

Miller was the liberal establishment's ideal of a business executive. Cummins was among the nation's most socially enlightened corporate citizens, one of the few that donated up to the limit of five percent of its pre-tax income a year. Miller was a member of the Committee on Economic Development, the elite, quasi-governmental advisory association of business leaders founded by Paul Hoffman and William Benton. He gave a high percentage of his yearly income to religious, political, and philanthropic organizations. He was a generous supporter of liberal Republicans like Lindsay and Scranton, but voted for Johnson over Goldwater. A patron of the arts, he commissioned the world's best modern architects to build in Columbus, transforming that small town into an intoxicating showcase of tastefully restored Victorian buildings and daring contemporary edifices. He was a highly cultured man who owned two homes designed by Eero Saarinen, read the New Testament in Greek, and relaxed by playing Bach on his Stradivarius violin—sometimes accompanied by his friend William Sloane Coffin on piano.

On the Yale Corporation the deeply religious Miller was effectively a member of the clerical bloc, along with Moore. Like Moore, he advocated clerical activism as a force for spiritual regeneration as well as for social change, particularly as a critical mass of the clergy became concerned with civil rights. Miller steered the National Council of Churches into the civil rights arena, over considerable opposition from within the organization, and helped organize the 1963 March on Washington. As one of the strongest allies of Martin Luther King's nonviolent protest, the council helped legitimize King and his movement.

In bringing his activism to his trusteeships, Miller motivated colleagues and institutions to seek progressive change. He put backbone into men like Brewster (and later Bundy), pushed them to modernize their organizations, and spurred them on to make the controversial decisions that they knew were the correct ones. He backed up his exhortation with his intelligence, personal example, and (not least) money; he was one of a handful of Yale's donors who gave over $1 million during the 1960s.

When Brewster received angry letters from alumni who felt that Yale, by honoring King, was fomenting communism, he pressed Miller into service to answer some of the critics. "The menace and threat of world-wide Communism is a very real one," Miller wrote. "In my opinion we combat it best by making our country so strong and healthy, so clearly superior to competitive societies that the Communist virus finds no fertile soil among us. This means, among other things, the elimination of persistent poverty, the reduction of unemployment to levels well below those of other societies, and the extension of equal freedom, dignity, and opportunity to every segment of our people."[125]

That kind of Cold War, establishment liberalism reached its high-water mark of hope and confidence in the mid-1960s. Miller had a metaphor for moderate leaders like Brewster (and himself) who tried to maintain the stability of their institutions and society while accommodating the energies of change: "I'm an engine builder. If you build an engine without a governor, you never know when it's going to explode. But if it has a governor, it can do good work, and never to the point of destruction."[126] As the political temper of the 1960s became hotter, though, such establishment governors would find it increasingly difficult to exert their moderating influence.

6

APPROACHING

THUNDER

O N MARCH I, 1965, Kingman Brewster and McGeorge Bundy and their
wives were sitting on a beach in the Bahamas. The couples usually
vacationed in Antigua, but this spring Pan Am president (and Yale Corporation member) Juan Trippe gave them the use of his Eleuthera home and
the well-manicured Cotton Bay Club. Lyndon Johnson had only grudgingly
given Bundy permission to take the vacation. During the Bundy–Brewster
vacation in Antigua the previous year, the president watched the flow of
White House paperwork slow to a trickle in the absence of his national security advisor.[1]

The talk on the beach that day was mainly about Vietnam. Three weeks
earlier, Bundy had made his first visit there, to take the measure of the floun-
dering South Vietnamese government. On his last day, Vietcong guerrillas
attacked a U.S. base near Pleiku, killing eight American soldiers, wounding
a hundred, and destroying ten American aircraft. Afterward, Bundy joined
Ambassador Maxwell Taylor and General William Westmoreland at the
military headquarters in Saigon. He called Vance at the White House Situation Room and recommended that the United States retaliate by bombing
North Vietnam, a step it had thus far refrained from taking.

Vance had conveyed Bundy's message to Johnson, who was meeting with
Bill Bundy, McNamara, Hubert Humphrey, George Ball, and other officials
in the Cabinet Room upstairs. Humphrey and Ball objected to the plan to
widen the war—Vance recalled that Ball "was particularly concerned about
the fact that [Soviet premier] Kosygin was then in Hanoi and felt that at
least the bombing should be held up until Kosygin left."[2] Johnson overruled
the dissenters, and, within hours, carrier-based jets were dropping bombs

on a North Vietnamese army camp. The United States had taken a large step into the war in Vietnam.[3]

Within days of Bundy's recommendation, Brewster began to feel its effects on his campus. Yale students and faculty formed an ad hoc committee to protest the air strikes and took part in a march for peace in downtown New Haven.[4] Senator Wayne Morse of Oregon, who had stood almost alone in his opposition to the Gulf of Tonkin Resolution the previous year, came to the university to blast the government's policy and to call for a halt to the war. The student newspaper published its first antiwar editorial, declaring that "the time has come to leave South Vietnam."[5]

YALE AND A handful of other universities were among the few places where significant antiwar sentiment could be detected, and protesters remained a minority even on the campuses for some time. The peace activities at Yale were countered by a sizable pro-involvement rally sponsored by the Buckley-inspired Young Americans for Freedom and the circulation of a heavily endorsed petition supporting the U.S. commitment in Vietnam.[6] Yale's traditional strains of patriotism and militarism were still evident. On his trip to Saigon, Bundy had crossed paths with Barry Zorthian, the student his friend Doc Howe had tapped for Skull and Bones after Brewster's refusal, who was now the chief U.S. information officer in Vietnam.[7] Already enough of the university's alumni were engaged in the war to form a Yale Club of Saigon, and death notices would crop up in the *Yale Daily News* that spring.[8] Even so, both Bundy and Brewster were concerned that the war might drive a wedge between the government and the intellectual community.

As the two men mulled over these matters on the beach at Eleuthera, the phone rang inside the beach house—an urgent call from the States. Everyone expected that it would be for Bundy, summoning him to deal with a national security crisis. Instead it was for Brewster. The phone trilled again and again throughout the day. "Every time the phone would ring I'd think it was the White House," Bundy recalled, "but it was always New Haven."[9] One of the nation's first mass student demonstrations had erupted at Yale. The next day the U.S. government implemented Operation Rolling Thunder, initiating sustained bombing of North Vietnam, and this time the phone began ringing for Bundy as well. For Brewster and Bundy, the 1960s had entered an entirely new phase.

To university administrators like Brewster, the beginning of the Free Speech Movement at the University of California at Berkeley, the previous semester, was an isolated episode. Few recognized it as the opening salvo in the so-called student revolution. In early September 1964, the *Oakland Tribune*, annoyed by Berkeley students protesting its racial hiring practices, notified the university that political activities were taking place on the strip of brick pavement where students had traditionally set up tables to advertise, recruit, and raise funds for various causes. The Telegraph Avenue strip, the *Tribune* complained, was university property, even though it was outside the university gates. Two weeks later, President Clark Kerr closed the strip, citing "historic policy" prohibiting political advocacy and fund-raising on campus property. The uproar that followed united groups of all political hues, from the Young Socialist Alliance to Youth for Goldwater, in defense of the First Amendment. A campaign was launched by students to restore and perhaps expand free speech on campus. The administration then suspended seven students who manned tables on the strip in defiance of the ban.

On October 1, when police arrested Jack Weinberg, a Congress of Racial Equality (CORE) worker and former graduate student, for violating the new "historic policy," hundreds of students spontaneously sat down around the police car in which he was held, touching off a thirty-two-hour rally and open speakers' forum. The protests that followed culminated in a December 2 sit-in of a thousand in Sproul Hall, Berkeley's main administration building. It was the first act of civil disobedience of the 1960s carried out by students against their own university. State police cleared the building the next day, making 773 arrests. A shocked faculty and student body rallied to the FSM's cause, and the discredited Kerr administration was forced to accede to the movement's demands.[10]

As nearly all commentators pointed out, there were structural reasons why the student movement began at Berkeley, the university that in 1964 practically defined the postwar idea of progress. The school, which epitomized the values of modernization toward which other universities were striving, was large, academically superior, meritocratic, and deeply integrated into the American system. It was a "knowledge factory" acting as a "servant of the larger society," in Kerr's memorable words, by training a generation of professionals, carrying out research for the public good, and providing expertise to government and corporations. But progress had come at a price. As Berkeley had expanded to accommodate the numbers of baby boomers who wanted an education, it had grown more bureaucratic and impersonal.

Until the 1960s, the drawbacks had appeared to be merely the by-products of progress and success, but the Free Speech Movement made it clear that the growth of the multiversity had the unintended consequence of breeding student unrest. In the analysis of the *New York Times* columnist James Reston, students were "in revolt against bigness and facelessness."[11] FSM spokesman Mario Savio put it this way: "Asking why it happened in Berkeley first is like asking why Negroes, and not Americans generally, are involved in securing access for all to the good which America could provide for all her people."[12] As Savio's comment suggests, the FSM escalated from an effort to restore the status quo ante into a movement that encouraged students to see themselves as a class, and perhaps an oppressed class at that.

In early 1965, Brewster commented that "the recent events at Berkeley certainly made me realize how fortunate we are in being able to really say that there is no single undergraduate who is not known to some member of the administrative group, and many members of the faculty, as a human being."[13] The university had remained small enough to be a fairly cohesive community. While this differentiated Yale from the faceless multiversities, Yale students were hardly quiescent. The 1960s witnessed the rise of student activism at Yale as well as at Berkeley, and for some of the same reasons.

CHANGE WAS INDEED in the wind in New Haven by the early 1960s. In the spring of 1961, undergraduate petitions against plans to build a house on Old Campus for the dean of the freshman year represented a considerable shift from past students' patterns of deference toward university authority. The protest led to the formation of the Committee on the Freshman Year, which Brewster encouraged to make significant alterations in Yale's admissions and educational structure.[14]

Students' attitudes everywhere were influenced by the civil rights movement, which captured the sympathies of young people across the country and gave new popularity to activism generally. The campuses were stimulated and politicized as they had not been since the debate over intervention, before Pearl Harbor, in Brewster's undergraduate years. While relatively few students played a direct role in civil rights activities, many others eventually came to share a broad, vicarious sense of participation in the movement. Many who had made the journey south became radicalized by their experiences, and applied the strategies of the movement to activism within the university. The Free Speech Movement at Berkeley was led by students and faculty members who had been involved in the civil rights movement. So, too, was the Yale student demonstration that disturbed the tranquillity of Brewster's vacation in early March 1965.

The protest was sparked by the denial of tenure to the popular philosophy teacher Richard Bernstein. It began as "a visible rumor you could see
moving across the campus as small groups of undergraduates gathered."
Students felt the Bernstein case was "the last in a series of unwarranted,
unexplained injustices in tenure appointments."[15] For two weeks, they
staged a series of meetings and actions, including a seventy-two-hour vigil
in front of Woodbridge Hall. Undergraduates and faculty alike felt the
soon-to-be-familiar high that commingled cause and comradeship. To one
student, the protest was "the most exciting, inspiring week of our four years
here." The English professor Richard Sewall declared, to a large and enthusiastic rally, that "we have established a sense of community here. Yale has
come alive this week."[16]

An administration dossier on the dramatis personae involved noted that
one Bruce Payne, a graduate student in political science, "went to Berkeley
as undergraduate, [was] very active in student affairs there and . . . also in
Civil Rights work in South." The dossier labeled him a "pro in the demonstration business."[17] The protests were supported and partially orchestrated
by Chaplain Coffin, Sewall, and several other faculty members who had also
been active in civil rights. Still, the protest was the first at Yale in years to
mobilize support from nearly all sectors of the student body, and not simply
the politically inclined core. As Brewster wrote later, "It was not just the
campus politicians and the agitators who took causes seriously. The out-
pouring of 'squares' and 'jocks' . . . was a sign for all but the blind to read."[18]

At many universities the first wave of student demonstrations was
greeted with suspicion, or worse, by administrators. Berkeley's response to
the Free Speech Movement featured police in riot gear dragging away nonviolent protesters, an image that for many students suggested parallels to
sheriffs beating up peaceful demonstrators in Mississippi. No police officers
were involved at Yale during the Bernstein affair, but at least one member
of the administration was sufficiently alarmed or curious (or both) to make
a record of every sign at the demonstration. Most were earnest appeals
such as WE HAVE A STAKE IN EDUCATION TOO, REVIEW TENURE POLICY, and
WHY *NOT* CREATIVE TEACHING? Others were more blunt or cryptic: DEAD
WOOD MAKES GOOD PAPER, WHY?, DAMN!, REPENT!, and BABIES FOR BERNSTEIN
(on a baby stroller).[19]

When the president returned to New Haven, his reaction to the demonstration was generally approving, despite the fact that Brewster's stringent
process of tenure appraisal was one reason for Bernstein's failure to pass the
newly empowered divisional review for the humanities. Brewster sought to

resolve the issue by sending the appointment back to the department to clarify its initial recommendation. A subsequent vote revealed a 5–2 split, attributable to academic reservations (outside reviewers found Bernstein's work unoriginal), intradisciplinary warfare between analytic and other approaches to philosophy, and personal and political squabbles between Bernstein's mentor Paul Weiss and other members of the department.

While Brewster genuinely regretted that a superb teacher like Bernstein had not made it through the appointments committee, he was not about to intervene and weaken one of his most significant contributions to Yale's academic excellence. Although it is within the president's power to make appointments independent of the faculty, Brewster's concern for process overrode whatever temptations he may have had to play the man on the white horse. "Ultimately the faculty must decide who the faculty shall be," he announced. "Appointments and promotions should not be made either by Presidential decree or by student ballot." He added, however, "I greatly appreciate the zeal, the good will, and the responsibility which have characterized the student protest over the failure to grant tenure to Mr. Bernstein."[20]

Brewster could generally accept and even encourage some expressions of undergraduate restlessness and activism. Perhaps reflecting on his own undergraduate experiences in the America First Committee, he observed that "using the campus as a forum for political affairs is a long tradition, and the democratic process cannot survive on apathy."[21] "In spite of the yearning for the quiet life on the part of all educators," he told the other New England college presidents, "we must not demand or expect surrender of a student's right to question authority if he thinks it is mean or thoughtless or unjust. . . . So I say, don't let education get in the way of enthusiasm. Don't let it override moral standards and don't let it smother the student's right to stand up for what he believes in."[22]

This attitude distinguished Brewster from many Americans. A more typical view was that of one Yale alumnus who asked protesters, "By what process of mental delusion can you imagine that your opinions are of value?"[23] Another saw in the Bernstein demonstration a consequence of dean of admissions Inky Clark's new approach, even though Clark had not actually admitted anyone yet. "Does Yale wish to produce and foster the kind of educational and moral climate that spawned riots at the University of California?" the alum demanded. "By placing all emphasis on scholarship and little on character, discipline, and moral stability this result seems inevitable."[24] While the students rallying for Bernstein considered themselves orderly, rational, and measured, one philosophy professor saw them as a mass of "chanting, protesting, bellicose demonstrators."[25] A. Bartlett Giamatti, who would succeed Brewster as president, captured the neoconservative academic distaste for student demonstrations when he wrote that the Free Speech Movement "was intended not only to free speech from middle-class constraints about uttering obscenities, for instance. It was also intended to free us from the shackles of syntax, the racism of grammar, the elitism of style. . . . The Free Speech Movement was where we first began to hear language mediated through the bullhorn into the formulaic chant of the crowd."[26]

Giamatti's point about obscenity was not completely off base. The Free Speech Movement broke up in March 1965 when it was overshadowed by the Filthy Speech Movement, which paraded a certain Anglo-Saxonism (allegedly an acronym for "Freedom Under Clark Kerr") as part of an "insanity campaign" to harass Kerr. A similar split between political and countercultural dissenters appeared at the same time at Yale, where some students insisted that the best response to the Bernstein situation was to drag a dead horse in front of Woodbridge Hall for passersby to kick.[27]

Such antilogic was beyond Brewster's ken, but he quickly recognized a situation in which well-meaning dissent could be channeled into either radical resentment or pragmatic reform. Characteristically, he attempted to get the protesters to work through the system to educate themselves about the standards and procedures for faculty appointment and promotion. The result was the creation of a series of committees, departmental as well as universitywide, in which students shared responsibility with the faculty for evaluating the quality of courses and instructors. "The most crucial aspect" of the protest, Brewster determined in hindsight, "was the message to the entire community, especially to the faculty, that we were henceforth in a new era in which students demanded and deserved respect for their views about how to improve Yale education."[28]

Several commentators pointed out that the Bernstein demonstration, like the Berkeley Free Speech Movement, stemmed from fears that teaching and students had become undervalued as universities headed toward modernization and the "publish or perish" tenure system. On another level, both protest movements were acts of generational self-assertion. Neither the Berkeley movement nor the Bernstein demonstration was about the growing scale of U.S. intervention in Vietnam; however, both protests pointed to an attitude of student restlessness and frustration on which antiwar sentiment would soon be superimposed. Kerr, appearing on television with Brewster and McGeorge Bundy, commented that universities are like the proverbial canary in a coal mine: the dissatisfactions produced by social change appear at universities long before they are apprehended by the larger society. Brewster and Bundy observed that the canary dies after detecting such atmospheric shifts, but the general point was valid.[29] As a 1965 *Yale Daily News* editorial declared, "Our generation is speaking for itself. American students are becoming a class of challengers. . . . After Mississippi and Alabama, after Vietnam, after Berkeley, and after Bernstein, they will not call us silent."[30]

STUDENT UNREST WAS only one of the engines of reform at Yale in the 1960s. Changes at the university did not occur because mobs of radical students ran roughshod over frightened professors; the questioning spirit of the 1960s affected adults as well as young people. It led Yale faculty members, administrators, and students to reexamine what they were doing and why. Sometimes the students played the major role in calling for change, but often the faculty, the trustees, or the president took the lead. Student unrest had played little part in the expansion and diversification of the faculty or the reforms in admissions policies, although these changes fed into and upon the rising tide of campus activism.

It was the faculty, for example, that decided to do away with mandatory classroom attendance—not because the professors were besieged by howling students demanding that lecture attendance requirements be abolished but because significant developments were occurring among the faculty. The new faculty, recruited from outside Yale, were more closely connected to national educational trends and took a dim view of the university's practices that were holdovers from an older, more parochial era. "A lot of Yale's way of doing things, like keeping class attendance and telling the student what to do," Brewster's assistant Sam Chauncey recalled, "was a product of tradition and history as much as educational philosophy. And in comes a guy like John Blum from a Harvard or a MIT. . . . I can remember him saying, 'I have no truck with this issue of people coming or not coming to my class. If they don't want to come, as far as I'm concerned, that's fine.'"[31] Such faculty members regarded students as individuals capable of making responsible choices about their lives and education, not as marionettes on a string. These professors were confident that their lectures were of such quality that intellectually motivated students would want to attend; if the students didn't come to class, it was their loss. Finally, more and more teachers agreed that the best education was self-directed. Course of Study

Committee chairman William Kessen, the driving force behind much of the academic reform in the mid-1960s, emphasized that growing numbers of teachers and educational theorists recognized that the student "is moved to learn for reasons of his own—delight in the solution of problems, pursuit of the orderly, joy in his own active enquiry, the relief and excitement of setting his own goals."[32]

And so the faculty shrugged off the remnants of the old pedagogical approach—taking attendance, giving cut marks, administering required summer reading lists to students on general warning, and so forth. In quick succession, the faculty created independent reading periods, abolished the convoluted system of distributional requirements, simplified the 0–100 grading scale, and reduced the number of credits required for graduation. Most departments eliminated mandatory comprehensive exams and replaced them with senior essays and independent projects.[33] Kessen said later that the idea that these reforms were forced on the faculty was "utter nonsense."[34] Certainly many students were in favor of the changes and agitated in favor of them. But as Brewster observed, "Many [reforms] were initiated by the faculty well before any student prodding. . . . Many of them would probably not have been pushed as fast without active student support. None of them would have been adopted . . . if they had been rammed down the throat of the faculty either by . . . administrative fiat or by the coercion of student threats."[35]

IN THE SPRING of 1965, protest over the Bernstein tenure case overlapped with antiwar demonstrations and civil rights activism. As the Bernstein case was receiving widespread media attention and Rolling Thunder was beginning in Vietnam, the nation witnessed the much-televised spectacle of Alabama policemen brutally clubbing, whipping, and gassing nonviolent marchers in Selma. Twenty Yale students and faculty members responded to Martin Luther King's call for a massive interracial pilgrimage to Selma, to be followed by a march to the state capital in Montgomery.

One of the emotional high points of the gathering in Selma was the interdenominational memorial service for James Reeb, a Unitarian minister from Boston who had gone there to protest and had been beaten to death by white hoodlums. Lieutenant Governor Richardson was there as Massachusetts' official representative "in respect to [the] memory of a citizen of this Commonwealth who died as a martyr to the cause of humanity," as he told a protest gathering on Boston Common a few days earlier.[36] Richardson stood on a platform in an African Methodist Episcopal chapel in Selma along with King and representatives of "virtually every other denomination and order in America," he remembered. "Facing us in the pews, in the aisles, the balconies, jamming the doorways and craning to see over window ledges, were hundreds of others—clergymen, dungaree-clad 'Snick' demonstrators, and plain citizens from all over the United States." The lieutenant governor clasped the hand of a black Methodist bishop on his left and a Greek Orthodox priest on his right when the congregation sang "We Shall Overcome." "In that small enclosed space," it seemed to him, "the voices were strong, ringing—full of promise."[37] In retrospect, it was the zenith of black–white togetherness in the civil rights movement.

Richardson was struck not only by the mix of races but by the unity of Americans of all faiths at Selma, a phenomenon that also impressed the news media. "The conscience of the nation had been outraged" at Selma, *Newsweek* commented, "and now the white religious leaders who regard themselves as guardians of that conscience were locked arm in arm with their Negro brethren in an unprecedented display of church unity." While some of the clerics at Selma had, like Paul Moore, a long commitment to the struggle, "most were merely outraged and ashamed establishment clergy seeking some kind of personal affiliation—and possibly redemption—in a movement they barely understood." At a deeper level, however, the clerical protesters were working out "the rudiments of a new role for the church militant in modern American society."[38]

Moore was the man *Newsweek* had wanted to put on the cover to illustrate the new militancy of establishment clergy involving themselves in the civil rights movement.[39] Since the police repression of the first march in Selma, Moore had cochaired a demonstration in front of the White House to persuade Johnson to protect the marchers. "The bodies of white men may be at liberty," he told a crowd of fifteen thousand that had gathered in front of the White House, "but to the extent of their prejudice their souls are in chains. The bodies of Negro Americans are in chains, but those who are in the movement are the freest men in the world, for their souls are free."[40] Moore and other leaders of the demonstration spent an hour with President Johnson, who later sent troops to Alabama. In a meeting with Hubert Humphrey, Moore told the vice president that "the civil rights movement and this administration have just about come to the parting of ways. . . . We just can't take very much more."[41] Moore remembered that "I was criticized in the press for being rude."

Within the civil rights movement, Moore was thought of as a moderate.

"I was never willing to risk losing my position as bishop or risk being considered a flake by moderate people of good will," he recalled. "A few times I pushed the edge of the envelope of liberal behavior, but by and large I felt my greatest influence would be within the system." In hindsight, he felt that "I was usually wrong when I became timid; history seemed to be on the side of boldness."[42] Moore's moderation, however, meant that he retained a foothold in both the movement and the establishment. He marched and picketed, but he also ministered to the powerful in Washington and socialized in his brother's financial circles—William Moore was chairman of the board of Banker's Trust. His perspective as a reasonable yet activist institutional leader made him a useful counselor to Brewster when both church and university began to evaluate the question of institutional neutrality.

Moore faced opposition throughout his priesthood from those who thought the church had to be neutral in politics, or above politics altogether. He observed that the opposition came largely from the middle and upper classes, who comprised much of the Episcopal Church's membership. They tended to be conservative, since "those who have power and financial security want to keep it." By contrast, Moore felt that the church's interest in social issues was a sign of its health and relevance. He believed that those who condemned church involvement in politics (aside from blessing the status quo) misunderstood the separation of church and state: "The purpose of the notion of separation is not only to protect the State from forcing any religion upon the people, but also to protect the Church's freedom to criticize the State." In the suffragan bishop's view, the church's critique ultimately helped society adapt to change. Arguably the silence of religious authorities in the face of poverty and injustice had contributed to the French and Russian revolutions, while "a more alert Anglican Church could have warded off the American War of Independence."[43]

BREWSTER BELIEVED DEEPLY that the university as an institution should not advocate political positions. "I resent as well as object to the statement 'Academic freedom and the traditional American freedom of speech are now found to apply only to those with the proper political and social views [at the university],'" he wrote to one alumni critic. "Pin that one on Yale and its President should resign."[44] At the same time, he strongly supported the right of faculty, students, and chaplain to responsibly speak their consciences on issues that concerned them, although he sometimes hedged a bit on what "responsible" might mean. As early as 1962, Brewster had told students that while dishonorable rebellion was "sabotage," honorable rebellion was "a precious right."[45] But who was to say which was which? Brewster worried over this question throughout the 1960s. How, he asked Coffin, could one determine the honorable from the dishonorable rebel? "By what litmus paper do you, do we, distinguish the two? Is it by our own preferences: the causes which seem to us subjectively more or less worthy? Is it by an inevitably subjective and intuitive sizing up of the young man, since two may follow similar paths for quite different reasons?"[46]

In the end, Brewster decided that in order to understand their motivations, one needed to know the activists and that the old Yale ideal of community provided the way to judge the motivations of its members. "There will always be those who will exploit idealism for wretched purposes," he told the alumni in early 1965, "and it's always tempting to be unfair to the idealist by associating him with those who may be exploiting him. The thing that makes it possible for us to deal with students is because we can fairly and personally know the motivation, the quality, and the individual quirks of those with whom we're dealing."[47] In the spring of 1965, Brewster defended the free speech of students and faculty members who sent an antiwar faculty petition to Lyndon Johnson and took part in an antiwar rally, but he also upheld conservative professor David Nelson Rowe's right to testify against the admission of Communist China to the United Nations.[48]

The question of Brewster's own freedom to speak out on controversial issues was more complicated. The notion that a university president is bound by institutional neutrality to be silent on political matters is something of a modern invention. Brewster remembered that Charles Seymour had not hesitated to speak out in favor of U.S. intervention in the European war in the late 1930s and early 1940s, following in the tradition of Yale presidents in previous wars. Brewster's position was that the university's leader ought not to enjoy less freedom of speech than his students and faculty, and that the public could distinguish between Brewster speaking as a private individual and as the Yale president. "You have a right to speak as yourself and as President," Paul Moore told him, although he added that "sometimes it is helpful *not* to clarify in which capacity you speak."[49]

On the other hand, political reality demanded that the president take into account the likely reaction of the alumni to his speeches. Coffin often tried to push Brewster toward more active spokesmanship. "If it is a matter of education," he wrote to Brewster, "then university presidents have a special opportunity, better termed perhaps 'obligation,' and no one can fulfill it for them. Lesser arguments yield only to greater ones, but greater ones have maximum effectiveness only when they are enunciated by great men."[50] Coffin rejected the idea forming on the left that leadership came from "the people" alone. His belief in the responsibility and even greatness of individual leaders represented common ground with men like Brewster and McGeorge Bundy, who were otherwise his ideological opponents.

In 1965, Brewster's old mentor Grenville Clark persuaded him to preside over a second conference on world peace through world law in Dublin, New Hampshire. Speaking as a private citizen, Brewster contended that "national government alone is no longer able to assure survival" and proposed international government as a substitute for "the horrifying prospect of nuclear anarchy."[51] The Yale student newspaper applauded Brewster for speaking out. "Few American university presidents are as qualified as he to approach the problem," the *News* noted, "and fewer still have done so. Those who disagree with him will say that a university president should mind the business of higher education. We would only reply that the concerns of a university's public spokesman should be as broad as the problems of the society his university serves."[52]

For Brewster, the experience provided useful preparation for dealing with student radicals. Part of being a moderate, as he saw it, was being able to be both idealistic and pragmatic without falling prey to the Scylla of impractical idealism or the Charybdis of cynical realism. "It is a long time since I have had the privilege of dwelling among those who are wholly free from the restraints imposed by practicality," he wrote to Clark after the conference. "Compromise, mutual adjustment, decent deference to the majority, all are so much part and parcel of practical accomplishment that it was a shock to witness again the arrogance and selfishness of the utopian ego. . . . I do not think that we can afford to placate the utopians if it means forfeiting all chance of political progress. . . . [F]or one small inch of practical progress toward the limited goal of survival in the nuclear age I would trade the self-satisfaction of being self-consciously 'radical.'"[53]

THE BIG QUESTION after 1965, of course, was whether Brewster would speak out against the war in Vietnam. As the scale of the U.S. commitment increased, the war became the engine that drove Americans into extremes of polarization and even violence. It throbbed beneath the surface even of seemingly unrelated phenomena such as the countercultural activities of the hippies and the racial riots in the cities. It underlay the feelings of alienation and disaffection that Yale students voiced in the contemporary film *To Be a*

Man. In that work, the producer Murray Lerner presented an implicit debate between Coffin and history professor John Blum over whether faculty members should preach or conceal their political views in the classroom; every frame alluded to Vietnam even though the name was never spoken. Because of the war, divisions in American society cut more deeply than they had since the Civil War. The universities were particularly affected because until mid-1968, students in college or graduate school received near-automatic exemption from the draft. As a result, the campuses turned into what Brewster called "cauldrons of tortured souls"; the universities had become holding pens for involuntary students caught between "the competing claims of national duty, moral conscience, and animal instinct for self-preservation."[54]

As Brewster later pointed out, the student unrest of the late 1960s had no single explanation, and Vietnam was not the only provocation. He cited the revolt against the impersonality of the multiversity and recognized that the student movement was motivated by some of the same frustrations that drove the civil rights movement and the antiwar movement. The university itself was its main target, if only because it was the nearest one. But the 1962 Port Huron statement of Students for a Democratic Society, the most important of the 1960s New Left groups, castigated the university for its "cumbersome academic bureaucracy" and its training and employment of the social and physical scientists who were working for "the corporate economy" or helping to accelerate the arms race. The university itself—which was thus to blame for the "apathy and inner alienation that remain the defining characteristics of American college life"—was part of the establishment's interlocking directorate, part of the same system of oppression that operated in Mississippi and in Vietnam.[55] The increase in the draft calls after July 1965 and the nightly body count in Vietnam propelled the apathetic into the ranks of the protesters and lent plausibility to the radical case against the university. While many academics claimed that politics and scholarship were wholly separate realms and that the university was and should be neutral, the radicals countered that neutrality amounted to a defense of the status quo.

The two most prominent antiwar spokesmen at Yale were Chaplain Coffin and assistant professor of history Staughton Lynd. Their arguments proceeded from somewhat different grounds. Coffin eloquently drove home the point that the war was immoral: it was in violation of international law, it employed ghastly weapons like napalm and horrific tactics like indiscriminate aerial bombing, and its brutality was dulling the moral sensibilities of Americans. To Coffin, the war amounted to a crime against humanity.

Lynd tended toward a more radical explanation of the war as a logical expression of capitalism's policy of racist, imperial domination. Quaker, Marxist, pacifist, and existentialist, Lynd was a soft-spoken, likable man with a sense of humor. He also had what Coffin called "a touch of fanaticism."[56] Son of Robert and Helen Lynd (authors of the famous sociological study *Middletown*), he had come to Yale in the fall of 1964 from Spelman College in Atlanta, where he was deeply involved in the civil rights movement. Even before his arrival, he had upset the alumni by attacking the Warren Commission's report on Kennedy's assassination. "We lied about the U-2," Lynd told a New York audience. "We lied about the Bay of Pigs. And in my judgment we are lying about the assassination of a President."[57] Brewster responded to the early critics by telling them that Lynd was undoubtedly "a liberal skeptic"—in Brewster's opinion, a term of praise—but not "a show-off agitator. . . . I err on the side of those who question the pap and poop of the 'official' or 'establishment' explanation of all things," the president continued. "Life needs more color than is provided by whitewash. I want more nose thumbing, provided it is genuinely responsible in its motivation, and thoughtful in its consideration. I think Lynd is both."[58]

Coffin spent a considerable amount of time debating politics with Lynd and his wife (who shared her husband's politics), usually in the company of a number of students who were attracted to Lynd's radicalism. "Conversations with them were always earnest, not to say tormented," the chaplain remembered, "and most took place on the hard floor of their austere living room." Their disagreements were significant. Publicly, Coffin would say only that "Staughton is purer. I am more willing to compromise, to work with the Establishment."[59] Privately, he winced "to hear the word 'imperialistic' used so confidently by a Marxist," although he suspected that Lynd was correct that the slogans of democracy were being used by the United States as a pretext for escalating the war in Vietnam. Coffin objected, as well, to aspects of the antiwar critique put forward by Students for a Democratic Society, for which Lynd became one of the older mentors. Coffin found the movement's claim to be "representing the people" to be so much loose talk, given that the preponderance of Americans solidly supported Johnson's actions in Vietnam. Coffin found SDS too ready to overlook Communist crimes, too quick to advocate anti-Americanism, too eager to march beneath the banners of totalitarian heroes like Mao, Ho Chi Minh, and Che Guevara. For these reasons, Coffin didn't go to SDS's April march on Washington, at which Lynd spoke.[60]

The 1965 SDS march, which drew between twenty and twenty-five thousand attendees, is often considered to be the beginning of the mass antiwar movement. In the closing speech, SDS president Paul Potter electrified the crowd with his indictment of "the system" that permeated American life and the Vietnam War, a dark manifestation of the system's institutions. The task of the movement, Potter said, was to "name the system," and over the next few years the New Left would name it corporate liberalism, and eventually imperialism, and associate it with whatever passed for the establishment. "I do not believe that the president or Mr. Rusk or Mr. McNamara or even McGeorge Bundy are particularly evil men," Potter told the gathered protesters. "If asked to throw napalm on the back of a ten-year-old child they would shrink in horror—but their decisions have led to mutilation and death of thousands and thousands of people. What kind of system is it that allows good men to make those kinds of decisions?"[61]

LARGELY BECAUSE HE had fought in the Second World War and knew first-hand what terrible means were required to defeat evil regimes, Moore was not so quick to leap to that level of moral accusation. In the spring of 1965, however, Moore ran into Bundy at a party in Washington. Since so many of Moore's old friends, like Bundy and Vance, were in positions of responsibility in the Kennedy and Johnson years, he "felt the government was in good hands. . . . I assumed that if they thought we were doing the right thing in Vietnam we probably were."[62] Indeed, Moore and his wife had enjoyed a pleasant dinner with the Vances on the day the Operation Rolling Thunder bombardment of North Vietnam began,[63] Many of his friends in the civil rights movement, though, had doubts. So at the party Moore decided to ask his friend Mac what the government's military strategy was in Vietnam. Bundy, he recalled, "began to speak about the cold war, the danger of Communist China, and so forth. I said I was not asking about the political or geopolitical objectives; I merely wanted to know what the military objective was. I was astonished when he had no answer."[64] After this conversation Moore moved into the orbit of the antiwar movement—partly because whites were increasingly pushed out of civil rights activities by blacks demanding leadership of their own movement and partly because Moore believed with Martin Luther King that "the two causes—peace and justice—were so interrelated that no true peace, domestic or international, could come about without justice and that justice could not be effected in a nation intoxicated by war."[65]

Lindsay was also beginning to question U.S. involvement. Although he had voted for the Gulf of Tonkin Resolution the previous year, he became one of the few members of Congress to speak out after the bombing of North Vietnam. "The President must define our policy in Vietnam," he insisted. "It is still apparent that we have no clear policy except an aimless patchwork of scotch tape and bailing wire that becomes more confused every day." There would be more strikes and counterstrikes, Lindsay predicted, "until the little remaining cover is totally stripped away and the involvement that is euphemistically known as military support becomes a naked U.S. war that has neither front lines nor back lines, nor beginning or ending, nor commitment by the very people we seek to defend."[66]

J. Irwin Miller, who crossed paths with William Bundy at the monthly Yale Corporation meetings, was unsettled to find that the deputy secretary of state shared Lindsay's bleak assessment. "I was a player a good deal of that time in the Johnson administration," Miller later recalled, and "because of a couple of remarks from the president to me [I knew] Johnson never believed in the war. The only thing was, he didn't know how in the hell to get out of it." Miller asked Bill Bundy to tell him about the situation in Vietnam, "and he said, 'The truth is, there is no such place as South Vietnam. There are a bunch of small villages composed of farmers whose only concern is to be allowed to grow some rice and not get shot up. It's not a nation, an ethnic group, or anything else. There is no leadership; there's no George Washington down there.' And I said, 'Well, that's a pretty dismal outlook, isn't it?' And he said, 'Yes, it is.' And that was the first sort of shedding of light on it."[67]

Publicly, however, Miller supported the Vietnam intervention until well into the 1960s, although with much squirming. The managerial outlook of men like Miller made it all but impossible for them to take issue publicly with friends' operations in their spheres of expertise. "I think anyone who's in a position of management is apt to be extremely reluctant to second-guess somebody else," Miller said, "because he knows that choices are not usually between the good way and the bad way to do something but almost always between two bad ways."[68]

Brewster found himself in a similar bind. His assistant Sam Chauncey recalled Brewster having serious arguments over Vietnam with Mac Bundy during the latter's years as Johnson's national security advisor.[69] In 1964, both men attended a discussion group at Robert Kennedy's home, Hickory

Hill, in Virginia. Bundy got into a debate on Vietnam with the author Peter Maas, and several people remembered Brewster interrupting to tell Bundy, "Maas is right, this Vietnam thing is headed for disaster."[70] Bundy's and Brewster's opposite positions in the 1939–41 debate over intervention had taught them different lessons. Bundy learned from the World War II experience that America should intervene where its participation could tip the balance against totalitarianism. He argued that it was necessary for the United States to fight Communist aggression in the third world, just as it should have intervened in Europe in the 1930s to stop Hitler and the Nazis.

Brewster retained the former isolationist's skepticism toward U.S. overcommitment abroad. He opposed the war quietly and on pragmatic rather than moral grounds: it was unwinnable, it was costing too many American lives, it was diverting resources away from the war on poverty at home, and it was dividing the nation. He also resented "the failure to present the issue for Congressional, let alone straightforward popular, debate"—another reminder of his early 1940s critique of Roosevelt.[71] Although Brewster would on occasion speak of "the communist threat," it was usually to suggest that Americans give priority to mending injustices at home rather than abroad; this view, too, was an echo of some of his pre–World War II thinking. Further, as long ago as 1951, Brewster had warned of "the fear of a new Western Imperialism" in Asia. He emphasized that "the historical experience of brutal exploitation by an alien race and the persistent spectre of literal starvation make quite clear that whoever would compete for the allegiance of the Asians must bid in revolutionary terms." This did not mean military intervention in Indochina or "the easy export of slogans and political institutions" but land reform and intensive economic assistance. Brewster worried that military intervention could augur "a deep and awful chasm between the yellow and white peoples" and cautioned that "an enduring bitterness between Orient and Occident can only forebode a greater and more terrifying division of the world, and set the stage for a war of racial vengeance."[72]

A variety of factors, however, inhibited Brewster from speaking out publicly against the war. Part of what tied him in knots on the subject was that for all his reservations, he did in fact share many of the Cold War beliefs that led most Americans to consider Vietnam a necessary war. When Vance was sworn in as secretary of the Army in 1962, McNamara foresaw a period of crisis because of Communist-bloc support for "what they call wars of liberation, but we know as covert aggression."[73] Brewster agreed that Kennedy's decision to intervene in Vietnam had at least been plausible: "To allow a war of national liberation to succeed in 1962 might have vindicated Chinese aggressive doctrine, and encouraged a worldwide rash of sponsored wars: civil in form, but imperial in global pattern."[74]

Having committed to Vietnam, he believed, the United States had to uphold its promise. As Brewster said in his 1965 speech at the world government conference in Dublin, nuclear peace depended on "the credibility of American resolution to resist aggression"—hence, "I for one do not think that we can risk impairing the credibility of that resolution in Vietnam or anywhere else."[75] Standing firm in South Vietnam might be "the only way to prevent a later global holocaust."[76] Nor did men like Brewster believe that the United States should abandon South Vietnam to the slaughter and reeducation camps that they (correctly) predicted would follow Communist victory. And so they were forced to accept the outrages of the American-backed regime—as Bundy put it, "This is what you get stuck with in this kind of an affair."[77] While Brewster didn't like the war, he didn't feel that he could offer a better alternative.

Bundy once commented that the Vietnam conflict "is not a war which explains itself."[78] Partly for that reason, he resorted to metaphors for the war when arguing about it with Brewster. He compared it to the Korean War, for instance, knowing that Brewster had wholeheartedly supported U.S. intervention in that struggle, both to defend another non-Communist Asian government from aggression and to prevent recourse to a nuclear exchange with the Soviet Union. (When the Korean War broke out, Brewster had actually advocated total mobilization as "the only way to forestall the ill-considered courses either of appeasement or of atomic aggression."[79]) Since Bundy and his allies in government had come through the Cuban missile crisis (seemingly a much more dangerous conflict) with flying colors, they appeared to be applying the same triumphant strategy to Vietnam. As Vance put it, "We had seen the gradual application of force applied in the Cuban Missile Crisis, and had seen a very successful result. We believed that, if this same gradual and restrained application of force were applied in South Vietnam, that one could expect the same result."[80] It may also have been in the back of Brewster's mind that in the debate over intervention in 1939–41, Bundy had been right and Brewster wrong. Might not Bundy be right in this debate as well?

Debates between Bundy and Brewster, then, usually ended with each meeting the other halfway. Brewster argued that American power was limited; Bundy agreed and opposed "the notion that the Americans are super-powered and should impose their will on all others." Brewster found the domino theory simplistic; Bundy agreed but pointed out that it was not "sensible either politically or historically to sneer at the notion that what happens in one country does affect what happens in another."[81] Because Bundy was such a subtle and flexible thinker, his friends found it difficult to disagree with him entirely. And who was to say that the continued stability of Thailand, for example, was not at least in part the result of U.S. involvement in Vietnam? When Bundy told his friends that the government had considered the moral and ethical issues behind intervention, they trusted him, as they did when he said that the Viet Cong could not be included in a coalition government because there was "no political situation in the last twenty years in which there has been greater polarization between Communists and all non-Communists than the one in South Vietnam."[82] As his friends knew, Bundy opposed what he considered the military's irresponsible demands for massive U.S. aggression that risked nuclear war with China and the Soviet Union. Given the alternatives of desertion or severe escalation, Bundy's advocacy of calibrated retaliation and flexible commitment seemed the moderate, prudent course, which naturally appealed to centrists like Brewster.

Brewster was also constrained in his criticism by his intense loyalty to Bundy, Vance, and other talented people who were prosecuting the war. Many, perhaps even most of the key policy makers of the intervention in Vietnam had ties to Brewster. Mac Bundy and Cy Vance were among his closest friends, as was Peter Solbert, who took leave from his corporate law practice in New York to work in the Pentagon. Vance's deputy Adam Yarmolinsky was a close associate from Harvard law days; other Harvard colleagues involved in the war included Abram Chayes, Joe Peck, Roger Fisher, and McNamara himself. One of McNamara's brightest whiz kids, John McNaughton, had been Brewster's fellow law student, Marshall planner, and law faculty colleague, and lived around the corner in Cambridge. Steuart Pittman (also in the Pentagon) and Barry Zorthian (U.S. minister of information in Vietnam) were Brewster's college classmates. Stanley Resor, a successor to Vance as secretary of the Army, had been Bill Bundy's roommate at Yale. Other Yale graduates deeply involved in the war included Walt Rostow, Eugene Rostow (who became undersecretary of state for political affairs shortly after Brewster had appointed him master of one of Yale's residential colleges), and senior advisors for whom Brewster had the greatest respect, including Harriman, Acheson, and Robert Lovett. Later in the 1960s, William Bundy wrote to Brewster that "I trust that no one will do any research on the reasons for the failure of US policies in Asia in the past decade, on George Pierson's lines"—Yale historian Pierson had recently completed a study of the college origins of American leaders. "If they were to do so, they would find that responsibility has been held for all but nine months by graduates of an institution in New Haven."[83]

Brewster knew better than anyone that what had drawn these men to Washington was public-spiritedness of the most laudable kind. During the 1950s, when he had promoted Solbert for various public positions, Brewster had written that Solbert had "an obvious itch to serve the Republic in some official Washington post."[84] He confided to Solbert that the "itch" was "not a disease to which I am immune myself."[85] It was really just chance, in the form of his from-the-blue appointment as provost, that enabled Brewster to put his ideals of public service into practice at Yale rather than in the government. As a result, he was spared the personal entanglement in Vietnam that ensnared many of the public-minded leaders in his generation. When he looked at his friends sinking deeper into the Vietnam quagmire, he may well have thought, "There but for the grace of God . . ."

For all these reasons, Brewster felt that he ought to disagree with his friends on Vietnam in person, privately, and as a gentleman, rather than speak out. This attitude increasingly caused him difficulties with antiwar activists like Coffin and students who wanted him to use his status to pressure his friends. Gregory Craig, a Yale law student who became an informal advisor to Brewster in the late 1960s and later served under Bill Clinton, felt that Brewster "had too much faith in the decency of people. For example, I do not believe that the people that were responsible for our policy in Vietnam were merely fools. I think there were some villains there as well. I think Kingman went to bed at night thinking that by and large they were just misguided. They were not only misguided, they were engaged in a conscious policy of deceit and violence and lying. My generation still hasn't gotten over it. To me, the Vietnam syndrome is not simply the idea of engaging American troops in places in the world where we don't have a vital national security interest and losing a lot of men and killing a lot of civilians in the process. To me, the Vietnam syndrome was the discovery that the American leadership was capable of deceiving the American public and lying to the American Congress in order to support and gain its political objectives abroad."[86]

Because Brewster was convinced of the decency of his friends, when he spoke about Vietnam he tried to convey a sense of the dilemmas that confronted people like Bundy, and the pressures they were under. In fact, the stress of the war on Bundy was plain to his friends, and evident in

McNamara's deterioration even by early 1965. One of Vance's aides wrote him to see if something could be done to relieve the "extreme mental pressure" on the defense secretary: "No one can quite forget Mr. Forrestal," McNamara's predecessor who had committed suicide.[87] When Brewster appeared on NBC's *Meet the Press,* he emphasized that Vietnam was "a most unhappy, unwelcome, reluctant war for everybody, even those who are in favor of it." The growing "unhappiness and the misgiving and the reluctance about the war . . . is shared by the official government administration as well," he noted.[88] Above all, Brewster sought to counter the impression that the president and his advisors were already dead set in their courses and impervious to counterarguments.

Indeed, some of the most effective criticisms of the U.S. war effort were made by McGeorge Bundy himself. On January 27, 1965, he and McNamara had sent Johnson a memorandum (later referred to as the "fork in the road" memo) in which they warned that "both of us are now pretty well convinced that our current policy can lead only to disastrous defeat." The two alternatives they saw were, first, to use military power in Indochina to force a change of Communist policy, or second, "to deploy all our resources along a track of negotiation, aimed at salvaging what little can be preserved with no major addition to our present military risks." Bundy and McNamara said they tended to favor the first course, "but we believe that both should be carefully studied and that alternative programs should be argued out before you."[89] In March, Bundy wrote to Johnson that he, Rusk, and McNamara would have to start thinking about the possibility of defeat. In deference to what Bundy called Rusk's belief "that when men even look as if they were planning for defeat, they make defeat even more likely," there would be no paperwork at all on the subject, "but simply some intensive discussion limited completely to the three of us and one subordinate each."[90]

Even more prescient was Bundy's memo to McNamara of June 30, 1965, in which he declared that the plan to Americanize the war by dramatically escalating the engagement was "rash to the point of folly." Bundy questioned every premise behind bombing the North and committing greater numbers of U.S. troops to a situation for which they were ill suited. Sending 200,000 ground troops, he observed, was "a slippery slope toward total US responsibility and corresponding fecklessness on the [South] Vietnamese side." He also pointed out that there was no upper limit on the U.S. commitment, no definite prospect of success, and no real consideration of alternatives if American casualties mounted sharply. More broadly, he asked, "What is the real object of the exercise? If it is to get to the conference table, what results do we seek there? Still more brutally, do we want to invest 200 thousand men to cover an eventual retreat? Can we not do that just as well where we are?"[91]

In short, while Bundy, like Brewster, considered Vietnam to be worth a commitment, he had serious questions about the size, extent, and cost of such a commitment. Bundy may also have taken heed of Brewster's criticisms of the means by which the war was waged. One of the persistent themes in Brewster's speeches throughout the 1960s was that America should be a voluntary society, in which an individual's path through life should be shaped as much as possible by his or her own decisions. A coercive military draft was the antithesis of a voluntary society. Perhaps such arguments resonated with Bundy when he suggested to Johnson that instead of saying to draftees, "You go to Vietnam and you fight in the rice paddies," he announce that "from now on, nobody goes to this task who doesn't volunteer." Bundy told the president that "I think we might turn around the atmosphere of our own people out there if it were a volunteers' enterprise. I suspect the Joint Chiefs won't agree to that. But I'd like to know what would happen if we really dramatized this as 'Americans Against Terror' and 'Americans Keeping Their Commitment' and 'Americans Who Have Only Peace as Their Object' and 'Only Americans Who Want to Go Have to Go.' You might change the temper of it some." Johnson asked whether the nation would be likely to end up with only "a corporals' guard" in Vietnam—that only the lowest-ranking military men would volunteer. "I just don't know," Bundy replied. "If that's true, then I'm not sure we're the country to do this job."[92]

Bundy was also sensitive to Brewster's criticism that the administration was not being open with the American people about the war and the scale of effort it would require. "At its very best," Bundy wrote to Johnson after Pleiku, "the struggle in Vietnam will be long. It seems . . . important that this fundamental fact be made clear to our people and to the people of Vietnam."[93] He pressed Johnson repeatedly to explain the war and its costs. The president refused, and the issue became what Bundy called "a basic, real disagreement" between the two men.[94]

His belief in the need to inform the public led Bundy to endorse a 1965 proposal for a citizen's committee to explain and defend the war. Kingman Brewster, Irwin Miller, and five other candidates were proposed as chairman. The committee would, as Johnson's assistant Douglass Cater wrote, "speak out in support of the Administration against both the appeasers and those who would take rash risks."[95] Bundy wrote to Johnson that "everyone is ready to go ahead with the Citizens Committee as soon as you give the signal," but the signal never came.[96]

BUNDY ACCEPTED AN invitation to participate in a national teach-in on the war in mid-May 1965, to be transmitted to college campuses across the country. He had not asked Johnson for permission to take part in the debate. The president, annoyed, instructed his national security advisor to tell the forum that the protest movement was Communist-inspired and was abetting the enemy, a crude reductionism that Bundy knew from Brewster was totally false.[97] Johnson and some of his advisors, indignant that Bundy would debate the war at all, believed that he would thereby legitimize the protest. As Bill Moyers told the president, "I don't think the White House ever has to debate. . . . You don't make decisions by debating. You make the decisions and then history will justify them."[98]

The relationship between Johnson and Bundy was always complicated, although more on the president's side than on his advisor's. According to Mac's Groton friend Louis Auchincloss, Bundy had "a certain distaste for the man" and never established the kind of personal tie with Johnson that he had had with Kennedy.[99] However, Bundy rarely let slip a negative remark about Johnson, even among friends. He would have given his wholehearted support to any president out of dedication to the office, but he seems, in fact, to have genuinely respected Johnson in his own right, an opinion that was shared by most of his circle. Richardson, who had encountered Johnson in his years as majority leader, was impressed by the sense he gave of being completely on top of the business of the Senate. Johnson handled even the most complex matters "crisply and with the sense and impression of being, as he was, fully in charge."[100]

Johnson, for his part, had immense respect for Bundy. Bundy's aide Francis Bator remembered that "Johnson really relied on Mac for all sorts of things after the [Kennedy] assassination. Mac's speed, range, competence, and energy made him invaluable—and not just on foreign affairs, but on lots of things during the transition. And Johnson never forgot that."[101] Nicholas Katzenbach, who like Bundy served under both Kennedy and Johnson (as attorney general and as undersecretary of state), believed that "Johnson relied even more heavily on Mac than Kennedy did," since Kennedy had felt better qualified to serve as his own foreign policy advisor.[102] As one of the last holdovers from the Kennedy administration, Bundy also had political value to Johnson and was useful as a go-between with Bobby Kennedy.

At the same time, Bundy bore the brunt of Johnson's suspicions and feelings of inferiority toward the Kennedys and their eastern intellectual circles. Johnson's view of establishmentarians like Bundy was not unlike Goldwater's. He called Martha's Vineyard "that female island," told Bundy that tennis was a sissy sport, parodied the imperious language and diction of Bundy's mentor Dean Acheson, and laughed at Bundy's squeamishness when summoned to confer with Johnson while the president was on the toilet. To Johnson, the establishment's web of friendships, backgrounds, and allegiances made it seem like a cabal. "If something works out, Joe Alsop will write that it was Bundy that brilliant Harvard dean who did it," he complained, "and if it falls flat he'll say it was the fault of that dumb ignorant crude baboon of a President."[103] Johnson's relationship with Bundy had long teetered between respect and distrust. Bundy's need to explain the war publicly, perhaps strengthened by his friend Brewster's needling, tipped the balance into distrust.

Hours before Bundy was supposed to take part in the teach-in on the war, the president sent him on a mission with Deputy Secretary of Defense Vance to stabilize the situation in the Dominican Republic, where Johnson had sent twenty thousand Marines in the wake of a coup. Bundy and Vance, good friends since undergraduate days, saw each other regularly to discuss policy at the president's Tuesday lunches and to coordinate the selection of bombing targets in Vietnam. This was not Vance's first trouble-shooting assignment for Johnson; he had helped quell rioting in the Panama Canal Zone the previous year. In the wake of that intervention, Vance wrote to his friend Congressman Jonathan Brewster Bingham that "one of the major problems we face is the lack of any strong or intelligent group on which to build."[104] It was the challenge that plagued nation-building efforts in Vietnam, and Bundy and Vance would encounter the same difficulties in the Dominican Republic. What was supposed to be a brief visit turned into a two-week stay; Vance quickly ran out of clean shirts. The two men entered lengthy negotiations with a series of would-be rulers, often in dangerous circumstances with firefights and snipers nearby. Years later they were still darkly amused that one of the militias had mulled over the idea of strengthening their position by shooting Vance.[105]

Bundy and Vance made an excellent negotiating team. Vance was proficient at finding common ground between opposing parties, while Bundy was able to confer in Spanish and brought to the table what one participant called "a clear crisp grasp of things—the strengths and weaknesses of the people on both sides, what each wanted, what each could, and could not, give up."[106] The *New York Times* reporter Tad Szulc, listening to a briefing in Santo Domingo, was "convinced that Mr. Bundy was probably the only high-ranking American official who had fully understood the complexities of the Dominican situation and the psychological problems inherent in it."[107]

In hindsight, Bundy believed that Johnson had sent him to Santo Domingo not so much to devise a solution to the impasse as "to keep me away from all those wild men" he was scheduled to debate.[108] Bundy probably would have been entertained to learn that SDS leader Todd Gitlin considered his absence to be the most significant aspect of the teach-in: "While we were arguing rights and wrongs, the men in power, heedless, were off settling the affairs of small, weak nations."[109] In fact, the leaders of the different factions would not accept U.S. proposals for a coalition government, and the mission failed, although a similar arrangement later succeeded under the mediation of the Organization of American States. To Bundy and Vance, the episode seemed to speak more to the limitations of U.S. power than its limitlessness.

On his return to the States, Bundy "heard a lot of talk that he had ducked out of the debate" on Vietnam, Bator recalled. "Mac had concerns for what he thought of as his own personal honor, and his relations with his old constituency were at stake."[110] Bundy accepted an invitation to discuss the administration's policies at Harvard. He also approached CBS producer Fred Friendly to set up another debate, this one to be televised, with University of Chicago professor Hans Morgenthau, who had told the *Washington Post* in mid-March that Bundy and McNamara were "devoid of sound judgment and understanding of foreign policy."[111]

At the Harvard debate, far from trying to dodge an argument, Bundy walked through a line of pickets outside the lecture hall and took questions from a student-faculty panel and members of the audience. Bundy's wife, who was in the auditorium, recalled that, before the debate, one of Bundy's government colleagues tried to calm what he thought would be her fears about her husband facing hostile questioning. "I remember thinking, 'I don't need that. He doesn't need that. Whatever his role in this, he has gone at it in an honorable way, and he will be dealing with it in an honorable way. And he can take care of himself.'"[112] The *New York Times* recorded that the debate was "a largely good-natured give and take" and that Bundy was applauded frequently and seemed to enjoy the exchange. When at one point a hiss came from the crowd, Bundy "said with a thin smile, 'That interesting noise is not an argument, let's go on.'"[113]

The televised debate a week later with Morgenthau was less good-humored. Bator recalled that "Mac was a brilliant debater, unfortunately. One of the things Johnson worried about Mac going on TV was that he would be too effective, in a sense. And Johnson was right to worry. Mac beat the hell out of Morgenthau, but he did it in a way that people would sort of back away rather than be empathetic."[114] Still, Bundy was uniformly judged to have won the debate, and several months later Morgenthau complained about "the tendency, noticeable on all levels of American society, not only to give the government the benefit of the doubt but to endow it with a near monopoly of truth and virtue."[115] That tendency soon would weaken as the war became less defensible.

In July 1965, U.S. deaths in Vietnam since the start of the conflict numbered fewer than five hundred, a high but tolerable toll restricted largely to career military personnel.[116] To the extent that most Americans knew about the intervention in Vietnam, they supported it. Even *New York Times* reporter David Halberstam, who would later castigate "the best and the brightest" for their hubris in plunging the country into a quagmire, emphasized in 1965 that "Vietnam is a strategic country in a key area. It is perhaps one of only five or six nations that is truly vital to U.S. interests."[117]

Even so, Johnson himself had doubts about the war, and so he asked some of the architects of America's Cold War policy to review U.S. involvement in Vietnam. Bundy had urged him to do so in a memo entitled "Backing from the Establishment."[118] The first gathering of the "Wise Men" (Bundy's term), on July 8, brought to the White House establishment heroes like Acheson, McCloy, and Lovett. Without much discussion of the situation, they endorsed Johnson's plans to send large numbers of troops into ground combat in Vietnam. Most of these men, like Bundy, suppressed their doubts about the wisdom of escalation—a response that puzzled them in hindsight. At the time, the Cold War logic of intervention seemed unassailable, the case for maintaining commitments and credibility too powerful. Perhaps there was simply too much deference in the air—too much mutual respect between the older members of the establishment and their younger protégés, too much willingness on the part of the supposedly independent Wise Men to give Johnson the support he wanted. None of Bundy's incisive questions from his June 30 memo to McNamara about the costs and limits of the intervention were discussed.

And so on July 16, Johnson told Vance that he would approve General William Westmoreland's request for a doubling of troops in Vietnam to bring the total commitment there to thirty-four battalions. About two weeks later, Johnson announced at the end of a routine press conference that American forces in Vietnam would rise to 125,000 "almost immediately." The president would double the monthly draft call but would not summon the reserves or ask Congress for additional funding.

Johnson's avoidance of public debate over escalating the war dismayed advisors like Bundy and also Cyrus Vance, who warned Bundy that the overall cost of mobilizing the forces needed to support 100,000 troops in Vietnam would likely be some $8 billion in the next year, rather than the several hundred million dollars then discussed.[119] Johnson thought it was politically impossible to ask for more, Vance wrote, since "if a larger request is made to the Congress, he believes this will kill [his] domestic legislative program."[120] Johnson evaded a candid national discussion of Vietnam in order to preserve his Great Society legislation, but in the end the evasion so eroded his credibility that it destroyed him.

Bundy suppressed any public mention of his doubts, both because he wished to retain influence and because he considered publicly opposing the president to be disloyal. By that point, however, Johnson had half-persuaded himself that Bundy was in fact not trustworthy. Johnson had talked of demanding his national security advisor's resignation after his debates at Harvard and with Morgenthau. Bundy knew that Johnson didn't want him to participate in the debates, but "I did it anyway." Bundy's friendship with Brewster and his own experience as Harvard dean had taught him "that not defending the damn war, or any policy, well, that was not the way to deal with these characters. They were a bunch of undergraduates and that was a breed I knew—the worst thing you could do was ignore them. . . . [Besides] they were entitled to hear what the hell the government thought it was doing." To Johnson, such liberal faith in open (or semiopen) dialogue was nothing short of betrayal. "I am not going to have anything more to do with the liberals," Johnson snapped to Moyers. "They all just follow the communist line—liberals, intellectuals, communists. They're all the same. . . . I'm going to get rid of everybody who doesn't agree with my policies. I'll take a tough line—put Abe Fortas or Clark Clifford in the Bundy job."[121]

The deterioration of his relationship with Johnson helped push Bundy to leave the government. As he had told his friend Doc Howe three years earlier, the jobs that he coveted outside government were at the helms of the *Washington Post* and the Ford Foundation. In early autumn of 1965, Katharine Graham offered him the editorial-page editor's job at the *Post;* a bit later on, Ford trustee Charles Wyzanski, an old mentor to Bundy, Brewster, Richardson, and many of their friends, offered him the foundation presidency.

The promise of more money (his annual salary would go from $30,000 to $75,000) and more independence helped sweeten the deal.[122] Bundy accepted the Ford offer, and told Johnson that he would leave at the end of February 1966.

AROUND THE TIME that Bundy was looking to get out of government, Brewster was becoming more involved with the administration. In July 1965, two days before he announced the Vietnam escalation, Johnson ordered the formation of a presidential commission to study crime in America and make recommendations about ways to reduce it. Brewster was a member, along with other national figures like *Los Angeles Times* publisher Otis Chandler, Urban League president Whitney Young, future secretary of state William Rogers, future Supreme Court justice Lewis Powell, and future Watergate prosecutor Leon Jaworski. The commission was headed by Attorney General Katzenbach, an old friend of Brewster's from Martha's Vineyard, who had graduated from Princeton, attended Yale Law School with John Lindsay, and taught there during the 1950s. The recommendation that Brewster serve on the commission came from Joseph Califano, a former student of Brewster's at Harvard who had become one of Johnson's closest aides. The Yale president also began to be invited to White House dinners and presidential conferences with other eminent citizens. Brewster wrote to Johnson on occasion, as in September of 1965 when he argued that the rationale for and administration of exemptions from military service were "arbitrary, often inexplicable, and encouraging to cynicism. . . . I do see this as a problem which impinges on the motivation and morale of the generations we are trying to educate at all levels."[123] The correspondence would lead to Brewster's appointment the next year to another presidential commission, on selective service and the draft. These were time-consuming commitments, without much in the way of public recognition—part of the reason, perhaps, that such presidential commissions have become scarce in recent years. Brewster took on the responsibilities not only to have influence but because doing so was in keeping with his dictum that a private office is a public trust.

Earlier that year, Brewster had participated in one of the premier establishment conclaves, the Bilderberg Meetings. This annual conference, sponsored by the royal family of the Netherlands, brought together respected, influential leaders from different fields to discuss matters of common European-American concern. Many of Brewster's mentors had attended in the past, men like Harriman, Acheson, McCloy, Herter, and Mason, as had some of their protégés, like Bundy and Rusk. The international character of the conference, combined with its elite participants and off-the-record discussion, made it irresistible to a colorful assortment of conspiracy theorists. As one wrote, "The Bilderbergers . . . lay secret plans to destroy the sovereignty of this nation, as well as all nations, and to control the world through a 'One World Government' which they will control. We 'little people' who are the producers of this world will be held in slavery."[124] As far as can be determined, Brewster did not take part in discussions on world enslavement at the Bilderberg conference, although he did talk to McCloy, David Rockefeller, George Ball, the New York Times columnist James Reston, and Lord Mountbatten. Much of his conversation, however, was with Lindsay, another participant in the conference, on the topic of urban renewal.

From his vantage point at Yale, Brewster had seen New Haven, a medium-size, unlovely city long past its heyday of industrial prosperity, become the nation's pioneer in urban renewal under its dynamic mayor, Richard C. Lee. A local boy who had grown up impoverished in a cold-water flat, Lee was a matchless politician equally at home at Yale (even though he never attended college) and in the wards. He was an intimate of the Kennedys who turned down cabinet-level appointments and opportunities for higher office to devote himself to the city he loved. Brewster had known Lee since he was a reporter for a local paper in the 1930s. In the small hours of the morning, Lee and Brewster would meet in the Yale Daily News building, drink Moxies, and plot "how we were going to take over the newspapers from the Jacksons," the ultraconservative family that owned the New Haven papers.[125]

After Lee identified himself with the cause of urban redevelopment in 1953, he won every election he ran in, and the Republicans never again held power in the city. He assembled an internationally renowned team of urban planners, academics, and administrators to remake large parts of the community. By the mid-1960s, New Haven ranked first among American cities in per capita urban renewal grants ($458 for each resident, compared with $31 for New York) and had undertaken ambitious redevelopment measures, from commercial construction to governance reform to welfare programs. The city allied with Community Progress, Inc., an antipoverty program supported by the Ford Foundation, to deal with social ills. Although urban renewal was already being faulted for dismantling neighborhoods and displacing the poor, New Haven, under Lee and his chief redevelopment aide,

Edward Logue, renovated thousands of units of dilapidated housing, built thousands of new low-income housing units, and undertook a large, relatively unpublicized relocation effort for families left homeless by slum clearance. Robert Weaver, secretary of the Department of Housing and Urban Development, declared that "New Haven is coming closest to our dream of a slumless city."[126]

In cold hindsight, Lee and Logue were unable to do more than slow the city's decay. Federal redevelopment funds ran dry, businesses and residents continued to flee to the suburbs, and the slums did not disappear. At the time, however, the uphill battle against decline was invigorating, and the revival of New Haven under Lee seemed to parallel the renewal of Yale under Brewster. When Brewster brought in the novelist John Hersey to be master of one of the residential colleges, part of the allure of the job for Hersey was that "New Haven happens to be one of the most exciting cities in the United States at the moment; in some ways it is *the* most exciting."[127]

Yale played a significant supporting role in the city's redevelopment, lending academic expertise, money, and influence to the effort. Brewster considered New Haven's renovation to be in the university's best interests, but he also believed that the university had a unique intellectual contribution to offer, particularly through the social sciences. "For Yale," he wrote, "New Haven is the laboratory for study and experimentation with better ways of evaluating physical renewal and human renewal problems." Cutting-edge social science would "provide the foundation for new concepts and skills essential to the understanding and appraisal of community action techniques."[128] While Brewster approved of action-oriented scholarship, as his predecessor did not—Griswold had feared that work on practical problems would turn the university into a "service station"—he thought that the university ought not to attempt, on its own, to put its solutions into effect. "We are," he wrote, "best equipped to be our brother's thinker."[129] Brewster, who had been warned off the social sciences by Acheson, remembered a conversation in which the former secretary of state had commented, "When I read a monograph by a member of our political science department which referred to me in the Korean crisis as a dependent variable, I knew I didn't believe in political science."[130] Still, Brewster had high hopes that academic rationalism could slice through any urban problem, no matter how tangled.

Among his other connections to the New Haven renewal effort, Brewster was vice chairman of the Citizens Action Committee, a group that included the city's top bankers, industrialists, business executives, educational leaders, and power brokers. Mayor Lee had created the commission partly to ensure that his urban redevelopment program had the bipartisan support of the local establishment and partly to forestall the creation of a citizen's council, traditionally the upper class's weapon against urban ethnic machines.

Yale Corporation member Jock Whitney had tried to form just such a good-government council in New York City in 1964 to attack the Democratic machine and combat the deterioration that beset the metropolis. However, prominent citizens such as David Rockefeller, whom he recruited to the committee, felt that Mayor Robert Wagner Jr. was sure to win a fourth term in the 1965 election and that they ought not to jeopardize their standing with him. Instead, Whitney's paper, the *New York Herald Tribune*, ran a series of articles on the city's physical rot and ossified bureaucracy under one-party rule, and the crime, poverty, pollution, congestion, and malaise that afflicted its citizens.[131]

Lindsay said later that the series provided him with a raison d'être to run for mayor. In some ways he saw it as his duty to run, for he believed he could reverse the city's decline. As Brewster's professor August Heckscher (later parks commissioner under Lindsay) pointed out, Lindsay was a man "impelled from within—by a dominant, rather cheerless compulsion—to act according to what he thought was right."[132] He announced his candidacy in May 1965.

Lindsay had never made a secret of his presidential aspirations; his congressional campaign slogan was "The District's Pride—the Nation's Hope." One of Richardson's acquaintances wrote to him during the campaign that "it is the feeling of a great many friends of John Lindsay that being Mayor of New York will not be his last political stop."[133] The New York City mayoralty seemed an unlikely stepping-stone to the presidency. And yet the mid-1960s was a time of high attention to what invariably was referred to as "the urban crisis." The dominant concerns of the liberal establishment— education, race relations, equal opportunity, environment, good government and administration—came together in the cities. As the Yale law professor Alexander Bickel wrote before the election, "the Great Society is going to be a Great City, or it will be nothing." Bickel further predicted that Lindsay, if elected, would bring "a conception of the mayor's office as a bully pulpit, such as Theodore Roosevelt first made of the Presidency," and his words proved an accurate prognostication.[134]

Lindsay's entrance into the mayoralty race led William Buckley to announce himself as a surprise candidate, running on the Conservative

Party ticket. Buckley was nothing if not colorful, but his campaign was quixotic at best, at worst viewed as a prank. When asked at his first press conference what he would do if he actually won, he laughed, "Demand a recount." Buckley was quite serious, however, about the need to arrest Lindsay's political ascent. "There will be those who will try to propel [Lindsay] towards the presidency," Buckley wrote just after the election. "If they do, they will find it especially hard, I think, thanks to the record I tried hard to publicize in the course of the campaign."[135]

Buckley's animus toward Lindsay did not proceed merely from the fact that the latter was a liberal Republican who had refused to endorse Goldwater, although Buckley hoped to remove liberals root and branch from the party. On some deeper level, Buckley identified Lindsay with the liberal establishment he both admired and despised and had attacked since his undergraduate days at Yale. His friend Norman Mailer once pointed out to Buckley that "we both detest the Establishment, we don't like the center, that's why we can talk though we are on opposite sides."[136] Somewhat to his surprise, Buckley became the tribune of those oppressed, without being quite able to say why, by Lindsay's good looks, patrician ease, and connections, as well as his progressive outlook. Stripped of its quirks, Buckley's campaign attacked any form of social change, which set him against challengers of existing arrangements (civil rights activists, antiwar protesters, intellectuals) and also against establishment reformers. The election provided a preview of the curious alliance of establishment leaders, youth, minorities, and the upper middle class against lower-middle-class and working-class white ethnics that would characterize the later 1960s.

For a while, all three mayoral candidates—Lindsay, Buckley, and Wagner—were Yale graduates. As the columnist Dick Schaap facetiously pointed out, while Buckley was in Skull and Bones, Lindsay and Wagner "were only in Scroll and Key. That makes them more sensitive to the aspirations of minority groups."[137] Lindsay's alma mater did not help his cause when, on Columbus Day, Yale scholars outraged Italian-Americans by announcing the discovery of the "Vinland" map, showing the New World lands explored by Norsemen long before Columbus. Further opportunities for Yale humor were reduced when Wagner unexpectedly declined to run for reelection, and the Democratic candidacy went to Abraham Beame, a colorless party loyalist. Lindsay bested Beame by over a hundred thousand votes, winning the year's biggest election "in a balloting pattern that crisscrossed party lines, ethnic prejudices and religious blocs all over town."[138] Lindsay shot to the top of political handicappers' presidential polls, and ensured that when he came up for Yale Corporation meetings (in Jock Whitney's limousine or by helicopter with Juan Trippe), he would bring the press in his wake. As the newest member of the Corporation, the mayor sat at a far end of the table, but was free to speak out as he pleased. "No, John Lindsay damn well hasn't been shy or quiet," an older member of the board would later tell a reporter.[139]

Brewster liked to say that he represented "the most independent politics in existence," so Lindsay—who ran as Lindsay rather than as a Republican—was a politician after his heart.[140] Lindsay became the most visible symbol of an establishment trying to rally the nation around the problems of the cities and black people. He pushed the city's gargantuan bureaucracy toward modernization and meritocracy. He hammered away at the closed ethnic fiefdoms that dominated the city's unions. He brought into public service a legion of bright, young activists. He drew on the learning of social scientists and the talents of the nation's experts in urban renewal. Lindsay also swiped some of New Haven mayor Lee's ablest staff for his own urban redevelopment efforts in New York, notably Edward Logue, Paul Ylvisaker, and Mitchell Sviridoff.

After he had been in office for a year, Lindsay came up to New Haven for a dinner honoring Mayor Lee, and Brewster and Lindsay spent much of the dinner collaborating on lyrics to commemorate the occasion. "They were laughing so hard," Lee recalled, "they were practically rolling on the floor."[141] Lindsay sang to Lee, "It's plain to see I much esteem / Your highly touted civic team / In view of all my staffing needs / I wonder if you'd have some leads?" Lee retorted, "I know full well what you admire / But wish that you'd just praise, not hire / We've now the staff to get our plans off / So keep your cotton-pickin' hands off." Lindsay serenaded Brewster: "My dearest King, I feel distress / That you should hog the New York press." Brewster responded, apropos of Lindsay's presidential ambitions: "I feel it would be quite a score / To paint the White House blue once more."[142] Lindsay served as a fount of advice for Brewster and Lee on the related questions of urban renewal, race relations, and unrest with which Yale and New Haven struggled during the later 1960s.

Lance Liebman, who first met Brewster in his provostial period (when Liebman was chairman of the *Yale Daily News*) and later served on the Yale Corporation under Brewster, was also an assistant to Lindsay during the late 1960s. He observed that although both men were from elite WASP backgrounds, "they were very forward-looking; they represented inclusivity and progress in the best way. John Lindsay was a good-looking, blue-eyed

WASP, and yet blacks and Puerto Ricans identified with him—it was very strange, in a way." Liebman noticed "a very similar dynamic at work with both of them: John Lindsay will fix the slums, and Kingman Brewster will fix Yale. They were both modernizing and overhauling outdated institutions, bringing in aspects of equality, making them inclusive." Liebman also knew that neither Brewster nor Lindsay was as rich as most people thought they were, and because they dedicated themselves to public service, "neither of them became rich later on, either. . . . [B]oth Kingman and John retained very skeptical opinions of the wealthy boys they had gone to school with, and the class that had produced them."[143]

ONE OF THE heroes of Brewster's circle was Supreme Court justice Oliver Wendell Holmes Jr. (1841–1935). Lindsay quoted him in speeches, Richardson carried *The Mind and Faith of Justice Holmes* with him everywhere throughout World War II, and McGeorge Bundy was raised to regard Holmes, for whom his father had clerked, as a sort of household god. Brewster had occasion to mull over Holmes's dicta on free speech and tolerance of dissent in the 1965–66 academic year when antiwar protest put Yale in the national headlines.

Brewster did not consider civil disobedience against the war to be morally equivalent to the civil rights protests in the Jim Crow South. He told an interviewer early in 1965 that he thought some antiwar demonstrations were "ludicrous mockeries, on the level of stuffing telephone booths and other expressions of egotism."[144] More to his taste was the October 1965 "Who Speaks for Yale?" demonstration opposing antiwar civil disobedience, after a series of antiwar demonstrations at Yale and across the country. Joe Lieberman, one of the organizers, criticized protesters who disobeyed laws and then tried to evade punishment. Borrowing a phrase from Brewster, Lieberman said the demonstration was intended "to show that those students who have yelled loudest are not the most numerous. I myself have yet to be convinced of any practical value these raucous minority protests have had other than to elevate the morale of Communist forces in Asia to fight on in the name of their totalitarian form of government."[145] Another organizer of the demonstration, Yale College senior John Kerry, presented Vice President Hubert Humphrey with a petition signed by over one thousand students insisting that "a reasonable debate on foreign policy must be kept free from fanaticism or emotional posturing and must show a fundamental loyalty to our political institutions. A position of protest justifies no one in an attempt to impede troop movements at home, to undermine morale abroad, and to encourage our generation to repudiate its military duties."[146]

At the same time, Brewster found much to praise about Americans for Reappraisal of Far Eastern Policy (ARFEP), a national antiwar group started at Yale by William Sloane Coffin. Believing that the time was not yet ripe for an outright assault on the nation's Vietnam policy, the chaplain created the group to press for U.S. recognition of the People's Republic of China, the admission of China to the United Nations, and a cease-fire and negotiated settlement to the war in Vietnam. Coffin joined forces with Allard Lowenstein, a 1954 Yale law graduate and prominent student organizer with extensive experience in the civil rights movement; the joint effort was an early indication that, by late 1965, the tide of white liberal protest was shifting from civil rights to antiwar activities. Coffin and Yale students would collect articles on American policy and suggestions for organizational work, then send them out to the chapters Lowenstein was establishing on campuses across the country. The ARFEP board of directors included older, respectable left figures like Norman Thomas, Norman Cousins, and Brewster's mentor Roger Baldwin.[147] A nationwide telephone hookup in October brought speeches from Coffin, Thomas, Michael Harrington, and others to twenty-five thousand listeners. Although Coffin pointed out that ARFEP never gained anything like the public and political support that the conservative organization the Committee of One Million Against the Admission of Communist China to the United Nations had garnered, the group received considerable press and was a harbinger of student antiwar protest to come.[148]

Brewster told an alumni audience that ARFEP and the "Who Speaks for Yale?" activities were "a most encouraging recoil from the shrill draft card burning, sloganeering, obstructionist, disruptionist techniques which have been found so much in evidence on some other campuses on this issue."[149] By the end of 1965, however, Brewster was hearing from the alumni about the activities of assistant professor of history Staughton Lynd. In August 1965, Lynd was the first of 350 participants in the Assembly of Unrepresented People, held in Washington, to be arrested for crossing police lines. The American Nazi Party, which was staging a counterprotest, hurled red paint at him. Photos of Lynd, with an apparently bloody shirt and clenched fist upraised in a revolutionary salute, landed in *Life* and many other magazines. John Blum, chairman of the Yale History Department at the time, recalled that many people in the 1960s "reached the point where they were mad, not in a clinical sense but in an emotional sense—excessively emotional, hyperbolically emotional, not subject to rational discourse about either urban racial issues or/and the war in Vietnam. . . . That photo of Lynd with blood across him and his arm raised really represents the mood he had cultivated within himself."[150]

Lynd gained notoriety in December, when he flew to Hanoi, along with SDS leader Tom Hayden and the Marxist historian Herbert Aptheker, to express sympathy for Vietnamese victims of U.S. imperialism and shame at being American. Many alumni could not understand why Brewster did not simply fire Lynd. "Lynd's publicity is almost entirely attributable to his connection with Yale," one group of alumni wrote to Brewster. "Without the prestige of this association, Lynd would be just another shouting far leftist and most people would pay no attention to him. . . . Why should loyal Americans and Yale permit its name to be used in such degrading activities, pay his salary and furnish a renowned platform of freedom for Lynd to consort with and aid the enemy?"[151]

Brewster may have wavered privately on how to respond to what he himself considered an unpatriotic act and to an antiwar movement that still puzzled him in many ways. He turned for advice to Paul Moore. "I do not feel the anti-Vietnam movement in this country is, in any noticeable way, inspired or guided by 'Communists,' although they no doubt rejoice in it," Moore told him. "However, I also feel that thinking of Communism as a monolith is fuzzy . . . I still feel Lynd is a man of integrity, not a knave. I think it was an error in judgment to speak as he did where he did. But you must realize that thousands of Americans passionately agree with what he said. . . . I do not think we can claim academic freedom when a person is disciplined because he goes beyond an arbitrary degree of difference with the Administration. (Such freedom is like being a little pregnant.)"[152] In the end, Brewster rejected demands to dismiss Lynd but publicly criticized his rhetoric and his visit behind enemy lines.

Coffin questioned Brewster's criticism of Lynd, asking, "Is it proper for you to take a stand on another man's words and deeds without taking a stand on the situation that prompts them? And if the situation is as serious as many of us believe, then the epithets of an assistant professor may not be as reckless as the silence of university presidents."[153] Brewster wrote back: "Let me turn to your criticism of my silence about the war. I have to confess it is more the result of quandary than of official inhibition. I have forborne to make statements or sign petitions even though urged to do so by spokesmen for a variety of positions. This is simply because I have not had a confident notion about what I would do tomorrow morning at nine o'clock if I had the responsibility for US policy. Until I do have such a confident notion, I do not find it appealing simply to say that war is horrible or that peace is desirable. Until I can find means to these ends which are convincing, I do not feel that I have a position worthy of public statement. In fact to pretend that ends without means constitute a position seems to me bad teaching and bad spokesmanship. . . . Maybe there is a clear way in Vietnam which has eluded me. If so, it has also eluded all the pronouncements and petitions which I have seen or heard, in the press or in open forums. But this is all the more reason to keep probing. If there is a convincing means to the end of peace, which doesn't buy peace here and now at the price of a greater war thereafter, then I can think of nothing more worthy to break the silence."[154]

The Lynd controversy was a taste of what was to come. Brewster would increasingly find himself caught in the crossfire between right and left, struggling to arrest the polarization that was dividing the nation. Just as the radicals said, the war was coming home.

7

THE GUARDIANS OF
EQUAL OPPORTUNITY

I N T H E spring of 1966, admissions director R. Inslee ("Inky") Clark was summoned before the Yale Corporation to report directly on the changes in policy he had implemented since his appointment by Brewster the year before. The thirty-year-old Clark walked over to Woodbridge Hall and climbed the marble stairs to the second floor. He entered the imposing room where Brewster and the Corporation were gathered in their high-backed leather chairs around a long, immaculately polished table beneath twin chandeliers and portraits of Elihu Yale and bygone presidents. Clark briefly described the process leading up to the admission of his first class, the Class of 1970, and the new emphasis he had placed on talent spotting, merit, and diversity. One of the Corporation members who had "hemmed and hawed" through Clark's presentation finally said, "Let me get down to basics. You're admitting an entirely different class than we're used to. You're admitting them for a different purpose than training leaders." Unspoken but understood by all was that the dean of admissions' new emphasis had rejected unprecedented numbers of wealthy, WASP applicants from preparatory schools, many of them alumni sons, who had been Yale's longtime constituency. Clark responded that in a changing America, leaders might come from nontraditional sources, including public high school graduates, Jews, minorities, and even women. His interlocutor shot back, "You're talking about Jews and public school graduates as leaders. Look around you at this table"—he waved a hand at Brewster, Lindsay, Moore, Bill Bundy, and the other distinguished men assembled there. "These are America's leaders. There are no Jews here. There are no public school graduates here."[1]

No aspect of Kingman Brewster's presidency stirred more anger and debate than the overhaul of Yale's undergraduate admissions during the 1960s. Admissions became a battleground over the university's purpose. The outcome of the battle, which was felt far beyond Yale, was part of a larger struggle in American society, the thorny debate over race, class, gender, and leadership. It caught up all the members of Brewster's circle, as in the second half of the 1960s, Brewster, Bundy, Lindsay, and the rest devoted themselves to the cause of equality of opportunity. Their efforts aimed to widen individual chances for social mobility, especially among disadvantaged African-Americans and other minorities. Like the Platonic guardians McGeorge Bundy had once studied at the Harvard Society of Fellows, they would become master threshers, separating society's wheat from the chaff. The act of raising up some from the bottom, however, implied casting others from the top. When the social churning set in motion by the liberal establishment encountered the energies and outrage unleashed by the 1960s, the results were often explosive.

THE PROCESS OF renovating Yale's admissions began placidly enough. Admissions director Arthur Howe had left the university in 1964 to become head of the American Field Service.[2] After an interim year, Brewster looked for a new dean to fill the five-year term. Clark, a younger staff member in the admissions department and dean of one of the residential colleges, was one of several candidates. A 1957 graduate, Clark had been president of the Inter-Fraternity Council and a member of Skull and Bones; he had taught at the Lawrenceville School after graduation. When Brewster interviewed Clark, he asked whether Clark thought of himself as an architect or an engineer. An architect, Clark replied: "I said I'd like to design a different student body than the one we have now. . . . And I told him what I would like to do, starting right in with a different kind of admissions staff, a much more diverse student body."[3] Clark felt that Yale's impressive faculty and facilities imposed an obligation to serve the nation by admitting the students who could most benefit from the institution: "the most able, the most motivated, those with the most potential."[4] Brewster liked the sweeping ambition hidden behind Clark's handsome and conventional exterior, and his appointment was announced in early 1965.[5]

Given that Clark would soon become a target of conservative wrath, it is ironic that he was initially opposed by faculty activists and progressives, like William Sloane Coffin, who had chafed at the slow pace of reform in admissions and to whom Clark looked like a stereotypical Yale achiever. As

English professor Richard Sewall wrote to Brewster, Clark's appointment was not well received by "those who looked for an EXCITING CHANGE, a move toward a New Image."[6]

The problem with the traditional image was that it was based on the view that Yale's purpose was to serve as a repository of the best of WASP culture and to educate men who would hold property and power in a society that deferred to upper-class leadership. Such a vision might barely have held true in Brewster's undergraduate years, but American society had shifted direction, and most universities were changing along with the society. Brewster could recite the reasons as well as anyone: the "jolt of the Depression, followed by the war's premium on brains; the tremendous increase in college applicants spurred by the G.I. Bill and then the birthrate; the high correlation between income potential and higher learning; finally the explosion of useful knowledge itself; all conspired to make the home of culture and rest into a community of driven men."[7] But Yale's admissions continued to be geared toward the older vision.

Consider the wall of biases against an applicant from an excellent, competitive public high school such as New York's Bronx High School of Science in the 1950s. The student came from a public high school, which Yale's admissions officers did not visit. He scored highly on aptitude tests, which Yale discounted. He had a specialized education, which many influential Yale faculty members thought unfitted him for the liberal arts. He focused on science or technology, which Yale had traditionally considered unsavory. He was almost certainly from a nonwealthy family, which handicapped him in the era before need-blind admissions. And he had no Yale alumni connection or feeder-school tradition to boost his candidacy.

Furthermore, even if the candidate from Bronx Science was not Jewish himself, he came from a school that was predominantly Jewish (partly because admission depended entirely on examinations), at a time when anti-Semitism in Yale's admissions was covert but active. Brewster's predecessor Whitney Griswold did not condone this kind of discrimination, but neither was he interested in rooting it out.

In the early 1950s, the college made little effort to reach beyond its traditional constituencies to recruit talent, and Yale regained a reputation for non-intellectual conformity that had partially dispersed during the veteran years. It is not surprising to find that during Griswold's first five years in office, Bronx Science sent only 7 graduates to Yale, while Andover (not nearly as selective) sent 275.[8] Over the same five-year span, almost all alumni sons who applied were accepted. As one Yale historian pointed out, "the generosity of the board may have helped to promote the belief among alumni that the admission of their sons was a right."[9] The point is not that all alumni sons and Andover students were intellectually inferior; rather, it didn't matter whether they were bright or dull, since Yale accepted virtually all minimally qualified legacies and graduates of favored schools. Whatever places remained were distributed among intellectually outstanding applicants from less favored backgrounds and social, ethnic, and racial groups—a neat reversal of the priorities to which Yale had long officially committed itself.

Clearly the admissions policy undercut the aim of making Yale a more intellectual enterprise. As an undergraduate, Inky Clark was disappointed to find that Yale was more homogeneous and had fewer "people who were very bright and motivated [than] I would have expected."[10] His classmate Calvin Trillin, a midwesterner and a high school graduate like Clark, conceded that the St. Grottlesex students set the social tone at Yale but argued that "there was widespread circumstantial evidence that, on the whole, we were smarter than they were."[11]

While the direction of undergraduate admissions started to change in the late 1950s and early 1960s, many faculty members and observers like Chaplain Coffin thought that the approach was excessively gradualist and Yale's efforts to diversify the student body small-scale and cautious. The Class of 1967, entering in 1963, was the first in which the number of high school students equaled the number of prep school students, a level of parity reached by Harvard in the 1940s and by Princeton as early as 1955.[12] Some of Howe's innovations, like the "ABC" rankings that offered early admissions to selected schools that sent large cohorts of students to Yale, Harvard, and Princeton, gave further advantage to the already advantaged.[13] In the early 1960s, Yale was found to accept a lower percentage of Jews than any other Ivy League college.[14] Alumni sons, by contrast, enjoyed a preference that meant that more than two-thirds of them were admitted, although a disproportionate number flunked out or were placed on probation.

These shortcomings were of particular frustration to the increasing number of faculty members who had not attended the college or one of the graduate or professional schools. By the early 1960s, Brewster had helped assemble, in many departments, a critical mass of "outside" professors who, together with some Yale-bred critics, were speaking out on the academic limitations rooted in admissions. The new faculty brought new priorities and a spirit of academic professionalism. Although most shared Yale's traditional concern for teaching—or at any rate could not escape the obligation to teach (the university mandated that all professors must instruct undergraduates)—they were more focused on their own research and less emotionally invested in their students' moral and social growth. They had little interest in polishing gentlemen. Several Yale-trained professors still advocated that students wear coats and ties in classrooms, while Harvard-trained John Blum dryly observed that "I have never discerned any direct correlation between the dress of a student and his intellectual performance."[15]

Brewster's assistant Sam Chauncey remembered that, as the president was considering candidates for the admissions deanship, he thought of Harvard's example of admissions diversification under president James Conant. Not only had Chauncey's father been Conant's right-hand man in establishing talent-searching programs, but several bright students from the provinces who were so identified and brought to Harvard were by then prominent on the Yale faculty, including the economist James Tobin, head of the President's Council of Economic Advisors under Kennedy.[16] When Brewster and McGeorge Bundy talked about admissions, Conant's was the model they had in mind. Bundy had been inspired by it during his time as dean of the Faculty of Arts and Sciences at Harvard. Brewster felt that Clark would be the candidate most likely to follow Conant's example at Yale. After Clark's hiring, he and Brewster accelerated the school's efforts to broaden its national base, diversify the student body, and raise the intellectual standard for admissions.

Investigating admissions policies at other selective colleges and universities, Clark found that they ran the gamut from completely by-the-numbers meritocracy to old-fashioned preferences. At one extreme was the University of California at Berkeley, which "did almost everything by the computer" in an impersonal process that admitted students almost wholly on the basis of grades and test scores. At the other was a traditional college like Williams, where the admissions approach was "personal, subjective, and weighted toward maintaining the kind of college that Williams was in the '50s and '60s: white, New England-y, genteel, very much the place for the well-rounded kind of person."[17] Neither approach would be favored by Brewster or Clark.

Back in New Haven, Clark initiated his restructuring of admissions by getting rid of nearly the entire admissions staff. Clark's new staff, doubled in size, included more public school graduates, individuals without Yale connections, and the first African-American admissions officer, W. C. Robinson. Their backgrounds, Clark felt, would provide fresh perspectives, enable the university to communicate with people suspicious of its received image, and eliminate bias and Yale's traditional insularity.

Within a year the number of schools visited by Yale admissions officers doubled to over a thousand. Clark's recruitment policy centered on talent searching, the process of actively seeking out "all those candidates who will benefit most from studying at Yale and who will contribute significantly to the life of the Yale community. . . . Very specifically, talent searching means penetrating deeper into at least two particular areas: the inner-city high school and the rural high school."[18]

Clark's elimination of the "ABC" system and of the old geographic criteria resulted in less emphasis on the central states with long Yale traditions (such as Ohio, Illinois, Minnesota, and Wisconsin) and much more attention to eastern urban areas, particularly the New York–New Jersey metropolitan region.[19] He also altered Yale's scholarship policy to increase the amount of outright gift aid, lessen the dependence on bursary jobs, and loosen the conditions that had prevented many scholarship students from playing a significant role in extracurricular activities.

Most important, in 1966 the Corporation approved Brewster's proposal for need-blind admissions, which removed information about financial resources from a candidate's admissions docket. No longer would the university reject otherwise qualified applicants who could not afford to attend Yale.[20] There would be no quota on the number of scholarship students to be accepted, nor any limit on the amount of money available for gifts and loans. While the most selective universities had become more meritocratic in the twentieth century, never before had any severed the connection between admissions and ability to pay. It was a revolutionary step.

The policy received relatively little attention at the time, and its financial implications were seriously underestimated, but need-blind admissions became one of the most important ways in which Yale attracted students from less affluent backgrounds. Brewster observed that the policy helped attract wealthy students as well, particularly during the 1960s. Now that "the pocketbook was no longer relevant to admission," he said, "the privileged took pride in the feeling that [they] had made it on the merits rather than on the basis of something ambiguously called 'background.'"[21]

In addition to developing remedial-education programs, Yale began to work more closely with referral agencies and professional recruitment groups to target minority students.[22] As the emphasis shifted to "developing a well rounded class rather than choosing one thousand similar individuals" and to selecting "the young men who will have a constructive impact on our society thirty years later in a variety of fields and endeavors," more recent notions of diversity, including racial diversity, came into consideration.[23]

McGeorge Bundy felt that the heightened emphasis on recruiting and admitting larger numbers of blacks to elite universities in the 1960s could be explained almost entirely by the ideals of university administrators. "Black demand, white awareness, riots in the cities, and the death of Martin Luther King" were all contributory factors, according to Bundy, but "the deeper and more durable cause was the growing conviction that there was a fundamental contradiction between an asserted opposition to racism and the maintenance, by whatever process of selection, of essentially all-white colleges and professional schools."[24] Bundy believed that the functional desegregation of Yale came about largely because Brewster, sensing that Yale had not convincingly demonstrated its commitment to the principle of equal opportunity, moved to remedy the failing.[25]

According to Brewster and Clark, Yale did not maintain an affirmative action program as such. Worth David, Yale's director of admissions for much of the 1970s, recalled that "we had a statement of goals, we tried to act as affirmatively as possible, but our search for the most talented people always overrode our consideration of numbers."[26] The assumption throughout Brewster's presidency was that wide-reaching, aggressive recruiting could expand the pool of minority candidates to the point where no preferences would be needed. Even so, both Brewster and Clark conceded that the admission of nontraditional students was an especially sensitive process calling for "some gambling, some risk-taking," and flexibility in interpreting SAT scores in light of background.[27] "We are going to try to make a subjective judgment about the potential of each student," Brewster told a skeptical alumni audience. "You use different evidence depending on what's available, and the evidence will often be different for a fellow from a disadvantaged background than it will be for a fellow from a highly organized high school or prep school."[28]

Diversity was not defined only in terms of race or ethnicity. Brewster—perhaps reflecting his own appreciation for contrasting types—believed that future leaders would come from a broader array of fields than in the past. And he believed that even future executives would benefit from greater exposure to scholars and artists.[29] He tried to fight Yale's traditional image as a place "sought chiefly by young men eager to succeed as lawyers, business men, bankers, advertisers, diplomats," in the words of one faculty report.[30] In his statement of admissions policy, Brewster wrote that "an excessively homogeneous class will not learn anywhere near as much from each other as a class whose backgrounds and interests and values have something new to contribute to the common experience."[31]

Brewster's basic view of Yale's undergraduate mission was quite traditional: "We want Yale men to be leaders in their generation. This means we want as many of them as possible to be truly outstanding in whatever they undertake."[32] Off the record, he vowed more bluntly that "I do not intend to preside over a finishing school on Long Island Sound." But, as one of his earliest advisors pointed out, there had long been an ambiguity "between the view that Yale's education is a genuine process which involves growth and change and the view that it is a mantle cast upon superior (by reason of selection) people."[33] Brewster thought the school's principles encompassed both these elements, but he could not agree with the alumni view that Yale's contribution to national leadership consisted of "taking a stupid young man and trying to prepare him for Life."[34]

Brewster tried to reassure the alumni that qualities of leadership and character would receive consideration in the admissions process alongside measurable intellectual capacities. But the same considerations would, he stressed, be granted to black applicants whose test scores seemed at variance with their personal and academic promise, and to students whose creativity and imagination seemed not to have been captured in their test scores. In short, Yale's new admissions policy embodied a subjective rather than an objective meritocracy. Clark and his colleagues attempted to evaluate for potential, took a flexible approach toward circumstances (particularly for minority applicants), and refused to set specific targets for representation of any group, be it athletes, minorities, or alumni children.

With these policies in place, Clark and his team of recruiters fanned out across the country, visiting schools where they sometimes had to apologize to administrators for having snubbed their graduates in the past. Clark recalled his frosty reception at academically competitive Catholic schools, and his interaction with principal Abe Lass at Abraham Lincoln High School near Coney Island, in Brooklyn: "He said, 'Don't expect me to give you my top Jewish student—he's going to City [College] or Columbia. Don't ask me for my best scientist—he's going to MIT. Where has Yale been for the last twenty years?' I said, 'If I come back next year or send somebody back next year, will you give us some candidates?' He said, 'Maybe, but it might take a while.'"[35]

CLARK'S FIRST CLASS, the Class of 1970, was selected in the spring of 1966. The recruiting effort produced slightly fewer applications than had arrived the year before —although the total, 5,781, was an increase of almost forty percent over what it had been just four years before.[36] Neither was it the most selective class, but the acceptance rate of twenty-seven percent indicated a considerable sharpening of the competition since the thirty-five percent acceptance rate four years earlier. In many other respects, however, it was a pathbreaking class: fifty-eight percent were public school students, the highest of any class in Yale history and a jump from fifty-two percent the previous year. The class drew on more public schools than any other class (478), but also more private schools (196). The admissions office revealed that the increased proportion of public school students resulted mainly from the fact that they had consistently outscored prep school students for the past dozen years, racking up an average grade of 81.1 the previous year versus 78.5 for prep school students.[37]

For the first time ever, the rate of matriculation of financial aid applicants was higher than for nonfinancial aid applicants. Financial aid jumped to nearly $1 million, thirty percent above what it had been the year before; gift aid from the university increased by almost fifty percent.[38] The class contained more minorities of every kind. Clark recalled that "nobody came to my office screaming for more Jews. It was just a matter of natural selection. When we were picking that first class in 1965, no one counted Jews, but I knew that [Jewish enrollment] was going up. It had to."[39]

The Class of '70 would enter with the highest SAT scores in Yale's history. A student who scored its mean SAT Verbal mark of 697 would have been in the ninetieth percentile of the Class of 1961, and the seventy-fifth percentile of the Class of 1966. In a national context, half the incoming freshmen scored in the top one percent on the Verbal SAT. These SAT marks were higher than those scored by the incoming class at Harvard, also a first for Yale.

Clark's policies accorded minimal consideration to the privileges of background, money, prep school training, and Yale relationships. Many applicants from traditional constituencies were excluded. The reaction set in before Clark had actually admitted or rejected anyone; it began when he visited Andover, Yale's largest feeder school, in October 1965. In the past, Yale's dean of admissions and his two top assistants had stayed at the school for several days, socializing with the faculty and headmaster and promising near-assured admission to many applicants. Clark, however, felt that a one-day visit to Andover with a large group of his newly minted staff members was sufficient. Later conceding that this was "a mistake which I will take full credit for," he remembered that the visit "didn't go well. . . . [F]or the counselor who had dealt comfortably before with Yale . . . , this was a very unsettling event. And I think word went out from that visit that Yale didn't care about Andover."[40]

Clark addressed a large group meeting, at which he was asked how Yale felt about the bottom quarter of the class at Andover. Unbeknown to him, the same question had been asked of a Harvard admissions officer the week before. At that time, for its own financial self-interest, Harvard was pulling away from its commitment to thoroughgoing meritocracy.[41] By 1966, the Harvard Admissions Office was again filling its "happy bottom quarter" with athletes, mediocre prep school students, and alumni sons. At Andover, Harvard's representative sent glad tidings of this policy to the weakest members of the senior class.

Clark gave a diametrically opposed answer, in effect that "Yale can do a lot better than the bottom quarter at Andover. We're looking for the top kids at Andover. If you haven't performed well at Andover, what makes us think you're going to perform well at Yale?" In recounting the story years later he added, "You can imagine what the reaction was."[42]

The response was not long in coming. Enraged alumni wrote letters to the administration and each other lambasting the perceived change in admissions policy. Overlooked in the years that followed was the fact that Andover continued to send large delegations to Yale (though smaller than in the past) and continued to be the college's largest feeder. Clark apologized and reverted to the pattern of extended personal visits to Andover and other prominent schools. By the next year Andover's director of college placement was writing to him that "all of us were extremely pleased with the Yale visit and are in accord with the fact that the Andover-Yale relationship is just where it should be."[43] But the damage was done.

One of the reasons for the furor over Yale's attitude toward prep schools was that Clark's policies did, in fact, drastically reduce admissions from smaller New England private schools, which were more concerned with social than intellectual education. The anger of these schools was compounded when Clark told the *Yale Daily News* that "the old notion of the 'feeder school' supplying most of the freshman class is no longer applicable"[44] and that the "ingrown" prep schools would be disappointed in the future.[45] Yale was now leading the meritocratic charge. In 1968, Harvard accepted 28 of 61 applicants from Choate, Princeton 17 of 30, but Yale only 5 of 28.[46] The record was much the same at St. Paul's and many other well-known prep schools.[47]

Almost immediately, Clark and Brewster were charged with bias against the preparatory schools, and—most explosive—against the sons of alumni.

As the policy shifts became widely known, many alumni determined that, as one put it, Brewster had initiated "a turn away from the Yale that all of us loved and respected."[48] "You will laugh," William F. Buckley wrote, "but it is true that a Mexican-American from El Paso High with identical scores on the achievement test, and identically ardent recommendations from the headmaster, has a better chance of being admitted to Yale than Jonathan Edwards the Sixteenth from Saint Paul's School."[49] Other critics asserted that Brewster and Clark preferred Jews over Christians, scholars over athletes, and intellect over leadership.

Some of the evidence brought forward to support this view may easily be laid to rest. Athletes were expected to meet intellectual standards similar to those of other applicants, but this shift that had occurred under Arthur Howe's deanship. Relations between the Athletic Department and the Admissions Office actually improved considerably during the Clark era. While the number of Jews at Yale increased dramatically in Clark's years, eliminating the discriminatory barriers that had kept them out hardly amounted to anti-Christian bias. Likewise, Clark's abolition of the "ABC" ratings, far from constituting discrimination against the prep schools, supported his contention that "the independent schools were now being placed on the same plane, in terms of the admissions process, as the public schools. Everybody was going to be dealt with the same; therefore, no more favoritism."[50]

The Brewster administration's troubles with the admission of alumni sons derived in large part from a demographic time bomb planted in the 1930s. The Admissions Office under Howe dealt mainly with the offspring of graduates who had attended Yale in the 1910s and early 1920s, at a time when alumni sons constituted about 15 percent of each class. The office under Clark was dealing with the offspring of graduates of the late 1920s, 1930s, and early 1940s, who had experienced legacy rates of twenty-five to thirty-five percent.[51] As competition for admission intensified in the 1960s, the demographic dilemma would have blown up in the face of any admissions dean, no matter how sensitive.

Still, it was a shock to the alumni when the percentage of alumni sons in each Yale class dropped from 24 percent in 1961 to half that in Clark's second year in office, considerably below the levels at Harvard and Princeton.[52] One of Clark's faculty admissions committee members recorded that "Yale sons have a much harder time of it than I thought. They won, it seemed to me, very little special consideration. If they were good enough, they didn't need it; if they were poor enough, we didn't think it wise to give it to them. The in-between range in which special consideration could be decisive turned out to be a very narrow range indeed."[53]

CLARK OFTEN CONTRASTED the cultural advantages alumni children enjoyed with the disadvantages endured by the poor and minorities, particularly as reflected in objective measures such as the SAT. "What's really the difference," he asked, "between a 550 [SAT score] for a favored Yale son who has gone to Choate and a 480 for a black kid from the inner city, who has no books in the home, no money, and no opportunity to go to plays or theater or opera? I'm not so sure the 480 doesn't represent more on that one indice than the 550."[54] Clark was prepared to argue that lower SAT scores among blacks and other disadvantaged groups might reflect cultural deprivation. (Such understandings were not often extended to businessmen's sons, whose cultural backgrounds could be equally negligible and who were taken by surprise by the shift in Yale admissions policy.)

The battle over admissions raised the old debate over whether the main purpose of the Ivy League institutions was learning or the preservation of a particular kind of WASPy culture. One Harvard conservative commented that "there is an unbridgeable gulph between the Harvard man and the vulgar [which is] composed of taste and style, not learning, which any graduate of the Universities of Ohio or Tennessee can get. Yet the fact remains that you can always tell a Harvard man; but it is usually difficult to tell the difference between an Ohio man and a bum. . . . What is it then that gives Harvard this advantage? The answer is breeding. . . . What the people who go to Harvard get is not a culture. They get their culture from their families, and they are born into it. What they get is polish."[55]

Although most Yale alumni would not have expressed it that way, they shared a sense that something important was changing. The novelist John O'Hara wrote in 1965 that the typical Yale man was "likely to be at least fourth generation of part-Yankee stock, financially well fixed, conservative in all his tastes, friendly and polite without making many new friends after college, loyally but not unswervingly Republican, tolerantly but unwaveringly Protestant, optimistic, patient, dependable, and good. . . . The remarkable thing is the patience of these men, especially as they see the university they loved being taken away from them."[56] It was a matter of considerable puzzlement to angry alumni that the initiators of the change were men like Brewster, who fit O'Hara's description of the typical Yale man quite closely. Indeed, Brewster understood the code of the northeastern upper class in ways that even O'Hara, who chronicled that class, did not. When someone once inquired why O'Hara, who wrote repeatedly and reverently about Yale in his novels and short stories, had not been awarded an honorary degree, Brewster replied: "Because he asked."

Yale's fund-raisers feared that the future financial contributions of students from economically disadvantaged backgrounds would not equal that of wealthier students. While Corporation members such as Irwin Miller, Paul Moore, Doc Howe, and John Lindsay often pressed Brewster to go further and faster in his policy of risk, a number of other board members had no sympathy with the idea that Yale should reach beyond its established channels. Corporation member Herbert Sturdy, for example, argued that "a crusade . . . to seek out and prefer the 'underprivileged'" would destroy Yale's "civilizing influence and inspiration for leadership." Sturdy offered the analogy of integration in California, in which blacks moved from slum neighborhood A into white neighborhood B. Within four or five years, neighborhood B had become an all-black slum, "and the negro residents of area B are just as discontented as they were before they moved. The change is then practically irreversible."[57] Clearly the implication was that admitting too many underprivileged, blacks or otherwise, could irreversibly turn Yale into a slum as well.

MCGEORGE BUNDY HAD not had significant contact with the underprivileged by the time he left the White House for the Ford Foundation at the end of February 1966. It would therefore come as a surprise to many when he reoriented the foundation's priorities in the direction of greater equality of opportunity, particularly for African-Americans. Bundy spent much of his tenure at Ford wrestling with some of the same problems that were preoccupying his friend Brewster.

According to some observers, Bundy's selection as Ford president was merely a case of the establishment hiring one of its own. The foundation's board of trustees was full of Bundy friends and admirers. One of them, John McCloy, had assisted Bundy from the time he wrote his Henry Stimson biography through his years at the White House. Judge Charles Wyzanski and the Minneapolis publisher John Cowles had been Harvard trustees when Bundy was dean, while MIT president Julius Stratton had been a fellow member of the Friday Evening Club. Irwin Miller had worked with Bundy at the White House as chairman of a presidential commission on trade with the Soviet bloc, and "I had heard a lot about Mac from Kingman

Brewster."[58] White-shoe lawyer Bethuel Webster had also been a mentor to Brewster and John Lindsay. So when word came that Bundy could be dislodged from government, the board of trustees extended the tap.

Actually, Bundy's selection was more likely the result of a power struggle within the board. Several Old Turks on the board had revolted against the previous president, Henry Heald, for his conservative conception of the foundation's purpose. Heald objected to the foundation's work overseas (particularly in India) in taking direct action to help the poor, rather than merely studying the problem of poverty. He had the same objection to the foundation's Gray Cities initiative, run by Ford's public affairs director, Paul Ylvisaker, which operated antipoverty programs in minority areas of cities like New Haven. Heald wanted to keep controversy at arm's length, and he "didn't like the foundation to be involved in political problems or social action," as one program officer observed. He preferred to make large block grants to universities, hospitals, orchestras, museums, and other uncontroversial organizations.[59] As Bundy had written to McCloy in 1962, "A machine filled with the conventional wisdom in 1950 would have produced about 80% of the results the Ford Foundation has produced. . . . But what really large and constructive forces has it let loose in our society?"[60]

By the mid-1960s, many of the trustees were fed up with Heald's avoidance of involvement. As the civil rights movement turned its sights from Jim Crow segregation in the South to de facto segregation in the North, as riots broke out in American cities, and as the problems of race, crime, poverty, and urban deterioration cut more sharply in New York and elsewhere, the Ford Foundation's aloofness seemed like dereliction of duty. The journalist Joseph Goulden observed that "in Detroit the simmering racial tensions among workers at his own motor company warned Henry Ford II of the crisis rapidly sweeping down upon urban America. . . . The Establishment knew it must regroup, not only to assure its own preservation but also to guarantee that it had a voice in the imminent rebuilding of urban government."[61] In this interpretation the board appointed Bundy because its members knew that his energy and activism would take the foundation into direct engagement with social ills, regardless of his lack of previous involvement in civil rights and urban problems.

THE BUNDYS MOVED to Manhattan in March 1966 and bought an apartment on Fifth Avenue, facing Central Park. Doc Howe had moved to Washington shortly before to become commissioner of education, and when

Bundy left for New York, he gave Howe all his liquor. "For some reason he couldn't transport it across state lines, and there was a lot of it, which worked out very nicely for us."[62] From the viewpoint of Bundy's family, his departure from government, with its eighteen-hour days and seven-day weeks, meant that "he came back to us," as his son Stephen remembered. "He became a presence in our lives again, because he'd been away."[63]

Bundy also had more opportunity to be in touch with old friends such as Richardson, who wrote that he was "more delighted than I can say that you're in the place where you are. You have uniquely and magnificently earned this opportunity for further (it could not be greater) public service."[64] In early May, Bundy went to New Haven to join Brewster at the *Yale Daily News* banquet. "Let me know when you are ready to form a partnership," Brewster scribbled in a note to his friend. "*Right now,*" Bundy wrote back. "Antigua Ancients Inc.—advice from the IRRESPONSIBLE."[65] The Bundys and Brewsters went on vacation again in the Caribbean, this time with their children along. The Beatles had recently recorded "We Can Work It Out," and Andrew Bundy remembered that on the croquet court, "Kingman's notion of high entertainment was to sing 'Wicket Work It Out' every time he smacked a ball through the wicket. It was that sense of silliness and play that was one of his most endearing qualities."[66]

When Bundy first arrived at the Ford Foundation, it seemed to many of the four-hundred-person staff that he was "coiled up very tight," as one put it. "He was really on a razor's edge."[67] It was clear to all that he had been through a period of great stress. There was already some uneasiness among the staff about Bundy's role in the Vietnam War, and uncertainty over the extent to which he would try to retain an unofficial position in government. Reassuringly, one of Bundy's first actions was to summon key foundation officers and tell them that he would not involve Ford in Vietnam and that they should not change their views on the conflict (or any other issue) on his account.[68] Still, Bundy had not lost his appetite for influencing Washington, and would continue to do so directly on his own and indirectly through the work of the foundation.

As time went by, Bundy warmed up to the staff, and most found him an excellent boss. He retained the antibureaucratic approach that had served him well at Harvard and the White House. As he had done at the National Security Council, Bundy replaced a corporate model with an academic one, nonhierarchical and based on merit and expertise. His door was open, and he reached across the chain of command to question low-ranking program officers who were experts in their domain. Sometimes the president's informality annoyed the middle management, but as one officer observed, "Bundy had the view that you talk to the people who know something about the subject, regardless of their rank."[69] "He never lost his edge of intolerance with fools, and with some people who were not fools," another officer remembered. "If you came in with some flabby or loose argument or suggestion and it was the wrong time of day, you'd hear about it. But overall he was really receptive to all kinds of things and people."[70]

Not long into Bundy's presidency, the foundation would move to new quarters on East Forty-third Street, an imposing glass and steel structure. Inside, a vast atrium extended eleven stories over a living forest, complete with magnolia trees and a pond. Although the building had been designed before the new president's arrival, it struck many of his intimates as an excellent metaphor for Bundy himself: life and warmth behind a steely exterior. Others suggested that the atrium, with glassed-in offices overlooking the jungle, helped Bundy establish openness and squelch intrigue within the organization; after all, why should staff listen to rumors about who was meeting with the president when they could look into his office and see for themselves? The luxurious appointments of the offices, with Honduran mahogany furniture and Klee and Picasso reproductions on the walls, projected an image of wealth joined with modernity, intelligence, and good taste.

Yet the surface was, unfortunately, deceiving. Bundy made an unpleasant discovery during his first weeks on the job: the Ford Foundation was spending itself into extinction. Because Heald and the trustees had disagreed so uncompromisingly on what the foundation should be doing, they had abandoned their responsibility to balance competing claims and simply funded any projects backed by the various combatants. Although it was by far the largest of America's seventeen thousand foundations—its $3 billion endowment was three and half times the size of its nearest competitor, the Rockefeller Foundation—Ford was spending more than twice its annual income. It was projected to run out of money in a decade or less from the time Bundy took over.

Several trustees were indifferent to this prospect. As Henry Ford II told one of the younger trustees, "You worry too much about this foundation. If we want to spend it out of existence tonight at the Century, we will."[71] Because Bundy decided that the foundation should be preserved, its commitments had to be reduced sharply—from $365 million in Heald's last fiscal year to $250 million.[72] Reducing expenditures would entail a significant reordering of the foundation's priorities.

May Day rally, May 1, 1970. The eyes of the nation were on New Haven, Connecticut, as one of the biggest—and potentially most explosive—campus demonstrations of the student-protest era took place outside the gates of Yale University. (*Lee Lockwood/Time-Life Pictures/Getty Images*)

Kingman Brewster Jr. at a press conference during the May Day weekend. Vice President Spiro Agnew had called publicly for his ouster as Yale president, and Brewster knew that his enemies would rejoice if the demonstration turned to disaster. (*Yale Picture Collection, Manuscripts and Archives, Yale University Library*)

ABOVE: Brewster with his governess. Brewster recalled that the highlight of his 1927 European visit was a flight to Paris "on Imperial Airways in a big trimotor biplane, and that seemed to me the most *dramatic* thing that life could afford." (*Courtesy of Mary Louise Brewster*)

ABOVE LEFT: Brewster, age eight, aboard the RMS *Franconia* in the summer of 1927. Brewster's mother took the children to Britain, France, and Switzerland. (*Courtesy of Mary Louise Brewster*)

BELOW LEFT: Brewster with his uncle, Arthur Besse, and cousin, Alden Besse, on Martha's Vineyard around 1930. Arthur Besse became a kind of surrogate father to Brewster after his parents divorced. Family and familiar places were an important part of Brewster's makeup; he spent part of every summer of his life on Martha's Vineyard. (*Courtesy of Mary Louise Brewster*)

BELOW RIGHT: Brewster, age twenty-one, testifying against the Lend-Lease Act before the Senate Foreign Relations Committee, February 1941. "We are willing, we are eager to give our lives and our deaths if need be, in the service of the nation," he told the senators. "But we do insist that those lives or those deaths not be wasted." (*AP/Wide World Photos*)

Cyrus Vance   McGeorge Bundy   Kingman Brewster

Paul Moore Jr.   Elliot Richardson   John Lindsay

Some of the biggest men on the Ivy League campuses in the late 1930s and early 1940s were among the greatest critics of their universities. TOP ROW: (left to right) Cyrus Vance, Yale Class of 1939; McGeorge Bundy, Yale Class of 1940; Kingman Brewster Jr., Yale Class of 1941; BOTTOM ROW: (left to right) Paul Moore Jr., Yale Class of 1941; Elliot Richardson, Harvard Class of 1941; John Lindsay, Yale Class of 1944. (*Elliot Richardson, Harvard College 1941 Yearbook; all others, Yale Picture Collection, Manuscripts and Archives, Yale University Library*)

LEFT: Brewster, age forty-four, at his inauguration as seventeenth president of Yale University in April 1964. It was pageantry with a purpose: the sweep and ambition of the ceremony declared that universities had become one of the major estates in American society. (© Alfred Eisenstadt/Time-Life Pictures/Getty Images)

BELOW: Paul Moore Jr. discussing the problems of the poor in Mississippi at a news conference in Washington, D.C., February 1966. As Episcopal bishop of Washington from 1963 to 1970, Moore was at the forefront of the movement for black civil rights, and his activism provoked controversy among both priests and parishioners. (AP/Wide World Photos)

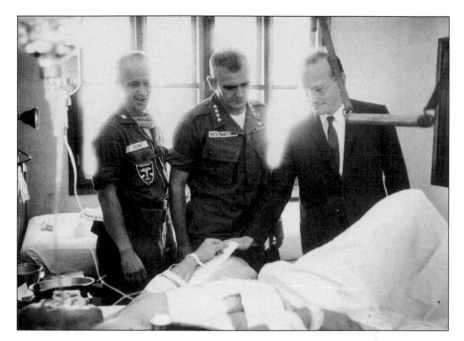

National security advisor McGeorge Bundy with General William Westmoreland in South Vietnam, February 1965, after a Viet Cong attack on a U.S. military base near Pleiku. Bundy would soon call Cyrus Vance at the White House and recommend that the United States retaliate by bombing North Vietnam. (*AP/Wide World Photos*)

Cyrus Vance and Lyndon Johnson, 1968. The former deputy secretary of defense believed that in the debates over Vietnam within the Johnson administration "there weren't evil men and good men—there were men with differing views as to what the best way was to try and bring the war to a conclusion." (*AP/Wide World Photos*)

John Lindsay debating William F. Buckley Jr. in the New York City mayoral election campaign, September 1965. Congressman Lindsay was the bright hope of the nation's liberal Republicans, while journalist Buckley galvanized a growing conservative movement. (*Cornell Capa/Magnum Photos*)

Lindsay in his office as mayor of New York, 1966. Lindsay brought charisma, concern, and social-scientific expertise to bear on the problems of the nation's urban poor—but those problems proved more resistant than anticipated. (*AP/Wide World Photos*)

TOP RIGHT: Yale College Dean of Admissions R. Inslee (Inky) Clark, October 1966. As dean from 1965 to 1970, Clark stoked alumni outrage with his new emphasis on merit, admitting greater numbers of high-achieving public school students, minorities, and (for the first time in 1969) women, breaking the college's 268-year male tradition. *(Yale Picture Collection, Manuscripts and Archives, Yale University Library)*

RIGHT: Brewster with Yale College Chaplain William Sloane Coffin Jr. at a May Day weekend news conference, May 1970. The two men clashed on numerous occasions, but Brewster refused alumni pressure to fire his activist chaplain even after Coffin's 1967 indictment on federal conspiracy charges. *(Yale Picture Collection, Manuscripts and Archives, Yale University Library)*

BELOW: Garry Trudeau's "Bull Tales" cartoons in the *Yale Daily News* in the late 1960s and early 1970s affectionately caricatured Brewster and his ability to frustrate student radicals like SDS's Mark Zanger. Brewster observed that Trudeau's cartoons meant that neither "the King or Megaphone Mark [could] take themselves as seriously as true controversy requires." *(DOONESBURY © 1971 G. B. Trudeau. Reprinted with permission of Universal Press Syndicate. All rights reserved.)*

LEFT: Elliot Richardson at his October 23, 1973, press conference at the Department of Justice after resigning as Richard Nixon's attorney general. Richardson's resignation, after his refusal to fire the Watergate special prosecutor Archibald Cox, led to Nixon's downfall. (*Bettmann/Corbis*)

BELOW LEFT: Brewster was presented to Elizabeth II in May 1977, and took part in the Jubilee Week festivities to celebrate the queen's twenty-fifth year in the monarchy. As ambassador to the Court of Saint James's from 1977 to 1981, Brewster would be a low-key but effective diplomat. (*Hulton-Deutsch Collection/Corbis*)

ABOVE: Secretary of State Vance swore in Brewster as ambassador to Great Britain in the backyard of the Yale president's house in May 1977. Brewster's wife, Mary Louise, held the bible on which her husband took the oath of office. (*Courtesy of Mary Louise Brewster*)

To the surprise and shock of the academic world, Bundy made most of his cutbacks in spending on higher education. Of the $1.5 billion in grants the Ford Foundation had made between 1950 and 1965, about $1 billion had gone to educational affairs, mostly as capital grants to college and universities.[73] Bundy shut off the tap for almost all such grants. Coming from a former Harvard dean, the cutoff seemed treasonous. "It is quite understandable," Bundy wrote in his first annual report, "that any given dean or president should feel sure that he needs our capital more than we do—when I was a dean, I felt that way myself. The trouble is in the arithmetic: the present needs of deans and presidents, strung end to end, would go three times around the endowment of the Ford Foundation, without a pause for breath."[74]

Bundy's cutoff of block-grant aid affected Yale less than those colleges and universities that relied almost as heavily on Ford's annual subsidy as on student tuition. Yale counted on Ford funding for particular program requests, such as the $6.3 million grant to the university in May 1966 for support of international studies.[75] In any case, Brewster did not desist from bombarding Bundy and his foundation with funding requests. A few months into his Ford presidency, Bundy wrote to Cornell president James Perkins that he had received Perkins's telegram requesting Ford funds and "read it to one of my most dispassionate advisors, a certain Kingman Brewster of New Haven, Connecticut. Even without a hint from me, he was able to observe the difficulties which your projection would create for any institution which had an early benefactor whose name began with a Y." Bundy reassured Perkins that Brewster was reworking the proposal in a way "which will somehow have the happy effect of producing still more money for universities located somewhere between Boston and New York and having only four letters in their name. He assures me, however, that he will not display the appalling extravagance of making his proposal by telegram. It will come instead in one of those cheap 60-page brochures with six colors and raised engraving for those who like to feel the future with their hands."[76] Ford officer Peter De Janosi remembered that Brewster once came into a colleague's office in New York and asked for $25,000 for what seemed a cockeyed scheme; the staffer approved it on the spot. After Brewster left, De Janosi "said to my colleague, 'That was a crazy idea. Why are you funding it?' He said to me, 'Peter, any time we can get Kingman Brewster out of the Ford Foundation for $25,000, we are making money.'"[77]

*　　　*　　　*

WHEN BREWSTER AND Bundy got together to talk about the institutions they led, they agreed that both Yale and the Ford Foundation were innovative forces in the so-called third sector, between government and business. Brewster liked to call it "the self-determined sector," and defined it as "the vast variety of activities and organizations which are not for profit and not for votes."[78] Universities and foundations were among the most important national entities in this sector, along with religious organizations, groups of concerned citizens (such as the Council on Foreign Relations), and to some extent the media.[79] The well-known publicist T. J. Ross described these entities in the early 1960s as "those who occupy the role of guardians, so to speak, in society."[80] A distinguishing characteristic of such organizations was that they were much less constrained than government or business. Foundations, as Bundy observed, "are unusually free. They do not have, as most other institutions have, the guidance of a specific mission. . . . Compared to nearly all other institutions, they are relatively free to shape their own courses of action. That freedom is at once a foundation's most precious asset and its most demanding condition."[81] With that autonomy, as Bundy saw it, came the responsibility to put the foundation's resources to use where they might have the most leverage, even at the cost of controversy.

Bundy's first major initiative, advanced five months after he assumed his post, was to put an ambitious program for public television before the Federal Communications Commission. Bundy had created a proposal with Fred Friendly, the former president of CBS News, who had resigned after the network broadcast *I Love Lucy* reruns instead of covering Senator William Fulbright's hearings on Vietnam. The Bundy–Friendly plan called for the FCC to create a public corporation that would own the communications satellite system and would fund noncommercial television by taxing the networks use of the system. Commercial interests including AT&T savaged the proposal, which ultimately died in Congress, but Bundy was instrumental in supporting the efforts that led to the creation of the Public Broadcasting Service (PBS).[82]

The uproar his proposal to the FCC produced left Bundy unrepentant. The agency had, after all, issued a call for public comment, "and we decided that to keep silent in such a situation would be irresponsible. . . . Can we be charged with 'interfering with other people's business,' when that business is concerned with a national decision on public policy?" The episode drove home to him the "public blandness" that had grown up in American institutions headed by executives less open to controversy than himself: "Neither in business, nor in the professions, nor in government is there enough encouragement to independent activities by young men." Bundy concluded that the "organization man" was a public menace because "he is not willing to annoy his organization by any action, and his organization is too easily annoyed. Foundations ought to stand against this kind of thing."[83]

Bundy's belief that responsibility demanded actions to face society's toughest problems led him to make equal opportunity, particularly as it related to the racial crisis, the defining theme of his presidency at Ford. By his own admission Bundy had spent little time thinking about black–white relations before he went to Ford. Doc Howe felt that "race was a whole new ball game for Mac, Kingman, John Lindsay and a whole lot of my friends." Bundy and Brewster became more involved because civil rights "was a moral issue that was appealing to Mac, and to Kingman too. They were smart people in dealing with customs and laws and rights, and they found themselves really uneducated on this subject."[84] Bundy educated himself by setting aside the first half of each workday morning for reading, and by meeting with black leaders, of whom the most influential was probably Whitney Young, the tough, pragmatic leader of the Urban League.

The day after he delivered his FCC proposal for public television, Bundy spoke before the annual banquet of Young's organization in Philadelphia to emphasize his commitment to the civil rights cause. Speaking on behalf of his foundation, Bundy declared that "full equality for all American Negroes is now the most urgent domestic concern in this country" and would henceforth be the most important priority of the Ford Foundation as well. He acknowledged that fulfillment of black equality—in terms of "improvement in skills and schools, in real opportunity, and in the quality of life itself"—would be more difficult than the mainly southern struggle for basic civil rights. While he believed that business and government could do far more than any foundation to elevate African-Americans, he saw a role for philanthropy in addressing the problems of urban life.

"The American city has been a scandal for three generations," he told his audience, "and it has constantly dwarfed our feeble efforts to remake it. Nothing would be more foolish, for both white men and Negroes, than any angry assumption that the cities of the future are the problems of one color only. We shall succeed or fail together, in our great cities as in our whole society." Bundy also believed that he and his peers shared a personal obligation: "a wider and deeper and stronger effort among white leaders is needed so that the white American can see the problem as it really is, and recognize *his* need to face it, and to act." Bundy was confident that the country's leaders could both win the war in Vietnam and mobilize the nation to expunge racism. "America is full of error," he concluded, "but she has always known how to reach beyond her failures toward greatness."[85]

One of the qualities that Bundy and Brewster and the others in their circle shared was a somewhat naive, patriotic belief in the capacity of their fellow Americans to do the right thing. John Lindsay would soon involve Bundy in a practical lesson on the difficulty of race and the urban crisis that would test their faith.

LINDSAY'S NEW YORK mayoralty got off to a rocky start. Four hours into his first day in office, January 1, 1966, the Transport Workers Union struck, shutting down buses and subways and strangling the city. The TWU leader, Mike Quill, a stage Irishman with a brogue and buckthorn cane, opted for class warfare as a negotiating technique, using Lindsay's Anglo-Saxon image to paint the mayor as an enemy of the white working class. (Other white ethnic labor leaders later would attack Bundy and Brewster in the same way.) Cursing Lindsay to his face and calling him a "pipsqueak," "juvenile," and "ass"—the 1960s contempt for authority was by no means limited to the young—Quill refused to moderate his demands, sneered at the city's budget deficit, and defied the law that made the strike illegal.[86]

Lindsay delivered his inaugural address at City Hall on the first day of what he called, in his speech, the "unlawful strike against the public interest." The strike was a useful illustration of Lindsay's view that "the public interest must prevail over special interests, the good of the community over the desires of any group." He positioned himself squarely in the tradition of progressive Republicans like Theodore Roosevelt and Fiorello La Guardia, men who "cared about the malignant effects of injustice, intolerance and indifference." And he pledged to bring moral and visible government to New York and hope to the downtrodden. "Our enemies in this battle," he warned, "are greed, ignorance, bureaucracy, prejudice, and defeatism in high places and low."[87] The address served notice that, like the Yankee reformers of old, Lindsay would take on the power brokers and party hacks, although he would add a concern for disadvantaged minorities that had been absent from past good-government movements.

The entrenched interests, however, proved difficult to dislodge. Lindsay cut a heroic figure during the transit strike, sitting through marathon bargaining sessions, giving lifts to pedestrians in his city limousine, and leaving reporters in his wake as he briskly strode the three miles from Gracie Mansion to City Hall each morning. But the strike was one of the costliest in history at that point, averaging over $100 million a day in lost business. The pressure to settle on any terms proved irresistible. After thirteen days, Lindsay paid tribute to the TWU in a budget-bending settlement—reportedly twice the size of any pact made by former mayor Robert Wagner—that opened the door to strikes by other municipal unions.

Lindsay had no greater initial success in taking on other power brokers, such as city planner Robert Moses or the New York legislature, which thwarted the mayor's proposal to tax commuters into the city. He pushed for the unions to admit minorities—apprenticeships were often handed down from father to son, and as late as 1960 there were only three hundred blacks out of fifteen thousand apprentices in the building trades—but most of the unions strenuously resisted any efforts to allow more blacks or Puerto Ricans into their ranks.[88] Reforming the bureaucracy also proved more difficult than expected. "The red tape and bureaucratic delay really send me through the roof," he told a reporter a hundred days into his administration. "The biggest frustration is getting things moved, getting things pushed through. The rigidity of civil service makes it incredibly difficult to move personnel around."[89]

As Vance and Brewster had already discovered, part of the problem in running large institutions in those years was their leaders' inability to keep track of revenues and expenses. Following the pattern laid down at the Pentagon and at Yale, Lindsay's staff adopted the Program, Planning, and Budgeting Systems (PPBS) approach, and embarked on an ambitious attempt to use technology and business methods to reorganize the city's departmental structure. PPBS and the superagencies that Lindsay created did not fulfill the high hopes he vested in them, but they dealt a severe blow to the old Tammany-esque culture of patronage and graft and at least took some halting steps to push the bureaucracy toward meritocracy and modernization.

Lindsay did succeed in attracting idealistic young people to the cause of public service, many of whom went on to later fame, including Sandy Berger, Steve Brill, Jeff Greenfield, Leslie Stahl, and Leon Panetta. He also brought to New York a talented generation of planners, social scientists, and experts in urban renewal. Budget planner Charles Morris, later author of the most clear-eyed assessment of Lindsay's mayoralty, confirmed that the atmosphere around City Hall was "one of heady excitement. If there was any place in the country where things were going to be done, where bright people would finally get a chance to show what they could do, it was Lindsay's New York City."[90]

The nation's future lay not in the suburbs but in its dynamic, diverse cities, Lindsay insisted. His first parks commissioner, Thomas Hoving, staged kite-flying "happenings" on windy days, put on plays, concerts, and psychedelic sidewalk-painting extravaganzas, and closed Central Park roads to traffic on weekends, opening them up to joggers, strollers, and bikers. Lindsay established the Mayor's Office of Film, Theater, and Broadcasting to lure the entertainment industry back to New York. Tourism picked up, and what had seemed a metropolis on the skids was soon being called "Fun City."

By opening "Little City Halls" around the city and by making a variety of symbolic visits and personal appearances, Lindsay attempted to bring government closer to the people. On one occasion he appeared at a fire in fancy dress, having come straight from a party; on another, he and his wife were seen picking up litter on a vacant lot in the South Bronx. Police officers at their stations learned that the late-night caller from City Hall might be the mayor himself. And sanitation workers loafing in a bar almost dropped their beers in shock when Lindsay barged in and ordered them back to their unattended trucks.

Above all, Lindsay was visible in the city's poorest neighborhoods, walking through the mainly black and Puerto Rican slums on hot summer nights without an entourage, his jacket slung casually over his shoulder. The mayor's visits came without advance publicity, and journalists and TV cameras were rarely in evidence. Lindsay carried no megaphone and made no speeches. Children flocked around him and adults called out from tenement windows. Laughing, joking, and bonding with the crowds, he never condescended and never drew back. Lindsay made these visits partly to gauge the temper and condition of the neighborhoods, and partly to convey to the people that he cared and was trying to help. "I think it's important for the people in the ghettos to see their mayor," Lindsay explained. "They've got to feel somebody is interested in them. You can tell from the double-takes how much the visits are appreciated."[91]

In the summer of 1966, race riots blazed in Chicago and Cleveland and appeared to be imminent in the gritty East New York neighborhood of Brooklyn. A gang of white ethnic youths calling themselves the Society for the Prevention of Niggers Getting Everything (SPONGE) engaged in low-level warfare with blacks and Puerto Ricans in the formerly white working-class area. In July, when trouble seemed certain, Lindsay and his team rushed to the scene as black and white crowds pushed and cursed, and sniper fire killed a black child and wounded another. A massive but restrained police presence brought the miniriot under control, making hundreds of arrests without incident. Lindsay and his aides brought fifty black, white, and Puerto Rican youths from the area for a marathon talk in City Hall. At times the session devolved into a shouting match but ended with handshakes between leaders from the different groups.

Hoping to head off similar disturbances, Lindsay created a task force under the direction of his young assistant Barry Gottehrer to go directly into trouble areas, identify the leaders, and open up lines of communication. Gottehrer, who became notorious for making his contacts in seedy locales with dubious characters like mobster Joey Gallo and black militant Charles 39X Kenyatta, told reporters that, in reality, most of his work was much less dramatic: "We get kids jobs, play ball with them, open street academies, arrange for bus outings. We've always got about fifteen young guys walking the streets of their home areas trying to cool it and listening for rumbles. They've got to trust us and we've got to trust them."[92]

Lindsay knew that these were only cosmetic solutions and that the problems of the ghettos were deep-rooted. One of the biggest headaches of his first year in office was the struggle over Intermediate School 201 in Harlem. At the start of the 1966 fall term, black activists boycotted the newly opened school, demanding either that it be forcibly integrated or that control of the school be turned over to the community. As the civil rights movement turned north, the spotlight shifted to the increasing numbers of all-minority schools, most of which were generally inferior. The trend toward segregated schools was a consequence of the 1950s, when more than 800,000 mostly middle-class whites had fled the city, to be replaced by almost equal numbers of poor blacks and Puerto Ricans.[93] By the mid-1960s, minorities were reading on average two years below grade level, and dropout rates in ghetto schools averaged seventy percent.[94] (There was a sense in which Lindsay's problem was also Vance's, since two-thirds of New York City's black students flunked the armed services intelligence test, depriving the military of much-needed recruits.) The ills that beset inner-city schools had many causes, although whether they stemmed from official neglect, white teachers' conviction that slum children couldn't learn, or the tangle of pathology in poor neighborhoods was a matter of hot debate.

*   *   *

SEGREGATION IN NORTHERN urban schools became a major issue in the early 1960s, and one of the politicians taking the lead in dealing with it was Lindsay's friend and fellow liberal Republican, Massachusetts lieutenant governor Elliot Richardson. When Martin Luther King came to Massachusetts to denounce de facto segregation, Richardson welcomed him at a mass rally on Boston Common and agreed that "we must take positive action to end racial imbalance in education wherever it may exist."[95]

As the state official in charge of health, education, and welfare, Richardson met with leaders of the mostly black Roxbury community to deal with school segregation; he supported a program of voluntary busing from overcrowded, mainly black schools to undercrowded, mainly white ones. He was also the primary advocate, on the governor's staff, of a 1965 law mandating that no school could have more than fifty percent nonwhite pupils. No other state passed such a law.[96] When the Racial Imbalance Act finally was enforced nine years later, white Boston exploded with rage. Already, however, involuntary busing promised to be a politically dangerous course of action.

In New York City, busing was nearly impossible; by 1966, fewer than half of all New York public school students were white. Further, with Black Power ideology gaining ground nationally, the ideal of integration had less appeal to black activists. So minority activists increasingly shifted their demands from integration to "community control," which might mean—depending on the speaker and the audience—anything from neighborhood participation to educational improvement to black control of black schools.[97] When blacks demanded outright control, including the power to hire and fire administrators and teachers, their desires put them on a collision course with the Board of Education, the United Federation of Teachers, and the law. But the worsening situation of the schools cried out for some remedy.

In the fall of 1966, the New York City Board of Education, looking for a way out of the crisis, proposed to establish a "Task Force to Advance Education in Disadvantaged Areas."[98] Lindsay urged that it go beyond attempts to settle immediate conflicts—that it seek to involve parents and the communities more directly in their children's education.[99] Most people agreed that decentralization was a necessary step, since by the mid-1960s, the school system had swollen to an unmanageable size—over 1.1 million students, 70,000 teachers, and 43,000 administrators, all governed by a rigid bureaucracy at 10 Livingston Street in Brooklyn. Plans to delegate some powers to local authorities had been under discussion since 1954 but had come to nothing. Lindsay's administration took up the subject with a new urgency in 1966: city officials and the New York legislature arranged a deal that would give the city $51 million in additional educational aid in return for decentralization.[100]

McGeorge Bundy's assistant Paul Ylvisaker, head of the Ford Foundation's National Affairs Division, was under consideration as the board's task force chairman, but it soon emerged that the board wanted Bundy himself for the role.[101] Bundy's interest in equal opportunity for blacks naturally included concern for education, the key to social mobility.

Bundy got most of his information on the decentralization debate from Ford Foundation program officer Mario Fantini, a go-between in the Harlem school battles. In October 1966, Fantini wrote to Bundy that the Lindsay administration's new Human Resources Division (set up with Ford money) was using the school controversy "as a lever for considering broader problems of urban education." The primary concern was how to break up the bureaucratic educational system, which Fantini pronounced "impervious to outside influence."[102]

Lindsay had lured Mitchell Sviridoff, the head of the new division, from Mayor Dick Lee's administration in New Haven, where he had been director of the city's Ford-sponsored antipoverty program.[103] Sviridoff wanted to replicate his success in New Haven by breaking up the centralized system into more-manageable clusters in which universities, businesses, teachers' unions, administrators, parents, and community leaders would cooperate to help run the schools.

Bundy expressed his sympathy with all sides in the Harlem debate. He empathized with those who protested from "the deep and right conviction that a school must somehow belong to its own community" and with those who "responded by defending professional standards." Acknowledging that the school system needed more money and resources, he added that "above all, we need functional decentralization."[104]

None of the Harlem activists would serve on the Board of Education's proposed task force, and when Bundy turned down the chairmanship, the idea died. The push for school decentralization gained momentum, however, and Lindsay soon named Bundy as chairman of the Mayor's Decentralization Advisory Panel.

Bundy's reputation for being a super-competent, honest broker made him an ideal candidate, and he seemed politically acceptable as well. In his first year of the Ford presidency, he had already made clear his broad sympathy with Lindsay's aims. Besides, Lindsay knew Bundy through Brewster, and he saw Mac's brother Bill nearly every month at meetings of the Yale Corporation. As one account recorded, "The mayor himself proposed Bundy as someone of unexceptionable status whose recommendations would command a hearing in all communities."[105]

"QUESTION AUTHORITY," RAN the slogan on the buttons and bumper stickers that began to pop up during the late 1960s. Many of the controversies of that era boiled down to arguments over authority and attempts by those who had less power (or none) to gain a greater share. But to a greater extent than is commonly realized, the late 1960s was a period when authority itself questioned authority. Pressured both by protests and by daily responsibilities, Brewster and his peers debated what leadership might mean in a less-deferential era.

Ever since they were undergraduates, of course, Brewster and his friends had criticized bad leaders and condemned bureaucratic thinking, dogmatism, self-righteousness, and corruption at the top. Stylistically there was often a major difference between the new men and the older generation of leaders they replaced—Bundy, for example, was the antithesis of the elderly, stuffy, and remote Henry Heald. Although Brewster and his peers tried to be leaders who would command respect because they were fair, competent, accessible, and accountable, not just because they occupied positions of power, they were also elitists. They believed strongly in the value of intelligence, professional knowledge, and expertise; they thought that the best men should make the decisions (a view that, after all, suggested the original definition of aristocracy). Until the late 1960s, they resisted the idea that elite authority should, in any substantive way, be devolved or dissipated.

The challenges to such a model of leadership bubbled up from two mostly separate sources. The first, emerging from New Left organizations like Students for a Democratic Society, was the idea of participatory democracy, defined in the SDS's 1962 Port Huron statement as letting "the individual share in those social decisions determining the quality and direction of his life."[106] Participatory democracy was always difficult to define, but for students it meant that, as the individuals affected by the educational process, they should have a greater say in their colleges and universities—sometimes, the ability to change those institutions. "Student Power" followed "Black Power" as a rallying cry in the latter half of the decade.

The other main challenge to the top-down model of leadership came from the activism of community organizers like Saul Alinsky, who attempted to raise the consciousness of the urban poor and mobilize them as a political force. Reformers theorized that efforts to improve the slums would fail unless the poor could be represented in the programs and institutions that affected them (be it welfare, the police force, or the school system) and overcome the entrenched power that blocked change. This concept of community action, involving the "maximum feasible participation" of poor people, was the operating logic of antipoverty programs run by the Office of Economic Opportunity under Brewster's friend Sargent Shriver.

Initially Brewster was highly critical of the populist notions that underlay the idea of maximum feasible participation. In early 1966 he turned down an OEO grant for one of Yale's compensatory-education programs because, he told an alumni audience, "their regulations required that it be called a National Community Action Program and therefore its board of directors must include representatives of the poor. I wonder what [the result] would be if we followed the same policy in the area of mental health?"[107] When Brewster and McGeorge Bundy attended the *Yale News* banquet in May, they heard the paper's outgoing chairman, Lanny Davis (later counsel to Bill Clinton), attack student apathy. A student's lack of interest in larger educational issues was, Davis claimed, "encouraged, if not completely provoked, by a general feeling that his opinions are considered unimportant and insignificant by the people who are determining policy in this university." His solution was to integrate the student into the administrative and decision-making machinery of the university, by allowing him to have closer contact with department problems and to "be represented on tenure committees and course of study committees; he should be given a significant role in considering appointments and promotions."[108] Brewster applauded the diagnosis of student apathy but not the remedy, commenting that "Mr. Davis missed the target—with a wet sponge." Bundy added that "Mr. Davis surely wouldn't let heelers write editorials."[109]

There was, however, an aspect of the critique of top-down leadership with which men like Brewster and Bundy agreed. Both extolled the virtues of decentralization, and in fact believed that their stance on the issue was part of what made them conservatives. It was a trumpet Brewster had been sounding since his law professor days. In his first speech as Yale president, he praised "dispersion of power and initiative rather than centralized power and planning to a single all-embracing design."[110] His commitment to decentralization would lead him to rethink his first, negative reaction to student demands for greater participation. It also provided common ground with conservatives who inveighed against the federal government's threat to local initiatives, the disappearance of town-hall democracy, and the dwindling significance of the individual citizen. Bundy, too, was wary of the inertia of large bureaucracies. He had purposely reduced the National Security Council's staff to keep it nimbler than the lumbering State Department. A key rationale for the Ford Foundation's involvement in economic and social issues addressed by the War on Poverty, said Bundy, was that as an independent institution, it had "a daring and flexibility not available to the government."[111]

Further testimony to the benefits of decentralization came from Richardson, who declared that "today we want to see government operate as close to the people as possible."[112] Richardson believed that suburban Americans as well as ghetto residents increasingly lacked purpose and identity: "Living in 'little houses made of ticky-tacky' in densely subdivided tracts . . . , overwhelmed by numbers and size, depressed by ugliness, besieged by advertising, they feel depersonalized and insignificant."[113] Decentralizing would strengthen the individual's ability to effect change. John Lindsay agreed. "Over past decades," he noted, "we've witnessed an increasing centralization of this country's power in big government, big business, big labor—big institutions of all kinds. We've become a more efficient and richer nation as a result, but we also have taken the power of government further and further away from the people it represents." City residents, in particular, were developing a deep mistrust of the established institutions of power, which often seemed to be "heedlessly closed to the individual who wants to better his position, to alter his place in society or to change his way of life."[114] Riots and repression could easily follow, with disastrous consequences for American society. Lindsay warned that the individual who lost faith in government institutions might lose faith in himself and turn toward some form of authoritarianism—the fascist specter that had haunted the men of the liberal establishment before World War II.

So, over time, a combination of events and influences would convince Brewster, Bundy, and the rest that bolder responses were necessary if the related problems of lack of equal opportunity and late 1960s anomie were to be overcome. These changes would require revision of their previously held beliefs and would anger many people, especially members of their own class. For instance, Bundy's activism upset business interests and other foundation leaders, who didn't want philanthropy to challenge the status quo. Moore's commitment infuriated conservative Episcopalians. Lindsay's policies made him "the target of the concerted wrath of the pillars of the Establishment—the same legal-banking-business fraternity that financed his campaign and helped put him in office," as one 1966 *New York Times* article commented.[115] Brewster's reworking of Yale's admissions policy stirred the alumni's ire. The controversies these leaders involved themselves in fractured what had been a more or less unified establishment, and separated the liberals from the conservatives. But as Brewster and the members of his circle saw each other responding to similar problems in similar ways, their belief that the activist course was right, even at the cost of controversy, was reinforced.

THEN, TOO, THE forthright leadership of Brewster and the rest brought them considerable national attention. Inky Clark, Brewster's dean of admissions, remembered that "to see a major Ivy League school—the one that was probably perceived to be amongst the most stuffy and least willing to do new things—suddenly engaged in activism and experimentation . . . was front-page news. We were in the front pages of the papers around the country, all the time, in a way that Yale had never been before and has never been since. And it was exciting."[116] These establishment leaders, with their blend of traditional backgrounds and modern views, seemed the right leaders for the times. James Reston Jr., the influential *New York Times* columnist, observed in mid-1966 that the most promising Republican presidential candidates were, "for some odd reason, Yale men," including Brewster, McGeorge Bundy, and Lindsay. "If Ronald Reagan of California is suddenly put on the list of Republican Presidential possibilities," he wrote, "why not Brewster of Yale, who may, though we will probably never find out, be another Woodrow Wilson?"[117]

But for leaders like Brewster, who thought deeply about equal opportunity, being a pioneering leader at this uncertain new frontier involved hard tradeoffs and real risks. The anger of many alumni over Yale's admissions policy, for example, was not motivated by mere prejudice. As Clark pointed out, the changes that he and Brewster implemented "represented a statement, really, about what leadership was going to be in this country and where leaders were going to come from."[118] The alumni were correct in their perception that admissions was a zero-sum game; like most other selective institutions, the university had not expanded to take in the new constituencies. Since access to income, power, and status was becoming increasingly dependent on higher education, the failure of an alumnus to get his son into Yale represented more than the breaking of a nostalgic tie— it raised the specter of downward social mobility for his family. While such fears were exaggerated (and many excellent although less selective institutions were eager to enroll the applicants alma mater rejected), Yale's new admissions policies threatened to change the way American institutions selected their leaders.

Brewster was convinced that American society had been permanently altered by the information explosion and the country's growth as a world power. Yale, he felt, should accommodate society's need for expertise by admitting students who had the intellectual capacity and motivation to make the most of Yale's resources. The university should give them the training to fit them for the evolving demands of leadership—otherwise, society would look for its leaders at Yale's competitors or beyond the universities altogether.[119]

Allied to this view was Brewster's belief that success based on inherited privileges could no longer be counted on and that knowledge and ability, rather than background, would now be the keys to achievement. As he wrote in a memo to himself, the future promised "increasing organization and professionalization of a society dominated by organized services rather than competition of truly independent proprietors and backers." In a time of "unpredictable change," Yale's leverage lay in attracting and educating students who had the "capacity to break new ground or at least adapt to it."[120] To those alumni who charged that "Yale took too many oddballs," Brewster insisted that "variety is a better context for mutual education than is homogeneity. One man's oddball is another man's square."[121] Brewster held that familiarity with diversity would be necessary for leaders who would be required "to mould disparate interests and ambitions into group effort."[122] The alumni argument that leaders would continue to come from "fine old families whose sons have gone to Yale for many generations and come from prep schools . . . with B & C averages and fine citizenship records" was open to question.[123] If Yale depended too much on past definitions of success, it might find itself without its share of leaders and patrons.

By the same token, it was to Yale's advantage to keep pace in a society in which minorities were winning an increased share of power and responsibility. As Clark remembered Brewster insisting at alumni gatherings, "'Yale wants to train the very best within the black community. We've got to turn out the black leaders of the future. The Martin Luther Kings of this world are going to come from Yale.' . . . It was very selfish for Yale, in the best sense. Yale was not for a minute changing its elitist approach to its role in world leadership."[124]

During the decade a heightened consciousness of the needs of minorities, the spirit of the Great Society, and widespread antipathy to elitism and privilege were important forces behind Yale's modernization and reorientation, as was the university's self-interest in changing its admissions policies. But there was nothing inevitable about Yale's move toward meritocracy and diversity, or its leadership among selective universities on these issues. These outcomes were a result of Kingman Brewster's enlightened stewardship of the institution, and his willingness to endure the opposition that came as a price for his idealism.

If Brewster's predictions were wrong, and power and influence would in fact continue to be passed down through tight networks of white males, then Yale would diminish its future importance (and financial contributions) by admitting Jews, blacks, intellectuals, women, and the underprivileged. But the fact that institutions like Yale determined, to some extent, who future leaders would be lent a circular quality to the question of how best to recruit leaders. By reducing the weight of inheritance, wealth, and social standing in admissions, Brewster was helping to shrink the power of the WASP elite, even while he was gambling that its influence would be redistributed to other, rising groups. Like Franklin D. Roosevelt, he tried to conserve the essence of the system by steering an evolutionary path between revolution and decay, and was damned as a traitor to his class.

8

A NEW SOCIETY
EMERGES

As the last notes from the pipe organ resounded through the cavernous, dimly lit Woolsey Hall auditorium on June 12, 1966, Kingman Brewster walked across the stage to deliver his baccalaureate address to the graduating seniors. Most presidential graduation speeches that year were the usual bland exhortations, no sooner heard than forgotten. Brewster, however, had stirred controversy from the Woolsey stage since he had introduced Charles Lindbergh to an America First rally more than a quarter century before, and he intended his baccalaureate to be nothing less than a national policy address. The capped and gowned students sat up straight when Brewster began to speak, clearly and critically, about the Selective Service System, a sword of Damocles hanging over young men in campuses across the land. He charged that the ideal of service was being mocked by a military draft that fell primarily on "those who cannot hide in the endless catacombs of formal education. . . . The result has been to encourage a cynical avoidance of service, a corruption of the aims of education, and a tarnishing of the national spirit."[1] His speech landed on the front page of the next day's papers.[2]

While his remarks had been crafted with a national audience in mind, Brewster was not out to provoke controversy for its own sake. The issue of the draft was relevant to his job, and he had already criticized the Selective Service System in previous statements to the Yale community.[3] As he was well aware, the draft exemption could distort young men's life choices, particularly by keeping students in college and graduate school when they didn't want to be there and by fostering guilt-driven activism.

"Privilege always carries its burden of guilt," Brewster observed. "In the late '60s guilt was compounded by the unparalleled affluence of those whose parents had made it; made more searing by awareness that education was a sanctuary from the obligations of military service."[4] Brewster had discussed the lack of a comprehensive manpower policy with Lyndon Johnson at a White House dinner; he wrote the president again to warn that "the rationale and administration of exemptions from military service seem somewhat arbitrary, often inexplicable, and encouraging to cynicism."[5] Further, his baccalaureate address articulated concerns shared by many other establishment leaders. Former secretary of defense and "Wise Man" Robert Lovett, for example, wrote to Brewster that "having worked on these problems for many years, starting with Colonel Stimson on the Civilian Military Training Camps and ending with the Universal Military Training concept, I found myself increasingly disillusioned with our draft system which by now has become, in my opinion, almost ludicrous. I am very glad you spoke out as you did."[6] On the other hand, some Yale alumni attacked Brewster for criticizing the head of the selective service, Lewis Hershey.

Brewster's speech led to his being named, a month later, to the President's National Advisory Commission on Selective Service, a twenty-person group headed by Burke Marshall, former head of the Civil Rights Division in the Justice Department under Kennedy and Johnson. Brewster's appointment to this, his second presidential commission, was boosted by the endorsements of the liberal Republican John Gardner (then HEW secretary) and of Brewster's former student Joe Califano (then an assistant to Lyndon Johnson).[7] Brewster was also a longtime friend and admirer of Marshall, who had been John Lindsay's classmate at Yale and had worked with Brewster on antitrust issues during the 1950s.[8] Joseph Lieberman, then in his last year at the law school, and several other students were hired to assist Brewster with the work of the commission. Through the fall of 1966 and the spring of 1967, Brewster would try, through the commission, to plan a more equitable system of national service, even while the tide of student anger against the draft continued to rise.

IN EARLY 1967, a reporter from the *New York Times* spent a day trailing Kingman Brewster as he went about the business of running Yale.[9] The president's day began with two meetings, in his office in Woodbridge Hall, with university officials concerned about government grants. The government's share of the Yale budget had grown from two percent in 1950 to ten percent in 1960 and to almost thirty percent by 1967; in effect, the state had replaced the alumni as the university's most important patron. At 10 A.M., Brewster met with the director of the Yale Summer High School, the largest of the university's compensatory-education programs for disadvantaged youth.

Next were two undergraduates from the *Yale Daily News*. Brewster set aside time for the chairman or the managing editor of the student paper once a week, partly to inform them about what the administration was doing and partly to keep himself clued in to the student mood. This week a reporter was also along to grill the former *News* chairman about the possibility of greater student involvement in areas previously reserved for faculty and administration, such as discipline, teaching, and promotions. After the journalists departed, a law student filed in to brief Brewster on the staff reports of the President's Commission on Law Enforcement and Administration of Justice, in preparation for the next commission meeting in Washington. (Brewster served simultaneously on the presidential commissions on crime and on the draft.) Then the chairman of the Geography Department came to discuss plans to merge into a broader department including oceanography, geology, and geophysics. Brewster's assistant for external relations, ex-CIA agent Howard Weaver, talked over plans for the national alumni meeting in Saint Louis, where the hot topic was bound to be all-male Yale's recently announced study of the possibility of merging with all-female Vassar College, bringing at least some kind of coeducation to Yale at last.

After noon, Brewster walked over to Mory's, the famous restaurant-club where oars hung from the ceiling and Yale memorabilia covered the walls, to lunch with a faculty committee searching for a new medical school dean. Brewster's working lunches were usually social occasions as well; as one of his officers observed, even when Brewster tried to diet, his lunch "was nearly always a huge shrimp cocktail with a couple of double martinis."[10] Back in Woodbridge Hall, the president met with his assistant Sam Chauncey and went over the day's mail. Brewster wrote all his own speeches and a surprising amount of his correspondence, particularly the longer letters he typed out in his office or in the Gothic study in the president's house. By the late 1960s, however, the volume of correspondence was such that routine acknowledgments and the like were drafted by staff and sent over to the Kingman Brewster signature machine; Brewster was the first Yale president for whom such a device was necessary. Later in the afternoon, provost Charles Taylor brought over a geologist Yale was trying to seduce away from a western university. "Everybody likes to see the head-waiter," Brewster quipped.

Brewster left his office at the end of the day to give a brief, informal speech to a meeting of senior class officers, describing the administrative machinery of the university, then walked the half mile back to his home on Hillhouse Avenue. Dinner at the president's house usually included Brewster's friends along with his family, and often people from whom Brewster wanted to learn something. As one of his Corporation members observed, the president "didn't really enjoy just sitting around and talking about nothing. Trivia didn't seem to satisfy him. When you were with Kingman, it wasn't long before you were examining some important question and he was asking you your views on it. He had a questing mind."[11] The *Times* reporter, in summing up Brewster's day, concluded that while the university president's job was usually compared with that of a corporate executive, "in fact, it probably involves more intellectual juggling, greater persuasive skills and social consequences of a much higher order."[12]

THE PLAN TO bring Vassar to Yale—"the Vassar flirtation," as it was inevitably referred to in the press—was one of the institutional changes contemplated by Brewster that also had wider potential consequences. Before the mid-1960s, the absence of women from Yale had never really been considered a handicap. Indeed, Yale and other prestigious all-male institutions had once been valued precisely as sanctuaries apart from the distaff side. They were academies for the cultivation of male intellect and leadership qualities, and oases where male friendships could flourish—places where, in the words of an inscription at the Princeton Club of New York, "the women cease to trouble and the wicked are at rest." Yale's residential colleges, with their heavy medieval doors, wooden paneling, dim lighting, and overstuffed leather chairs, exuded the air of exclusive men's clubs.

Although women had been part of Yale's community since 1875, as graduate students or members of the faculty, they were treated as second-class citizens. No woman held the position of full professor on the Yale College faculty before 1961. The University Health Service had no gynecologist. Women's access to the Payne Whitney gymnasium was severely restricted, lest they end up in the parts of the gym where males walked around in the buff. (A group of women getting off the elevator on the wrong floor once came face-to-face with a nude Mayor Lee, on his way to his daily massage.) Women were denied membership in Mory's, the unofficial faculty club, and were allowed in only at certain times (and usually only in the private dining room, on the second floor). This restriction made it difficult for Yale's few women administrators and faculty members to participate in university business conducted at the club.

Undergraduates and faculty alike had opposed coeducation. When women graduate students were finally admitted to the luxurious Linonia and Brothers Room in the Sterling Memorial Library in the fall of 1963, undergraduates complained that they would be unable to concentrate in the presence of a feminine form. Professors asked that the room's comfortable chairs be replaced with austere wooden furniture to prevent fornication.[13] As one undergraduate commented, "If you allow girls here during the week, they will begin to feel they have a prescriptive right to be here, a feeling that they are equal—and this will lead to destructive integration, the destruction of Yale grades and male independence."[14]

One of Brewster's acquaintances remembered that shortly after the future president had been named provost, he said that the only basis on which the Corporation would agree to admit women undergraduates would be "if an angel appeared with $50 million dollars and it could be established that this money would not be given to the university for any other purpose."[15] Obviously, it was difficult for Kingman Brewster and other men in his circle to consider the exclusion of women from places like Yale an injustice comparable to discrimination against (male) Jews or blacks. The subject was too close to home: Mary Louise Phillips had left Vassar midway through her junior year to marry Brewster, and she never returned to complete her degree. Brewster regarded this as something less than a tragedy. "If I can't offer her as much as Vassar," he joked to Whit Griswold shortly after his wedding, "what the hell good am I?"[16]

For Brewster and his peers, as for most Americans in the 1950s and 1960s, women's primary roles were as wives and mothers. Because higher education for women was often considered akin to icing on the cake and because the notion that women should occupy positions of power and responsibility in society had little currency, Brewster could be flippant about coeducation, a pose he never would have dreamed of taking toward civil rights. But then, as Brewster's assistant Elga Wasserman remarked, Brewster never felt guilty about women the way he did about blacks.[17] One undergraduate remembered Brewster referring to women in a speech as "attractive nuisances."[18] In a similar vein, a Ford Foundation staffer recalled McGeorge Bundy, addressing a predominantly female audience, setting their teeth on edge with the same sort of ingrained, unconscious sexism.

On the other hand, Brewster had grown up around strong, accomplished women like his mother and her friends, including the social activist Evelyn Preston Baldwin and the civil rights crusader Judge Dorothy Kenyon. Brewster's mother adamantly believed that "the great company of scholars" was "made up of both men and women from all areas of the world," and all evidence suggests that her son agreed.[19] Wasserman, the woman in the Yale administration who had the most contact with Brewster, felt that while his social interactions with women were colored by old-fashioned chivalry, he had no problem entrusting women with power.

Further, Brewster and other Yale administrators began to wonder whether the enforced separation of the sexes was healthy. Brewster often said that he thought coeducation had been unnecessary for students' moral development in the era when he was an undergraduate—although a skeptic might point out that the gang rape of a prostitute in the Chi Psi fraternity house in 1940 was a running public joke during those years.[20] But he realized that Yale's social life was, in his words, "quite abnormal, because it is concentrated in a rather frenetic focus on the weekends, very largely populated by strangers through the barbaric device of the mixer. This has long been, I think, a fundamentally crude and degrading form of social activity during the ages of seventeen to twenty-one."[21]

Most important, Brewster had a keenly developed sense of fairness. He recognized that "there is a dramatic shortage of first-rate university colleges for women."[22] He also was well aware that even in nominally coeducational institutions like Cornell, the University of Michigan, Duke, and Stanford, places for women were far fewer than those for men, and the competition for those places more severe.[23] As Bernice Sandler of the Women's Equity Action League later would testify before Congress, "Girls need far higher grades for admission to many institutions. Numerous studies have shown that between 75 and 95 percent of the well-qualified students that do not go on to college are women."[24]

Moreover, as Brewster knew, institutions like Yale acted as gatekeepers to the professions and were part of the old-boy network of personal contacts among male leaders. Culturally and symbolically, Yale helped to define the college experience as primarily male—at public universities, for instance, men were called "college students" and women were frequently referred to as "coeds." Yale and other prestigious all-male institutions and traditions—such as Rhodes scholarships, gentlemen's clubs, and stag dinners at the White House—also served to define excellence and leadership in male terms. As long as the nation's power structure was all-male, women and their concerns would not be taken seriously. As the *New York Post* columnist Jimmy Cannon put it more crudely, "What makes a dumb broad smart all of a sudden? They don't even let broads in a joint like Yale."[25] The sense that the exclusion of women from the opportunities Yale offered was simply unfair weighed more heavily on Brewster as the 1960s progressed.

Faculty and undergraduate opinion also started to change as Yale's single-sex status became a disadvantage in recruiting professors from outside Yale and the Northeast. The sociology professor Kai Erikson, a Californian, found Yale's all-maleness "strange beyond all imagining. I didn't like it. . . . I thought it was very peculiar. I had never met people who had gone to single-sex schools. It's an odd idea in the West."[26]

By the mid-1960s, more students declared themselves in favor of coeducation than opposed to it. Public school graduates, by then, outnumbered private school graduates at Yale, although preppies continued to set the tone on campus. While most of the latter considered single-sex education to be the norm, the former, accustomed to studying and socializing with women, increasingly thought Yale's monosexuality to be aberrant. One admissions official confirmed that "virtually every candidate who turns Yale down goes to a coed school—we are hard put to defend our monastic atmosphere."[27] Likewise, football coach Carmen Cozza and other athletic heads were losing their most coveted recruits to coeducational institutions.[28] The absence of women not only hurt Yale's admissions but was increasingly resented by the students that Yale did attract. Even prep school graduates were annoyed by Yale's lack of a nearby coordinate women's college, such as Radcliffe to Harvard or Pembroke to Brown.

Most students favoring coeducation wanted richer social lives, but many also said that the separation of their intellectual and social lives was unhealthy and that they wanted to get to know women outside of weekend activities. In the spring of 1966, the *Yale Daily News* ran a series of statements on coeducation from about twenty educators and eminences, most in favor. McGeorge Bundy told the *News* that coeducation "works and the smart people want it. It's nothing but a dull question of money."[29] Students told various polls that women would make classes more interesting, provide a more natural social environment, and would not seriously distract men from their studies.[30] Sexual mores were changing—even before counterculture sentiment set in. The civil rights movement offered a precedent for rethinking social arrangements as well.

The national tide was also turning against single-sex education. By 1976, men's and women's colleges would represent only four and five percent of the total, respectively.[31] Almost half the nation's 268 single-sex colleges for women would become coeducational or close their doors between 1960 and 1972, and an increasing number of preparatory schools abandoned single-sex education.[32] Internationally, it was the same story. In 1965, New College announced that it would become the first male college at Oxford to admit women.[33] Coeducation was the norm in the Australian and Japanese universities that Brewster visited in the mid-1960s. Sam Chauncey emphasized that one of the forces driving Brewster toward coeducation was "the pragmatic reason: the snowball was rolling, and there was not a hell of a good way to stop it."[34]

In December 1966, Julius Stratton—Vassar trustee, Brewster's friend from the Friday Evening Club, and chairman of the Ford Foundation board under McGeorge Bundy—invited Brewster and Vassar president Alan Simpson to dinner at his Manhattan apartment. After dinner, according to one account, Stratton "turned to his two guests, saying, 'Kingman, you want to introduce women to Yale. Alan, you're looking for new dimensions for Vassar. You should have a lot to talk about.'"[35] Stratton then ushered the two presidents into his library and left them alone with a bottle of brandy. Brewster and Simpson had already met several times to discuss the problems of their institutions and the possibilities of alliance, but not until that night did they agree to put the matter to their respective boards.[36] Later that month, the two institutions announced that they had agreed to conduct a joint study to investigate the possibilities of cooperation, including "the desirability and feasibility of relocating Vassar College in New Haven."[37]

The great advantage, as far as Brewster was concerned, was that a coordinate arrangement would bring undergraduate women to Yale without upsetting conservative alumni. Other advantages included the consideration that the move could be financed by Vassar's sale of its holdings in Poughkeepsie, the convenience of having Vassar handle the administration of its students and faculty, and Vassar's $63 million endowment. Institutions and foundations concerned with women's education might be more likely to support Vassar, the oldest and perhaps best known of the women's colleges, than they would a coeducated Yale, or a coordinate women's college created by Yale.[38]

Brewster hoped, too, that coeducation might come to Yale in a way that would be innovative, distinctive, and take account of the difference between the sexes. For this reason, he found the idea of simply admitting women to Yale College and treating them as normal students unappealing, and made him stick to the Vassar merger despite the opposition of his closest advisors. Sam Chauncey recalled that "I wanted straight coeducation. I thought the Vassar thing, frankly, was stupid."[39] At the time, though, the merger announcement was hailed as a bold reform, and satisfied one of the key grievances of an increasingly restive student body on the New Haven campus.

BREWSTER FOUND IT difficult to read the political temperature of under-graduates in the mid-1960s with any precision. There was no unanimity of student opinion even on the war in Vietnam. In late 1966, Robert McNamara was surrounded and forced from his car by protesters at Harvard, some of whom yelled that he was a murderer and a fascist. But nearly three thousand students signed a letter of apology to the defense secretary.[40] A poll that year of one thousand Yale upperclassmen revealed that over sixty percent believed the United States should maintain or increase its commitment to Vietnam. Less than ten percent favored immediate withdrawal.[41]

But Brewster believed that the significant development in the antiwar movement was the increasing activism among the campus leaders. A case in point was Strobe Talbott, of the Class of '68, a serious, intelligent young man who chaired the *Yale Daily News* in 1967. (Later he was Bill Clinton's housemate at Oxford and deputy secretary of state in the Clinton administration.) Talbott was the kind of thoughtful, moderate activist Brewster understood best. Nelson Strowbridge Talbott IV had arrived at Yale from Hotchkiss, following in the path of his father, grandfather, and numerous uncles and cousins. Talbott was related to George Mead, the fallen war-hero friend of Brewster, Vance, and Moore, and Brewster had worked with his father on a proposal for a bipartisan council on American foreign policy during the late 1950s.[42] With his dark hair and regular features, Talbott even looked strikingly like Brewster had at the same age.

Years later, Talbott would remember that the Yale president was "one of the most important teachers that I ever had, even though I never had Brewster in a class." In the midst of "impassioned hostility on all sides of all issues," Brewster "was able to preserve a level of civility that was both a corrective for all the incivility around him and also a real model that we could all study, absorb, and (I'd like to think) apply to many other situations that we encountered later on."[43]

Talbott was among the one hundred student body presidents and news-paper editors from major universities who signed a letter to Lyndon Johnson in late 1966 lamenting the "increasing confusion [surrounding] both our basic purpose and our tactics" in Vietnam. The campus leaders wrote of their "increasing fear that the course now being pursued may lead us irrevocably into a major land war in Asia—a war which many feel could not be won without recourse to nuclear weapons."[44] The letter, striking a tone of moderation and earnest concern, made the front page of the *New York Times*. (It was part of a campaign by the peripatetic youth organizer Allard Lowenstein to build the antiwar movement on the broadest base possible and have it "reflect the mainstream of American students."[45])

About half the signers, including Talbott, were invited to meet with Dean Rusk in Washington in early 1967, a disastrous encounter in which the secretary of state stonewalled the students' request for an explanation of why the war was in the national interest and implied that the U.S. might use nuclear weapons in Vietnam. Harvard student leader Greg Craig said that Rusk "transformed the makeup of the antiwar movement with a single stroke. It was no longer SDS and Port Huron people and Tom Hayden and those folks. It became a mainstream student movement . . . that went straight into the 'dump Johnson' movement."[46] When the student presidents and editors returned to their campuses, Talbott wrote, "the doubts and disaffection with US policy which had brought us to Washington were unrelieved and in many cases intensified."[47]

In the spring of 1967, the *New York Times* columnist James Reston noticed that campus leaders like Talbott had changed: "The Strobe Talbotts at Yale, serious, patriotic, progressive Republican types, might be the first to be expected to respond to General Westmoreland's noble appeal, but they don't. They are not marching in the anti-Vietnam parades, but they are dissenting, and the dissent of this clean-cut, solemn, middle-class crowd of campus leaders may be much more significant than the sign-carrying protesters on the front pages."[48] Talbott agreed that most of the war's opponents at the university were not radicals but "people more of my stripe: people who were clearly doomed to end up in three-piece suits. . . . You know, very Yale, in a way."[49]

BY THE MID-'60S, the increased volume of Vietnam call-ups was having an impact on most young men outside the universities. Full-time students in good standing, however, were deferred even at the peak of troop commitment to Vietnam. The resulting tensions were complex. The Yale SDS leader Mark Zanger later stated bluntly that "I did not belong in college in those years. I was a mess. I was there because otherwise there was this guy named Lyndon Johnson trying to kill me, and college was the best place to hide." The fact that the university was saving students like Zanger from the draft "made us hate it. That was another side of its hypocrisy."[50] Although he opposed Zanger on many matters, Talbott agreed that the student deferment was "morally intolerable because it discriminates along class and income lines. . . . It is wrong to use economic standards to determine who should die in the 'national interest.'"[51]

In March 1967 the National Advisory Commission on Selective Service, of which Brewster was a member, issued its report, recommending elimination of student and occupational deferments, endorsing a random lottery selection, and calling for greater consistency in the local draft boards' decisions to exempt and defer. Brewster and a minority of the commission called for the recognition of selective conscientious objectors—that is, individuals who were against a particular war; they differed from pacifists, who opposed war in any form. In language taken almost verbatim from Brewster's speeches on student dissent, the minority distinguished between "responsible students" caught between their consciences and their sense of duty to country, and "the handful of irresponsible individuals whose opposition to particular wars is simply part of a broader revolt against organized society."[52] Brewster thought the selective conscientious objectors should be excused from combatant service but be required to serve in a nonmilitary capacity. However, the majority outvoted Brewster and his allies in favor of the status quo.

Even the majority's recommendations proved too much for selective service director Hershey and his mainly southern and conservative congressional allies such as Mendell Rivers, chairman of the House Armed Services Committee. Not only did Congress fail to act on the commission's recommendations; it even stood some on their head—by making college undergraduate deferments mandatory, for example. The *New York Times* lamented that Congress was "yielding to the ugly spirit of some of its least enlightened members." Nevertheless, there would be no draft reform for the next several years.[53] When the fact became evident, draft resistance would increase and turn violent.

Anxious to head off an angry response, Brewster and McGeorge Bundy set up a conference, shortly after the release of the commission's report, for the student body presidents who had met so unproductively with Rusk in January. Talbott, Craig, and the other disillusioned campus leaders from around the country met in New York, at a hotel outside Kennedy Airport, to talk with Bundy about the war and with Burke Marshall (who had led the commission on selective service) about the draft. The Ford Foundation picked up the tab. Brewster began by saying that he hoped that a more extended dialogue with Bundy and Marshall might show that people in government made their decisions in good faith based on a coherent logic—although the students might still think the policy makers fools or knaves. Talbott remembered that, in addressing the war, Brewster "was more memorable for the way in which he articulated values, standards, principles, and that kind of thing than he was for taking a clear-cut position on the 'yes' and 'no' of the issue at hand." His presentation had to do with "his sense of place, and his obligation to be a unifying rather than a dividing factor, and to educate us by the way in which he addressed issues."[54] Bundy talked with the students for about three hours. Craig was "surprised at Bundy's gentleness, his willingness to listen to the concerns of all the students. . . . I think in a way the Bundy waspishness was under control because he was performing for his friend Kingman."

Craig felt that Brewster, perhaps naively, believed that the people he liked could work out any problem, no matter how opposed their views. Brewster liked and respected Bundy, "and he was troubled that other people he liked and respected didn't have the same view of McGeorge Bundy that he did." This distaste for conflict was "something that I think was typical of all the people in Brewster's circle. . . . They were uncomfortable when their friends disagreed. They were most comfortable when, as all gentlemen should, they ultimately got to the right answer to the question, and that would be the same one. The application of intelligence, and the same principles and values of life, would result in the right answer—the same answer—to all the tough questions. That was their doctrine."[55]

THE DRAFT CONTINUED to erode the consensus within Yale's faculty as well. In early 1967, some 264 of its members signed a letter to Johnson urging the cessation of the bombing of North Vietnam. When the document was published as an ad in the *New York Times,* it gained major exposure and further irritated many of the university's conservative alumni.[56] Shortly after, Robert Cook, a political activist and assistant professor in the Sociology Department, withheld his class grades, in protest against the use of grades and class standing in the Selective Service System. Cook believed that grading created an "authoritarian" relationship between teachers and students that was "incompatible with real education."[57] While few other faculty members agreed with his stance, all were uncomfortably aware that a failing grade might literally mean the difference between life and death for a student. The draft also affected the disciplinary system. Eli Clark, a law professor and master of one of Yale's residential colleges, remembered giving a one-term suspension to a student, the son of a man he knew, which exposed him to the draft and led to his being sent to Vietnam. "That student was killed, and I have always felt that in some way I was to blame for that."[58]

DEBATES OVER THE war, whether in faculty gatherings or around the dinner table, became sharper, and took a toll on personal relations. In the summer of 1967, Brewster was outraged by an advertisement placed in the *Vineyard Gazette* by well-known local cultural figures, including Jules Feiffer, John Hersey, William Styron, and Yale Drama School dean Robert Brustein. The ad criticized Chilmark summer resident Nicholas Katzenbach, recently appointed undersecretary of state, for his defense of the Gulf of Tonkin resolution before the Senate Foreign Relations Committee.

In response, Brewster wrote a critical letter to the literati. He did not defend his friend Katzenbach's position, but called the ad "bad manners at best" and "an offensive infringement of the long standing ethic of the Vineyard as a place where even a public man's life can be lived quietly."[59] That summer, Brewster and Mac Bundy criticized Brustein over cocktails for breaching long-held (though unwritten) gentlemanly rules of etiquette. Brustein retorted that to keep silent in the face of the war was tantamount to being a "good German."[60] Katzenbach, for his part, avoided the signers and resented the incident for the rest of his life. "I didn't think you did that sort of thing to people," he said. "The individuals who put that ad in the paper were not gentlemen. They purported to be gentlemen."[61]

The resistance to Vietnam was altering many lives. William Sloane Coffin was now a nationally controversial figure, an early member (along with Paul Moore) of the interfaith group that came to be known as Clergy and Laymen Concerned About Vietnam. CALCAV's goals were moderate, calling for negotiations and a halt to the bombing of North Vietnam and advocating neither immediate withdrawal nor civil disobedience. In early 1967 the group sponsored an "education-action mobilization" that brought 2,400 clergy to Washington for a silent demonstration in front of the White House and mostly futile meetings with members of Congress. According to a report, participants received "the general impression that most of the congressmen feel powerless to determine the direction in which the nation will go," having "abdicated that responsibility when they passed the Gulf of

Tonkin Resolution."[62] Coffin decided, in retrospect, that "it was the passivity of Congress as much as anything else that pushed me and many like me toward civil disobedience."[63]

Coffin and Moore, among others, later addressed a CALCAV gathering in Washington at the New York Avenue Presbyterian Church. Coffin would recall that the attendees were "deeply moved just to be jammed against one another in the pews, an experience of solidarity which contrasted so sharply with others we had shared. . . . Now instead of feeling alone and isolated, we were all together in the church."[64] Before returning to New Haven, Coffin and six other CALCAV representatives met with Secretary of Defense Robert McNamara, who assured them that he "understood" their unhappiness and was trying to exercise restraint in the war's conduct and resist pressures for escalation. As much as he disagreed with McNamara, the Yale chaplain was disconcerted to find him to be a fundamentally decent man. He reflected afterward that "it was a dangerous world when so much evil could be done by a man who was really 'a nice guy.'"[65]

Coffin returned to Washington a month later to speak at a conference on civil disobedience, which he considered a justified reaction to public unresponsiveness. College and university presidents, he claimed, "are always saying, 'We are ready to reason, but we will not knuckle under to pressure,' [but] they generally prove far more responsive to pressure than invitations to reason. . . . [W]hile no one has the right to break the law, every man upon occasion has the duty to do so. I think the war is such an occasion." Coffin proposed that seminarians and young members of the clergy should surrender their draft exemptions and declare themselves conscientious objectors, while the older clergy should counsel, aid, and abet draft resisters and so become subject to the penalties of the Selective Service Act.[66]

The backlash at Yale was huge. One member of the Class of '48 wrote to demand, "How long must we, as Yale alumni, be subjected to treasonable suggestions by such as Mr. Coffin, Mr. Lynd, and the like, in the guise of academic freedom? How long is Yale, under the leadership of Kingman Brewster, going to sit idly by, and with its silence repudiate the greatness of men like Nathan Hale?"[67] Coffin resisted the urge to write back that Yale's Revolutionary War spy was hanged as a traitor. He did respond to the alumni that "if there is such a thing as a just war, then there is such a thing as an unjust war; and whether just or unjust is finally a matter of individual conscience."[68]

Brewster told the alumni that Coffin was not calling for students to resist the draft. He knew from his son Kingman III, who was a conscientious objector and a friend of Coffin's, that the chaplain actually bent over backward not to pressure students into draft resistance.[69] Coffin emphasized that "the last thing in the world I would ever tell you to do is turn in your draft card. That's such an eminently personal decision that you have to make it yourself."[70]

In addition, Brewster pointed out, Coffin's Washington exhortation was addressed to individuals sheltered from service by age or exemption. As Brewster saw it, the chaplain was not urging others to flout the law but asking those with a conscientious objection to the war "to stand up and be counted as men should, taking the full consequences which the law provides." But Brewster strongly disagreed with Coffin's belief that civil disobedience was a legitimate way to call attention to a problem. Like most of Coffin's critics, he preferred orderly change to the disorderly variety: Brewster felt that conscientious noncompliance with the law was justifiable only when the law was obviously questionable on constitutional grounds, such as the Jim Crow segregation laws in the South. But he agreed with Coffin that national unhappiness over the Vietnam War "faces the present student generation with a tension between duty to conscience and duty to country which goes to the depths of moral judgment."[71]

Religious critiques of Vietnam, such as Coffin's, troubled the conscience of Cyrus Vance. In May 1967 the deputy secretary of defense delivered one of his longest and most considered statements on the war, to the convention of the Episcopal Diocese of West Virginia—a group he wanted to address because of his West Virginia and Episcopalian background. Not long before, General William C. Westmoreland had remarked that dissent on Vietnam undercut the American cause, prompting one thousand divinity students from twelve eastern seminaries to write to McNamara, Vance's boss. They criticized Westmoreland's position and stated that many divinity students "cannot support the war in Vietnam because they believe this war is neither in the religious tradition of just wars nor in the national interest."[72]

Vance was particularly uncomfortable with moral arguments against the people who waged the war. He later stressed that when civilians in the Pentagon first became disaffected with the bombing policy, "there were honest differences of opinion . . . [T]here weren't evil men and good men—there were men with differing views as to what the best way was to try and bring the war to a conclusion."[73] He tried to cool the students' anger by defending their right to express their views, but he also said that the dialogue on Vietnam had become "heated and intolerant." Both supporters and opponents, he believed, were hewing to lines that were too sharply drawn. "Vietnam has been viewed too often in absolutes of black and white," he told the assembled Episcopalians. "There are gray tones. The issues are complex and sometimes ambiguous."

Vance conceded that political affairs in South Vietnam were turbulent, that the Vietnamese armed forces were often ineffective, that the United States had inflicted civilian casualties in both South and North Vietnam, and—in what amounted to a significant admission—that the war in the South was in some measure a civil war. But he argued that U.S. objectives in Vietnam were limited, that American forces were using restraint, and that Hanoi had run the insurgency in the South even before the United States intervened. In a complex and interdependent world, he concluded, "the national interest of the United States is international. Our role of leadership is inescapable. We cannot fulfill a meaningful destiny as an affluent but passive witness to great principles in contest."[74]

Still, Vance conceded that the war was not going well. By the start of 1967, more than six thousand U.S. soldiers had been killed. Bombing had failed to halt the North Vietnamese flow of troops and matériel to the south. And the public was beginning to turn against the war. Some of Vance's friends were writing with increasingly sharp criticisms. "Are we really reduced," wrote one, "to acceptance of our prime national goal as the killing of the miserable inhabitants of a miserable little country attached to the flank of China? Must we accept the pouring out of our youth and national treasure into a rat hole we have not subdued in three years of war?"[75]

Along with McNamara, Vance was quietly looking for an exit strategy— opposing the military's requests for additional troops, calling for a halt to the bombing of North Vietnam, and pursuing a variety of peace explorations. Upper-level State and Pentagon officials opposed to the hawkish counsels of Rusk and Walt Rostow (McGeorge Bundy's successor as national security advisor) met for secret strategy sessions on Vietnam. Undersecretary of State Nicholas Katzenbach referred to it as "the only secret I know in government." The "nongroup," as it was called, used their "nonmeetings" on Thursday evenings in Katzenbach's office to voice doubts about the direction of the war that could not be expressed openly around Johnson and his tightening inner circle.[76] The "nonmembers" included Vance, Katzenbach, Bill Bundy, Averell Harriman, defense counsel and Brewster classmate Paul Warnke, and Pentagon civilian staffer John McNaughton, Brewster's former colleague at the Harvard Law School.

McNaughton crystallized the discontent furtively expressed in these meetings when he wrote in 1967 that "a feeling is widely and strongly held that the 'Establishment' is out of its mind. The feeling is that we are try-ing to impose some US image on distant peoples we cannot understand (any more than we can the younger generation here at home)." For McNaughton, "the increased polarization" caused by the war signaled "the worst split in our people in more than a century." He lamented that McGeorge Bundy, George Ball, and Bill Moyers, all of whom had at least been able to ask the hard and necessary questions about the U.S. commit-ment in Vietnam, had resigned. "Who next?" he wondered.[77]

As it turned out, Vance would be next. He had requested to leave in 1966, but McNamara asked him to stay on until the summer of 1967. His reasons for going were partly related to disillusion with the war and partly to his health and finances. In 1962, Vance had ruptured a spinal disk; four years later he tore cartilage in his knee, which eventually put pressure on his spinal column and caused another disk to rupture. He ended up in the hospital again in February and March of 1967. Vance also had five children approaching college age, and having depleted his savings after six and a half years in government service, "I simply had to get back out and earn some money."[78]

The praise given to Vance on his departure was unusually heartfelt. Joseph Alsop wrote that "in more than three decades of public experience, I have seldom seen a public servant work so well and so selflessly."[79] "In our materialistic times," wrote one of Vance's assistants, "it is exceptionally rare to encounter men who obviously want nothing for themselves and fight for causes rather than personal advancement. . . . The word aristocratic is a most antiquated, very old-fashioned term, but it clearly and fortunately still holds a deep meaning for you."[80]

Vance left on good terms with Lyndon Johnson. The president had always seen him as a "Johnson man," and the defense deputy came from the Wall Street lawyer wing of the establishment that Johnson was most comfortable with. Califano remembered that "Johnson understood the establishment world; he'd get annoyed at it frequently, but he understood it. He could wheel and deal with Eddie Weisl and Cy Vance and Arthur Krim and whoever. It wasn't the world of Texas, but Johnson was really a Washingtonian. Christ, he'd lived there for thirty-five years by the time he became president."[81] As Vance departed, Johnson awarded him the Presi-dential Medal of Freedom, the nation's highest civilian honor, declaring, "He has always placed his country before himself." Although Vance would return to his law firm in New York, Johnson continued to call on him for a variety of assignments. He would be neither in the government nor fully out of it.

MCGEORGE BUNDY OCCUPIED a similar ambiguous position. Bundy spent his first six months in the Ford Foundation presidency immersed in the job. He saw Lyndon Johnson "only a few times. . . . My only relation to the White House now," he insisted to a reporter, "is that I know a number of phone numbers."[82] However, the White House still thought of Bundy as being on tap, even for particular positions. In early December 1966, for example, he was under consideration as ambassador to South Vietnam, to succeed Henry Cabot Lodge.[83] Bundy also continued to advise Johnson on the course of the Vietnam War.

Later in December, Johnson summoned Bundy to the White House and asked him to "explore the possibilities of establishing a permanent forum for the exchange of management knowledge with the Soviet Union and all other advanced societies."[84] The project that Bundy led for the next several years resulted in the creation of the International Institute for Applied Systems Analysis (IIASA), in which social scientists, engineers, and technicians from East and West worked together on their shared problems, ranging from urban planning to transportation to pollution.

The fame of the systems analysis approach that McNamara and Vance had pioneered in the Pentagon had spread worldwide. Francis Bator, Bundy's former assistant who had persuaded Johnson to make the appointment, wrote the president that "there is great demand—in Russia and Yugoslavia as well as the UK and Germany—for the new techniques of management designed to cope with these problems."[85] Bundy became a roving ambassador, meeting with Western and Eastern bloc diplomats, academics, and business leaders. In May and June of 1967, he visited London, Paris, Bonn, and Rome, and made a special visit to Moscow with his former assistant Carl Kaysen, who by then was director of the Institute for Advanced Study in Princeton.

When the Six Day War erupted in the Middle East, in June 1967, Bundy actually went back, briefly, to his old job in the White House. The government was "terribly overloaded, especially with Vietnam," Bator recalled. The Israeli–Arab war threatened to embroil the nations' respective patrons, the United States and the Soviet Union, in a larger war that could go nuclear. Bundy returned to Washington for about three weeks, reestablished working relations with Johnson, and helped pull the government together. "No one else conceivably could have done that," Bator emphasized. "For Mac it was not only a matter of ability but also the fact he had done that job for a very long time, and so there was nothing new about his being around."[86] Because Bundy's continuing involvement in the Johnson administration, however, was conditional on his demonstrated loyalty to the president, he was obliged, in his public speeches, to support the war in Vietnam more loudly and more often than he likely would have otherwise. His position would eventually cause him difficulties within the foundation and affect his public image.

Bundy's more immediate concern, however, was the Mayor's Decentralization Advisory Panel, which he had led since April in an examination of ways to make the New York City school system more accountable. Bundy insisted that he was on the panel as a private individual and not as president of the Ford Foundation, but here, too, his status was ambiguous. Ford gave financial aid to the panel, Bundy's lieutenant Mario Fantini headed the staff, and clearly many of the interested parties were hoping that some of Ford's $3 billion endowment might support whatever arrangements came out of the panel's work.

Contrary to later accusations, Bundy seems not to have gone into the study with many preconceptions, let alone a precooked plan for handing power over the schools to the black community. Richard Magat, a Ford officer delegated to help with the work of the panel, pointed out that "Bundy knew very, very little about the New York City schools" when he began the project, and in fact had no direct experience of public schools either as student or parent (he sent his four sons to Groton). "He didn't know too much about New York City, for that matter. But . . . he was a very quick study, and it was a great learning experience for him."[87]

Bundy educated himself by delving deeply into the problems plaguing the schools and by considering the implications of various models for reorganization. Mostly he learned by talking to representatives from every group that might conceivably be affected by decentralization, particularly the teachers' union, the Board of Education, and various community groups. Aware from the start that decentralization was likely to raise tensions between minorities in ghetto communities and the ninety percent white, predominantly Jewish teachers' union, Bundy rather enjoyed the high-wire aspect of it all. He felt that he could find an acceptable middle ground. In any case, minority militants were already on a collision course with the teachers' union and the Board of Education, so inaction seemed the worst option.

Unfortunately, Bundy had no more success than Lindsay in persuading the city's power brokers and entrenched interests to follow a course of enlightened reform. The teachers' union (the United Federation of Teachers) and school administrators resisted his panel at every turn. As Bundy penetrated deeper into the bureaucracy, school officials' intransigence increased. Things heated up further when the president of the Assistant Principals Association told Bundy that she would not accept any community participation in education, in any form. "Bundy turned white when he heard this," Magat recalled. "I think he finally realized that the supervisors weren't serious, that the system would not reform itself, and that some outside impetus was needed."[88] Magat observed that while Bundy initially believed that the people at the top knew best, after a while he concluded that "the people who were running the system were not people of good will." It was "kind of a '60s discovery, in a way."[89]

Even while Bundy was in the midst of rethinking the school system, events were outflanking his plans. In April 1967 the Board of Education, anxious to bring an end to the demonstrations against it, announced that it would "experiment with varying forms of decentralization and community involvement in several experimental districts of varying size."[90] With very little forethought, the board established three "demonstration" districts in poor minority areas in Harlem, Manhattan's Lower East Side, and Ocean Hill–Brownsville, setting the stage for disaster. (The board's failure to approve a fourth district, in the racially integrated Upper West Side of Manhattan, contributed to the public image of decentralization as black-only.)

The Bundy panel's report, issued in the fall, was a moderate plan that aimed to meet some of the demands of community advocates while reassuring union and school officials that the reforms would safeguard teachers and retain central oversight. Unsurprisingly, the community control forces attacked it for being too conservative, while school and union officials condemned its radicalism.

Having put the decentralization plan together, Bundy submitted it without thinking much about how to get it accepted politically. In a sense, it wasn't his job to do so, or the foundation's role, any more than the Carnegie Foundation had done political follow-up after it supported the publication of Gunnar Myrdal's *An American Dilemma*. But his inaction reflected what Magat saw as both the foundation's lack of political clout and its parochial view that "we deliver the truth and others will be wise enough to follow." Further, while Lindsay supported the panel's recommendations, Magat thought the mayor's staff was "scared of the whole thing": "a lot of people around him just thought it was a no-win situation."[91] Lindsay removed key aspects of the plan, such as its inclusion of high schools in the decentralization process and its call for parents-only board elections, and sent it on to the legislature.

As the Bundy-Lindsay plan (as it then became known) moved through the legislature, it would become hostage to the conduct of the three demonstration districts, which began to career out of control almost as soon as they were created. Because Bundy chaired the decentralization panel and the Ford Foundation supported the demonstration districts with small grants, the districts would be portrayed as the joint creations of Ford and black militants. But they had been established before the Bundy panel had even held its first meeting.

The image would gain credence from the fact that Ford was supporting other programs aimed at improving the situation of black Americans. Bundy had doubled the foundation's spending on black issues, to $40 million during his first two years in office. One of his most controversial donations was a $175,000 grant, in July 1967, to the Cleveland chapter of the Congress of Racial Equality for support of voter registration and community organization. CORE had transformed itself into a Black Power outfit after the splintering of the civil rights movement in 1966, purging its membership of whites and removing multiracial concerns from its social agenda. (Its national leader, Floyd McKissick, declared nonviolence "a dying philosophy," while CORE's Brooklyn chapter leader, Sonny Carson, made racist threats against white teachers in Bedford-Stuyvesant.[92])

Still, Bundy thought that enfranchising blacks in the political process was beneficial no matter who ran the registration effort. The fact that CORE's drive likely would mobilize black support exclusively for Carl B. Stokes, a black candidate opposing Seth Taft (of the Yale Tafts), was an equally positive development, however much it might upset the city's political establishment. One of Ford's officers on the scene concluded that the Stokes campaign was part of what kept Cleveland cool that summer.[93] Stokes won the election, becoming the first black mayor of a major American city. "Motherhood, boy scouts, voter registration," Bundy joked with reporters, "everyone's for it, as an alternative to rocks and fire bombs."[94] Taft, the losing candidate, wrote later that "I chose not to conclude that the Ford Foundation had provided the margin of difference in the election . . .

in good part because at the time what the Foundation did produce was such a reaction in the white community that its efforts were pretty well offset. If that is true, one could fairly conclude that on the whole the community benefited by more people being registered and interested in government."[95] However, Ford's critics were far less generous, and castigated what they saw as Bundy's partisanship and his support of black-nationalist groups like CORE.

Bundy declared that Ford had made the decision to give money to CORE's Cleveland project "on the merits, not on the question whether other actions or statements from other members of CORE are 'too controversial.' . . . The national officers of CORE have dealt with us on this matter in a businesslike way, and neither Mr. Floyd McKissick nor I supposes that this grant requires the two of us—or our organizations—to agree on all public questions."[96] Or, as Henry Ford II more laconically expressed it, "If you're going to work in civil rights, you can't stop at Roy Wilkins and Whitney Young."[97]

PAUL MOORE HAD long experience working with civil rights leaders outside the mainstream. Ever since becoming bishop of Washington, Moore had been critical of the city's power structure and what he considered its lack of will to eliminate poverty and enforce proper police treatment of juvenile delinquents. More important, however, was the need for home rule for the city, which was run (and chronically underfunded) by Congress. Moore believed that District of Columbia residents' interests "in better schools, more affordable housing, sufficient welfare benefits, and a police department more sensitive to race all depended on their being able to elect their own officials, who in turn would direct tax revenues toward their needs."[98] It was a view that had many parallels with arguments being put forward for community control in New York.

While the case for self-government made intuitive sense, its success would depend on the black community's electing the sort of moderate, responsible leaders who were in short supply in the ghettos. More typical was Marion Barry, an undeniably intelligent, charismatic Washington civil rights leader who would eventually run the city into the ground when he was elected mayor in the 1980s. Moore remembered that Barry in the 1960s, when he was head of the local chapter of the Student Nonviolent Coordinating Committee (SNCC) and of the PRIDE antipoverty program in the District of Columbia, "was something of a rough diamond. He did not adopt the dress or manners of the black bourgeoisie that liberals were accustomed to dealing with. Rather, he talked and dressed like the poor black people he served."[99] Barry and leaders like him helped widen the split in the civil rights movement between whites and blacks and also between middle-class and lower-class blacks.

Moore and Barry became cochairmen of the Free D.C. movement, which advocated home rule and campaigned against the U.S. government and the District of Columbia Board of Trade, which lobbied the government to keep taxes (and therefore public spending) at low levels. The movement started a boycott of stores that were members of the Board of Trade. Some of the canvassers, many of them young members of PRIDE, demanded that merchants contribute to the Free D.C. movement as well as sever ties to the Board of Trade. Moore recognized that "this sort of shakedown was illegal," but the *Washington Star* nonetheless editorialized: "Bishop Moore blackmails merchants."[100] An angry backlash came forth from many Episcopalian clergy and laity in Washington. One parish announced that it was halving its financial contribution to the diocese, and Moore narrowly escaped censure at a meeting of parish wardens.[101] Still, Moore believed that part of his vocation "was to be a steward of power, to use my office to empower those who were too weak to achieve the modest goals of economic and political justice."[102] He felt that the Free D.C. movement, excesses and all, at least represented a positive channeling of unfocused black anger into the political process. As his friend McGeorge Bundy acknowledged, there was truth to the cliché that "picketing is better than rioting."[103]

Vance could testify to the violent consequences that followed when blacks did not become enfranchised in the American process: he saw them in the dreadful riots that summer in Detroit, at that time the county's fifth-largest city. Vance had left the government in late June, but on July 24, Vance received a phone call from McNamara, who said that Johnson wanted Vance to be his personal representative in Detroit, where violence had broken out the day before. What would become the worst American riot in a century began when police raided an illegal after-hours club, setting off hundreds of blacks who burned and looted across fourteen square miles of ghetto. The massive riot that had broken out two weeks earlier in Newark, New Jersey, had also started with a clash between blacks and white police officers, just as the riot in Watts, a section of Los Angeles, had two years earlier. Johnson's aide Califano recalled that Detroit presented an "incredibly complicated political situation," since Michigan's liberal

Republican governor, George Romney, was considered a likely candidate in the 1968 presidential race.

"Romney wanted the guard to be federalized," Califano remembered, "but he would not declare that he couldn't control the situation, and we didn't want to commit troops until we got the declaration. . . . [W]e needed somebody we could totally trust, who had enormous discretion, and who was bright enough and tough enough to deal with Romney. I thought Vance was perfect for that role."[104] Vance—"secretly pleased," his wife thought—agreed to the mission after securing permission to bring his wife along to help with his shoes and socks, since his back was still too painful to allow him to bend over. "Nothing like being out of government," Grace Vance somewhat acidly wrote to her daughter.[105]

As Vance and his wife flew into an airfield outside Detroit, enormous troop carriers were landing and disgorging men and vehicles. Huge fires were blazing across the city, and smoke drifted across the sky. Vance had arrived during a lull in the riot, and when he and Army general John Throckmorton toured the city, they saw no looting and heard no sniping. Although Governor Romney and Detroit mayor Jerome Cavanaugh wanted troops sent immediately, "we felt the evidence did not sustain their request," Throckmorton wrote.[106] Vance knew that the National Guard could do more harm than good, since guardsmen were virtually all white (only 1.15 percent were black) and poorly trained for riot control.[107] "I believed it was not wise or prudent to commit Federal troops until we saw whether or not the local and State authorities could handle the situation," Vance told a press conference a few days later. "I thought it might inflame the situation rather than quiet it down." Having been through similar crises in the South and the Dominican Republic, he knew that "over-commitment of force tends to produce a counter result."[108] By nightfall, however, the incident rate was rising—60 at 7 P.M., 85 at 9 P.M., 124 at 11 P.M.—and the sheer nihilism of the violence demanded a response. Vance recommended to Johnson that federal troops be deployed in the city and that the National Guard be federalized.[109] The president was extremely reluctant and challenged Vance's assessment of the situation, but Vance insisted. He told Johnson that there was no time to drop leaflets on the mob urging them to disperse before troops were sent in.[110]

The Detroit riot caused widespread devastation and left behind a smoking wreck of a city: 43 people dead, 7,000 arrests, 1,300 buildings destroyed, and 2,700 businesses looted. The riot might have gone on longer if Vance and General Throckmorton had not persuaded the National Guard to unbarricade the Twelfth Street thoroughfare. Both men courageously walked bareheaded down the middle of the street for several blocks to convince people that sniper fire was no longer a threat.[111] Afterward, Vance wrote to McNamara that "from start to finish, our basic approach was to apply the minimum amount of force required to achieve the objective."[112] Vance's report on the crisis became the "black book" standard guide for handling urban riots with the least possible bloodshed.

The Detroit riot was the worst of many outbreaks of urban violence in 1967: 164 racial disorders occurred in the first nine months of the year.[113] New Haven was not immune from the virus of unrest. State police had to be called in after fires and looting broke out in the mainly black and Hispanic neighborhood known as the Hill, bordering the Yale Medical School. The disturbance, which began after the white proprietor of a small restaurant shot a Puerto Rican customer, lasted for five nights. No one was killed, but police arrested 621 people, while rioters ransacked 63 businesses (including half of the city's liquor stores), racking up over a million dollars in damages.[114]

There was little agreement on the meaning of the riots, if any. One of New Haven's black radicals declared that "this was a rebellion against the white man, a rebellion which started 400 years ago. The only way to get action from the white man is to kill him. This was just a little scratch on the surface."[115] To many white liberals, the riot was evidence that "the political structure has not been in contact with neighborhood people," as one Yale Divinity School student put it. "The clergy hasn't been in touch with the reality of poverty."[116] But to many other observers, the New Haven riots demonstrated the limits of even the best antipoverty programs and were a black eye for Mayor Lee's administration and New Haven's renowned program Community Progress, Inc., which had once been run by Lindsay's Human Resources Administration director, Mitchell Sviridoff. (Days before the riot, Sviridoff had announced his resignation from the Lindsay administration to become McGeorge Bundy's vice president for national affairs at the Ford Foundation.[117])

The limits of liberal efforts to reach out to ghetto blacks were also evident in Yale's Upward Bound program, which attempted to remedy the educational shortcomings of impoverished New Haven children and help send them to college. The participants ended the 1967 summer session by destroying every article of furniture in the common rooms of the Yale residential colleges where they were taught. John Hersey, one of the official sponsors of the project, wrote that its organizers "recognized that there were serious risks, both material and human, involved in it, particularly inasmuch as the program was to deal with hard-core cases rather than docile and already motivated young people." Hersey speculated that the damage to Yale "will have served some of us in the university a glancing education in the desperation which vented itself, alas, in recent days."[118] Some whites concluded that more assistance to blacks was necessary, but others felt that the lesson was to stop throwing good money after bad.

Vance was on the side of doing more. After the Detroit riots were brought under control, he returned to Washington to meet with Johnson and the newly appointed members of the National Advisory Commission on Civil Disorders. According to Califano, the president had established the commission to preempt congressional investigation into the Newark and Detroit riots, which would give the left an opportunity to criticize Johnson for not having done enough for black communities and the right a chance to condemn him for having done too much. Johnson "wanted this commission to help whites understand the plight of black ghetto dwellers and help assure blacks that he was working to alleviate their plight."[119]

Although the group was nominally chaired by Illinois governor Otto Kerner, its moving force would be vice chairman John Lindsay, who had managed to keep New York City cool for a second summer. Other members included Senator Edward Brooke, Richardson's political ally in Massachusetts, and Roy Wilkins, executive director of the NAACP. Vance briefed the commission on his experiences in Detroit, and exchanged congratulations with Lindsay, a friend he saw every few years at Scroll and Key reunions. Vance then appeared at a press conference with Califano and described the carnage in Detroit. "At the root of this shattering disturbance," he told the media, "lie problems of enormous magnitude. These problems will require thoughtful analysis, contemplation, and action."[120]

Kingman Brewster had already contemplated some of the broader ideas of law and order through his service on the President's Commission on Law Enforcement and Administration of Justice, headed by Nicholas Katzenbach, which had produced its report earlier in 1967. *The Challenge of Crime in a Free Society* was largely an operational report, with two hundred specific recommendations, some of which led to the creation of the 911 emergency number and a more systematic structure for recording crimes nationally. The commission called for new ways of dealing with offenders, increased attention to eliminating unfairness in the justice system, better personnel at all levels, and more use of the techniques of social science in researching and administering justice. But the thrust of the report was that politicians' demands for law and order would be of no avail without "assuring all Americans a stake in the benefits and responsibilities of American life."[121] As Moore said in one of his sermons, "Violence springs from the inequality of justice. . . . The unanimity of the Crime Commission on the causes of crime underscores what a few voices have been saying, that the ultimate answer to violence is not more stringent police power, but the eradication of the roots of violence in poverty and frustration."[122]

ELLIOT RICHARDSON WAS one of the more interested readers of the crime commission's report. By 1967 he had become attorney general of Massachusetts, the winner of a wrenching election the previous year. He could easily have remained lieutenant governor, which would have kept him on the succession track for the governorship, but the Republicans wanted him to run for the attorney general position, which Richardson himself found appealing. Henry Shattuck, then in his late eighties, advised his nephew that he should strive for the "position [which] would give you, in [Harvard] President Charles W. Eliot's words, more 'durable satisfaction.'"[123]

Richardson opted for the attorney general contest, and was comfortably ahead with five days left before the election when he was given documents showing that his Democratic opponent, Francis X. Bellotti, had received a $6,000 annual retainer from an out-of-state insurance company while holding public office. Richardson's campaign staff begged him not to go public with the documents, knowing that to do so would look like a last-minute, unanswerable charge that would be perceived as a Yankee patrician attacking an Italian-American. But his assistant Jonathan Moore remembered that Richardson "felt that it couldn't be kept from the public. Saying nothing would be failing to disclose something he felt the electorate deserved to know. He knew it would cost him votes, and it did."[124]

Richardson's sizable lead evaporated, and he eked out a victory while the rest of the Republican ticket won with huge margins. The next day, the journalist Christopher Lydon wrote, "when Richardson took his place at the giant round table of the downtown Tavern Club in Boston, the son of Webster Thayer, the Massachusetts judge in the notorious Sacco-Vanzetti trial of 1921, upbraided Richardson for using tactics against an Italian-American that he would never have considered against a member of their own class."[125] But Richardson felt he had done the right thing, and his gamble that he could throw away perhaps half a million votes and still pull out a victory thrilled him as only combat in World War II had.

As attorney general, Richardson used the crime commission report as a blueprint for some of his own initiatives, including the creation of a special unit to deal with a rash of gangland slayings in Boston connected to organized crime. (In taking on the mob, Richardson also persuaded the state legislature to pass wiretapping measures that had been deemed too controversial to include in the commission's report, as well as a witness immunity bill.) He was particularly enthusiastic about "the role visualized by the National Crime Commission for the 'community service officers' who, under the Commission's recommendation, would operate out of storefront headquarters in slum areas."[126]

More generally, Richardson shared a concern for the underlying causes of crime and a belief that social science allied to popular resolve could do something about them. "Crime, juvenile delinquency, structural unemployment, bad housing, racial discrimination, the urban ghetto—these are deeply disturbing and stubbornly resistant manifestations of our continuing failures," he told an audience in 1967. "There is good reason to hope, nevertheless, that they will eventually yield to massive applications of techniques and resources we now know how to use."[127] He emphasized the commission's message that neither force nor criminal justice was a cure for the cities' problems. He didn't mince words in taking on those who thought it would be enough to crack down on criminals, or simply to abandon the cities to the minority poor and let them rot. "Our cities are truly sick," he declared. "They are suffering from the diseases of poverty, discrimination and hopelessness, and their illnesses have been all but ignored by the rest of society. The sickness will not cure itself—it will not simply go away if left alone—rather, it will get worse and infect the entire body of our society."[128]

"WE KNOW THE country is in trouble," Brewster told freshmen as the 1967 fall term began. "The sick society probably seems sicker precisely because it is in such mocking contrast to the pretentious sloganeering about the Great Society." He believed that Vietnam protest and racial unrest were symptoms rather than causes. The deeper problems were lack of opportunity, lack of world order, and a lack of purpose that afflicted both authority and individuals. Amid outrage and unrest, Brewster called for moderates to resist the nation's drift into extremism.

"White power is not an acceptable alternative even if you find black power wrong," he told the freshmen. "Sabotage and obstruction is not the only course for those who cannot acquiesce in official policy. Uncritical endorsement of whatever Israel wants to do is not the only alternative to anti-semitism. . . . Tossing constitutional values to the winds is not an acceptable alternative to condoning of rampant crime."[129]

Most protest at Yale was still moderate. When Lady Bird Johnson came to the university in early October to give a speech on "The Beautification of America," fifteen hundred students jammed the plaza outside the hall where she was speaking to demonstrate against her husband's war. The protest, however, was silent, so as not to disrupt the first lady's speech. Yale's chapter of SDS held a noisier, less chivalrous protest outside Brewster's house, along with a lone black protester calling for increased minority hiring at Yale.[130]

William Sloane Coffin remembered 1967 as an enormously frustrating year—for hawks because the country couldn't win the war in Vietnam and for doves because the fighting didn't stop. "Bitterness grew, making it more and more difficult to resist doing things that made you feel better but didn't necessarily improve the situation. On both sides the name-calling and violence increased."[131]

Coffin tried to make a positive contribution to the protest by putting himself on the line. He would violate the codicil of the Selective Service Act that mandated prison or a fine for anyone "who knowingly counsels, aids or abets another to refuse or evade registration or service in the armed forces."[132] Three events in October led to the chaplain's arrest. Early in the month, he chaired a press conference in New York announcing the manifesto "A Call to Resist Illegitimate Authority," challenging the legality of the war and pledging to support draft resisters. In mid-October, he spoke at a church service at the Arlington Street Unitarian Church in Boston, part of a national protest in which young men would turn in their draft cards and announce that they were resisting induction. It was a beautiful ceremony, which made for irresistible television when it was broadcast nationally.[133] The penalties that likely awaited draft resisters—not merely arrest and imprisonment but a felony conviction that could bar an aspiring lawyer from licensure or a scientist from government clearance—imbued the proceedings with an air of great solemnity. As Yale's draft resisters gave their draft cards to the chaplain, he recognized a law school student among the group. "Don't be a fool," Coffin told the student, trying to give him back his card. "Never mind," came the reply. "I've changed my mind about being a lawyer."[134]

A week later, at a large antiwar rally in Washington that would culminate with a march on the Pentagon, Coffin, together with the well-known pediatrician Dr. Benjamin Spock and three antiwar activists, turned over to the attorney general's office the draft cards gathered by resistance groups. If the conscientious objectors were arrested for failing to comply with the law, Coffin told reporters on the steps of the Justice Department, "we too must be arrested, for in the sight of the law we are now as guilty as they."[135]

If Yale's conservative alumni had been angry at Coffin before, now they were furious. Brewster had mixed feelings. He did not agree that widespread civil disobedience could or should change national policy on the draft, although he supported Coffin's right to speak his mind. At the Parents Day assembly at the end of October, Brewster sharply criticized Coffin's tactics in protesting the war. "The Chaplain's effort to devise 'confrontations' and 'sanctuaries' in order to gain spot news coverage," he said, "seems to me unworthy of and to detract from the true trial of conscience which touches most of your sons and preoccupies so many." But as he told the parents, he refused to forbid Coffin from following his conscience, because "I have great confidence in your sons' ability to keep their own counsel and to sort out the true from the false if they are allowed to make up their own minds. I would have no confidence in them at all if they were protected from exposure to all argument and sheltered from the risk of error." Praising Coffin for helping to make rebellion at Yale "affirmative and constructive," he added, "I feel that the quality of the Yale educational experience and the Yale atmosphere has gained greatly from his presence."[136]

Brewster's measured position did not please Coffin's student supporters, who attacked Brewster's "unremitting dedication to the 'radical center.'"[137] Nor were the Coffin-hating alumni satisfied. "Our President is afraid to stand firm," charged one member of the Class of 1913. "He slaps Coffin in the face with his right and then pats him on the head with his left."[138] Publicly, Coffin told reporters that "I'm grateful for a president with whom one can disagree and still remain good friends. . . . [M]y quarrel is with President Johnson not with President Brewster." Privately, the chaplain seethed, believing that "Kingman was simply swaddling his uncertainty in rectitude."[139]

But Brewster was uncertain not merely about the war but about the very question of institutional neutrality. To what extent did the university president have a responsibility to speak out or keep silent when basic issues of national policy, which might be far removed from academic life, became the dominant concerns of the academic community? Although he realized that the war was so pervasive "that the guy on top looks like some kind of faceless or two-faced character if he doesn't take a stand on it," he recognized that his institutional responsibilities in some measure inhibited him from speaking out.[140] But at what point did that argument become a cover for conformity?

Coffin and Brewster clashed again that fall when the chaplain announced his intention to offer Battell Chapel as a sanctuary for draft resisters.[141] Brewster insisted that the chaplain had no legal right to declare Yale's chapel a safe haven. When faculty deacons came down on Brewster's side, a furious Coffin accused them "of behaving more like 'true blues than true Christians.' They squirmed," he recalled, "but weren't about to change their minds. Finally one of them said quietly, 'Bill, on this issue we're not as certain as you and the students are that your wills are that clearly aligned with the will of the Lord.' Kingman smiled. I realized I was licked."[142]

Still, when Coffin was indicted on charges of conspiring to aid and counsel draft resisters, Brewster emphasized that respect for due process of law required that the accused be presumed innocent until found guilty. "Therefore, the fact of the indictment itself does not warrant any change in Mr. Coffin's status at Yale."[143] Brewster maintained this position, in the face of considerable alumni opposition, even after the chaplain was found guilty of the charges.

In Brewster's opinion, Coffin played a valuable role on campus, although he understood that supporting him would arouse alumni ire and cost Yale donations. Brewster also was "impressed and not a little surprised at the extent to which personal admiration is bestowed upon [Coffin] by under-graduates who are completely opposed to his views."[144] Indeed, one of Yale's graduates who volunteered for service in Vietnam and was killed there had also believed, according to his father, that Coffin's antidraft activism was "right and important."[145]

Paul Moore, who understood Coffin well, described the chaplain to Brewster as "a man passionately caught up in a cause which he feels to be—and which actually is—of the most overwhelming importance. . . . He approaches this, by his particular vocation, from the moral, 'religious' not the pragmatic or prudential perspective. This means he moves from a dif-ferent *priority* in his values. He also seeks a different kind of impact on events than do those who move from other positions of responsibility." And, Moore pointed out, Coffin should go on being heard on the war, despite the "very real sacrifice" his doing so would entail for Yale, since the govern-ment's voice was in no danger of being silenced.[146]

As two former chairmen of American Veterans Committee chapters—Brewster at Harvard, Coffin at Yale—they shared several idealistic traits, although Coffin was usually more able to express his idealism freely. The chaplain used to needle the president by telling him that "it is a good thing you have me to say some things you can't say."[147] But Coffin, too, had his constituencies that he hesitated to offend. The reverend attended the nominally left-liberal New Politics Convention in Chicago in the fall of 1967, at which the two thousand or so delegates kowtowed to a caucus of a couple hundred Black Power separatists under the new SNCC head, H. Rap Brown. The blacks produced a hateful, racist, and anti-Semitic manifesto that they forced through over the tepid protest of white liberals. According to one observer, Coffin was "bewildered and ineffective in his opposition to the manifesto," and later tried to play down and explain away the ugliness of the document.[148] Brewster may have had Coffin in mind when he lamented that "the liberals among us, especially the academic liberals, are sometimes tempted to rationalize and excuse a call to hate or violence if it is uttered in the name of the victims of poverty or discrimination."[149]

One of the few times Brewster was seen to lose his temper occurred during a meeting with Coffin in the Corporation room, at which each man seemed to accuse the other of lacking the courage of his convictions. Brewster growled at the chaplain, "Your remarks are certainly ungrateful addressed as they are to one who spends an inordinate amount of time defending you to Yale alumni." Coffin shot back, "The amount of time you spend defending me to the right, I spend and more defending you to the left, and I'd be more worried if I were in your shoes."[150]

John Wilkinson, an assistant dean of Yale College, recalled the scene and Brewster's anger. "I think everyone sitting around the table thought, 'Good.' Most of us were good and admiring friends of Bill, but Bill had gone beyond the pale," Wilkinson said. "Bill had a way of forcing you to go further than you wanted to go lest you be accused by him of being pusillanimous, though that's not a word that I think he would use—'cowardly' is the word he would use—and so you felt yourself being pushed by him all the time. And Kingman really went after him. It was a good moment."[151] Brewster could be goaded by Coffin but not intimidated by him.

BREWSTER AND COFFIN were examples of how the privileged members of the World War II generation struggled in very different ways to reform the institutions and social order that had produced them. While Coffin threw himself directly into movements and confrontation, Brewster worked with moderates to bring about change within the system. Theirs was a tense but symbiotic relationship. Each had enormous respect for the other, although they disagreed often and sometimes vehemently. When Coffin expressed skepticism about Yale, Brewster replied: "You are a distinctive product of this institution. You might have happened elsewhere, but not bloody likely. Now you are having an impact on your generation and those to follow which is precisely in the Yale tradition which I proclaim and which you deny."[152]

Each man in his own way posed the question of what styles and tactics would be most effective in bringing about change. Brewster's assistant Sam Chauncey believed that Coffin was an example of "the modern liberal who has no Victorian pull on him, none at all. So he went off in directions in which it was not possible to accomplish anything because he was so far out. What made Kingman so successful was the tension between the Victorian pull on one hand and the pragmatic push on the other."[153] But Coffin, like Brewster, was marked by the tradition in which he was raised, even as he rebelled against it. The novelist Norman Mailer, watching Coffin speak at the Washington protest in the fall of 1967, wrote that "the Yale Chaplain had one of those faces you expected to see on the cover of *Time* or *Fortune,* there as the candidate for Young Executive of the Year, he had that same flint of the eye, single-mindedness in purpose, courage to bear responsibility . . . that same suggestion of an absolute lack of humor once the line which enclosed his true Wasp temper had been breached. He was one full example of the masculine principle at work in the cloth."[154]

Wilkinson remembered the occasion when Coffin, after being released from a Baltimore jail where he had been imprisoned for civil rights protests, raced up the New Jersey Turnpike to attend a formal party at Jock Whitney's Long Island estate. "Yale was well served by the WASP ascendancy during that period," Wilkinson observed. "It was absolutely right and maybe even necessary to have these thirteenth-generation *Mayflower* Americans running the place. . . . They were to their class as Franklin Roosevelt was to his people in the New Deal, and it was no accident that so many conservative Republicans hated Kingman Brewster and despised Bill Coffin, because they belonged to all the right clubs and associations."[155]

On most Sundays during the academic year, Brewster would sit in the president's chair—the counterpart of the bishop's throne in the Episcopal Church—to hear Coffin preach. Battell was usually full to overflowing on those occasions, with students from Yale and even other colleges crowding in to hear Coffin's electric, moving sermons. Once Yale had forced its students to come to this chapel under pain of expulsion; now they came of their own accord.

One of the students close to Coffin pointed out that "there's a whole legacy of people who went through Yale during Bill's years who have remained committed to religion as a result of his influence, who might not have been interested in religion at all had he not galvanized them."[156] In his way, Coffin was a conservative force, keeping angry and alienated young people connected to established religion. Strobe Talbott, who served as one of Battell's deacons, told a reporter that "one of the first things Coffin showed me was that you could be a liberal and a political activist and still be in church."[157]

In doctrinal terms, Coffin was indeed a conservative, even an orthodox one. He retained the traditional Protestant liturgy, from the opening prayer to the confession to the benediction, resisting the wave of reform that swept over most denominations in the 1960s. His congregation sung the powerful old New England hymns; the one that spoke most directly to him was "Once to Every Man and Nation," whose title he would take for his autobiography. The civil rights and antiwar activism of the 1960s seemed part of a much older American history when set to the hymn's ominous, rolling cadences and the spine-tingling words of McGeorge Bundy's ancestor, the nineteenth-century poet James Russell Lowell: "Once to every man and nation / Comes the moment to decide, / In the strife of truth with falsehood, / For the good or evil side; / Some great cause, God's new Messiah / Off'ring each the bloom or blight, / And the choice goes by forever / 'Twixt that darkness and that light."

EVEN AMID THE crises of the late 1960s, the leaders of large institutions spent most of their time dealing with quotidian operational matters. On any given day, Paul Moore, for example, was less likely to be involved in civil rights or antiwar protest than to be ministering to the parishes of his diocese, from the battered chapels of inner-city Washington down to the graceful brick church in Saint Mary's City, Maryland, on Chesapeake Bay, whose honorarium to the bishop was a quart of fresh oysters. And at the Ford Foundation, McGeorge Bundy was more likely to receive pleas for funds from his friend Kingman Brewster than from black nationalists.

Brewster himself was mainly preoccupied with the mundane matters of running a university: recruiting faculty, making appointments, pondering budgets, planning strategic initiatives. As much as Brewster was interested in and affected by the antiwar protests and civil disorders of 1967, he spent more time on his continuing efforts, which ultimately proved unsuccessful, to lure Vassar College to New Haven. It was difficult to find sufficient space for a new college (although Brewster reportedly toyed with displacing the divinity school), and professors from both institutions doubted that Vassar's teaching-oriented faculty would integrate comfortably into a university where scholarship was of crucial importance. Vassar's alumnae and faculty were also too attached to the rural tranquillity of their spacious campus to abandon it. Finally in November, Vassar's trustees voted overwhelmingly that "the college should remain in its birthplace" and proposed establishing a coordinate men's college in Poughkeepsie instead.[158] But the merger had fallen apart largely because, as Yale's associate provost Alvin Kernan observed firsthand, the practical difficulties of coordinate arrangements had become too difficult while their intellectual justifications had ceased to be compelling. In the end, Vassar would become a coeducational school, in the process losing what Kernan called "the mystique of high society and the strange accent that had been its distinctive mark."[159]

Having argued the merits of coeducation for a year and having raised student expectations for its imminent arrival, Brewster could hardly drop the idea after Vassar's refusal. But the advantage of the Vassar arrangement had been that it not only would stop short of full coeducation but would pay for itself. Brewster announced that Yale would establish its own coordinate women's college but estimated the cost for facilities and endowment to be somewhere between $50 and $80 million, and where would the money come from? A subterranean rumor circulated among the faculty that Brewster had persuaded McGeorge Bundy to underwrite the cost. Shortly thereafter, Bundy came up to New Haven for a dinner with Brewster that left both of them fizzing with booze. One professor remembered that as the limousine taking Bundy back to New York was pulling away, he leaned out the window and said, "You ain't never going to get that money, Kingman," leaving his friend blinking in surprise.[160] So the plan for a coordinate women's college became another claimant on a budget that was already stretched to the breaking point.

Time magazine put Brewster on its cover in June 1967, but the article made no mention of student unrest or the war. Instead it dwelt on universities' financial troubles. Brewster said that his institution "has never had a more difficult financial prospect—and a serious strain on resources for Yale is a crisis for other places."[161] Costs were rising faster than revenues for colleges and universities because of increased competition for faculty, the proliferation of specialized studies, the accelerating expense of everything from computer systems to building maintenance, and the competition private universities faced from public universities. Some formerly private universities, such as Temple, Buffalo, Pittsburgh, and Houston, threw in the towel and became affiliated with state systems. The financial crunch, ironically, was hitting the universities at a time when the federal government was providing unprecedented levels of financial support. Johnson sent more than fifty bills dealing with higher education through Congress, culminating in the $10 billion Higher Education Amendments of 1968. But a largely unspoken worry among the university presidents was that the demands of the Vietnam War would squeeze out the federal funds that had recently become available.

For this reason, the university world had reacted angrily to Bundy's announcement, early on in his presidency, that Ford, the largest source of new funds for universities besides the government, would be cutting back on its grants to higher education. Bundy remained sympathetic to his old colleagues, however, and promoted various ideas for overcoming the financial crisis. He gathered the presidents of the Ivy League and other major universities to lobby the government for higher rates of reimbursement. He declared that alumni should contribute more to the universities that had set them on the road to prosperity. (The historian Jonathan Spence puckishly responded that Yale should dun Chairman Mao Tse-tung for its support of the Communist leader when he was a librarian at a Yale-run school in China.[162]) Above all, Bundy thought, the universities should publicize their "imminent bankruptcy," but doing so would require efforts that no university had undertaken: "to learn and to tell the whole story of their resources and obligations, their income and their expenses, their assets and their debts, in such a way that the public can fully and fairly judge their economic position."[163]

Under Brewster, Yale had gone further down this road than any other university, making bold innovations in its endowment management and applying systems analysis and new management techniques to keep its costs under control. Bundy put Brewster on a Ford-sponsored committee that would study these ideas and recommend some of them to a broader audience of nonprofit institutions. But, as Brewster had told Bundy on a train ride back from the funeral of former secretary of state Christian Herter, Yale needed to raise much more money if it was to have any hope of paying for his ambitious hopes for the university. "I think Yale is an imaginative, energetic, national institution," he wrote Bundy. "It is excellent and broke. . . . We now need the chance to experiment effectively with ways of enhancing our power to gain the support we deserve."[164]

Later in 1967, Brewster put together a proposal to the Ford Foundation for support of experimental methods of fund-raising. He pointed to his university's accomplishments in its nonacademic infrastructure and its changes in programs, faculty appointments, and admissions policies. "The inherent controversy which these changes involve has of course brought on a chorus of nay-sayers, particularly among the older alumni," he wrote Bundy. While he was convinced that most alumni welcomed the institution's new liveliness, "the spectre is always raised that controversy will breed a decline of capital support."[165] Ford's aid would strengthen Brewster's hand against the forces of conservatism.

In late November, Ford gave $5 million to Yale for experimental use in university development. It was a highly unusual donation in that Yale was given, in effect, an "internal foundation" with almost unrestricted freedom in how to apply the money. As the university's development director pointed out, the grant represented "a tremendous endorsement of Yale, President Brewster, his administration, and his style."[166] It is unlikely that the grant would have been made if Brewster and Bundy had not been presidents of Yale and Ford—some faculty members thought it a consolation prize to Brewster for Ford's failure to support coeducation—and in any case Ford never made a similar donation to any other university.

The internal foundation did in some measure leverage alumni donations in creative ways. After 1967, however, what seemed at stake was not so much Yale's prosperity as its very survival. Increasingly, funds from the internal foundation would go toward efforts to keep the peace in New Haven, reaching out to the sullen ghettos to help prevent a larger and more deadly riot than that of August 1967. The concern of establishment leaders like McGeorge Bundy and Kingman Brewster for the welfare of higher education, on the one hand, and for the elimination of urban violence, on the other, was evolving in ways that neither had anticipated.

9

HEAVY TURBULENCE

I N LATE 1967, Kingman Brewster decided that the members of the Corporation should have breakfast with small groups of undergraduates and faculty in Yale's twelve residential colleges. He hoped that in an intimate and informal setting, the trustees "would get a more vivid sense of what makes the student generation tick" than they were getting from the media's sensationalistic coverage.[1]

On the designated Saturday morning in December, Brewster farmed out the trustees to their appointed destinations: Paul Moore to Saybrook College, John Lindsay to Berkeley, and so forth. The investor and philanthropist John Hay Whitney—one of the Corporation's longest-serving trustees, and certainly the richest—had spent Friday night at Brewster's home and came downstairs after a sleepless night. The multimillionaire, who did not like confrontation, had developed a bad case of nerves at the prospect of dealing with angry students face-to-face. Usually Jock Whitney walked with his shoulders thrown back, as resolute as the championship polo player he had been in his youth, but now he slumped. "I don't want to go," he told Brewster.[2] The president refused to let his university's greatest benefactor off the hook. "I assured him that the students of the present generation were not interested in asking him questions, they were only interested in telling him what they thought," Brewster recalled. "That seemed to relieve him to some extent."[3] Brewster finally got Whitney under way, a process he compared to sending a small child off to his first day at school.

Whitney, in no mood for breakfast, had no sooner sat down in his chair at Morse College than the confrontation he had dreaded began. Armstead Robinson, a leader of the university's black student organization, opened up on him about Yale's failure to address "the black experience." Robinson, the son of a Memphis preacher, was gaunt and fiery, with an unkempt Afro, unpressed dashiki, and black rectangular glasses—the very model of an angry young black scholar.[4] He had intellect to match his passion, and, fortunately, Whitney had the sensitivity to engage him in serious conversation rather than patronize or take offense. As the trustee listened intently, his appetite returned. He invited Robinson to address his concerns to the administration, and reported back to Brewster (his customary swagger restored) after several hours of animated conversation with the students.

Whitney's breakfast encounter with Robinson led to further meetings between black students and Brewster, and eventually to the creation of a formal program of instruction in Afro-American studies. The president and the black students at Yale had begun a dialogue, for which Brewster would be extremely grateful in the turbulent times that lay ahead.

AFTER YALE HAD been recruiting minority students for several years, Brewster wrote to McGeorge Bundy that Yale's selectivity and standards had "made it possible for us to give hope to disadvantaged minorities. Thanks to our efforts," he continued, "there is beginning to be a feeling that there is room at the very top of the American university ladder for any minority student who is worthy of the opportunity."[5]

Brewster's self-congratulatory tone was not unmerited. The number of blacks matriculating at the college rose from three in 1960 to forty-three by 1968, and Yale's progressive image was attracting increasing numbers of minority applicants. One of the university's black undergraduates remembered that "the most significant single factor which influenced my decision [to apply] was the media image that Yale received during the late 1960s— namely that of an institution which sought out and listened attentively to the voices of change."[6]

Until the mid-1960s, Yale had largely confined itself to recruiting more black students without resorting to an egregious double standard. Few administrators gave much thought to the social or intellectual experiences of black students once they were on the campus. While there was a vague awareness of unique adjustment problems, the assumption was that, in the end, the new additions would be Yale students much like the uncomplaining middle-class black students who had arrived since 1870, when Edward Alexander Bouchet became the first African-American admitted to Yale

College. (He later became the first black member of Phi Beta Kappa and the first black Ph.D.[7])

Black political consciousness at Yale intensified in the fall of 1964, when the fourteen black freshmen in the Class of '68 helped start an informal organization for African-American students on campus. The group was created mainly to coordinate social gatherings, but it brought with it the first hint of racial awareness. "We got together because we felt a need to assert our sense of positive self-identification," said Robinson, one of the founders.[8]

The organization gradually enlarged its focus to deal with broader issues. The Black Student Alliance at Yale (or BSAY), as it came to be called, sponsored its first issue-oriented conference in the spring of 1966 as interest in African-American history developed along with the stirrings of a black consciousness. By the next school year, BSAY members were giving lectures on black history to New Haven schoolchildren. Even so, black students' efforts to change Yale began in earnest only when the young men first negotiated with Brewster and other members of the administration.

The February 1968 parley between BSAY representatives and Yale's president and other administrators, arranged after Whitney's breakfast with Robinson, was an eye-opener for Brewster. Some of what the students told him reflected their own ambivalence: most were guiltily aware that the racial pride proclaimed in the late 1960s was in some measure compromised by attendance at an elite, predominantly white institution. Robinson told a reporter that "Yale is by definition white; in many respects it is the epitome of whiteness. To be black here . . . is a fundamental contradiction for anyone with a positive black identification."[9] With rioting in the ghettos and militancy on the rise, the claim to be in the university but not of it was a necessary part of many black students' psychic armor.

But there was reality behind the rhetoric. The black students, viewing Yale with critical outsiders' eyes, found shortcomings of which the administrators were unaware. Brewster was told that much of the curriculum lacked significant engagement with the history, culture, and even existence of black people. He learned that black students walking across campus were likely to be confronted by the university police, while whites (even those without any obvious Yale connection) were allowed to pass freely. Robinson and Donald Ogilvie, another BSAY leader at the meeting, also recalled "numerous confrontations . . . between black Yalies trying to get into college and fraternity parties, and white students questioning our 'right' to be on campus."[10] Like most administrators, Brewster had never given a thought to how black students might perceive the Confederate battle flags and crossed bullwhips that hung above the fireplace in the lounge of Calhoun College, named for the famous secessionist and slave owner. And he had never noticed that the Payne Whitney gymnasium, the massive Gothic palace given to Yale by Jock Whitney, was decorated with nineteenth-century sporting prints showing grotesque depictions of blacks.

Although Brewster did not fit the stereotype of the guilty white liberal, Robinson and Ogilvie remembered his "pained expression of patrician disbelief" upon hearing about the racial caricatures in the gym. Within days, the prints came down. "A symbolic act, to be sure," the two BSAY members commented. "Yet it proved deeply revealing."[11] Brewster recognized that the institution had been deficient in its dealings with blacks, and he took steps to address the students' concerns.

It helped that, in his encounters with black students, he was a skilled diplomat and negotiator. Brewster was both personally sympathetic to black students and not intimidated by them, and students were often relieved to deal with authorities as responsible adults rather than resort to violent rhetoric or mau-mauing. Brewster recalled that on one occasion, when a black drama student loomed over him and said, "I think irresistible force has just met immovable object," the president merely smiled and pleasantly asked why. The student "almost audibly sighed with relief," he said, and sat down to talk for the next three hours.[12]

When a group of black students marched to Brewster's house to demand that Yale do more to increase the number of minorities admitted, Brewster came off his sickbed to meet with them. Undergraduate William Farley remembered that he charmed nearly all the group. "Some people never wavered in negative feelings about Brewster, about Yale, about many things. But I think many of us were just greatly impressed by the way in which he handled the affair." From the meeting came a recruiting campaign in which Yale paid for minority students to visit their hometowns and bring in prospective applicants.

While he appreciated the outcome of the meeting, Farley was also impressed by Brewster's knack for "taking a protest or something that was in opposition to him and converting it, completely flipping it. They used to call it co-option. All of a sudden it became his movement or his issue or his problem, and he would come out of it looking very good and smelling like a rose."[13] Kurt Schmoke, a black freshman in the spring of 1968 who later became mayor of Baltimore, recalled that "Brewster was absolutely a master at co-opting the student body. There is no other way of putting it."[14]

Yale's black students were not exactly eager to be co-opted. "Co-option," according to student government leader Ray Nunn, "assumes that when you offer a black man a bigger bone you've got him, he's your nigger for life."[15] But the benefits of dialogue for both the BSAY and the administration were several. For the black students, it provided a route through the system to express their needs. The BSAY and the administration reached agreements on scholarship funds, tutorials, new job training programs, ethnic counselors, support for black student recruiting trips, racial awareness seminars for campus and city police, university backing for selected black New Haven programs, the hiring of black faculty members, and the inauguration of a black cultural center. From Brewster's point of view, personal relationships with the leaders of the BSAY ensured that grievances could be handled in an orderly manner. It was also useful that the administration could deal with one strong organization instead of ten weak ones. The relationship between Brewster and the BSAY strengthened the hand of moderates in the organization and helped to prevent frustrations from boiling over, guaranteed that reform proposals would be well considered rather than radical and hasty, and showed that change could occur through the system.

Yet the administration did not quail in supine surrender before any demand from the BSAY. Brewster felt that "in the case of black power . . . it is terribly important to have your non-negotiable principles, but your non-negotiable principles will be listened to, providing you are willing, within those principles, to be as flexible, as responsive, and as affirming as you can be."[16]

In the case of the creation of an academically credible Afro-American studies major, it was vital to achieve the same curricular standard and involve the same faculty appointment process as for all other majors in Yale College. After the February summit, a committee composed of four leading faculty members and an equal number of BSAY members began meeting to discuss the design of a formal program. The Ford Foundation underwrote a conference that brought nearly all the leading scholars in the field to Yale, including Harold Cruse, Nathan Hare, Alvin Poussaint, and even radicals like Maulana Ron Karenga. The BSAY invited 150 attendees, mainly federal officials and educators, most of them white.

Although Brewster knew that some of the faculty believed that black issues ought to be incorporated into a broader, less racially oriented course of studies, he saw a parallel with the programs in Irish and other ethnic studies that had been set up in the 1950s. Henry Shattuck had given Harvard a professorial chair in Irish studies expressly to heal the rift between

Irish-Americans and Yankees. According to Richardson, his uncle realized that the way to promote understanding between the two cultures was to proclaim the identity of Boston's Irish heritage rather than subordinate it: "Such appreciation, he felt, would directly enhance the significance of the Irish contribution as perceived by other segments of the community, including the Yankees. It would also increase the value of their heritage in the eyes of the Boston Irish themselves. The result, Uncle Harry hoped, would be to diminish Yankee smugness and boost Irish self-esteem."[17] Obviously, then, there was a political element in the liberal establishment's use of the curriculum to reconcile with blacks as their predecessors had done with the Irish. But the key question was whether the politics would warp the academic dimensions of the major. When McGeorge Bundy addressed the gathering at Yale, he praised the new program but warned against using it primarily as a vehicle for black identity politics.[18]

As Brewster said later, "One of Yale's great good fortunes" was that "we were working on this problem before Martin Luther King was assassinated, and this had a great deal to do with the credibility of our efforts."[19] In fact, Yale's program in Afro-American studies, as it finally developed, may have been unique in heeding Bundy's warnings against egregious ideological and identity politics. Almost every other university in the country tried to develop an African-American studies program after King's assassination, but those panic-stricken efforts resulted in programs that were deformed by politicization, fear of blacks, and capitulation to student protest.

At Harvard, for example, an African-American Studies Department was created that allowed students to vote on term and tenure appointments—a privilege that had not hitherto been extended even to junior faculty members. As a consequence, no reputable scholar would go near the department. Roger Rosenblatt, who was then teaching African-American literature at Harvard, contended that the department was victimized by liberals who were only too willing to give students whatever they wanted, and conservatives who knew that the student demands would end in disaster but wanted to see African-American studies destroy itself. The faculty failed to defend its principles and "tell the students, black and white, that they thought too much of the future of black studies to allow it to go to hell at the hands of incompetents. But instead, they put on their most sympathetic faces and let the mob rule."[20]

In New Haven, by contrast, the black students who helped establish the program took pride in the fact that while it had been created with significant student input, it was as strong academically as other Yale departments, met the same standards as other majors, and was fully integrated into the academic structure. Certainly in its early years, the program was more racially integrated than most such departments at other universities. Brewster delighted in the fact that his students "were quite gleeful . . . that a systematic study of the black experience would be at least as valuable if not more valuable for white students than it would be for black students."[21] As a result, Yale's was among the first and for many years the best program of African-American studies in the country, while most similar majors created elsewhere at that time have long since dried up and blown away.

TO YALE'S CONSERVATIVE alumni, Brewster's special attention to black students was emblematic of what was going wrong at their alma mater. After years of complaining, they finally found an outlet for their anger when, in late 1967, William F. Buckley Jr., scourge of the establishment and the nation's premier right-wing celebrity, declared himself a petition candidate for the Yale Corporation.

Buckley was not motivated by a desire for fellowship with trustees such as his onetime mayoral opponent, John Lindsay, or William Scranton (who had taken on Barry Goldwater at the Republican primary in 1964). He aimed to arrest or reverse the changes Brewster had brought about. Buckley envisioned restoring traditionalism in the classroom, applying an ideological litmus test to faculty appointments, ending competitive faculty recruitment, and cutting back federal monies to Yale and other private universities.[22] He criticized anew Yale's award of an honorary degree to Martin Luther King, "who more clearly qualifies as a doctor of lawbreaking."[23] He advocated firing radical faculty members such as Staughton Lynd, since to retain him would be "to assume that the University ought to serve as base for the revolution." While he didn't quite call for Coffin's resignation, Buckley commented that "if in fact it's impossible to go to church at Battell Chapel without being hectored by Mr. Coffin to send blood to the Viet Cong or whatever, then it seems to me that fanaticism would be getting in the way of his duties as a spiritual counselor."[24]

Above all, Buckley called for spiking Inky Clark's "democratic leveling guns" and halting Yale's outreach to talented boys from nontraditional backgrounds. He claimed that Clark, by holding alumni sons to the same standard as other applicants, was actively discriminating against "the older families—the members of what the English, in tones increasingly hushed, refer to as 'the governing class.'"[25] Buckley demanded the admission of all minimally qualified alumni sons, even if legacies would then constitute half of Yale's entering classes and minorities would be largely squeezed out.

Brewster was personally rather fond of Buckley, despite their vast political differences, but believed that it would be disastrous to have him on the Corporation and acted accordingly. The president's assistant Sam Chauncey recalled that the administration "couldn't control" Buckley's nomination, but "we did everything we could to defeat him." Chauncey studied the history of alumni fellow elections and concluded that they operated according to predictable rules—a candidate who was famous would defeat someone who was not, the younger of two people of equal fame would always win, and so on. "I had a whole series of formulas, so that I knew how to structure an election so that I could get the winner out of it," Chauncey recalled.[26] After running their calculations, Brewster and Chauncey decided that Buckley's opponent should be Cyrus Vance.

Vance had been given scant opportunity to enjoy a placid readjustment to civilian life at his New York law firm. Shortly after his troubleshooting mission to the Detroit riots, he was preparing to visit his daughter at her school in Virginia when he got a call from Undersecretary of State Nicholas Katzenbach. Turkey and Greece were about to go to war over the island of Cyprus, and Johnson was desperate to avert armed conflict between the two NATO nations. Katzenbach asked Vance to fly to Ankara that afternoon as Johnson's personal representative, with instructions to prevent a war.[27] Vance called his wife to inform her of his change of plans. "After a considerable silence," he recalled, "she finally accepted the fact that I was not joking and that indeed I was going to the Eastern Mediterranean sometime that afternoon."[28]

Over the next week and a half, Vance would log ten thousand miles flying back and forth between the Greek, Turkish, and Cypriot capitals, in some respects inventing the concept of shuttle diplomacy. In an incredible display of patience and stamina, he went without sleep for most of that time while devising a four-point settlement calibrated to meet each party's needs and to allow Greece and Turkey to back away from the brink without losing face. Finally, in early December, he convinced both countries to sign an agreement that would remove Greek troops from the island and guarantee the rights of the Turkish minority. It was not a durable peace, as the Turks would invade Cyprus seven years later. Vance himself conceded after the accord was signed that "the situation is still held together with paste and glue, and more paste than glue."[29] Still, he had helped avert an almost certain war, and he well deserved the tributes he received. ("Cyrus Fixes Cyprus," proclaimed the cover of the *Economist* magazine.[30])

Vance resolved conflicts by mastering the facts as a lawyer would, listening patiently to all sides and trying to understand their positions, ensuring that all parties understood the principles involved in a solution, and refusing to give up. Strobe Talbott, the *Yale Daily News* chairman who was in his senior year at Yale during the Cyprus crisis, later interviewed Vance and found him to be the most unquotable public figure he ever encountered, "allergic to the first person singular and prone to wooden understatement," with "little knack for explaining what he is up to in terms of grand theories of history, strategy or geopolitics."[31]

But these same qualities made Vance an ideal mediator. Unflappable, indestructible, uninterested in taking credit and unwilling to take sides, he obtained the trust and esteem of the contending parties. He was soft-spoken, courtly, secure enough not to be bothered by bluster, bad behavior, or threats. His skill at negotiation was a product of his endurance and genuine respect for everyone he dealt with, as much as it was of sound judgment and lawyerly cunning.

On his return to the United States, Vance turned down Johnson's offer to become secretary of defense, succeeding Robert McNamara, who had left his post literally in tears. By 1968, Vance's longtime friend and superior had reached a point of disillusion with the war where he was all but asking to be fired. Johnson announced that McNamara would become president of the World Bank. According to the columnist Joseph Kraft, McNamara left office "under a cloud that casts a dark shadow across the qualities and values of the best men" in the country. His departure signaled "a failure in the managerial faith, a crisis of the whole postwar generation."[32]

From Vance's point of view, Kraft's conclusions were overdrawn. Vance was not a technocrat but a believer in public service and the need to take on problems, even without assurance that a solution could be reached. Vietnam had not shaken that faith. Vance told a group of legal scholars in early 1968 of his "very deep conviction that it is the duty of each individual, if he is to fulfill himself as a human being, to become involved in the issues of his time. The cardinal sin is to stand aside—what each of us must do is to participate to the best of his abilities in wrestling with the problems of our time, and to contribute in some measure to improving the welfare of one's fellow man."[33] Vance defended his participation in public service, even in the prosecution of the Vietnam War, in virtually the same language of religious obligation that clerics like Moore and Coffin used to oppose the war.

In February 1968, Johnson turned again to Vance: a North Korean commando squad had attempted to assassinate the South Korean president, Chung Hee Park, and two days later the paranoid Communist state seized the USS *Pueblo*, an American intelligence-gathering ship. Preoccupied as it was with Vietnam, the United States could not afford to support South Korea in another war. Vance insisted that South Korea refrain from retaliation, reassured Park that the United States would provide money for military assistance, and persuaded the president to accept South Korea's exclusion from U.S.–North Korean negotiations over the release of the *Pueblo*'s crew.[34] He managed to keep the peace, and again received plaudits from Johnson and the press. Shortly afterward, Vance would accompany the president to Honolulu for conferences with Park and American military commanders in Vietnam.

By the spring, Vance was one of the most newsworthy, distinguished members of Brewster's circle of informal advisors and friends, and Brewster persuaded him to stand against Buckley in the Yale Corporation election. On learning who his opponent would be, Buckley told reporters, "I'm sure Mr. Vance is a very nice man, and I hope that he will be more successful against me than he has been against the Viet Cong, but my guess is that I will probably win."[35]

MCGEORGE BUNDY HAD reviewed America's Vietnam policy at the second gathering of the "Wise Men," at the White House in November 1967, along with former secretary of state Dean Acheson, ambassador-at-large Averell Harriman, former Treasury secretary Douglas Dillon, and other aging establishment luminaries. Most of the briefings seemed to show sustained military progress, buoying optimism that the war could be won.

Bundy, the youngest of the Wise Men, spoke for the group when he declared that "getting out of Vietnam is as impossible as it is undesirable."[36] He and most of the others also agreed that the bombing of North Vietnam should be continued but not escalated and that more of the military effort should be shifted to the South Vietnamese. In a considerably less upbeat report to Johnson after the meeting, however, Bundy acknowledged that "public discontent with the war is now wide and deep. One of the few things that helps us right now is public distaste for the violent doves—but I think people really are getting fed up with the endlessness of the fighting."[37]

Then, in late January 1968, the North Vietnamese launched the Tet offensive, a massive surprise assault on South Vietnam's cities and towns, seeking to spark a popular uprising. American television viewers saw the gruesome spectacle of Saigon's police chief executing a suspected Viet Cong prisoner at point-blank range and Communist commandos occupying the U.S. embassy. Although the Viet Cong and North Vietnamese forces suffered heavy casualties in their failed effort to spur a revolt in the South, the Tet offensive destroyed the Johnson administration's credibility among much of the American public. Elite figures such as media commentators, liberal business executives, members of the clergy, academics, and foundation heads were the most likely to feel misled and even betrayed by the administration's claims of progress and impending victory in the war. Walter Cronkite, the nation's leading newscaster, returned from Saigon in late February to foretell that "the bloody experience of Vietnam is to end in a stalemate." Public approval of Johnson's handling of the war fell from forty to twenty-six percent in the six weeks following Tet.[38] More bad news came with the leaked announcement that Westmoreland would request 206,000 additional troops, a story that "churned up the whole Eastern Establishment," according to the national security advisor, Walt Rostow.[39]

In mid-March, McGeorge Bundy returned to Harvard to deliver a series of lectures on government and to debate the war with government professor Stanley Hoffman, his onetime teaching assistant. As Bundy took the stage of the Sanders Theater, filled to capacity with a tense, largely hostile crowd, few knew that his personal views on the war had changed drastically in recent weeks: Tet had completed his conversion. A week after the debate, he would urge Johnson to find a way out of Vietnam. But on that night he remained a loyal soldier, defending the war as vigorously as when he was in the administration, two years earlier. In later years, when the discrepancy between his public and private views became known, the contradiction puzzled many people who knew him, even his own family. His son Andrew—in 1968 an adolescent opponent of the war—found it "an eye-opener" to realize that his father "was not merely defending the position with which he disagreed, he was publicly *advocating* it. What was that about?"[40]

Bundy stated clearly that he was no longer responsible for the formation of policy or informed about the day-to-day conduct of the war. He told his audience that "I know the administration's position well enough so that I could give you a speech of nearly any desired length on that point. But I have a brother, whose Yale and Harvard education is superior to mine in

every way, who does this for a living, and it's not in my view my most constructive function."[41] (In David Halberstam's hostile account in *The Best
and the Brightest*, this statement became Bundy's arrogant refusal to discuss
administration policy "because I have a brother who is paid to do that."[42])

Bundy emphasized, moreover, that he would not speak out against the
administration's policy because of his inherited Stimsonian inhibitions
against public criticism of the presidents he served. "I have very little sympathy with those who write criticisms which appear over the heading 'former White House Assistant,'" he said. "I think that in the main when
people do that they have taken a gun provided by someone else and aimed
it at him, and I'm against it."[43]

Bundy's former assistant James Thomson Jr., on leave from the State
Department and sitting in the audience, wondered if he was the target of
that barb. Thomson had been at a black-tie party at the home of Bundy's
friend Kingman Brewster the previous year and, on his way out to catch a
train back to Boston, made a passing remark about the disastrous escalation taking place in Vietnam. "Oh, I hear you, Jim, I hear you," he recalled
the Yale president responding, "but no one has ever proposed a viable alternative, has he? There never were any." Of course there were viable alternatives, Thomson thought, and on the train he wrote a letter to the *New York
Times* decrying Brewster's fatalistic attitude and describing missed opportunities when the United States could have left Vietnam. The letter was
what Thomson called "my first public break with the establishment," a
break that would become irreparable with the publication of his article
"How Could Vietnam Happen?: An Autopsy" in the *Atlantic Monthly* a few
weeks after Bundy's Harvard debate.[44] In that article Thomson would suggest that his unnamed but clearly identifiable boss had harbored serious
doubts about American war policy but, fearing to lose his effectiveness,
failed to resign in protest as he should have.

However much Bundy disagreed with the course of the war, though, he
believed that the United States had been right to aid the South Vietnamese;
that conviction was as powerful as other motivations in keeping him on
board with the administration. During the debate at Sanders Theater, he
listened grimly as Hoffman lambasted the government's lack of candor in
acknowledging its mistakes, the administration's wishful thinking about
escalation, and the overall political ineffectiveness of American policy in
Vietnam. Bundy recognized these criticisms very well, having made them
himself when he was in government. He even had a significant overlap of

view with the undergraduates who lined up at the microphone to denounce him, although he told one that his friend Brewster thought the essence of such student comments was, "You're a liar. Let's have a dialogue."

Bundy conceded that advocates of Westmoreland's recently announced escalation had not yet made a persuasive case, but he could not accept the proposition that the war was immoral because the effort had turned out badly. He continued to feel that the Korean War was the closest (though inexact) analogy to the Vietnam conflict, and he admonished the Harvard gathering that South Korea, "little as it may please you to respect and acknowledge the fact," was a successful society offering vastly greater freedom and opportunity to its people than any Communist state. Such talk failed to win over his audience, many of whom agreed with one student who told Bundy, "I do not consider you a liar. . . . The problem, sir, is that you are deaf."[45]

IN MARCH 1968, the newly appointed defense secretary, Clark Clifford, had been in touch with Bundy and shared his view that the time had come to disengage the United States from the Vietnam quagmire. He also knew that other Wise Men, particularly Acheson, had become similarly disenchanted with the war. After only two weeks in office, Clifford recalled, he became persuaded that the war could not be won, and his desire to pull back grew from opinion to conviction to passion.

"We were losing thousands of men and billions of dollars in an endless sinkhole," Clifford said later. "If I ever knew anything, I knew that we had to get out."[46] But wary of losing his friendship and influence with Johnson, he resorted to an indirect strategy: he suggested that the president reconvene his committee of senior advisors. "We should get the benefit of their substantive opinion," Clifford proposed on March 19. Johnson agreed that the idea was a good one, and insisted that the group include Cyrus Vance this time (he had been in Cyprus during the previous Wise Men's meeting in November).[47]

The next morning Clifford called to let Johnson know that he had spoken with an "exceedingly friendly and cooperative" McGeorge Bundy. Wouldn't it be a fine thing to have Mac come down and help Johnson with the important speech he was planning to give on Vietnam? Johnson agreed, although he was in a particularly self-pitying mood, complaining to Clifford that John Lindsay's antiwar speech had garnered a four-column story on the *New York Times*'s front page. ("Mayor Urges Youths to Aid War Resistance," read the headline—misleadingly, for Lindsay was actually calling for antiwar insurgency within the major political parties, not draft resistance.) The country was really in a fix, Johnson said, "when the head of the biggest city goes to doing things of that kind."[48]

BUNDY MET WITH Johnson and his principal advisors in the Cabinet Room on March 20 and again on March 22. But unfortunately, from Bundy's perspective, the president refused to include any reference to a peace initiative in his planned address. Bundy warned Johnson that another bellicose speech like the one he had given the previous week would cost him the election.[49] The president could not carry the American people with him for much longer "if all we seem to offer is more of the same, with stalemate at a higher cost as the only prospect." The time had come, Bundy insisted, to end the bombing and rethink the whole U.S. commitment in Vietnam. "This damned war is really much tougher than—and very different from—World War II and Korea," he wrote to the president, "and I just don't think the country can be held together much longer by determination and patriotism alone."[50]

The Wise Men came to Washington for their third and final gathering on March 25. The Cold War brethren dined by candlelight in the eighth-floor dining room of the State Department. Vance was at the table this time, along with Bundy, Acheson, Harriman, UN representative and former Supreme Court justice Arthur Goldberg, former undersecretary of state George Ball, generals Matthew Ridgway and Omar Bradley, and other distinguished men who had helped project American power and influence across the globe in the postwar era. Over dinner Clifford outlined the three options facing the United States in Vietnam: expanding the war effort, "muddling along" with current policy, or reducing participation in the war and ending the bombing. In the past, most of these moderates had been drawn to whatever option was posed between two extremes. In the briefing that followed dinner, however, it became clear that the Wise Men were finally prepared for the country to cut its losses and pull back from Vietnam.

The change occurred, in part, because the briefings were considerably more pessimistic than the sunny projections heard less than five months earlier. In November the group had been told that victory was only a year away. Now their briefers estimated it would take five to ten more years to expel the North Vietnamese from the South. The senior advisors also posed searching questions they had failed to ask in the past: when Major General

William DePuy told the group that U.S. forces had killed 80,000 North Vietnamese troops during Tet, Ambassador Goldberg wanted to know the ratio of enemy wounded to killed. Three to one, the general replied. Since the military also maintained that there were only 230,000 enemy troops in the field before Tet, Goldberg shot back in exasperation, then "who the hell are we fighting?"[51]

While Johnson subsequently blamed the briefing officers for turning around the Wise Men, Vance thought the reports were accurate and not unduly pessimistic. "Most people came to that meeting with their minds fairly well made up," he remembered. "We were weighing not only what was happening in Vietnam, but the social and political effects in the United States, the impact on the U.S. economy, the attitude of other nations. The divisiveness in the country was growing with such acuteness that it was threatening to tear the United States apart."[52]

National security advisor Walt Rostow, an unshakable advocate for the war, became increasingly alarmed as the briefings went on into the night and the consensus for pullback solidified. In his opinion these Cold War architects were unmaking their own creation. "I thought to myself," he declared with more than a touch of melodrama, "that what began in the spring of 1940 when Henry Stimson came to Washington ended tonight. The American Establishment was dead."[53] But the context these men dealt with was no longer that of a prosperous, unified country after World War II and the black-and-white simplicities of U.S.–Soviet confrontation. "Gray is the color of truth," McGeorge Bundy once said of the Vietnam War, and the same sort of complexity and uncertainty permeated the problems of race, unequal opportunity, and unrest that the younger generation of the establishment had to address in the late 1960s.[54] The members of the establishment had always thought of themselves as pragmatists, not ideologues, and by 1968 they had come to the pragmatic conclusion that Vietnam was costing more than its worth relative to America's other needs.

"THERE IS A very significant shift in our position," Bundy told Johnson when the Wise Men met with him the next afternoon in the Cabinet Room. "Dean Acheson summed up the majority feeling when he said that we can no longer do the job we set out to do in the time we have left and we must begin to take steps to disengage."[55] Bundy added that he had come to agree with George Ball that the bombing of North Vietnam was eroding domestic support for the war more than it was harming the enemy.[56]

Despite a few dissenters, most of the men endorsed Bundy's conclusion that the United States should deescalate and negotiate. "We cannot build an independent South Vietnam," Acheson emphasized. "Unless we do something quick," Vance warned, "the mood in this country may lead us to withdrawal."[57] Johnson seemed greatly surprised by these negative conclusions.[58] He recorded in his memoirs that these were "intelligent, experienced men," most of whom he had always regarded as "very steady and balanced. If they had been so deeply influenced by the reports of the Tet offensive, what must the average citizen be thinking?"[59] In the less reflective aftermath of the meeting, the president cursed that "the establishment bastards have bailed out."[60]

On March 31, Johnson delivered his much-anticipated televised address, announcing that he would limit the bombing of North Vietnam, end all bombing if Hanoi reciprocated U.S. restraint, and seek to open peace talks, naming Harriman as his personal representative. Then Johnson dropped the bombshell announcement that he would not let partisanship interfere with his quest for peace: "Accordingly, I shall not seek, and I will not accept, the nomination of my party for President."[61]

THE WISE MEN's turn was one of many factors influencing Johnson's decision, but it wasn't the only factor: the "dump Johnson" movement within the Democratic Party had been gathering momentum since the previous summer, and the indefatigable campus organizer Allard Lowenstein helped bring moderate, mainstream student leaders like Yale's Strobe Talbott into the fold. In the fall of 1967, Talbott had written that the movement offered "a chance to crystallize sentiment against Johnson in a useful way—a way which might both help end the war and preserve the political order which the war is eroding." He predicted that "if Johnson's control over the party can be successfully contested in three or four primaries, there is a good chance either he will be defeated at the convention or will bow out before the convention in favor of someone like Eugene McCarthy."[62]

Sure enough, the cerebral, articulate antiwar Minnesota senator won forty-two percent of the New Hampshire primary vote in mid-March, a stunning total for a near-unknown running against a sitting president. McCarthy's campaign succeeded partly on the strength of thousands of eager young activists "getting clean for Gene," including Paul Moore's oldest son, Paul III, then a junior at Yale, and John Lindsay's daughter Eleanor.

McCarthy's victory emboldened New York senator Robert Kennedy to leap into the presidential race in mid-March. But Lindsay had also indirectly helped push Kennedy into the race. The National Advisory Commission on Civil Disorders (the Kerner Commission), of which Lindsay was vice chairman, had released its report. Lindsay was responsible for its fiery and much-quoted conclusion that "our nation is moving toward two societies, one black, one white—separate and unequal. . . . What white Americans have never fully understood—but what the Negro can never forget—is that white society is deeply implicated in the ghetto. White institutions created it, white institutions maintain it, and white society condones it." More than two million copies of the report were sold, and the effectiveness of its conclusion came from the fact that it was drawn by what the *New York Times*'s Tom Wicker called "representatives of the moderate and 'responsible' Establishment—not by black radicals, militant youth or even academic leftists."[63]

Conservatives attacked the report, with Richard Nixon castigating its emphasis on white racists rather than black rioters and other politicians accusing the commissioners of advocating appeasement rather than law and order. But Lindsay's conclusions were much in line with the thinking of other liberal establishment leaders. McGeorge Bundy, whose foundation had assisted the commission in its work, wrote shortly before the report was issued that "the most deep-seated and destructive of all the causes of the Negro problem is still the prejudice of the white man."[64]

Richardson endorsed the report's conclusion that "compassionate, massive, and sustained" spending would be required to overcome the problems of the ghettos.[65] He wrote that "public officials must be as concerned with eliminating the conditions which breed violence as they are with controlling the disorders that result from them." He acknowledged that the Kerner Commission's recommendations to create millions of jobs, build homes, upgrade schools, implement a guaranteed minimum income, break the discriminatory building trades unions, and eliminate segregation would be very expensive. But, he pointed out, "we are presently paying an inordinately high price for poverty and discrimination in our country. Misery generates social chaos and social chaos requires substantial sums of money just to police it, just to keep it from becoming so explosive that it destroys our nation."[66]

While Robert Kennedy saw the report as a blueprint for action, Johnson refused to accept it. Johnson also spurned Kennedy's suggestion that a blue-ribbon commission of distinguished outsiders—Kennedy mentioned

Kingman Brewster as a possible chairman—review American policy in Vietnam.[67] "This means," Kennedy concluded, "that he's not going to do anything about the war and he's not going to do anything about the cities either."[68] Kennedy announced his candidacy on March 16.

ON APRIL 4, 1968, Paul Moore was at a meeting to discuss Operation Connection, an interfaith program to channel some $10 million to urban black communities, with the aim of linking emerging black leaders to the power structure in the cities.[69] While the group, which Moore would soon be named to lead, was huddled around a table, someone burst in to say that the Reverend Martin Luther King Jr. had been assassinated in Memphis. Moore had often crossed paths with King, most recently the previous year, when they led a march on the White House for Washington home rule. "We were speechless," Moore recalled.

"Dr. King had been a symbol of all the hope and idealism of the movement," Moore wrote later.[70] Now his dream of nonviolence appeared to die with him as a rage-filled rampage of violence burst out in over 130 cities around the nation. Washington, which had thus far escaped the worst urban rioting, was the hardest hit, with looters and arsonists torching commercial districts in black sections. In what seemed a metaphor for the collapse of American order, machine guns had to be mounted outside the White House to protect it from the mob; it was, Dean Acheson wrote, "the kind of thing one reads about in Gibbon."[71]

Moore made his way across the burning city to lead a Mass that evening at Saint Stephen's of the Incarnation, an Episcopal church on the edge of the ghetto in Washington's decaying Mount Pleasant neighborhood. Saint Stephen's was the city's most integrated church, and its rector, Bill Wendt, was one of the city's leading social activists: the previous year, he had invited H. Rap Brown to speak at the church just after the Black Power leader had been indicted for starting a riot in Cambridge, Maryland. "Violence is necessary, it is as American as cherry pie," Brown told his black audience in Saint Stephen's, urging them to "get you some guns" and "burn this town down" if militant black demands were not met.[72] Moore, who had sanctioned the event, pointed out that the police thanked Wendt for offering Brown a hall when even the black churches feared to do so, thereby keeping him off the streets and possibly preventing a riot. Even so, the incident had contributed to the general uneasiness in Moore's diocese.[73]

Now the grief-stricken, frightened worshipers crowding into the church included people from all parts of the city: blacks, whites, clergy of all faiths, government workers still in coat and tie, even leaders like Senator Ted Kennedy, many with tears streaming down their cheeks. Although the church was packed to overflowing, "when the prayers began a reverent silence enveloped the congregation, and we could plainly hear the wail of sirens, the sound of gunshots, and the fearsome sound of men running as fast as they could, soles beating on the pavement."

When prayers were offered at the intercessions, individuals came forward to pray for Dr. King, the repose of his soul, his family, the nation's cities, the civil rights movement, and racial justice. Then a man at the back stood and shouted in a slurred, angry voice, "Why don't you motherfuckers stop this crap of prayers and get out in the street and fight with the brothers!" A shocked silence stilled the church until Reverend Wendt came to the microphone and replied, "Johnny, you go on out and do your thing—we are staying here to do our thing." Moore recalled that the crowd gave a good-humored "Amen" and the service proceeded.[74]

That night the federal government summoned Cyrus Vance from his law practice in New York to deal with the Washington riots. He was given a bedroom in the White House and acted as an advisor to the recently appointed Walter Washington, whom the Johnson administration (in response to pressure from Moore and the Free D.C. movement) had plucked from Lindsay's administration to serve as the city's first black mayor.[75] Together with Attorney General Ramsey Clark, Vance devised a plan to restore order that was noted for its humanitarian restraint.

When the riots died down three days after they began, nine people were dead, a considerably lower total than had been feared. Vance believed that the tighter discipline enforced on a more integrated National Guard kept the casualty figures low. Vance's restrained approach was criticized—usually by the same people who praised Chicago mayor Richard Daley's order that police "shoot to kill" arsonists and "shoot to maim or cripple" looters—for leading to undue looting.[76] Nonetheless, "I personally feel that it's better to save a life than to shoot a fourteen-year-old kid who's taking a loaf of bread," Vance said later, "and I think that by and large most police chiefs now agree with that."[77]

Lindsay's response to King's death was, some thought, his finest hour. When news of the assassination hit the city's black neighborhoods, "things almost blew clear across the city," his police chief recalled. "We had serious incidents all at the same time in Harlem, Brownsville, Bedford-Stuyvesant, the Bronx, and Coney Island."[78] But Lindsay headed straight into the center of the storm. His aides felt it was too dangerous for him to venture into Harlem, but Lindsay insisted. "Somebody just has to go up there," he argued. "Somebody white just has to face that emotion and say that we're sorry." So he took his media consultant David Garth with him. As they got out of the mayor's car and headed directly into a heaving mob of people on 125th Street, Garth thought, "My life is over."

"I kept moving," Lindsay remembered, "but finally I was hemmed in from all sides. Occasionally, I could hear my name shouted, and at other times I could hear men and women weeping or moaning." The mayor spoke to the people of his sorrow and sympathy, and his words and presence seemed to calm the crowd.[79] Lindsay remembered that on that troubled night in Harlem, the local leaders and operators whom he and his team had worked with over the previous long, hot summers "were with us in trying to keep the city calm, to prevent mobs from gathering, to keep people off the streets. They helped because they trusted us, and it took long months of work to create that trust."[80]

Lindsay was as much a believer in the policy of restraint as Vance. During discussions in connection with the Kerner Commission, each reinforced the other's belief. While there was more property damage in New York in the nights following King's assassination than initial press reports suggested—police counted six hundred separate incidents across the city—there were none of the violent confrontations between troops and ghetto residents that had turned Newark and Detroit into battlegrounds the year before. The police cordoned off the worst disturbances and brought them under control without overreacting. Sanitation workers moved in to clean up the worst of the broken glass and debris before daybreak. The city administration prevented press and television coverage from sensationalizing the disturbances—not merely so that Lindsay would look good but to keep the separate incidents from creating a chain reaction that would reduce the city to ashes. As former Lindsay official Charles Morris observed, other cities that tried to squelch riots with force in the wake of King's death quickly found that they had to adopt the Vance-Lindsay policy of containment and restraint: "Meeting the disturbances with force and firepower merely caused events to escalate out of control."[81]

*   *   *

WHEN WORD OF King's assassination spread through New Haven on April 4, a group of about two thousand people, mainly black, marched to the Green to mourn and protest. Two days later, Brewster and Coffin led a larger, mainly white group to the same place and for the same purpose. The university canceled classes to honor King's memory, and thousands of members of the community signed a petition urging Congress to pass immediate civil rights legislation. On the day after King's funeral, Brewster issued a long statement acknowledging that "the message of the Kerner Report applies to Yale just as it does to any other American citizen or institution." The university could and should do more, he wrote, about the discrimination, poverty, inadequate education, and poor housing that afflicted many of the city's minority citizens. At the same time, "Yale cannot solve the problems of New Haven, nor can it be its banker or redeveloper. It would be immoral to raise such false expectations."[82]

The university already was engaged in efforts to improve the situation of the city and its minorities through affirmative action employment and compensatory-education programs. The law school provided free legal services to the indigent, while the medical center offered health care at no cost. Brewster's assistant Joel Fleishman was a coordinator of these activities; since the August 1967 riots he had been meeting with black New Haveners to discuss their problems and consider how Yale might help. On April 1 he had written to Brewster urging that the university establish a community corporation to work with the city and its residents on antipoverty efforts.[83]

Brewster also vowed that Yale would work closely with and help fund the Black Coalition, a moderate-led umbrella group of organizations and neighborhood associations that had worked to keep the city cool in the wake of King's assassination. The president saluted the coalition and its leaders Henry Parker and Hugh Price (who would later head the National Urban League) for inspiring hope for constructive solutions in New Haven "when so many other cities have been reduced to arson, looting, and martial law. Failure to respond to this hope could only encourage the ugly belief that violence or its threat is the only way the powers that be can be moved."[84]

That same belief led Brewster to seek to rescue the Poor People's March in Washington, which had been planned by King and was carried forward after his assassination by his allies Ralph Abernathy and Jesse Jackson. Abernathy set up a shantytown in the capital and promised to "plague the Pharaohs of this nation . . . until they agree to give us meaningful jobs and a guaranteed income."[85] The protest quickly devolved into a sodden morass of mud, crime, and disorder. Before Brewster was to give a speech in Washington, he sent telegrams to David Rockefeller, Henry Ford, Thomas Watson of IBM, and other business leaders in his circle, asking them to help rescue the march. "I feel that it is terribly important that Abernathy and Jackson who are constructive non-violent leaders should not be shamed by a festering frittering end to the Poor People's March," he wrote. "If they become the laughingstock of the militants then there will be a literal fiery hell to pay." He suggested that an establishment group propose a negative income tax policy and work to commit all presidential candidates to support it, at least in principle.[86] Although nothing came of his proposal, it was evidence of his alarm at the national situation and of the policies he thought might ameliorate it.

Back in New Haven, Brewster designated his personal assistant C. Tracy Barnes to head the new Yale Council on Community Affairs. It was an inspired choice. Barnes was a blue-blooded ex-CIA official, a cousin of John Hay Whitney's whose vertiginous rise through the agency had come to a crashing halt with the failure of the Bay of Pigs invasion. Hired by Brewster in 1966 in the hope that his old-school manner and connections would soothe disgruntled alumni, Barnes had grown bored with the Old Blues. His new responsibility suited both his liberal idealism and his taste for danger and intrigue.

Barnes served the same role for Brewster that Barry Gottehrer served for John Lindsay, seeking out the most militant black activists in order to keep a step ahead of any tensions that might flare up. Sometimes he met with his contacts after midnight in deserted ghetto walkups just to accentuate the spookiness of it all.[87] Barnes could not be intimidated by those who tried to threaten or shake down the university. On one occasion, a woman picked up a heavy glass ashtray off his desk and hurled it at his head. It whizzed past his ear and shattered against the wall behind him. Barnes was relieved, because he knew then that she had meant to miss.[88] His fearlessness with community activists, like Brewster's with black students, helped all parties get beyond posturing and deal with substantive issues. Once the black community determined that Barnes was an honest broker, a man they could trust to tell them clearly what they could and could not expect from the university, there was less need to take a radical or threatening stance.

One of the reasons Barnes was so effective, Brewster's assistant Jon Fanton recalled, was that he looked the part. He was "tall, well-spoken, with a patrician accent and all the rest. When Tracy went down to talk to Fred Harris on the Hill, the community leaders said, 'We're seeing Yale.

This is what we expect Yale to look like. We're dealing with the Man.' Tracy did a lot of good in building bridges very quickly to the black community. And one of the reasons Yale, and New Haven for that matter, came through this very difficult late '60s period as smoothly as we did owes to the relationships and trust that Tracy developed."[89]

AS BREWSTER WAS worrying about the threat to Yale from outside, he was becoming alarmed by student revolutionaries within. The New Left had not had much of a foothold at Yale in the mid-1960s. In the fall of 1965, the university's handful of radicals included the students around Peter Countryman and the Northern Student Movement, the Yale Council on Civil Rights, and the members of Yale's first chapter of Students for a Democratic Society.[90] At that time, a small group of undergraduates in SDS obtained Yale's permission to move off campus; after much debate within the administration, they relocated to the Hill ghetto of New Haven, where they concentrated on community organizing.[91] Together with their mainly black and Hispanic neighbors, they formed the Hill Neighborhood Union and engaged in voter registration drives, rent strikes, picketing (often directed at urban redevelopment efforts), and other attempts at grassroots democracy and community activism. Although their efforts received considerable attention, the SDS made little impression at Yale.

The SDS that revived in the fall of 1967, however, was more influenced by antiwar politics and the counterculture than by the civil rights movement. The difference was manifest in the undergraduate career of Mark Zanger, the most prominent leader of SDS at Yale in the late 1960s. (He was caricatured as Megaphone Mark in Garry Trudeau's *Yale Daily News* comic strip *Bull Tales*, which was later nationally syndicated as *Doonesbury*, while Brewster was immortalized as President King.)

Zanger came to Yale in the fall of 1966 with Inky Clark's first class, the Class of 1970. On paper, at any rate, the cherubic-looking Zanger seemed an unlikely candidate to become a leading radical, having graduated from Brewster's father's prep school, the Williston Academy, and been recommended by John Hay Whitney. But Zanger recalled that his "notoriously precedent-breaking class . . . was really sort of the turning point in the baby boom attitudinally. . . . [W]e felt a lot of division between ourselves and the older undergraduates. And a lot of stuff changed as we walked over it."[92]

In the 1966–67 academic year, New Haven residents complained about Yale "beatniks," with "their beards, long hair, dirty slovenly clothes and sockless feet," as one citizen put it.[93] Zanger remembered that "our class arrived and basically marijuana and LSD arrived with us." (He guessed that there were only a dozen or so upperclassmen "who used and liked drugs and embraced the counterculture."[94]) That same year, in a neat metaphor for the changing zeitgeist, students broke into the bomb shelters set up in Yale basements in the 1950s and dosed themselves with the phenobarbital stored there for the survivors of nuclear Armageddon.[95]

In his freshman year Zanger wrote drug-influenced *Yale Daily News* columns on the fictional adventures of Joe the Clod, Louie the Anarchist, and the Nutmeg Freak. He was "not into SDS at that point," he recalled. "I was just a humorist and a hippie."[96] By the fall of the next year, however, he was a member of Yale Provo, a group that staged antiauthority happenings such as smashing a piano, holding a "read-in" at Beinecke Library (where students were forbidden to study), and wearing boxers and garish cardboard ties at a "tie-in" protesting mandatory coats and ties in the residential college dining halls.[97] (The coat-and-tie rule would be abolished soon afterward.)

The revived chapter of SDS that Zanger joined that fall consisted mainly of graduate students who combined political discussions of a social-democratic variety with pickets against Lady Bird Johnson's visit to Yale, CIA recruitment on campus, and the New Haven draft induction center.[98] The group, calling for governance reforms in the name of student power, expressed general distaste for Yale as an institution. One article noted that SDS member Howard Shrobe '68 (who had also been a member of Provo) "was more anti-Yale than anti-war. 'I regard this place as a mess. There are ivy-covered walls, but that's all there is to it,' he said."[99]

In late April 1968, Zanger covered the SDS-led student rebellion at Columbia University for the *Yale Daily News*. The Action Faction of the Columbia SDS, under the soon-to-be-notorious Mark Rudd, rallied students to protest the university's planned construction of a gym in an adjoining minority neighborhood (among other issues) and occupied a series of buildings. When Columbia president Grayson Kirk, after much dithering, ordered the police to clear the buildings, something close to a police riot broke out. The New York City police, stretched taut by Lindsay's policy of restraint in handling civil unrest, lashed out at what they saw as spoiled, privileged students. Numerous injuries resulted, and previously moderate students became radicalized. Final exams were canceled amid widespread calls for a fundamental restructuring of the university, and Columbia was effectively shut down. In August, Kirk announced his early retirement.[100]

Partly because of media coverage, these events greatly influenced the development of campus radicalism nationally. The Columbia crisis also reflected the atmosphere of polarization and sharpening ideological differences stemming from the ongoing war in Vietnam, the urban riots, and King's assassination. The Columbia "revolution" produced a quantum leap in the volume and temperature of the rhetoric of both New Left and New Right. Even at the time, the events were viewed as a convenient measure of the distance that student activism had traveled since the Berkeley Free Speech Movement in 1964: from nonviolence to violence, from civil disobedience to direct action, from humanitarianism to Che-styled radicalism. The SDS of the early 1960s criticized the university as a source of student alienation and apathy; the SDS of the late 1960s indicted it as an agent of racist imperialism at home and abroad. Zanger believed that the police bust "was the war come home. This was the true face of American hypocrisy displayed to the people from whom it was supposed to be hidden. . . . Grayson Kirk didn't care if we lived or died; we were an impediment to his business operation."[101]

Lindsay had not been inclined to get involved in the Columbia crisis. In fact, once the Columbia trustees filed a formal complaint of trespass against the building occupiers, he had no authority to hold back the police.[102] According to Lindsay's aide Barry Gottehrer, Brewster warned the mayor that "the very future of the American university depended on punishing the strikers. If Columbia gave amnesty to students who had occupied buildings, willfully destroyed records and defied every authority, it would be impossible to run any university."[103]

Brewster was more resolutely opposed to student power than his student-friendly rhetoric usually revealed. He was not instinctively antagonistic to the SDS's concept of participatory democracy and welcomed the benefits of self-determination and "meaningful participation in the decisions which affect you." But, he told an audience in the spring of 1968, SDS "is still to me more adequately described as Students to Destroy Society . . . because they are so long on disruption and so short on positive programs." The problem with participatory democracy as applied to student power was that even in the most politicized years of the 1960s, most undergraduates were more interested in getting an education and developing themselves than in running the university. Since the majority of students would probably not be involved in participatory democracy, Brewster predicted that "spokesmanship will fall to a most unrepresentative minority group," those motivated by political ego.[104]

But Brewster recognized that such legalistic admonitions would not make the problem of student unrest go away. An unruly, questioning spirit had taken hold among the younger generation. As Richardson put it, "the weakening of parental authority has encouraged challenges to all authority. . . . 'it's so because I say it's so' has become an unacceptable answer."[105]

Archibald Cox, who had taught law to Brewster and Richardson at Harvard, headed a fact-finding commission on the Columbia disturbances; he found that part of what had brought on the crisis was the unconscious authoritarianism by which universities had traditionally operated. In part it was a governance problem—Columbia, like Yale, had no effective student government—but in part it was a matter of style. Cox's commission observed that Columbia students were affronted to be told "that an influential University official was no more interested in student opinion on matters of intense interest to students than he was in their taste for strawberries."[106]

Evidence of changing student attitudes confronted Brewster when a protest percolated in April over the architectural plans for Yale's new underground library. The protest was in some part aesthetic—the plans called for large glass skylights that would reduce the size of the students' much-loved Cross Campus lawn—and in some part political—students were outraged at not having been consulted.[107] But the university had never previously thought it necessary to seek out student opinion on such matters, and Brewster, no doubt, found it odd to have to deal with student protesters proclaiming, "Grass Not Glass—Grass Has Class."[108] Then again, although the university had never asked for the opinion of the community before constructing buildings in ghetto neighborhoods, Yale was now working closely with the Black Coalition and Hill Parents Association toward that end. The plans for the library were changed, and it was clear that the university's conception of authority would have to change as well.

BREWSTER HAD ALREADY been moving toward a more open, visible model of leadership by taking a page from Lindsay. Cyrus Vance observed that "John did an excellent job in walking the streets and going out during that very difficult time when there was high racial tension within the United States. There was a similarity there, the same way that Kingman was willing to walk the streets and try to keep the peace by his own personal strength."[109] Most of the other Ivy League presidents were invisible men, who seemed to believe that the dignity of office required them to remain aloof from the rest of the community. By contrast, almost everyone who was at Yale in the late 1960s has a memory of Kingman Brewster and his wife, Mary Louise, walking their black Labrador and golden retriever across the campus, dropping in at random on administrators, college masters, and undergraduates. Or they remember Brewster in the stands at the football games, in the presidential pew at Battell Chapel, or driving in his Jaguar with the Yale license plates and the dogs in the backseat.

Brewster succeeded in conveying an impression of ubiquity, when in fact by the mid-1960s he had become Yale's first jet-setting president. As a semipolitical public figure and media favorite, he was in constant demand around the country. He delivered two to three dozen major addresses yearly, took on major outside responsibilities like the presidential commissions on crime and the draft, and was scheduled to the hilt—in contrast to his predecessor, whose weekday calendar usually had one appointment in the morning and one in the afternoon.[110] It would not be atypical for Brewster to drive to New York to meet with alumni, fly to Washington to testify before a Senate committee, spend the night at billionaire alumnus Paul Mellon's estate in Virginia horse country, fly overseas the next day for a meeting of the executive board of the International Association of Universities, and be back in New Haven in time for the football game. It was all the more important, then, that when he was on campus he had multiple channels of information.

Brewster's reasons for lessening the distance between students and the administration were partly in the interest of community and communication, and partly political. He talked with undergraduates as he made his rounds with the dogs, and held regular, casual forums in the residential colleges. When the political climate began to heat up, he jokingly referred to these visits as "rural pacification missions." Such informal meetings on the streets, in the colleges, in his Woodbridge Hall office, and occasionally at dinners in his house or in the colleges were useful to the president and the students alike. Since the president was able to keep abreast of what students were thinking, he could sometimes act to alleviate discontent before it festered. The students, for their part, could argue with a flesh-and-blood leader rather than a faceless bureaucracy. Students called Brewster "a charismatic listener."

This made him an unusual figure among college and university presidents. A University of Pennsylvania student wrote that while Brewster had weekly meetings with student leaders, Penn's president, Gaylord Harnwell, had "little or no connection with the students; most of them see him only twice in their college careers—at Opening Day exercises and Commencement."

The Penn reporter complained that Harnwell, like the aging Chairman Mao, had vanished from public view, and speculated that "perhaps the Office of the President will soon issue a picture of Harnwell swimming in the Schuylkill, to prove he really exists."[111]

At Yale, by contrast, undergraduates had a sense that authority was accessible—taking student concerns seriously and making sincere efforts to deal with their grievances. Students never got the seat on the Corporation or the voice in academic policy and faculty hiring that many of them wanted, and a number of governance reforms effected in the 1960s petered out in the exhaustion of the 1970s. But for the first time, students were given a say in matters that affected them, including the disciplinary system, admissions policies, the curriculum, and life in the residential colleges.

Thanks in part to Brewster's efforts, the residential colleges (which had been less important when Yale was dominated by the preparatory schools) experienced a revitalization in the 1960s. As longtime Silliman College master Eli Clark observed, "Students from Andover, St. Paul's, and Hotchkiss didn't need the colleges; they had support systems they came in with." But for the student who came in alone from Cheyenne High School, "the colleges did a wonderful job," and their role as centers of community grew as the percentage of public high school students increased.[112] The colleges' displacement of the fraternities as the hub of student social life had a significant effect in breaking the exclusive, preppy culture that had characterized Yale.

Because of the decentralization of the decanal system that Brewster accomplished earlier, each residential college now had a dean whose responsibility was to advise and counsel all students in the college (previously, only the best and worst students had any real contact with the dean's office). The result, Assistant Dean John Wilkinson remembered, was to transform the colleges into "places that really established an identity." When he attended student debates, Wilkinson was impressed that "students would stand up . . . and say, 'I'm Bill from Silliman,'" a form of self-identification that none of his 1950s contemporaries could comprehend. "The '60s was a time when students lost their surnames, and because for the first time they were able to take leaves of absence, their class didn't count so much. But they created surnames for themselves; their surnames were their residential colleges."[113]

The small scale and social intimacy of the residential communities were an important part of students' affection for Yale in moments of crisis. Zanger's dislike of Yale as an institution was compromised by his affection for Silliman College and its master, Eli Clark. In the late 1960s, Zanger and other members of SDS stayed in the college instead of going home over the holiday break, and Clark invited them to his house for Christmas dinner. He was amused to remember Zanger and some other would-be revolutionaries dressed in coat and tie, playing games with Clark's young children, and behaving "like perfect gentlemen."[114]

Until the 1960s, the residential colleges had never fulfilled the hope that they would become intellectual as well as social communities. The situation would change when students grew dissatisfied with what they considered the irrelevant department-based curriculum. "Relevance" in education has long been a matter of debate. Some students demanding curricular relevance wanted courses that would cater to their passing political and countercultural interests, but by no means all. "Too many administrators and teachers interpret the call for 'relevance' as a demand for political action and entrance into the public arena," senior Derek Shearer told a group of alumni in the spring of 1968. "In my mind, relevance connotes not immediacy, but relation to the real world as it actually is. . . . Education is not just filling one's head with facts, getting right answers and learning to take tests. Education means learning how to think for oneself, to experience beauty for oneself, to choose one's own actions."[115]

By the mid-1960s, students had already started to run their own noncredit seminars from within the residential colleges. Displaying his genius for co-option, in 1968 Brewster made the students' cause his own by supporting the creation of for-credit residential college seminars. College masters, fellows, and students participated jointly in selecting courses and instructors, which then had to be approved by the faculty. At its peak the college seminar system was a laboratory where faculty and outside instructors could experiment with courses and teaching methods, and students could influence the shape of their studies. Talented nonacademic experts brought fresh air from the external world, student–fellow relations became closer, and an intellectual element was introduced into residential college life.[116]

Many faculty members severely distrusted the program: however liberal the faculty may have been politically, Brewster observed, its members were hardbitten reactionaries when it came to their own departmental prerogatives. They were prepared to tolerate the seminars for their good effects on the residential college community and for their role in dampening down student frustrations. But many of the faculty gradually realized that students had legitimate intellectual justifications for their grievances. The Yale curriculum was indeed narrow and inflexible in some areas, with little emphasis on writing, and even less attention to matters of race, ethnicity, and gender. The faculty's suspicion of newness extended even to artistic forms such as film and photography. The sociology professor Kai Erikson, who studied the seminar system, found that, over time, much of the innovation in the residential college seminars passed into the regular curriculum.[117] The college seminar program, like the creation of the Afro-Am studies program, demonstrated that there were good intellectual as well as social and political reasons for giving students a voice in the decision-making process.

THE LAW STUDENT Greg Craig, who became one of Brewster's closest student advisors in the late 1960s, had been the Harvard Class Day speaker at his graduation in 1967. Students in the 1960s, he said then, were "a generation that is up for grabs, for their hope could easily turn to hate, and their passion for building a more equitable society could easily surrender to the temptation to tear down an unjust and oppressive society."[118] "The generation *was* up for grabs," Craig reminisced later. "I was fighting desperately with other people like me to keep it within the American system."[119] But Brewster was one of the relatively few leaders who really engaged with the students, who met their skepticism before it could turn to cynicism. What made Brewster successful was that he embodied the concept that would be carved on his tombstone: "the presumption of innocence." It was a quality that made him as effective a diplomat, in his way, as his friend Cyrus Vance. Brewster's assistant Sam Chauncey felt that "Kingman really believed the best and not the worst about a person he didn't know. So if he went into a meeting with a radical group and they were looking awful and yelling obscenities, Kingman could genuinely see each one of them as a human being who had something to offer. . . . He really did presume innocence in others. And that made him very good at dealing with hostile groups and difficult people, because he was disarming in his ability to show respect."[120]

To be sure, some of Brewster's success resulted from other factors, including plain old good luck. For example, SDS once was staging an angry rally on Beinecke Plaza when Mary Louise Brewster came walking by with the dogs, who broke their leash and became involved in a wild four-way dogfight. That was all for the rally.[121] Brewster had the kind of luck that enabled him to blithely sail without maps, confident that the rocks would strike the boats of those less favored by Providence. "I was never sure if Kingman believed in God," Coffin observed, "but I was sure that God believed in Kingman."[122] Gary Johnson, a freshman in 1968, remembered that "Brewster's luck" was a common phrase on campus, a force of nature that dictated that it would never rain on official events like commencement but would always rain on protest rallies. "As people planned meetings and demonstrations," he recalled, "they would shake their heads and say, 'Brewster's luck—it's going to rain on us.' It would enter into their plans. It was a widely held belief, a fact of life."[123]

It was Brewster's good fortune that Yale was located in a small city that had only a small contingent of the drug-soaked nonstudents who added to the volatility of campus demonstrations in places like New York, Boston, and Berkeley.[124] Brewster also believed that "happily the bright people at Yale were not knaves and the knaves were not very bright, whereas there were some very bright knaves elsewhere."[125]

But Brewster also was a better tactician than many other university presidents. Zanger recalled that Brewster "would never do the stupid thing that would put everybody on our side. He wouldn't call the cops to smash our heads. . . . I spent a lot of time trying to fathom this guy in order to be able to embarrass and defeat him. And I really did come to admire his cleverness."[126] Brewster and Chauncey used to speculate about how *they* would bring down a university president if they were student radicals. They concluded that the radicals lacked mastery of more subtle terrorist tactics; because the radicals' program was completely out front, it was easier to handle.[127]

Brewster's undergraduate experience with America First came in handy, as he could recognize and respond to activist attitudes when he saw them reappear a generation later. Unlike many adult observers during the 1960s, Brewster believed that most student protest involved actual issues and was not simply an extension of students' egos and psyches. Because of his undergraduate involvement, he recalled, he had "more appreciation of the motivation of those [who] other people tend to think are just trouble-makers."[128]

Charles Taylor pointed out that Brewster "knew from experience that students could sometimes have a gut feeling for something that was more correct than the older generation. That gut feeling was not always wise, not always well understood. But Kingman did not assume that the students were always wrong."[129] On the other hand, Strobe Talbott believed that Brewster's experience of having been on the wrong side of a defining moral issue "gave him a sense of irony and the fallibility of student activism. . . . I always felt that Kingman was saying two things to us when we would debate the [Vietnam] war. It was, 'You guys are terrific, and I love your conviction and your idealism and your passion and your willingness to put yourself on the line for what you believe in . . . but don't be so goddamn sure you're right.'"[130]

BREWSTER WOULD NOT look back fondly on the spring of 1968. Along with the terrible national events, such as King's death and urban riots, he had to deal with significant local upheaval, including the Cross Campus affair, racial protest in the law school, and a short but angry labor strike. The troubles extended to his own family when his oldest son, twenty-year-old Kingman III, was arrested in early April, along with twenty others, for "being present where a narcotic drug [i.e., marijuana] was illegally kept or deposited," at a party on Martha's Vineyard.[131] The New York Times carried a brief description of the arrest, while a longer account, in the New Haven Register, noted that young Kingman, who had dropped out of Occidental College after one semester and had recently been classified as a conscientious objector, appeared in court with long hair and sideburns, wearing a brown turtleneck sweater, striped pants, and boots.[132]

When the local paper called the accused's father for comment, he told the reporter he was going to resign as university president, then stalked over to his assistant Sam Chauncey's house to give him the news. Chauncey was dumbfounded. He pointed out that Brewster himself had not been arrested for marijuana and that plenty of other sons of well-known men of his generation (a list that soon would include Robert F. Kennedy Jr. and R. Sargent Shriver III) had been busted on the same charge. "But he said that it was, in fact, ultimately his fault, and therefore he should resign as president of Yale. Well, we got him over that pretty quickly, but that represented the sort of moralistic streak that was part of his makeup."[133]

William Sloane Coffin was also considering resigning from Yale. While Coffin was fighting his conspiracy indictment in a Boston courthouse, his marriage was falling apart. After he filed for divorce, he went to the president's house to submit his resignation. The Brewsters talked Coffin out of resigning, and Kingman asked the chaplain if he would like to move into the president's house for a while. "I was hard pressed to hold back the tears," Coffin remembered. The chaplain and president were at swords' points on many issues, and "I would hardly be his favorite house guest. Yet his offer of hospitality was totally spontaneous."[134] It was a comforting gesture in an awful time.

Then in early June, Robert Kennedy was assassinated just after winning the California Democratic primary. Talbott, who graduated five days later, remembered that "there was a real sense of heading towards oppressiveness."[135] Paul Moore, delivering the commencement invocation in place of the absent Coffin, painted a picture in words of a nation falling apart: "We see strange forms appearing. Inner depths split open the sudden emptiness of trusted symbols, and we are afraid. The once strong structures of our civilization are giving way. Our nation, which we love, staggers like a blind giant under blow upon blow and in the staggering often crushes those it seeks to help."[136]

Richardson attended Kennedy's funeral at Saint Patrick's Cathedral in New York City. He thought better of his old enemy by now; time and the experience of his brother's assassination, he believed, had made Kennedy a wiser, more sensitive leader. McGeorge Bundy was also there in the pews; his later authorization of travel and research grants to Kennedy's grieving aides would get him into hot water with his political enemies. Lindsay was at the service as well. Kennedy and Lindsay, as the two highest-profile politicians in New York, had been uneasy rivals, all but certain to contend in a future presidential race. Arthur Schlesinger Jr. observed that Lindsay privately considered the New York senator a publicity hound, while Kennedy thought Lindsay something of a lightweight and was jealous of the mayor's good looks and charisma. "But they agreed on most things, especially on the importance of racial justice, and each essentially respected the other."[137] The two men also worked together and with McGeorge Bundy on the creation of a community development corporation in the depressed Bedford-Stuyvesant neighborhood, an effort that became a model of its kind.

Now, Kennedy's death presented Lindsay with a political dilemma. It fell to New York governor Nelson Rockefeller to appoint a replacement for Kennedy, whose term ran until 1970. Although Lindsay and Rockefeller were both liberal Republicans, they had sniped at each other over the years, and their egos got in the way of compromise on New York City–State issues. Nonetheless, most political observers thought the governor was obliged to offer the Senate position to the mayor, but Rockefeller was too proud to offer without being asked, and Lindsay was too proud to ask. One of the few people Lindsay called for advice was New Haven mayor Dick Lee, who counseled him to stay put.[138] In the end, Lindsay let it be known that he would rather stay on as mayor than take the Senate seat. He instructed the journalist Nat Hentoff to tell Rockefeller that "in terms of power, complexity, and responsibility, my job dwarfs even his and that he ought to keep that in mind."[139]

One observer who felt Lindsay should have asked Rockefeller for the Senate position was Vernon Jordan, the dynamic young leader of the United Negro College Fund. Lindsay offered Jordan the job of running New York's Model Cities program. "John," Jordan remembered replying, "I just found out that the Kennedy Airport is in Queens. I've never been to Brooklyn or Staten Island. The only thing I know about the Bronx is that it has a zoo." Lindsay swept aside his objections. When he went to lunch with some of Lindsay's assistants, they told him, "Jordan, you've got to get on board this train." Where, he asked, was it going? "1600 Pennsylvania Avenue!" The problem, Jordan felt, was that "Lindsay had a mandate to take care of the city, not the nation. The young people around him had convinced him to look beyond his mandate, and it was the wrong decision. When Rockefeller telephoned, he should have taken the call."

Kingman Brewster, another able spotter of talent, also had his sights on Jordan, who was a fellow of Ezra Stiles College at Yale and had worked alongside Brewster on the draft commission. Brewster proposed that Jordan leave the UNCF to become the vice president in charge of Yale's minority issues. He replied, "Kingman, why should I give up being Chancellor of the Exchequer for forty black colleges to be your Deputy for the Colored?" Brewster "howled" with laughter, Jordan recalled affectionately. "Kingman was a hell of a man."[140]

BREWSTER'S DIFFICULT YEAR was unfurling against the backdrop of Bill Buckley's campaign to best Cyrus Vance in the Yale Corporation election. Brewster and his trustees had added fuel to the fire by reappointing Chaplain Coffin, still under indictment for conspiracy, to an unlimited term; Coffin doubted "that many other university corporations would have taken so courageous and generous a stand."[141] Buckley's Yale supporters had mounted a vigorous campaign, mailing thousands of letters to friends and classmates supporting the insurgency. The candidate had pressed his effort through his column and articles; the April *Atlantic Monthly* carried a typically insouciant Buckley interview with himself on his reasons for wanting to become a Yale trustee.

Privately, Vance thought "that with all the fuss and publicity that Bill Buckley was pumping out to get himself elected that he would probably be elected."[142] Publicly, he said only that "I think we should get the best student body possible, no matter where they come from. As for the dangers of liberalism, I consider myself basically a liberal, and you can draw your own conclusions."[143] Brewster maintained an official silence, although behind closed doors he occasionally indulged in an imitation of Buckley's affected British drawl. But when Brewster awarded Vance an honorary degree at the 1968 commencement ceremonies, he did laud his friend for exemplifying the Yale tradition of citizen service to the nation. "Your understanding of the realities of power," he told Vance, "has equipped you to serve more effectively the universal aspiration for peace."[144]

A week later, after a record 32,000 votes had been cast—representing almost half of the university's living alumni—Brewster stood up on the final day of class reunions to make a one-sentence announcement. "Gentlemen," he said with a poker face, "I have the privilege to tell you that Cyrus Vance, Class of '39, has been elected to the Corporation." While the vote tallies were not released, one Corporation member told a friend, "I thought Cy would win but I never thought he'd win as big as he did. It wasn't even a contest. He just creamed Bill."[145] The election result, and that year's record-setting alumni donations to Yale, convinced Brewster that most of the alumni were still with him despite the upheavals of recent years.

Vance would have a busy summer before returning to New Haven in the fall for his first Corporation meeting. Johnson had asked him to serve as Harriman's deputy negotiator, with the rank of ambassador, in peace talks with the North Vietnamese.[146] The seventy-six-year-old Harriman "could be a loose cannon," according to Undersecretary of State Nicholas Katzenbach, "and we wanted somebody who was a good deal younger and would steady Averell down." Harriman's partner had to be someone the older man respected, "and he respected Cy a great deal."[147] So Vance was pressed into service yet again. "He has a serious physical problem and a serious financial problem," Johnson told a group of *Washington Star* reporters before Vance set out on his mission, "and I keep him working just as much of that time that the body will bear and the bank will permit."[148]

Vance and his wife spent several nights in early May in the Lincoln Bedroom at the White House before departing for Paris, the designated site of the talks. The Vances arrived in the French capital in time to witness the student and labor protests that shut down the country and nearly toppled the de Gaulle government, a salutary reminder that the 1960s unrest was an international phenomenon.

Hope ran high for a rapid resolution to the Vietnam War, so much so that the American delegation took suites on the fifth floor of the luxurious Hotel Crillon in the expectation that a settlement could be reached in a matter of months. But the North Vietnamese, perceiving that Tet had drained

Americans' will to fight, had no intention of halting their military advance. When the United States insisted that the North Vietnamese withdraw their forces from the South, the Communists demanded that the United States call a total bombing halt before they would even consider negotiations. As the talks reached an impasse, the American negotiators moved to cheaper rooms on the first floor. Vance visited Washington at the end of May to report to the president and congressional leaders that the Americans had made no tangible progress. He characterized the North Vietnamese as polite and proper, "but their words are very strong."[149] He believed the enemy was using the talks as a propaganda device, in pursuit of a "fight-and-talk strategy."[150] And so the talks wore on through the summer.

When Gay Vance joined her husband in Paris, their twelve-year-old son would stay with the Bundys at their apartment in Manhattan. Cyrus Jr. impressed Mary Bundy as the most organized child imaginable; each night he would place his completed homework in a briefcase outside his door.[151]

For the past year, Mac Bundy and Cy Vance had been working together at Johnson's behest to create an independent, nonprofit research institute that would provide independent analysis of government performance and data-driven research on urban questions. Both served on a six-man panel, chaired by Ford Foundation and Yale trustee J. Irwin Miller, that was responsible for nominating a board of directors and drafting incorporation papers for what became the Urban Institute.[152]

Johnson's assistant Joseph Califano recalled that "at the height of the Great Society initiative, we passed at least a hundred laws a year, so we were choking the government with new programs."[153] The Urban Institute would be a means of objectively assessing those programs, of bridging what Johnson called "the gulf between the . . . scholar in search of truth and the decision-maker in search of progress."[154] Califano worked closely with Bundy to get sufficient Ford funding and government contacts in place for the institute to survive after the Johnson team left office. Onto its board, in the fullness of time, went Bundy, Vance, Brewster, and Richardson. Califano later remembered the creation of the Urban Institute as an example of the kind of government partnership with nongovernment establishment figures that largely ended with the Johnson era. "It was a lot easier in those days. There were fewer rules and regulations, so it was simpler for people in government to have those kinds of dealings with trusted individuals like Bundy outside the government."[155]

In April 1968, Nicholas Katzenbach was casting about for an individual who could serve secretly as the president's personal representative on a trip to the Middle East, still in turmoil after the war the previous year. Such an individual, he wrote Johnson, "should be a private person in whom you have confidence rather than a government official. . . . The emissary should have some ostensible reason for the visit other than the actual purpose."[156] Not surprisingly, Johnson chose McGeorge Bundy, who set off on the trip in early July, nominally to review Ford Foundation matters in the region.

Bundy had a ninety-minute conversation with Egypt's leader, Gamal Abdel Nasser, on July 3 and, his debriefer recorded, came away from the meeting with the impression that there was "no prospect for early improvement in the Middle East situation." On the subject of relations with the Israelis, Nasser was intransigent. When Bundy suggested that Nasser's remarks indicated an underlying belief that no political solution was in sight, the Egyptian leader remarked, "Then there is only one other solution." Nasser assured Bundy that his country would fight more effectively the next time, since he had taken the initiative to obtain Soviet military advisors and made other improvements. When Bundy asked if he had any message for the Israeli leaders Bundy would soon visit, Nasser said, "Tell them we are patient."[157] Bundy spent July Fourth in Beirut, then moved on to Israel and Jordan, where he found the leaders more reasonable. However, he frankly advised Jordan's King Hussein "that the US was heavily preoccupied with the war in Viet-Nam and with elections, and that there was little incentive to expend energy on a no-result exercise in the Arab-Israel contest."[158]

By the time Bundy returned to the States, in late July, Richard Nixon had largely secured the Republican nomination. Vice President Hubert Humphrey had little chance of beating him, Bundy thought, unless he separated himself from Johnson's position on Vietnam. Bundy and McNamara informed Humphrey that if he was prepared to break with Johnson's approach to the war and work to disengage the United States, the two former architects of the war would publicly support Humphrey's position.[159] But when the vice president went to the West Wing for his appointment to discuss the plan with Johnson, the president—probably guessing what Humphrey wanted to talk about—kept him waiting long enough that Humphrey lost his nerve.

While his brother was in the Middle East, Bill Bundy was in Paris, meeting with Harriman, Vance, Katzenbach, and Philip Habib from the State Department (who had been one of the briefers at the last Wise Men meeting). There had been a lull in Communist military activity in Vietnam at that point, which Vance felt strongly that the negotiating team should interpret "as an action which was both political and military, and that this might be used as a basis for trying to find a proper formula on which to stop the bombing."[160] The five men drafted what became Harriman and Vance's July 29 cable appealing to Johnson to end the bombing unilaterally. Without such a dramatic move, they warned, "the month of August, and particularly the Democratic convention, will produce a further division of domestic US opinion which will severely weaken the base which is necessary for the long, hard negotiations required to achieve a just solution."[161] The day after the proposal arrived, Johnson summoned Bill Bundy to his office and, Bundy remembered, "the President just *absolutely* flatly rejected it."[162] In so doing, Johnson destroyed what Vance believed to have been an important opportunity for peace.[163]

At the Democratic convention in Chicago, Johnson blocked a proposed compromise plank recommending an unconditional bombing halt along the same lines as the Harriman–Vance cable. Humphrey went along rather than jeopardize his nomination, tearing the convention apart and sparking the angry antiwar demonstrations outside that led police to club and gas the demonstrators—a sordid spectacle that all but guaranteed victory for the Republicans in the fall presidential election.

While Lindsay was touted in some quarters as the GOP presidential nominee, the mayor himself had set his sights on 1972. Talk then turned to the possibility that Lindsay might be offered the vice presidential spot on Nixon's ticket, but Lindsay was ambivalent and the southern conservatives Nixon was courting were actively opposed to his nomination. Instead, Nixon selected the little-known Maryland governor, Spiro Agnew. At Nixon's request, Lindsay gave Agnew's seconding speech at the Republican convention, although he mentioned the candidate only three times and dwelt mainly on the urban crisis. That Lindsay would recommend the person who would become Nixon's hatchet man against the liberal establishment was not quite as strange as it would later seem. William Scranton remembered that Agnew had originally been known as a Rockefeller supporter and a civil rights liberal, elected with black support, who "did a very good job with education and other fields that we 'liberal' Republicans felt were important." During the riots in Baltimore that followed King's assassination, however, a black delegation had met with Agnew in his office. Scranton said that the encounter "was a very traumatic experience for him, because as he described it to me, they were unruly and adamant; there was no reasonableness there at all. And that changed Spiro Agnew. From then on he became a totally different person."[164] But the depth of Agnew's apostasy was not yet fully appreciated.

Richardson's first choice for the GOP presidential nomination was Nelson Rockefeller. When Johnson announced he would not run for reelection, Richardson wrote to Brewster's aide David Martin that now Rockefeller would be forced to become an active candidate "in response to the accumulative weight of polls indicating that Nixon just can't beat RFK."[165] Rockefeller did finally enter the race, but with Humphrey rather than Kennedy as the opposing candidate, the case for a liberal Republican nominee collapsed. Rockefeller made no headway at the convention, and neither did Richardson's second choice, liberal Senator Mark Hatfield, from Oregon. The increasingly conservative makeup of the Republican Party was driven home to Richardson in the platform committee's rejection of his proposed planks on gun control, community service, and a massive jobs and housing program to "change the system of failure and frustration that now dominates the ghetto and weakens our society."[166] Still, Richardson hoped that the liberal wing of the party might prosper under the non-ideological and pragmatic Nixon, who since the 1950s had provided encouragement to Republicans of all stripes, including Richardson and Lindsay. *Newsweek* even printed a rumor that Nixon had informally enlisted Kingman Brewster and Irwin Miller as foreign policy advisors, although Brewster denied it.[167]

YALE'S SDS LEADER Mark Zanger witnessed the chaos of the Democratic convention in August; the peace advocates' frustration and police beatings merely confirmed his radical views. When he returned to Yale in the fall, Zanger cut his hair, stopped using drugs, and became a committed Maoist hewing to the Worker-Student Alliance faction within SDS. His *News* column was now entitled "Up against the Wall"—short for "Up against the wall, motherfucker," the stickup artist's announcement that had been adopted as the rallying cry of the Columbia revolutionaries. Zanger started searching for issues that would mobilize and polarize the campus as Mark Rudd had done at Columbia. The most promising issue seemed to be Brewster's stalled commitment to coeducate the college.

After Vassar had rejected Yale's proposal, Brewster appointed a three-person committee, consisting of his cousin Janet Murrow, the Boston banker Thaddeus Beal (who had married a cousin of Mac Bundy's), and Rosemary

Park of UCLA, to help him develop a program for coordinate coeducation. From the committee's deliberations and Brewster's own ideas came his ludicrous plan in May 1968 for "cluster-coordinate" coeducation, which would establish an affiliated college where women could study the arts, health care, and urban planning, areas "for which women would seem to have special potential."[168] By July almost all the president's advisors were counseling a change of course. The only justification that Sam Chauncey could see for the three-cluster scheme was "its value in bringing about academic reform which we probably could not bring about with Yale College as it now is. Every time I think about this problem," he wrote to Brewster, "I return to the thought that women should be admitted to Yale College as regularly enrolled students. I do not believe that there should be any difference between the education of men and women at the undergraduate level."[169]

By now, Brewster was persuaded that equity demanded that Yale admit women. The sticking point for him was that coeducation should not reduce the number of male graduates. Women, he thought, would not be likely to follow male graduates in becoming the nation's scholars and artists as well as "those who will rise to a significant level of responsibility in private enterprises and in the professions as well as in public service."[170] After all, women were still a tiny presence in most professions: only three percent of the country's lawyers, for example, and seven percent of physicians. Most professional women were confined to "sex-typed" occupations: legal aid jobs rather than private practice, pediatrics rather than surgery, "women's page" writers rather than feature reporters, and so on.[171] If even the best-qualified women were destined to be primarily wives and mothers, or at best leaders of women, would Yale's coeducation really be a contribution to society if it meant admitting fewer men? As one Yale professor told the campus newspaper in 1968, "Until society makes its role assignments equal, I can't help feeling a deeper satisfaction and sense of accomplishment teaching all-male classes. . . . As a professor, I feel a greater sense of accomplishment when I direct my efforts toward those who will one day have a greater role in society—men."[172]

But since institutions like Yale helped shape society by producing leaders, women's exclusion was part of a vicious cycle. Yale would not admit women until women could be leaders in the establishment, but the establishment would not admit women until they had graduated from places like Yale. The university's admission of blacks on a large scale in the mid-1960s reflected Brewster's belief, influenced by the civil rights movement as well as his own ideals, that blacks would play a more important social role in the future. If in 1968 he didn't anticipate the coming transformation in women's opportunities, neither did most of the men in his circle or the vast majority of cultural and political opinion makers. Even student radicals like Zanger were basically sexist. Coeducation, the SDS hoped, would demolish "the 'mission' of the university as seen by the established power structure: to turn out as many 'public service minded' State Department and corporation officials as it can, and who, in this society, happen to be men." The SDS did not suppose that if women were given the same opportunities as men, they might become part of the establishment as well; coeducation, the male radicals imagined, would make the university "a meaningful arena for personal development."[173]

A rush of events in the fall of 1968 helped push Yale toward coeducation. In September a committee at all-male Princeton University released a report calling for complete coeducation rather than coordination and recommending that Princeton admit one thousand women to the college, at an estimated cost of $24.7 million.[174] Princeton and Yale were caught in a kind of prisoner's dilemma; each could remain all-male if the other did, but if one went coed, the other would come under intense pressure to follow. More important, as the head of the Princeton committee told Brewster at a panel discussion, the university intended to coeducate because it was betting that "women are abandoning penny-ante aspirations with respect to their lives outside the home," although he conceded that "if it isn't true, then we're making a mistake, I think."[175]

In October, Brewster met with the members of the SDS's coeducation committee; he told them, as Zanger remembered the conversation, that Yale had a traditional mission of educating "a thousand male leaders a year." Zanger recalled that "I knew right then that that was what we were going to come out of the meeting with. I had even then a suspicion that he was playing us, that he wanted us to disseminate that quote."[176]

Zanger believed that coeducation was part of Brewster's larger scheme for university expansion, in concert with New Haven's ongoing urban renewal plans. Indeed, Brewster would later write to John Hay Whitney that "the importance of this move in the long run will not seem to be so much in the advent of women as in the deliberate decision to expand Yale College by about 30 to 50 per cent."[177] In the slightly paranoid but not entirely illogical reasoning of the SDS, Brewster calculated that he would have an easier time getting coeducation past the alumni if he made his move in response to a big undergraduate protest movement rather than on his own initiative.

At the same time, coeducation would allow him to expand the university into New Haven with undergraduate backing rather than opposition. "He had a lot of different agendas at once," Zanger explained.[178]

The SDS held a series of demonstrations trumpeting Brewster's "thousand male leaders" quote and demanding immediate coeducation.[179] Unfortunately for Zanger, "within weeks, as tended to happen, a larger and broader spectrum of people captured this issue from the Yale SDS."[180] A more moderate group of undergraduates led by junior Aviam Soifer planned a "Coeducation Week," to bring 750 women from twenty-two schools to the campus for integrated classes and socialization. Although university officials had initially opposed the operation, when Soifer presented Brewster with a fait accompli, Brewster's instructions to the administration to help with management of the event further marginalized SDS.[181] "No doubt about it," one student columnist wrote, "no school is more Establishment than Yale. The proof is the way the administration (read: Establishment) absorbed Coeducation Week. All these groovy radicals thought they had a way to put Kingman up against the Woodbridge Hall wall and then they got absorbed. Now all their demands are checked out by John Wilkinson, he's checked out by the King, and everybody is on a committee. It's beautiful."[182]

On November 4, the day the first visiting women arrived on campus, the Corporation met at the Yale Club of New York to vote on coeducation. According to the provost, Charles Taylor, "Nearly everybody on the Corporation was by then convinced that we had to do it—just do it, even though it would cost us money we didn't really have." Even so, the group deliberated the decision at length, with most of the trustees weighing in on the affirmative side. Juan Trippe, the president of Pan American Airlines and one of the more conservative trustees, had just begun to speak on the negative side when a helicopter flew noisily overhead. At that time, John Lindsay was battling Trippe over the heliport on the Pan Am Building, arguing that the choppers were too loud and dangerous to be allowed to take off and land from the midtown skyscraper. "As Juan was trying to get worked up to his case," Taylor remembered, "John leaned across the table and said in a loud voice, 'Speak up, Juan, I can't hear you!' And the meeting just broke up in laughter, because it was so well understood what this was about. And it was like it just took all the air out of Trippe's balloon. He never even finished his speech."[183]

The Corporation voted to accept women to Yale College on a full coeducational basis beginning in the fall of 1969. Five hundred women would be admitted—half sophomore and junior transfers, half first-year students in the Class of '73—with the number of women at Yale to rise incrementally to fifteen hundred once suitable housing became available. The number of men accepted would not be reduced. Brewster estimated the cost of the expansion to be $55 million, although he anticipated that the first year's increase in operating expenses (about $4 million) would be covered by tuition and fees. Later that weekend, Brewster told a coeducated rally outside his house that "in 1972 it will be Lindsay versus [Ted] Kennedy and there will be women at Yale."[184] On November 14, Brewster presented the proposal to the faculty, who approved 200–1, and the news was splashed across the nation's papers the next day.

The timing of the decision was affected by Brewster's desire to capitalize on what he called the "responsible optimism" of the Yale community and by his fear that delay would scuttle the chance of admitting women by the next fall.[185] The swift announcement of the decision helped steal Princeton's thunder (Old Nassau finally decided to coeducate in January 1969). It also reflected the judgment of admissions officers and faculty members like Ronald Dworkin that "if we admitted young women immediately, we would get the best women in the United States," a strategy that, in turn, might impress the donors who would underwrite the move.[186] As one undergraduate wrote of Brewster's attitude toward coeducation, he "bowed to the inevitable and embraced it as his own. Thus he was able to maintain a semblance of control over the flow of events."[187]

Brewster referred to Yale's decision to coeducate as "precipitate," a surprising statement considering that proposals to admit women had been in the air since 1956.[188] Still, the decision was hasty in that it was made before anyone in the administration knew how women would fit into Yale, how Yale would adjust to accommodate women, what problems would be created by women being outnumbered eight to one, where and how the new students would be housed, how the alumni would react, how Yale would pay for the costs of expansion, and so on. The decision also left unanswered the questions that one administrative aide posed to Brewster: "What does Yale expect of its women—as competitors in the admissions process, as students and as graduates? . . . What provisions have we made for women to become 'leaders' in the traditional sense?"[189] In the end, these questions would not be answered so much as worked out in practice by the women themselves.

*   *   *

FOR LINDSAY, THE Corporation's meeting on coeducation was the bright spot in the otherwise dismal autumn of 1968. In the spring, after he had helped keep New York calm in the wake of King's death, his national stature reached its highest point; by November, his face would be on the cover of *Time* magazine under the headline "The Breakdown of a City."

The unmaking of Lindsay's reputation stemmed partly from increased exposure to problems that had been brewing throughout his mayoralty: rising crime, soaring taxes, burgeoning debt, fudged budgets, delayed construction, resistant bureaucracy, and assorted scandals. Welfare rolls ballooned, the result of a movement aimed at destroying the welfare system by overloading it and bringing about New York's financial collapse; the movement did at least cause the city's welfare spending to rise from $400 million to $1 billion during Lindsay's first term.[190] The fact that most of the new dependents were minorities sharpened a growing white backlash against what seemed the mayor's disproportionate attention to minority concerns. On one of Lindsay's 1968 walks in the predominantly white ethnic Bay Ridge section of Brooklyn, a reporter observed a resident asking the mayor "why all the taxes came out of the white pockets only to be spent in black neighborhoods. 'We have three hundred years of neglect to pay for,' Lindsay said, and half the sidewalk audience was shuffling in impatience."[191] Lindsay continued to take an unbending attitude toward the city's municipal unions, and slowdowns and sick-outs by the police and firemen in the autumn contributed to the feeling that the city's order was eroding.

By far the ugliest problem to confront Lindsay was the series of teacher strikes that shut down nearly all the city's schools for much of the fall, in response to black harassment of unionized teachers in Ocean Hill–Brownsville, one of the three experimental decentralized school districts. One journalist called the strikes "the worst disaster my native city has experienced in my lifetime," depriving children of their education and pitting union against city, whites against blacks, and the middle class against the poor.[192]

The flash point of the crisis came in May 1968, when the Ocean Hill–Brownsville governing board, intoxicated with hubris and Black Power ideology, dismissed thirteen teachers and six administrators for alleged incompetence and "sabotage." Since Rhody McCoy, the administrator of the eight-school district, could have had the staff legally transferred out of the district, the move was taken explicitly to create a controversy and to assert black control over the schools that the law and the Board of Education would not permit. A murky stew of motivations went into the governing board's action, including opposition to the teachers' union and to the Bundy–Lindsay decentralization bill then under consideration in the New York legislature (since it stopped well short of community control). Racism was also a factor, since only one of the fired teachers was black, most were Jewish, and the charges against all were without substance. Some 350 unionized teachers in the district walked out to protest the action, and the governing board upped the ante by vowing that none of the strikers would be taken back.

The situation in Ocean Hill simmered during the summer, then boiled over again at the start of the fall term when McCoy announced that he had hired permanent replacements for the 350 teachers who had struck in the spring. Since McCoy and the governing board had no legal basis for their coup, they played the race card, claiming that the district had become a symbol of minority self-determination and that to oppose its actions was ipso facto racism. The gambit worked, at least to the extent that many white liberals pledged support and the Board of Education hesitated to enforce the law on its wayward creation.

The United Federation of Teachers and its unyielding leader, Albert Shanker, matched the governing board's intransigence. In early September, 54,000 UFT teachers went on strike for two days until the Board of Education agreed that the 350 teachers McCoy had replaced would get their jobs back. When those teachers returned to Ocean Hill and were terrorized by the black militant Sonny Carson and his intimidators, with McCoy's connivance, the UFT shut down the city's schools again, this time for over two weeks. Lindsay reentered the negotiations and brokered a peace agreement, but it, too, fell apart because Shanker did not trust the mayor or the Board of Education to enforce it. The third strike lasted five weeks, and Shanker refused to accept anything less than the dissolution of the Ocean Hill–Brownsville district. In the end, the governing board, which had refused all compromise, lost everything. For the UFT it was a Pyrrhic victory, since the strikes stirred such racial hatred that the union was blamed for shredding the city's delicate social fabric.

The strikes damaged Lindsay not only because they caused havoc but because they made him seem indecisive. His history of awkward relations with unions meant that the UFT effectively refused to accept his leadership. Hesitant to offend his minority constituencies, he exposed himself to charges of hypocrisy when he tried to minimize the indefensible actions of the governing board. Lindsay's friend Kingman Brewster had emphasized all along that in dealing with Black Power issues, one should be flexible but maintain nonnegotiable principles. By not making clear that the experiment would end if the governing board did not follow proper procedures, Lindsay set back the cause of decentralization. He knew that "the centrists and the moderates have to keep fighting to keep the extremist elements from colliding head on and killing each other," but he couldn't pull off the balancing act required.[193]

McGeorge Bundy, on the other hand, believed that "it could still turn out that New York, because its engagement is deepest, and because it is now in full-scale, open debate over fundamental questions, has actually begun to move ahead of the country."[194] Bundy also came under fire for his role in decentralization. He had ready rebuttals to all charges: the Board of Education (not Ford) had created the demonstration districts, ninety-seven percent of the districts' funds came from the board and the New York public school system, it wasn't the foundation's responsibility to run the districts, and so on. "I have regrets about the tempestuous situation, as I think any citizen should have," he acknowledged, but he still believed that "the problem deserved the best effort we could give it."[195]

To their detractors, however, Lindsay and Bundy represented a paradoxical alliance of the WASP patriciate and the black and Hispanic underclass against the embittered white working classes. Shanker found both men to be convenient scapegoats and symbols, and he drew elaborate parallels between what he saw as Bundy's failures in Vietnam and in the schools debate. While there was an element of truth to the caricature, such demonization was a way of averting one's gaze from the real failures in urban education. Shanker breezily admitted, "Sure, 80 to 85 percent are coming out of the slum schools as illiterate as when they started. But the 15 percent who are making it are not a negligible number. At least it's something."[196] Bundy and Lindsay both wanted to do better, and their admirers respected them all the more for taking on the complex, controversial problems that others preferred to sweep under the rug.

WITH THE NOVEMBER elections approaching, Bundy for the first time spoke out in public against the course of the war—in an attempt, some thought, to encourage Hubert Humphrey to distance himself from Johnson's Vietnam policies. At a DePauw University memorial for his former aide John McNaughton, who had been killed with his family in a plane crash, Bundy said publicly what he had long been saying privately: "this war cannot continue at its present level of cost and sacrifice, not only because of what it means in Southeast Asia, but still more because of what it means in the United States."[197] He endorsed an unconditional bombing halt, supported negotiations (while remaining skeptical about North Vietnam's willingness to compromise), and envisioned reducing the number of troops in Vietnam to 100,000 from the current half a million.

Bundy's call for a de-Americanization of the war put him in the familiar position of being attacked by those who thought his plan went too far and those who didn't think it went far enough. But his new willingness to publicly consider different policies and, in effect, to criticize Johnson at least had some impact in freeing other establishment figures, such as Brewster, to speak out against the war.

Nixon's victory in the fall election did not signal a complete end to liberalism; although he had courted the right in the campaign, Nixon was ideologically hard to pin down, and would include some liberal initiatives in an agenda that was conservative overall. Some evidence of his trickiness, however, had already become clear to Cyrus Vance in Paris. The North Vietnamese, worried about the prospect of Nixon as president, at last agreed to begin formal negotiations, with the National Liberation Front as well as the Hanoi government present at the table. But the South Vietnamese, secretly encouraged by Nixon and his emissary Henry Kissinger to hold out for a better deal under a new administration, reneged on their previous commitment to negotiate with the NLF. "In my mind," Vance said later, "this was one of the great tragedies in history, that the South Vietnamese double-crossed the United States, which I clearly feel they did."[198] The war would drag on for five more years; in the end, the United States would settle for terms no better than those Vance could have secured in 1968.

With Johnson's exit from the political scene, an era had ended for the liberal establishment. The men in Brewster's circle often referred to themselves as the "interface," borrowing a term from systems analysis for the point at which two or more processes interconnect. They were the human links between the interrelated worlds of government, communications, academia, and other centers of power and influence in society. Under Nixon, who feared and resented the establishment even more than his predecessor had, men like Brewster, Bundy, and Vance would no longer move as easily between the public and private worlds as they had during Johnson's presidency. Ideological hardening in both parties would marginalize the men of the center, while the storm in New York over school decentralization paralleled the national crack-up of the New Deal coalition that had empowered their kind of pragmatic liberalism. Fallout from the school wars also sharply cut back the ability and inclination of government leaders like Lindsay to play an activist role and helped bind McGeorge Bundy's wings at the Ford Foundation. In hindsight, the men of the liberal establishment would look back to the fall of 1968 as the moment when their influence had passed its zenith.

10

INTO THE STORM

O N THE evening of May 1, 1969, Kingman Brewster and the members of his Corporation gathered in their chambers in Woodbridge Hall, preparing for the university-wide meeting to debate the place of the Reserve Officers' Training Corps at Yale. That spring, student activists had been fomenting a movement to expel ROTC, through which, they claimed, the university contributed to the ongoing carnage in Vietnam. A little more than two weeks earlier, the ROTC conflict had led students at Harvard to take over the central administration building, resulting in a brutal police bust and a divisive strike. The faculty splintered into enemy caucuses, the Harvard administration was almost completely discredited, and the university was still in chaos by early May. Seeking to avoid a similar fate, Brewster had called the meeting, to be held in the capacious Ingalls Rink, to direct student and faculty anger over ROTC into a more constructive outlet. But fearing that the meeting might go disastrously awry, he had summoned the Corporation to be with him in his hour of danger.

Lindsay had arrived from New York by helicopter; in that sort of urgent situation, he remembered, "Brewster called and you came."[1] Bill Bundy, who flew up from Washington—despite severe burnout from the stress of his involvement with Vietnam—agreed: "You had to stand up and be counted; this was *it*."[2] Brewster was in an atypically tense and self-doubting mood. "Am I doing the right thing?" he asked the group. Paul Moore, Cyrus Vance, William Scranton, John Hay Whitney, and the other Corporation members assured him that they would stand behind him, however the meeting turned out.[3]

"Gentlemen, the limousines are waiting," the university secretary, Ben Holden, announced, provoking a burst of nervous laughter; in this moment of antiestablishment tumult, what would be the symbolism of arriving at the rink in high capitalist style? The group decided to walk—even Whitney, with his dangerous heart condition.

As the Corporation neared the rink, surrounded by throngs of under-graduates, graduate students, and faculty members heading for the meeting, Scranton sensed that one of the things worrying Brewster was the possibility that he would lose control of the meeting. There had been rumbling discontent among the undergraduates all week at the restrictive rules Brewster had put in place, specifying a fixed slate of speakers and limited opportunity to speak from the floor. "Kingman," Scranton told his friend, "have faith in the students of this university. They respect you, and they are very decent and obviously intelligent people." Scranton remembered that Brewster looked at him and asked, "You mean I shouldn't run it?" "That's just what I mean," the former Pennsylvania governor replied.[4] Vance and Moore had earlier counseled the same course of action. The president fell silent as he mulled over the idea that he should sail into unknown waters without compass or charts. Then they were at the doors of the rink, and the entire university, it seemed, was inside waiting for them.

WHEN ANTIWAR STUDENTS began to examine the ways in which the universities were complicit in the war in Vietnam, they focused their attention, not surprisingly, on the Reserve Officers' Training Corps units. Although Yale's SDS chapter had agitated against ROTC since the fall of 1967, not until the 1968–69 academic year did ROTC become the prime target of antiwar activity on campuses around the country.

At Yale, ROTC was something of a hangover from the First World War, when faculty members had reluctantly agreed to adopt the program even though it was at odds with their academic ideals.[5] Further, ROTC was an anomaly in the curriculum. Its instructors were the only teachers who were not appointed or approved by the faculty; although its courses were unquestionably vocational training rather than liberal education, they were awarded full academic credit. As one youthful firebrand wrote, the ROTC course "is not art, it is not history, it is not letters, it is not even science in the academic sense."[6] "Let the powers that be rescind the favor of equal credit status for ROTC or abandon the sham of liberal arts purpose and go all the way down the line for a trade-school curriculum."[7] Who was that young critic? It was Kingman Brewster—writing in 1940.

More than two decades later, many faculty members thought that ROTC students were subject to outrageous restrictions. They were forbidden from majoring in subjects such as history of art or anthropology, for example, and if they withdrew from ROTC, they immediately became eligible for the draft. Undoubtedly, too, the faculty felt pressure from students who wanted to end a program that supported the military effort in Vietnam.

But ROTC's status presented such a contradiction to Yale's professed ideals that the university was vulnerable to charges of hypocrisy. McGeorge Bundy, speaking in a televised panel discussion with Brewster in 1969, observed that "part of the game" for student activists was "to roust through the closets of university life for things that have been sitting there a long time and have gotten way out of date and nobody got around to throwing them away."[8] Further, Brewster was hard-pressed to tell undergraduates they could not get academic credit for social action in the ghetto while allowing credit for military practice. "They sort of have us on the ropes in terms of the credibility of the principles that we assert," he commented, and he thought it "folly" to let SDS and other radicals cash in on the inconsistency.[9]

So in January 1969, after months of study and debate, the faculty voted to require the military programs to meet Yale's standards of academics and appointments. ROTC could continue at Yale, but as an extracurricular activity rather than as part of the course of study.[10] The services would still have to accept this demotion of ROTC, but Brewster didn't think that obtaining their support would be a serious obstacle. After all, Army secretary Stan Resor and Navy secretary John Chafee were both good Yale men, and General William Westmoreland had told one of Brewster's assistants, "Hell, we don't give academic credit to ROTC at West Point!"[11]

The change in ROTC's status, coming on the heels of the coeducation decision and Chaplain Coffin's conspiracy conviction, further inflamed the alumni. Many wondered whether Yale's purpose was still service to God and Country, in the words of the school motto. Later that year, alumnus Julien Dedman, who had previously called for Coffin to be executed for treason, would publish a short screed entitled "The Rape of Yale." The ROTC issue was prominent in his compendium of Brewster's crimes, and he noted darkly that in the faculty discussions, "unmentioned went the fact that abolition of ROTC is a longstanding goal of the Students for a Democratic

Society."[12] But the faculty had not abolished ROTC. Indeed, Brewster enraged SDS by insisting that ROTC would remain for as long as the services maintained contracts with the university, and contracts then in effect would not expire until June 1970. And of course the Vietnam War continued unabated under Richard Nixon. In the end, the services would reject the faculty's conditions and would decline to renew their contracts, but ROTC remained a live issue at Yale during the spring of 1969.

SINCE THE PREVIOUS spring, Brewster had been at work on a proposal that he thought might assuage some of the undergraduates' anger at being forced to choose between student deferment and military service in a war they hated. He chaired a United Nations–affiliated, Ford Foundation–supported policy panel examining UN peacekeeping as a means of controlling conflicts like the Vietnam War. Young men who objected to fighting in Vietnam might welcome the opportunity to fulfill their service requirement, Brewster thought, by serving as UN peacekeepers in other trouble spots.[13] Because Cyrus Vance, Irwin Miller, and other panel members thought the idea a bit radical, the Brewster panel put forward, instead, a plan for a large UN standby force, ready to intervene rapidly and backed with a sizable peace fund to support its operations.[14] Brewster and Vance lobbied Congress and the administration to support this plan, starting with their old friend Elliot Richardson, who had been named Nixon's undersecretary of state.[15]

Richardson owed his new position to his friendship with Secretary of State William Rogers, with whom he had worked in the Eisenhower administration. But his appointment allowed Nixon to demonstrate his statesmanship by naming liberal northeastern Republicans of great ability to his team, along with his California cronies. Although Richardson was unhappy to leave Massachusetts and the attorney general's office, he wrote to his mentor Judge Charles Wyzanski that "the opportunity to play a part in the attainment of peace and the preservation of our national security is an opportunity to serve humanity at the highest level."[16] His confirmation hearings became bumpy when his Massachusetts political enemies spread the word, once again, about his driving record, coupled with "at least an implication that I am an alcoholic," Richardson told the Senate Foreign Relations Committee. The charge was "absolutely without foundation," he insisted, and the committee chose not to pursue the matter.[17]

The new undersecretary of state had no previous experience with foreign policy (although he had been president of the Boston World Affairs Council for three years), but he viewed its challenges as merely another set of problems to be mastered by his steel-trap lawyerly mind. "I approach any job in essentially the same way," he once said. "I don't consider that the subject matter makes any particular difference. If I don't know it, I learn it. I try to find out what it is necessary to do, and then do it."[18] Since his wife and children remained in Massachusetts until the end of the school year, Richardson was free to stay late every night poring over briefing papers in his grand, blue-carpeted office overlooking the Potomac, decorated with Asian tapestries, an ornate globe, and photographs of Richardson's past and present bosses—no photo of Nixon, though. His appetite for work won him the admiration of State Department aides, particularly after they found that Richardson would, when presented with a thousand-page report, return it the next day with underlining and commentary.[19]

Moreover, Richardson sought advice from his predecessors in the Johnson administration, particularly Vance, the Bundy brothers, and Katzenbach (who advised him to bring blacks into State "regardless of exams—reserve, transfer laterally," Richardson noted).[20] "Nobody in Washington has ever thought of me as a politician at all," he recalled. "In fact, however, I had more full-time experience in politics than almost anybody on Nixon's staff."[21] He demonstrated his political savvy by winning a seat on the National Security Council (becoming the first undersecretary to join the group) and making an ally of national security advisor Henry Kissinger, who exercised near-total control over foreign policy. "Richardson's at least as smart as I am," Kissinger once said, putting the Bostonian in a highly select group, indeed, in Kissinger's estimation.[22] "I think the things I'm best at don't show much," Richardson once observed. "Nobody ever asked how I could be the political appointee closest to the career service in 1969–70, but at the same time also be the person in State who worked most closely with Kissinger, without any strain or incompatibility between those roles."[23]

To his critics, however, his versatility could look like excessive flexibility. Vietnam had now become a major part of Richardson's responsibilities, and as it became clear that Nixon and Kissinger had no "secret plan" for exiting the conflict—as they had claimed before the election—some of Richardson's friends wondered when he would speak out against the war. "This Administration is responsible neither for the initial commitment to Viet-Nam nor for the depth of our existing involvement," he wrote to one acquaintance—but that argument could not be sustained for long.[24] Withdrawing from Vietnam, he told a reporter, "would deal a very damaging blow to the credibility of the United States commitment"—but even Vance and Mac Bundy had advised him that this was no longer an adequate reply to the war's critics.[25] Richardson would enjoy a honeymoon with the press while he adjusted to his job, and most reporters initially were less interested in his role in the war than in his wilderness vacations, his watercolors, and his habit of doodling incessantly through conversations, telephone calls, and cabinet meetings.[26] (Richardson and Brewster had framed examples of each other's doodles; Richardson tended to draw abstract geometrical designs, while Brewster sketched flags, letters, and portraits.) But the honeymoon would be brief.

AMONG HIS OTHER nongovernmental duties, Richardson was a member of the Harvard Board of Overseers, along with other Harvard worthies including David Rockefeller, C. Douglas Dillon (part of the Wise Man group), and former education commissioner Francis Keppel (a member of the Bundy Panel on New York City school decentralization). While most of the board's business was usually pro forma, Richardson and the other trustees were jolted by the events at the university in April 1969.

Trouble had been bubbling at Harvard ever since the spontaneous sit-down in November 1966 that had trapped defense secretary Robert McNamara. Yale SDS leader Mark Zanger praised Harvard for having "a generally more [ideologically] developed student body" than Yale, with "a far larger chapter of SDS."[27] Harvard's radicals regularly staged strikes, sit-ins, and protests around issues such as ROTC, campus recruiting visits from Dow Chemical and the CIA, and university expansion into low-income neighborhoods. Once, when Richardson was meeting with Harvard president Nathan Pusey, their discussion was interrupted by a telephone call with the latest bad news. The president uttered a soft "Damn," then resumed the conversation. Even when he was made aware of impending crisis, Pusey was not sufficiently alert or agile to diffuse the situation by reaching out to disaffected undergraduates. "I don't have any time to see students," he blustered in the spring of 1969. "I have a whole university to run." The president's aloofness permeated much of the administration. When McGeorge Bundy played tennis with trustee Hooks Burr at the beginning of the 1968–69 academic year, Burr assured the former dean that finances, not unrest, were the university's main problem and that "the student thing" would soon dissipate.[28]

Then on April 9 a Maoist faction of SDS occupied University Hall, the central administration building in Harvard Yard, forcibly expelling the deans and administrators. Pusey and his closest advisors decided to call in the cops. Shortly after five o'clock the next morning, hundreds of Boston troopers poured into the Yard and the occupied building, bloodying onlookers along with radicals and venting generations of Irish resentment against what they saw as the university of the Brahmins.

Pusey's decision to summon the police was a colossal blunder. It made martyrs of SDS, turned moderate students against the administration, sundered the faculty, and polarized the entire university community. One of Brewster's residential college deans, who witnessed the raid by the police, wrote to Yale College dean Georges May that the Harvard administration's action led previously nonradical students "to believe the conspiracy theory of the university (the university represses blacks, colludes with the CIA on Vietnam, etc.). . . . Many moderate students felt they owed SDS 'a debt of gratitude' for revealing the university's true nature."[29] The bust unleashed poisonous resentments among the faculty as well. Franklin Ford, McGeorge Bundy's successor as dean, suffered a stroke two days after a philosophy professor called him a liar at a meeting of the faculty. While some alumni condemned Pusey's actions, others insisted that meritocratic policies of faculty and student recruitment were ultimately responsible and had to be reversed; one alumnus wrote to the Board of Overseers demanding "an elimination of riff-raff, no matter how talented."[30] Nationally, conservatives used the events at Harvard to stoke outrage against students and the young. "What happened at Harvard is the destruction of all humane values," Kissinger charged. "It is fascism."[31] What the events did at least show was the essential fragility of even the greatest academic communities.

The incident at University Hall reflected an administration that was out of touch and felt no need to consult before plunging ahead. Pusey believed that in acting quickly, he was following the advice of Brewster's law professor Archibald Cox, who had examined the student occupations at Columbia the year before and told the Harvard president and trustees that the crisis had become more serious as the Columbia administration dithered. But Pusey didn't bother to consult with Cox before calling in law enforcement. Cox said later that his observation about administrative delay "was not supposed to be a prescription to get the police as fast as you can, regardless of how many people there were occupying the building. . . . I thought the 'bust' was all wrong."[32] Neither had Pusey made any attempt to engage the majority of moderate students. Yale law student Greg Craig, an advisor to Brewster, informed him that moderates in the Harvard student government had opposed the SDS takeover and even "proposed a procedure by which police action would least disrupt the working of the university. Needless to say, none of these suggestions was followed by the administration at Harvard."[33]

Richardson returned to his alma mater on April 14 for the regularly scheduled meeting of the Board of Overseers. The trustees met with Pusey, set up committees to look into the events of the previous week, and issued a statement "unequivocally" endorsing Pusey's action. "A tiny minority has tried to impose its will on an institution which belongs to all of us," the board declared.[34] Nonetheless, the board debated a motion of no confidence in the president, and the Harvard Corporation, the university's other governing body, asked Pusey to resign. Several months later Pusey would announce his retirement, two years ahead of schedule.[35] After the trustees' meeting, Richardson spoke with a deeply concerned Mac Bundy, who warned that the administration had to try to reach out to alienated students and faculty. "Pres./Univ. dangerously isolated," Richardson scrawled on a legal pad as he talked with Bundy.[36] To men like Bundy and Richardson, the events at their institution were a tragedy, the more so because they were avoidable.

TEN DAYS AFTER the student takeover at Harvard, black students at Cornell University occupied the student center; their action turned into an armed occupation when they brought in rifles. President James Perkins resisted government pressure to let the National Guard clear out the building, a course that almost certainly would have resulted in deaths. But he recalled, "a good many of the faculty lost their confidence in me because I refused to bring in the police."[37] The Cornell administration agreed to all the black students' demands, which included an autonomous black studies institute, amnesty for the building occupiers, protection for separate black residences, and the elimination of the disciplinary system the faculty had created the previous year. The triumphant students emerged draped in bandoliers and brandishing their weapons—an image that provoked national outrage.

The Cornell faculty rejected the deal the administration had made under duress, but the professors wavered when thousands of students occupied the gymnasium to protest their decision. On April 23, the black student leader Tom Jones went on the radio to threaten that Perkins and several professors would "die in the gutter like dogs." If the faculty did not reverse its previous decision, he warned, "Cornell University has three hours to live."[38] The faculty reversed itself, letting the occupiers off without punishment and acceding to their demands.[39] While the deal ended the state of siege on campus, a number of prominent professors resigned in protest at what they saw as "abject capitulation." Others campaigned to remove Perkins, and Cornell's reputation suffered serious damage. By the end of the academic year, the trustees would pressure Perkins into resigning.[40]

From Brewster's perspective, the Cornell drama offered a number of lessons. The root of the disturbances, he believed, was the university's affirmative action policy of admitting blacks without regard to their academic qualifications. Lacking confidence in themselves, Cornell's black students never became part of the university and submerged their individuality in a hostile, uncompromising black separatism. It was almost inevitable that they would "resort to violent efforts to compensate for [their] own insecurity," Brewster believed.[41] Because blacks at Cornell had never been disciplined for a series of increasingly disruptive actions, it was also unsurprising that they became contemptuous of university authority and saw violence as a successful strategy.

In counterpoint to the events at Harvard, Cornell showed that student unrest could demolish even liberal, in-touch university administrations. Perkins was an intelligent, progressive, nationally visible leader very much like Brewster. "Brewster and I were activists," Perkins remembered. "We thought the universities had very pressing public responsibilities, and we wanted to see to it that they discharged them. . . . The two of us were probably the most outward-looking of the Ivy League presidents."[42] Perkins had appeared several times in public forums with Brewster and McGeorge Bundy, and Bundy sent the Cornell president an emergency grant of $50,000 during the crisis.[43] But Perkins's good intentions and his refusal to call in the police were not enough to save the situation or himself. For radicals who considered liberalism to be the enemy, bringing down a progressive like Perkins was a greater achievement than overturning a conservative president like Pusey.

THE EVENTS AT Harvard and Cornell were only the most prominent of dozens of student protests that broke out on the nation's campuses that spring, from sprawling public universities like Wisconsin and Berkeley to tiny women's colleges like Briarcliff and Sarah Lawrence. There was no reason to think Yale would be spared. Besides SDS agitation over ROTC, a group of nearly a hundred seniors was planning to walk out of McGeorge Bundy's speech at the class dinner. Students at the School of Art and Architecture were mounting guerrilla theater actions demanding increased financial aid; the Black Workshop, a combination of urban planning group and community outreach program, was importing toughs from New York in an attempt to extort money from Yale; a confederation of student groups calling itself the Coalition for a New University was pressing for "serious change in University structures, philosophy, and processes of decision-making."[44] Students were protesting Nixon's plans for an antiballistic missile system and, of course, the war in Vietnam. Any one of these potential tinderboxes, or unforeseen others, might provide the spark that would send the university up in smoke.

To prepare for whatever might happen, Brewster worked with Paul Moore and other informal advisors to craft a policy statement regarding student disruptions. Moore, drawing on his civil rights experiences, warned the president that "it is often impossible for the most responsible leadership to maintain control when things heat up. . . . Goals escalate *during* the process of demonstrating."[45] For this reason, Brewster thought it was better to head off student disruption before it materialized. However, if there should be any forcible interference with normal university activities, Brewster told a Yale faculty meeting on April 16, the administration would deal with it "speedily and firmly. . . . I see no basis for compromise on the basic proposition that forcible coercion and violent intimidation are unacceptable."

Brewster offered a plan for dealing with a building takeover or similar crisis. Disrupters would be offered the opportunity to meet with Brewster for unrestricted discussion and be warned that continuing the disruption would lead to suspension. Those who would not desist would be identified, suspended, and disciplined by the faculty. If the campus police could not handle the disorder, Brewster reserved the right to secure a court order and call in outside assistance as a last resort. The Brewster scenario attracted wide publicity because it was a strong statement against disruption but also affirmed "the encouragement of controversy, no matter how fundamental" and "the protection of dissent, no matter how extreme."[46] The future of the country, Brewster felt, hinged on being able to maintain balance between dissent and disruption.[47]

Mark Zanger of the SDS thought the scenario reflected what radicals in the 1960s termed "managerial liberalism." In his view, Brewster and his confreres, like those in the previous generation of the establishment, saw to it that "the same guys made the decisions [and] more or less the same decisions got made." The modern twist was that they also "believed that you had to maintain this machinery of communication and pseudo-inclusion to make it work." The Brewster scenario was managerial liberalism in action: "You follow the due process, you have all the options in your pocket."[48] Success for the SDS would depend on breaking free of the constraints Brewster laid down. Another SDS member commented that "we've got nothing against Brewster personally, he's a nice enough fellow; but to the extent that he has become an idol, he has to be destroyed."[49]

Throughout most of the spring term, Zanger recalled, the SDS "had been running a low-key, ineffectual anti-ROTC campaign." Then, in late April, "all of a sudden it was galvanized by eighteen seniors, unconnected to SDS."[50] For the radicals, it was glumly reminiscent of what had happened the previous fall when moderates had hijacked their movement for coeducation. Indeed, the leader of Coed Week, Avi Soifer, also emerged as one of the non-SDS leaders on the ROTC issue, along with Paul Moore's oldest son and Tom Gerety, nephew of a Catholic bishop and Moore's future son-in-law. The members of this new coalition, although passionately opposed to ROTC, were not enemies of the university.[51] If they were not doctrinaire radicals, however, neither were they necessarily friendly to the administration, and they objected strongly to Brewster's proposed means of debating the ROTC issue.

At the faculty's request, Brewster had planned two meetings to be held in Ingalls Rink, one on ROTC and the other on university governance. At the first meeting, on May 1, a prearranged set of speakers would debate ROTC in a sort of parliamentary manner, and provost Charles Taylor would moderate.[52] "One of Kingman's failings," law student Greg Craig recalled, "was that in trying to deal with conflict and trying to channel energy and dissent in constructive ways, he frequently set up situations in such a fashion that they had the appearance of being over-controlled. He was reluctant, understandably, to go with the flow."[53] Students demanded changes to Brewster's rigid format. "What the faculty requested was a truly open meeting, not a cynical attempt to pacify student sentiment against ROTC," coalition spokesman Gerety declared. "We'll bring it to the floor."[54] Rumors flew that the SDS would use bullhorns to drown out any speeches that displeased its members, and that there might be disruption and violence.

At the mass meeting on May 1, 1969, some four thousand people were in attendance, including many faculty and graduate students, a sizable fraction of the undergraduate body, and some outside observers (notably including the sportscaster Howard Cosell and the well-known columnist Stewart Alsop). Brewster's entrance into the rink was greeted with a standing ovation. Brewster took his place behind the speaker's platform, with the Corporation sitting "solemnly in a row on either side of the president," Moore remembered, "looking frighteningly Establishment."[55]

Provost Taylor called the meeting to order at 8:15 P.M., and almost immediately lost control of it. Michael Medved (then a leftist, later a conservative media critic) rushed up to the stage, shirttails flapping. He was one of the seniors who had organized the protest, and his proposal to get rid of Brewster's plan for a fixed slate of speakers and open the debate to speeches from the floor met with a great roar of approval. Political science professor Robert Dahl replaced Taylor as chairman of the meeting, and the meeting proceeded according to Medved's proposal. One of Brewster's great strengths as a tactician was that he knew when to lose, and he let the meeting go forward without opposition. "We'd had our little coup d'état, and Kingman had been overthrown," Craig remembered. "But Kingman won, because the debate went on in exactly the way he wanted it to go on, in a civilized, cogent, powerful sort of parliamentary democratic way."[56]

The SDS introduced the group's motion to expel ROTC from Yale, and debate began. One of the emotional high points of the meeting, in most participants' recollections, was a speech by law student Stephen Cohen, part of the group of student leaders Brewster had taken to meet McGeorge Bundy the previous fall. Cohen articulated what no one had thus far mentioned: that the debate over ROTC came about "because of Vietnam and what Vietnam represents in American society."[57] Cohen said this "quietly but passionately," Craig reminisced, "and the place went absolutely bonkers."[58] If the community wished to send a message to the policy makers in Washington, Cohen added, there were no better people to send it through than Corporation members Cyrus Vance and Bill Bundy, who were both in attendance. He challenged them to respond to the students' criticism, quoting the Spanish antifascist educator Miguel de Unamuno: "To be silent is to lie."[59] Bundy, who was sitting by Vance, recalled that "neither of us stirred." Bundy was not inclined to answer the students, since "I was an awful dead doughnut by that time. . . . And Cy Vance, although they didn't know it of course, had really knocked himself out to keep peace talks going in Paris."[60]

Brewster, one of the last speakers, reiterated that the university would not break its legally enforceable contracts with the military. "I happen to respect and even honor those who decide to serve their country in the military forces," he said. "I also hope that, if we are to have a military establishment, it will not be deprived of a chance to draw on the student body of the best educational institutions. I also hope that we can make it possible for individual students to make individual choices as to whether and how they will serve."[61] Brewster's statement attracted boos and cheers from the students. (Alsop, who heard only the boos, scribbled furiously in his notebook, "Young jerks terrified of the draft. Spocked when they should have been spanked."[62]) The president, declaring that the meeting had made him both "profoundly depressed and at other times profoundly exhilarated" and observing the palpable feeling of community in the rink, challenged the students to create a new system of governance. It would be, he thought, a tremendous contribution not only for Yale "but for others who hope there are better ways than confrontation."[63]

As one reporter commented, the debate was "filled with fiery speeches, ovations, boos, cheers, a few hearty insults, and great goodwill." It was Yale's good fortune, he thought, that Brewster and his aides were "determined to achieve some sort of direct communication with the students," while the students were "apparently happier to talk and try to influence the Establishment than to riot."[64] For a night, at least, the generation's sense of powerlessness lifted.

A nonbinding vote on whether to expel ROTC resulted, implausibly, in a tie vote, 1,286–1,286.[65] As Moore remembered, when the vote count was announced, "Everyone gasped, then roared with laughter and went home. Thus ended student rebellion over ROTC at Yale."[66] "Brewster's luck," the radicals muttered. "It was the best possible result," then-freshman Gary Johnson thought, "because neither side had won and neither side had lost."[67] The outcome of the rink meeting, *Washington Post* reporter Alan Barth wrote, was "a strong sense that democracy had prevailed, that the administration was not scared of its students but rather respected them— and that therefore, in return, the students could reasonably respect the administration."[68] Brewster's gamble had paid off, and the contrast with events at Harvard and Cornell could not have been sharper.

The wonderfully absurd tie vote did not put an end to unrest at Yale that spring. In early May, SDS staged a "mill-in" in the treasurer's office to protest ROTC, after campus police foiled an attempt to occupy Woodbridge Hall. The demonstration, which lasted only an hour, fizzled when it became obvious that the administration was serious about putting the Brewster scenario into effect and that most students did not support further disruption on ROTC.

Two weeks later, Bobby Seale, the founder and national leader of the paramilitary Black Panthers, delivered a threatening, obscenity-laden address in Battell Chapel, vowing that the Panthers would "cross out the racist pig ruling class. . . . Today's pig is tomorrow's bacon."[69] Paul Moore's daughter, Honor, a drama student who had become caught up in black revolutionary politics, had arranged the visit. She had first asked drama school dean Robert Brustein to allow Seale to speak in the University Theatre; he wrote later that when he refused, "she took this as confirmation of my racial 'insensitivity.'"[70] Honor Moore prevailed on William Sloane Coffin to allow Seale to speak in Battell, but the chaplain "almost called the deal off," he recalled, "when I was frisked in my own church, as everyone was that night."[71] Seale's actions later that evening would become a matter of intense significance to everyone in the Yale administration; Moore's daughter, in hindsight, was the catalyst for dangerous events. At the time, however, Brewster was mainly upset by the "inexcusable" frisking by Seale's bodyguards and the offensive language that did "grave discredit to the sponsors of the occasion and to those who gave it sanction in the Chapel."[72]

Black Power politics surfaced again in late May when the City Planning Department in the School of Art and Architecture presented Brewster with a constitutional crisis. The department faculty, in a burst of egalitarianism, had decided to share with students, on an equal basis, their powers of budgeting, student admissions, and faculty hiring—although they neglected to inform the administration of this arrangement. The new governing body, called the City Planning Forum, resolved that half the incoming master's degree class should be black, and delegated responsibility for recruiting the students to the Black Workshop, a nonuniversity group. Few of the students the forum accepted through this process were, by normal standards, remotely qualified.

When he found out what the department faculty had done, Brewster hit the roof. Their actions directly contradicted his deeply held principles that the faculty should have ultimate responsibility for admissions and appointments and that there should be no racially separate and unequal program in any part of the university. He countermanded the black student admissions, relieved the City Planning teachers of their administrative responsibilities, and largely dismantled the program by reassigning its courses to other departments. In early June, still angry at the debacle, Brewster delivered the commencement address at Johns Hopkins University. "No sentimental egalitarianism, racial or otherwise," he snapped, "can be permitted to lower the standards for the relatively few institutions which are capable of really superior intellectual accomplishment."[73]

Later that month an intense fire broke out in the art and architecture building, gutting much of the interior. Although most people at the university believed that disgruntled students had torched the structure, the city fire marshal found no evidence of arson; the students' work spaces contained plenty of highly flammable materials that could have set off the conflagration. The students themselves retorted that they would sooner have set Woodbridge Hall ablaze than their home base. As one of the Black Workshop participants remembered, "When that building burned, everyone that I knew was in shock. You hated the building; there were all kinds of problems with the architecture school; but that was your building."[74]

Even before the fire, however, the whole City Planning episode left Brewster with a bad taste, and he wondered in hindsight whether he had acted precipitately. His gut reaction to disruption was to strike back at the offenders. One journalist noticed that the Yale president "appalled the more timid members of the faculty by passing the word that, if militants stormed his office, he would do his best to distribute a few bloody noses, and he expected the faculty to behave likewise."[75] But Brewster's combative instincts conflicted with his more measured judgment, which counseled patience in dealing with insecure students and blacks. In such matters, Chaplain Coffin advised, "it's better for the administration to be right than wrong; better to be wise and sensitive than right."[76]

STUDENT DISCONTENT OVER the Vietnam War permeated the Yale commencement in mid-June. Two large WE WON'T GO banners hung over the black-robed seniors as they marched into the sea of chairs set up on the Old Campus. Seventy-seven percent of the class had signed a petition, opposing U.S. policy in Vietnam, which ended with the pledge "that we will act in our public and private lives to assure that the tragic mistakes of Vietnam will not be repeated in our country's future." The class orator, John O'Leary, told parents and alumni that the dissent sweeping the country's colleges and universities was "not the work of a small group of campus radicals" but "a symptom of our deep and widespread frustration at this nation's reluctance to right its wrongs."[77]

In response to undergraduate requests, Brewster allowed the class secretary, William McIlwaine Thompson, to deliver a commencement address; Michael Medved, one of the organizers of the anti-ROTC movement, helped write the speech. Stephen Cohen, who helped publicize it, remembered that Thompson "was politically ideal. He came from several generations of Presbyterian ministers who had attended Yale, and he came across as conservative and all-American."[78] Thompson pointed out that opposition to the war united students of all political persuasions, not only because of the draft but because of students' "deep and overriding concern with the welfare of this country." He did not call the war immoral, and he did not condone the campus violence that had shocked the public that year. But, he emphasized, "the violence at home will not end while the violence abroad continues. The one feeds the other." The war was destroying the United States as well as Vietnam, he said, as the country poured its money and energies into war rather than the decaying cities and chaotic universities.[79] Thompson was interrupted a dozen times with applause, and virtually the whole gathering rose to give him a standing ovation when he concluded.

THOMPSON'S FRUSTRATION WITH the lack of public commitment to renewal echoed that of John Lindsay, who spoke at the Yale Law School alumni weekend that spring. The mayor criticized the disruptions on campus but observed that, for many students, the university had little more right to restore order than radicals had to disrupt it. The loss of respect for the university as an institution, he believed, was rooted in a spirit of defeat, "a sense that the processes of peaceful change really do not work." And the confidence of all Americans, not just youth, was shaken by the sense that many of society's key institutions were not performing humanely. In response to the country's upheavals, he pointed out, a commission was appointed (such as the riot commission on which he served or the commissions on crime and on the draft in which Brewster participated) to untangle the problems. And "each time," Lindsay observed, "we have asked moderate, pragmatic, eminently successful and respectable men to examine the causes. And each time, they have indicated not a conspiratorial minority or a breakdown of morality, but the failure of institutions to act decently." The reason that men like Lindsay, Brewster, and Bundy listened to radicals, he suggested, was not that they were in the grip of "radical chic" but that the radicals were often at least partially right. Lindsay concluded by asking his audience to understand that "change does not come through calls for it. It comes from a society that is in fact engaged in the long, difficult, hard, often unrewarding struggle to bring itself into line with the values it professes."[80]

Lindsay's counsel of struggle and self-criticism was uncongenial to conservatives, who had a more simple answer for what was wrong with the country: campus radicals, encouraged by a permissive elite. Vice President Spiro Agnew was emerging as the spokesman for the scapegoating point of view. In June 1969, speaking at the Ohio State University commencement, he charged that "a society which comes to fear its children is effete. A sniveling, hand-wringing power structure deserves the violent rebellion it encourages."[81] Agnew's speech received little attention, but the vice president had discovered the value of populism as a hammer with which to batter the liberal establishment. The lines in a larger battle were being drawn.

"HAVE A GOOD summer," one of Brewster's undergraduate friends wrote to him after commencement, "next year is going to be hell."[82] Brewster did have a good summer, traveling to Finland and the Soviet Union for business with the International Association of Universities, visiting Bonn and Bad Godesberg for a conference of German university rectors, and vacationing for the better part of July in Salzburg, the Italian lakes, and Paris before returning to the States on the *Queen Elizabeth 2*. The revolt of students was rarely far from his mind, however, since it was a phenomenon that his European counterparts also had to cope with; the airports were full of restless kids with guitars and bare feet, and even Russia had its rebellious youth, the *stilyagi*.

When Brewster returned to New Haven, he found that the journalist David Halberstam had written a slashing attack article, "The Very Expensive Education of McGeorge Bundy," for the July 1969 issue of *Harper's*. Halberstam blamed the Vietnam War on Bundy and, by extension, the class of public service aristocrats to which he belonged. The article enraged Bundy's friends partly because they disagreed with its conclusion; they believed that American involvement in Vietnam had come about because of Cold War policies that most of the country endorsed, not because John Kennedy and Lyndon Johnson had been manipulated by hawkish advisors. They also felt that Halberstam, in relying on hearsay evidence and blind quotes to paint his portrait of Bundy, distorted Mac into a barely recognizable caricature. Robert McNamara, who by this time had become one of Bundy's trustees on the Ford Foundation, remembered that when he first read the article, "I was absolutely exploding with anger at the way Halberstam characterized Mac. . . . I got so goddamned mad I spent all day long calling people to try to get them to do something about it."[83]

The president of Yale was furious because Halberstam quoted him telling an official in the Eugene McCarthy presidential campaign that Bundy should be left off a list of establishment supporters because "Mac is going to spend the rest of his life trying to justify his mistakes on Vietnam." Brewster may in fact have believed the assertion, but to voice the opinion to anyone outside his circle would be, to him, rank disloyalty. While he also thought it perfectly acceptable to criticize Bundy for his decisions, the personalization of such criticism was anathema to him. He wrote to *Harper's* denying the statement and damning Halberstam's technique of blind, unattributed quotation as "a very low form of journalistic deception."[84] As bad as he considered Halberstam's account, however, Brewster could not deny that the war Bundy had helped set in motion was grinding on, that opposition to it was infecting every aspect of the university, and that the pressure on leaders like Brewster to speak out against the war was becoming increasingly intense.

THE MAIN EVENT on the Yale campus at the start of the 1969–70 academic year was the presence, for the first time, of undergraduate women. History professor Donald Kagan, who arrived at Yale that year from Cornell, remembered being "overwhelmed" by the intellectual caliber of the undergraduates. In hindsight, he thought "it might have been the most brilliant total class that Yale ever had. The best women in the country wanted to come to Yale that year, and transferred in or came in as freshmen. The talent of the women was so extraordinary as to bring the whole standard up."[85] The media swarmed the campus to interview "the Superwomen," a label most found difficult to carry. Coeducation brought other concerns as well: crowding, the continued importation of Smith and Vassar students for mixers, and the seven-to-one male-female ratio, which led the women to feel that they were living a fishbowl existence and made it a challenge to develop close friendships among themselves. The (usually) unconscious sexism of male professors and students also grated on the new undergraduates. Still, they had been selected for character as well as intellect, and for the most part the women adjusted well to Yale.[86]

One student analyst predicted that the presence of women would make radical politicking more likely at Yale, since "women jump onto causes more quickly than men."[87] For both men and women alike, however, the overriding cause in the fall of 1969 was opposition to the war in Vietnam. The most important protest taking shape was the National Vietnam Moratorium, a plan to stage antiwar rallies across the country on October 15. The organizers of the New Haven protest were many of the same liberal-to-moderate students who had worked to keep the rink meetings peaceful in May, including Michael Medved (then in the law school), Stephen Cohen, and Greg Craig. Cohen remembered that "we tried to build as broad a coalition as possible. . . . We were trying to show that the moderate majority of Americans opposed the war."[88] Not surprisingly, the Yale SDS opposed the protest. The moratorium committee lined up centrist political figures— including Allard Lowenstein, Mayor Richard Lee, local AFL-CIO head Vincent Sirabella, former interior secretary Stewart Udall, Republican businessman Malcolm Baldrige, and Kingman Brewster—to speak.

A sea of people—black and white, old and young, mostly mainstream and moderate—filled the New Haven Green on October 15, a warm day under blue skies. The protesters waved American flags, sang "The Star-Spangled Banner," and listened respectfully to Coffin's opening invocation. Before the speeches began, however, Yale's Black Student Alliance leader Glenn DeChabert leaped onto the speaker's platform to denounce "murderous police practices" against minorities before the startled crowd.[89]

The seemingly spontaneous outburst had been secretly arranged by Brewster and DeChabert. Black sophomore William Farley recalled that "Glenn was kind of pushed forward by the radical element in the organization" to seize the microphone and make a statement against police harassment. "He kind of had to gird his loins and go out there and do it. . . . Brewster was letting Glenn speak to get him out of a jam. He didn't have to let him speak; he could easily have made it very difficult. But he knew the position Glenn was in, and he knew that by letting him go ahead and speak, not only would he let the idea out (which was important), but it would also help Glenn and would help him maintain his credibility and his position."[90]

Brewster was one of the last speakers. While his speeches could sometimes be orotund, on this occasion he had reduced his message to a few eloquent phrases. It was the president's first public statement against the war. "As we make our choice for withdrawal from Vietnam," he said, his words echoing across the Green, "let us speak in terms of candid confession rather than in terms of blame. . . . Let us say simply that our ability to keep the peace also requires that America once again become a symbol of decency and hope, fully deserving the trust and respect of mankind. . . .

We meet here not so much in protest as in dedication, rededication to the end of destruction abroad and to the end of decay at home."[91] To the *New York Times* columnist Anthony Lewis, Brewster's remarks were "almost Gettysburg-like in their simplicity after so much oratory."[92]

"New Haven yesterday was a moving experience," Lewis wrote to Richardson, "and I wish you could have been there. I know it was not representative of the whole country, but no one who saw those 50,000 people on the Green could mistake the feelings there."[93] But Richardson's boss, Nixon, made it known that he had watched a football game rather than pay any heed to the hundreds of thousands who protested around the nation. Vice President Agnew insulted them as "an effete corps of impudent snobs who characterize themselves as intellectuals." It was a "particularly disgusting phrase . . . that got you hot under the collar," Craig remembered.[94] "The President has indicated that he will not allow policy to be made 'in the streets,'" Craig and the other members of the New Haven Moratorium Committee shot back. "And yet if the government chooses to ignore the profound convictions of the American people concerning the continuation of the war in Vietnam, it does so not only at its own peril—but at the peril of our entire democratic system."[95]

Nixon declared himself equally unmoved by the next month's Mobilization Day, which brought immense crowds to Washington and other cities. William Sloane Coffin traveled to the capital a day early to take part in an antiwar service at the National Cathedral sponsored by Clergy and Laymen Concerned About Vietnam. A huge crowd, mainly of young people, filled nearly every square foot of the majestic space. They prayed with Paul Moore and sang with the folksinger Pete Seeger. Coffin remembered that when the service was over, no one moved: "Like the giant columns around us the more than five thousand people stood motionless, their fingers raised in the V sign of the peace movement. The silence was awesome."[96] The next day, Moore celebrated his fiftieth birthday by marching at the head of what was, at that time, the largest demonstration in United States history; it brought over half a million people to Washington. But the sense of unity of the previous day's service was missing. The Weathermen (the most extremist offshoot of SDS), attempting to disrupt the rally, waved Viet Cong flags, set fires, and drew media attention from the larger, peaceful protest. The antiwar movement was fracturing as disillusioned youth, convinced that the government would not respond to participants from the mainstream, turned to violent alternatives.

This prospect deeply alarmed Brewster, who wrote of his concern in a sharp exchange with Attorney General John Mitchell. Writing on behalf of the International Association of Universities to protest the administration's refusal of entry to the Belgian socialist scholar Ernest Mandel, Brewster told Mitchell that "I have been doing my best to convince restless students that their best chance to improve the quality of society is to work within, not against, the political and legal system, even if the objective is radical reform. . . . Your ruling is one more nudge which tends to drive constructive reformers into the ranks of the destructive radicals." Brewster could barely conceal his contempt for what he considered Mitchell's un-American conservatism. "When the nation's senior legal officer shows a fear of freedom," he charged, "I fear for the freedom of the nation."[97]

MCGEORGE BUNDY SHARED Brewster's distaste for the populist conservatism that was gaining ground both in Nixon's administration and in the country as a whole. Bundy had encountered it earlier in 1969 when he testified before the House Ways and Means Committee inquiry into foundation activities. The members of Congress blasted the Ford Foundation's travel grants to Robert Kennedy's staffers, its support of CORE's election activities in Cleveland, its support of La Raza and other Hispanic advocacy groups, and the foundation's other controversial activities. (Although the committee members grilled Bundy for almost an entire day, they made little mention, surprisingly, of the foundation's participation in the New York City school decentralization controversy.)

Bundy gave no ground at all. Refusing to concede that foundation activities were in any measure political as well as charitable, he denied that the foundation's role in foreign aid and urban issues was comparable to that of the government. He was resolutely unapologetic about his grants to Kennedy's ex-staffers, provoking the members of Congress by informing them that "the board of trustees of the Ford Foundation could give $3 billion tomorrow to any one of thousands of institutions . . . [or] individuals."[98] Losing his temper, he barked at one of the members that "I don't presume to think I can change your mind when others have obviously failed."[99] Former Danforth Foundation head Merrimon Cuninggim, who was in the room when Bundy testified, felt that Bundy's manner "just made some members of that committee livid—the positioning in the chair, the slouch, as if to say, 'Now you little people, what are you doing with us big people?'"[100]

Bundy knew that he had not put on a good performance. "I didn't behave, did I?" he said with a small smile to his staffers on his way out of the hearing.[101] Even the *New York Times* scolded his unbending defense of foundations: "The fact of the matter is that foundations often function as second governments in the shaping of controversial social policies."[102] By the end of the year, Congress prohibited foundations from giving grants that would influence elections, and enacted a four percent tax on foundations' net annual income, which cost the Ford Foundation $10 million a year. While the congressional conservatives almost certainly would have passed the legislation even if Bundy had been meek and lamblike, many of his colleagues at other foundations blamed him for stoking rather than soothing conservative anger. The episode did show that Bundy could neither tolerate nor comprehend conservatism. There was truth to Norman Mailer's complaint that year that centrist liberals tended to "think that anyone who does not subscribe to their ideas is seriously deranged."[103]

Bundy was also afflicted by a hard-right, anti–Ford Foundation organization, Families Opposed to Radical Donations (F.O.R.D.), that brewed up out of California, boycotting Ford automobile dealerships in protest against the foundation's "acting as a motivating and funding catalyst for the militants who demand that our system be destroyed." The conservative activists claimed that "the Ford Foundation has become a destructive power to foster Socialism, One Worldism, anti-Americanism, disunity, violence and revolution." The movement also drew in evangelicals like the Reverend Billy James Hargis, who charged that Bundy's organization was "the single Foundation that is doing more to undermine our country and destroy Christian freedom than any other."[104] Bundy attributed the anti-Ford sentiment to a growing McCarthyism of left and right, as well as to "the general malaise with the Eastern Liberal Establishment."[105]

IN EARLY NOVEMBER 1969, the Yale SDS—by this time dominated by its Worker-Student Alliance faction, under Zanger—found the issue it had been waiting for. Colia Williams, a black employee in one of the residential college dining halls, had been fired for arguing with the student managing her and throwing a glass of juice in his face. The SDS proclaimed Williams a victim of "speed-up" and institutional racism in the dining halls, held a rally on her behalf, and resolved to "confront the people who did this," as Zanger put it.[106] The door of Woodbridge Hall was locked, so the protesters moved on to the office of the business manager in the basement of Wright Hall, one of the freshman dormitories on the Old Campus.[107] Zanger remembered that "as word spread that something was happening, more people joined. So we probably went from twenty to thirty to sixty to one hundred or so (at various levels of involvement) by the time we actually got to the building."[108] John Embersits, the university business manager, agreed to review the case, but the students, denouncing his proposal as a stalling tactic, forced their way past the campus police into the offices, forcibly preventing Embersits and other supervisors from leaving.[109]

When Coffin arrived, in an attempt to impress on the students the gravity of their actions, he was shouted down. According to Zanger, the occupiers were incensed that the chaplain "showed up wearing a blue-jean jacket and pants, the official uniform of the civil rights movement" and began "trying to persuade us not to do stuff that we thought was just. We really thought he was playing the game of saying that every institution in society is subject to criticism except the one that you are in, which was a common game."[110] The dean of undergraduate affairs, John Wilkinson, recalled one of the moralistic SDS members yelling, "Who are *you* to tell us anything, Mr. Coffin? You're a divorced man!"[111] By now the radicals regarded even Coffin as part of the corrupt establishment. Charles Taylor, the provost, had the responsibility of putting the Brewster scenario into effect: he warned the students of the penalties that awaited them, summoned the residential college deans to identify the disrupters, and prepared a court injunction against the occupation. Finally the students left of their own accord.

The day after the SDS staged the first and only building takeover at Yale during the 1960s, Brewster went to a black-tie, stag dinner at the White House in honor of the Duke of Edinburgh. He spent much of the dinner with old friends like Acheson and Jock Whitney, but he also talked to Nixon and Kissinger. "I tried to get through to them about what's happening on the campuses," he told a reporter afterward. "I don't think I did. Kissinger was mainly worried about what the right wing would do if we failed to get an honorable settlement in Vietnam."[112]

The next morning Brewster appeared before the Senate's Administrative Practice and Procedure Subcommittee to testify on draft reform. The Yale president acerbically informed the senators that what particularly distinguished "the draft muddle" from other great policy failures, such as the Vietnam War and urban decay, was that its cause and cure were known and would not require any money—and "still we have done nothing to correct the situation."[113] His tour de force summary of the draft's defects, which he had diagnosed as a member of the presidential commission on the selective service, shamed and cajoled the senators into agreeing to pass a bill to allow random lottery selection of draftees. As one reporter observed, Brewster "accomplished singlehandedly what congressional leaders had been unable to do—find a compromise to get action this year on a major reform of the draft laws."[114] It would be difficult to find a similar example of an active university president having such a direct impact on legislation.

Back at Yale, Brewster dealt with the immediate cause of the Wright Hall occupation, the Colia Williams case, by working with the Black Student Alliance. By way of thanks for Brewster's having let him address the October moratorium rally, BSAY leader Glenn DeChabert agreed to be a witness at a job hearing for Mrs. Williams. She was reinstated, and the BSAY helped defuse the racial dimension of the protest. Brewster was pleased to tell a group of alumni that the black students "were much more rational about the issues" than the white radicals, and "so clear that Mrs. Williams and the blacks in general were being exploited by the SDS."[115] Zanger lamented that "the administration legitimized [the BSAY] and delegitimized us at every turn."[116]

More worrisome by far for Brewster were the developments in the faculty that followed the occupation of Wright Hall. Although Brewster had hoped the faculty's Executive Committee would deliver stiff penalties, the committee, after holding a hearing for each of the forty-seven students charged, suspended all of them but simultaneously commuted the sentences to disciplinary probation for the remainder of the school year. Wilkinson said that the "unprecedented situation" meant that "this time and this time only we decided to show mercy" and that the Brewster scenario would remain unchanged.[117] Yale College dean Georges May recalled that "I started out being much more on the side of harsh treatment, but as I saw all these kids [at the hearings], I had the feeling that what they needed most was to be spanked and sent back home to their colleges, and that they did not deserve anything more severe. They were mostly followers of the rhetoric of people who managed not to be caught."[118] Zanger confirmed that the list of accused building occupiers included some who were not present and omitted others who were. "Some people who were there and weren't on the list wondered if they should turn themselves in; it was an era of high conscience. I, as a Marxist cynic, told them not to."[119]

There followed three tempestuous faculty meetings at which the decision of the Executive Committee was opposed by those who thought it too lenient. Indeed, law professor Alexander Bickel declared that since the students had detained two Yale employees against their will, the events in Wright Hall "bore certain similarities to kidnapping and for this, according to the laws of Connecticut, the penalty might be death."[120] The faculty eventually united behind a consensus statement crafted by a group of professorial "mandarins" close to Brewster, but the debate highlighted incipient divisions within the faculty and the possibility of fracture if events took a turn for the worse, as they had at Harvard in the spring.[121]

TIME MAGAZINE NAMED "Middle Americans" its Man and Woman of the Year for 1969.[122] While there was no hard-and-fast definition of the term, the Middle Americans were usually white, working-class to middle-class, culturally if not economically conservative people alienated by the sweeping, confusing changes of the 1960s. Joseph Kraft, a discerning political writer, observed that Middle America was also defined by its opposition to the liberal establishment: the universities that incubated unsettling new ideas, the foundations that lavished concern on threatening blacks and browns, the media that gave "unstinted publicity to the cultural revolution fostered by the universities and foundations," and the politicians who "developed sophisticated foreign and economic policies at odds with the traditional notions native to Middle America." From Kraft's vantage point, Middle America was wrong on almost all the major issues, but the fault line between the elite and the mass struck him as being as dangerous as the medieval battle between church and state.[123]

John Lindsay had never had an easy relationship with the middling sort, and his standing among the hardhats and Catholics and unionists sunk to a low point in 1969. In February, when a freak storm dumped nineteen inches of snow on New York, it took days for an incompetent, unprepared Sanitation Department to clear the streets outside Manhattan. Touring the unplowed streets of eastern Queens, Lindsay was confronted with the venom of the people he usually overlooked, literally as well as figuratively. "There were a number of suggestions about what I might do with myself," he recalled, "and there was a good deal of fascinating speculation about my ancestry."[124]

In June, Lindsay lost the Republican mayoral primary to Staten Island state senator John Marchi. It was his first political defeat, and it seriously jeopardized his chances for reelection. Nixon's conservative aide Patrick Buchanan exulted that Lindsay's loss dealt "a permanent blow to the Dewey-Rockefeller, Eastern Liberal Establishment coalition."[125] Lindsay tried to regroup by running as an independent on the Liberal Party ticket, making peace with the unions, and mounting a highly sophisticated, media-savvy campaign. Swallowing some of his pride, he admitted that "I guessed wrong on the weather before the city's biggest snowfall last winter. And that was a mistake." The 1968 school strike, he conceded, "went too far." But, he pointed out, he had put more police on the streets, brought in jobs, reduced pollution, "and we didn't have a Newark, a Watts or a Detroit."[126] While the campaign lacked the celebrity vibe of Lindsay's 1965 run, solid supporters like Cyrus Vance and Jock Whitney rallied to his side.[127] Lindsay tilted further toward the antiwar movement, making several speeches on Moratorium Day blaming the war for diverting resources from the urban crisis.

To Lindsay's great good fortune, the New York Mets, baseball's perennial cellar-dwellers, miraculously won the World Series in October, lifting the entire city's mood. Photos of the players dousing a grinning Lindsay in a champagne celebration helped humanize his public image. Further good luck came in the form of Lindsay's Democratic opponent, city comptroller Mario Procaccino, a shiny-suited stereotype of a ward heeler who ran one of the decade's more incompetent campaigns. His one effective thrust was to add "limousine liberal" to the political lexicon, a term suggesting what the middle class saw as Lindsay's Manhattan glitz and celebrity, privilege and moral high-handedness, and insulation from the practical consequences of reforms like school decentralization.

Procaccino and Marchi split the backlash ballots and Lindsay emerged the victor with forty-two percent of the vote. "A great personal victory," Richardson congratulated Lindsay via telegram. "Enlightenment lives."[128] The mayor would not abandon his liberal beliefs, but the chastened tone of his second inaugural address ("We are all human, we are all fallible. The test is whether we have learned from the mistakes we have made") suggested that the era of visionary, highly ambitious liberalism had come to an end in New York.[129]

BY THE TIME of Lindsay's election, Paul Moore had been taking part in a more decorous, yearlong campaign to become bishop of New York. It was the foremost Episcopal diocese, and its bishop was generally considered the leading advocate for the Church. Moore traveled from Washington periodically to meet with different congregations, not only in the city but in the suburbs and distant counties included in the diocese. Some of his conservative opponents questioned whether Moore had sufficient theological sophistication for the post. "I am not a theologian," Moore agreed, "in the sense that I do not have academic credentials in theology. . . . I believe theology is best taught by bishops and parish priests through action accompanied by the spoken and written word . . . by leading movements for justice rather than analyzing the books of the Old Testament."[130] In the crisis-ridden atmosphere of the late 1960s, a committed man of the cloth seemed, to many, a more suitable spokesman for the church than what Moore called the "pipe-smoking Anglophile rector, steeped in interesting and esoteric books."[131]

Moore attended the Yale Corporation's meeting in mid-December, which, as customary, began with Brewster asking, "Will the Bishop pray?" Moore requested the Lord's guidance for the group "as the problems before us become more complex and the conflicts about us more intense."[132] On December 12, Moore was taking time out from Corporation business to meet with the trustees of an Episcopal seminary affiliated with the Yale Divinity School when the phone rang in the kitchen. It was Horace Donegan, the bishop of New York, informing Moore that he had been elected as Donegan's successor.[133] Moore told a reporter a few minutes later that he was "thrilled by the honor but a little scared" by the responsibility that would soon be his.

Moore had been elected on the second ballot. Two speeches by his supporters after the first, inconclusive ballot had put him over the top. The Reverend Clifford Lauder, spokesman for the diocese's Union of Black Clergy and Laymen, told the gathering that "Paul Moore, in our estimation, is the best representative in the white establishment of the truly liberal point of view." Then R. Keith Kane—Wall Street lawyer and Harvard trustee—swayed hesitant laymen by reassuring them that he had known Moore for years and found him to be "a prudent man."[134] Moore's coalition of minorities, liberals, and establishment bigwigs mirrored the coalition that had returned Lindsay to office a month earlier. When Moore moved to New York early the next year, Lindsay threw a dance party at Gracie Mansion to welcome him and his family. McGeorge Bundy and Cyrus Vance also met with Moore, who was not only their friend but now their bishop as well.

AFTER THE BISHOP relocated to New York, he, Lindsay, and Vance occasionally came up together to the Yale Corporation meetings. It was a jumpy time for the trustees, because Brewster's skill in handling the student movement was making him a target while it was bringing him national acclaim. In the fall of 1969, Jerry Rubin and other radicals gathered in Max's Kansas City bar and restaurant in New York to plot Brewster's downfall. As

Flora Lewis later reported, "They decided that the time had come to 'get Yale,' since it was one of the few major campuses which had yet to experience a massive, unruly demonstration."[135] The radicals needed a plausible cause, and they found it in the trial of the Black Panther founder and national chairman Bobby Seale that, almost unnoticed, was attracting activists to New Haven.

The chain of events that led to Yale's greatest crisis began with a young black man named John Huggins Jr., whose father was the steward of the Fence Club fraternity at Yale—a respectable job that gave the Huggins family prominence in New Haven's West Indian community. John Jr. was in line for the stewardship of the Faculty Club at Yale, but, intoxicated by violent black nationalism, he joined the Black Panthers in California, where he was killed in a shoot-out with a rival gang in the UCLA cafeteria. In January 1969 his widow, Ericka Huggins, along with a dozen or so Black Panthers, brought his body back to his hometown for burial. And so New Haven had a Black Panther chapter at a time when there were few Panthers east of the Mississippi.[136]

The Black Panther Party is still a difficult group to define.[137] Although the inner leadership consisted mainly of charismatic criminals and psychopaths, the Panthers also attracted able individuals who in less troubled times would have put their talents to use in more moderate organizations. In the overheated political atmosphere of the late 1960s, the Panthers' fetishization of guns, leather, and confrontations with the police made them romantic figures, and they gained a dominant position in leftist politics by being the only black-nationalist group willing to work with white radicals. The New Haven chapter created a positive image for itself by offering an honestly run free breakfast program for children, while at the same time stockpiling an arsenal and placing wiretaps on top of the phone taps already operated by the FBI and the New Haven police.[138] The Panthers scared and intrigued black and white Yale students as they stood in front of Liggett's drugstore urging passersby to purchase the *Panther Newsletter*, "'cause tha revolution will not be televised!"

When Seale came to speak in New Haven in the spring of 1969, at Honor Moore's invitation, he went to the local Panthers headquarters on Orchard Street after his speech in Battell Chapel. Upstairs was sometime-member Alex Rackley, whom the Panthers suspected of being an informant and were torturing with boiling water, lit cigarettes, and an ice pick. Following Seale's alleged order to "off the pig," the Panthers took Rackley out of town, shot him in the head, and dumped the corpse in a river, where it was discovered the next day. Most of the New Haven Panthers were arrested, and Seale eventually was extradited to stand trial in the city, where he and three other Panthers faced the death penalty.[139] In the autumn, mainly nonlocal activists staged protests on behalf of the Panthers, and in early March 1970, the New Haven Panther Defense Committee (NHPDC) was organized "to inform people of the trial and events connected with it." More than a dozen of its members were reputed to be Yale students or dropouts.[140]

By at least March 1970, the radicals' plan to "get Brewster" had merged with the Black Panthers' intention to stage a massive protest in New Haven on the May 1 weekend. News of the anticipated demonstration circulated on leaflets and through word of mouth, although the purpose of the protest was never clearly defined. A poster announced such invited speakers as David Hilliard (chief of staff of the Black Panther Party), the radical French playwright Jean Genet, and the Chicago Seven, the defendants in the notorious trial for conspiracy to riot at the 1968 Democratic convention. It warned participants to "come prepared," but also advertised "Jazz festival. Rock. Santana & other groups. Dancing."[141] Most of the activists intended the May Day weekend primarily as a protest against the trial of Seale and the other Panthers. The Black Panthers contended that Seale was a political prisoner, and that the Rackley murder trial was being used as a way to break up the Panthers. Seale had recently been tried with the Chicago Seven; when he was too vocal in his demands to his right to self-representation, Judge Julius Hoffman ordered him shackled to his chair and gagged. It was a horrific image, which made it all too easy to picture Seale in the electric chair. For the radicals, however, the announced goal of the weekend was not to protest the trial but to "Free Bobby" and "Burn Yale."

The link between Yale and the Panther trial was suggested rather than established. Zanger heard a story that Brewster's ex-CIA assistant Tracy Barnes had helped facilitate Seale's visit to New Haven on the day of Rackley's murder. Furthermore, "the Black Panther organization was riddled with informers. . . . And then you had this decision made to discipline this comrade, and Bobby Seale was asked for an OK, like the Mafia condoning a hit—already the FBI's model of how a command organization works. And lo and behold, Seale happens to be in New Haven at the right time. So it attract[ed] a certain amount of speculative attention to who in the Yale administration might have been horsing around with this."[142]

The NHPDC's mistrust of Yale ran deep. Another poster they produced emphasized that "we have to work to educate people about the role of the

Yale Corporation in New Haven so everyone can see clearly how responsible Yale is for the kinds of oppression that exist in the black community."[143] The poster also commented that "it could not have been an accident that the same Establishment which thrives on institutions such as Yale chose New Haven as the site" of the Panther trial.[144] As the New Left journalist Andrew Kopkind wrote, Yale is "much more than a run-of-the-sty Pig. In a real way, Yale denies power to the people, for it organizes and keeps power unto itself. Yale did not put Bobby Seale in the New Haven County jail; but it is a designer, supporter and executor of the system that led him to that place."[145] Destroying Yale seemed to many radicals like a promising step toward a more just social order, as well as payback for one of the few universities in its class that, as Brewster said, "hadn't had any experience with the gratuitously ugly types bent on violence, as well as on the destruction of established institutions."[146]

Rumors began to circulate that anywhere from fifty thousand to half a million demonstrators would be coming to town on the May 1 weekend. In early April an undergraduate wrote to Brewster that he had recently become aware of the Black Panthers and Seale. "Soon you will be very aware of them," he warned. "You will be caught up in the crisis in the days ahead—as a symbol of an institution, as a leader, as a man. As you know, many students are now questioning the values and the purposes of institutions, such as Yale. Can the universities such as Yale be a relevant moral force, or are they merely controlled by the force of narrow interests? . . . In short, what is Yale going to do about the Bobby Seale trial?"[147]

Brewster knew about the Panthers through undergraduate contacts but also because many people close to him, including several members of the Corporation, were concerned that the government crackdown on the Black Panthers, and the fear and loathing the group inspired among the public, posed a threat to the nation's democratic and legal processes. Not until mid-April, however, did Brewster and his assistants realize that the Panther trial might blow up in their faces. On April 14, Harold Mulvey, the presiding judge, punished two Black Panthers for talking to each other in the visitor's section of the courtroom; he sentenced them to six months in jail for contempt of court. Until then, one of the two, David Hilliard, had been the highest-ranking Panther who was not in jail or in exile.[148] "What more is there to talk about?" read a poster that went up after the contempt sentence. "The time for discussion and passive resistance has run out. Unless we relate to action today, it will be too late for all of us tomorrow."[149]

Before that episode, Brewster recalled, "we were aware that there was a general concern about the trial, but I don't think there was a widespread feeling that the trial was going to be almighty unfair, or a miscarriage, until the dramatic event of those two contempt citations."[150] The sentences were grossly disproportionate to the offense and imposed without a hearing in a manner that echoed the conduct of Judge Hoffman in the Chicago Seven trial. In addition, Brewster's recognition of the impending threat from outside was crystallized when, at an April 15 rally in Boston, Abbie Hoffman publicly asserted that, in two weeks, radicals would go to New Haven to burn Yale down; Hoffman's audience then marched on and trashed Harvard Square. "So we knew that this wasn't the typical problem of student unrest or disruption internally," the president observed. "Essentially it was the use of the Bobby Seale trial to bring together a great radical 'happening,' and Yale was clearly one of the announced targets."[151]

In mid- to late April, Brewster laid out a strategy for handling the crisis. He cooperated with state and city officials (particularly police chief James Ahern) to develop a coordinated response.[152] With some of his assistants, Brewster drove up to Sturbridge, Massachusetts, to meet with his old Harvard law professor Archibald Cox, who had headed the investigations into the 1968 disturbances at Columbia and was Harvard's executive officer in dealing with student disruptions.[153] Cox was most impressed by Brewster's panache in the face of potential disaster. The president drove out to a scenic spot overlooking a brook and took out an English wicker picnic basket from the trunk of his sports car. "The top layer was martini cocktails," Cox remembered. "The next layer was ice. The next layer was white wine. More ice. The next layer was something like Cornish rock hen—awfully good. So we sat there and discussed Bobby Seale day."[154] Brewster was mildly relieved to find that the Harvard authorities "really were somewhat less sophisticated than we were" at reacting to student rebellion.[155] Cox gave the president information on Boston "uglies" and troublemakers who might show up in New Haven, and Brewster made similar arrangements with Columbia University officials. "But there wasn't much else we could do except then focus on our own policies," Brewster concluded.[156]

One of Brewster's most important decisions was to take the unorthodox step of welcoming the demonstrators to Yale rather than closing the university and ringing it with armed guards, as many were urging. He knew it was a potentially dangerous move, but felt that locked buildings would be a provocation and an invitation to ransack Yale.[157] Persuading some of the residential college masters to open their colleges to outsiders took considerable lobbying, but Brewster accomplished his goal through near-continual meetings and the assistance of student allies like Stephen Cohen, Greg Craig, and William Farley on the Strike Steering Committee. The other major decisions came at an extraordinary meeting of the Yale College faculty on April 23. At its meeting a week earlier, the faculty had discussed the upcoming trial along with academic matters. "Over the years I had taken the position that the faculty should not be a forum for questions outside its duties," Georges May had said afterward. "Now I was afraid under the circumstances that our silence might be taken for indifference. We are certainly not indifferent."[158] Since the president and three-quarters of the faculty had been absent on April 16, no formal action was taken, and May announced that Brewster would be present at the next week's meeting.

At the April 23 meeting, a record four hundred people—over half the members of the college faculty—were present. Brewster had the floor first but yielded to Roy Bryce-LaPorte, the designated leader of the black faculty. In his talk of nearly half an hour, Bryce-LaPorte stressed Yale's deficiencies in dealing with blacks and the New Haven community rather than the trial, an indication of the direction in which the May Day bandwagon was rolling. The black faculty resolution he presented called for an indefinite "suspension of normal academic functions" during which instructors "should suspend their classes" and for a reassessment of the university's relationship with the city and the black community. The acting provost, Alvin Kernan, felt that "none of the blacks trusted us or had any interest in identifying with the old Yale. But we controlled the money, the appointments, the prestige, and with enormous practicality they saw that Yale would still be in place, and still rich, long after the Black Panthers . . . were gone."[159] The black faculty's resolution boiled down to a request for university engagement with black issues that stopped short of active support of the Panthers; the professors were signaling their willingness to make a deal.

Dean May then moved to adjourn the meeting to permit undergraduate Kurt Schmoke to address the faculty, the first student ever to do so. Undergraduates who had been put in similar situations at Harvard and Cornell in the spring of 1969 had threatened the faculty and polarized the university, and the Yale professors waited tensely, expecting another out-of-control militant. But they were pleasantly surprised when Schmoke began by thanking the faculty and then by assuring them that he would not ask the professors to endorse any particular proposition. "There are a great number of students on campus who are confused and many who are frightened," he told them. "They don't know what to think. You are our teachers. You are the people we respect. We look to you for guidance and moral leadership. On behalf of my fellow students, I beg you to give it to us."[160] The relieved faculty responded to Schmoke's brief address with warm applause. Despite the political undercurrent to Schmoke's plea—he was asking the professors to bend customary institutional neutrality, in regard to the Panther trial, just enough so that black students could support the university—his respectful rather than threatening stance made it far more likely they would agree. His good judgment also reflected that of Brewster and his associates, who knew Schmoke personally and trusted him to use the opportunity in a positive way.[161]

Brewster took the stage to deliver a statement about the trial and Yale's relation to the community. Yale, he insisted, must remain neutral. Yale could not contribute money to the Panther Defense Fund, as many were urging. But no member of the Yale community, including the president, would be inhibited from speaking his or her conscience on the trial or the broader questions of race relations.

Brewster then attempted to give personal force to this generality, in a sentence that would follow him for the rest of his life: "So in spite of my insistence on the limits of my official capacity, I personally want to say that I am appalled and ashamed that things should have come to such a pass in this country that I am skeptical of the ability of black revolutionaries to achieve a fair trial anywhere in the United States." He added that "in large part this atmosphere has been created by police actions and prosecutions against the Panthers in many parts of the country. It is also one more inheritance from centuries of racial discrimination and oppression."

In the remainder of his speech, Brewster asked for suggestions as to how the Yale community might make a greater contribution to New Haven's needy neighborhoods, endorsed the strike supporters' announcement that they would not interfere with those who wished to go to class, and assured the faculty that the administration would "do our best to prevent and to cope with violence if it should threaten."[162] Although Brewster's "skeptical" remark provoked an audible gasp from the faculty, the professors burst into thunderous applause at the end of the speech.[163]

In the discussion that followed, Brewster strove to find a middle ground that the black faculty would accept and the rest of the faculty could agree to. Instead of Bryce-LaPorte's "suspension of the normal academic functions," for example, the "normal expectations" of the university would be "modified." Rather than state that the faculty "should suspend their classes," the resolution would declare that the faculty "should be free to suspend their classes." These were not mere semantic distinctions; they spelled the difference between a university shutdown and a situation in which most classes continued, albeit in a context affected by the extraordinary circumstances. Brewster remembered that the black faculty resolution in its original form contained "the one thing that I could not buy, which was . . . the notion that there was an official policy against teaching. You can't do that."

Aside from this issue, however, Brewster realized that the black proposal was generally compatible with the opposing motion of a group of white faculty members around psychology professor Kenneth Keniston. "And so I made those proposals on the spur of the moment, and in presenting them got the acquiescence from the floor of the black spokesmen." The most important need, he felt, was to hold the faculty together. Brewster followed up his amendment by adding that if this resolution was to be voted, he would emphasize that professors could continue to meet their classes and would reaffirm the university's unwillingness to condone violence or disruption.[164] Brewster then sided with the black faculty's insistence that no time limit be set on the suspension of normal activities, against the Keniston resolution's call for classes to resume on a fixed date.

Brewster's unspoken calculation was that if Yale passed through May Day unscathed, he could bring off a return to normal operations, just as it was the tacit assumption of radically inclined faculty members, like the black faculty strategist Kenneth Mills, that the students' strike action could be continued indefinitely. Brewster also believed that the black faculty, having compromised on the shutdown issue, would not back down on the issue of a limitation. Indeed, while Keniston was on the floor pressing for a fixed limit, Mills stage-whispered to Keniston's henchman Peter Brooks, "You're playing with fire. We'll walk out."[165] When Brewster saw that a preponderance of the faculty was persuaded by Mills's pragmatic explanation for the necessity of an open-ended suspension, he took the unusual step of calling for an end to the debate, over some objections that several of the subsidiary items on the black faculty resolution (dealing with Yale's relation to the Black Student Alliance and the New Haven community) had not been discussed. The faculty then passed the amended black faculty resolution by an overwhelming voice vote.

Later, Brewster conceded that "I took the risk of much more of a steamroller approach than I ever had before on anything. And God knows, the

tension was high because it was just the kind of issue on which other institutions like Cornell, Harvard and so on had split wide open, not only
between the faculty and administration, but within the faculty." But the
president believed that "to have prolonged that discussion not only at that
meeting, but to have held something over for another meeting, and to try to
hold meetings between then and May Day, would have been a disaster, and
would have taken us into May Day in exactly the condition I most feared,
which would have been a kind of internal dissension and polarization. So
there's no doubt at all that the steamroller or bulldozer effort was to avoid
the necessity of having contentious faculty meetings between then and the
invasion."[166]

While one historian characterized the black faculty resolution as "radical" and the Keniston resolution as "liberal," such labels were of limited use
in the days leading up to May Day because the ground shifted so quickly.
The very fact of the Yale president's "skeptical" statement forced a redefin-
ition of what a "radical" position was. It is significant that there were no
"conservative" proposals presented at the April 23 meeting. The presump-
tive conservative position—continuing normal operations and academic
expectations unclouded by questions about the Panther trial or community
relations—was simply not a realistic possibility, as virtually everyone recognized.

By the time the faculty met, New Haven was already enveloped in a
miasma of fear. The city's inhabitants were bombarded with rumors of the
impending invasion of up to 100,000 bomb-throwing radicals, right-wing
motorcycle gangs, and anarchist saboteurs. Arsonists set fires in the law
library and several other spots on campus, and persons unknown stole a
truckload of rifles and a sizable amount of mercury (used in blasting caps).
Connecticut's governor announced that the National Guard would be sent
to New Haven, backed up by a reserve force of four thousand marines and
paratroopers who had just returned from Vietnam. Amid this atmosphere of
impending disaster, something like a third of the undergraduate body and
an indeterminable number of professors left town in the week before May
1. "What do you mean, am I leaving?" one undergraduate snarled at a
reporter while packing his car. "What the hell does it look like I'm doing?
You think I'm gonna stay around and watch this damn place burn down—
with me in it?"[167]

To the extent that there was a conservative position, it was to cancel the
semester, shut the university down completely, and flee. And yet a host of
conservative commentators claimed then (and still claim) that Brewster,

by keeping the university functioning on a modified basis, had betrayed academic principles and institutional neutrality. At the height of the culture wars of the 1990s, the journalist Roger Kimball declared that if not for Brewster's "liberal capitulation" in May Day, "the history not only of Yale's involvement in that sordid affair but also of American higher education in the decades that followed might well have been different. . . . Brewster aided in selling out the American university to forces that were inimical to its very essence."[168] Since the conservative alternative response to the invasion from outside was not the normal operation of the university but the complete cessation of its educational activities, such criticisms are essentially dishonest. One might with equal logic accuse the New Haven merchants who boarded up their shops and left town of betraying capitalism.

"May Day was a fucking zoo," Zanger remembered. "I was really glad not to be involved in May Day. Really insane people had taken over at May Day, at all levels."[169] The major problem, as far as Brewster was concerned, was finding out exactly who was organizing the demonstration. On April 30 he called his classmate William Kunstler, the controversial lawyer who was scheduled to speak as part of the protest. "I understand you're favoring your alma mater with your presence on the Green tomorrow," he recalled saying to Kunstler. "Would you mind telling me who the hell is in charge?"[170] With Kunstler's assistance Brewster arranged a meeting after midnight at the president's house with the Chicago Seven defendants David Dellinger, SDS founder Tom Hayden, John Froines, and Froines's wife, Ann. William Sloane Coffin also came along. Brewster had summoned his friend Cyrus Vance to advise him on how to handle the crisis, and was amused when the radicals greeted Vance warmly; they had met him two years earlier at the Paris peace talks. Brewster secured an agreement with the group that if they would counsel their followers against violence that weekend, the president would try to move the National Guard off the Green. Unbeknown to the radicals, Brewster had already arranged with New Haven police chief James Ahern to do just that.

Brewster's assistant Sam Chauncey and Chief Ahern had made other secret arrangements. When Brewster met with Cox a week earlier, he learned that the Weathermen had chartered two buses from Boston and would be coming to New Haven to raise havoc. Chauncey and Ahern took out an insurance policy on the buses and replaced the drivers with undercover state police officers. As the buses loaded with radicals drove down the Massachusetts Turnpike in the early hours of the morning, the lead bus pulled over as if with mechanical difficulties. The second pulled up behind it, and both drivers huddled underneath the hood. "All of a sudden," Chauncey recounted, "a police car came and picked the two up and just left the Weathermen right there on the Mass Turnpike. They picked a place where you could walk five miles in any direction and still not get anywhere. They all got out and went left and right and were never seen again, as far as New Haven was concerned."[171]

Many people in New Haven were praying for rain on May 1, and when the day dawned bright and clear, it seemed as though Brewster's luck had finally run out. But it soon became evident that his advance work and his policy of openness had paid off. Somewhere between ten thousand and twenty thousand demonstrators came to New Haven, fewer than anticipated. Yale housed and fed them, and student volunteers served as marshals, medics, and even day-care attendants. The mood remained fairly cheerful. As Pierson College master John Hersey observed, "The provocateur's basic requirement, an inflammable majority, simply was not there."[172] True to their pledge to Brewster and Vance, the rally's organizers preached nonviolence, at least as a temporary strategy. The most inflammatory speeches on the Green took place early in the day, and when the organizers opened the microphone in late afternoon, the speakers blurred the focus of the demonstration by talking about "women's rights, gay rights, and any other cause you can practically think of," one witness remembered. "You got these long, long speeches for things that had nothing to do with the issue at hand, and that had to help make it calm. People got a little bored."[173]

The event was more tightly managed by Yale authorities than appeared on the surface. Much of its success resulted from planning, cooperation, and control by the city police, the New Haven black community, the students, and the Panthers themselves, who worked hard to keep the event nonviolent. Aside from the bombing of the rink, several minor fires, and some skirmishes between the hard-core crazies and the police, there was little destruction and few arrests. Yale made it through the weekend and the rest of the academic year, even after Nixon's announcement of the U.S. incursion into Cambodia provoked a nationwide student strike. By Sunday most of the demonstrators were gone from New Haven. Disappointed violence seekers graffitied two messages on a statue on Old Campus: PANTHERS PLUS YALE EQUALS SELLOUT and WE WAS HAD.[174] As one New Left journalist put it, "A peaceful demonstration marred an otherwise promising holocaust."[175] A fatigued Brewster held a press conference at which he confessed that a mixture of relief, exhaustion, and exhilaration made it hard for him "to think straight or speak clearly. My most profound feeling is one of admiration and gratitude to everyone concerned, with the exception of a small group of roving willful troublemakers."[176] Classes resumed on Monday morning, May 4. Later that afternoon, National Guardsmen on the campus of Kent State University in Ohio fired into a crowd of students, killing four. Two more students were shot and killed at Jackson State College in Mississippi. The killings were terrible testimony to what could have happened at Yale.

MAY DAY AT Yale and the shootings at Kent State marked the end of the era of widespread national student protest. Between 1964 and 1970, nearly every major American university had experienced severe disruption. The list includes Harvard, Berkeley, Columbia, Cornell, Brown, Chicago, Wisconsin, Duke, Buffalo, Stanford, San Francisco State, and on and on. Student protest was also a worldwide phenomenon, experienced across Europe, South America, and Asia. Although the role of French university students in bringing about the political crisis of 1968 is perhaps the best-known example, there were massive fatalities in the Mexican protests of the same year, and the Japanese university system has had great difficulty recovering from the damage done in the 1960s.[177] It is impossible to overstate the bitterness that the disruptions produced and that still linger at many of the universities and among participants on all sides. Yale's experience was therefore all the more remarkable. Why did Yale remain unified and nonviolent when flames arose nearly everywhere else?

The answer is that Brewster helped prevent liberals from turning into radicals. By keeping Yale a community, by encouraging peaceful dissent, by facilitating student participation in decision-making processes, and by opening multiple channels of access, he defused the radical charge that change through the system was impossible. At Yale's moment of greatest crisis, Brewster relied on the intellect, maturity, and responsibility of his students as well as of his faculty, and was rewarded handsomely.

That kind of trust between students, faculty, and administration was rare on campuses in the 1960s. The main reason it existed in New Haven was that Brewster was more successful than most other presidents in maintaining Yale as a close-knit environment. Community had been one of Yale's traditional virtues, but in the past it had come from homogeneity. In the 1960s, Yale absorbed new kinds of faculty, new kinds of students, and new kinds of tensions. Diversity can be the enemy of community, but Brewster made it an ally.

Part of Brewster's purpose in preserving community, in a sense, was thereby to link the university's past to its present. His persistent challenge, he told a group of alumni, was "to keep Yale Yale and still keep it up to date."[178] According to Jonathan Fanton, the president once remarked that university secretary Ben Holden was not fully sympathetic to the changes Brewster had been making. "But what he doesn't understand is that in order to preserve the Yale he cares about, the values that are very important to Yale, we have to make these changes. And if we didn't, we would lose much more."[179]

Even forward-looking students of the 1960s, in their turn, enjoyed being part of a university that was modern yet remained a community and was still identifiably Yale. Jay Gitlin, of the Class of 1971, remembered that "Yale in those years was like Kingman himself. He embodied the university for us. [He was] Old Blue reshaped: manners, civility, leadership responding to change. It was still a fairly preppy campus. We didn't want to lose the Old Yale, but we all felt the burden of bringing the university into a new era. The Whiffs flirted with guitars. Everyone went to the prom; some in white tie and tails, others in psychedelic formal wear. In all of this, Kingman was both an anchor, a lifeline to an age of deference, and a lightning rod, safely conducting the currents of change into our student homes. . . . In short, the students felt a sense of common mission with the faculty and the administration."[180]

On the rare occasions when Brewster analyzed his position in quasi-philosophical terms, he saw the university from two perspectives: one, of the fair and meritocratic processes governing undergraduate admissions and faculty appointments and promotions; the other, the free interplay of ideas, both in and outside the classroom. To his critics, this position seemed an intolerably hands-off approach to student radicalism. "Kingman was so caught up in lawyer-like concerns of the process," according to his law classmate David Acheson (son of Dean Acheson), that "the result didn't interest him that much. Or he thought the result, good or bad, was either a reward or a penalty you had to pay for what he regarded as correct process."[181] Even Yale law student advisor Greg Craig thought Brewster's stance was dangerous. The president "called himself a 'due process radical,'" Craig remembered. "He thought that if you put some faith in the process, everything would work its way out." Craig, who "had spent a good deal of [his] time at Harvard and at Yale fighting the New Left," knew that "these guys didn't care about process. They exploited it. They used it. And so for Kingman to take that position, I thought, was rather naive. In fact, I think it saved the university."[182]

Brewster also emphasized the principle of institutional neutrality, the idea that the university should not be the captive or the champion of any one ideology or political position—a difficult balancing act in a period of rapid change and national discord. At the same time, he argued, the leaders of institutions had a responsibility to express their views, without being seen to speak for their institutions as a whole. Students who came to see that reform was possible, he felt, would recognize that their grievances could be redressed through the system and that the system itself was capable of reform. If the process was unfair or the leaders obstructed reform, the impediments to change would turn reformers into radicals. This quasi-political position, to which Brewster adhered throughout his career, reflected the experiences of the liberal wing of the establishment.

For a variety of reasons, the viewpoint and the liberal establishment itself incurred powerful opposition in the 1960s. There are few better illustrations than the reaction to Brewster's handling of May Day and his statement that he was skeptical of the ability of black revolutionaries to achieve a fair trial. Denounced in editorials from coast to coast, Brewster soon found himself on Richard Nixon's enemies list. Vice President Spiro Agnew called for Brewster's resignation.[183] In fact, most of Brewster's critics garbled his statement and claimed that he had said, "no blacks can get a fair trial," a misinterpretation that continues to be cited. According to William F. Buckley, George H. W. Bush said that Supreme Court chief justice Warren Burger "considered King Brewster's the most rhetorically seditious statement he had heard in his public lifetime; i.e., that [Brewster] had done more to endanger the processes of faith in American justice by that statement, given his own eminence, than anybody he could compare to."[184]

In light of what is now known about the FBI's clandestine, unconstitutional actions against the Black Panthers, it is hard to credit charges that Brewster's statement damaged respect for the law.[185] But there is a persistent feeling that even if the statement was true, Brewster ought not to have said it—that institutional neutrality requires that leaders not make controversial statements, particularly assertions critical of the system. Brewster replied to one such detractor, "We badly need more willingness to admit the weaknesses of our processes and institutions and a resolve to deal with them. Only if we do so will we deserve and command the respect of the considerable and growing number of young skeptics and critics."[186] When he was a boy, Brewster remembered, the president of Harvard had put his institutional authority behind the prosecution in the Sacco and Vanzetti trial, a trial that ultimately was viewed as more about the ethnicity and political beliefs of the accused than it was about justice. When his mother and Felix Frankfurter and other friends discussed the case at the table, they argued that it was the prejudice of the authorities and an inflamed public, not the protests of the critics, that caused millions of Americans to lose faith in the system. Brewster did not want to see history repeat itself.[187]

There is no doubt that Brewster's statement angered many alumni and cost Yale a considerable amount in lost donations. But Brewster never went back on his statement or apologized for having made it. In December 1970, one alumnus wrote to him that "in all honesty you must have many times regretted your now notorious 'fair trial' statement." If Brewster, when speaking with the alumni in Chicago, had simply admitted that he had made a mistake, the alumnus continued, "you would have brought down the house with the heaviest applause."[188] Brewster answered: "On the fair trial statement. What I replied in Chicago was what I feel. The statement was not a ploy. It was not erroneous. It in fact is said to have helped the fairness of the trial, and certainly made it clear that even those who shared my skepticism would do well to 'cool it' rather than heat things up the way the radicals were trying to. So, I'll have to pass up the applause which you quite correctly assume might have followed the recantation you urge. Sorry. While I regret the inevitable cost of the statement, particularly as it was stated from the Vice President on down . . . I don't think I can turn it on and off to suit the applause meter."[189]

One of the anti-Panther actions Brewster had in mind in formulating his statement was the December 1969 Chicago police raid that killed Panther leader Fred Hampton and another party member while they slept in bed; although none of the Panthers had fired a shot, the survivors were tried for attempted murder and other specious charges. When the accusations were shown to be false and the Panthers acquitted, the presiding judge remarked, "This is a direct answer to a careless and sad comment made by the president of Yale University that he was skeptical of the ability of black revolutionaries to achieve a fair trial."[190]

Brewster's private response to the verdict and the judge's comment goes far to explain why the president's statement was more than a tactical ploy. "The Panther shoot-out turns out to be a police shoot-in," he wrote to a friend, "and the dismissal of fabricated charges against the Panther defendants is celebrated by the Judge as proof that the President of Yale University is wrong in his skepticism! Splendid; I'm glad to be proved wrong. Meanwhile, the victims of that shoot-in are still dead, and the police officers who killed them will apparently not be prosecuted—in part because the living victims of the shoot-in so despair of justice at the hands of white society as to be unwilling to appear before a grand jury." In Brewster's opinion, the fault for unrest in the campuses and the streets did not lie with minorities and the young. "If it lies anywhere, it lies with us, with our generation," he wrote. "One of the reasons the young and downtrodden create their disturbing commotions is that people our age delude themselves about the quality of existing institutions and hence put off and put down those who seek orderly change. We also delude ourselves if we pretend that liberty is not in danger. It is always in danger, and the danger is greatest when 'respectable' people are cowed into silence by national epithets directed against dissent."[191]

The skepticism Brewster had expressed earlier may have had the effect he intended—to show disaffected Americans that the establishment was listening, shared some of their concerns, and was open to change. Certainly this was the way many people interpreted the message. Lindsay, a supporter of Brewster's statement, attacked Agnew's "intemperate" criticism of Brewster. Paul Moore came up to Yale on May Day to support Brewster, and defended his statement from the pulpit, asking rhetorically: "Could Jesus, a revolutionary, have a fair trial in the United States today?"[192] Corporation fellow J. Irwin Miller commented that "Kingman Brewster, among those in positions of major responsibility in America, has been exceptional in his willingness to criticize from within (which gives hope to the young that the Establishment may be more responsive than they think). He has been willing to listen to criticism from without, and willing to espouse change when he thought change called for. . . . When concerned young people find equal concern in their elders, they are given hope about the vigor and future of the society, where they are now too prone to despair."[193]

Many of the letters sent to Brewster during and after the May Day crisis supported Miller's argument. One young woman pleaded that the president continue to speak out, since "men like you and Mayor Lindsay . . . are all that some of us who believe in reform rather than revolution—at least violent revolution—have to look to."[194] J. Otis Cochran, chairman of the Black American Law Students Association, wrote Brewster that "I believe I would have made a more emphatic statement about what is happening to the Panthers. But what you said did go far toward restoring my confidence and the confidence of others that every member of the establishment is not insensitive to the problems, the inequities, and the injustices that plague so many Americans, particularly black Americans."[195]

On the other hand, Brewster received numerous excoriating letters accusing him of being a Communist, a coward, an appeaser, a "white nigar [*sic*]" and a "Judus [*sic*] goat."[196] Brewster told one of his advisors that many of the alumni letters he received should have been printed on asbestos.[197] "I would rather have seen Yale burned to the ground than capitulating to the Black Panthers and other radicals," wrote one representative critic. "Words cannot express my contempt + disgust for you as a person for destroying Yale."[198] While the abuse that came from right-wing politicians and editorial writers might have been expected, even some moderate or mildly liberal politicians ran from Brewster like scalded dogs. Prominent moderate Republicans like Lowell Weicker and George H. W. Bush turned against him. David Boren, an Oklahoma state representative and later a U.S. senator, resigned as an Alumni Fund agent and declared publicly that "I feel morally compelled as a responsible individual to withdraw from the University my support, financial or otherwise."[199]

The alumni were angry about many things besides Brewster's statement and the radical activity on campus. In the eyes of many, Brewster's admissions policies were to blame for the disturbance, particularly the admission of blacks and women. But the May Day weekend offered ample testimony to Yale's wisdom in broadening its definition of community. For example, a turning point in the events leading up to May Day occurred when a Black Panther leader was hectoring a Yale audience to prove its radicalism by picking up a gun. One brave woman student stood up and retorted, "We don't have to prove our masculinity," a crucial moment in moving the demonstration toward nonviolence.[200] Likewise, the negative reactions of many alumni to the May Day affair as a whole—building on their anger over Martin Luther King's honorary degree, Coffin's civil rights activities, and the increasing number of black admissions—suggest that race was perhaps the most important factor distancing Yale's alumni from their alma mater. The files contain too many letters from the alumni castigating what one called "Brewster's new version of the bulldog, with its Afro, kinky black coat and fat lips drooling treason."[201]

But the black students helped save their university at a time when students elsewhere were attacking theirs. Black Student Alliance secretary Henry Louis Gates Jr. realized early on that black students had to "protect our common Mother, Yale . . . from the Panther's most ardent desire to see the police bust our heads."[202] Black students pressured the Panthers into nonviolence, helped keep the peace in New Haven's minority neighborhoods, and kept the white crazies in check. The experience vindicated the admissions rhetoric about the benefits of interracial dialogue in the education of future leaders. Student leaders like Bill Farley and Kurt Schmoke became Rhodes scholars, and Gates, now an eminent scholar, is one of the most influential African-American men in the United States. In their own pioneering way, many of the black students at Yale fulfilled the university's ancient dreams of leadership in a way that even the hoariest alumnus ought to have applauded.

Brewster had staked his reputation on the behavior of students in the crucible of the May Day crisis, and from an internal standpoint, he won a huge victory. Agnew's criticism of Brewster helped unite the campus around its president, and three thousand students signed a petition of support for "the King" that had been set in motion even before Agnew's blast. When Brewster and Vance walked back to the president's house after the first night of the May Day rally, Brewster had reason to believe that he had demonstrated that "taking the risk of latitude for freedom" was superior to conservative crackdown and polarization.[203] A Yale administrator would later tell the journalist Nora Sayre that "in 1970, there was the notion that the nation would listen to Yale. That the country would follow the elite. The touching naiveté of the students: they despised elitism and yet partook of it."[204] Yet the country as a whole did not draw the same lesson and would not follow the liberal establishment in the years after 1970.

Brewster's emphasis on openness and community allowed him to make students peaceful adversaries, and even allies at times. This approach proved to be Yale's salvation in the May Day affair. Yale had its share of turmoil and tumult, but it was fortunate to have responsible students and responsive, adept leadership. Kingman Brewster knew that the university's and the nation's leadership must adapt to a changing America if it was to fulfill its traditional missions. His vision of excellence, community, and relevance provides an alternative model of the 1960s, one in which adult perspective worked with youthful energy and imagination to make progress. In the national context, Yale's history under Brewster still represents the path not taken.

11

NEW BEGINNINGS

AND ENDINGS

O N A May afternoon in the early 1970s, President Richard Nixon was having lunch with his good friend the shah of Iran in the Persian despot's guesthouse in Tehran. While the shah's liveried servants brought delicacies to the table, the two rulers discussed a subject of mutual interest: the irrationality of student protests. The shah, who would later distinguish himself as one of the era's least successful handlers of student protest, cited various instances of students' senseless misbehavior in Iran, while Nixon regaled the gathering with similar examples in the United States and elsewhere. Both leaders heartily agreed that no nation should tolerate such outrageous performances. "The terminology and attitudes expressed," one luncheon participant observed, "were right out of hard-hat Middle America."

To be fair, Nixon amended, perhaps the students were not entirely to blame for their actions. They were, after all, young and impressionable, and were egged on by older authority figures who should have known better. Nixon exclaimed that even Kingman Brewster, the head of Yale University, was known to have incited students, participated in anti-Vietnam causes, and made antiwar statements. "What can we expect of students," the president concluded, "if a person in that position and of that stature engages in such acts?" Henry Kissinger, sitting a few chairs down the table, confirmed that Brewster had visited him in Washington to criticize the war and that the secretary of state had given up trying to change the minds of academics on the Vietnam issue.

Nixon and Kissinger had forgotten that the tendrils of the liberal establishment extended everywhere. Seated below the salt with Kissinger was the

U.S. deputy chief of mission in Iran, a smooth diplomat named L. Douglas Heck, who was Brewster's Yale classmate, friend, and fraternity brother. Word filtered back to the Brewsters that Kissinger mused aloud that if the United States would benefit from the assassination of any public figure, it would be Kingman Brewster.[1]

IT WAS NOT only Brewster's handling of the May Day demonstrations but his actions after the crisis that made him a target of the Nixon White House. In the polarized political atmosphere of 1970, Nixon felt threatened by the efforts of Brewster and other members of his circle to preserve the moderate center.

Brewster opposed the national student strike that had been announced by Tom Hayden from the New Haven Green on the second day of the May Day rally. Yale remained open and functioning for the rest of the school year, which, as Paul Moore wrote to a disgruntled alumnus, was "quite remarkable" given that some five hundred colleges and universities shut down in May 1970 in response to the Cambodian invasion and the killings at Kent State.[2] Nearly two million students went on strike, their bitterness intensified by Nixon's characterization of activists as "these bums . . . blowing up the campuses" and the White House's callous comment on Kent State that "when dissent turns to violence it invites tragedy."[3] Believing that students' striking against educational institutions was irrational and counterproductive, Brewster warned that "the clenched fist and the 'shut it down' rhetoric simply help Mr. Agnew and Mr. Nixon to sterilize the political influence of universities, their faculties and students."[4]

However, Brewster knew that students had struck in part because they felt isolated and helpless. He told a national television audience that the situation put "the burden on us of the so-called establishment" to give students "a chance to get through, get heard, make a difference through the regular political process."[5] And so Brewster and Cyrus Vance went to Washington with a small delegation of professors and student class officers to talk with Yale graduates in Congress about "how to stop the war and how to counter the White House effort to make scapegoats of the universities and their students."[6] A larger group of students went down at the same time to lobby members of Congress against the war. His trip to Washington, Brewster admitted, skirted "the outer limits of permissible presidential activity." But as he told an alumni audience, he felt "very deeply" that the future of the country and the university alike would "depend upon the confidence that students have that the political process is a better avenue for action than action in the streets."[7]

At the height of the national student strike, Brewster met with his law student advisors Gregory Craig and Stephen Cohen. "All this rage and anger," Craig thought, "needed some channel."[8] While they were sitting at the kitchen table in the president's house, Craig recalled, "Brewster said, 'Maybe what we need is some kind of intergenerational strategy to end the war.' We started talking about members of his circle—in the legal community, the business community, some of his fellow university presidents—who would work together with students on a sensible plan to change policy."[9] Brewster put the two students in touch with other troubled moderate leaders including Irwin Miller, Joseph Califano, the Washington lawyer Lloyd Cutler, Common Cause founder John Gardner, and Francis Plimpton, the president of the New York City bar association. Craig and Cohen helped launch Project Pursestrings, linking grassroots activists with older supporters to endorse the Cooper-Church and McGovern-Hatfield bills, bipartisan legislation to shut off funding for military operations in Southeast Asia.

Other members of Brewster's circle spoke out in the tumultuous days of May. At a conference at the University of Texas, McGeorge Bundy warned that further unilateral presidential decisions like the Cambodian incursion "would tear the country and the Administration to pieces. At the very least Congress would stop money for the war, and the chances of general domestic upheaval would be real." Bundy insisted that the administration stop the draft, which was "tearing a generation apart," and desist from polarizing the country by attacking "such honorable and moderate men as Brewster of Yale."[10]

Bundy saw the polarization at close range that spring. A delegation of Ford dealers, pressured by the conservative boycott of their automobiles, met with Bundy to complain about the Ford Foundation's leftism. At the same time, left-leaning foundation officers angry about Cambodia went on what was in effect a one-day strike in May, stopping work for a mass meeting in the foundation's auditorium. George Zeidenstein, one of the organizers of the meeting, recalled that Bundy was a major target of the protest. "Were we trying to get Bundy to accept responsibility" for events leading to Cambodia, Zeidenstein wondered, "or tell us whether he knew about it? . . . I don't quite remember what the hell we were doing. But I know we were very upset." Bundy handled the protest with aplomb. He sat on the stage and, without notes, gave a detailed exposition of the events that had led the country into its involvement in Southeast Asia and his own role in that process. He answered questions from the audience as best he could, and kept his temper in check. "He was respectful, interested, not defensive, prepared to hear us out," Zeidenstein remembered.[11]

Just as the May Day rally had broadened beyond its initial agenda, so, too, the Ford Foundation protest gave vent to multiple sources of dissatisfaction. Ford's few women program officers rose to complain about the foundation's limited attention to women's issues and the difficulties they themselves encountered within the foundation.[12] Blacks echoed the criticism of personnel policies. Lamenting a general lack of information and openness, other staff members called attention to the limited opportunities for input into decision making. "Communications within the Foundation are *not* good," Bundy scribbled on a notepad as he listened.[13] Later, one of his officers admonished that "an open door is not reaching out."[14] As a result of the meeting, Bundy and some of his colleagues drafted policies to include lower-ranking staff in decisions, make aggressive efforts to hire and promote women and minorities, and devote significant program resources to women's issues. Siobhan Nicolau, one of the few women officers at Ford, pointed out that it was typical of Bundy that once he accepted their arguments about gender inequity at Ford, "he battled against many of his colleagues . . . [and] put pressure on very reluctant people to really start looking for women. He took a strong stand when others would not, and he was a real hero to women in the foundation."[15]

PAUL MOORE'S INSTALLATION as coadjutor bishop (he would automatically succeed Bishop Donegan upon the latter's retirement in 1972) took place on May 9, in a colorful but somber ceremony in the grand, unfinished Cathedral of Saint John the Divine on Manhattan's Upper West Side. Donegan interrupted the ceremony to offer a prayer for the dead at Kent State and Cambodia, and the two bishops called on the government to protect the right to dissent and halt the Cambodian invasion. In his former city of Washington, Moore observed, "young people from all over the land are converging with cries of rage and grief. . . . We older people do not fully understand what is happening around us. I am sure our President does not understand."[16]

John Lindsay went from Moore's installation to an emergency meeting with police officials to deal with the previous day's riot by hundreds of helmeted construction workers. A mob of several hundred hardhats, mainly

Lindsay-hating white ethnics, had marauded through lower Manhattan, bludgeoning antiwar demonstrators and men with long hair. The mob then marched to City Hall, where Lindsay had ordered the flag to be flown at half-mast in memory of the Kent State dead, stormed the building, and forced officials there to raise the flag to full-staff. Police officers stood by while the construction workers beat students from a nearby college. Lindsay, appalled by the violence and police negligence, ordered a thorough investigation.[17] Over the next several weeks, flag-waving hardhats returned to the streets for lunch-hour prowar demonstrations, praising Nixon and Agnew and denouncing the antiwar mayor as "a Commy rat, a faggot, a leftist, an idiot, a neurotic, an anarchist, and a traitor," as a reporter noted.[18] At a well-publicized White House meeting days after the initial riot, the leader of the local construction workers' union presented Nixon with an honorary hardhat. The president saluted the emblem of backlash as a "symbol, along with our great flag, for freedom and patriotism to our beloved country."[19]

Other citizens, however, viewed the hardhat hooliganism as the sort of street brawling that led to the collapse of the Weimar Republic. For a large number of well-established Manhattan lawyers, the *New York Times* recorded, "the actions of what some called 'labor fascists'" were "one of the last straws that moved many members of major law firms to take a stand on the war issue." Over a thousand attorneys stopped work and traveled to Washington to meet legislative and other government officials to urge "immediate withdrawal from Indochina." The group's sponsors included Mayor Lindsay, Cyrus Vance, and Francis Plimpton, all of them "decidedly members of the Establishment," as the group's spokesmen put it.[20]

The Nixon administration, mostly through Spiro Agnew, struck back at its critics in the liberal establishment. Agnew applauded the *Wall Street Journal*'s charge that over the past decade, "the American elite has not been protecting [the nation's] social bonds. It has been systematically assaulting them." The vice president alerted his constituency to the danger posed by those "elitists" who "were born on the social ladder and have a very great say about who is to climb on which rung. . . . For the first time in history a great nation is threatened not by those who have nothing—but by those who have almost everything."[21] Turning his guns on Cyrus Vance, Agnew branded him a "failure"—one of the "dandies of the old school tie" who, he implied, had betrayed his country in the Paris negotiations.[22] Agnew was considerably more adept at making stab-in-the-back charges than at defending the administration's substantive policies in Cambodia and elsewhere.

The Cambodian incursion put Elliot Richardson in an extremely difficult position. The State Department had been cut out of the planning, and Richardson himself had been overseas when the decision was made. His assistant Jonathan Moore, who headed an ad hoc committee in State on Cambodia and Laos, knew nothing about the impending military action and quit when it was announced. "My feeling, which I can't document," Moore recalled, "was that Elliot also was deeply opposed to the invasion."[23] On the day Nixon announced that troops had been sent into Cambodia, Richardson spoke at a Soviet-American convocation in New York. He put forward an ambitious plan to foster superpower relations through better United Nations peacekeeping, regional self-policing, and "spheres of restraint" in which both the United States and the Soviet Union would refrain from participating in local disputes.[24] When Richardson was asked whether his vision ought not to apply to the United States and Cambodia, reporter Flora Lewis recorded, the undersecretary of state, "in a tired and unhappy voice," said the policy "couldn't apply where one of the big powers was already 'too involved.'"[25]

Many of Richardson's friends, viewing his assertion as equivocation at best, urged him to follow his assistant's example by resigning in protest. "I hope you will desist from idiotic speeches about 'spheres of restraint,'" the *New York Times* reporter Christopher Lydon wrote to him, "and engage yourself openly and ardently against the galloping lunacy in Vietnam, Cambodia and the White House. Just as I was hopeful at your appointment, I am appalled at your silence and—now—the sanctimonious, irrelevant quality of remarks like these." On the basis of his record to date, Lydon warned, "you will be remembered as one more over-educated, morally constipated Boston Yank, who . . . stood by as a speechless ornament for men and policies that extended mass murder in Asia. . . . Think, and act, *boldly*, for God's sake, before it is too late."[26] Richardson heard a similar message, more politely expressed, from a delegation of Harvard faculty members who visited him and Kissinger in Washington in early May. Kissinger told Richardson that the group consisted of "people who won't believe we have a foreign policy problem until the Russians land north of San Francisco"; nevertheless, he misled the professors into thinking that he shared their unhappiness with the Cambodia policy.[27] Richardson, who privately had grave misgivings about the policy, stonily defended it. "Elliot Richardson told us this afternoon, 'I'm still a rational man,'" government professor Richard Neustadt remarked. "I wanted to say, 'But so was McGeorge Bundy.'"[28]

Like Bundy, Richardson defended policies with which he disagreed so that he could retain influence—not just for himself personally but for responsible leaders and policies. Shortly after Richardson took office as undersecretary of state, he and Kissinger met for dinner at the Cosmos Club with Cyrus Vance and a small working group from the Council on Foreign Relations who had devised a formula that might break the deadlock in the Paris peace talks. Building on an idea Vance had put forward when he was a negotiator in the talks, the group proposed a standstill cease-fire in Vietnam and a division of power based on territory controlled by the Saigon government and the Viet Cong. Kissinger wasn't interested, but Richardson was, and he and Vance moved the proposal forward. In the fall of 1970, Nixon would announce a peace initiative that included the first U.S. proposal for a standstill cease-fire and settlement based on "the existing relationship of political forces in South Vietnam." After Nixon laid out the proposal in a televised address, Kissinger telephoned Vance, Brewster, and Lindsay, as they were having dinner at Gracie Mansion, to get their reactions.[29] The plan bore sufficient similarity to that of the Council on Foreign Relations working group that Vance could say, "I think we had some influence."[30] Although Nixon and Kissinger had set their standard against the establishment and its ways, they still felt a need, on occasion, to sound out its chieftains.

Because Richardson had shown himself to be a talented wrangler of bureaucracies and a loyal Nixon man, the president appointed him secretary of the Department of Health, Education, and Welfare in June 1970. Although Richardson was now a cabinet officer, he assumed the new post with great reluctance. "I thought I had no real choice," he told his uncle. He was leaving behind a considerable amount of unfinished business at State, and he recognized that HEW would be "an administrative headache."[31] The department employed 110,000 people and spent more than $50 billion annually; its three hundred major programs reached into the life of almost every American. Richardson told an acquaintance that returning to HEW after working there in the 1950s was "like seeing an old friend who has gotten enormously fat."[32]

Like Yale and the Ford Foundation, HEW was rife with internal dissension, with some twenty separate employee groups issuing demands on everything from Cambodia to the antiballistic missile to minority hiring and promotion within the department. Much of the staff was openly hostile to Nixon, particularly after he fired education commissioner James Allen in early June for criticizing the Cambodian invasion. Leaders of the militant, mainly black National Welfare Rights Organization broke into and occupied the office of Robert Finch, Richardson's predecessor as HEW secretary, to demand more generous welfare benefits than those under consideration by the administration.[33]

Many in Congress considered HEW to be essentially unmanageable, even by the man editorial writers said was "regarded as probably the most effective administrator in the federal government in the last decade."[34] The basic cause of the department's turmoil, Richardson said at his confirmation hearing, was that it was "charged with dealing with problems that are difficult and intractable, while the people's expectations of success are rising. We now see poverty as something that can be conquered and disease as something to be eradicated, and people want it all done right now."[35] Only a few weeks after he was sworn in, Richardson rescued Nixon's ambitious welfare reform bill, the Family Assistance Plan, from sure defeat. In a marathon six-day testimony before the mostly hostile Senate Finance Committee, Richardson dazzled the panel with his familiarity with every clause and subclause of the complex, 153-page bill.[36] As always with Richardson, what he said was given force by how he said it. When he addressed a group of college and university presidents in one of his first HEW speeches, one president reportedly turned to another and remarked, "You know, it took three hundred years of training in Boston to develop that style."[37]

As he had in the past, Richardson reached out to friends for advice on the transition to his new post. McGeorge Bundy counseled him to discuss educational matters with former education commissioner Doc Howe (then serving as the Ford Foundation's educational advisor in India) and suggested Lindsay's Yale classmate John Chafee as Richardson's replacement at State. "He has a lot of qualities," Bundy said of Chafee, who would soon join Yale's board of trustees. "He's not quick, but he is savvy." Richardson agreed that Chafee was "a sensible fellow" but decided that "he's not quick enough. There's too much of it here."[38]

Richardson's domestic responsibilities brought him into closer contact with Bundy, Lindsay, and Brewster, all of whom in some measure depended on government programs now under Richardson's control. Later that summer, Richardson met with Bundy and Lindsay at an American Bar Association conference on the upcoming problems of the 1970s. Bundy spoke for all of them when he declared that "On the campus, in our cities, in our waters and our atmosphere, the crisis of today is not the crisis of yesterday, and the more we learn, the deeper and more difficult underlying troubles appear to be."[39] Yet all were hopeful that people of goodwill could handle the challenges the decade would present.

*   *   *

"OUR SOCIETY EXPERIENCED something approaching a national nervous breakdown in the years 1967–70," John Gardner wrote to McGeorge Bundy a few years later.[40] Many of the problems that convulsed America in the late 1960s persisted into the 1970s, but intense public sympathies for those problems, such as poverty, waned, as did the civil rights and antiwar movements. While the Nixon administration pursued some liberal initiatives, there was nothing like the symbiosis that had existed between the Johnson administration and the liberal establishment. As the political climate cooled, Brewster and most of the other members of his circle had less of a sense that they were dealing with the same burning, nationally significant issues. Economic pressures forced most of these leaders to scale back their ambitions, and the themes of the decade would be consolidation and retrenchment rather than advance.

When undergraduates returned to the nation's campuses in the fall of 1970, faculty and administrators bracing for further disruptions found that the student movement had largely burned itself out in the furor of the spring. "Nobody could have tolerated the excitement very much longer," Yale sociology professor Kai Erikson recalled. "You needed calm after the turmoils of May Day."[41] To Brewster, the campus mood was one of "eerie tranquility," brought about by drought in the job market, disenchantment with political protest, and scorn for established authority.[42] The faculty was eager to return to something like normality. Many agreed with Yale College dean Georges May, who announced he would step down at the end of the year, that "the huge amount of energy spent" in overcoming crises "has been denied to a host of pending problems which are crying for attention. . . . [W]e probably are in less strong and healthy a position than was the case in the recent past."[43] The university's financial situation had worsened considerably, mainly because of a sputtering national economy and academic expansion that had outpaced available resources.

Alumni backlash was also a factor, and while the annual alumni fund solicitation had set another record, it had brought in less than anticipated. The backlash worried Brewster, and he requested a formal review of his tenure by the Corporation. Taking up residence in the guest suite in one of the residential colleges, William Bundy canvassed a cross section of faculty members on their opinions of Brewster's first seven years. "It was so clear that the faculty was one hundred percent behind Kingman," he remembered.

Undergraduates and administrators were equally vehement in their support. "Certainly you'd have to say that the university wanted Kingman," he judged. "There was no possible doubt or question about it."[44] Among the alumni, however, there was much anger and confusion, particularly concerning the events of May and student activism generally. Yale was not alone in the challenges it faced; New York University's president James Hester, for example, observed that he and his peers were regarded "as establishment spokesmen by the young and as apologists for a generation of revolutionaries by those outside."[45] But clearly Brewster's major shortcoming was that he had not been as effective a fund-raiser as some other university presidents.

So Brewster borrowed a private jet from a wealthy supporter and embarked on a series of barnstorming visits to Middle America. With a rotating cast of students, faculty members, and university officials, he met with alumni, community leaders, and the general public in half a dozen midwestern cities. He sought to convince his audiences that the conservative politicians who were, in effect, campaigning against the universities in the fall elections—including Agnew, Ronald Reagan, and San Francisco State University president S. I. Hayakawa—were peddling a misleading, vitriolic caricature. While fund-raising concerns were an obvious consideration in the visits, Brewster was looking more to change minds than to rattle the tin cup. "If the alumni don't believe in us," he said, "the free university is going to have a hell of a time surviving in a controversial era."[46] Brewster's assistant Jonathan Fanton felt that the president "had a charming belief that the alumni body was better than it really was, more broad-gauged and broad-minded . . . and if they only had the facts, they would see things clearly and wouldn't be critical, and this great Yale family wouldn't be divided."[47]

Kai Erikson, part of Brewster's entourage on a visit to Cleveland, remembered that while some of the most critical alumni had been won over by Brewster and the other participants, it was also an exhausting experience. On the ride back to New Haven, however, Brewster and Vance were positively radiant, buoyed up by the success of the event as well as by their rock-ribbed constitutions. "These two guys, Vance and Kingman," Erikson observed, "were stronger at six in the evening than they had been at six in the morning. . . . It was almost as if my battery had been drained by the activities of the day, and their batteries had been charged."[48]

Brewster's energies were not limitless, of course, and many of his friends thought he was running on adrenaline in the year after the May Day crisis, which had visibly aged him. With the Corporation's approval, Brewster and his wife went to London in June 1971 for a six-month sabbatical. They rented a little town house in Knightsbridge, not far from Hyde Park. Although they made side trips to Greece and met up with McGeorge Bundy and his wife in Paris, they remained in London for most of the time. "Privacy and serenity unbounded," Brewster wrote to his assistants back in New Haven. "Totally disqualified for useful service."[49] The Brewsters spent their days reading, taking long walks through Hyde Park and other favorite parts of the city, going to the theater, and tooling about in a splashy new XJ-6 Jaguar sports car.

When Brewster returned to Yale, his job now centered on economic rather than social and political issues. Provost Charles Taylor, who served as acting president during the sabbatical, had convinced Brewster that the budget crisis required him to make major cutbacks. "Kingman clearly didn't want to do it," Taylor recalled, but in the end he agreed it was unavoidable.[50] The two men "tried to have a process that was as thoughtful about what we dropped as it had been about what we added," according to Taylor.[51] Some departments suffered only minor pruning, while the budgets of others were slashed by twenty-five percent or more. While he knew it was necessary, cutting back was at odds with Brewster's ebullient, expansionist nature. The job also became less enjoyable when Taylor resigned as provost in 1972, turning down several college and university presidencies to become a Jungian analyst. The economist Richard Cooper agreed to fill the position for two years. His "primary responsibility," Cooper recalled, "was to balance the budget while doing as little damage to the institution as possible."[52] The reductions were painful, but Brewster had no regrets about the investments he had made in Yale during the flush years. "The most expensive thing for a university," he emphasized, "is mediocrity. It costs almost as much, and it doesn't get any support."

Even before the university launched an ambitious fund-raising campaign in the mid-1970s, Brewster spent considerable time on the road, trying to cajole the alumni into supporting an institution with which many of them were still at odds. "The conversation was no longer 'What do we do about Coed Week?'" his friend John Hersey remembered. "It was about missing three planes and getting back late from Texas."[53] While Brewster did not stop thinking of ways to reform the university, his new initiatives would be of interest primarily to the university world; they lacked the wider social significance that had put Yale in the headlines during the 1960s.

All was not quiet on the home front, however. According to Fanton, conservative faculty members opposed to the president's reforms staged a comeback, and "Kingman never quite had as much leverage internally after May 1970."[54] In 1972 the faculty rejected an ambitious plan for reorganizing undergraduate education, which would have entailed longer semesters (to allow students to graduate in three years) and a network of college counselors to provide individualized guidance, something like the tutorial system at Oxbridge. The proposal was utopian and expensive, and as then-junior faculty member Peter Brooks observed, "By that time the spirit of change had died out."[55] An innovative summer term foundered, as did a visionary scheme underwritten by the Ford Foundation to have students repay tuition loans as a percentage of their postgraduation income. As dismal job prospects gave rise to a new academic competitiveness, students as well as faculty members lost interest in curricular experimentation. Taking note of the undergraduate "herd instinct for law and medicine," Brewster decried what he called "grim professionalism."[56] William F. Buckley's son, Christopher, a member of the Class of 1975, wrote that "the term quickly entered the Yale consciousness and became a buzz phrase for all that was lowly, bourgeois and mean in human nature. 'Grim professional!' replaced 'Eat my shorts' as the epithet of choice."[57]

Yet Brewster's situation was far from bleak. He continued to draw plaudits, in many quarters, for having brought Yale through the 1960s without the violence seen on other campuses. Harvard's selection of Derek Bok as its new president in 1971 was widely viewed as a tribute to Yale's leader. Not only was Bok a Brewster protégé but, as dean of the law school during the 1969 spring crisis, he had been one of the few Harvard administrators to respond with anything like Brewster's wisdom and sensitivity. Because Yale had been spared the kind of polarization that hit other universities and its faculty remained strong and relatively united, its popular reputation received a boost, particularly after professors Erich Segal and Charles Reich topped the fiction and nonfiction bestseller lists, respectively, with their books *Love Story* and *The Greening of America*. Recognition of Yale's faculty strength also came in the NEH's grant to establish the National Institute for the Humanities at the university, which brought some of the country's leading scholars to New Haven for a year in residence.[58] A *Harvard Crimson* editorial even expressed palpable envy of Yale—surely a first.

Even so, Brewster began to think seriously about resigning the Yale presidency. "I don't think he was ever quite the same after that sabbatical," Fanton remembered. One evening when Fanton was at Brewster's house on Martha's Vineyard, Brewster wondered aloud, as the sun set into the ocean, "whether the criticism, among the alumni especially, had been so severe that wouldn't it really be better for Yale if he were to retire. . . . I was a young man, and this was my hero, so what do I say?" Fanton tried to reassure the president that his positives outweighed his negatives, and "it's not whether you don't have support, but whether you feel like doing the job."[59] Brewster sat silently in the darkness, and only the glow from his tiny Danish cigar indicated that he was listening.

JUST AS BREWSTER'S ambitions for Yale were reined in by financial austerity, so, too, were McGeorge Bundy's at the Ford Foundation, and for much the same reason. Brewster and Bundy had both signed off on the foundation's much-publicized 1969 report counseling colleges and universities to manage their portfolios less timidly than they had in the past. It was a valid long-run strategy, but as both Yale and Ford moved more heavily into stocks, the market slump and stagflation of the early 1970s seriously eroded their endowments. Ford's dropped from over $4 billion in 1964 to $1.7 billion a decade later, which in real terms was only a quarter of what it had been at its peak.[60] The financial downturn made the vindictive 1969 congressional tax on foundations sting even more. Still, neither financial setbacks nor political backlash deterred Bundy from his activist course.

In the early 1970s the Ford Foundation encouraged the growth of the consumer and environmental movements, and helped create the field of public interest law, which permitted class action suits on behalf of those movements and other causes. Securing a legal opinion that endorsement of public interest law would not violate the provisions governing foundations in the 1969 Tax Act, Bundy set up a committee of four past presidents of the American Bar Association to advise on grants and insulate the foundation from criticism. According to Patricia Wald, an activist lawyer whom Bundy appointed to the board in 1972, the public interest law sector "was almost entirely supported by the Ford Foundation."[61]

The foundation not only provided start-up funds for a public interest firm, such as the Natural Resources Defense Council, but helped structure it through negotiations with its founders, whom Ford officer Sandy Jaffe described as "five fellows who had just graduated from Yale Law School [and] didn't even know where the courthouse was yet." Ford demanded that the NRDC hire an executive director and establish a board of trustees, consisting of experienced lawyers who could provide guidance and counsel.

Bundy and his officers imposed similar accountability measures in their grants to other public interest law firms they supported, including the Center for Law and Social Policy, the Environmental Defense Fund, the Institute for Public Interest Representation, and many more. As Jaffe pointed out, "These were fairly significant grants that had great potential to annoy lots of people, and we wanted to make sure we were doing things right."[62]

Many businesses were indeed annoyed when the public interest law firms Bundy supported sued the federal government (often Richardson's HEW) to enforce corporate compliance with consumer and environmental legislation such as the Clean Air Act. Although Bundy heard criticism even from members of his board, he insisted that the activists were needed as long as many Americans thought that "there is one law for the rich and another for the poor, one for the well-organized institution . . . and another for the ordinary citizen, one for those with economic power and another for the individual believer in fresh air or clean water."[63]

Another of Bundy's significant initiatives in the early 1970s was a $100 million grant to minority education, half to predominantly black colleges and half to scholarship and study awards for minorities. Because of the size of the award, four-fifths of the foundation's aid to higher education would, for the remainder of Bundy's tenure, be devoted to minorities, as compared to one-fifth in 1968.[64] Kingman Brewster criticized his friend's decision to spread so much of the foundation's support of minorities across a large number of historically black institutions, few of which would ever measure up to the standards of the nation's best universities. While Brewster obviously had Yale's self-interest in mind, he suggested that the Ford president was responding to the siren song of populism rather than supporting the institutions that were most likely to produce black leaders. "I realize that my counsel is one of 'elitism,'" Brewster wrote to Bundy. "So be it. But while you cannot support the bottom and middle of the pyramid, you can and should support the top."[65] An unrepentant Bundy replied, "In spite of my own experience in places like Yale and Harvard, I do not find it certain that there is a clear case for what you yourself describe as a 'counsel of elitism.'"[66]

Bundy, Brewster, and Cyrus Vance (as chairman of the board of the Rockefeller Foundation) engaged in parallel efforts to recruit younger, more diverse members to their boards of trustees. In short order, all brought aboard their first black and women trustees. Many of the appointments reflected the establishment's tendency to tap outsiders who had inside connections. One of the two women who joined the Yale Corporation in 1971, for instance, was University of Chicago history professor Hanna Holborn

Gray. The daughter of an eminent Yale historian, she had grown up around the university in the 1930s and 1940s; as a child, she had been escorted to a Christmas dinner by undergraduate McGeorge Bundy, whom she shot with a water pistol. She studied at Harvard with Myron Gilmore (a member of Brewster's and Bundy's Friday Evening Club) and got to know Brewster at a conference at the Rockefeller Foundation's Italian villa in the late 1960s.[67] Children's Defense Fund head Marian Wright Edelman, who joined the Yale Corporation at the same time as Gray, had graduated from the Yale Law School and served as an assistant to Martin Luther King Jr. She was married by William Sloane Coffin in a ceremony that included Paul Moore.[68] Her husband, Peter Edelman, a former aide to Robert Kennedy, received one of McGeorge Bundy's controversial study grants. Urban League president Vernon Jordan, whom Vance recruited to the Rockefeller Foundation board in 1971, was already linked to the men of the liberal establishment through a variety of connections; both he and Richardson, for example, had attended the Bilderberg meetings for the first time in 1969 and 1970.

BY TRAVELING TO South Vietnam to meet with the peace movement there, Moore served notice, shortly after moving to New York, that he would not desist from controversy in his new role. When Moore's delegation took part in a protest march in Saigon with South Vietnamese students, police fired tear-gas canisters and broke up the demonstration in what Moore called "one of the most brutal police actions I've seen."[69] On his return to the States, his old battalion commander Lewis Walt wrote to ask how a good marine like Moore could have participated in such an unpatriotic act.[70] Moore ruffled more feathers by pressing for women's ordination; the Episcopal Church was by that time the only major U.S. Protestant denomination that did not ordain women to the priesthood, but the issue remained a political land mine. More controversy followed the bishop's decision to allow the cathedral to be used for a raucous antiwar demonstration, which featured an obscene skit by Norman Mailer and clouds of what the bishop initially took to be a new incense but had to be told was in fact marijuana.[71] At the same time, Moore continued to exert his influence from within the power structure. Meeting with a group of wealthy laymen who feared that appointing blacks to the directorship of an Episcopal mission society would alienate their prep school and college classmates, he eventually lost his patience. "Don't give me any more stuff about Groton and Princeton," he shouted. "St. Paul's and Yale tell me different." His credential-flashing worked, as one participant testified: "One of the bishop's strong points is that the elite can't just dismiss him as some kind of nut."[72]

Moore's enthronement as the thirteenth Episcopal bishop of New York, in an exuberant eight-and-a-half-hour ceremony in September 1972, blended the modern and the medieval. Preceded by trumpet fanfare, Moore marched down the 601-foot central aisle of the Gothic nave, leading a long procession of clerics in bright vestments. Following a ceremony of established ritual and prayer, he took up the pastoral staff and ring of the diocese to the accompaniment of electric guitars and a choir performing the "Gloria in Excelsis" from a rock mass in F by the composer of the musical *Hair*.[73] Moore's installation sermon, delivered to a packed audience of five thousand that included John Lindsay and other political as well as religious leaders, enjoined his affluent parishioners to rebuild the city by observing Christ's commandment to "Love thy neighbor." Doing so would mean, he emphasized, "low-cost housing in *your* neighborhood, built with *your* taxes," and ultimately "some kind of redistribution of our national resources." Some of Moore's parishioners fumed, but Mayor Lindsay praised the bishop as "a man who is willing to lead at a time when most are crawling under rocks."[74] Cyrus Vance supported Moore's programs through his role as a vestryman at the posh Fifth Avenue Church of the Heavenly Rest.

"I DON'T THINK the Establishment is dead," Vance told the British journalist Godfrey Hodgson in the early 1970s. "I think it will continue to function, and usefully."[75] Vance occupied himself usefully throughout the Nixon years as he waited for an opportunity to return to government. In addition to his legal work, he joined the boards of IBM, Pan Am, and the *New York Times*, and became president of the New York bar association. His Rockefeller Foundation board trusteeship took him abroad several times a year— on one occasion, to a conference in Italy on world hunger to which he invited Moore. Brewster asked Vance to negotiate with New Haven city officials who were denying Yale permission to build two residential colleges to relieve crowding caused by coeducation; the mission failed, forcing Brewster to reduce male admissions. (Vance thought the immovable obstacle to the deal was not Yale-hating mayor Bartholomew Guida but the town's political boss, Arthur Barbieri.[76]) Lindsay appointed Vance to the four-member Knapp Commission to look into police corruption; the investigation presented a major headache for the mayor as the commission turned up evidence of widespread police graft and inaction on the part of City Hall.[77]

Lindsay attended his last Yale Corporation meeting in July 1970, when his term as alumni fellow expired. "I can't stand goodbyes," he wrote to Brewster, "so I had no conscience about slipping out of the last meeting a few minutes early. But even having checked all sentiment at the door of City Hall five years ago—along with conscience—I count my six years on the Corporation as the most enjoyable and in some ways most rewarding experience I have had. . . . The leadership, skill and decency you supplied throughout was, and is, an inspiration."[78] Lindsay and Brewster continued to see each other socially (often at Jock Whitney's Long Island estate) and at ceremonial occasions such as Prescott Bush's funeral (at which Moore helped officiate). But the period of close collaboration between them had come to an end.

The mayor's second term was less tempestuous than his first, but many of the same problems continued to haunt him. Welfare rolls mounted, health and education programs proved ruinously expensive, and Moore became an inadvertent symbol of rising crime when he was mugged in Central Park by three teenage boys. (The bishop, typically, told a reporter that "my ultimate concern is what can be done about the causes that bring kids into this kind of situation."[79])

In the summer of 1971, Lindsay switched his party affiliation from Republican to Democrat, calling his decision a necessary response to "the failure of 20 years in progressive Republican politics."[80] The GOP and the Nixon administration, he charged, had abandoned their commitment to cities, minorities, and civil liberties. He also recognized that his prospects for political advancement as a Republican were slim. In December 1971, a month after his fiftieth birthday, he declared he would run for the presidency. Yale Corporation member J. Irwin Miller became Lindsay's most important backer, as the mayor had lost some of his longtime financial supporters when he switched parties.

Lindsay's 1972 presidential campaign turned out to be embarrassingly short. Running on an antiwar, urban, and feminist platform, Lindsay came in second in the Arizona primary but a poor fifth in Florida, with a meager seven percent of the vote, after which he threw in the towel. With the suburbs draining population and vitality from the big cities, the country did not want to hear Lindsay's message about the urban crisis. And while new party rules had subordinated the influence of white ethnic leaders like Chicago mayor Richard Daley in favor of women, blacks, and youth, even the latter groups proved suspicious of a man who had been in the party for only four months before announcing his campaign. Lindsay returned to New York with his tail between his legs. His last year in office proved to be his most successful, with falling crime rates and welfare rolls and a brighter economic picture, but there was no question of Lindsay running for a third term. Although the *New York Times* praised him as "a mayor of vision" and "an eloquent spokesman for the cities," when Lindsay left office at the end of 1973, he passed into what would be lifelong political exile.[81]

PERHAPS LINDSAY HAD his friend Elliot Richardson in mind when he complained that the Republican Party had marginalized its liberals. Richardson's major political function in the Nixon administration seemed to be to lose gracefully. The president undercut the HEW secretary by disavowing busing and desegregation plans Richardson had brokered and vetoing a child care bill Richardson had shepherded through the Senate. Although Richardson believed that "medical care should be treated as a right," White House indifference and lobbying by the American Medical Association sunk his plan for national health care.[82] His most frustrating defeat was over the Family Assistance Plan. The welfare reform measure passed twice in the House by comfortable margins, but Richardson could not get Senate Finance Committee chairman Russell Long to let it go to the floor. It later emerged that Nixon's chief of staff H. R. Haldeman recorded in his diary: "About Family Assistance Plan, [Nixon] wants to be sure it's killed by Democrats and that we make a big play for it, but don't let it pass, can't afford it."[83]

Richardson's willingness to swallow these losses and his mastery of the labyrinthine HEW bureaucracy commended him for further responsibilities in the administration, which Nixon reshuffled after his crushing defeat of George McGovern in the 1972 election. The Bostonian became secretary of defense, a position that required him, once again, to defend the war in Vietnam. Asked at his Armed Services Committee confirmation hearing whether he favored the Christmas bombing of North Vietnam then taking place, he replied, "I think it would be more accurate to say I support it."[84] Two days before Richardson took office in late January 1973, the United States signed a peace agreement with North Vietnam; as defense secretary, he oversaw the end of the deeply unpopular draft. Richardson also expressed shock at the absence of women and minorities in the top civilian and military jobs in the armed services; he set in motion an ambitious effort to identify and promote them.[85]

Three months after taking office, Richardson changed jobs yet again, this time to become head of the Justice Department. Emerging revelations about the break-in at the Democratic National Committee headquarters at the Watergate office building during the 1972 campaign forced the president to appoint an attorney general of unquestionable integrity to restore public confidence. Richardson fit the bill, although he was reluctant to assume the job and uneasy about taking charge of the Watergate investigation. "What if the president did know about the cover-up?" he wrote in a note to himself. "Do you have the stomach for it?"[86] But Nixon assured Richardson he was innocent, and Richardson wanted to believe him. He took the position, he said publicly, "because I have an overriding duty to do so."[87]

As a condition of his confirmation, Richardson pledged to the Senate Judiciary Committee that he would appoint an independent investigator with complete authority to look into the Watergate crimes. After the attorney general and his team sorted through a number of candidates, Richardson asked Vance to serve as special prosecutor, even though some of the staff at the Justice Department thought Vance too closely identified with the establishment and too moderate to be credible with Hill Democrats.[88] Vance turned down the offer, perhaps fearing it might put an end to his political viability. Richardson graciously thanked Vance for "the consideration you gave to my request that you undertake the job of Special Prosecutor. I appreciate the thought you gave to it, and I want you to know that I understand the reasons you felt you could not accept."[89] But Vance had been one of the relatively few acceptable candidates, and one of Richardson's aides recalled him grumbling that "we had become a nation where the only heroes were rock singers and ball players and that there were no large men of probity who could be called upon for the task."[90]

In the end, Richardson offered the special prosecutor job to Archibald Cox, his former law professor at Harvard and fellow trustee on the Board of Overseers. Nixon later complained in his memoirs that Richardson could not have made a worse choice.[91] Certainly Cox would have seemed to Nixon like the epitome of the eastern establishment the president hated: a lean New England patrician; a graduate of St. Paul's School and Harvard College and law school, and, like Richardson, a clerk for Learned Hand and a sometime lawyer with the Boston firm Ropes, Gray. Cox shared a variety of ties to other establishment figures, having been a colleague of

Kingman Brewster at the Harvard Law School and of McGeorge Bundy in the Kennedy government; his mother was godmother to one of Paul Moore's children.

Having chosen Cox for his unshakable integrity, the attorney general erroneously believed that Nixon would welcome him as special prosecutor. But the president, in his turn, believed that the Watergate controversy was nothing short of an establishment conspiracy against him. "There is a lot of Watergate around the town," Nixon told his cronies in March 1973, "not so much our opponents, even the media, but the basic thing is the Establishment. The Establishment is dying, so they've got to show that despite the success we have had in foreign policy and in the election, they've got to show that it is just wrong, just because of this."[92]

Vice President Spiro Agnew had not offered a cease-fire in his battle with the liberal establishment. Although a presidential commission on campus unrest chaired by Yale Corporation member William Scranton found the Kent State shootings to be "unnecessary, unwarranted and inexcusable," Agnew dismissed the report as "pablum for permissiveness."[93] Attorney General Richardson, however, was sufficiently impressed to reopen the Justice Department's investigation into Kent State. He could not give much attention to the case, however, because of the twin crises of Watergate and the parallel but unrelated investigation into corruption charges against Agnew.

Barely a month after Richardson took office, Maryland's attorney general advised him that a probe of corruption in Baltimore County had implicated Agnew. It emerged that Agnew had not only accepted bribes and kickbacks as governor but had continued to do so even after becoming vice president. As the nation's chief law enforcement official, Richardson supervised the investigation and informed Nixon and Agnew in early August that the vice president faced criminal charges of extortion, conspiracy, bribery, and tax evasion. Richardson pressed the case skillfully and inexorably, and on October 10, 1973, he secured Agnew's resignation and plea of nolo contendere (no contest) to a single charge of income-tax evasion, with all other charges dropped. Many observers were upset that Agnew avoided prison— Richardson's friend Anthony Lewis charged that the attorney general had "played God" in making the deal[94]—but because Richardson thought it paramount that Agnew resign, particularly in view of the possibility that he might succeed Nixon in the presidency while still under indictment, the Justice Department pursued the course that led most certainly to that end.[95]

Although none of the members of Brewster's circle gloated over Agnew's fall, they must have felt considerable satisfaction that the instrument of his removal from public life was their upright friend Elliot Richardson. Brewster was pleased that Agnew's replacement as vice president was Gerald Ford, an amiable Yale law graduate who had been an early associate of Brewster's in the America First Committee in 1940.

The Watergate investigations revealed that Nixon and his henchmen had compiled an enemies list that included Brewster (under the category "Establishment types"), Bundy, Lindsay, Irwin Miller, John Gardner, Edwin Land, and other prominent, well-placed liberals.[96] John Dean had proposed that the administration "determine what sorts of dealings these individuals have with the federal government and how best we can screw them (e.g., grant availability, federal contracts, litigation, prosecutions, etc.)."[97] At the time the list became public, Yale was fighting the government's imposition of numerical quotas for hiring women and minorities. Provost Richard Cooper recalled that HEW "targeted Yale," intending to make the university a "showcase" trial of its intention to force institutions to meet affirmative action mandates. Yale eventually prevailed, demonstrating a good faith effort to meet hiring targets,[98] but Brewster pointed out that the government's leverage over universities could potentially be used to coerce political conformity, and "revelations of the 'enemies list' gave a pungent reality to this fear."[99] He may also have been thinking of Kissinger's alleged wish to see the Yale president meet an untimely end when he denounced the list's loose talk of "assassination."[100]

The Watergate probes revealed, as well, that Nixon had been secretly taping his Oval Office conversations. When special prosecutor Cox subpoenaed eight tapes, the president refused to hand them over. On October 15, chief of staff Alexander Haig informed Richardson that Nixon would supply summaries of the tapes to Democratic senator John Stennis for authentication; Cox rejected that arrangement. On Saturday, October 20, Nixon insisted that Richardson fire Cox. The attorney general had promised in his confirmation hearings that he would discharge the special prosecutor only for impropriety, and he believed there was nothing improper about Cox's request for tapes. Richardson entered the Oval Office at 4:00 P.M. and tendered his resignation. Nixon urged him to hold off, arguing that the Yom Kippur War raging in the Middle East made it essential that nothing undercut the president's stature vis-à-vis the Soviets. When Richardson insisted, Nixon disparagingly told him, "I'm sorry, Elliot, that you choose to put your purely personal obligations ahead of the national interest." Richardson icily replied, "Mr. President, it would seem we have differing views of the national interest."[101]

Deputy Attorney General William Ruckelshaus (who had served as the government's liaison to Brewster at the 1970 May Day demonstration) also refused to dismiss Cox, and was fired in turn. Solicitor General Robert Bork then fired the special prosecutor, but Richardson and Ruckelshaus talked him out of resigning, since there needed to be continuity in the Justice Department. Richardson called Cox and relayed the sequence of events. Toward the end of their conversation, Richardson recited in Greek a passage from Homer that their common mentor Learned Hand had cherished: "Now, though numberless fates of death beset us which no mortal can escape or avoid, let us go forward together, and either we shall give honor to one another, or another to us."[102] That evening FBI agents took over Richardson's and Cox's offices. Richardson's secretary drove away in tears, believing American democracy was over.[103]

News of what the media dubbed the Saturday Night Massacre produced a firestorm of public shock and indignation. Angry citizens sent three million messages protesting what many viewed as an attempted coup d'état. Editorial writers and columnists praised Richardson and Cox and denounced the president for plunging the nation into the worst constitutional crisis of the twentieth century. Some 2,400 Yale students signed a petition calling for Nixon's impeachment, as did students on many other campuses.[104] Paul Moore said at an afternoon service that he was "stunned by the arrogance of power displayed by the President," and called for Congress to "take action to restore the balance of power."[105] Eighty-four members of Congress introduced resolutions for impeachment, while ninety-eight called for legislation to establish a new office of special prosecutor.[106]

Richardson held a press conference at the Great Hall of the Justice Department on October 23 to explain his actions. When he and his wife stepped through the blue velvet curtain, along with Ruckelshaus, the crowd of employees responded with wave upon wave of a "thunderous, thrilling" ovation, as one person there recalled.[107] Bleary-eyed and overcome with exhaustion and emotion, Richardson seemed almost bewildered by the adulation. His columnist friend Mary McGrory remembered that "what he regarded as his greatest failure to find a solution to a government problem had brought him the acclaim he always craved."[108] Resisting whatever "demagogic impulse" he might have had, the former attorney general read a prepared statement urging moderation, duty, and restraint.[109]

The Saturday Night Massacre doomed Richard Nixon's presidency. Public outrage galvanized Congress and forced Nixon to appoint a new special prosecutor, which led eventually to the handover of tapes documenting the president's crimes against the Constitution. In August 1974, when he realized that impeachment was inevitable, Nixon resigned. While it was fashionable to say in the aftermath of his departure that the system had worked, the crisis had produced a corrosive public cynicism about government and politicians. As Kingman Brewster pointed out, had it not been for an alert night watchman in the Watergate, Nixon and his crew would have gotten away with their foul deeds.[110] And Richardson observed that the amorality of the president and his staff reflected a wider degradation in America's culture and the growing dominance of its "get-ahead, go-along" ethos.

Amid the whole sordid business, however, Richardson and Cox stood out as shining examples of public virtue, defenders of a government of laws not men, and representatives of an older, less crass and self-centered tradition of American leadership. After his resignation as attorney general, Richardson held a fellowship at the Woodrow Wilson Center for International Scholars in Washington and embarked on a series of lecture appearances, with an eye toward boosting his presidential chances. Initially welcomed rapturously by his audiences, he refrained from giving them the red-meat condemnation of Nixon they craved, dwelling instead on constitutional complexities. When asked in 1974 if he was qualified to become president, Richardson replied, "Better than anyone I can think of."[111] But his style of speaking in painstakingly considered paragraphs played poorly on television. "We can't use your kind of careful, deliberative statement," the television correspondent Daniel Schorr told him. "We just don't have time."[112] The medium gave men like Richardson and Brewster a reputation for being squarer and stiffer than they were. In the spring of 1974, for example, when Richardson and Brewster emerged from Battell Chapel after Richardson spoke there to find several hundred naked students streaking across the Old Campus, they were not "holding on to their brandy snifters for dear life" (as Christopher Buckley imagined) but cracking each other up with observations on untethered breasts and male underendowment.[113]

Richardson's White House hopes largely ended when President Gerald Ford named him ambassador to Great Britain, in 1975. As ambassador to the Court of Saint James's (the traditional name for the post), Richardson spent much of his free time working on the book he had begun at the Wilson Center, a dense, eat-your-spinach tract on the individual's relation to government, published the next year. By that time, Ford had appointed him secretary of commerce, making Richardson the only person in the nation's history to hold four cabinet posts.

WHEN JIMMY CARTER defeated Ford in the 1976 presidential election, the Georgia governor's advisors were an uneasy coalition of populists and establishment figures. Carter, who had won the election largely on the strength of his moralistic, outsider's appeal to a public still reeling from Watergate and the Vietnam defeat, presented his lack of foreign policy experience as an asset. As president, however, he would need foreign policy expertise and credibility in Washington and abroad.

Carter chose Cyrus Vance as his secretary of state. The president-elect said that he had received "almost unanimous recommendations from around the country" and even from overseas for the seasoned, sixty-year-old diplomat.[114] The two had met in the early 1970s when Vance was involved in promoting the United Negro College Fund.[115] Meetings of the Trilateral Commission, a private foreign policy group of elites from North America, western Europe, and Japan, had provided further contact. Vance and Carter shared a view of U.S. foreign policy that joined pragmatism and internationalism, with an emphasis on diplomacy, multilateral cooperation, and international law; they agreed that human rights should be a consideration in foreign relations, that the United States should move beyond rigid Cold War thinking about the Soviet Union, and that the need to reduce the threat of nuclear war was paramount.[116] According to Vance, Carter's positions, "although largely unformed, were in the centrist mainstream in which I felt comfortable."[117] Culturally and temperamentally, however, the gap between the Georgia populist and the polished statesman was wide. "Vance was very much a part of the Washington–New York establishment," HEW secretary-designate Joseph Califano remembered. "Carter not only was not part of it, he wanted no part of it, even in office."[118]

Although most commentators praised Vance's credentials and reputation as "the perfect consensus man," one anonymous New Republic critic sniped that Vance had reached the secretary's post "by the want of competition in a decaying establishment." Vance's discretion—he appeared on only three pages of David Halberstam's sweeping antiestablishment indictment, The Best and the Brightest—meant that he was the only one of the half-dozen principal executors of the Vietnam War who could be considered for any government role, let alone secretary of state.[119] While Vietnam had not tarnished Vance's reputation to the same extent as McGeorge Bundy's or Robert McNamara's, several senators on the Foreign Relations Committee asked him, during his confirmation hearings, about his role in the war. In hindsight, Vance admitted, "it was a mistake to intervene in Vietnam," a mistake he now thought required fundamental reforms in the conduct of foreign policy. The lessons of Vietnam, as he saw it, were that the United States could not prop up a regime lacking popular support, Western institutions could not be imposed on other cultures, and the superpowers had to understand the limitations of military power against guerrilla forces. He continued to believe, however, that "the motivations and initial involvement [in Vietnam] were not based on evil motives but were based on misjudgments and mistakes as we went along."[120]

Bundy had also experienced a change of heart on Vietnam. When the Pentagon Papers were published in 1971, revealing much more of Bundy's role in the war than had been known, once again he subjected himself to the anger of his staff in the Ford Foundation auditorium. "He was neither defensive nor apologetic, at least not in any fawning way," program officer Terry Saario remembered. "But the man had indicated that he had been wrong."[121] As Bundy conceded, "All sorts of things have been wrong about the war in Vietnam, and its critics have been right—and too little heard—on many issues. It may be that the whole course of action was unwise, and as one who had a role in some of the critical decisions of 1963–65, I am neither unsympathetic to the critics nor insistent that what was done was right." But like Vance, he would still feel that "precisely the hardest problem of those years was to find an acceptable third course between escalation or desertion. We failed in that search, but I do not think we *had* to fail."[122]

In an act of atonement, perhaps, Bundy sponsored a task force to study draft evaders and deserters from the Vietnam War. He worked with the University of Notre Dame president, Theodore Hesburgh (sometimes referred to in the press as "the Catholic Kingman Brewster"), who had been a member of Gerald Ford's temporary, limited-scale Presidential Clemency Board. Hesburgh had found that, contrary to the popular image, only a tiny minority of cases that came before the board were college-educated men whose refusal to fight resulted in exile or imprisonment. The great majority were deserters, most of whom had been in the military for a year before going AWOL. They tended to come from educationally and economically disadvantaged backgrounds; minorities were disproportionately represented among the group. Bundy lamented that a "very large number of relatively guiltless Americans" were "permanently stigmatized" by their convictions and undesirable discharges. They were denied veterans' benefits and often employment and other opportunities. As Hesburgh recalled, "Mac felt that this was a sad and sorry conclusion to the whole Vietnam business, to have these deserters and draft evaders hanging from the ropes. He did tell me that he felt in some way responsible for their situations."[123]

Two weeks after Carter's election, Bundy and Hesburgh met with the president-elect in Washington. Reviewing with Carter the task force's evidence on draft evaders and deserters, the two presented what they called a program of reconciliation. Furthermore, Bundy met with military officials to press the case for pardoning nonviolent military offenders. Vance, whom Hesburgh would succeed as chairman of the board of the Rockefeller Foundation, helped with the lobbying campaign. On January 21, 1977, Carter's first full day in office, the president granted "a full, complete and unconditional pardon" to almost all draft evaders of the Vietnam era. The government also dropped its cases against remaining draft fugitives, allowed draft evaders who had fled abroad to return, and assured nonregistrants that they no longer faced prosecution. In all, the decision affected some 265,000 men. Typically, Bundy made no effort to draw attention to his role in the pardon, and the public never learned of the efforts that one of the architects of the Vietnam War had made in behalf of some of its victims.

DURING HIS PRESIDENTIAL campaign, Carter had promised that his ambassadorial appointments would go to men and women of ability and stature, not just wealthy supporters. Early in 1977, Cyrus Vance selected Elliot Richardson as ambassador-at-large and the president's special representative to the Law of the Sea Conference, a legislative assembly of 156 countries under United Nations sponsorship to negotiate all international aspects of the oceans.[124] To Vance, "there was only one person to take hold of that" negotiating responsibility, because only Richardson could handle "one of the most difficult tasks that anybody has ever had put before them."[125] Richardson, who was one of the few Republicans to serve in high office during the Carter presidency, later called his four years as chief of the U.S. delegation to the conference "my longest and most demanding tour of duty in any government job."[126] Comparing the complex diplomacy to four-dimensional chess, the author Martin Mayer wrote that Richardson "kept himself sane through the years of negotiations by drawing hundreds of thousands of beautiful owls with a blue felt-tip pen on yellow legal pads."[127]

For ambassador to Britain, one of the most prestigious diplomatic posts, Vance proposed Kingman Brewster. "As far as the Court of St. James's was concerned," Vance recalled, "I felt that Kingman would be ideally suited for it, because he was very much of an Anglophile. In addition, I felt he would fit in with the British in a very good way, yet would be very straightforward in his reporting on what was happening on the political issues, and whatever he wrote and cabled would be crystal clear and eloquently stated."[128] Vance prevailed on Carter to make the appointment, even though Brewster had voted for Yale alumnus Ford in the election.

Carter called Brewster in March 1977 and offered him the ambassadorship. The two men had met several times before, as long ago as Brewster's visit to Atlanta in 1971 and as recently as the previous month, when Brewster, as president of the Association of American Universities, discussed higher education with Carter and sought to rebuild "some bridges that had been blown up during the Nixon period," as Brewster put it. The Yale president asked the White House to let him mull over the offer for a day. "It wasn't because I had any doubts at all," Brewster recalled. "It was just that it didn't seem that self-respecting to be that eager."[129] He called back the next day to accept, and Carter permitted him to delay his departure from Yale until after commencement in mid-May.

The ambassadorial appointment allowed Brewster a graceful exit from the Yale presidency, which he had planned on leaving in any case. The difficulties of fund-raising grated on him, and he joked to aides that he would kick-start the laggard campaign begun in 1974 by auctioning off his departure for $100 million. Although in the 1970s he had continued to push his initiatives, such as the creation of the innovative School of Organization and Management, his achievements as president were largely behind him. William Sloane Coffin had already left, in late 1975, complaining that the university had become boring; he had gone on to head New York City's Riverside Church.[130] Brewster also was looking for fresh challenges. As one student observed, when the president was asked in the late 1970s why students could not sit in on Corporation meetings, "Brewster sighed, smiled, decided not to give his tape recorded answer on the 'advisory' role of students and instead said something like, 'Look. A few years ago I wrote what I thought were masterpiece tracts on this subject and now nobody reads them anymore. I've already answered those arguments.'"[131]

Even so, despite some rumors to the contrary, the Yale Corporation was reluctant to see Brewster go. "We never would have asked him to resign, no way," Paul Moore emphasized. "We were one hundred percent loyal to Kingman."[132] Brewster, too, told the Yale community that he had "mixed emotions" about leaving. While both he and Mary Louise looked forward to their new role with anticipation, "Yale has been our total life for seventeen demanding and exhilarating years. Nothing will ever match the rewards of this experience."[133]

Brewster took a fond farewell from Yale, especially during what history professor John Blum called "an adoring luncheon" the senior professors put on for Kingman and his wife. The occasion was full of good cheer, affection, and old friends. The faculty gave the departing president a silver pillbox for his aspirins, and later that evening Mac and Mary Bundy came up from New York to help stage a hilarious skit about the Brewsters, with university administrator Howard Weaver playing Kingman and Mary Bundy playing Mary Louise. "Everybody put on a little performance to honor the King and the Queen," Blum remembered. "And it was a great day, when everybody who felt so indebted to Kingman and who was so fond of Kingman had a chance—without it mattering any longer in the Yale context, because he was leaving—to exhibit those feelings."[134]

Brewster's voice cracked as he began his last baccalaureate address in Woolsey Hall, confessing to what he called "anticipatory nostalgia." The president did not mention the controversial changes he had brought to the institution, and he minimized his role in keeping Yale nonviolent during the late 1960s. He metaphorically tipped his hexagonal hat to a number of administrators and students, including Garry Trudeau, whose cartoons ensured that neither "the King or Megaphone Mark [could] take themselves as seriously as true controversy requires."[135] The graduating seniors rose in a standing ovation at the end of his speech, and did so again the next day at the commencement exercises, when Brewster received a surprise honorary degree. "Long live the King!" the students chanted. "You have been the disturber of placid assumptions and preserver of the peace," the honorary degree citation for Brewster read in part. "Your patience with the academic process has strengthened it; your impatience to attain its goal has made it move." James Reston, who witnessed the ceremonies and received an honorary degree along with Gerald Ford and the blues guitarist B. B. King, reflected that "there is a continuity in our national life and . . . the university has a great part to play in it."[136]

Cyrus Vance was on hand to watch his son, Cyrus Jr., and Brewster's son Alden receive their undergraduate degrees. After the ceremony Vance and Brewster walked over to the backyard of the president's house on Hillhouse

Avenue, where, amid blooming tulips and azaleas, Brewster was sworn in as ambassador to Great Britain. The secretary of state told the small gathering that it was "with affection and greatest joy that I administer the oath of office."[137] While Mary Louise held the Bible, Kingman swore to protect and defend the Constitution of the United States against all enemies, foreign and domestic. The departing president gave a bouquet to former trustee Hanna Gray, who had become provost in 1974 and was now acting head of Yale. Afterward there was applause, champagne, kisses all around, and some tears. Few of those present could quite put it into words, but all knew that an era had ended.

BREWSTER FLEW TO London and was presented to Elizabeth II almost immediately, so that he could take part in the Jubilee Week festivities to celebrate the queen's twenty-fifth year in the monarchy. He had no trouble getting his London tailors to prepare the elaborate diplomatic costume he would need for his part in the pageant, but no shop in the city had a top hat large enough to fit his enormous head, and one had to be made specially by a hatter. The new ambassador rode to Buckingham Palace in a coach, with the traffic lights on his route synchronized to turn green as he approached. As Brewster bowed to the queen in the cavernous golden reception hall, it occurred to him that there was considerable irony in the descendant of a fugitive from Elizabeth I returning to represent his republican nation at the court of Elizabeth II.[138]

Brewster followed Richardson as ambassador and as resident of Winfield House, an enormous redbrick Georgian-style mansion that serves as the emissary's residence in London, the best piece of real estate in the city other than Buckingham Palace. Built in 1935 by Woolworth heiress Barbara Hutton (the "Million Dollar Baby" of the Bing Crosby song), the estate sprawls over twelve acres of lawns and gardens, ponds, and fields of flowers—a country manor set in the midst of a metropolis. The Brewsters shared the grounds with ducks, swans, roosters, cranes, peacocks, rabbits, and the occasional fox, in addition to the family's two dogs. The house was equally magnificent, particularly the sixty-foot-long Green Room, covered in delicate green, hand-painted Chinese paper taken from an Irish castle.[139] As ambassador, Brewster presided over a staff of close to eight hundred employees, including scads of servants at Winfield House. Living in such grandeur and being addressed as "Excellency" was disconcerting at first, but Brewster found the experience "rather corrupting," and soon felt at home.

Inside the atrium of the embassy on Grosvenor Square, the portrait of the fifty-fourth envoy joined the portraits of past ambassadors, including presidents John Adams, James Monroe, John Quincy Adams, Martin Van Buren, and James Buchanan. Most of Brewster's predecessors were well-established easterners, such as his distant relative Winthrop Aldrich and his friends Richardson, John Hay Whitney, Averell Harriman, and David Bruce. Like them, Brewster was impressive in a way the British easily understood. They appreciated his crisp Connecticut Valley accent and his baritone growl, his elegant phrasing and knack for understatement, his bespoke tailoring, and his dry, sardonic sense of humor. One British observer underscored that the "pure East Coast Establishment" ambassador was "as close as you can come in the United States to being an aristocrat."[140]

However, Brewster was unlike many recent ambassadors in that he was not rich and was unable to dip into his own funds to lay out the lavish spreads to which the London press had become accustomed. For this reason, he was not a favorite of many British journalists, who preferred Walter Annenberg, the endearingly inarticulate *Daily Racing Form* magnate who spent millions of dollars of his own money during his time as ambassador, in the early 1970s. Nor did Brewster provide "color," as Annenberg did (in both senses of the word) by dressing up in a cardinal's red satin robes when he dined alone in Winfield House, a practice that led delighted journalists to describe him as "richly absurd as well as absurdly rich."

What Brewster did provide to the post was substance and seriousness. More adept than any ambassador since Bruce, he studied the nation's leadership, attitudes, and concerns, to enhance his position as the interface between British society and the United States government. Brewster had daily contact with politicians and spent more time in the gallery of the House of Commons than his predecessors, assessing the effectiveness and conviction of various leaders. He also met frequently with civil servants, church officials, industrialists, academics, journalists, heads of think tanks, and trade union leaders. At the same time, he was aware that the ambassador lives in a fairly circumscribed realm; to broaden his experience, he asked the fifteen members of Parliament who had attended Yale to introduce him to some of their constituents. Through this connection he spent time with pensioners in old-age homes, workers in farms, factories, and pubs, and young people in schools and recreation centers.

Brewster also invested considerable time and effort in writing his own speeches for his public appearances. One such address, delivered in Saint George's Chapel in Windsor Castle, compared the nature and problems of the advanced welfare state in Britain and the United States.[141] As the *New York Times* reporter R. W. Apple Jr. commented, "It was a characteristic performance—moderate, thoughtful and a bit dull, perhaps, for the requirements of newspaper headlines."[142] Occasionally Brewster's friend McGeorge Bundy would vet his more political speeches. Once Bundy advised him that his description of British policy toward the racial turmoil in its former colony Rhodesia as "paranoid" might get him into trouble: "this is a word that can be taken from context and gossiped over."[143]

On many occasions Brewster's experience in international antitrust law at Harvard came into play, notably when he sought to persuade the British to adhere to U.S. sanctions on particular countries and to end the practice of allowing companies to write off bribes as business expenses. At other times his many years as Yale president came to bear on the new job. As ambassador he was on parade much as he had been as university head. He had to deal with a flow of issues, events, and personalities he was not necessarily familiar with or expert in, and he needed to know when to trust the judgments of intellectuals and when to be skeptical of them. Whereas at Yale he was ultimately responsible for the welfare of the institution, as ambassador he was, as he liked to say, only one link in a long chain.[144]

As a Harvard law professor in the 1950s, Brewster wrote that diplomacy had ceased to be the exclusive province of ambassadors and "an elite corps of experts."[145] He was right, in that by the 1970s, much of the relationship between the United States and Britain had become dominated by multilateral, nongovernmental, or personal connections, to the extent that the margin for an ambassador was narrower than it once had been. In the opinion of his political officer Thomas Simons, however, it was precisely the old-fashioned, elite diplomacy that Brewster did best: he "quietly offered a few people useful ideas backed by American power in timely fashion on various subjects. It may not be what he thought he was or should be doing . . . but it was the heart of his achievement."[146]

Brewster's relationship with Secretary of State Vance enhanced his impact as ambassador. While his immediate predecessor, Anne Armstrong, had been excluded from Kissinger's meetings with the prime minister and foreign secretary, Brewster was an active participant at such talks. And, as he said, "there was no doubt at all that if there was some crunch, I could pick up the phone and talk to Cy directly. And it was understood by my staff, and by the British, that I did have a hotline to Secretary Vance. I didn't use it very often, but the fact that it was there made me much more effective."[147] On one such occasion, Brewster helped broker a settlement to the Rhodesian crisis by intervening with Vance and Carter to secure American support for an agricultural development fund to facilitate land reform.[148]

Politics aside, many aspects of Brewster's life as ambassador were just plain enjoyable. The backdrops to many of his meetings with British dignitaries were frequently such exquisite venues as the Painted Hall at the Royal Naval College or White's Club in Saint James. The Brewsters rented a cottage deep in the Berkshire countryside, where Kingman would spend his weekends reading, thinking, and taking the dogs for long walks across the hills overlooking the downs. As his deputy recalled, Brewster could have dinner with anyone in British society who interested him, "from Dame Margot Fontaine to the street sweeper. . . . One of the things we enjoyed was the ability to put together people who didn't really belong together, and so create new relationships among the British which hadn't existed before."[149] Brewster also entertained prominent visiting Americans who came through London, from Bishop Paul Moore to touring rugby teams.

The ambassador had entree to All Soul's College at Oxford, a welcome at the Jockey Club, a box at Glyndebourne, and an invitation to "the Annual Banquet to meet the Right Honourable the Lord Mayor and Lady Mayoress, the Sherriffs and their Ladies, given by the Worshipful Company of Scientific Instrument Makers at Scientific Instrument Makers Hall in the City of London: Dress, Evening Dress with Decorations."[150] Brewster once went to the Royal Courts of Justice to see the Queen's Remembrancer receive a quitrent payment of six horseshoes and sixty-one nails for a plot of waste ground in Shropshire, a ceremony performed annually since 1211. And on one beautiful Indian summer day, he took part in an antique car race from London to Brighton, riding (and on occasion getting out and pushing) a 1904 Speedwell Dog Cart.[151]

Brewster's ambassadorship overlapped with the last two years of the Labour government under James Callaghan and the first two years of the Tories under Margaret Thatcher, a period marked by a drive toward political extremes that in some ways echoed the late 1960s in the United States. When Brewster had his first extensive conversation with Callaghan on arriving in London, he told the prime minister that the difference between Britain in 1977 and 1971, when Brewster had been in London on sabbatical leave, was the recent tendency toward polarization. Continuing inflation and lack of economic growth, combined with class and racial antagonisms, had made British life less generous and considerate than it had been, and now "ideology was raising its intemperate head." Within the Labour Party, the "militant tendency" came to the fore led by Sir Anthony Wedgwood-Benn—"that patrician populist," as Brewster referred to him. Angry labor strikes disrupted Britain during the 1978–79 "winter of discontent," when garbage rotted in the streets, rats ran rampant, hospitals shut down, and bodies piled up in the morgues.

Radicalism of the left paved the way for radicalism of the right, as Thatcher became prime minister in the spring of 1979. "She was dogmatic and dogged," Brewster remembered, "a true Friedmaniac."[152] From Thatcher's point of view, Brewster was an American counterpart of the "wet" establishment she hoped to dismantle. Raymond Seitz, then a political officer in the embassy, believed that "Thatcher thought that Brewster represented all the worst aspects of the Carter administration."[153] Brewster, in his turn, felt that Thatcher's hard-line Tory ideology, which repudiated traditional British pragmatism, ended up deepening the gulfs between classes, regions, and political partisans. While Thatcherism raised unemployment in the short term, the long-run damage of ideology, Brewster thought, was not to the economy so much as to social tolerance, patience, and decency.[154]

Nonetheless, Brewster forged a reliable working relationship with Thatcher and the new Conservative government. He was even able to secure some important diplomatic breakthroughs. When Thatcher came to power, the embassy devised a conscious strategy to persuade her that her opposition to the ongoing Strategic Arms Limitation Talks was unnecessarily rigid. Brewster and his officers sought to reach her indirectly, through her advisors. Doing so was not difficult, since Brewster and his talented deputy chief of mission, Edward Streator, had assiduously cultivated the Conservative leadership when the Tories were out of power; when the government changed, Brewster noted, "we weren't dealing with strangers, we were dealing with friends."[155]

Over breakfasts, lunches, and dinners, Brewster and his team held a series of roundtable discussions with Thatcher's senior ministers on strategic weapons and arms control. The ambassador, a master of the peculiar alchemy required to bring people together for informal meetings, facilitated discussions so that the British understood the rationale behind the U.S. approach. He brought to London some of the leading experts on arms control, including his friends McGeorge Bundy and Stanley Resor. Over time, Brewster and Streator determined that Thatcher's most trusted advisor on nuclear arms was Sir Geoffrey Pattie. Once they brought him around, Thatcher followed.[156]

*　　*　　*

BY 1979, BREWSTER'S conversations with Vance were no longer as upbeat as they had been when the secretary of state took office. The Carter administration's first years had included such foreign policy accomplishments as the Panama Canal treaty, normalization of U.S. relations with China, strategic arms negotiations with the Soviets, and the peace accord signed at Camp David by Egypt's Anwar Sadat and Israel's Menachim Begin. Vance, a moving force behind all these achievements, found his position increasingly undercut by his rival, national security advisor Zbigniew Brzezinski.

The Polish-born, fiercely anti-Soviet Brzezinski had long been acquainted with the liberal establishment; he had served as translator when Kingman Brewster and other Harvard law professors traveled to Poland in 1958 and had been a member of the government department throughout McGeorge Bundy's deanship. To Brzezinski, Vance was "a quintessential product of his own background: as a member of both the legal profession and the once-dominant white, Anglo-Saxon, Protestant elite, he operated according to their rules and values, but those values and rules were of declining relevance not only in terms of domestic American politics but particularly in terms of global conditions."[157] Brzezinski saw the liberal establishment's reluctance to use force as an outcome of its outdated courtly ideals and its recent experiences with domestic turmoil in the 1960s and the war in Vietnam.

Brzezinski himself had no gentlemanly inhibitions about using power plays to advance his position, through leaks, hostile off-the-record interviews, memos for the president that distorted discussions between Brzezinski and Vance, and a host of other hardball tactics. As State Department spokesman Hodding Carter III later wrote, Vance put himself in a disadvantageous position in these bureaucratic battles because "he wouldn't fight dirty if his life depended on it. In many ways, his effectiveness in the Carter Administration's infighting was severely hampered precisely because he was instinctively so straight."[158] Years later, Vance acknowledged that he had erred in agreeing to Brzezinski's appointment. "I had some reservations about him," he said, "but I knew the president wanted him very badly. I now realize my instinctive feeling on that was right."[159]

The security chief's hand was strengthened by a series of disruptive events in 1979, including the fall of the Somoza dictatorship in Nicaragua and of the shah in Iran, the seizure of the American embassy and its personnel in Tehran, and the Soviet invasion of Afghanistan. The public saw, in these developments, a resurgent Soviet Union, not an empire in its death throes, and the long captivity of the American hostages in Iran symbolized what seemed to be U.S. impotence and ineffectiveness on the part of the Carter administration. Brzezinski used this sense of drift to persuade Carter to build up the military and take a hard anti-Soviet line.

In the case of Iran, Brzezinski counseled the deployment of force to free the hostages; he poured contempt over Vance's arguments that to do so would sabotage ongoing diplomatic efforts, endanger the hostages, and worsen U.S. relations with the Islamic world. The national security advisor wrote later that he was bothered by Vance's failure to stand up for what Brzezinski considered to be American honor: "I wondered what this indicated about the current American elite and whether we were not seeing here symptoms of a deeper national problem."[160] As far as "honor" was concerned, Vance was aghast to discover that Brzezinski maintained his own secret channel of communication with Iran and that he had lied to the president in denying its existence.[161]

On April 10, 1980, when Vance and his wife were in Florida on a rare weekend away, Brzezinski used his rival's absence to persuade the president to undertake a military rescue mission. Appalled by this duplicity and what he considered the folly of the decision—and unable, on his return, to dissuade Carter—Vance informed the president that he would announce his resignation when the mission was over, regardless of its outcome.

On April 27, after the rescue attempt had failed, with eight servicemen killed in a collision after the mission had been aborted, Vance made his resignation public, becoming the first secretary of state since William Jennings Bryan to resign on a matter of principle. As one commentator observed of Vance, "He may be an Establishment lawyer . . . but at core he is a gentleman, and he left the service of his country like a gentleman."[162] In his letter to Carter, Vance said he was leaving "with a heavy heart" and he was aware that his departure constituted a major embarrassment for the president.[163] However, as the *Washington Post* pointed out, Vance's decision reflected the lessons he had learned in government in the Vietnam era: "he evidently came to feel that force should be used only in the most dire circumstances and that an official out of sympathy with a major policy should resign no matter what the cost to his chief."[164] As with Nixon's misjudgment of Richardson, Carter had underestimated an establishment baron's independence and fidelity to principle, and he paid a heavy political price.

Brewster, of course, was sorry to see his friend depart, and although he established a cordial relationship with Vance's successor, Edmund Muskie, he no longer had a hotline to power. In any case, the last few months of his ambassadorship became his most prominent diplomatic moment, as he joined with British authorities in efforts to secure the hostages' release from Iran. Brewster worked closely with Carter's chief negotiator, Lloyd Cutler, who by coincidence had been Brewster's lawyer and chief fund-raiser at Yale and lived a few doors down Hillhouse Avenue during the university's capital campaign.[165]

The endgame of the hostage release drama occurred when Bank of England officials, working through the Algerian government, transferred into an escrow fund the Iranian assets the United States had frozen after the hostage seizure. Deputy chief of mission Streator remembered that "some of the legal issues were quite complex with respect to this question of Iranian assets, and [Brewster] played a very important role in that particular process."[166] On January 20, 1981, Iran freed the hostages from their 444-day captivity. Brewster took to the airwaves to thank the British government for its cooperation and held a boisterous celebration at Winfield House. In so doing, he raised his public profile higher than it had been at any point in his tenure. "The American ambassador in London has suddenly become a radio star," one article noted.[167]

By that time, however, Brewster's time in office was nearing its end, as Ronald Reagan had won the presidential race. Brewster took a predictably dim view of "the first ideological campaign since the Goldwater defeat, and the first election of a president since Roosevelt's re-election in 1936 who had reason to think he had an ideological mandate."[168] The conservatives under Reagan loathed Brewster and the establishment from which he sprang, so there was no question of his staying on. But it was still a wrench to leave the ambassadorship. "It was wonderful," he later recalled of his time in office, "just a dream we didn't want to wake up from."[169] Reagan replaced Brewster with a wealthy businessman whose main qualification for the post, as one retired career diplomat acerbically observed, was that he spoke English.[170]

BREWSTER AND HIS wife returned to New Haven and rented a house near campus. Although Brewster had hoped that his provost Hanna Gray would succeed him, the Corporation felt the alumni reaction would be formidable. One representative alumnus had refused to donate to Yale "until I see that a woman isn't President," he told the campus newspaper in 1977. "Yale just isn't psychologically prepared for a woman."[171] Gray endured a frustrating year as acting president, then departed to become a highly successful president of the University of Chicago. After the Corporation offered the presidency to Harvard dean Henry Rosovsky, who embarrassed the university by publicly spurning the offer, the trustees elected Yale English professor A. Bartlett Giamatti.

The affable, highly articulate "Bart," one of the university's more conservative professors in the 1960s, had tilted against many of Brewster's reforms. As president, however, he found it impossible, as well as undesirable, to reverse any of his predecessor's major initiatives, from admissions to investment policies to the curriculum. Giamatti also lacked Brewster's personal and political skills, and his presidency was not a happy one. Brewster's former assistant Sam Chauncey, who stayed on as university secretary, recalled that while working for Brewster had been fun even at the tensest times, his dominant memory of working for Giamatti was "Bart yelling and screaming" at his provost while the president's wife cried on the stairway. It was "agony."[172] While many faculty members were personal friends of Giamatti, quite a few were openly nostalgic for Brewster, which to some degree complicated the former president's situation in New Haven.

Brewster, who had returned to the United States unemployed, soon found that fulfilling opportunities for a sixty-one-year-old former Yale president and ambassador were scarce. What was more, many men of his class closed their doors to him because of his actions as president of Yale in the late 1960s. Jonathan Fanton believed that Brewster "got marked as somehow a traitor to his class, or too far left of center, and then in his post-presidential period a lot of people who could have been helpful to him were not. . . . Why wasn't he chairman of some major commission? Why wasn't he on this board or that board? I think that he was being paid back, in a way, for having been too far out ahead."[173]

Brewster finally secured a position of counsel to the New York–based law firm Winthrop, Stimson, Putnam & Roberts, and commuted there from New Haven on a part-time basis. The rest of his time was taken up with writing what he self-deprecatingly called "a pretentious, tell 'em how to save the world book," supported by a grant from the Sloan Foundation.[174] By reworking some of his speeches as Yale president and ambassador, Brewster hoped to produce a volume about "the difficulty in maintaining a voluntary society in the face of pressures from government and large corporations."[175] Brewster discussed his ideas about the independent (or third) sector of society, mediating between government and business, as chairman of the advisory committee of Yale's Program on Non-Profit Organizations (PONPO), which he had helped create with McGeorge Bundy's support in the late 1970s. It was his last official Yale connection.

PONPO's director, John G. Simon, felt that his friend "was not fully engaged in either of those half-time jobs." Brewster could not bring his book to completion, Simon believed, because he lacked some degree of scholarly narcissism. "The idea that the Brewster corpus of thought was something to mature, fertilize, and bring to fruition wasn't terribly important to him, partly because I don't think he took himself all that seriously."[176] Brewster's Yale and Harvard law classmate Peter Solbert felt that although Brewster was pleased to be part of Henry Stimson's law firm, "He looked down on the daily practice, and hence didn't ever understand it." While Brewster grasped the legal issues, "Kingman could never have drawn up a checklist of what to do in an acquisition between a French and an Italian company. He just would not have known where to turn."[177] Neither of Brewster's part-time jobs paid well, either. Simon remembered him once coming into the PONPO office to make sure that he got a grant check into the bank so his quarterly tax payment wouldn't bounce.[178]

In 1984, Brewster returned to London as an overseas partner of Winthrop, Stimson, and declared himself delighted to be back.[179] He was able to return to his habit of spending weekends in the country by buying a thatched-roof cottage in the Berkshire hamlet of Combe. His neighbors there included his friend Sir Nicholas Henderson, the former British ambassador to the United States. During his two years with the London office, Brewster had some interesting legal assignments. Because of his reputation for fairness, he was named special master to arbitrate labor grievances in the National Basketball Association. He attributed his successes in the job to the fact that he was "totally ignorant of basketball."[180] Still, Brewster's time in London was fraught with many of the difficulties that had bedeviled his law practice in New York.

Then in 1986, through the intervention of former Yale law professor Ronald Dworkin, Brewster was elected master of University College, one of the oldest of the quasi-independent foundations that make up Oxford University. The college fellows hoped that Brewster would bring the administrative and fund-raising savvy that had suddenly become necessary as Thatcher imposed draconian cutbacks on the Oxbridge establishment.[181]

The Brewsters settled into the Victorian-Gothic master's house on Logic Lane, and the new master met with students and fellows, attended university administrative meetings in the Sheldonian Theatre and evensong services in the college chapel, and delivered the Latin prayer from the high table at college dinners. Brewster's friend Frank Norall, an American living in London, observed that the mastership "was a sufficiently prestigious job that Brewster could meet or at least maintain contact with practically anyone he wanted to," so Brewster could keep up some kind of political and social involvement in British life.[182]

Lesley Hazleton, a young Englishwoman writing a book on change in Thatcher-era Britain, met with Brewster in his elegant wood-paneled study, surrounded by leather-bound tomes and venerable stone walls. She thought him an English aristocrat in all but accent, complete with "a house in the rolling Berkshire countryside, and the good-natured ease and elegance of an Oxford mastership." She was astonished to find that he did not share her enthusiasm for the booming London stock market, but instead "shook his head at the idea of greed run rampant in the City. Speaking in his clipped New England accent . . . and with a frown as disapproving as that of the most dowager of English duchesses, he said: 'It's not British, you know. It's just not British.'" Hazleton was less surprised to find that "like the best of the old English elite, Brewster detested" the Conservative prime minister, and "attacked 'the politics of self-interest' and in particular, Thatcher's 'vendetta' on the universities."[183]

Brewster's ability to defend Oxford and University College from Thatcher's antiestablishment populism, however, was hampered when he suffered a stroke early in his mastership. Typically, Brewster tried to compensate for his physical disabilities by pushing himself even harder. He met with McGeorge Bundy in April 1987 on a trip back to the States to raise funds for University College. "You scared me," Bundy wrote to his friend afterward. "It did look as if you had just given yourself a hell of a day—or week—or how long? . . . [I]f I'd been your doctor I'd have been frantic— and I was a little frantic as a non-voting friend. You were brave as a lion, but I kept thinking 'this guy has a *circulation* problem—I don't think he should *do* this to himself.'"[184]

Neither Bundy nor anyone else could prevent Brewster from burning the candle at both ends; it was in the nature of the man. In early 1988, he suffered a second stroke, although neither he nor his wife could bring themselves to acknowledge its severity. Norall went out to Oxford to see Brewster and found him "quite disabled." One arm was blue and without feeling, and he was partially paralyzed in one leg and had to walk with a cane. "Kingman's mind, as far as one could tell, was functioning pretty close to normal," Norall thought, but he had difficulty speaking.[185] Brewster told the University College fellows to begin a search for his successor; he was still in the mastership when he suffered a massive cerebral hemorrhage on November 8, 1988, and died at age sixty-nine in a hospital near Oxford.

At Brewster's memorial service at the University Church of Saint Mary the Virgin in Oxford, his friend and former Corporation trustee J. Irwin Miller spoke of the president's courage and conviction, but also of his fundamental decency. "You could gossip with him, but you could not be petty," Miller remembered. "You could laugh, but you could not ridicule. . . . He was a patrician who could see and who esteemed the worth in every person."[186]

The crowd at Brewster's memorial service in Battell Chapel in New Haven included students, faculty, alumni, friends, strangers, and people from every race and age group. Most of the members of Brewster's Corporation were in the pews, including John Lindsay and Cyrus Vance. A surprising number of Old Blues attended; many still disagreed with the changes Brewster had brought to Yale, but in the end they were prepared to send him off as one of their own. McGeorge Bundy spoke of his friend's ability to find four-leaf clovers, referring both to Brewster's luck and to his ability to pick promising young people; several of his former assistants had by then gone on to university presidencies, including Hanna Gray at Chicago and Jonathan Fanton at the New School, while Joel Fleishman was senior vice president at Duke. Paul Moore delivered a prayer, and William Sloane Coffin offered a brief benediction.

Brewster's ashes were interred in the Grove Street Cemetery in New Haven, traditional resting place of Yale's presidents and senior faculty. In the coping around his gravestone, Brewster's friends had carved a quote from his 1971 Yale baccalaureate address that seemed to exemplify his humanity and his belief in ordered freedom. "The presumption of innocence is not just a legal concept," it reads. "In commonplace terms, it rests on that generosity of spirit which assumes the best, not the worst of the stranger."

EPILOGUE

IT WAS part of Paul Moore's job to attend memorial services, and over the years after Brewster's death, he attended the final rites for the other members of their circle. In one or another venerable Protestant church, the people they had touched gathered to sing the old hymns, offer the traditional prayers, and come to grips with the larger meaning of the lives of these uncommon men.

MCGEORGE BUNDY DIED of a heart attack in September 1996 at age seventy-seven. When he retired from the Ford Foundation presidency in 1979 on reaching sixty, his involvement in the Vietnam War continued to dog him, ruling out a return to high government office or even appointment to a major university presidency. Instead, he became a professor of history at New York University, despite the protests of some department faculty members over his Vietnam culpability. Through articles and speeches Bundy continued to play a role in public debates, advocating affirmative action and calling for restraint in the nuclear arms race. In 1988 he published *Danger and Survival: Choices about the Bomb in the First Fifty Years,* a masterly account of the use of, and controversy surrounding, nuclear weapons that combined scholarship with its author's insights from government service.

When he reached the faculty retirement age, Bundy became scholar-in-residence at the Carnegie Corporation; he began work on a memoir about his involvement in the Vietnam War. He had no doubt that committing combat troops to the war constituted the greatest U.S. foreign policy debacle since the failure to resist Hitler's rise in the 1930s. He was still wrestling with the question of how much blame attached to him and how much to Lyndon Johnson when he died, with the manuscript largely unfinished.[1] At his memorial service in New York's Saint James Church, the ranks of dignitaries, including Vance and Moore, heard Francis Bator defend his former boss's record. "The United States made a lot of good things happen during Mac's five-year watch," Bator insisted, and "he had a lot to do with it. With the one *very bad* thing that happened he had much *less* to do than the common version of the Vietnam story would have it."[2]

ELLIOT RICHARDSON DIED in Boston of a cerebral hemorrhage on December 31, 1999, at age seventy-nine. His career following his ambassadorship to the Law of the Sea conference turned out to be anticlimactic. Richardson had secured multinational agreement on all major conference issues when he stepped down after Ronald Reagan's 1980 presidential victory. The Reagan administration shocked the world by abandoning the negotiations and refusing to sign the final treaty, largely because Republican business interests opposed its restrictions on deep-seabed mining. The Republicans spurned Richardson for his liberalism as well as his role in undoing Nixon's presidency. His former chief of staff Jonathan Moore felt that the longtime public servant "was exiled, a national public resource wasted, during the Reagan and Bush years. He was still useful, and he would have been happy to serve in direct ways. But most people in Washington don't want that kind of intellect and ability shining a bright light on their dealings, and Elliot couldn't be manipulated."[3]

Richardson joined the Washington office of the New York law firm Milbank, Tweed, Hadley & McCloy, and continued to be involved in quasi-public service through organizations such as the United Nations Association of the United States, serving as cochair of its national council with Cyrus Vance. When Richardson ran for the Massachusetts Republican nomination for U.S. Senate in 1984, he received a painful lesson in how badly the GOP had canted to the right since the early 1970s. After he spoke out, at the party's national convention, against the fiscally irresponsible tax-cutting championed by supply-side Republicans, his Reaganite populist opponent savaged him as a free-spending liberal. Richardson sank stonelike in the polls and lost the primary election by twenty-five percentage points. "The '84 loss was very traumatic [for Richardson]," one of his supporters recalled, and "it really did change his life. But the politics never won out over his conscience."[4] Ironically, it was a Democratic president, Bill Clinton, who granted the lifelong Republican Richardson the nation's highest civilian honor, the Presidential Medal of Freedom.

In 1996, Richardson published a book, *Reflections of a Radical Moderate*, that, like his *The Creative Balance*, eschewed autobiography in favor of high-minded ideas about government and citizenship expressed in elaborate prose. But the book accurately reflected Richardson's emphatic belief that "every American who cares about this country—every one of us who is proud of what it has achieved and looks forward to what it may yet attain—shares responsibility for keeping its values alive."[5]

Richardson's memorial service took place in the National Cathedral, where Moore had served at the height of the civil rights era. The former bishop and more than a thousand other attendees sang "Once to Every Man and Nation," and listened to Jonathan Moore read "The Truly Great" by the British poet Stephen Spender. Many of those present smiled in wry recognition when Richardson's former assistant Richard Darman remembered his boss looking at his dogs sleeping in the sun and wondering aloud whether "they might prefer to be hitched to a plow. . . . [Richardson] saw work as a service and the opportunity to serve as a precious gift."[6]

TO AN EVEN greater extent than Richardson, John Lindsay had wandered in the political wilderness before his death, in December 2000, at age seventy-nine. After bowing out of the mayoralty in 1973 and spending the better part of a year in Europe on what he called a sabbatical, Lindsay returned to his partnership in the Webster, Sheffield law firm. He became a television commentator, wrote articles, and published a poorly regarded novel. His reputation took another beating when New York City slid into bankruptcy in April 1975. Although Lindsay had signed off on ill-advised financial gimmickry to balance the budgets in his last years, the massive borrowing and chicanery of his successor, Abe Beame, was more directly responsible for the city's fiscal collapse. Even so, Beame and the next mayor, Ed Koch, continued to blame Lindsay for the city's problems. Koch particularly enjoyed scapegoating the patrician ex-mayor, bragging that he "tortured [Lindsay] at every opportunity. He deserved it."[7] Lindsay made one more fling at office, entering the 1980 New York Democratic primary for the U.S. Senate, but came in a distant third.

Lindsay's last years proved difficult, as he suffered from strokes, heart problems, and Parkinson's disease, while the two law firms he was associated with folded. Left without a pension or health insurance, Lindsay was rescued from personal financial disaster through the intervention of friends, including New York mayor Rudolph Giuliani and City Council speaker Peter Vallone.[8]

Lindsay's memorial service took place in the Cathedral of Saint John the Divine, where a series of speakers remembered the energy and excitement he had brought to the mayoralty. Lindsay's administration was "one of the most magical moments in public life that this country has ever known," former chief of staff Peter Goldmark Jr. testified, "and he let us all be part of it. We would have walked through flames for this guy." Paul Moore presided over the ceremonies, and recalled that in their prep school days at St. Paul's, the future mayor was "a youngster of some charm and promise and a great deal of mischief." The boy grew up to be "an icon for my generation," the bishop said, "a leader in confusing and troubled times" who was never "quite given in his day the glory he deserved."[9]

CYRUS VANCE DIED in January 2002, at age eighty-four, after struggling for several years with Alzheimer's disease. After resigning from Carter's cabinet, the former secretary of state went back to the Simpson, Thacher law firm in New York. By the end of the 1980s, he had returned to the international arena as a troubleshooter for the United Nations. Acting as the personal envoy of the secretary-general, he helped broker a peace agreement in the Nagorno-Karabakh dispute between Armenia and Azerbaijan, and in 1992 traveled to South Africa to assist with the transition to black majority rule. His last high-profile assignment came between 1991 and 1993, when he worked with former British foreign secretary David Owen to broker a cease-fire in Croatia and attempted to halt the ethnic slaughter in what had been Yugoslavia. The Clinton administration rejected the Vance-Owen plan for partitioning Bosnia into ethnic "cantons" under weak central authority, claiming it rewarded the Serbian aggressors. Vance retired from the foreign policy arena and returned to the practice of law until Alzheimer's began to incapacitate him.

Vance's funeral took place at the Church of the Heavenly Rest in New York, with representatives from six presidential administrations present. Paul Moore, who took part in the ceremony, felt that its most moving moment came at the end. The pawl covering Vance's coffin was removed and replaced with an American flag, and the flag-draped coffin was carried out of the church shoulder-high.[10] It was an appropriate send-off for Vance, whose onetime deputy Warren Christopher remembered him as "an old-fashioned patriot."[11] Secretary of State Colin Powell described Vance as "the pride of a generation of Americans who valued public service as the highest good."[12]

PAUL MOORE DIED in May 2003, at age eighty-three, of complications from lung and brain cancer. Moore had served as bishop of New York until his retirement in 1989, and had continued to be embroiled in controversy throughout his tenure. He led the fight for women to be ordained, and in 1977 risked censure by ordaining a declared lesbian to the priesthood. He compared business executives leaving New York to rats abandoning a sinking ship, criticized Mayor Ed Koch's "naive and dangerous" views on homelessness, and protested the nuclear arms race of the 1980s. In 1982, he visited Moscow to discuss disarmament with Soviet leaders; his international work also took him to Nicaragua and South Africa. After his retirement, with Vance's encouragement, he took up the cause of human rights in East Timor.[13] In March 2003, Moore returned to the Cathedral of Saint John the Divine to denounce President George W. Bush and the impending war in Iraq. Although he was barely able to mount the steps of the pulpit, the aging lion roared eloquently against Bush's fundamentalist presumption that he had divine sanction for the war, contrasting "the religion that says, 'I talk to Jesus and therefore I am right'" with "millions and millions of people of all faiths who disagree."[14]

Moore's funeral took place in the cathedral less than two months later, in a swirl of the pageantry and ritual that he had so much enjoyed. Men and women of all races and many faiths gathered to pay tribute. Speakers testified to his passion for justice and the rights of the oppressed, and his commitment to New York City, which took physical form in his opening the cathedral to artists, performers, poets, neighborhood residents, and spiritual seekers. There was music in abundance, and many of the hymns Moore had sung as a schoolboy in the chapel of St. Paul's, including "The New Jerusalem," "Once in Royal David's City," and "In Christ There Is No East or West." Although "Once to Every Man and Nation" had by that time been removed from most hymnals, because of its stubbornly male-centric language, on this occasion it served as a tribute to Moore and other leaders like him who had taken unpopular stands for what they saw as right. "Then it is the brave man chooses," the congregation sang, "while the coward stands aside, / till the multitude make virtue / of the faith they had denied."

*   *   *

WHAT SHOULD TODAY'S Americans make of the lives of Kingman Brewster and the others in his circle? Although most obituary writers recognized that with the passing of these men, a certain tradition of establishment leadership had drawn to a close, they were hard-pressed to assess its legacy.

Brewster's record as university president can be addressed straightforwardly. His friend Cyrus Vance thought Brewster would have liked to be remembered as "somebody who brought to Yale the vigor, the wisdom, and the willingness to change that he so much admired."[15] The university experienced more changes and more controversy under Brewster in the 1960s than in any other period in its history. Those were the years when the patterns were created that still determine the shape of Yale's faculty, curriculum, finances, and admissions policies, and Brewster's example influenced many other major universities.

Brewster brought a new emphasis on merit to the university and opened its gates to minorities, women, and people from nonprivileged backgrounds. He moved the institution away from its deeply conservative tradition and turned it into a modern international university, one that remained a close-knit community while broadening its focus to embrace a wider world. None of the changes were reversed by his successors, and structurally the university has altered little since the late 1960s. Even some alumni who had protested the developments the loudest realized, later, that Brewster had anticipated the evolving shape of society and moved to adapt his institution to its needs.

Over time, many former critics also recognized that Yale was one of the few American institutions of any description that were strengthened rather than damaged by the upheavals of the 1960s, in large measure because of Brewster's deft responses to the tensions produced by the civil rights movement, the war in Vietnam, and student activism. Even so, when in 1994 a *New York Times* reporter sought to determine why university presidents had ceased to be public figures, he found that "many academic leaders recall with a wince the ordeal of Kingman Brewster Jr." Brewster's efforts to give disaffected youths hope in the establishment were forgotten; what survived, in memory, was the "howl that nearly drove him from office."[16]

The individuals who succeeded the likes of Brewster at Yale and Bundy at Ford concentrated on the tasks of managing their institutions—often quite successfully—while shunning the high-risk arena of leadership. "When was the last time you saw a university president on the front page of the *New York Times* with an argument or a statement?" asked Notre Dame's Theodore Hesburgh in 2000. "Nowadays I can't name any of the presidents of the Ivy League, or of Stanford, and I don't think most people can. Neither could I tell you who's in charge of the major foundations, or a lot of the other institutions that used to play a prominent role in public life." The generation of institutional heads who followed in the 1970s and 1980s avoided controversy, built up bureaucracies, and focused on the bottom line. The absence of widespread student unrest or intense public debate over subjects like race and war also made it unlikely that institutional leaders would emerge. As Hesburgh remembered, for a select number of university presidents and other leaders, the turmoil of the 1960s "put some steel in our souls."[17]

As it became clear that the liberal establishment lacked successors, commentators in the 1990s and early years of the twenty-first century expressed nostalgia not only for the vanished university and foundation presidents but for the Wise Men of old. What had happened to the establishment and its tradition of moderate, independent public service? Had Brewster and his peers, for all their accomplishments, somehow dropped the baton passed from the previous generation of Wise Men like Dean Acheson and John McCloy?

The obvious answer is that Brewster's generation lived in a different America and had to deal with social realities undreamed of by their elders. By the 1960s, no sphere of authority, even foreign policy, could any longer be formulated behind closed doors by a group of elites and accepted by the rest of the nation. As Halberstam correctly pointed out, the Vietnam War not only tarnished the reputations of the individuals who had planned and executed it; the period also "saw a major challenge to the right of the elite to rule. . . . The years had made all the other political groups in the country aware of just how little a part they played in foreign policy, and by the end of the decade, the outlanders—Negroes, women, workers—were determined to play a greater role; they had reached the moat and were pushing on."[18]

The paradoxical defining truth of the liberal establishment, however, is that its members did not oppose this change—they welcomed it, and actually devoted themselves to carrying it forward. In a development that their mentors never could have anticipated, the theme of their careers became one of increasing equality of opportunity. They agreed with their elders that responsible elites had to uphold a standard of disinterestedness. In the 1960s, however, they came to think of this concept not only as the ability to rise above ties of region and party but as the responsibility of elite white males to uphold wider opportunity for those who were not elite, white, or male. They were not resisting the outsiders' entry into the castle—they were lowering the drawbridge and lifting the gate.

It is no slur on the civil rights movements to point out that the liberal establishment worked with the grass roots to increase social mobility and equality and that a failure to remember the critical role of elites has hampered the development of American democracy. As the political commentator John Judis has pointed out, "At their best, elites and elite organizations have promoted an idea of the national interest that could bind together citizens and unite conflicting interest groups. . . . Trust in their wisdom and expertise has been essential to trust in government itself."[19]

McGeorge Bundy resisted the idea that the country was dominated by a unified establishment. Even as an undergraduate, he believed that science and the media had a far greater impact on public thinking and the course of American history than the little band of lawyer-statesmen around Henry Stimson.[20] "We have a great many establishments, not one, and they are very strong," he observed in 1970. The hallmark of these varied establishments could be seen in "the rigidity of the university faculty with respect to curriculum or the rigidity of school superintendents with respect to the way schools are organized. You find parallel rigidity in every other field." Ultimately, he thought, frustration with this sort of rigidity was at the root of the 1960s unrest and the questioning of values that went with it.[21] But Bundy's argument provides an apt definition of the liberal establishment of which he and Brewster were part. They were the "guardian critics," as the columnist Tom Wicker called them, who tried to break down the power of the smaller establishments by speaking from the heart of the American tradition in the name of the national interest.[22]

It is a misreading of history to say, as one of Bundy's obituarists did, that "the Vietnam War did to America what the Somme did for Britain: it destroyed the confidence of the public in the elite, and destroyed the confidence of the elite in itself. The personal tragedy of McGeorge Bundy's life reflected a much broader failure of his class, of his beliefs, of his whole concept of public affairs. The wisdom of Harvard Yard and Martha's Vineyard had turned out not nearly adequate to deal with the modern world."[23] On the contrary, Bundy and Brewster and their peers did help define the modern world. By reorienting themselves and their establishment institutions to the landscape whose contours had been reshaped by the civil rights movement, they were among the writers of a new chapter in the history of social mobility. While it was not a struggle for which they had consciously prepared, the lessons and ideals they had grown up with assisted them along the way. They were old-fashioned men who nonetheless became modernizing leaders, establishmentarians who helped pave the way for a postestablishment world.

If the members of the liberal establishment successfully influenced the shape of the modern world, however, they lost the political battle against the hard right, and the loss of public trust in government and the elite after Vietnam played a role. So, too, did their failure to reach the broad American middle, whether defined in terms of class or of outlook. Although they tried to act in the best interests of the country as a whole, the leaders in Brewster's circle often proved to be dividers more than uniters.

Former attorney general Nicholas Katzenbach felt that Brewster and his peers "were the successor generation to the Wise Men, and were cut from much the same cloth. I think they probably achieved more than their predecessors," since the Wise Men had dealt only with foreign policy, while "the big domestic problems of the 1960s were in many ways harder than the foreign policy problems. I'm not sure that anyone really understood them."[24] But in domestic as in foreign affairs, the liberal elite in the 1960s raised expectations of progress that proved impossible to satisfy, and underestimated the resentments that they provoked. "The truth is, of course," Elliot Richardson wrote with calm assurance in 1967, "that there remains little philosophical disagreement between the major parties on the old issue of governmental responsibility for the general welfare." All responsible individuals, he continued, knew that "those significant problems which still persist—problems such as crime, juvenile delinquency, structural unemployment, racial discrimination, and the urban ghetto—will yield to massive applications of techniques and resources we already know how to use."[25]

Reality proved thornier and more intractable than anticipated. By 1973, a sadder and wiser Richardson called on his fellow Americans to "recognize, as we have with both foreign affairs and natural resources, that resources we once thought were boundless—human, financial, and intellectual resources—are indeed severely limited."[26] By that time, the bipartisan political consensus on which the liberal establishment depended had broken against the rock of late-1960s turmoil. A backlash against the elite and its assumptions gave rise to a bitter, anti-intellectual, populist form of conservatism that shattered the old New Deal coalition and constrained the ambitions of the liberal establishment. The social problems with which Brewster and his circle struggled had not disappeared, but the national will to deal with them had.

The journalist T. H. White, in writing about the "action intellectuals" of the 1960s, concluded his mostly admiring account with a cautionary quotation from the Athenian historian Thucydides. "It was," he warned, "frequently a misfortune to have very brilliant men in charge of affairs; they expect too much of ordinary men."[27] Brewster and his circle were set apart from the mass not just by their intellect and sophistication but by the freedom and independence that came from their deep American ancestry, comfortable financial status, and certainty of their authority. When they were confronted with the challenges of the 1960s, they were able to take a measured view of the upheavals that frightened less-secure individuals. Brewster learned to listen and respond to the concerns of student rebels in the 1960s, while along with the others in his group he came to a new understanding of the needs of previously dispossessed groups. Because the liberal establishment lacked a lived sense of the passions and fears of most ordinary people, however, they overestimated the ability of their fellow citizens to respond in an equally measured way to unsettling new roles for women, racial and ethnic self-assertion, student activism, and the rights revolution. And because they were most at home on an elevated level of debate and discourse, they had difficulty responding to the multitude in a language that most could understand, particularly as the national dialogue coarsened.

Their disconnection from the multitude, and their unwillingness to pander to the lowest denominator, meant that their enemies could portray them as enemies of the common people—the remnants of a decaying WASP aristocracy clinging to power. McGeorge Bundy's combination of breeding, intellect, and arrogance made him a perfect target for both left and right, for those who hated him for his role in Vietnam as well as those who hated his attempts to bring social change. But the other members of Brewster's circle provoked similar resentments. Their deep identification with the nation was perceived as a sense of ownership. Their austere code of personal integrity, faith in process, and public service was a reproach to a swaggering, commercial era in which the new leaders increasingly were brash upstarts from the South and the West.

The country's tectonic shift to the right in the 1980s meant that when the protégés of the liberal establishment came to power during Bill Clinton's administration—people like Strobe Talbott, Gregory Craig, Vernon Jordan, Joseph Lieberman, and Derek Shearer—their ability to bring progressive change was drastically circumscribed. As Elliot Richardson observed in 1997, "Most people don't really get the fact that the Nixon administration was to the left of the Clinton administration. Even the Eisenhower administration was to the left of the Clinton administration."[28]

Left-leaning critics would charge that the country's conservatism in the 1980s and 1990s owed in some measure to the liberal establishment's failure to take a bolder course in the 1960s and 1970s. "The liberal establishment," Bill Coffin laughed in hindsight, "they all fooled themselves. Irwin Miller bankrolled John Lindsay's 1972 presidential campaign. I asked, 'Why'd you do that, Irwin?' He said, 'John Lindsay was the only populist in the race.' I said, 'John Lindsay! If he's a populist, Joe Namath is a virgin.' Irwin looked quite shocked. But that's what they thought; you know, this was as far as you could go."[29] The moderate, incremental approach of men like Brewster was marginalized in the storms of political reaction and counterreaction that have racked the nation since the 1960s.

Coffin was aware that the nation lost something when it no longer had wise and independent leaders like Brewster and Lindsay and the other members of their circle. But he did not feel that their loss justified a return to the quasi-aristocratic system that had produced them. "The virtues of the few," he noted, "did not outweigh the inertia of the many."[30] The passing of the old system was inevitable. As Garry Wills observed, the "Establishment was built up on structures of privilege—the right prep schools and colleges, the right clubs and relatives and law firms, the long experience derived from a semi-monopoly of prestigious positions. These things were not created overnight, and even they had to crumble in a vast sea of social change."[31] Perhaps the most remarkable aspect of the transition was not that the old order passed away but that the change occurred so peacefully. Civil wars have been fought over less.

Brewster and his peers had helped along the process of social change in the 1960s, and in so doing undercut some of the sources of their own authority. As the leaders of universities, foundations, and mainline religious denominations ceased to be important public figures, as the media succumbed to increasing commercialism, as poll-driven expediency replaced political independence, and as special interests displaced the old tradition of public service, Americans found out what it was to live in a society without guardians. Commentators argued over whether the change empowered the everyday citizen or amounted to replacing shepherds with wolves.

American society has always had a way of frustrating the intentions of its guardians. The Massachusetts Bay Colony did not long remain the godly commonwealth envisioned by the Elder Brewster and the other leaders of the *Mayflower.* Many of the Founding Fathers were unsettled and disillusioned by the developments that followed in the wake of the American revolution. While Thomas Jefferson and his fellows had anticipated an enlightened populace led by geniuses and great-souled men, instead they saw the growth of a society characterized by materialism, evangelical religion, sectarianism, anti-intellectualism, and vulgarity. The historian Gordon Wood remarked that the generation that followed the founders was "no longer interested in the revolutionaries' dream of building a classical republic of elitist virtue out of the inherited materials of the Old World." What developed on the new continent was a society dominated by "common people with their common interests in making money and getting ahead."[32] In the long view, it was all but inevitable that Brewster and his peers would end up mostly disregarded by a populace that barely registered their achievements.

The liberal establishment is gone and will not return. Rooted as it was in the dominant position of the Northeast and its upper-class culture, united by a shared ethos and experience, it could not survive the political, social, and cultural changes that followed its moment in the 1960s. Without overlooking the failures of Brewster and his circle, however, it is possible to have a clear-eyed appreciation of their successes and their service. A new generation of leaders may someday measure itself against their example.

NOTES

The following abbreviations and shortened forms are used in the notes.

ARCHIVES AND COLLECTIONS

AFC Papers: America First Committee Papers, Hoover Institution on War, Revolution, and Peace, Stanford, California

Brewster Personal Papers: Kingman Brewster Jr. Personal Papers, Yale University

Brewster Presidential Records: Kingman Brewster Jr. Presidential Records, Yale University

Buckley Papers: William F. Buckley Jr. Papers, Yale University

Bundy Records: Office of the President, Records of McGeorge Bundy, Ford Foundation Archives, Ford Foundation Headquarters, New York City

Conrad Papers: Albert G. Conrad Papers, Yale University

CUOHA: Columbia University Oral History Archives, Butler Library, Columbia University

DeVane Records: Records of the Dean (William Clyde DeVane) of Yale College, Yale University

Ford Foundation Archives: Ford Foundation Archives, Ford Foundation Headquarters, New York City

Griswold Personal Papers: A. Whitney Griswold Personal Papers, Yale University

Griswold Presidential Records: A. Whitney Griswold Presidential Papers, Yale University

LBJ Library: Lyndon B. Johnson Library, University of Texas, Austin

Lindsay Papers: John V. Lindsay Papers, Yale University

Moore Papers: Paul Moore Jr. Papers, property of the Moore family, New York City

Nixon Presidential Materials: Richard M. Nixon Presidential Materials, National Archives, College Park, Maryland

Richardson Papers: Elliot Lee Richardson Papers, Library of Congress

Vance Papers: Cyrus R. Vance and Grace Sloane Papers, Yale University

Williams Papers: John R. Williams Papers, Yale University

PERIODICALS

BG: Boston Globe

NHJC: New Haven Journal-Courier

NHR: New Haven Register

NJ: New Journal
NYHT: New York Herald Tribune
NYT: New York Times
NYTM: New York Times Magazine
WP: Washington Post
YAM: Yale Alumni Magazine
YDN: Yale Daily News

INTERVIEWS

Interviews with an asterisk are part of the McGeorge Bundy Oral History Collection at the John F. Kennedy Library in Boston. With some exceptions, the rest are part of the Griswold-Brewster Oral History Project at the Yale Manuscripts and Archives Library in New Haven.

Alice Acheson: 2 October 1990
David Acheson: 4 October 1990
Edward Adelberg: 5 December 1996
Noël Annan: 5 July 1991
Robert Arnstein: 1 October 1991
Eric Ashby: 19 June 1991
Elisha Atkins: 7 April 1992
Lawrence Baskir: 25 November 2002*
Francis Bator: 19 June 2002*
Peter Bell: 24 January 2001,* 20 November 2002*
Samuel Beers: 15 July 1997
William S. Beinecke: 14 August 1991
G. d'Andelot Belin: 10 April 1992
Daniel Bell: 7 February 1996
Robert Berliner: 30 March 1992
Susan Berresford: 9 July 2002*
Richard Besse: 10 December 1991
Brewster Bingham: 5 September 1994
Richard Bissell Jr.: 19 April 1991
Boris Bittker: 19 March 1992
John Blum: 18 March 1991, 11 February 1992, 4 March 1992, 28 April 1992
Charles Bockelman: 20 April 1992
Edgar Buell: 29 October 1991, 5 November 1991
Derek Bok: 19 November 1996
Mary Louise Brewster: 27 November 1994
Richard Broadhead: 18 March 2000
D. Allan Bromley: 27 May 1992
Cleanth Brooks: 1 November 1991
Harvey Brooks: 22 October 1991
Peter Brooks: 5 August 1992
Ralph S. Brown: 30 April 1992
Robert Brustein: 24 October 1991, 12 November 1991
William F. Buckley Jr.: 25 March 1991
Andrew Bundy: 23 May 2002*
Mary Bundy: 26 September 2001*
McGeorge Bundy: 29 April 1991, 22 May 1991

Stephen Bundy: 5 September 2001*
William P. Bundy: 11 May 1991, 24 April 1992
Joseph A. Califano Jr.: 16 January 2003
Robert Campbell: 22 June 2000
Wallace Campbell III: 5 December 1991
Beekman Cannon: 18 March 1992
Alfred Chandler: 25 June 1997
Melville Chapin: 13 April 1992
Henry Chauncey Jr.: 20 March 1992, 13 July 1993, 22 July 1993
Lincoln Chen: 6 February 2003*
Elias Clark: 5 March 1992, 11 March 1992
R. Inslee Clark Jr.: 5 April 1993, 13 May 1993
William Sloane Coffin Jr.: 9 December 1991, 26 June 2000
Stephen B. Cohen: 5 August 2003
Richard N. Cooper: 13 November 1991, 8 April 1992
Archibald Cox: 13 November 1991
William C. Coughlan: 6 October 1990
Gregory Craig: 9 April 1991, 13 April 2001
A. Dwight Culler: 29 April 1992
W. Jack Cunningham: 6 July 1992
Lloyd Cutler: 9 April 1991
Robert Dahl: 19 November 1991, 9 March 1992
Gibson Danes: 4 May 1992
Worth David: 22 June 1992, 27 July 1992
Peter De Janosi: 8 November 2002*
Donna Diers: 29 June 2001
J. Richardson Dilworth: 26 March 1991, 10 May 1991
William Doering: 5 September 1991
Leonard Doob: 6 November 1990, 9 November 1990
Arthur Ebbert: 14 April 1992
John Ecklund: 8 June 1992, 16 June 1992
Alvin Eisenman: 4 August 1992
James R. Ellis: 27 February 2001*
John Embersits: 15 June 1992
Kai Erikson: 9 March 1992
Jonathan Fanton: 17 April 1992, 18 July 1993
William Farley: 16 December 1991
James Fesler: 11 September 1990
Alfred Fitt: 10 April 1991, 27 May 1992
Roger Fisher: 25 October 1990
Joel Fleishman: 17 May 2002
Charles Forman: 1 May 1992
Joseph Fruton: 1 August 1991, 20 August 1991
Arthur Galston: 22 April 1992, 30 April 1992, 12 May 1992
David Gergen: 23 April 1998
T. Keith Glennan: 2 January 1991
Robert Goheen: 26 March 1991
Hanna Gray: 17 December 1991
Thomas Greene: 13 December 1999
Erwin Griswold: 10 April 1991

Mary Griswold: 18 April 1990, 25 April 1990, 4 December 1991, 4 April 1992
John Whitney Hall: 3 June 1991
Ralph Halsey Jr.: 21 April 1992
David Hamburg: 9 May 2001*
Caryl Haskins: 5 October 1990
J. Bryan Hehir: 5 November 2001*
Nicholas Henderson: 18 July 1999
John Hersey: 13 August 1991
Willard Hertz: 6 November 2002*
Theodore Hesburgh: 16 December 1991, 4 February 2000,* 4 December 2000*
Reuben A. Holden: 1 June 1990, 2 March 1991
William Horowitz: 7 May 1991
Arthur Howe Jr.: 1 April 1991, 18 July 1992
Harold Howe II: 23 October 1990, 22 December 2000,* 14 December 2001*
William Jackson: 10 September 1991
Louis Jaffe: 14 November 1991
Sandy Jaffe: 24 January 2001*
Gary Johnson: 7 January 2000
Vernon Jordan: 9 January 2001*
Donald Kagan: 9 June 1992
Benjamin Kaplan: 15 November 1991, 16 March 1996
Nicholas Katzenbach: 4 June 2003
Milton Katz: 13 August 1990
Carl Kaysen: 11 November 1996, 9–10 May 2002*
Kenneth Keniston: 12 November 1991
Duncan Kennedy: 19 September 1996
Mary Kennedy: 24 October 1991, 14 November 1991, 8 April 1992, 31 July 1992, 10 August
    1997
Roger Kennedy: 8 February 2001*
Alvin Kernan: 11 May 1991
Chester Kerr: 10 July 1990
William Kessen: 2 June 1992
Spencer Klaw: 15 October 1990
Howard Lamar: 28 April 1992, 6 May 1992
Robert Lane: 28 June 1991
Louis Lapham: 13 April 1998
Robert A. Lawrence: 6 April 1992
Richard C. Lee: 5 September 1990, 12 September 1990, 19 November 1990, 18 November 1991
Edward Levi: 19 December 1991
Anthony Lewis: 6 October 1998
Theodore Lidz: 15 May 1992
Joseph Lieberman: 7 July 1992
Lance Liebman: 22 January 1999
Charles Edward Lindblom: 3 June 1991
John Lindsay: 12 March 1992
Leon Lipson: 28 July 1992
Maynard Mack: 16 October 1990, 20 February 1991, 13 July 1992
Richard Magat: 20 July 2001*
Burke Marshall: 27 April 1992
William McChesney Martin: 6 October 1990

Louis Martz: 2 October 1991, 29 October 1991
Georges May: 19 March 1991, 20 February 1992, 16 March 1992, 22 April 1992
Myres McDougal: 31 January 1991
Robert S. McNamara: 5 July 2001*
Paul Mellon: 12 May 1990
Tom Mendenhall: 7 August 1990, 14 August 1991
Cord Meyer: 10 March 1995
John Perry Miller: 19 September 1990, 26 April 1991
J. Irwin Miller: 18 December 1991, 17 February 2001*
Spencer Miller: 21 April 1992
Jonathan Moore: 2 December 2002
Elting Morison: 26 August 1991
Edmund Morgan: 21 March 1991
Paul Moore Jr.: 15 January 2000, 5 February 2002
Paul Mott Jr.: 15 August 1997
Siobahn Nicolau: 9 February 2001*
Frank Norall: 14 June 1991, 20 June 1991
Luther Noss: 2 July 1992
Alvin Novick: 17 December 1999
Merton Joseph Peck: 11 February 1997
Jim Perkins: 20 May 1992
Charles Phillips: 12 June 1997
Lawrence Pickett: 10 December 1991
George Pierson: 24 May 1990, 4 April 1991, 22 April 1991, 14 July 1992
Louis Pollak: 18 May 1992
John Pope: 23 April 1991
Stanley Resor: 30 May 1999
Lloyd Reynolds: 2 October 1990
Frederic M. Richards: 11 December 1996
Elliot Richardson: 22 June 1997
David Riesman: 15 August 1997
S. Dillon Ripley: 4 January 1991
Marshall Robinson: 31 December 2001
Edna Rostow: 3 January 1991
Eugene Rostow: 21 November 1990
Harry Rudin: 2 November 1990
Terry Saario: 28 October 2002*
Jack Sandweiss: 1 May 1992
John Sawyer: 12 August 1991
Arthur Schlesinger Jr.: 8 July 2002*
Kurt Schmoke: 22 May 1992
Enid Curtis Bok Schoettle: 4 November 2002*
George Schrader: 9 December 1991
William Scranton: 16 July 1992
Vincent Scully: 6 May 1991
Raymond Seitz: 12 July 1999
Richard Sewall: 13 February 1991
John Simon: 22 June 1992
William Simpich: 22 June 1997
Albert Sloman: 21 June 1991

Gaddis Smith: 18 March 1991, 28 July 1992
John Smith: 21 July 1992
Aviam Soifer: 6 September 1991
Peter Solbert: 25 February 1992
Arthur Solomon: 6 February 1997
J. William Stack Jr.: 3 August 1992
Edward Streator: 20 June 1991, 25 July 1999
Zeph Stewart: 26 November 1991
Stuart Sucherman: 23 October 2001*
Robert Douglas Stuart Jr.: 6 March 1995
Clyde Summers: 19 May 1992
Francis X. Sutton: 12 February 2001*
Strobe Talbott: 11 April 1991
Charles H. Taylor: 2 March 1992, 12 May 1992
Frank Thistlethwaite: 11 June 1991, 22 June 1991
Frank Thomas: 7 June 2002*
Jim Thomson: 13 August 1990, 27 October 1990
Catherine Tilson: 12 March 1991
James Tobin: 20 March 1991, 19 March 1992
Donald Trautman: 24 October 1990
John Trinkaus: 27 April 1992
Amy Vance: 28 February 2002
Cyrus Vance: 19 August 1993
Florence Wald: 8 June 1992
Patricia Wald: 31 July 2001*
Charles A. Walker: 29 April 1992
F. Champion Ward: 3 October 2001*
John H. Ware Jr.: 1 June 1991
Elga Wasserman: 7 May 1992
Peter Wegener: 20 July 1992
Paul Weiss: 28 May 1992
H. Brad Westerfield: 28 October 1991
Harold B. Whiteman: 22 March 1991, 2 May 1991
Amos Wilder: 23 October 1990
John Wilkinson: 19 May 1992
Frank O. H. Williams: 24 September 1990, 11 October 1991
Norman Winik: 15 September 1990
Mary Wolff: 9 April 1992
C. Vann Woodward: 5 November 1991
Mark Zanger: 7 April 1992
George Zeidenstein: 13 August 2001*
Felix Zweig: 6 November 1991

INTRODUCTION

1. Jeff Greenfield, *No Peace, No Place: Excavations along the Generational Fault* (Garden City, N.Y.: Doubleday, 1973), p. 212.
2. Kingman Brewster Jr., Statement at the Yale College Faculty Meeting, 23 Apr. 1970. Brewster Personal Papers I-21:4.
3. Interview with William Bundy, 24 Apr. 1992.

4. "Transcript of President's Address to the Nation on Military Action in Cambodia," *NYT,* 1 May 1970, p. 2.

5. James Nuzzo, interview with Kingman Brewster Jr. [nd (1974)]. Brewster Personal Papers I-45:4.

6. Interview with Jonathan Fanton, 17 Apr. 1992.

7. Quoted in Rupert Cornwell, "Elliot Richardson," *Independent,* 3 Jan. 2000.

8. McGeorge Bundy, "One Day Before," *Yale Alumni Magazine,* June 1970, p. 26.

9. Paul Moore Jr., *Presences: A Bishop's Life in the City* (New York: Farrar, Straus and Giroux, 1997), p. 210.

10. Otto Kerner et al., *Report of the National Advisory Commission on Civil Disorders* (New York: Bantam Books, 1968), p. 1.

11. Spiro Agnew, Address to the American Retail Federation, 4 May 1970. In John R. Coyne Jr., *The Impudent Snobs: Agnew vs. the Intellectual Establishment* (New Rochelle, N.Y.: Arlington House, 1972), p. 324.

12. James Nuzzo, interview with Kingman Brewster Jr. [nd (1974)]. Brewster Personal Papers I-45:4.

13. Interview with Jonathan Fanton, 17 Apr. 1992.

14. James Nuzzo, interview with Kingman Brewster Jr. [nd (1974)]. Brewster Personal Papers I-45:4.

15. Brewster, Yale University Inaugural Address, 11 Apr. 1964. Brewster Personal Papers I-2:5.

16. Plato, *The Republic* (trans. Richard W. Sterling and William C. Scott) (New York: W. W. Norton, 1985), Book III 415c (p. 113).

17. William F. Buckley Jr., "Capitulation of Kingman Brewster," *New York Journal-American,* 1 May 1970.

I : ORIGINS

1. Deed of Gift of Prince of Wales Cup, 1 Aug. 1931. Brewster Personal Papers II-1, "Vineyard Haven Yacht Club."

2. Brewster, "Autobiographical Data for Dean Halfdan Gregersen," 18 July 1941. Brewster Personal Papers II-72, "United World College."

3. Kingman Brewster Jr. to Lawrence Henry Gipson, 11 Apr. 1968. Brewster Presidential Records RU 11 I-24:4.

4. Interview with John Blum, 11 Feb. 1992.

5. James Rice, J. H. Bisbee, and Charles Kingman Brewster, *History of the Town of Worthington, from Its First Settlement to 1874* (Springfield, Mass.: Clark W. Bryan, 1874), p. 23.

6. "Charles Kingman Brewster," *Berkshire Eagle,* [July] 1908. Source courtesy of Mary Kennedy.

7. Brewster, Address to the Eastern Fairfield County Yale Alumni Association, 5 Feb. 1970. Brewster Personal Papers I-20:1.

8. Entry for Lyman W. Besse, *National Cyclopedia of American Biography,* v. 41 (New York: James T. White, 1956), pp. 284–85.

9. Interview with Mary Kennedy, 24 Oct. 1991; interview with Richard Besse, 10 Dec. 1991.

10. Interview with Mary Kennedy, 24 Oct. 1991.

11. Interview with Mary Kennedy, 14 Nov. 1991.

12. Brewster, "Excerpt from an Uncompleted Book," in *Kingman Brewster: Remembrances* (New Haven: Yale University, 1997), pp. 75–76.

13. Interview with Henry Chauncey Jr., 13 July 1993.

14. Interview with John Blum, 11 Feb. 1992.

15. Brewster, Yale Baccalaureate Address, 8 June 1969. Brewster Personal Papers I-16:12.

16. Interview with Mary Kennedy, 24 Oct. 1991.

17. Florence Besse Ballantine, "Personal Creed" [nd]. Brewster Personal Papers II-76.

18. John Bainbridge, "Our Far-Flung Correspondents: Excellency," *New Yorker* 12 Dec. 1977, p. 142.

19. Brewster, "Autobiographical Data for Dean Halfdan Gregersen," 18 July 1941. Brewster Personal Papers II-72, "United World College."

20. *Ibid.*

21. Entry for Arthur Besse, *Dictionary of American Biography*, Supp. 5 1951–55 (New York: Charles Scribner's Sons, 1977), pp. 54-55; entry for Arthur Besse, *National Cyclopedia of American Biography*, v. 39 (New York: James T. White, 1954), p. 509.

22. Interview with Richard Besse, 10 Dec. 1991.

23. "L. W. Besse Left $4,544,996 Estate," *NYT*, 16 Aug. 1930, p. 22.

24. Brewster, "Excerpt from an Uncompleted Book," p. 76.

25. Brewster, Address at the Yale National Alumni Meeting, Chicago, 10 May 1969. Brewster Personal Papers I-16:1.

26. Brewster, Address at the Yale Regional Alumni Meeting, Boston, 13 Feb. 1975. Brewster Personal Papers I-36:1.

27. Brewster, Address at the Yale National Alumni Meeting, Seattle, 15 Mar. 1970. Brewster Personal Papers I-20:9.

28. Brewster, Address at the Yale National Alumni Meeting, Pittsburgh, 22 Jan. 1966. Brewster Personal Papers I-6:12.

29. Evan Thomas, "The Once and Future Kingman Brewster" (unpublished article, 1 Sep. 1977), p. 10. Source courtesy of Mary Louise Brewster. Brewster Sr.'s major works were *Federal Tax Appeals* (1927), *Outline of the New Deal* (1934), *Distraint under the Federal Revenue Laws* (1934), and *Excise Profits Tax* (1940).

30. Interview with Mary Kennedy, 10 Aug. 1997.

31. "Report to the Sioux Nation, from the Attorneys for the Sioux Nation," 30 Sep. 1932. Brewster Presidential Records RU 11 I-124:1.

32. Interview with Mary Kennedy, 24 Oct. 1991.

33. "Universities: Anxiety behind the Façade," *Time,* 23 June 1967, p. 80.

34. Kingman Brewster Jr. to Sisson [nd]. Brewster Personal Papers II-1, "KB's Typed Originals."

35. Brewster, Amherst College Commencement Address, 2 June 1967. Brewster Personal Papers I-9:3.

36. FBI report on Kingman Brewster, 15 May 1942. FBI FOI file 65-30981, "Kingman Brewster, Sr."

37. Lothrop Stoddard, *The Revolt against Civilization: The Menace of the Under-Man* (London: Chapman & Hall, 1922), p. 226.

38. Interview with Mary Kennedy, 10 Aug. 1997.

39. Interview with Mary Louise Brewster, 27 Nov. 1994.

40. Interview with Mary Kennedy, 14 Nov. 1991.

41. Interview with Mary Kennedy, 24 Oct. 1991.

42. Celia Goodhart, interview with Kingman Brewster Jr., 1986. Source courtesy of Mary Louise Brewster.

43. Brewster, "Excerpt from an Uncompleted Book," pp. 75–76.

44. Kai Erikson, "Reflections," in *Kingman Brewster: Remembrances,* p. 65.

45. Brewster, "Excerpt from an Uncompleted Book," p. 75.

46. Interview with Mary Louise Brewster, 27 Nov. 1994.

47. Roger F. Duncan, *The Story of the Belmont Hill School 1923–1983* (Boston: Howard Kirshen, 1985), pp. 2–12.

48. "Universities: Anxiety behind the Façade," p. 80.

49. "President Brewster," *New Yorker* 11 Jan. 1964, p. 23.

50. Brewster, address at the fiftieth anniversary of the Belmont Hill School, 19 May 1973. Brewster Personal Papers I-32:1.

51. "Universities: Anxiety behind the Façade," p. 80.

52. Interview with William Bundy, 10 May 1991.

53. Thomas, "The Once and Future Kingman Brewster," p. 11.

54. *The Panel*, 18 May 1972, p. 2. Brewster Personal Papers I-32:1.

55. Thomas, "The Once and Future Kingman Brewster," p. 11.

56. Brewster, "The Deeper Unrest," Address at Ford Hall Forum, 6 Dec. 1970. Brewster Personal Papers I-25:2.

57. "The Marketplace of Ideas," *Boston Herald Traveler* 22 Sep. 1969, p. 12.

58. "President Brewster," p. 23.

59. Brewster, "The Deeper Unrest."

60. Thomas, "The Once and Future Kingman Brewster," p. 14.

61. Interview with Mary Kennedy, 24 Oct. 1991.

62. Claude Moore Fuess, *Stanley King of Amherst* (New York: Columbia University Press, 1955), pp. 153-55.

63. Thomas, "The Once and Future Kingman Brewster," p. 10.

64. "President Brewster," p. 23.

65. Brewster, "Autobiographical Data for Dean Halfdan Gregersen," 18 July 1941. Brewster Personal Papers II-72, "United World College."

66. See Richard Lowitt, *George W. Norris: The Making of a Progressive, 1861–1912* (Syracuse, N.Y.: Syracuse University Press, 1963); Lowitt, *George W. Norris: The Triumph of a Progressive, 1933–1944* (Urbana, Ill.: University of Illinois Press, 1971); Richard L. Neuberger and Stephen B. Kahn, *Integrity: The Life of George W. Norris* (New York: Vanguard Press, 1937); George W. Norris, *Fighting Liberal* (New York: Macmillan, 1945).

67. Brewster, "Excerpt from an Uncompleted Book," pp. 76–77.

68. Quoted in Neuberger and Kahn, *Integrity*, p. 317.

69. See Edson Blair, "Presidential Possibilities: Steiwer," *Barron's* 25 May 1936, p. 12; *Martindale and Hubble* listing for Brewster & Steiwer, 1938.

70. Congress at that time also included 8 Progressives and 7 Farmer-Laborites, in addition to 409 Democrats and 106 Republicans.

71. Brewster, "Excerpt from an Uncompleted Book," p. 77.

72. Brewster, Yale Baccalaureate Address, 14 June 1964. Brewster Personal Papers I-2:16.

73. Celia Goodhart, interview with Kingman Brewster Jr., 1986.

74. Bainbridge, "Our Far-Flung Correspondents," p. 142.

75. Interview with Mary Kennedy, 14 Nov. 1991.

76. Celia Goodhart, interview with Kingman Brewster Jr., 1986.

77. Brewster, Yale Baccalaureate Address, 8 June 1969. Brewster Personal Papers I-16:12.

78. Brewster, "Autobiographical Data for Dean Halfdan Gregersen," 18 July 1941. Brewster Personal Papers II-72, "United World College."

79. Mitchel Levitas, "Present and Future of Kingman Brewster," *NYTM*, 12 Feb. 1967, p. 75.

80. Quoted in Duncan, *The Story of the Belmont Hill School 1923–1983*, p. 49.

81. Interview with Mary Kennedy, 24 Oct. 1991; Brewster, "Autobiographical Data for Dean Halfdan Gregersen," 18 July 1941. Brewster Personal Papers, II-72, "United World College."

82. Interview with John H. Ware Jr., 1 June 1991.

83. Interview with Elliot Richardson, 22 June 1997.

84. Elliot Richardson, foreword to Ken Gormley, *Archibald Cox: Conscience of a Nation* (Reading, Mass.: Addison-Wesley, 1997), p. xii.

85. E. Digby Baltzell, *The Protestant Establishment: Aristocracy and Caste in America* (New Haven: Yale University Press, 1964), pp. 116–20.

86. Kai Bird, *The Color of Truth: McGeorge Bundy and William Bundy: Brothers in Arms* (New York: Simon & Schuster, 1998), p. 39.

87. *Ibid.*, p. 31.

88. Interview with McGeorge Bundy, 29 Apr. 1991.

89. Interview with Mary Bundy, 26 Sep. 2001.

90. Interview with Elliot Richardson, 22 June 1997.

91. Juan Cameron, "A Boston Brahmin in 'Heartbreak House,'" *Fortune,* Oct. 1971, p. 162.

92. Interview with Amy Vance, 28 Feb. 2002.

93. Lloyd Shearer, "Cyrus Vance: The Nation's No. 1 Troubleshooter," *Parade,* 23 June 1968, p. 5.

94. Bird, *The Color of Truth,* p. 36.

95. Interview with Stephen Bundy, 5 Sep. 2001.

96. Dorothy McCardle, "The Making of a Manager," *WP,* 3 Jan. 1971, p. F1; interview with Elliot Richardson, 22 June 1997.

97. As related to William F. Buckley Jr. Quoted in John Judis, *William F. Buckley, Jr.: Patron Saint of the Conservatives* (New York: Simon & Schuster, 1988), p. 27. The quotation is without attribution in the book, but the source is clearly McGeorge Bundy; see John Judis to Buckley, 19 Sep. 1983. Buckley Papers III-I:42.

98. Interview with Elliot Richardson, 22 June 1997.

99. Paul Moore Jr., *Presences: A Bishop's Life in the City* (New York: Farrar, Straus and Giroux, 1997), p. 27.

100. McGeorge Bundy, "They Say in the Colleges . . . ," in *Zero Hour: A Summons to the Free* (New York: Farrar and Rinehart, 1940), p. 88.

101. Richard Hofstadter, *The Age of Reform: From Bryan to F.D.R.* (New York: Vintage, 1955), p. 139.

102. Christopher Lydon, "Richardson and Justice," *NYTM,* 20 May 1973, p. 97; Henry L. Shattuck, *Some Experiences of My Political Life* (Portland, Me.: Athansen Press, 1952).

103. Interview with Elliot Richardson, 22 June 1997.

104. John T. Galvin, *The Gentleman Mr. Shattuck: A Biography of Henry Lee Shattuck* (Boston: Tontine Press, 1997).

105. David Reich, "Profile: Elliot Richardson—a Late Encounter with Mr. Clean," *World,* Jan.–Feb. 1997, p. 22.

106. Lydon, "Richardson and Justice," p. 97.

107. Richardson to Henry Shattuck, 23 July 1967. Richardson Papers I:46, "Family—Shattuck, Henry L.—1924–68."

108. David Halberstam, *The Best and the Brightest* (New York: Random House, 1972), p. 49.

109. William H. Harbaugh, *Lawyer's Lawyer: The Life of John W. Davis* (New York: Oxford University Press, 1973), pp. 389–90.

110. Dwight Macdonald, "The Defense of Everybody—I," *New Yorker,* 11 July 1953, p. 54.

111. Dwight Macdonald, "The Defense of Everybody—II," *New Yorker,* 18 July 1953, p. 32.

112. *Ibid.*, p. 46.

113. *Ibid.*, p. 31.

114. Brewster, honorary degree citations. *YAM,* July 1969, p. 16.

115. Peggy Lamson, *Roger Baldwin, Founder of the American Civil Liberties Union: A Portrait* (Boston: Houghton Mifflin, 1976), p. 125. Emphasis in the original.

116. *Ibid.,* p. 192.

117. John P. Marquand, *The Late George Apley* (Boston: Little, Brown, 1937), p. 150.

2 : BRIGHT COLLEGE YEARS

1. McGeorge Bundy, "The Yale Spirit," *YDN*, 23 Feb. 1938, p. 2.

2. "Seymour Acclaimed at Mammoth Rally in His Initial Appearance as President," *YDN*, 30 Sep. 1937, p. 1.

3. Owen Johnson, *Stover at Yale* (Boston: Little, Brown, 1912), p. 8.

4. Interview with Mary Kennedy, 24 Oct. 1991.

5. Johnson, *Stover at Yale,* pp. 2, 13.

6. *Ibid.* p. 10.

7. F. Scott Fitzgerald, *This Side of Paradise* (New York: Charles Scribner's Sons, 1920), p. 33.

8. Douglass Campbell, "Freshman Year," in *History of the Yale College Class of 1941* (New Haven: Yale University, 1941), p. 212.

9. "Thy Brother's Keeper," *YDN*, 27 Sep. 1940, p. 4.

10. See, for example, George Santayana, *The Genteel Tradition at Bay* (1931; Cambridge, Mass.: Harvard University Press, 1967).

11. E. Digby Baltzell, *The Protestant Establishment: Aristocracy and Caste in America* (New Haven, Yale University Press, 1964), chapter 5.

12. J. W. B., Letter to *YDN*, 6 March 1940, p. 4.

13. Roger Starr, "John V. Lindsay: A Political Portrait," *Commentary*, Feb. 1970, p. 27. My thanks to Jim Sleeper for bringing this source to my attention.

14. Quoted in Jim Sleeper, "Alan Dershowitz's Chutzpah: The Making of a 'Race Man,'" *Reconstruction* 1:4 (1992), p. 86. I owe this quote, too, to Jim Sleeper.

15. George Wilson Pierson, *Yale: The University College 1921–1937* (New Haven: Yale University, 1955), p. 489.

16. "Educational Provincialism," *Harvard Alumni Bulletin*, 12 Feb. 1937, p. 601; "President Conant's Annual Report," *Harvard Alumni Bulletin*, 28 Jan. 1938, p. 473.

17. Nicholas Lemann, *The Big Test: The Secret History of the American Meritocracy* (New York: Farrar, Straus and Giroux, 1999), p. 39.

18. "The Steady Hand," *Time*, 11 June 1951, p. 75.

19. William Benton, "Start a Business, Young Man," 10 Apr. 1941. AFC Papers, box 58, "William Benton."

20. Griswold wrote that "I think it [the Political Union] will be serving well the cause of sending college men into politics and of ballasting the academic study of government with stimulating practical contacts." A. Whitney Griswold to Thomas Swan, 6 Jan. 1937. See correspondence from Griswold and Dean Acheson to Thomas Swan, Jan. 1937 and Apr. 1937, in Brewster Presidential Records RU 11 I-233:16.

21. Kirby Simon, interview with Kingman Brewster Jr., 1985. Source courtesy of John G. Simon.

22. Interview with McGeorge Bundy, 29 Apr. 1991.

23. Kingman Brewster Jr., Address to the Yale Club of Boston, 22 Apr. 1964. Brewster Personal Papers I-2:7.

24. Mitchel Levitas, "Present and Future of Kingman Brewster," *NYTM*, 12 Feb. 1967, p. 76; "Abolish the Dean's List?" *YDN*, 16 Jan. 1940, p. 2.

25. Brewster, Autobiographical Data for Dean Halfdan Gregersen, 18 July 1941. Brewster Personal Papers II-72, "United World College."
26. Interview with William E. Jackson, 10 Sep. 1991.
27. Interview with Robert Arnstein, 1 Oct. 1991; interview with William E. Jackson, 10 Sep. 1991.
28. Interview with William E. Jackson, 10 Sep. 1991.
29. Evan Thomas, "The Once and Future Kingman Brewster" (unpublished paper, 1 Sep. 1977), p. 12. Source courtesy of Mary Louise Brewster.
30. William E. Jackson, "Valentines Indiscriminately Bestowed," *YDN*, 13 Feb. 1940, p. 2.
31. Interview with Wallace Campbell III, 5 Dec. 1991.
32. Interview with Mary Griswold, 4 Dec. 1990.
33. Campbell, "Freshman Year," p. 213.
34. Interview with McGeorge Bundy, 29 Apr. 1991.
35. McGeorge Bundy, "Visions & Revisions," *YDN*, 26 Jan. 1938, p. 2.
36. "Richardson's Driving Record Holds Up Senate Approval," *Berkshire Eagle*, 16 Jan. 1969.
37. Paul Moore Jr., *Presences: A Bishop's Life in the City* (New York: Farrar, Straus and Giroux, 1997), p. 43.
38. *Ibid*, p. 207.
39. *Ibid.*, p. 16.
40. *Ibid.*, p. 51.
41. Paul Moore Jr., "A Touch of Laughter," in Diana Dubois (ed.), *My Harvard, My Yale* (New York: Random House, 1982), p. 202.
42. Leslie H. Gelb, "A Skilled and Realistic Negotiator," *NYT*, 4 Dec. 1976.
43. Interview with Amy Vance, 28 Feb. 2002.
44. Pierson, *Yale: The University College 1921–1937*, p. 423.
45. Albert G. Conrad, "As It Was" (unpublished memoir, ca. 1979), pp. 215–17. Conrad Papers, box 1.
46. Interview with H. Bradford Westerfield, 28 Oct. 1991.
47. Brewster, Autobiographical Data for Dean Halfdan Gregersen, 18 July 1941. Brewster Personal Papers II- 72, "United World College."
48. Interview with McGeorge Bundy, 29 Apr. 1991.
49. McGeorge Bundy, "Visions and Revisions," *YDN*, 18 Mar. 1938, p. 2.
50. DeLaney Kiphuth, Remarks at Parents' Day Assembly, Yale University, 17 Oct. 1970. Brewster Personal Papers I-24:4.
51. George Wilson Pierson, *A Yale Book of Numbers: Historical Statistics of the College and University 1701–1976* (New Haven: Yale University, 1983), pp. 127–29.
52. William E. Jackson, "Wake, Freshmen, Wake!," *YDN*, 23 Sep. 1940, p. 14.
53. "This Place You've Come To," *YDN*, 16 Sep. 1953, p. 2.
54. Arthur M. Borden, in *Yale College Class of 1940, 25-Year Record* (New Haven: Yale University, 1965).
55. Quoted in Jacqueline Van Voris (ed.), *College: A Smith Mosaic* (West Springfield, Mass.: Smith College, 1975), p. 120.
56. "'Esquire' Editor Says Yale Dress Affects Fashions," *YDN*, 6 Oct. 1939, p. 3.
57. "Eight Elis Praised for Dapper Attire," *YDN*, 9 Feb. 1940, p. 1.
58. *Boston Herald*, 14 Mar. 1940.
59. Ernest Earnest, *Academic Procession* (New York: Bobbs-Merrill, 1953), p. 232.
60. A signed poster from the event hangs in the Signet Society.
61. Interview with Elliot Richardson, 22 June 1997.
62. Brewster, "Pre-War Uncertainty," in James C. Thomson (ed.), *75: A Generation in Transition* (New Haven: Yale University, 1953), p. 66.

63. *Ibid.*
64. "Overture," *YDN,* 22 Jan. 1940, p. 2.
65. Quoted in Thomas, "The Once and Future Kingman Brewster," p. 9.
66. William Harlan Hale, "I Can't Afford to Be a Communist," *Harkness Hoot,* May 1933, p. 20.
67. Brewster, "Pre-War Uncertainty," p. 65.
68. William Proxmire, "Blind Man's Bluff," in Diana Dubois (ed.), *My Harvard, My Yale,* pp. 183, 187.
69. Louis Auchincloss, "New Haven for a Film Fan," in Diana Dubois (ed.), *My Harvard, My Yale,* p. 192.
70. Jackson, "Wake, Freshmen, Wake!," p. 14.
71. Newbold Noyes, "Yale and the War," *YDN,* 24 Feb. 1940, p. 1. Noyes was describing the leaders of the anti-interventionist movement at Yale, but his characterization applies broadly to the individuals under discussion.
72. McGeorge Bundy, "Lincoln Day Speeches," *YDN,* 14 Feb. 1938, p. 2.
73. Johnson, *Stover at Yale,* p. 386.
74. "Educational Menus," *YDN,* 29 Feb 1940, p. 2.
75. William E. Jackson, "Words on Education," *YDN,* 2 Mar 1940, p. 2.
76. Quoted in Kai Bird, *The Color of Truth: McGeorge Bundy and William Bundy: Brothers in Arms* (New York: Simon & Schuster, 1998), p. 58.
77. A cursory review of the Harvard and Princeton student newspapers reveals essentially the same preoccupations with tutoring schools, ghost writers, hour tests, gut courses, etc. See also "'Princetonian' Heads Crusade to Rid Tiger Campus of Cramming Schools," *YDN,* 19 Apr. 1940, p. 1; "Cantab Drive on Tutoring Schools Sounds Death Knell for Wolff's," *YDN,* 24 May 1940, p. 1.
78. Interview with Elliot Richardson, 22 June 1997.
79. McGeorge Bundy, Donald Schmechel, and Charles C. Glover to the Yale Economics Department, 24 May 1938. DeVane Records 2:31. Source courtesy of Harold Howe II.
80. McGeorge Bundy to George DeVane, 6 Nov. 1938. DeVane Records 2:31. Source courtesy of Harold Howe II.
81. "Yale and the Whole People," *YDN,* 4 Dec. 1939, p. 2.
82. "Where Unity Counts," *YDN,* 6 Nov. 1940, p. 2.
83. McGeorge Bundy, "Bread and Circuses . . . or Else—II," *YDN,* 12 Oct. 1938, p. 2.
84. "Overture," *YDN,* 22 Jan. 1940, p. 2.
85. Brewster, Remarks at the Yale Forum in Cincinnati, 19 Oct. 1970. Brewster Personal Papers I-24:5.
86. A dissertation dedicated to uncovering evidence of leftist dissent at the university in the 1930s indirectly reveals how little radical activity there was and how little impact the radicals made. See Deborah Sue Elkin, "Labor and the Left: The Limits of Acceptable Dissent at Yale, 1920s to 1950s" (unpublished Ph.D. diss. in History, Yale University, 1995).
87. "Exposé," *YDN,* 25 Jan. 1940, p. 4.
88. Interview with Elliot Richardson, 22 June 1997.
89. "Reform or Revolt?" *YDN,* 5 Mar. 1940, p. 2.
90. Godfrey Hodgson, "Cord Meyer: Superspook," in Philip Agee and Louis Wolf (eds.), *Dirty Work: The CIA in Western Europe* (Secaucus, N.J.: Lyle Stuart, 1978), p. 63.
91. Brewster, "Excerpt from an Uncompleted Book," in *Kingman Brewster: Remembrances* (New Haven: Yale University, 1997), p. 80.
92. Richard M. Weissman, "Our Brave New World," *YDN,* 30 Sep. 1939, p 2.
93. Robert L. Griffiths III, "The Boom for Bartlett: II," *YDN,* 13 Dec. 1939, p. 1.

94. "Paradise Regained," *YDN*, 1 Mar. 1940, p. 4.

95. W. Liscum Borden Jr., "What Every Educator Knows," *YDN*, 23 Feb. 1940, pp. 4–5.

96. Quoted in Dan A. Oren, *Joining the Club: A History of Jews at Yale* (New Haven: Yale University Press, 1982), p. 82.

97. "Why Help the German Refugees?" *YDN*, 14 Dec. 1938, p. 2.

98. McGeorge Bundy, "Visions and Revisions," *YDN* 28 Sep. 1938, p. 6.

99. "Debating," *YDN*, 16 May 1940, p. 4.

100. William E. Jackson, "State of the Union—I," *YDN*, 13 Apr. 1940, p. 2.

101. William E. Jackson, "The Yale Political Union," in *History of the Yale College Class of 1941*, p. 108.

102. Interview with Elliot Richardson, 22 June 1997.

103. Christopher Lydon, "Richardson and Justice," *NYTM*, 20 May 1973, p. 98.

104. Brewster, Commencement Address, Carleton College, 11 June 1970. Brewster Personal Papers I-22:10.

105. McGeorge Bundy, "For the Defense," *Yale Literary Magazine*, Feb. 1939, p. 8.

106. Starr, "John V. Lindsay: A Political Portrait," p. 27.

107. Brewster, Yale Baccalaureate Address, 11 June 1967. Brewster Personal Papers I-9:5.

108. Henry Seidel Canby, *Alma Mater: The Gothic Age of the American College* (New York: Farrar and Rinehart, 1936), pp. 73–74.

109. McGeorge Bundy, "The Senior Societies—I," *YDN*, 6 May 1939, p. 3; William Jackson, "Senior Societies: I—The Yale Angle," *YDN*, 27 Apr. 1940, p. 2.

110. "Finale," *YDN*, 9 May 1940, p. 4.

111. Interview with Harold Howe II, 23 Oct. 1990.

112. Brewster, introduction to *Stover at Yale*, 1968. Brewster Personal Papers I-13:17.

113. "Is the Ivy League Still the Best?" *Newsweek*, 23 Nov. 1964, p. 68.

114. Michele Flynn Stenehjem, *An American First: John T. Flynn and the America First Committee* (New Rochelle, N.Y.: Arlington House, 1976), p. 9.

115. See Laura McEnaney, "He-Men and Christian Mothers: The America First Movement and the Gendered Meanings of Patriotism and Isolationism," *Diplomatic History* 18 (Winter 1994), pp. 47–57.

116. See, for example, Robert Cohen, "Revolt of the Depression Generation: America's First Mass Student Protest Movement, 1929–40" (unpublished Ph.D. diss., University of California at Berkeley, 1987); Robby Cohen, *When the Old Left Was Young: Student Radicals and America's First Mass Student Movement, 1929–1941* (New York: Oxford University Press, 1993); Eileen Eagan, *Class, Culture, and the Classroom: The Student Peace Movement of the 1930s* (Philadelphia: Temple University Press, 1981); and James Wechsler, *Revolt on the Campus* (New York: Covici, Friede, 1935). One may also include, in the list of antiwar campus organizations, the satirical Veterans of Future Wars, founded in the spring of 1936 by Princeton senior Lewis J. Gorin Jr. See "Lewis J. Gorin Jr., Instigator of a 1930's Craze, Dies at 84," *NYT*, 31 Jan. 1999, p. 33.

117. A poll of students before the 1940 presidential election, for example, drew only 5 votes for Earl Browder, compared with 1,457 for Willkie and 592 for Roosevelt. "Traditional Yale Republicanism Gives Willkie Nearly 3–1 Margin in 'News' Poll," *YDN*, 2 Nov. 1940, p. 1.

118. Herbert Winer, quoted in Elkin, "Labor and the Left," p. 489.

119. Brewster, Testimony before the Senate Foreign Relations Committee Hearings on S. 275, Part 2 (Feb. 4–10, 1941) (Washington: Government Printing Office, 1941), p. 613.

120. For example, an October 1939 poll of about 1,500 Yale undergraduates revealed that while 95 percent were "against our entrance into the conflict at this time," 96 percent said that they "would fight in defense of the United States proper," and 77 percent

declared themselves willing to fight "in defense of its possessions." "Huge Majority Votes against Joining War," *YDN*, 4 Oct. 1939, p. 1.

121. Charles Seymour, "War's Impact on the Campus," *NYTM*, 29 Sep. 1940, p. 3.

122. Moore, *Presences*, p. 56.

123. William E. Jackson, "These Perilous Days," *YDN*, 26 Sep. 1939, p. 4.

124. "The Duty to Understand," *YDN*, 2 Oct. 1939, p. 4.

125. Brewster, Testimony before the Senate Foreign Relations Committee Hearings, p. 614.

126. Snowden T. Herrick, "A Truism to Remember: Deflation Follows War," *YDN*, 27 Sep. 1939, p. 1.

127. "Faculty Cooperation Urged," *YDN*, 18 Apr. 1940, p. 2.

128. Brewster, "The Generation of Reappraisal," Latham Blair Memorial Lecture, 1 Aug. 1968. Brewster Personal Papers I-13:3.

129. Interview with Elliot Richardson, 22 June 1997. See also Richard D. Edwards, "Harvard Views the War," *History of the Harvard College Class of 1941* (Cambridge, Mass.: Harvard University, 1941), pp. 252–61.

130. Brewster, "Pre-War Uncertainty," p. 66.

131. McGeorge Bundy, "Visions & Revisions," *YDN*, 14 Nov. 1938, p. 2.

132. McGeorge Bundy, "A Gloss on Our Days," in *Yale College Class of 1940, 25th Reunion Book* (New Haven: Yale University, 1966), p. xi.

133. Ruth Sarles, "A Story of America First" (unpublished manuscript, 1942, on deposit at the Hoover Institution, Stanford, California), p. 41. For descriptions of America First's beginnings and early activities at Yale, see Wayne S. Cole, *America First: The Battle against Intervention 1940–1941* (Madison: University of Wisconsin Press, 1953), esp. pp. 8–16; Justus Doenecke (ed.), *In Danger Undaunted: The Anti-Interventionist Movement of 1940–1941 as Revealed in the Papers of the America First Committee* (Stanford, Calif.: Hoover Institution Press, 1990), esp. pp. 6–40; Sarles, esp. pp. 41–70; and Stenehjem, *An American First,* esp. pp. 13–23.

134. Interview with Richard C. Lee, 19 Nov. 1990.

135. Sarles, "A Story of America First," p. 41.

136. *Ibid.,* p. 43.

137. "Yale Christian Association to Sponsor Appeal for Peace," *YDN* 23 May 1940, p. 1; "Y.C.A. Peace Proposal Nets 1486 Signatures as Whitridge Flays Petition in Open Meeting," *YDN* 25 May 1940, p. 1.

138. "Barbed-Wire, Tank, Phoney Dead Soldier Pop Up as Students Rally against War," *YDN* 27 May 1940, p. 1; Arnold Whitridge, "Where Do You Stand?: An Open Letter to American Undergraduates," *Atlantic Monthly,* Aug. 1940, pp. 133–34.

139. Robert Douglas Stuart Jr. to Kingman Brewster Jr., July 26, 1940, AFC Papers, box 65, untitled folder. Brewster's lack of formal position in the AFC, other than a temporary chairmanship of the Yale chapter, belies his importance in the organization, particularly during its early phase. Brewster resisted Stuart's invitation to join the AFC's national committee; see Brewster to Robert Douglas Stuart Jr., 1 Oct. 1940, AFC Papers, box 66, "Senate Foreign Relations."

140. Thomas Rankin to Robert Douglas Stuart Jr., 9 Sep. 1940, AFC Papers, box 65, untitled folder.

141. Robert Douglas Stuart Jr. to Kingman Brewster, Jr. [nd (July 1940)], AFC Papers, box 65, "Lists of Proposed Committee"; Arthur Ballantine Jr. to Robert Douglas Stuart Jr. [nd (Aug. 1940)], AFC Papers, box 65, untitled folder. Ballantine also suggested Brewster's uncle, Arthur Besse, the head of the National Wool Manufacturer's Association, for the national committee of the still-nameless organization.

142. Quoted in Sarles, "A Story of America First," p. 53.

143. A. Scott Berg, *Lindbergh* (New York: G. P. Putnam's Sons, 1998), p. 413.

144. Kingman Brewster Jr. to J. M. Patterson [nd (1940)], AFC Papers, box 65, "Lists of Proposed Committee."

145. See folder "Moore, Richard A.," AFC Papers, box 64.

146. Brewster, "Pre-War Uncertainty," p. 66.

147. Kingman Brewster Jr. and Spencer Klaw, "We Stand Here," *Atlantic Monthly,* Sep. 1940, p. 277.

148. Brewster, Testimony before the Senate Foreign Relations Committee Hearings, p. 614.

149. William E. Jackson, "Class History," in *History of the Yale College Class of 1941,* p. 316.

150. Brewster, Address to the National Meeting of Yale Alumni, Seattle, 15 Mar. 1970. Brewster Personal Papers I-20:9.

151. Brewster, unpublished speech [nd (1940?)]. Emphasis in the original. Source courtesy of Mary Louise Brewster.

152. Interview with Charles H. Taylor, 12 May 1992.

153. Anne Morrow Lindbergh, *War Within and War Without* (New York: Harcourt Brace Jovanovich, 1980), pp. 193–94. Stanley Flink used part of this quotation in "The Passing of a President," *YAM,* Feb. 1989, p. 32.

154. Berg, *Lindbergh,* p. 412.

155. Brewster, Testimony before the Senate Foreign Relations Committee Hearings, p. 614.

156. Murrow had married Brewster's cousin Janet Huntington Brewster on October 27, 1934. Kingman was one of about twenty-five guests present. See Joseph E. Persico, *Edward R. Murrow: An American Original* (New York: McGraw-Hill, 1988), p. 84. See also Alexander E. Kendrick, *Prime Time: The Life of Edward R. Murrow* (Boston: Little, Brown, 1969), pp. 128–29.

157. Seymour, "War's Impact on the Campus," p. 3.

158. Charles Seymour to Fred T. Murphy, 29 May 1940. Cited in "The Book of Documents, v. I—to 1950" (reference materials to accompany Gaddis Smith's DeVane Lectures 194a, fall 1998), p. 169.

159. "Independence and Responsibility," *YDN,* 30 Sep. 1940, p. 2.

160. Brewster, "Pre-War Uncertainty," p. 66.

161. Paul Fussell, *The Great War and Modern Memory* (New York: Oxford University Press, 1975), p. 21.

162. Doenecke (ed.), *In Danger Undaunted,* p. 5.

163. See esp. Laura Kalman, *Legal Realism at Yale, 1927–1960* (Chapel Hill: University of North Carolina Press, 1986); Morton J. Horwitz, *The Transformation of American Law 1870–1960: The Crisis of Legal Orthodoxy* (New York: Oxford University Press, 1992); and Wilfred E. Rumble Jr., *American Legal Realism: Skepticism, Reform, and the Judicial Process* (Ithaca, N.Y.: Cornell University Press, 1968).

164. Horwitz, *The Transformation of American Law 1870–1960,* p. 169.

165. "Judge Not . . ." *YDN,* 2 Feb. 1940, p. 4.

166. Interview with William Scranton, 16 July 1992.

167. Louis M. Starr, "Hip-Hip Hurrah, Legionnaire!" *YDN,* 1 Dec. 1939, p. 2.

168. "Paradise Regained," *YDN,* 1 Mar. 1940, p. 4. The occasion of this and related editorials was Hutchins's visit to Yale in late February 1940 to address the Phi Beta Kappa banquet. Brewster's editorial of February 27, 1940, had puckishly welcomed Hutchins to campus—in Latin.

169. McGeorge Bundy, "They Say in the Colleges . . ." in *Zero Hour: A Summons to the Free* (New York: Farrar and Rinehart, 1940), pp. 92–3.

170. *Ibid.,* p. 98.

171. *Ibid.,* p. 97.

172. Brewster, "Pre-War Uncertainty," p. 175.

173. Arthur Schlesinger Jr., *A Life in the 20th Century* (Boston: Houghton Mifflin, 2000), p. 241.

174. Interview with Gregory Craig, 9 Apr. 1991.

175. See Doenecke (ed.), *In Danger Undaunted*, pp. 35–37.

176. Brewster to Robert Douglas Stuart Jr. [nd (Apr. 1941)], AFC Papers, box 58, "B—Jan. to Apr. [1941]."

177. Brewster, "Excerpt from an Uncompleted Book," p. 75.

178. *Ibid.,* p. 76.

179. Brewster, "Pre-War Uncertainty," p. 175.

180. Quoted in *ibid.*

181. See, for example, the exchanges between Ed Koch and Patrick Buchanan in the *New York Post* in June 1997.

182. Brewster to Robert Douglas Stuart Jr. [nd (July 1940)]. Quoted in Doenecke (ed.), *In Danger Undaunted*, p. 89.

183. Brewster, "Bosanquet's Philosophy of the State: A Clue to a More Adequate Liberalism" (senior essay in the History, Arts, and Letters major, Yale College, 1941), p. 2. Emphasis in the original. Source courtesy of Mary Louise Brewster.

184. *Ibid.,* p. 1.

185. Brewster, Address at the Yale National Alumni Meeting, Denver, 20 Jan. 1968. Brewster Personal Papers I-11:7.

186. Brewster, to Robert Douglas Stuart Jr. [nd (March? 1941)], AFC Papers, box 58, "B—Jan. to Apr. [1941]."

187. For an example of this supposed contrast, see James Fallows, "What Did You Do in the Class War, Daddy?" *Washington Monthly*, Oct. 1975.

188. Edwards, "Harvard Views the War," pp. 252–53.

189. "Our Real Enemies," *YDN*, 29 Sep. 1939, p. 4.

190. Thomas, "The Once and Future Kingman Brewster"; interview with Jackson, 10 Sep. 1991; Jackson, "Class History," in *History of the Yale College Class of 1941*, p. 316.

191. *Yale Record*, 7 Dec. 1940, p. 21.

192. "Excerpts from Alumni Day Speeches Given in Woolsey and Commons," *YDN*, 22 Feb. 1941, p. 8.

193. Brewster, "Class Oration," in *History of the Yale College Class of 1941*, p. 317.

194. William Bundy, "Class Oration," in *History of the Yale College Class of 1939* (New Haven: Yale University, 1939), p. 192.

3: THE LEADERS OF THE GI GENERATION IN WAR AND PEACE

1. Thomas Rankin to Robert Douglas Stuart Jr., 31 Oct. 1940. AFC Papers box 65, unmarked folder; Jacob K. Javits (with Rafael Steinberg), *Javits: The Autobiography of a Public Man* (Boston: Houghton Mifflin, 1981), pp. 57–58.

2. "Opportunity Knocks," *YDN*, 17 Oct. 1940, p. 4.

3. Interview with McGeorge Bundy, 29 Apr. 1991.

4. Kai Bird, *The Color of Truth: McGeorge Bundy and William Bundy: Brothers in Arms* (New York: Simon & Schuster, 1998), p. 69.

5. Javits, p. 58.

6. Kingman Brewster Jr., "Autobiographical Data for Dean Halfdan Gregersen," 18 July 1941. Brewster Personal Papers II-72, "United World College."

7. Joe Alex Morris, *Nelson Rockefeller: A Biography* (New York: Harper & Brothers, 1960), pp. 150–55; interview with Leonard Doob, 6 Nov. 1990. See also Cary Reich, *The Life of Nelson Rockefeller: Worlds to Conquer, 1908–1958* (New York: Doubleday, 1996).

8. "Opportunity Knocks," *YDN,* 17 Oct. 1940, p. 4.

9. Brewster did comment that the CIAA "was one of those situations where one agency was stumbling over every other, where a bureaucratic mountain was bringing forth a mouse of results." William G. Bardel, "Kingman Brewster: Yale's New Educator," *YDN,* 21 Nov. 1959, p. 2.

10. Interview with Frank Norall, 14 June 1991.

11. Interview with Frank Norall, 20 June 1991.

12. Quoted in Stanley Flink, "The Passing of a President," in *Kingman Brewster: Remembrances* (New Haven: Yale University, 1997), p. 23.

13. See the histories of the Yale College Class of 1905.

14. Edward Tenner, "Environment for Genius?" *Harvard Magazine,* at http://www.harvard-magazine.com/issues/nd98/genius.html

15. Quoted in John T. Galvin, *The Gentleman Mr. Shattuck: A Biography of Henry Lee Shattuck* (Boston: Tontine Press, 1997), p. 295.

16. Interview with Elliot Richardson, 22 June 1997.

17. Paul Moore Jr., *Presences: A Bishop's Life in the City* (New York: Farrar, Straus and Giroux, 1997), pp. 54, 61.

18. Stanley Weintraub, *Long Day's Journey into War* (New York: Dutton–Truman Talley, 1991), pp. 308–9.

19. Interview with Wallace Campbell III, 5 Dec. 1991.

20. Brewster, Address at the Navy League Dinner Honoring Trubee Davison and the Members of the First Yale Unit, 26 Oct. 1966. Brewster Personal Papers I-7:15.

21. See Walter Isaacson and Evan Thomas, *The Wise Men: Six Friends and the World They Made* (New York: Simon & Schuster, 1986), pp. 90–93; Kai Bird, *The Chairman: John J. McCloy: The Making of the American Establishment* (New York: Simon & Schuster, 1992), pp. 40–46.

22. A photo of the unit appears in *YAM,* 20 Mar. 1942.

23. John C. Ripley to Geoffrey Kabaservice, 26 Sep. 1990.

24. Interview with Norman Winik, 15 Sep. 1990; interview with William C. Coughlan, 2 Sep. 1990; Arthur N. Turner to William C. Coughlan, 6 Oct. 1990, source courtesy of Arthur N. Turner; Brewster, Address at the Navy League Dinner, 26 Oct. 1966. Brewster Personal Papers I-7:15.

25. Brewster to A. Whitney Griswold, 9 Sep. 1942. Griswold Personal Papers I-2:23.

26. See Michael Gannon, *Operation Drumbeat: The Dramatic True Story of Germany's First U-Boat Attacks along the American Coast in World War II* (New York: Harper & Row, 1990); and Harald Busch, *U-Boats at War* (New York: Ballantine Books, 1955).

27. Brewster to A. Whitney Griswold and Mary Griswold, 23 Dec. 1942. Griswold Personal Papers I-2:23.

28. McGeorge Bundy, "A Gloss on Our Days," in *Yale College Class of 1940, 25th Reunion Book* (New Haven: Yale University, 1965), p. xiii.

29. Interview with John Blum, 11 Feb. 1992.

30. Brewster to A. Whitney Griswold, 6 Aug. 1944. Griswold Personal Papers I-3:25.

31. Brewster to Charles Ream, 3 Oct. 1963. Brewster Personal Papers II-3, "Personal—Miscellaneous."

32. See the entries for Charles Morgan Perry (p. 316), Wilfrid Lee Simmons (p. 364), William Scott Snead Jr. (p. 318), and George Raymond Waldmann 2nd (p. 249) in

Eugene Kone, *Yale Men Who Died in the Second World War: A Memorial Volume of Biographical Sketches* (New Haven: Yale University Press, 1951).

33. Brewster "Excerpt from an Uncompleted Book," in *Kingman Brewster: Remembrances* (New Haven: Yale University, 1997), p. 77.

34. Interview with William C. Coughlan, 2 Sep. 1990; interview with Norman Winik, 15 Sep. 1990. See also Isaacson and Thomas, *The Wise Men*.

35. E. Digby Baltzell, "The Protestant Establishment Revisited," *American Scholar* 45 (Autumn 1976), pp. 505–6.

36. Brewster, "Excerpt from an Uncompleted Book," p. 77.

37. Mark F. Goldberg, "An Interview with Harold 'Doc' Howe II: 'Stirring the Pot,'" *Phi Delta Kappan,* Oct. 2000, p. 160.

38. Brewster, Speech Notes [1945]. Brewster Personal Papers II-31, "A."

39. Paul Moore Jr., "A Time of Testing," in *Yale College Class of 1941, 50th Reunion Book* (New Haven: Yale University, 1991), p. 12.

40. Moore, *Presences,* p. 56.

41. Interview with Elliot Richardson, 22 June 1997.

42. Elliot Richardson, "The Day Paris Was Liberated," *BG,* 16 Oct. 1966, p. A 16; Richardson memo [nd (Oct.? 1966)], Richardson Papers I:50, "Fourth Infantry Division."

43. Interview with Elliot Richardson, 22 June 1997.

44. Bird, *The Color of Truth,* p. 82.

45. Interview with McGeorge Bundy, 29 Apr. 1991.

46. Theodore H. White, "The Action Intellectuals," *Life,* 9 June 1967, p. 76.

47. Brewster, Speech at the Dublin Conference, Nov. 1945. Brewster Personal Papers II-31, "A."

48. Brewster, to Lyman Besse Burbank [nd (1945)]. Brewster Personal Papers II-31, "I–J."

49. Brewster, Speech at the Dublin Conference, Nov. 1945. Brewster Personal Papers II-31, "A."

50. Brewster to A. Whitney Griswold, 22 Dec. 1943. Griswold Personal Papers I-2:24.

51. Brewster to A. Whitney Griswold, 6 Aug. 1944. Griswold Personal Papers I-2:25.

52. "President Brewster," *New Yorker,* 11 Jan. 1964, p. 23.

53. Mark W. Foster, "Kingman Brewster, Jr.: No Water-Treading," *YDN,* 30 Apr. 1963, p. 4.

54. Brewster, Address to Yale National Alumni Meeting, Pittsburgh, 22 Jan. 1966. Brewster Personal Papers I-6:12.

55. Interview with William Sloane Coffin Jr., 26 June 2000.

56. Moore, *Presences,* p. 85.

57. Paul Moore Jr., "A Time of Testing," p. 12.

58. Nat Hentoff, *A Political Life* (New York: Alfred A. Knopf, 1969), p. 53.

59. *Ibid.,* p. 55.

60. James Fallows, *More Like Us: Making America Great Again* (Boston: Houghton Mifflin, 1989), p. 159. James Patterson notes that an additional 3.5 million returning veterans went to technical schools below college level under the GI Bill, and 700,000 to agricultural instruction on farms. The GI Bill spent $14.5 billion on educational benefits between 1944 and 1956. See Patterson, *Grand Expectations: The United States, 1945–1974* (New York: Oxford University Press, 1996), p. 68.

61. Michael J. Bennett, *When Dreams Came True: The GI Bill and the Making of Modern America* (Washington: Brassey's, 1996), p. 243.

62. "S.R.O.," *Time,* 18 Mar. 1946, p. 75.

63. Quoted in *ibid.*

64. Michael C. C. Adams, *The Best War Ever: America and World War II* (Baltimore: Johns Hopkins University Press, 1994), esp. chapters 6 and 7. Paul Fussell makes similar points about the war's myths of unity in *Wartime: Understanding and Behavior in the Second World War* (New York: Oxford University Press, 1989).

65. Helen Lefkowitz Horowitz, *Campus Life: Academic Cultures from the End of the Eighteenth Century to the Present* (Chicago: University of Chicago Press, 1987), pp. 184–85.

66. Dan A. Oren, *Joining the Club: A History of Jews and Yale* (New Haven: Yale University Press, 1985), p. 162. One may parenthetically observe that the veterans' progressivism did not extend so far as to open up and demystify the society system, as Brewster had advocated before the war.

67. Quoted in Keith W. Olson, *The G.I. Bill, the Veterans and the Colleges* (Louisville, Ky.: University Press of Kentucky, 1974), p. 51.

68. Christopher Jencks and David Riesman, *The Academic Revolution* (Garden City, N.Y.: Doubleday, 1968), p. 280.

69. Interview with John Pope, 23 Apr. 1991.

70. Paul Moore Jr., "Above—Looking Down," in *Yale College Class of 1941, 25th Reunion Book* (New Haven: Yale University, 1966), p. xxii.

71. William Jackson to Kingman Brewster Jr., 25 May 1945. Brewster Personal Papers II-31, "C."

72. McGeorge Bundy to Thomas Erickson, 1942. Letter courtesy of Harold Howe II.

73. Clark's firm was originally Root, Clark, Buckner & Howland; by the time Arthur Ballantine died, in 1960, the firm had mutated into Dewey, Ballantine, Bushby, Palmer & Wood.

74. Brewster, "Grenville Clark: Operator Extraordinary," in Norman Cousins and J. Garry Clifford (eds.), *Memoirs of a Man: Grenville Clark* (New York: W. W. Norton, 1975), pp. 159–60.

75. Elliot Richardson, *The Creative Balance: Government, Politics, and the Individual in America's Third Century* (New York: Holt, Rinehart & Winston, 1976), p. 343.

76. John Bantell, "Grenville Clark and the Founding of the United Nations: The Failure of World Federalism," *Peace and Change* X:3–4 (Fall–Winter 1984), p. 97.

77. Eleanor Fowle, *Cranston* (San Rafael, Calif.: Presidio Press, 1980), p. 81.

78. Lawrence S. Wittner, *Rebels against War: The American Peace Movement, 1941–1960* (New York: Columbia University Press, 1969), p. 113.

79. Quoted in Fowle, *Cranston,* p. 79.

80. Paul Hendrickson, "Behind the Scenes of One CIA Agent's Life," *WP,* 7 Feb. 1978, p. B1.

81. Brewster, Address at the Second Dublin Conference, 2 Oct. 1965. Brewster Personal Papers I-5:11.

82. Cord Meyer Jr., *Peace or Anarchy* (Boston: Little, Brown, 1947), p. 3.

83. Declaration of the Dublin Conference, 16 Oct. 1945. Brewster Presidential Records RU 11 I-85:12.

84. Brewster, "World Aims Held Not Met," *NYT,* 2 Jan. 1946, p. 7.

85. Entry for Gilbert A. Harrison, *Current Biography Yearbook 1949* (New York: H. W. Wilson, 1949), pp. 253–54.

86. American Veterans Committee, "10 Questions and Answers on AVC," Feb. 1946.

87. American Veterans Committee, "Statement of Intentions," 1945.

88. American Veterans Committee, "10 Questions and Answers on AVC," Feb. 1946; "AVC Summarizes Past Projects on Yale Campus," *YDN,* 24 Sep. 1946, p. 1.

89. Entry for Endicott Peabody, *Current Biography Yearbook 1964* (New York: H. W. Wilson, 1964), pp. 342–44.

90. "A.V.C. Plans Public Meeting Shortly," *Harvard Service News*, 25 Jan. 1946, p. 1.
91. American Veterans Committee, "10 Questions and Answers on AVC," Feb. 1946; William Sloane Coffin Jr., letter to *YDN*, 4 May 1948, p. 2.
92. "AVC Not Limited to Students—Bolte," *Harvard Service News*, 12 Feb. 1946, p. 1.
93. Interview with John Blum, 11 Feb. 1992.
94. Edgar J. Driscoll and Brian Mooney. "Endicott Peabody, Former Governor, Dead at 77," *BG*, 3 Dec. 1997, p. A1.
95. "Cambridge Chapter of A.V.C. Chooses Permanent Officers," *Harvard Service News*, 15 Feb. 1946, p. 1.
96. "Student Federalists to Hold Meeting," *YDN*, 27 Sep. 1946, p. 1.
97. Wittner, *Rebels against War*, p. 137.
98. Charles DeBenedetti, *The Peace Reform in American History* (Bloomington: Indiana University Press, 1980), pp. 149–50; "Federalists Plan National Merger," *YDN*, 24 Feb. 1947, p. 1.
99. Cord Meyer Jr., *Facing Reality: From World Federalism to the CIA* (New York: Harper & Row, 1980), p. 45. See also Joseph Preston Baratta, *Strengthening the United Nations: A Bibliography on U.N. Reform and World Federalism* (Westport, Conn.: Greenwood Press, 1987).
100. Dexter Perkins, *The American Approach to Foreign Policy*, rev. ed. (Cambridge, Mass.: Harvard University Press, 1962), p. 113.
101. Brewster, "World Aims Held Not Met," p. 7.
102. See McGeorge Bundy, *Danger and Survival: Choices about the Bomb in the First Fifty Years* (New York: Vintage Books, 1990), pp. 130–96.
103. Bird, *The Color of Truth*, p. 423.
104. Meyer, *Facing Reality*, pp. 51–55.
105. McCarthy's attack on "one-worlders" offered an opportunity for the conservative wing of the Republican Party to attack the party's liberals. The term "one world" had, after all, been popularized by Wendell Willkie's 1943 bestseller of that name.
106. Wittner, p. 222.
107. Meyer, *Facing Reality*, p. 51.
108. Brewster, Notes for an Address at the Harvard Business School, 10 July 1978. Brewster Personal Papers I-50:17.
109. Interview with Roger Fisher, 25 Oct. 1990.
110. Brewster, Notes for a Speech at the Harvard Law School, 10 June 1964. Brewster Presidential Records 11 I-110:1.
111. Interview with Elliot Richardson, 22 June 1997.
112. Interview with Benjamin Kaplan, 16 Mar. 1996.
113. Hugh Calkins to Geoffrey Kabaservice, Nov. 25 1999.
114. Interview with Elliot Richardson, 22 June 1997.
115. Quoted in Thomas Vance, "Elliot Richardson: Man of Principle," available at http://www.trustingov.org/research/books/richardson/chap2htm, accessed 11 Feb. 2002.
116. *Harvard Alumni Bulletin*, 12 Apr. 1947, p. 545; interview with Elliot Richardson, 22 June 1997. See also F. O. Matthiessen, *From the Heart of Europe* (New York: Oxford University Press, 1948), pp. 9–66, and the Salzburg Seminar, "President's Report 1996/97." My thanks to Sir Michael Palliser and Jesse Lee Kabaservice for helping me to obtain this information.
117. Brewster, Notes for an Address at the Harvard Business School, 10 July 1978. Brewster Personal Papers I-50:17.
118. Brewster, American International College Baccalaureate Address, 4 June 1961. Brewster Personal Papers I-1:5.

119. Many histories focus on the transition from crisis to consensus in particular fields. These include Peter Bachrach, *The Theory of Democratic Elitism: A Critique* (Boston: Little, Brown 1967); Alexander Bloom, *Prodigal Sons: The New York Intellectuals and Their World* (New York: Oxford University Press, 1986); Howard Brick, *Daniel Bell and the Decline of Intellectual Radicalism* (Madison: University of Wisconsin Press, 1986); Lewis Coser, *Men of Ideas: A Sociologist's View* (New York: Free Press, 1965); Peter Novick, *That Noble Dream: The "Objectivity Question" and the American Historical Profession* (Cambridge [U.K.]: Cambridge University Press, 1988); Richard Pells, *Radical Visions and American Dreams: Culture and Social Thought in the Depression Years* (New York: Harper & Row, 1973); and Michael Rogin, *The Intellectuals and McCarthy: The Radical Specter* (Cambridge, Mass.: MIT Press, 1967). Godfrey Hodgson analyzed the most prominent works that codified the postwar political and ideological consensus in *America in Our Time* (New York: Vintage Books, 1976).

120. See Michael Ignatieff, *Isaiah Berlin: A Life* (New York: Metropolitan Books, 1998), pp. 197–207.

121. Joseph Kraft, "The Two Worlds of McGeorge Bundy," *Harper's*, Nov. 1965, p. 106.

122. Philip Hamburger, "The Great Judge," *Life*, 4 Nov. 1946, p. 117.

123. Elliot Richardson, memo 16 Jan. 1952. Richardson Papers I:51, "Hand, Learned."

124. Elliot Richardson, *The Creative Balance*, pp. xxvi–xxvii.

125. Elliot Richardson, "He Died, As He Lived, in Kindness," *BG*, 28 Feb. 1965, p. A-2.

126. Seymour R. Linscott, "His Boston Background," *BG*, 23 Feb. 1965.

127. Brewster, "Excerpts from an Uncompleted Book," p. 77.

128. *Ibid.*, p. 87.

129. Brewster, Address at the Yale Law School Sesquicentennial, 25 Apr. 1975. Brewster Personal Papers I-36:10.

130. Brewster, Remarks at the Ceremonies to Celebrate the Deanship of Albert M. Sacks [nd]. Source courtesy of Mary Louise Brewster.

131. Interview with Duncan Kennedy, 19 Sep. 1996.

132. Interviews with Archibald Cox, 13 Nov. 1991; Roger Fisher, 25 Oct. 1990; Erwin Griswold, 10 Apr. 1991; Louis Jaffe, 14 Nov. 1991; Benjamin Kaplan, 15 Nov. 1991 and 16 Mar. 1996; Milton Katz, 13 Sep. 1990; Duncan Kennedy, 19 Sep. 1996; and Donald Trautman, 24 Oct. 1990.

133. Brewster, "International Legal Studies in the Law School Curriculum," *Harvard Law School Bulletin*, Apr. 1960, p. 3.

134. Interview with Benjamin Kaplan, 16 Mar. 1996.

135. Interview with Duncan Kennedy, 19 Sep. 1996.

136. Brewster, Article on Milton Katz for Harvard Law School Yearbook [nd (1977?)]. Brewster Personal Papers II-69, "D."

137. Donald L. M. Blackmer, *The MIT Center for International Studies: The Founding Years 1951–1969* (Cambridge, Mass.: Massachusetts Institute of Technology, 2002), p. 45.

138. Interview with Milton Katz, 13 Sep. 1990.

139. Walter LaFeber, *The American Age: United States Foreign Policy at Home and Abroad, v. II—Since 1896*, 2nd ed. (New York: W. W. Norton, 1994), p. 479.

140. Alexander E. Sharp II, "A Man of Eminence," *YDN*, 12 Oct. 1963, p. 1.

141. Interview with Roger Fisher, 25 Oct. 1990.

142. Christopher Lydon, "Yale President Recalls Harvard Years," *BG*, 20 Oct. 1963, p. 5.

143. Interview with Roger Fisher, 25 Oct. 1990.

144. Michael Hogan, *The Marshall Plan: America, Britain, and the Reconstruction of Western Europe, 1947–1952* (Cambridge [U.K.]: Cambridge University Press, 1987).

145. *Ibid.*, pp. 4–18.

146. See, for example, Joyce Kolko and Gabriel Kolko, *The Limits of Power: The World and United States Foreign Policy, 1945–54* (New York: Harper & Row, 1972), pp. 359–83, 428–76.

147. Evan Thomas, *The Very Best Men: Four Who Dared: The Early Years of the CIA* (New York: Simon & Schuster, 1995), p. 97.

148. Brewster, Address at the National Alumni Meeting, Seattle, 15 Mar. 1970. Brewster Personal Papers I-20:9.

149. Rudy Abramson, *Spanning the Century: The Life of W. Averell Harriman, 1891–1986* (New York: William Morrow, 1992), p. 431.

150. Interview with Mary Louise Brewster, 27 Nov. 1994.

151. Interview with Roger Fisher, 25 Oct. 1990.

152. Brewster to A. Whitney Griswold, 21 Feb. 1949. Griswold Personal Papers I-3:32.

153. Mitchel Levitas, "Present and Future of Kingman Brewster," *NYTM,* 12 Feb. 1967, p. 77.

154. Interview with Milton Katz, 13 Sep. 1990.

155. Brewster, Address at Max Millikan Memorial, 17 Feb. 1970. Brewster Personal Papers I-20:6.

156. Interview with John Blum, 11 Feb. 1992.

157. Evan Thomas, "The Once and Future Kingman Brewster" (unpublished paper, 1 Sep. 1977), p. 14. Source courtesy of Mary Louise Brewster.

158. *Ibid.*

159. Interview with Mary Kennedy, 14 Nov. 1991.

160. Quoted in Driscoll and Mooney, "Endicott Peabody, Former Governor, Dead at 77," p. A1.

161. Elliot L. Richardson, "Poisoned Politics," *Atlantic Monthly,* Oct. 1961, p. 78.

162. Quoted in Vincent J. Cannato, *The Ungovernable City: John Lindsay and His Struggle to Save New York* (New York: Basic Books, 2001), p. 585.

163. *Ibid.*

164. Bird, *The Color of Truth,* p. 103.

165. Interview with Carl Kaysen, 9–10 May 2002.

166. Brewster to Fred Wacker, 21 Dec. 1970. Brewster Presidential Records RU 11 I-219:16.

167. Quoted in Driscoll and Mooney, "Endicott Peabody, Former Governor, Dead at 77," p. A1.

168. Brewster to Alan Steinert, 12 May 1958. Brewster Personal Papers II-8, "Peabody Campaign Fund."

169. Thomas, "The Once and Future Kingman Brewster," p. 14.

170. Interview with William Scranton, 16 July 1992.

171. Thomas, "The Once and Future Kingman Brewster," p. 14.

172. Brewster to Milton Katz, 18 Feb. 1952. Brewster Personal Papers II-34, "Brewster— correspondence, 1952."

173. See Edward Levi to Kingman Brewster Jr., 5 Oct. 1967. Brewster Presidential Records RU 11 I-133:8.

174. Howard B. Schaffer, *Chester Bowles: New Dealer in the Cold War* (Cambridge, Mass.: Harvard University Press, 1993), p. 41.

175. White, "The Action Intellectuals," p. 76.

176. *Ibid.*

177. Interview with M. Joseph Peck, 11 Feb. 1997.

178. *Ibid.*

179. Celia Goodhart, interview with Kingman Brewster Jr., 1986. Source courtesy of Mary Louise Brewster.

180. Interview with John Blum, 11 Feb. 1992.

181. Interview with George Zeidenstein, 13 Aug. 2001.

182. Derek Bok to Kingman Brewster [nd (Aug.? 1955)]. Brewster Personal Papers II-1, "Bok, Derek."

183. Thomas F. Eagleton to Kingman Brewster Jr., 6 July 1967. Brewster Personal Papers I-9:6.

184. G. E. Hale to L. L. Callaway Jr., 21 Dec. 1964. Brewster Personal Papers I-3:13. See also Brewster, *Antitrust and American Business Abroad* (New York: McGraw-Hill, 1958). See also James R. Atwood and Kingman Brewster, *Antitrust and American Business Abroad,* 2nd ed. (New York: McGraw-Hill, 1981). Brewster also produced a pioneering casebook in international legal studies with Milton Katz, *The Law of International Transactions and Relations: Cases and Materials* (Brooklyn, N.Y.: Foundation Press, 1960).

185. McGeorge Bundy to Mary Louise Brewster, 3 July 1946. Brewster Personal Papers II-31, "I–J."

186. Henry Stimson and McGeorge Bundy, *On Active Service in Peace and War* (New York: Harper & Brothers, 1948), p. 672.

187. Isaacson and Thomas, *The Wise Men,* p. 624.

188. Harold Howe II, "McGeorge Bundy: A Man for All Seasons," 20 Sep. 1996. Source courtesy of Harold Howe II.

189. Interview with Arthur Schlesinger Jr., 8 July 2002.

190. Transcript of WGBH, "Vietnam: Bundy and Hoffman," 14 Mar. 1968. Ford Foundation Archives, box 41835.

191. Stimson and Bundy, *On Active Service in Peace and War,* p. 406.

192. Interview with Peter Bell, 24 Jan. 2001.

193. Interview with McGeorge Bundy, 29 Apr. 1991.

194. Interview with John Blum, 11 Feb. 1992.

195. Interview with McGeorge Bundy, 29 Apr. 1991.

196. Bart Barnes, "Anne Richardson Dies; Literacy Leader Was Cabinet Spouse," *WP,* 28 July 1999.

197. Ken Gormley, *Archibald Cox: Conscience of a Nation* (Reading, Mass.: Addison, Wesley, 1997), p. 87.

198. Elliot Richardson, "Freedom of Expression and the Function of the Courts," *Harvard Law Review,* Nov. 1951; see also Richardson Papers I:79, "Writings—'Freedom of Expression and the Function of the Courts'—Corr."

199. Interview with Elliot Richardson, 22 June 1997.

200. Elliot Richardson, Lowell Lecture at the Massachusetts General Hospital, 9 Mar. 1966. Richardson Papers I:72, "Speeches—Lowell Lecture, Massachusetts General Hospital—Mar. 1966."

201. Juan Cameron, "A Boston Brahmin in 'Heartbreak House,'" *Fortune,* Oct. 1971, p. 162.

202. Charles Saunders, Speech at Cosmos Club Dinner for Elliot Richardson, 16 Jan. 1960. Richardson Papers I:76, "Dinner Honoring Richardson—1959."

203. Quoted in John Gunther, *Inside U.S.A.* (New York: Harper & Brothers, 1947), pp. 477–78.

204. Elliot Richardson, Saltonstall Dinner Speech, 19 Apr. 1966. Richardson Papers I:68, "Saltonstall, Leverett—General."

205. Interview with John Blum, 11 Feb. 1992.

206. Interview with McGeorge Bundy, 29 Apr. 1991.

207. Max Millikan to Kingman Brewster Jr., 9 July 1964. Brewster Presidential Records RU 11 I-142:5.

208. Quoted in James R. Killian Jr., *The Education of a College President: A Memoir* (Cambridge, Mass.: MIT Press, 1985), p. 68.

209. "The Nature and Objectives of the Center for International Studies" [nd (1952?)] Brewster Personal Papers II-13, "International Legal Studies."

210. Interview with Elting Morison, 26 Aug. 1991.

211. Jerome Bruner, *In Search of Mind: Essays in Autobiography* (New York: Harper & Row, 1983), p. 223.

212. Victor K. McIlheny, *Insisting on the Impossible: The Life of Edwin Land* (Reading, Mass.: Perseus Books, 1998), p. 17.

213. Roger Baldwin to Kingman Brewster Jr., 28 May 1946. Brewster Personal Papers II-31, "I–J."

214. Victor Weisskopf, *The Joy of Insight: Passions of a Physicist* (New York: Basic Books, 1991), p. 160.

215. Bruner, *In Search of Mind,* pp. 224–25.

216. "Admission to the Law School," *Harvard Alumni Bulletin,* 22 Jan. 1937, p. 476.

217. Interview with M. Joseph Peck, 11 Feb. 1997.

218. William H. Harbaugh, *Lawyer's Lawyer: The Life of John W. Davis* (New York: Oxford University Press, 1973), p. 234.

219. Erwin O. Smigel, *The Wall Street Lawyer* (Glencoe, Ill.: Free Press, 1964), p. 37.

220. Interview with M. Joseph Peck, 11 Feb. 1997.

221. Milton Katz, "Kingman Brewster, Jr.," in *Century Yearbook 1989* (New York: Century Association, 1989), p. 220; interview with Milton Katz, 9 Aug. 1990.

222. Interview with Duncan Kennedy, 19 Sep. 1996. See also Laura Kalman, *Legal Realism at Yale, 1927–1960* (Chapel Hill, N.C.: University of North Carolina Press, 1986), p. 220.

223. *Ibid.,* p. 57.

224. Seymour Martin Lipset, "Political Controversies at Harvard, 1636 to 1974," in Lipset and David Riesman, *Education and Politics at Harvard* (New York: Carnegie Commission on Higher Education, 1975), p. 179.

225. White, "The Action Intellectuals," p. 76.

226. Interview with Carl Kaysen, 11 Nov. 1996.

227. Richard Norton Smith, *The Harvard Century* (New York: Simon & Schuster, 1986), p. 186.

228. Bird, *The Color of Truth,* p. 118.

229. Interview with Carl Kaysen, 9–10 May 2002.

230. John Richardson to *BG,* 3 Mar. 1965, Richardson Papers I:50, "Frankfurter, Felix—General—1954–67"; entry for Elliot Lee Richardson, *Current Biography 1971* (Bronx, N.Y.: H. W. Wilson, 1971), p. 343.

231. McGeorge Bundy, "The Attack on Yale," *Atlantic Monthly,* Nov. 1951, p. 51.

232. William F. Buckley Jr., "The Changes at Yale," *Atlantic Monthly,* Dec. 1951, p. 82.

233. Peter Viereck to Henry Regnery, 28 Nov. 1951. Buckley Papers 97-M-160:4, "Corr.—1950s [1]."

234. William F. Buckley Jr. to Peter Viereck, 12 Dec. 1951. Buckley Papers 97-M-160:4, "Corr. —1950s [1]."

235. Bundy, "The Attack on Yale," Nov. 1951, p. 52.

236. William Bundy to Elliot Richardson [nd (Nov. 1950?)] Richardson Papers I:43, "'B' miscellaneous."

237. Kraft, "The Two Worlds of McGeorge Bundy," p. 112.

238. Peter Viereck, "Conserving Is Not Conforming," address to the American Historical Association, 28 Dec. 1954. Source courtesy of Peter Viereck.

239. Finis Farr to William F. Buckley Jr., 25 July 1956. Buckley Papers I-2, "Farr, Finis."

240. William Frank Buckley, "Proposed Speech by Billie at Yale," in "Memorandum Regarding Data That May Be Used in Part in Writing an Article on 'God and Man at Yale'" [nd (1952?)]. Buckley Papers III/411:214, "GAMAY—Epilogue material."

241. Bundy, "The Attack on Yale," p. 50.

242. McGeorge Bundy, "Bread and Circuses or Else—I," *YDN*, 10 Oct. 1938, p. 2.

243. Bird, *The Color of Truth*, p. 119.

244. Harvard University, Minutes of the Faculty of Arts and Sciences, 12 Dec. 2000.

245. Phyllis Keller, *Getting at the Core: Curricular Reform at Harvard* (Cambridge, Mass.: Harvard University Press, 1982), pp. 20–22.

246. David Riesman, Address at Quincy House Senior Dinner, 7 May 1968. Brewster Personal Papers II-60.

247. McGeorge Bundy, A Report from Academic Utopia," *Harper's*, Jan. 1962.

248. Henry Kissinger, *White House Years* (Boston: Little, Brown, 1979), p. 14.

249. Interview with McGeorge Bundy, 29 Apr. 1991.

250. Quoted in Bird, *The Color of Truth*, p. 134.

251. Brewster, Statement [nd (1953?)]. Brewster Personal Papers I-18, "Civil Liberties Union of Mass.—1953 [1]."

252. See, for example, Richard Hofstadter, *Anti-Intellectualism in American Life* (New York: Knopf, 1963), pp. 12–14.

253. Elliot Richardson to Henry Cabot Lodge, 21 Mar. 1950. Richardson Papers I:60—"'L' miscellaneous."

254. Elliot Richardson to Kingman Brewster Jr., 10 Feb. 1954. Brewster Personal Papers II-18, "Civil Liberties Union of Massachusetts—1954."

255. Scott Donaldson, *Archibald MacLeish: An American Life* (Boston: Houghton Mifflin, 1992), pp. 431–33.

256. Interview with McGeorge Bundy, 29 Apr. 1991.

257. Kingman Brewster, Draft of a Letter for Nathan Pusey, Apr. 1958. Brewster Personal Papers II-15, "Harvard."

258. William P. Bundy, "Class Oration," *History of the Yale College Class of 1939* (New Haven: Yale University, 1939), p. 12.

4 : NEW FRONTIERS

1. Robert Kaiser, "Snooping Around," *YDN*, 20 Sep. 1963, p. 2.

2. There were other candidates for the provostship, both at Yale and outside, but Griswold's preferences were almost certainly Stewart, Brewster, and Brooks. The paper trail of Griswold's provostial negotiations with Stewart is clear and unambiguous, but Griswold's interest in Brooks is harder to trace. Brooks turned down an apparent offer to join Yale's Physics Department in 1954, and also Griswold's offer of a college mastership and "tangible opportunities and responsibilities for Yale science." Mary Griswold confirmed that Griswold was interested in making Brooks his provost, though Brooks did not recall a concrete offer of the job. See A. Whitney Griswold to Harvey Brooks, 17 Mar. 1954, Griswold Presidential Records 42:397; Harvey Brooks to A. Whitney Griswold, 30 Mar. 1954, Griswold Presidential Records 42:397; interview with Mary Griswold, 4 Apr. 1992; interview with Harvey Brooks, 22 Oct. 1991.

3. Interview with Zeph Stewart, 25 Nov. 1991.

4. *Ibid.*

5. Fred M. Hechinger, "Yale's New President Picked as Aide by Dr. Griswold in 1960," *NYT,* 13 Oct. 1963, p. 83.

6. *Ibid.*

7. Interview with John Blum, 18 Mar. 1991.

8. Interview with McGeorge Bundy, 29 Apr. 1991.

9. *Ibid.*

10. Brewster, "Excerpt from an Uncompleted Book," in *Kingman Brewster: Remembrances* (New Haven: Yale University, 1997), p. 78.

11. Evan Thomas, "The Once and Future Kingman Brewster" (unpublished article, 1 Sep. 1977), p. 15. Source courtesy of Mary Louise Brewster.

12. Brewster, "Excerpt from an Uncompleted Book," p. 78.

13. Mitchel Levitas, "The Present and Future of Kingman Brewster," *NYTM*, 12 Feb. 1967, p. 77.

14. McGeorge Bundy, untitled poem, 28 Apr. 1960. Brewster Personal Papers II-3, "Friday Evening Club."

15. Alonzo Hamby, *Liberalism and Its Challengers: From F.D.R. to Bush,* 2nd ed. (New York: Oxford University Press, 1992), p. 183.

16. Interview with Elliot Richardson, 22 June 1997.

17. Interview with Alfred Chandler, 25 June 1997.

18. Levitas, "The Present and Future of Kingman Brewster," p. 80.

19. Leo Damore, *The Cape Cod Years of John Fitzgerald Kennedy* (Englewood Cliffs, N.J.: Prentice-Hall, 1967), p. 40.

20. Brewster to Peter Solbert, 29 June 1954. Brewster Personal Papers II-34, "Brewster—correspondence, 1954."

21. Kai Bird, *The Color of Truth: McGeorge Bundy and William Bundy: Brothers in Arms* (New York: Simon & Schuster, 1998), p. 150.

22. Interview with Arthur Schlesinger Jr., 8 July 2002.

23. Robert Dallek, *An Unfinished Life: John F. Kennedy 1917–1963* (Boston: Little, Brown, 2003), p. 91.

24. Paul Moore Jr., *Presences: A Bishop's Life in the City* (New York: Farrar, Straus and Giroux, 1997), p. 166.

25. Interview with Stephen Bundy, 17 Feb. 2001.

26. Cyrus R. Vance Oral History Interview, 3 Nov. 1969, LBJ Library.

27. "Cyrus Roberts Vance," *Current Biography 1962* (Bronx, N.Y.: H. W. Wilson, 1962), p. 432.

28. Grace Vance, memo 28 July 1962. Vance Papers I-3:33.

29. Lloyd Shearer, "Cyrus Vance: The Nation's No. 1 Troubleshooter," *Parade,* 23 June 1968, p. 5.

30. Interview with Joseph A. Califano Jr., 16 Jan. 2003.

31. David Barnett, "Top Man of the Army," *Grumman Horizons,* Autumn 1962, p. 19.

32. Interview with Joseph A. Califano Jr., 16 Jan. 2003.

33. Barnett, "Top Man of the Army," p. 19.

34. Shearer, "Cyrus Vance: The Nation's No. 1 Troubleshooter," p. 4.

35. Cyrus Vance, Address at the Kent School Prize Day, 3 June 1962. Vance Papers III-38:289.

36. Marilyn Berger, "Cyrus R. Vance, a Confidant to Presidents, Is Dead at 84," *NYT,* 13 Jan. 2002.

37. "Elliot Lee Richardson," *Current Biography 1971* (Bronx, N.Y.: H. W. Wilson, 1971), p. 344.

38. "Closeup: Richardson Once Too Busy to Ghost Ike's Talks," *BG,* 10 Sep. 1959.

39. Elliot Richardson, *The Creative Balance: Government, Politics, and the Individual in America's Third Century* (New York: Holt, Rinehart & Winston, 1976), p. 122.

40. *Ibid.*

41. Juan Cameron, "A Boston Brahmin in 'Heartbreak House,'" *Fortune*, Oct. 1971, p. 162.
42. Roger Rosenblatt, *Coming Apart: A Memoir of the Harvard Wars of 1969* (Boston: Little, Brown, 1997), p. 126.
43. Elliot Richardson, *Reflections of a Radical Moderate* (New York: Pantheon Books, 1996), p. 8.
44. "Closeup: Richardson Once Too Busy to Ghost Ike's Talks."
45. John Lindsay to Elliot Richardson, 18 Nov. 1959. Richardson Papers I:75, "U.S. Attorney—Congratulations on Appointment—1959."
46. John Lindsay to Robert A. Forsythe, 15 Jan. 1960. Richardson Papers I:76, "Dinner Honoring Richardson—1959."
47. Ted Sorensen, "To Elliot," Sep. 1959. Richardson Papers I:76, "Dinner Honoring Richardson—1959."
48. Richardson, *The Creative Balance*, p. 306.
49. Interview with Elliot Richardson, 22 June 1997.
50. Elliot L. Richardson, "Poisoned Politics: The Real Tragedy of Massachusetts," *Atlantic Monthly*, Oct. 1961, pp. 80–81.
51. Interview with Elliot Richardson, 22 June 1997.
52. Elliot Richardson, memo 10–13 May 1961. Richardson Papers I:75, "Replacement as U.S. Attorney."
53. Interview with Elliot Richardson, 22 June 1997.
54. Elliot Richardson to Richard Nixon, 19 Jan. 1961. Brewster Personal Papers II-74, "Brewster, Kingman—Personal."
55. Elliot Richardson to Colgate S. Prentice, 27 Dec. 1961. Richardson Papers I:66, "'P' miscellaneous."
56. John Lindsay to Elliot Richardson, 18 June 1962. Richardson Papers I:60, "'L'—misc."
57. Quoted in Vincent J. Cannato, *The Ungovernable City: John Lindsay and His Struggle to Save New York* (New York: Basic Books, 2001), p. 3.
58. Nat Hentoff, *A Political Life: The Education of John V. Lindsay* (New York: Alfred A. Knopf, 1969), chapters 1–3.
59. Noel E. Parmental Jr., "John V. Lindsay: Less Than Meets the Eye," *Esquire*, Oct. 1965, p. 101.
60. Hentoff, *A Political Life*, p. 49.
61. Interview with Leon Lipson, 28 July 1992.
62. Brewster, "A. Whitney Griswold," in *Yale College Class of 1929, 40th Anniversary Yearbook* (New Haven: Yale University, 1969), p. 3. Reprinted in *Style, Pluck and Integrity* (Stamford, Conn.: Overbrook Press, 1969).
63. Interview with David Acheson, 4 Oct. 1990; interview with Alice Acheson, 2 Oct. 1990.
64. Interview with Mary Griswold, 18 Apr. 1990.
65. Reuben A. Holden, *Profiles and Portraits of Yale University Presidents* (Freeport, Me.: Bond Wheelwright, 1968), p. 132.
66. Charles Beard to Leonard Labaree, 8 Feb. 1947. Griswold Personal Papers I-3:26.
67. Interview with James Perkins, 20 May 1992.
68. Interview with Mary Griswold, 18 Apr. 1990; Holden, *Profiles and Portraits of Yale University Presidents*, pp. 131–41.
69. Robert Maynard Hutchins to A. Whitney Griswold, 12 Sep. 1942. Griswold Personal Papers I-2:23.
70. A. Whitney Griswold to Francis Bronson, 16 July 1949. Griswold Personal Papers I-3:33.
71. Interview with Zeph Stewart, 12 June 1991.
72. Roger L. Geiger, *Research and Relevant Knowledge: American Research Universities since World War II* (New York: Oxford University Press, 1993), p. 89.

73. See Edward Corn, "Dean Calls Classrooms 'Disorderly,'" *YDN,* 25 Feb. 1952, p. 1; "Faculty Votes Coats in All Dining Halls," *YDN,* 29 Feb. 1952, p. 1.

74. Dan A. Oren, *Joining the Club: A History of Jews and Yale* (New Haven: Yale University Press, 1983), p. 183.

75. A. Whitney Griswold to Francis Bronson, 16 Jul. 1949. Griswold Personal Papers I-3:33.

76. Interview with Mary Wolff, 9 Apr. 1992.

77. "Is the Ivy League Still the Best?" *Newsweek,* 23 Nov. 1964, p. 68.

78. Brewster to A. Whitney Griswold, 7 Jan. 1943. Griswold Personal Papers I-2:24. Emphasis in the original.

79. Polly Stone Buck to Geoffrey Kabaservice, 15 Sep. 1990.

80. David B. H. Martin to Elliot Richardson, 20 Feb. 1961. Richardson Papers I:60, "Martin, David B. H."

81. Interview with Harold Howe II, 23 Oct. 1990.

82. Levitas, "The Present and Future of Kingman Brewster," p. 75.

83. Interview with John Perry Miller, 19 Sep. 1990.

84. "President Brewster," *New Yorker,* 11 Jan. 1964, p. 24.

85. A. Whitney Griswold to Wilmarth S. Lewis, 25 Oct. 1962. Griswold Presidential Records 140:1278.

86. Brewster to Edwin Land, 30 Apr. 1963. Brewster Presidential Records RU 11 I-187:1.

87. John Hay Whitney to Kingman Brewster Jr. and Mary Louise Brewster, 1 Nov. 1961. Brewster Personal Papers II-1, "Provost—Personal—B-2."

88. Georges May, "Durability and Self-Renewal during Ten and a Half Years," *YDN,* 12 Oct. 1973, p. 10.

89. "Universities: Anxiety behind the Façade," *Time,* 23 June 1967, p. 80.

90. Interview with Elliot Richardson, 22 June 1997.

91. Maitland A. Edey to Kingman Brewster Jr., 7 Dec. 1960. Brewster Personal Papers II-74, "Brewster, Kingman—Personal."

92. Theodore Sorensen, *John F. Kennedy* (New York: Harper & Row, 1965), pp. 253–57.

93. Arthur Schlesinger Jr., *A Thousand Days: John F. Kennedy in the White House* (Boston: Houghton Mifflin, 1965), p. 128.

94. David Halberstam, *The Best and the Brightest* (New York: Random House, 1972), pp. 39–41.

95. Sorensen, *John F. Kennedy,* p. 252.

96. Carl M. Brauer, *John F. Kennedy and the Second Reconstruction* (New York: Columbia University Press, 1977), pp. 68–71.

97. Cynthia Harrison, *On Account of Sex: The Politics of Women's Issues, 1945–1968* (Berkeley: University of California Press, 1988), p. 79.

98. Interview with Amy Vance, 28 Feb. 2002.

99. Joseph Kraft, "The Two Worlds of McGeorge Bundy," *Harper's,* Nov. 1965, p. 106.

100. "JFK's McGeorge Bundy—Cool Head for Any Crisis," *Newsweek,* 4 Mar. 1963, p. 20.

101. Arthur Schlesinger Jr., "McGeorge Bundy: The End of an Era," *WP,* 27 Feb. 1966, p. 1.

102. Interview with Stephen Bundy, 5 Sep. 2001.

103. Interview with Carl Kaysen, 9–10 May 2002.

104. Interview with Francis Bator, 19 June 2002.

105. Evan Thomas, *The Very Best Men: Four Who Dared: The Early Years of the CIA* (New York: Simon & Schuster, 1995), p. 266.

106. "JFK's McGeorge Bundy—Cool Head for Any Crisis," p. 24.

107. Quoted in Richard Reeves, *President Kennedy: Profile of Power* (New York: Simon & Schuster, 1994), p. 113.

108. Schlesinger, "McGeorge Bundy: The End of an Era," p. 1.

109. Quoted in E. Digby Baltzell, *The Protestant Establishment: Aristocracy and Caste in America* (New Haven: Yale University Press, 1964), p. 79.

110. McGeorge Bundy, *Danger and Survival: Choices about the Bomb in the First Fifty Years* (New York: Vintage, 1988), p. 391.

111. Bird, *The Color of Truth*, p. 232.

112. Arthur Schlesinger Jr., *Robert Kennedy and His Times* (New York: Ballantine Books, 1978), p. 546.

113. Bundy, *Danger and Survival*, pp. 399–400; Bird, *The Color of Truth*, p. 234.

114. Interview with Carl Kaysen, 9–10 May 2002.

115. Meg Greenfield, *Washington* (New York: Public Affairs, 2001), p. 90.

116. Todd Gitlin, *The Sixties: Years of Hope, Days of Rage* (New York: Bantam, 1987), p. 94.

117. Bird, *The Color of Truth*, p. 436.

118. Gitlin, *The Sixties*, p. 96.

119. Todd Gitlin to A. Whitney Griswold, 26 Jan. 1962. Griswold Presidential Records 116-1804.

120. Bird, *The Color of Truth*, p. 190.

121. McGeorge Bundy, Address at the National Urban League Annual Banquet, 2 Aug. 1966. Ford Foundation Archives, box 41834.

122. William Manchester, *The Death of a President* (New York: Harper & Row, 1967), p. 581.

123. McGeorge Bundy to Dean Rusk, 8 Jan. 1963. Available at http://www.yale.edu/lawweb/avalon/diplomacy/forrel/cuba/cuba264.htm

124. Interview with Joseph A. Califano Jr., 16 Jan. 2003.

125. Robert McNamara, LBJ Library oral history interview, 8 Jan. 1975.

126. Interview with Joseph A. Califano Jr., 16 Jan. 2003.

127. Quoted in Schlesinger, *Robert Kennedy and His Times*, p. 348.

128. Interview with Nicholas Katzenbach, 4 June 2003.

129. Interview with Joseph A. Califano Jr., 16 Jan. 2003.

130. McGeorge Bundy, "Were Those the Days?" *Daedalus*, Summer 1970, p. 566.

131. Moore, *Presences*, p. 93.

132. Paul Moore Jr., "A Touch of Laughter," in Diana Dubois (ed.), *My Harvard, My Yale* (New York: Random House, 1982), p. 103.

133. Moore, *Presences*, pp. 109, 113.

134. "Bishop Moore: A Leader of the New Breed," *Newsweek*, 29 Mar. 1965.

135. Moore, *Presences*, p. 122.

136. *Ibid.*, p. 129.

137. *Ibid.*, p. 140.

138. Brewster to Hugh Calkins, 15 Oct. 1953. Brewster Personal Papers II-2, "Brewster—Correspondence (1953)."

139. Benjamin Bradlee, "A Churchman of the Street," *WP*, 28 Mar. 1965, p. E2.

140. Moore, *Presences*, p, 153.

141. "Paul Moore, Jr." *Current Biography 1967* (Bronx, N.Y.: H. W. Wilson, 1967), p. 303.

142. "Make Room for the Martyrs," *YDN*, 22 Feb. 1960, p. 2; "Eight Yale Students Picket Downtown Woolworth Store; Five of Group Apprehended by City Police Officers," *YDN*, 22 Feb. 1960, p. 1.

143. Jodi Lynne Wilgoren, "Black & Blue: Yale Volunteers in the Civil Rights Movement, 1963–65" (unpublished senior essay in history, Yale College, 13 Apr. 1992), p. 15.

144. "Summer Integration Program Devised to Supplement Sit-Ins," *YDN*, 6 Apr. 1962, p. 1; Stephen Bingham, "Nationwide NSM Drive Nov. 6 to Aid SNCC," *YDN*, 2 Nov. 1962, p. 1.

145. William Sloane Coffin Jr., *Once to Every Man* (New York: Atheneum, 1977), p. 81.
146. *Ibid.*, p. 86.
147. *Ibid.*, p. 90.
148. Quoted in Wilgoren, "Black & Blue," p. 5.
149. Interview with Arthur Howe Jr., 18 July 1992.
150. Brewster, "Excerpts from an Uncompleted Book," p. 78.
151. *Ibid.*
152. John M. Payne, "Senior Year," *Yale Banner 1963* (New Haven: Yale Banner Publications, 1963), p. 270.
153. Interview with John Blum, 18 Mar. 1991.
154. *History of the Yale College Class of 1964* (New Haven: Yale University, 1964), p. 286. See also "A Wise and Witty Fighter Is Dead," *Life*, 3 May 1963, pp. 34–35.
155. Dean Acheson, *Present at the Creation: My Years in the State Department* (New York: W. W. Norton, 1969), p. 373.
156. Leonard Doob et al., "The Education of First Year Students in Yale College" (New Haven: Yale University, 1962), p. 12.
157. *Ibid.*, p. 5.
158. Interview with Howard Lamar, 28 Apr. 1992.
159. John Q. LaFond, "Yale Raises Tuition $250 to $1800, Adopts 'Unique' Scholarship Policy," *YDN,* 29 May 1963, p. 1.
160. "The Quiet Revolution," *YDN,* 10 June 1963, p. 1.
161. Interview with David Gergen, 23 Apr. 1998.
162. "The Quiet Revolution," p. 4.
163. Mark W. Foster, "Kingman Brewster, Jr.: No Water-Treading," *YDN,* 30 Apr. 1963, p. 1.
164. Interview with Harold Howe II, 23 Oct. 1990.
165. Wilmarth S. Lewis to A. Whitney Griswold, 10 July 1959. Griswold Presidential Records 68:648.
166. Wilmarth S. Lewis, American Law Institute Dinner Speech, 24 May 1963. Griswold Presidential Records 140:1278.
167. Wilmarth S. Lewis, *One Man's Education* (New York: Alfred A. Knopf, 1967), pp. 425–26.
168. Brewster to Joseph S. Jones, 23 Dec. 1969. Brewster Presidential Records I-124:15.
169. "Aide Says Wallace Considering News Parley Instead of Speech," *NHR,* 1 Oct. 1963, p. 1.
170. The 1975 report of the Committee on Freedom of Expression at Yale, chaired by historian C. Vann Woodward, declared the Wallace affair to have been the first of several violations of free speech during Brewster's presidency. The committee did not, however, do any research into the episode apart from consulting back issues of the *Yale Daily News.* Tom Cavanagh, writing on the Wallace affair in 1975, interviewed James Wood, the president of the Political Union in 1963, and Rollin Osterweis, the union's faculty advisor, neither of whom had been contacted by the Woodward committee. On the basis of their testimony, Cavanagh concluded that the *YDN*'s 1963 coverage, and the Woodward report's interpretation of that coverage, were faulty: "Contrary to almost universal belief, George Wallace was never disinvited by the Political Union. Nor did the University administration attempt to persuade the officers of the Union to disinvite him. For a variety of reasons, some commendable, some not, the administration successfully persuaded the Union merely to postpone Wallace's visit. . . . [T]hese actions in no way represented an abridgment of freedom of speech. The use of the incident in this context by the Woodward Committee, while

understandable in light of inadequate research, is thus spurious." Cavanagh, "George Wallace in '63: Disinvited or Postponed?" *YDN*, 5 Feb. 1975, p. 2; Woodward et al., "Report of the Committee on Freedom of Expression at Yale" (New Haven: Yale University, 1974), pp. 10–13.

171. Alan Boles, "Dixie's Darling George," *YDN, FRIDAY Magazine*, 20 Oct. 1967, p. 11.

172. Arthur L. Singer and Jonathan F. Fanton, "A Bill of Obligations for Yale University" (New Haven: Yale University, 1968), Brewster Presidential Records RU 11 I-187:5.

173. Interview with Jonathan Fanton, 2 Feb. 1993.

174. Interview with Harold Howe II, 23 Oct. 1990.

175. Brewster, "Informal Reflections on the Yale Delegation's Trip to the Soviet Union in March 1961." Brewster Personal Papers I-1:3.

176. David Halberstam, *The Best and the Brightest*, p. 44. Emphasis in the original.

177. "Washington 'Post' Says Bundy Rejects 'Feeler,'" *YDN*, 30 Apr. 1963, p. 1.

178. Bird, *The Color of Truth*, p. 268.

179. There is no evidence of such an offer in the archives. The nine members of the Corporation that elected Brewster who were still alive in the 1990s—including Bill Bundy—all denied that Mac had ever been offered the Yale presidency. Interview with William P. Bundy, 10 May 1991; interview with J. Richardson Dilworth, 26 Mar. 1991; interview with T. Keith Glennan, 2 Jan. 1991; interview with Caryl Haskins, 5 Oct. 1990; interview with Harold Howe II, 23 Oct. 1990; interview with William McChesney Martin, 6 Oct. 1990; interview with J. Irwin Miller, 18 Dec. 1991; interview with Amos Wilder, 23 Oct. 1990; interview with Frank O. H. Williams, 24 Sep. 1990. The other six members of the Corporation had died or were unreachable by the time I began my interviewing. McGeorge Bundy denied that he had been offered the Yale presidency, in my interview with him of 22 May 1991. However, when I asked Miller whether Bundy had been offered the presidency before Brewster, he replied, "No. I've heard that, certainly, and I know something else—that Mac believes it. But he was never offered the presidency."

180. Interview with Harold Howe II, 23 Oct. 1990.

181. Interview with McGeorge Bundy, 29 Apr. 1991.

182. Lewis, *One Man's Education*, pp. 437–38.

183. Brewster to Daniel B. Hodgson, 27 June 1966. Brewster Presidential Records RU 11 I-113:14.

184. Interview with Harold Howe II, 23 Oct. 1990.

185. Interview with Edward Levi, 19 Dec. 1991.

186. R. Thomas Herman, "The Inscrutable King of Yale" (unpublished paper, 7 Aug. 1968), p. 28. Brewster Presidential Records RU 11 I-47:14.

187. Interview with Mary Louise Brewster, 18 June 1998.

188. "Provost Succeeds Griswold at Yale," *NYT*, 13 Oct. 1963, p. 1.

189. "A President for Yale," *NYT*, 14 Oct. 1963, p. 28.

190. Dean Acheson to Kingman Brewster Jr., 16 Oct. 1963. Brewster Presidential Records RU 11 I-68:3.

191. Interview with Mary Bundy, 26 Sep. 2001.

192. John M. Van Dyke, "New President Holds First Press Conference, Cites Necessity to Maintain Yale's Standards; Brewster to Continue Griswold Tradition," *YDN*, 14 Oct. 1963, pp. 1–2.

193. Herman, "The Inscrutable King of Yale," p. 11.

194. Brewster, Address at the Buckingham School, 8 Nov. 1966. Brewster Personal Papers I-7:17.

195. Brewster, Address on "The Strategy of a University," Hall of Graduate Studies, Yale University, 21 Sep. 1965. Brewster Personal Papers I-5:9.
196. Moore, *Presences*, p. 164.
197. *Ibid.*, p. 166.
198. McGeorge Bundy to Kingman Brewster Jr., 21 Nov. 1963. Brewster Presidential Records I-42:2.
199. Bird, *The Color of Truth*, p. 264.
200. Godfrey Hodgson, *America in Our Time* (New York: Vintage Books, 1976), p. 167.
201. Bird, *The Color of Truth*, p. 266.
202. *Ibid.*, p. 267.
203. William B. Stanberry Jr., "Freshman Year," *History of the Yale College Class of 1966* (New Haven: Yale University, 1966), p. 252.
204. Coffin, *Once to Every Man*, p. 200.

1. Brewster, Yale University Inaugural Address, 11 Apr. 1964. Brewster Personal Papers I-2:5.
2. Interview with Edward Adelberg, 5 Dec. 1996.
3. Interview with McGeorge Bundy, 29 Apr. 1991.
4. Noël Annan, *Our Age: The Generation That Made Post-war Britain* (New York: Fontana, 1991), p. 4.
5. Yale University, inauguration press kit, 11 Apr. 1964. Records of the Office of the Secretary (Reuben A. Holden) of Yale University 1:15.
6. Interview with William Bundy, 10 May 1991.
7. Richard Nixon to Kingman Brewster Jr., 3 Aug. 1964; Kingman Brewster Jr. to Richard Nixon, 17 Aug. 1964. Brewster Presidential Records RU 11 I-162:1.
8. Brewster, Commencement Address at Case Institute of Technology, 15 June 1965. Brewster Personal Papers I-5:5.
9. McGeorge Bundy, "The Faculty and the President," 8 May 1968. Ford Foundation Archives, box 41835.
10. William Clyde DeVane, "Report of the Dean of Yale College," July 1963, p. 3.
11. Quoted in Jeremy Weinberg, "Long Live the King's Yale: How Kingman Brewster's University Survived and Thrived in the 1960s" (unpublished senior essay in history, Yale College, 13 Apr. 1992), p. 10.
12. See Dan A. Oren, *Joining the Club: A History of Jews and Yale* (New Haven: Yale University Press, 1985), chapter 6.
13. Richard Bissell Jr. to A. Whitney Griswold, 21 Feb. 1942. Griswold Personal Papers I-2:22. Italics in the original.
14. President's Committee on the Natural Sciences and Mathematics, Interim Report, Sep. 1959. Griswold Presidential Records 184:1667.
15. "Another Blow," *YDN*, 11 Apr. 1961, p. 2.
16. Interview with Edward Adelberg, 5 Dec. 1996.
17. Brewster, Address to the Yale Club of Washington, 12 Feb. 1965. Brewster Personal Papers I-4:5.
18. Interview with Edward Adelberg, 5 Dec. 1996.
19. Interview with William von Eggers Doering, 5 Sep. 1991.
20. Interview with Jack Sandweiss, 1 May 1992; Kingman Brewster Jr. to Edward Roberts, 12 July 1963. Brewster Personal Papers II-1, "Bills."

21. Interview with D. Allan Bromley, 27 May 1992; D. Allan Bromley to Stuart Symington Jr., 28 Sep. 1966. Brewster Presidential Records RU 11 I-2:10.

22. Minutes of the Visiting Committee for the MIT Center of International Studies, Sep. 1962. Brewster Personal Papers II-1, "Visiting Committee—Center for International Studies (MIT)."

23. Interview with John Perry Miller, 19 Sep. 1990.

24. Brewster, Statement before the Subcommittee on Science, Research, and Development of the House Committee on Science and Astronautics, 26 May 1964. Brewster Personal Papers I-2:11.

25. Interview with Edward Adelberg, 5 Dec. 1996.

26. Brewster, "Problems and Perspectives in Yale Science," *YAM*, June 1961, p. 10.

27. Interview with Frederic M. Richards, 11 Dec. 1996; interview with Arthur Solomon, 6 Feb. 1997.

28. Interview with Edward Adelberg, 5 Dec. 1996.

29. Interview with Charles Bockelman, 20 Apr. 1992.

30. Interview with Henry Chauncey Jr., 22 July 1993.

31. Nicholas Lemann, "The Structure of Success in America," *Atlantic Monthly*, August 1995, and "The Great Sorting," *Atlantic Monthly*, Sep. 1995.

32. Interview with Henry Chauncey Jr., 22 Mar. 1992.

33. Brewster to McGeorge Bundy, 18 Oct. 1967. Brewster Presidential Records RU 11 I-98:8.

34. Brewster, Address on "The Strategy of a University," Hall of Graduate Studies, Yale University, 21 Sep. 1965. Brewster Personal Papers I-5:9; interview with Lloyd Reynolds, 2 Oct. 1990.

35. Kingman Brewster Jr. to Yale Corporation Committee on Educational Policy, 12 Oct. 1962. Brewster Presidential Records RU 11 I-93:19.

36. John Perry Miller, *Creating Academic Settings: High Craft and Low Cunning* (New Haven: J. Simeon Press, 1991), p. 104.

37. Interview with William von Eggers Doering, 5 Sep. 1991.

38. David Riesman, "Educational Reform at Harvard College: Meritocracy and Its Adversaries," in David Riesman and Seymour Martin Lipset, *Educational Politics at Harvard* (New York: McGraw-Hill, 1975), p. 300.

39. Sample letter, Director of the Division of Sciences [nd (1964)]. Brewster Presidential Records RU 11 I-94:4.

40. Edgar J. Boell, "Goading Science to a New State of Excellence," *YAM*, June 1977, p. 18.

41. Interview with Charles Bockelman, 20 Apr. 1992.

42. Clark Kerr, Address at the Pre-Inauguration Luncheon for Kingman Brewster Jr 11 Apr. 1964. Brewster Personal Papers I-12:7.

43. Interview with John Blum, 28 Apr. 1992.

44. Robert Brustein, *Making Scenes: A Personal History of the Turbulent Years at Yale, 1966–1979* (New York: Limelight Editions, 1984), p. 9.

45. Kai Erikson, "Reflections," in *Kingman Brewster: Remembrances* (New Haven: Yale University, 1997), p. 64.

46. Brewster, Address to the Yale Class Officers and Alumni Fund Agents, 11 Oct. 1963. Brewster Personal Papers I-1:13.

47. George Wilson Pierson, *A Yale Book of Numbers: Historical Statistics of the College and University 1701–1976* (New Haven: 1983), p. 608.

48. Interview with D. Allan Bromley, 27 May 1992.

49. Pierson, *A Yale Book of Numbers*, pp. 358, 360–61.

50. Kingman Brewster to McGeorge Bundy, 18 Oct. 1967. Brewster Presidential Records RU 11 I-98:8.

51. Interview with Henry Chauncey Jr., 22 July 1993.
52. Interview with M. Joseph Peck, 11 Feb. 1997.
53. Interview with Henry Chauncey Jr., 13 July 1993.
54. Kingman Brewster to Marshall Robinson, 18 Sep. 1967. Brewster Presidential Records RU 11 I-98:8.
55. "Universities: Anxiety behind the Façade," *Time*, 23 June 1967, p. 82.
56. "The Needs of Yale: The Ten Year Plan" (New Haven: Yale University, 1967). Records of the Office of the Provost (Kingman Brewster Jr.) of Yale University RU 19 III-279:985.
57. Interview with John Embersits, 15 June 1992.
58. Interview with Joseph A. Califano Jr., 16 Jan. 2003.
59. Cyrus Vance, Address to the Army Tactical Mobility Symposium in Fort Benning, Georgia, 19 Nov. 1963. Vance Papers I-5:49.
60. Richard M. Bissell Jr. to Kingman Brewster Jr., 24 Aug. 1965. Brewster Presidential Records RU 11 I-44:9.
61. Interview with M. Joseph Peck, 11 Feb. 1997.
62. Alain C. Enthoven and K. Wayne Smith, *How Much Is Enough?: Shaping the Defense Program, 1961–1969* (New York: Harper & Row, 1971), p. 33.
63. Robert S. McNamara, LBJ Library oral history interview, 8 Jan. 1975.
64. Quoted in H. R. McMaster, *Dereliction of Duty: Lyndon Johnson, Robert McNamara, the Joint Chiefs of Staff and the Lies That Led to Vietnam* (New York: HarperCollins, 1997), p. 20.
65. L. P. Curtis to Kingman Brewster Jr., 13 Dec. 1963. Brewster Presidential Records RU 11 I-113:11.
66. Interview with M. Joseph Peck, 11 Feb. 1997.
67. Paul Moore Jr., *Presences: A Bishop's Life in the City* (New York: Farrar, Straus and Giroux, 1997), p. 177.
68. "Honorary Degree Citations," *YAM*, July 1964, pp. 15–16.
69. Martin Luther King Jr. to Kingman Brewster Jr., 24 June 1964. Brewster Presidential Records RU 11 I-63:14.
70. J. D. Stetson Coleman to Kingman Brewster Jr., 19 June 1964. Brewster Presidential Records RU 11 I-126:14.
71. "The Union of States Undermined," *The Register* (Danville, Virginia), 15 June 1964.
72. Erwin L. Baldwin to Edward Swenson, 29 May 68. Brewster Presidential Records RU 11 I-41:13.
73. Kingman Brewster Jr. to Frank E. Block, 12 Aug. 1964. Brewster Presidential Records RU 11 I-126:14.
74. Kingman Brewster Jr. to Tom Brady, 25 June 1964. Brewster Presidential Records RU 11 I-126:14. Brady graduated from Yale College in 1927.
75. Kingman Brewster Jr. to Spruille Braden, 9 June 1967. Brewster Presidential Records RU 11 I-46:14.
76. Interview with Nicholas Katzenbach, 4 June 2003.
77. Oren, *Joining the Club*, p. 206.
78. Brewster, Address to the Yale Freshman Class, 14 Sep. 1964. Brewster Personal Papers I-3:6.
79. William F. Buckley Jr., "Prayermongering against Goldwater," *New York Journal American*, 23 Sep. 1964.
80. "Buckley and/or Yale," *YDN FRIDAY Magazine*, 29 Oct. 1967, p. 2.
81. "Brewster: Little Choice in November; 'No Victory' for Liberals," *NHR*, 29 Sep. 1964; Brewster, Address to the Yale Political Union, 28 Sep. 1964. Brewster Personal Papers I-3:7.

82. Cyrus Vance, Address to Cleveland VFW Convention, 27 Aug. 1964. Vance Papers I-4:47.

83. "William Warren Scranton," *Current Biography 1964* (Bronx, N.Y.: H. W. Wilson, 1964), p. 398.

84. Conservative Society of America, "Where Scranton Really Stands," 1964. Buckley Papers I-29, "Coudert-Courtney (1964)."

85. "Signs of Revolt over Goldwater Policy," *Times* (London), 12 July 1964. Buckley Papers I-30, "Goldwater, Barry—Newsclippings, articles (1) (1964)."

86. William F. Buckley Jr. to John Judis, 3 Mar. 1990. Buckley Papers III/1-42, "John Judis, 1990."

87. Leonard Silk and Mark Silk, *The American Establishment* (New York: Basic Books, 1980), pp. 6–7.

88. Hugh Thomas, "The Establishment and Society," in Hugh Thomas (ed.), *The Establishment* (London: Anthony Blond, 1959), p. 20.

89. Richard H. Rovere, "Notes on the Establishment in America," *American Scholar* (Autumn 1961), p. 490.

90. *John Birch Society Bulletin*, 1 Mar. 1961, pp. 6–7. Buckley Papers I-14, "John Birch Society (2 of 2) (1961)."

91. William F. Buckley Jr. to Charles Harding II, 23 Aug. 1961. Buckley Papers I-14, "Hacker–Hayes (1961)."

92. William F. Buckley Jr., "The Genteel Nightmare of Richard Rovere," *Harper's*, Aug. 1962, p. 54.

93. Kevin Phillips, *The Emerging Republican Majority* (New Rochelle, N.Y.: Arlington House, 1969), p. 38.

94. Tom Wicker to William F. Buckley Jr., 1 June 1965. Buckley Papers I-36, "*New York Times* (1965)."

95. Dick Mooney to Kingman Brewster Jr., 21 Feb. 1966. Brewster Presidential Records RU 11 I-161:19.

96. William F. Buckley Jr., "The Genteel Nightmare of Richard Rovere," p. 54.

97. M. Stanton Evans, *The Liberal Establishment* (New York: Devin-Adair, 1965), pp. 15–16.

98. "Buckley Hits Liberal Ideas of Education," *Harvard Crimson*, 5 May 1960, p. 1.

99. Elliot Richardson to Leverett Saltonstall, 16 July 1963. Richardson Papers I:68, "Saltonstall, Leverett—General."

100. Rick Perlstein, *Before the Storm: Barry Goldwater and the Unmaking of the American Consensus* (New York: Hill and Wang, 2001), p. 384.

101. Moore, *Presences,* p. 177.

102. *Ibid.,* p. 179.

103. Joseph Lieberman to Kingman Brewster Jr., 6 Aug 1964. Brewster Presidential Records RU 11 I-134:11.

104. Todd Gitlin, *The Sixties: Years of Hope, Days of Rage,* rev. ed. (New York: Bantam, 1993), p. 161.

105. Moore, *Presences,* p. 181.

106. Paul Moore Jr., "A Long Hot Week" [nd (1964)]. Paul Moore Jr. Papers.

107. Thomas Hughes, in Ted Gittinger (ed.), *The Johnson Years: A Vietnam Roundtable* (Austin, Tex.: Lyndon Baines Johnson Library, 1993), pp. 33–34.

108. William Conrad Gibbons, *The United States Government and the Vietnam War: Executive and Legislative Roles and Relationships,* part 2 (Princeton, N.J.: Princeton University Press, 1986), p. 283.

109. Lyndon Johnson, *The Vantage Point: Perspectives on the Presidency, 1963–1969* (New York: Popular Library, 1971), p. 113.

110. Gibbons, *The United States Government and the Vietnam War*, part 2, p. 290.

111. Chester Cooper, in Gittinger (ed.), *The Johnson Years*, p. 34.

112. McGeorge Bundy, in Gittinger (ed.), *The Johnson Years*, p. 31.

113. Quoted in James Patterson, *Grand Expectations* (New York: Oxford University Press, 1996), p. 559.

114. Juan Cameron, "A Boston Brahmin in 'Heartbreak House,'" *Fortune*, Oct. 1971, p. 167.

115. Interview with Elliot Richardson, 22 June 1997.

116. Daniel E. Button, *Lindsay, a Man for Tomorrow* (New York: Random House, 1965), p. 40.

117. M.S. Handler, "Negro Vote Rises as a Key in the South," *NYT*, 9 Nov. 1964, p. 21; Bill Minataglio, "Living with a Legacy: Famous Family and Its Achievements Have Shaped George W. Bush," *Dallas Morning News*, 17 Oct. 1999.

118. Murray Kempton, "They Got Him," *The New Republic*, 25 July 1964, p. 9.

119. Kirkpatrick Sale, *Power Shift: The Rise of the Southern Rim and Its Challenge to the Eastern Establishment* (New York: Random House, 1975), p. 8.

120. "Is the Ivy League Still the Best?" *Newsweek*, 23 Nov. 1964, p. 67.

121. "WASP-land," *Newsweek*, 16 Nov. 1964, p. 89.

122. Kingman Brewster, Address to the Yale Club of Washington, D.C., 12 Feb. 1965. Brewster Personal Papers I-4:5.

123. Interview with Harold Howe II, 7 Nov. 2000.

124. John Hay Whitney, Address at Colby College, 12 Nov. 1964. Brewster Presidential Records RU 11 I-221:9.

125. J. Irwin Miller to John McKay Jr., 2 Oct. 1964. Brewster Presidential Records RU 11 I-126:15.

126. Interview with J. Irwin Miller, 18 Dec. 1991.

6: APPROACHING THUNDER

1. Kai Bird, *The Color of Truth: McGeorge Bundy and William Bundy: Brothers in Arms* (New York: Simon & Schuster, 1998), p. 297.

2. Cyrus Vance, LBJ Library oral history interview, 9 Mar. 1970.

3. Stanley Karnow, *Vietnam: A History* (New York: Viking Press, 1983), pp. 411–13.

4. Boris M. Baczynski, "Professors Condemn US Vietnam Policy," *YDN*, 12 Feb. 1965, p. 1; Richard Van Wegenen, "Students Hold Two Rallies for, against Vietnam War; 250 March for Peace Saturday," *YDN*, 15 Feb. 1965, p. 1.

5. "The Time Has Come," *YDN*, 12 Feb. 1965, p. 2.

6. Frank W. Clifford, "Students Hold Two Rallies for, against Vietnam War; YAF Urges Continuation of Fighting," *YDN*, 15 Feb. 1965, p. 1; Victor H. Ashe, "925 Students Support US Stand in Vietnam," *YDN*, 2 Mar. 1965, p. 1.

7. *YAM*, Feb. 1969, p. 20.

8. *YAM*, Feb. 1964, p. 50; *YDN*, 14 Apr. 1965, 1 May 1965.

9. Mitchel Levitas, "Present and Future of Kingman Brewster," *NYTM*, 12 Feb. 1967, p. 75.

10. See W. J. Rorabaugh, *Berkeley at War: The 1960s* (New York: Oxford University Press, 1996).

11. James Reston, "New York: The Computers That Bloom in the Spring, Tra La!" *NYT*, 31 Mar. 1965, p. 38.

12. Godfrey Hodgson, *America in Our Time* (New York: Vintage Books, 1976), p. 288.

13. Brewster, Address to the Yale Club of Philadelphia, 15 Jan. 1965. Brewster Personal Papers I-4:2.

14. "Corporation Delays Decision on House for Dean Whiteman," *YDN*, 10 Apr. 1961, p. 1; "Freshmen Riot Attempt Fizzles into Seminar with Whiteman," *YDN*, 11 May 1961, p. 1.

15. John H. Garabedian, "Class History," in *History of the Yale College Class of 1965* (New Haven: Yale University, 1965), p. 309.

16. Steven Schatzow, "Junior Year," in *History of the Yale College Class of 1966* (New Haven: Yale University, 1966), p. 262.

17. Memo [nd, ns (Apr. 1965)]. Brewster Presidential Records RU 11 I-44:2.

18. Brewster, "Excerpt from an Uncompleted Book," in *Kingman Brewster: Remembrances* (New Haven: Yale University, 1997), pp. 78–79.

19. Memo [nd, ns (Mar. 1965)]. Brewster Presidential Records RU 11 I-44:2.

20. Yale University News Bureau, New Release #302, 8 Mar. 1965. Brewster Presidential Records RU 11 I-44:2.

21. Eric Ludvigsen, "A Blue Blast at Teach-Ins," *Detroit News*, 7 May 1965.

22. Kingman Brewster Jr., Address to the Association of New England Colleges, 4 Dec. 1964. Brewster Personal Papers I-4:1.

23. Holloway Kilbourn to *YAM*, July 1966, p. 3.

24. Phillip Fairbanks to R. Inslee Clark, 6 May 1965. Brewster Presidential Records RU 11 I-2:15.

25. Schatzow, "Junior Year," p. 262.

26. A. Bartlett Giamatti, "Sentimentalism," *YAM*, Apr. 1975, p. 18.

27. *YDN*, 11 Mar. 1965; Garabedian, "Class History," p. 310.

28. Brewster, *Report of the President, 1967–68* (New Haven: Yale University, 1968), p. 20.

29. Channel 13, "The Future of the University," 12 Mar. 1969. Brewster Personal Papers I-14:9.

30. "Your Generation," *YDN*, 15 Sep. 1965, p. 2.

31. Interview with Henry Chauncey Jr., 22 July 1993.

32. William Kessen, "The Student in Search of Education," *YAM*, May 1967.

33. See Daniel Catlin Jr., *Liberal Education at Yale: The Yale College Course of Study 1945–1978* (Washington: University Press of America, 1982), pp. 163–90.

34. Interview with William Kessen, 2 June 1992.

35. Brewster, *Report of the President, 1967–68*, p. 19.

36. Elliot Richardson, Notes for a Meeting on Boston Common, 14 Mar. 1965. Richardson Papers I:72, "Speeches—NAACP Legal Defense Fund—Detroit—May 1968."

37. Elliot L. Richardson, "Lt. Gov. Richardson at Selma: 'A Sense of Unity,'" *Boston Herald*, 21 Mar. 1965.

38. "Selma, Civil Rights, and the Church Militant," *Newsweek*, 29 Mar. 1965, p. 75.

39. A mockup of the March 29, 1965, cover of *Newsweek* with Moore's photo had been prepared but was bumped at the last minute by the image of a Russian cosmonaut, the first human to walk in space.

40. "Bishop Moore: A Leader of the New Breed," *Newsweek*, 29 Mar. 1965, p. 77.

41. Drew Pearson, "Humphrey into the Breach," *WP*, 14 Mar. 1965, p. E7.

42. Paul Moore Jr., *Presences: A Bishop's Life in the City* (New York: Farrar, Straus and Giroux, 1997), pp. 183–84.

43. *Ibid.*, pp. 190–91.

44. Kingman Brewster Jr. to Frank E. Block, 12 Aug. 1964. Brewster Presidential Records RU 11 I-126:14.

45. Brewster, Fessenden School Commencement Address, 8 June 1962. Brewster Personal Papers I-1:7.

46. Kingman Brewster Jr. to William Sloane Coffin Jr., 24 Feb. 1964. Brewster Presidential Records RU 11 I-61:6.

47. Brewster, Address to the Yale Club of Philadelphia, 15 Jan. 1965. Brewster Personal Papers I-4:2.

48. Dennis T. Jaffe, "Faculty Criticizes US in Vietnam Conflict," *YDN,* 7 Apr. 1965, p. 1; "Lynd Tells Marchers He Won't Pay Taxes," *YDN,* 15 Apr. 1965; Richard Van Wegenen, "Local Group to Join March on Washington," *YDN,* 16 Apr. 1965, p. 1; "SDS Call for March on Washington," *YDN,* 16 Apr. 1965, p. 2; Kingman Brewster Jr. to Mrs. George Sidenberg Jr., 14 Apr. 1965. Brewster Presidential Records RU 11 I-182:16.

49. Paul Moore Jr. to Kingman Brewster Jr., 13 Jan. 1966. Brewster Presidential Records RU 11 I-150:18.

50. William Sloane Coffin Jr. to Kingman Brewster Jr., 7 Jan. 1964. Brewster Presidential Records RU 11 I-61:6.

51. Brewster, Statement at the Second Dublin Conference, 1 Oct. 1965. Brewster Personal Papers I-5:11.

52. "The Dublin Conference," *YDN,* 4 Oct. 1965, p. 2.

53. Kingman Brewster Jr. to Grenville Clark [nd]. Brewster Presidential Records, RU 11 I-85:12

54. Brewster, "Excerpt from an Uncompleted Book," p. 80.

55. Quoted in Allen J. Matusow, *The Unraveling of America: A History of Liberalism in the 1960s* (New York: Harper & Row, 1984), p. 312.

56. William Sloane Coffin Jr., *Once to Every Man* (New York: Atheneum, 1977), p. 209.

57. J. William Stack Jr. to Kingman Brewster Jr., 21 Feb. 1964. Brewster Presidential Records RU 11 I-113:11.

58. Kingman Brewster Jr. to J. William Stack Jr., 28 Feb. 1964. Brewster Presidential Records RU 11 I-113:11.

59. Garry Wills, "Buckley, Buckley, Bow Wow Wow," *Esquire,* Jan. 1968, p. 73.

60. Coffin, *Once to Every Man,* pp. 210–12.

61. Judith Clavir Albert and Stewart Edward Albert (eds.), *The Sixties Papers: Documents of a Rebellious Decade* (New York: Praeger, 1984), p. 222.

62. Moore, *Presences,* p. 207.

63. Cyrus Vance, appointment book, 1965. Vance Papers I-6:67.

64. Moore, *Presences,* p. 207.

65. *Ibid.,* p. 208.

66. *Congressional Record,* v. 111, p. 2155.

67. Interview with J. Irwin Miller, 18 Dec. 1991.

68. Steven V. Roberts, "Is It Too Late for a Man of Honesty, High Purpose and Intelligence to Be Elected President of the United States in 1968?" *Esquire,* Oct. 1967, p. 183.

69. Henry Chauncey Jr. to Geoffrey Kabaservice, 9 Mar. 1999.

70. Jeff Greenfield, *No Peace, No Place: Excavations Along the Generational Fault* (Garden City, N.Y. Doubleday, 1973), p. 239.

71. Brewster, "Excerpt from an Uncompleted Book," p. 80.

72. Brewster, Address to the George C. Stone Dinner, Brockton, Mass., 31 Jan. 1951. Brewster Personal Papers II-44, "Foreign Policy."

73. "2 Pentagon Aides Sworn to Posts," *NYT,* 6 July 1962, p. 7.

74. Brewster, Commencement Address at State University of New York at Buffalo, 28 May 1967. Brewster Personal Papers I-9:1.

75. Brewster, Statement at the Second Dublin Conference, 1 Oct. 1965. Brewster Personal Papers I-5:11.
76. Brewster, Commencement Address at State University of New York at Buffalo, 28 May 1967. Brewster Personal Papers I-9:1.
77. Transcript of WGBH, "Vietnam: Bundy and Hoffman," 14 Mar. 1968. Ford Foundation Archives, box 41835.
78. McGeorge Bundy, Address to the American Society of Newspaper Editors, 20 Apr. 1967. Ford Foundation Archives, box 41834.
79. Kingman Brewster Jr. to *New York Herald Tribune,* 12 Dec. 1950. Brewster Personal Papers II-44, "Foreign Policy."
80. Cyrus Vance, LBJ Library oral history interview, 9 Mar. 1970.
81. Transcript of WGBH, "Vietnam: Bundy and Hoffman."
82. McGeorge Bundy to Jonathan B. Bingham, 10 Mar. 1966. Bundy Records III-23:271.
83. William P. Bundy to Kingman Brewster Jr., 10 Apr. 1969. Brewster Presidential Records RU 11 I-47:2.
84. Kingman Brewster Jr. to Christian Herter Jr., 29 June 1954. Brewster Personal Papers II-34, "Brewster—correspondence, 1954."
85. Kingman Brewster Jr. to Peter Solbert, 29 June 1954. Brewster Personal Papers II-34, "Brewster—correspondence, 1954."
86. Interview with Gregory Craig, 9 Apr. 1991.
87. DeWitt C. Smith to Cyrus Vance, 9 Jan. 1965. Vance Papers I-3:33.
88. Brewster on NBC-TV's *Meet the Press,* 25 Sep. 1966. Brewster Personal Papers I-7:11.
89. Gibbons, *The United States Government and the Vietnam War,* part 3, pp. 47–48.
90. McGeorge Bundy to Lyndon Johnson, 6 Mar. 1965. *Foreign Relations of the United States, 1964–1968,* vol. 2 (Washington: Government Printing Office, 2002), p. 405.
91. McGeorge Bundy to Robert McNamara, 30 June 1965. Reprinted in Larry Berman, *Planning a Tragedy: The Americanization of the War in Vietnam* (New York: W. W. Norton, 1982), pp. 187–89.
92. Michael R. Beschloss, *Taking Charge: The Johnson White House Tapes* (New York: Simon & Schuster, 1997), p. 372.
93. McGeorge Bundy to Lyndon Johnson, 7 Feb. 1965. Quoted in Berman, *Planning a Tragedy,* p. 43.
94. Bird, *The Color of Truth,* p. 325.
95. Douglass Cater to Lyndon Johnson, 10 July 1965. Quoted in Gibbons, *The United States Government and the Vietnam War,* part 3, p. 397.
96. McGeorge Bundy to Lyndon Johnson, 19 July 1965. Quoted in Gibbons, *The United States Government and the Vietnam War,* part 3, p. 398.
97. Michael Beschloss, *Reaching for Glory: Lyndon Johnson's Secret White House Tapes, 1964–1965* (New York: Simon & Schuster, 2001), p. 306.
98. *Ibid.,* p. 321.
99. Bird, *The Color of Truth,* p. 299.
100. Elliot Richardson, LBJ Library oral history interview, 31 Jan. 1974.
101. Interview with Francis Bator, 19 June 2002.
102. Interview with Nicholas Katzenbach, 4 June 2003.
103. Walter Isaacson and Evan Thomas, *The Wise Men: Six Friends and the World They Made* (New York, Simon & Schuster, 1986), pp. 643–44.
104. Cyrus Vance to Jonathan Bingham, 10 Feb. 1964. Vance Papers I-3:25.
105. David S. McLellan, *Cyrus Vance* (New York: Rowman and Allanheld, 1982), p. 12; interview with Mary Bundy, 5 Feb. 2002.

106. John Barlow Martin, *Overtaken by Events: The Dominican Crisis from the Fall of Trujillo to the Civil War* (Garden City, N.Y.: Doubleday, 1966), p. 697.

107. Tad Szulc, *Dominican Diary* (New York: Delacorte Press, 1965), p. 265.

108. Bird, *The Color of Truth*, p. 320.

109. Todd Gitlin, *The Sixties: Years of Hope, Days of Rage*, rev. ed. (New York: Bantam, 1993), p. 188.

110. Interview with Francis Bator, 19 June 2002.

111. Bird, *The Color of Truth*, p. 318.

112. Interview with Mary Bundy, 26 Sep. 2001.

113. John H. Fenton, "Bundy Says Policy Is Widely Backed," *NYT*, 15 June 1965, p. 26.

114. Interview with Francis Bator, 19 June 2002.

115. Henry Morgenthau to *Harper's*, Jan. 1966, p. 8.

116. Beschloss, *Reaching for Glory*, p. 388.

117. Isaacson and Thomas, *The Wise Men*, p. 656.

118. *Ibid.*, p. 28.

119. McGeorge Bundy to Lyndon Johnson, 21 July 1965. Gibbons, *The United States Government and the Vietnam War*, part 3, p. 415.

120. Cyrus Vance to Robert McNamara, 16 July 1965. Gibbons, *The United States Government and the Vietnam War*, part 3, p. 381.

121. Bird, *The Color of Truth*, p. 322.

122. Joseph Goulden, *The Money Givers* (New York: Random House, 1971), p. 243.

123. Kingman Brewster Jr. to Lyndon B. Johnson, 20 Sep. 1965. Brewster Presidential Records RU 11 I-124:17.

124. Eugene M. Daugherty to William F. Buckley Jr., 2 July 1991. Buckley Papers III-III:118.

125. Brewster, Address to the New Haven Citizens Action Commission, 12 Apr. 1966. Brewster Personal Papers I-6:19.

126. David J. Narot, "The Prime Mover: Mayor Richard C. Lee," *YAM*, May 1966.

127. John Hersey, "What Am I Doing Here?" *YAM*, Jan. 1966, p. 12.

128. Kingman Brewster Jr. to Mott Foundation, 1965. Brewster Presidential Records RU 11 I-7:5.

129. Brewster, *Report of the President, 1967–68* (New Haven: Yale University, 1968), p. 29.

130. Brewster, Remarks at a Panel Discussion on the ISS, Development Board Convocation, 15 Nov. 1968. Brewster Presidential Records RU 11 I-79:7.

131. Vincent J. Cannato, *The Ungovernable City: John Lindsay and His Struggle to Save New York* (New York: Basic Books, 2001), pp. 22–23.

132. *Ibid.*, p. 27.

133. William T. Glidden to Elliot Richardson, 30 June 1965. Richardson Papers I:60, "'L'—misc."

134. Alexander M. Bickel, "Liberals and John Lindsay," *The New Republic*, 3 July 1965, p. 18.

135. William F. Buckley Jr. to Russell Kirk, 11 Nov. 1965. Buckley Papers I-35, "*Educational Reviewer* (1965)."

136. Michael Harrington, "Pro-Vest & Anti-Guitar: The Sad Truth about Campus Conservatism," *Nugget*, Oct. 1962, p. 37.

137. Dick Schaap, "Lux et Veritas," *NYHT*, 7 June 1965.

138. "Incitement to Excellence," *Time*, 12 Nov. 1965.

139. William Borders, "Lindsay among U.S. Leaders on the Board," *NYT*, 13 Mar. 1967, p. 39.

140. "Den uafhaengige amerikaner," *Berlingske Tidende,* 27 June 1964.

141. Interview with Richard C. Lee, 3 Mar. 2000.

142. Sung on the occasion of the New Haven Advertising Club dinner, 9 Mar. 1967; lyrics supplied courtesy of Richard C. Lee.

143. Interview with Lance Liebman, 22 Jan. 1999.

144. Ludvigsen, "A Blue Blast at Teach-Ins."

145. Joseph Lieberman, Letter to Chairman, *YDN,* 21 Oct. 1965, p. 2.

146. Andrew P. Garvin, "Responsible Action Urged," *YDN,* 22 Oct. 1965, p. 1; "Tide Turns against Protesters," *Los Angeles Herald Examiner,* 24 Oct. 1965.

147. William H. Chafe, *Never Stop Running: Allard Lowenstein and the Struggle to Save American Liberalism* (New York: Basic Books, 1993), pp. 248–49.

148. Coffin, *Once to Every Man,* pp. 213–15.

149. Brewster, Address to the Yale Club of Southern California, 10 Nov. 1965. Brewster Personal Papers I-6:5.

150. Interview with John Blum, 4 Mar. 1992.

151. Independent Group of Yale Alumni to Kingman Brewster Jr., 15 June 1966. Brewster Presidential Records RU 11 I-138:10.

152. Paul Moore Jr. to Kingman Brewster Jr., 13 Jan. 1966. Brewster Presidential Records RU 11 I-150:18.

153. William Sloane Coffin Jr. to Kingman Brewster Jr., 5 May 1966. Brewster Presidential Records RU 11 I-59:1.

154. Kingman Brewster Jr. to William Sloane Coffin Jr., 5 May 1966. Brewster Presidential Records RU 11 I-59:1.

7: THE GUARDIANS OF EQUAL OPPORTUNITY

1. Dan A. Oren, *Joining the Club: A History of Jews and Yale* (New Haven: Yale University Press, 1983), p. 272; interview with R. Inslee Clark, 13 May 1993.

2. "Admissions Dean Howe to Take Year Off; Replaced by Hyatt," *YDN,* 12 Feb. 1964, p. 1; "Dean of Admissions Howe Resigns Post, Elected AFS Head," *YDN,* 20 Oct. 1964, p. 1.

3. Interview with R. Inslee Clark, 8 Apr. 1993.

4. Oren, *Joining the Club,* pp. 208–09.

5. "Clark Named Admissions Director; To Form a Policy Advisory Board," *YDN,* 3 Feb. 1965, p. 1.

6. Richard B. Sewall to Kingman Brewster Jr., 12 Feb. 1965. Brewster Presidential Records RU 11 I-2:9. See also Paul Weiss to Kingman Brewster Jr., 12 Feb. 1965. Brewster Presidential Records RU 11 I-2:9; C. Vann Woodward to Kingman Brewster Jr., 4 Feb. 1965. Brewster Presidential Records RU 11 I-2:9; interview with William Sloane Coffin Jr., 9 Dec. 1991.

7. Brewster, Address at the 100th Anniversary Dinner of the Cincinnati Yale Club, 8 Feb. 1964. Brewster Personal Papers I-2:1.

8. Author's calculations from *The Old Campus* series (New Haven: Yale University), 1950–54.

9. Brooks M. Kelley, *Yale: A History* (New Haven: Yale University Press, 1974), p. 407.

10. Interview with R. Inslee Clark, 8 Apr. 1993.

11. Calvin Trillin, *Remembering Denny* (New York: Warner Books, 1993), p. 41.

12. "High Schools' Percentage Up at Princeton," *YDN,* 21 Sep. 1955, p. 3.

13. "University Inaugurates Policy to Standardize Admissions Procedures," *YDN,* 10 Oct. 1958, p. 1.

14. Oren, *Joining the Club,* pp. 189-97. According to the Hillel directors of the other Ivy League colleges, the percentage of Jewish undergraduates at their institutions ranged from a high of 45 percent at Columbia to a low of 12 percent at Yale. Even Princeton and Dartmouth had a higher proportion of Jewish undergraduates than Yale.
15. "Class Dress Habits Are Much Improved, According to Faculty," *YDN,* 24 Sep. 1957, p. 1.
16. Henry Chauncey Jr. to Geoffrey Kabaservice, 2 Mar. 1999.
17. Interview with R. Inslee Clark, 13 May 1993.
18. R. Inslee Clark, "Admission to Yale: Policies and Procedures," *YAM,* Oct. 1966, p. 35.
19. Strobe Talbott, "Brewster Attacks Harvard's Ratings as Unfair to Public Schools," *YDN,* 31 Oct. 1966, p. 1.
20. Strobe Talbott, "Admissions Office to Install New Financial Aid Policies," *YDN,* 22 Feb. 1966, p. 1.
21. Brewster, "Excerpts from an Uncompleted Book," in *Kingman Brewster: Remembrances* (New Haven: Yale University, 1997), pp. 79–80.
22. R. Inslee Clark Jr. to John Burke, 21 May 1968. Brewster Presidential Records RU 11 I-3:4.
23. Clark, "Admission to Yale," p. 36.
24. McGeorge Bundy, "The Issue before the Court," *Atlantic Monthly,* Nov. 1977, p. 42.
25. Interview with McGeorge Bundy, 2 Mar. 1993.
26. Quoted in Jennifer Kaylin, "The Changing Face of Affirmative Action," *YAM,* Summer 1994, p. 40.
27. Interview with R. Inslee Clark Jr., 2 Apr. 1993.
28. "Helping the Alumni Keep in Touch," *YAM,* Jan. 1969, p. 37.
29. Brewster, typed statement [nd (1966)]. Brewster Presidential Records RU 11 I-47:17.
30. Henri Peyre et al., "Report to the President of Yale University on the Role of the Arts in Undergraduate Education at Yale" (New Haven: Yale University, Jan. 1967). Brewster Presidential Records RU 11 I-177:8.
31. Kingman Brewster Jr. to John Muyskens, 15 Mar. 1967. Reprinted in "Yale Alumni Schools Committee Handbook" (New Haven: Yale University, 1995), p. 31. This document is widely known as "the Muyskens letter."
32. *Ibid.*
33. Sam Babbitt to Kingman Brewster Jr., 20 Nov. 1964. Brewster Presidential Records RU 11 I-41:4.
34. Malcolm Weiskel to Kingman Brewster Jr., 7 July 1967. Brewster Presidential Records RU 11 I-220:8.
35. Interview with R. Inslee Clark, 8 Apr. 1993.
36. The decreased number of applications, according to Clark, reflected a new policy of discouraging applications from students who did not meet Yale's minimum requirements. See Richard W. Goldman, "Class of 1970: Accent on Variety," *YDN,* 15 Apr. 1966, p. 3.
37. R. Thomas Herman, "Class of '70 Reflects Admissions Changes," *YDN,* Summer 1966, p. 1.
38. Statistics courtesy of Yale Office of Institutional Research.
39. Oren, *Joining the Club,* p. 211.
40. Interview with R. Inslee Clark, 8 Apr. 1993.
41. Penny Hollander Feldman, *Recruiting an Elite: Admission to Harvard College* (New York: Garland, 1988), p. 100.
42. Interview with R. Inslee Clark, 8 Apr. 1993.

43. Robert Hulburd to R. Inslee Clark, 21 Oct. 1966. Brewster Presidential Records RU 11 I-2:10.
44. Quoted in R. Thomas Herman, "New Concept of Yale Admissions: Diversity," *YDN*, 16 Dec. 1965, p. 6.
45. Quoted in Goldman, "Class of 1970," p. 3.
46. Peter S. Prescott, *A World of Our Own: Notes on Life and Learning in a Boys' Preparatory School* (New York: Coward-McCann, 1970), p. 200.
47. Matthew Warren to Kingman Brewster Jr., 4 May 1966. Brewster Presidential Records RU 11 I-2:9.
48. Interview with Ralph Halsey Jr., 21 Apr. 1992.
49. William F. Buckley Jr., "What Makes Bill Buckley Run," *Atlantic Monthly*, Apr. 1968, p. 68.
50. Interview with R. Inslee Clark, 8 Apr. 1993.
51. Yale historian Gaddis Smith points out that many students of the earlier period were the first generation to go to college, an observation corroborated by my study of the Class of 1916. Further, he notes that the earlier classes were smaller and so did not produce as many offspring as their counterparts in later years.
52. George Wilson Pierson, *A Yale Book of Numbers: Historical Statistics of the College and University 1701–1976* (New Haven: Yale University, 1983), p. 88; C. Tracy Barnes to Howard Phelan, 13 Feb. 1968. Brewster Presidential Records RU 11 I-6:2.
53. Memo by Charles E. Lindblom, 30 Mar. 1966. Brewster Presidential Records RU 11 I-2:4.
54. Interview with R. Inslee Clark, 8 Apr. 1993.
55. John Wisner to Millie, 20 Apr. 1966. Buckley Papers I-41, "Wisner, John (1966)."
56. John O'Hara, "The Situation Up at Yale," *Denver Post*, 1 Jan. 1965, p. 31.
57. Herbert Sturdy to Kingman Brewster Jr., 22 June 1966. Brewster Presidential Records RU 11 I-2:10.
58. Interview with J. Irwin Miller, 17 Feb. 2001.
59. Interview with Francis X. Sutton, 12 Feb. 2001.
60. Kai Bird, *The Color of Truth: McGeorge Bundy and William Bundy: Brothers in Arms* (New York: Simon & Schuster, 1998), pp. 377-78.
61. Joseph Goulden, *The Money Givers* (New York: Random House, 1971), p. 242.
62. Interview with Harold Howe II, 22 Dec. 2000.
63. Interview with Stephen Bundy, 5 Sep. 2001.
64. Elliot Richardson to McGeorge Bundy, 18 Mar. 1966. Bundy Records II-23:271.
65. Written on announcement of the formation of Heald, Hobson and Associates, 29 Dec. 1965. Brewster Presidential Records RU 11 I-48:15.
66. Interview with Andrew Bundy, 23 May 2002.
67. Interview with Richard Magat, 20 July 2001.
68. Martin Mayer, "Washington's Grant to the Ford Foundation," *NYTM*, 13 Nov. 1966, p. 142.
69. Interview with Peter De Janosi, 8 Nov. 2002.
70. Interview with Richard Magat, 20 July 2001.
71. Interview with James Ellis, 27 Feb. 2001.
72. Interview with Francis X. Sutton, 12 Feb. 2001.
73. Goulden, *The Money Givers*, p. 244.
74. *Ford Foundation Annual Report, 1966.*
75. Gerald Bruck, "Yale Receives $6.3 Million Grant," *YDN*, 3 May 1966, p. 1.
76. Kingman Brewster to James Perkins, 7 Nov. 1965. Brewster Presidential Records RU 11 I-98:7.

77. Interview with Peter De Janosi, 8 Nov. 2002.

78. Brewster, "The Voluntary Society" (unpublished manuscript, 25 Feb. 1983 draft), p. 102. Source courtesy of John G. Simon.

79. See Benjamin Barber's description of civil society in *Jihad vs. McWorld* (New York: Ballantine, 1995), p. 281.

80. T. J. Ross, "The Public Relations Function," lecture at the New School for Social Research, 4 Feb. 1963. Source courtesy of William Simpich.

81. Quoted in Richard Armstrong, "McGeorge Bundy Confronts the Teachers," *NYTM*, 20 Apr. 1969, p. 27.

82. Interview with Stuart Sucherman, 23 Oct. 2001.

83. *Ford Foundation Annual Report, 1966.*

84. Interview with Harold Howe II, 22 Dec. 2000.

85. McGeorge Bundy, Address at the Annual Banquet of the National Urban League, Inc., 2 Aug. 1966. Ford Foundation Archives, box 41834.

86. Emanuel Perlmutter, "Strike Was Felt 'In Air All Week,'" *NYT,* 2 Jan. 1966, p. 58.

87. "Text of Lindsay's Inaugural Address at City Hall," *NYT,* 2 Jan. 1966, p. 56.

88. *Ford Foundation Annual Report, 1968,* p. 9.

89. Terence Smith, "Mayor Lindsay's First 100 Days: Satisfactions and Frustrations," *NYT,* 10 Apr. 1966, p. 67.

90. Charles R. Morris, *The Cost of Good Intentions: New York City and the Liberal Experiment* (New York: W. W. Norton, 1980), p. 31.

91. Vincent J. Cannato, *The Ungovernable City: John Lindsay and His Struggle to Save New York* (New York: Basic Books, 2001), p. 121.

92. Larry L. King, "Lindsay of New York," *Harper's,* Aug. 1968, p. 38.

93. Diane Ravitch, *The Great School Wars: New York City, 1805–1973* (New York: Basic Books, 1974), p. 261.

94. Mario Fantini, Marilyn Gittell, and Richard Magat, *Community Control and the Urban School* (New York: Praeger, 1970), p. 103.

95. Elliot Richardson, Address at the Rally on Boston Common Honoring Dr. Martin Luther King Jr., 23 Apr. 1965. Richardson Papers I:72.

96. Martin A. Linsky to A. A. Michelson [nd (1966?)]. Richardson Papers I:66; Ronald P. Formisano, *Boston against Busing: Race, Class, and Ethnicity in the 1960s and 1970s* (Chapel Hill: University of North Carolina Press, 1991), p. 35.

97. Ravitch, *The Great School Wars,* p. 272.

98. New York City Board of Education, "Proposals for Improving Education in Schools in Disadvantaged Areas," 19 Oct. 1966. Bundy Records II-13:164.

99. John Lindsay to Lloyd Garrison, 24 Oct. 1966. Bundy Records II-13:164.

100. Morris, *The Cost of Good Intentions,* p. 109.

101. Ravitch, *The Great School Wars,* p. 307; Bernard E. Donovan to McGeorge Bundy, 9 Nov. 1964. Bundy Records II-13:164.

102. Quoted in Cannato, *The Ungovernable City,* p. 275.

103. "Sviridoff to Run New N.Y. Agency," *YDN,* 7 Jan. 1966, p. 1.

104. McGeorge Bundy, "Statement on New York Schools," 29 Dec. 1966. Bundy Records II-13:163.

105. Fantini, Gittell, and Magat, *Community Control and the Urban School,* p. 108.

106. Students for a Democratic Society, "The Port Huron Statement," 1962. Quoted in James Miller, *Democracy Is in the Streets: From Port Huron to the Siege of Chicago* (Cambridge, Mass.: Harvard University Press, 1994), p. 333.

107. Brewster, Address at the Yale National Alumni Meeting, Pittsburgh, 22 Jan. 1966. Brewster Personal Papers I-6:12.

108. Lanny J. Davis, "From the Chairman's Desk," *YDN*, 4 May 1966, p. 2.
109. Lanny Davis to Kingman Brewster Jr., 27 Apr. 1969. Brewster Presidential Records RU 11 I-68:1.
110. Brewster, Address at Butler University, 7 Feb. 1964. Brewster Personal Papers I-1:20.
111. McGeorge Bundy, NBC-TV *Meet the Press*, 25 Dec. 1966. Ford Foundation Archives, box 41834.
112. "Panel at Yale Agrees on Need for Federal Decentralization," *NHR*, 7 Mar. 1967.
113. Elliot L. Richardson, "Beyond the Marlboro Man," *The Ripon Forum*, May 1967, p. 1.
114. John Lindsay, Address to Liberal Party of New York State Dinner, 11 Oct. 1967. Lindsay Papers XVI:349-251.
115. Smith, "Mayor Lindsay's First 100 Days," p. 67.
116. Interview with R. Inslee Clark, 8 Apr. 1993.
117. James Reston Jr., "Washington: The Tragedy of the Republicans," *NYT*, 13 June 1966.
118. Interview with R. Inslee Clark, 13 May 1993.
119. Kingman Brewster Jr. to John Muyskens, 15 Mar. 1967.
120. Brewster, typewritten notes from Yale Corporation Educational Policy Committee meeting, 11–12 Mar. 1966. Brewster Presidential Records RU 11 I-88:2.
121. Kingman Brewster Jr. to Herbert Sturdy, 11 Aug. 1966. Brewster Presidential Records RU 11 I-2:8.
122. Brewster, "Report of the President, 1965–66," p. 3.
123. Reference to letter by Burton Closson; Charles M. O'Hearn to Burton Closson, 20 July 1966. Brewster Presidential Records RU 11 I-163:14.
124. Interview with R. Inslee Clark, 13 May 1993.

8: A NEW SOCIETY EMERGES

1. Brewster, Yale Baccalaureate Address, 12 June 1966. Brewster Personal Papers I-7:6.
2. William Borders, "Brewster Scores U.S. Draft Policy," *NYT*, 13 June 1966, p. 1.
3. Brewster, Statement to the *Yale Daily News*, 18 May 1966. Brewster Personal Papers I-7:4.
4. Brewster, "Excerpt from an Uncompleted Book," in *Kingman Brewster: Remembrances* (New Haven: Yale University, 1997), p. 80.
5. Kingman Brewster Jr. to Lyndon B. Johnson, 20 Sep. 1965. Brewster Presidential Records RU 11 I-124:17.
6. Robert Lovett to Kingman Brewster Jr., 15 June 1966. Brewster Presidential Records RU 11 I-41:10.
7. *YDN*, 12 Sep. 1966; interview with John Gardner, 28 June 1996.
8. Brewster had, in fact, offered Marshall the deanship of the Yale Law School when he left the government in 1965.
9. Mitchel Levitas, "Present and Future of Kingman Brewster," *NYTM*, 12 Feb. 1967, p. 78.
10. Interview with John Ecklund, 8 June 1992.
11. William S. Beinecke, *Through Mem'ry's Haze: A Personal Memoir* (New York: Prospect Hill Press, 2000), p. 450.
12. Levitas, "Present and Future of Kingman Brewster," p. 78.
13. John H. Garabedian, "Women in L&B," *YDN*, 28 Oct. 63, p. 1; interview with Arthur Galston, 22 Apr. 1993.

14. George A. Brown, "Female Integration," *YDN,* 3 Oct. 1964, p. 2.

15. Robert Joost to Kingman Brewster Jr., 21 Nov. 1968. Brewster Presidential Records RU 11 I-124:10.

16. Kingman Brewster Jr. to A. Whitney Griswold, 23 Dec. 1942. Griswold Personal Papers I-1:23.

17. Interview with Elga Wasserman, 7 May 1992.

18. Brewster was punning on the legal term for dangerous properties, such as the nineteenth-century railway roundhouses that often injured children who were attracted to them as playhouses; interview with Aviam Soifer, 6 Sep. 1991.

19. Florence Besse Ballantine, quoted in *Wellesley Alumni Magazine,* 1973.

20. Kingman Brewster Jr. to Holland [nd]. Brewster Personal Papers II-1; interview with Lawrence Pickett, 15 Dec. 1991.

21. Brewster, Address at Yale Development Board Convocation, 15 Nov. 1968. Brewster Personal Papers I-13:12.

22. Brewster, Address at the Yale Alumni Day Luncheon, 18 Feb. 1967. Brewster Personal Papers I-8:10.

23. See Charlotte Williams Conable, *Women at Cornell: The Myth of Equal Education* (Ithaca, N.Y.: Cornell University Press, 1977).

24. Bernice Sandler, in *Equal Rights for Men and Women: Hearings before Subcommittee No. 4 of the House Committee on the Judiciary,* sec. no. 2, 1971 (Washington: Government Printing Office, 1971), pp. 263–72. Cited in Blanche Linden-Ward and Carol Hurd Green, *Changing the Future: American Women in the 1960s* (New York: Twayne, 1993), p. 67.

25. Quoted in David Remnick, "American Hunger," *New Yorker,* 12 Oct. 1998, p. 64.

26. Interview with Kai Erikson, 9 Mar. 1992.

27. Quoted in Liva Baker, *I'm Radcliffe, Fly Me!: The Seven Sisters and the Failure of Women's Education* (New York: Macmillan), p. 26.

28. Charles M. O'Hearn, Address at the Westchester Yale Alumni Association Dinner, 20 Nov. 1968. Brewster Presidential Records RU 11 I-42:10.

29. "88th NEWS Banquet Honors Bundy; Brewster, Moffett, Davis Address 350," *YDN,* 3 May 1966, p. 1.

30. Frederick I. Taft, "Poll Results: Yale Men Want Women," *YDN,* 18 May 1966, p. 1.

31. Barbara Miller Solomon, *In the Company of Educated Women: A History of Women and Higher Education in America* (New Haven: Yale University Press, 1985), p. 44.

32. Linden-Ward and Green, *Changing the Future,* pp. 69–70.

33. "Admission of Women to New College," *Oxford,* Dec. 1964. See also Joseph Soares, *The Decline of Privilege: The Modernization of Oxford University* (Stanford, Calif.: Stanford University Press, 1999), pp. 96–99.

34. Interview with Henry Chauncey Jr., 13 July 1993.

35. Barbara Foote, "A Royal Marriage" (unpublished paper). Source courtesy of Harold Howe II.

36. Interview with Henry Chauncey Jr., 14 Apr. 1996; Strobe Talbott, "Coordinate Women's College Considered by Corporation," *YDN,* 14 Mar. 1966, p. 1.

37. Quoted in Stanley J. Vendit, "Yale, Vassar Link under Study; Girls' College May Move Here," *NHR,* 17 Dec. 1966, p. 1.

38. Mount Holyoke was founded as a female seminary in 1837, long before Vassar College opened, in 1865, but was not chartered as a full-fledged college until 1888.

39. Interview with Henry Chauncey Jr., 22 July 1993. See also interview with Charles Taylor, 12 May 1992; J. Richardson Dilworth to Kingman Brewster Jr., 8 Mar. 1966. Brewster Presidential Records RU 11 I-4:5.

40. Richard Norton Smith, *The Harvard Century* (New York: Simon & Schuster), p. 244.
41. "Student Views Polled by Political Union," *YDN,* 10 Mar. 1966, p. 1; "Poll Shows Most Students Favor US Vietnam Policy," *YDN,* 23 Nov. 1965, p. 1.
42. Hugh Calkins to Geoffrey Kabaservice, 25 Nov. 1999; "Proposal for a Bipartisan Council on American Foreign Policy," 8 July 1957. Brewster Personal Papers II-2, "Council on Foreign Relations."
43. Interview with Strobe Talbott, 10 Apr. 1991.
44. Terence Smith, "Student Lenders Warn President of Doubts on War," *NYT,* 30 Dec. 1966, p. 1; William H. Chafe, *Never Stop Running: Allard Lowenstein and the Struggle to Save American Liberalism* (New York: Basic Books, 1993), pp. 251–52.
45. Chafe, *Never Stop Running,* pp. 250–51.
46. *Ibid.,* p. 252.
47. Strobe Talbott, "'The Secretary of State Said Nothing New,'" *YDN,* 1 Feb. 1967, p. 1.
48. James Reston, "New Haven: God and War at Yale," *NYT,* 26 Apr. 1967, p. 46.
49. Interview with Strobe Talbott, 10 Apr. 1991.
50. Interview with Mark Zanger, 7 Apr. 1992.
51. Strobe Talbott, "Wartime Draft: Dilemma and Lesson," *YAM,* Apr. 1967, p. 30.
52. Burke Marshall et al., *In Pursuit of Equity: Who Shall Serve When Not All Serve?: Report of the National Advisory Commission on Selective Service* (Washington: Government Printing Office, 1967), p. 50.
53. "Backward Step on the Draft," *NYT,* 21 June 1967, p. 46.
54. Interview with Strobe Talbott, 10 Apr. 1991.
55. Interview with Gregory Craig, 13 Apr. 2001.
56. "Continuing Concern about the War in Vietnam," *YAM,* Feb. 1967, p. 8.
57. Robert Cook to Grant Robley, 18 Jan. 1967. Brewster Presidential Records RU 11 II-317:17.
58. Interview with Elias Clark, 11 Mar. 1992.
59. Kingman Brewster Jr., to Jules Feiffer et al., 26 Aug. 1967. Brewster Personal Papers II-74, "Brewster, Kingman—Personal."
60. Robert Brustein, *Making Scenes: A Personal History of the Turbulent Years at Yale, 1966–1979* (New York: Limelight Editions, 1984), pp. 43–44.
61. Interview with Nicholas Katzenbach, 4 June 2003.
62. Kyle Haselden, "Concerned and Committed," *The Christian Century,* 15 Feb. 1967, pp. 197–98.
63. William Sloane Coffin Jr., *Once to Every Man* (New York: Atheneum, 1977), p. 234.
64. *Ibid.,* p. 225.
65. *Ibid.,* pp. 228–29.
66. William Sloane Coffin Jr., "On Civil Disobedience," lecture for the Washington Seminar, "Law, Order, and Civil Disobedience," sponsored by the American Enterprise Institute for Public Policy Research, 21 Feb. 1967. Brewster Presidential Records RU 11 I-149:17.
67. *YAM,* Mar. 1967, p. 4.
68. "Chaplain Coffin Explains His Position," *YAM,* Mar. 1967, p. 8.
69. "Yale President's Son Deferred as Objector," *BG,* 11 Mar. 1968.
70. Transcript of *Meet the Press,* 28 Jan. 1968. Brewster Presidential Records RU 11 I-62:9.
71. Kingman Brewster Jr. to Beckwith R. Bronson, 5 May 1967. Brewster Presidential Records RU 11 I-149:17.
72. George C. Wilson, "Vance Asks End of 'Intolerance' in War Debate," *WP,* 7 May 1967, p. A1.
73. Cyrus Vance, LBJ Library oral history interview, 9 Mar. 1970, p. 9.

74. Cyrus Vance, Address to the 90th Annual Convention of the Diocese of West Virginia, 6 May 1967. Vance Papers I-5:49.

75. Brooke Hindle to Cyrus Vance, 15 Aug. 1967. Vance Papers I-7:88.

76. LBJ Library oral history interview with Nicholas Katzenbach, 23 Nov. 1968; Walter Isaacson and Evan Thomas, *The Wise Men: Six Friends and the World They Made* (New York: Simon & Schuster, 1986), p. 684.

77. Deborah Shapley, *Promise and Power: The Life and Times of Robert McNamara* (Boston: Little, Brown, 1993), p. 418.

78. Cyrus Vance, LBJ Library oral history interview, 9 Mar. 1970, p. 13.

79. Joseph Alsop to Cyrus Vance, 13 June 1967. Vance Papers I-3:34.

80. Fritz G. A. Kraemer to Cyrus Vance, 12 June 1967. Vance Papers I-3:35.

81. Interview with Joseph A. Califano Jr., 16 Jan. 2003.

82. Martin Mayer, "Washington's Grant to the Ford Foundation," *NYTM*, 13 Nov. 1966, p. 142.

83. Robert Komer to Lyndon Johnson, 1 Dec. 1966. *Foreign Relations of the United States, 1964–1968*, vol. 4, p. 883.

84. Max Frankel, "Trading of Skills Suggested by U.S.," *NYT*, 16 Dec. 1966, p. 1.

85. Francis Bator to Lyndon Johnson, 30 Nov. 1966. Quoted in Alan McDonald, "International Institute for Applied Systems Analysis (IIASA): Systems Analysis as a Bridge across the Cold War Divide," paper presented to the New York Academy of Sciences, available at http://www.ciaonet.org/conf/nya02/nya02ab.html, accessed 1 Sep. 2002.

86. Interview with Francis Bator, 19 June 2002.

87. Interview with Richard Magat, 20 July 2001.

88. Joseph Goulden, *The Money Givers* (New York: Random House, 1971), p. 252.

89. Interview with Richard Magat, 20 July 2001.

90. Mario Fantini, Marilyn Gittell, and Richard Magat, *Community Control and the Urban School* (New York: Praeger, 1970), p. 143.

91. Richard Magat, Ford Foundation Oral History Project interview, 14 Mar. 1974.

92. David Burner, *Making Peace with the 60s* (Princeton: Princeton University Press, 1996), p. 67.

93. S. M. Miller, "Cleveland Escapes a Riot," 26 Sep. 1967. Bundy Records I-2:26.

94. Kai Bird, *The Color of Truth: McGeorge Bundy and William Bundy: Brothers in Arms* (New York: Simon & Schuster, 1998), p. 381.

95. Seth Taft to David K. Ford, 17 Mar. 1970. Bundy Records II-23:279.

96. McGeorge Bundy, "Grants for Improving Race Relations and Opportunities for Minority Groups in Cleveland," 14 July 1967. Ford Foundation Archives, box 41834.

97. Goulden, *The Money Givers*, p. 260.

98. Paul Moore Jr., *Presences: A Bishop's Life in the City* (New York: Farrar, Straus and Giroux, 1997), p. 186.

99. *Ibid.*, p. 187.

100. *Ibid.*

101. "Paul Moore, Jr.," *Current Biography 1967* (Bronx, N.Y.: H. W. Wilson, 1967), pp. 303-04.

102. Moore, *Presences*, p. 210.

103. Mayer, "Washington's Grant to the Ford Foundation," p. 150.

104. Interview with Joseph A. Califano Jr., 16 Jan. 2003.

105. Grace Vance to Elsie Vance, 25 July 1967. Vance Papers I-4:42.

106. John Throckmorton, Memorandum on Detroit [nd (1968)]. Vance Papers I-4:42.

107. Cyrus Vance to Lyndon Johnson, 9 Aug. 1967. Vance Papers I-4:42.

108. Cyrus Vance, Remarks at Press Conference, 29 July 1967. Vance Papers I-4:42.
109. Cyrus Vance, Memorandum for the Secretary of Defense [nd (Aug.? 1967)]. Vance Papers I-4:42.
110. Joseph A. Califano Jr., *The Triumph and Tragedy of Lyndon Johnson* (New York: Simon & Schuster, 1991), pp. 216–17.
111. John Throckmorton, Memorandum on Detroit [nd (1968)]. Vance Papers I-4:42.
112. Cyrus Vance, Memorandum for the Secretary of Defense [nd (Aug.? 1967)]. Vance Papers I-4:42.
113. Allen J. Matusow, *The Unraveling of America: A History of Liberalism in the 1960s* (New York: Harper & Row, 1984), p. 362.
114. Paul Moore, "Riots Mar City's Summer," *YDN,* 15 Sep. 1967, p. 1.
115. *Ibid.*
116. Alan Boles, "The Aftermath of August," *YDN FRIDAY Magazine,* 29 Sep. 1967, p. 4.
117. Charles G. Bennett, "Sviridoff Resigning His Post with City to Join Ford Fund," *NYT,* 16 Apr. 1967, p. 1.
118. John Hersey to Charles Taylor, 30 Aug. 1967. Brewster Presidential Records RU 11 I-191:5.
119. Califano, *The Triumph and Tragedy of Lyndon Johnson,* p. 219.
120. Cyrus Vance, Remarks at Press Conference, 29 July 1967. Vance Papers I-4:42.
121. "Text of Summary of 18-Month Study Made by a Special Presidential Commission," *NYT,* 19 Feb. 1967, p. 68.
122. Paul Moore Jr., "Sermon for National Cathedral Service on Poverty as a Moral Crisis," 15 Jan. 1967. Paul Moore Papers.
123. Henry L. Shattuck to Elliot Richardson, 6 Jan. 1966. Richardson Papers I:46, "Family—Shattuck, Henry L.—1924–68."
124. Interview with Jonathan Moore, 2 Dec. 2002.
125. Christopher Lydon, "Richardson and Justice," *NYTM,* 20 May 1973, p. 98.
126. Elliot Richardson, C. R. Musser Lecture at the University of Chicago Law School, 26 Apr. 1967. Richardson Papers I:72, "Speeches—Musser Lecture, University of Chicago Law School—April 1967."
127. *Ibid.*
128. Elliot Richardson, "Urban America, State Government and the Kerner Commission," [University of Massachusetts] *Bureau of Government Research Bulletin* II:2 (1968), p. 2.
129. Brewster, Address to the Freshman Class of 1971, 11 Sep. 1967. Brewster Personal Papers I-10:1.
130. *YDN,* 9 Oct. 1967; Timothy Bates, "Negro Demonstrates: Charges Eli Employment 'Apartheid,'" *YDN,* 10 Oct. 1967, p. 1.
131. Coffin, *Once to Every Man,* p. 230.
132. Coffin, "On Civil Disobedience."
133. "Boston Card Party Protests Draft War," *YDN,* 16 Oct. 1967, p. 1.
134. Coffin, *Once to Every Man,* p. 243.
135. *Ibid.,* p. 247.
136. Brewster, Address to the Yale Parents Day Assembly, 28 Oct. 1967. Brewster Personal Papers I-10:7.
137. Quoted in *ibid.*
138. Quoted in R. Thomas Herman, "The Inscrutable King of Yale" (unpublished paper, 7 Aug. 1968), p. 9. Brewster Presidential Records RU 11 I-47:14.
139. Coffin, *Once to Every Man,* p. 256.

140. "Brewster on Drugs, Dissent, Development," *YDN FRIDAY Magazine,* 1 Dec. 1967, p. 6.
141. Paul Moore, "Coffin Gives Yale CO's Sanctuary," *YDN,* 3 Oct. 1967, p. 1.
142. Coffin, *Once to Every Man,* p. 258. See also interview with Lawrence Pickett, 10 Dec. 1991.
143. Brewster, Coffin Postindictment Statement, 8 Jan. 1968. Brewster Personal Papers I-11:5.
144. Kingman Brewster Jr. to Thomas Kempner, 20 May 1968. Brewster Presidential Records RU 11 I-63:2.
145. John C. White Jr. to Kingman Brewster Jr., 11 Nov. 1968. Brewster Presidential Records RU 11 I-221:2.
146. Paul Moore Jr. to Kingman Brewster Jr., 13 Dec. 1967. Brewster Presidential Records RU 11 I-150:18.
147. Lincoln Richardson, "Yale's Controversial Chaplain," *Presbyterian Life,* 1 Apr. 1967.
148. Fred C. Shapiro, "God and That Man at Yale," *NYTM,* 3 Mar. 1968, p. 62; Lanny Davis to *YDN,* 26 Sep. 1967, p. 2.
149. Brewster, Address to the New Haven Chamber of Commerce Breakfast, 4 Oct. 1966. Brewster Personal Papers I-7:12.
150. Coffin, *Once to Every Man,* p. 255.
151. Interview with John Wilkinson, 19 May 1992.
152. Kingman Brewster Jr. to William Sloane Coffin Jr., 24 Feb. 1964. Brewster Presidential Records RU 11 I-61:6.
153. Interview with Henry Chauncey Jr., 22 July 1993.
154. Norman Mailer, *The Armies of the Night* (New York: Signet, 1968), p. 87.
155. Interview with John Wilkinson, 19 May 1992.
156. Interview with Gary Johnson, 7 Jan. 2000.
157. Richardson, "Yale's Controversial Chaplain."
158. *YDN,* 21 Nov. 1967.
159. Alvin Kernan, *In Plato's Cave* (New Haven: Yale University Press, 1999), p. 154.
160. Background interview.
161. "Universities: Anxieties behind the Façade," *Time,* 23 June 1967, p. 78.
162. Jonathan Spence, *YDN,* 1 May 1967.
163. McGeorge Bundy, "In Praise of Candor," Address to the American Council on Education, 13 Oct. 1967. Ford Foundation Archives, box 41834.
164. Kingman Brewster Jr. to McGeorge Bundy, 2 May 1967. Brewster Presidential Records RU 11 I-98:7.
165. Kingman Brewster Jr. to McGeorge Bundy, 18 Oct. 1967. Brewster Presidential Records RU 11 I-98:8.
166. *YDN,* 4 Jan. 1968.

9: HEAVY TURBULENCE

1. Kingman Brewster Jr. to Thomas Bergin, 16 Nov. 1967. Brewster Presidential Records I-43:11.
2. E. J. Kahn, *Jock: The Life and Times of John Hay Whitney* (Garden City, N.Y.: Doubleday, 1981), p. 303.
3. Brewster, Address to the Yale Alumni Club of Philadelphia, 14 Feb. 1969. Brewster Personal Papers I-14:4.
4. Henry Louis Gates Jr., "Parable of the Talents," in Gates and Cornel West, *The Future of the Race* (New York: Alfred A. Knopf, 1996), pp. 6–7.

5. Kingman Brewster Jr. to McGeorge Bundy and Ford Foundation trustees, 19 Mar. 1970. Brewster Presidential Records RU 11 I-100:3.

6. Jesse Allen Young, "A Century of Blacks at Yale, 1874–1974" (unpublished Scholar of the House essay, Yale College, 1974), p. 45.

7. Robert Austin Warner, *New Haven Negroes: A Social History* (New Haven: Yale University Press, 1940), p. 176.

8. "How Black Studies Happened," *YAM,* May 1969, p. 23.

9. Armstead L. Robinson, Raymond S. Nunn, Glenn DeChabert, and Larry E. Thompson, "On Being Black at Yale," *YAM,* May 1969, p. 28. Reprinted in Immanuel Wallerstein and Paul Starr (eds.), *The University Crisis Reader,* vol. 1 (New York: Random House, 1971), pp. 378–91.

10. Armstead L. Robinson and Donald H. Ogilvie, "Old Blues in Black and White," *YAM,* Summer 1993, p. 27.

11. *Ibid.,* p. 28.

12. Evan Thomas, "The Once and Future Kingman Brewster" (unpublished paper, 1 Sep. 1977), p. 19. Source courtesy of Mary Louise Brewster.

13. Interview with William Farley Jr., 16 Dec. 1991.

14. Interview with Kurt Schmoke, 22 May 1992.

15. Robinson, Nunn, DeChabert, and Thompson, "On Being Black at Yale," p. 32.

16. Brewster, Address to the Yale Club of Philadelphia, 14 Feb. 1969. Brewster Personal Papers I-14:4.

17. Elliot Richardson, *The Creative Balance: Government, Politics, and the Individual in America's Third Century* (New York: Holt, Rinehart & Winston, 1976), p. 281.

18. McGeorge Bundy, "Some Thoughts on Afro-American Studies," in Armstead L. Robinson, Craig C. Foster, and Donald H. Ogilvie (eds.), *Black Studies in the University: A Symposium* (New Haven: Yale University Press, 1969), pp. 171–77.

19. Brewster, Address to the Yale Club of Philadelphia, 14 Feb. 1969.

20. Roger Rosenblatt, *Coming Apart: A Memoir of the Harvard Wars of 1969* (Boston: Little, Brown, 1997), pp. 155–56.

21. Brewster, Address to the Yale Club of Philadelphia, 14 Feb. 1969.

22. William F. Buckley Jr., "Should U.S. Aid Private Colleges?" *New York Post,* 19 Oct. 1967.

23. William F. Buckley Jr., "What Makes Bill Buckley Run," *Atlantic Monthly,* Apr. 1968, p. 69.

24. "Buckley and/or Yale," *Yale Daily News FRIDAY Magazine,* 29 Oct. 1967, p. 2.

25. Buckley, "What Makes Bill Buckley Run," p. 68; Buckley, "Should U.S. Aid Private Colleges?"

26. Interview with Henry Chauncey Jr., 22 July 1993.

27. Interview with Nicholas Katzenbach, 4 June 2003.

28. Cyrus Vance, LBJ Library oral history interview, 29 Dec. 1969, p. 2.

29. Memorandum for the record, Meeting of the National Security Council, 29 Jan. 1968. *Foreign Relations of the United States, 1964–1968,* vol. 16 (Washington: Government Printing Office, 2000), p. 740.

30. *Economist,* 9 Dec. 1967.

31. Strobe Talbott, "The Ultimate Troubleshooter," *Time,* 9 Mar. 1992, p. 37.

32. Deborah Shapley, *Promise and Power: The Life and Times of Robert McNamara* (Boston: Little, Brown 1993), p. 448.

33. Cyrus Vance, Address to Root-Tilden Scholars, New York University Law School, 14 Mar. 1968. Vance Papers III-38:289.

34. Cyrus Vance, LBJ Library oral history interview, 29 Dec. 1969, pp. 8–10.

35. William Borders, "Buckley Opposed by Cyrus Vance in Yale Election," *NYT,* 9 Mar. 1968, p. 31.
36. President's Assistant (Jones) to Lyndon Johnson, 2 Nov. 1967. *Foreign Relations of the United States, 1964–1968,* vol. 5 (Washington: Government Printing Office, 2002), p. 958.
37. McGeorge Bundy to Lyndon Johnson, 10 Nov. 1967. *Foreign Relations of the United States, 1964–1968,* vol. 5 (Washington: Government Printing Office, 2002), p. 1013.
38. Stanley Karnow, *Vietnam: A History* (New York: Viking Press, 1983), pp. 546–47.
39. Walter Isaacson and Evan Thomas, *The Wise Men: Six Friends and the World They Made* (New York: Simon & Schuster, 1986), p. 690.
40. Interview with Andrew Bundy, 23 May 2002.
41. Transcript of WGBH, "Vietnam: Bundy and Hoffman," 14 Mar. 1968. Ford Foundation Archives, box 41835.
42. David Halberstam, *The Best and the Brightest* (New York: Random House, 1972), p. 625.
43. Transcript of WGBH, "Vietnam: Bundy and Hoffman."
44. Interview with James Thomson Jr., 13 Aug. 1990.
45. Transcript of WGBH, "Vietnam: Bundy and Hoffman."
46. Quoted in Isaacson and Thomas, *The Wise Men,* pp. 690–91.
47. Notes of the President's Meeting with His Foreign Advisers at the Tuesday Luncheon, 19 Mar. 1968. *Foreign Relations of the United States, 1964–1968,* vol. 6 (Washington: Government Printing Office, 2002), pp. 413–14.
48. Telephone conversation between Lyndon Johnson and Clark Clifford, 20 Mar. 1968. *Foreign Relations of the United States, 1964–1968,* vol. 6 (Washington: Government Printing Office, 2002), pp. 428–31.
49. Notes of meeting, 22 Mar. 1968. *Foreign Relations of the United States, 1964–1968,* vol. 6 (Washington: Government Printing Office, 2002), p. 445.
50. Lloyd C. Gardner, *Pay Any Price: Lyndon Johnson and the Wars for Vietnam* (Chicago: Ivan R. Dee, 1995), pp. 449–50.
51. Larry Berman, *Lyndon Johnson's War: The Road to Stalemate in Vietnam* (New York: W. W. Norton, 1989), pp. 194–95.
52. Cyrus Vance, LBJ Library oral history interview, 9 Mar. 1970, p. 14; Townsend Hoopes, *The Limits to Intervention* (New York: David McKay, 1969), pp. 215–16.
53. Isaacson and Thomas, *The Wise Men,* p. 700.
54. McGeorge Bundy, Address to the Cosmos Club of Washington, 8 May 1967. Source courtesy of Stephen Bundy.
55. Notes of meeting, 26 Mar. 1968. *Foreign Relations of the United States, 1964–1968,* vol. 6 (Washington: Government Printing Office, 2002), p. 471.
56. George W. Ball, *The Past Has Another Pattern: Memoirs* (New York: W. W. Norton, 1982), p. 408.
57. Notes of meeting, 26 Mar. 1968, pp. 472–73.
58. *The Pentagon Papers: The Senator Gravel Edition,* vol. 4 (Boston: Beacon Press, 1971), p. 592.
59. Lyndon Johnson, *The Vantage Point: Perspectives on the Presidency, 1963–1969* (New York: Popular Library, 1971), pp. 408–09.
60. George C. Herring, *America's Longest War: The United States and Vietnam 1950–1975,* 2nd ed. (New York: Alfred A. Knopf, 1986), p. 206.
61. James Patterson, *Grand Expectations: The United States, 1945–1974* (New York: Oxford University Press, 1996), p. 685.
62. Strobe Talbott, "'Dump Johnson': Making Dissent Work," *YDN,* 8 Nov. 1967, p. 2.

63. Otto Kerner et al., *Report of the National Advisory Commission on Civil Disorders* (New York: Bantam Books, 1968), pp. v, 1–2.
64. *Ford Foundation Annual Report, 1967*, p. 2.
65. Kerner et al., *Report of the National Advisory Commission on Civil Disorders*, pp. 1–2.
66. Elliot Richardson, "Urban America, State Government and the Kerner Commission," [University of Massachusetts] *Bureau of Government Research Bulletin* II:2 (1968), p. 2.
67. "Text of Kennedy's Statement on Talks," *NYT*, 18 Mar. 1968, p. 50.
68. John Morton Blum, *Years of Discord: American Politics and Society, 1961–1974* (New York: W. W. Norton, 1991), pp. 267–69, 295.
69. William R. Mackaye, "Bishop Moore Heads Ghetto Project," *WP*, 17 Apr. 1968, p. C8.
70. Paul Moore Jr., *Presences: A Bishop's Life in the City* (New York: Farrar, Straus and Giroux, 1997), p. 199.
71. Isaacson and Thomas, *The Wise Men*, p. 708.
72. Ben A. Franklin, "S.N.C.C. Head Advises Negroes in Washington to Get Guns," *NYT*, 28 July 1967, p. 14.
73. Moore, *Presences*, p. 199.
74. *Ibid.*, pp. 199–200.
75. Affidavit of Cyrus Vance, 24 Feb. 1970. Vance Papers I-7:89.
76. Allen J. Matusow, *The Unraveling of America: A History of Liberalism in the 1960s* (New York: Harper Torchbooks, 1984), p. 396.
77. Cyrus Vance, LBJ Library oral history interview, 3 Nov. 1969.
78. Charles R. Morris, *The Cost of Good Intentions: New York City and the Liberal Experiment, 1960–1975* (New York: W. W. Norton, 1980), p. 77.
79. Vincent J. Cannato, *The Ungovernable City: John Lindsay and His Struggle to Save New York* (New York: Basic Books, 2001), pp. 211–12.
80. John Lindsay, Address at the University of Illinois, 30 Apr. 1968. Lindsay Papers V:77–632.
81. Morris, *The Cost of Good Intentions*, p. 77.
82. Brewster, Memorandum to the Yale Community, 9 Apr. 1968. Brewster Personal Papers I-11:19.
83. Joel Fleishman to Kingman Brewster Jr., 1 Apr. 1968. Brewster Presidential Records RU 11 I-217:7.
84. Brewster, Memorandum to the Yale Community, 9 Apr. 1968.
85. Matusow, *The Unraveling of America*, p. 397.
86. Kingman Brewster Jr. to David Rockefeller, 1968. Brewster Presidential Records RU 11 I-150:5.
87. Evan Thomas, *The Very Best Men: Four Who Dared: The Early Years of the CIA* (New York: Simon & Schuster, 1996), p. 335.
88. Interview with John Blum, 11 Feb. 1992.
89. Interview with Jonathan Fanton, 17 Apr. 1992.
90. Richard Van Wegenen, "Meeting Will Consider SDS Chapter at Yale," *YDN*, 23 Nov. 1965; John G. Brim, "Yale Students Consider Forming SDS Chapter," *YDN*, 23 Nov. 1965; Paul Booth, "SDS: Build, Not Burn," *YDN*, 23 Nov. 1965, p. 2.
91. Joshua Civin, "Educating Activists: Moving Off-Campus in 1966," *YDN Magazine*, Feb. 1994.
92. Interview with Mark Zanger, 7 Apr. 1992.
93. *NHR*, 9 Jan. 1967.
94. Interview with Mark Zanger, 7 Apr. 1992.

95. Douglas P. Woodlock, "Students Steal Drugs from Bomb Shelters," *YDN*, 10 Nov. 1967, p. 1.

96. Interview with Mark Zanger, 7 Apr. 1992.

97. Peter Gordon, "15 Provos Protest the Tie That Binds," *YDN*, 22 Sep. 1967, p. 3.

98. George B. Reid Jr., "SDS Plans Yale Chapter, Sets Student Power Goal," *YDN*, 3 Oct. 1967, p. 1; Paul Taylor, "SDS Teach-In Condemns US Economy, Universities," *YDN*, 19 Oct. 1967, p. 1; Reid, "First Lady's Visit Sparks Protest; Protesters Jam Beinecke Plaza," *YDN*, 10 Oct 1967, p. 1; Joe Gelles, "CIA Presence at Yale Draws SDS Protesters," *YDN*, 9 Nov. 1967, p. 4; Timothy Bates, "Two Say No to Army; 60 Join Protest," *YDN*, 11 Oct. 1967, p. 1; Gelles, "300 Picket Inductions; 30 Arrested," *YDN*, 11 Dec. 1967, p. 1.

99. George B. Reid Jr., "New SDS Forms, Will Demonstrate," *YDN*, 4 Oct. 1967, p. 1.

100. See Jerry L. Avorn et al., *Up against the Ivy Wall: A History of the Columbia Crisis* (New York: Atheneum, 1970).

101. Interview with Mark Zanger, 7 Apr. 1992.

102. Avorn et al., *Up against the Ivy Wall*, p. 180.

103. Barry Gottehrer, *The Mayor's Man* (Garden City, N.Y.: Doubleday, 1975), p. 169.

104. Brewster, Address at the George Washington University Commencement, 2 June 1968. Brewster Personal Papers I-12:8.

105. Elliot Richardson, Address to the Second Unitarian Church of Boston, 17 Nov. 1968. Richardson Papers I:71, "Speeches—Second Unitarian Church of Boston—Nov. 1968."

106. Archibald Cox et al., *Crisis at Columbia: Report of the Fact-Finding Commission Appointed to Investigate the Disturbances at Columbia University in April and May 1968* (New York: Vintage Books, 1968), p. 193.

107. Robert Irving, "The Heart of the University: Renewal or Requiem?" *NJ*, 14 Apr. 1968.

108. *YDN*, 9 May 1968.

109. Interview with Cyrus R. Vance, 19 Aug. 1993.

110. Interview with Henry Chauncey Jr., 22 Mar. 1992.

111. Stephen Marmon, "The Vanishing President," *Daily Pennsylvanian*, 1 Mar. 1967, p. 1.

112. Interview with Elias Clark, 11 Mar. 1992.

113. Interview with John Wilkinson, 19 May 1992.

114. Interview with Elias Clark, 11 Mar. 1992.

115. John Hersey, *Letter to the Alumni* (New York: Alfred A. Knopf, 1970), p. 120.

116. See John Hall et al., "Report of the Committee on the Educational Potentialities and Responsibilities of the Residential Colleges at Yale" (New Haven: Yale University, 1968).

117. Interview with Kai Erikson, 9 Mar. 1992.

118. Gregory Stone and Douglas Lowenstein, *Lowenstein: Acts of Courage and Belief* (New York: Harcourt Brace Jovanovich, 1983), p. 114.

119. Interview with Gregory Craig, 9 Apr. 1991.

120. Interview with Henry Chauncey Jr., 22 July 1993.

121. *YDN*, 14 Apr. 1969.

122. Interview with William Sloane Coffin Jr., 9 Dec. 1991.

123. Interview with Gary Johnson, 7 Jan. 2000.

124. See Hunter S. Thompson, "The Nonstudent Left," *The Nation*, 27 Sep. 1965. Reprinted in Hunter S. Thompson, *The Great Shark Hunt: Strange Tales from a Strange Time* (New York: Warner Books, 1979).

125. Celia Goodhart, interview with Kingman Brewster Jr., 1986. Source courtesy of Mary Louise Brewster.

126. Ruth Conniff, "Adventures in Doonland," *NJ*, 2 Feb. 1990, p. 21.

127. Interview with Henry Chauncey Jr., 22 July 1993.

128. Celia Goodhart, interview with Kingman Brewster Jr., 1986.

129. Interview with Charles Taylor, 12 May 1992.

130. Interview with Strobe Talbott, 10 Apr. 1991.

131. "Brewster's Son Faces Drug Count in Massachusetts," *NHR*, 31 Mar. 1968.

132. "Young Brewster Pleads Innocent to Dope Charge," *NHR*, 2 Apr. 1968.

133. Interview with Henry Chauncey Jr., 13 July 1992.

134. William Sloane Coffin Jr., *Once to Every Man: A Memoir* (New York: Atheneum, 1977), p. 288.

135. Interview with Strobe Talbott, 10 Apr. 1991.

136. Paul Moore Jr., Yale University Commencement Invocation, 10 June 1968. *YAM*, July 1968, p. 34.

137. Arthur Schlesinger Jr., *Robert Kennedy and His Times* (New York: Ballantine Books, 1978), p. 847.

138. Interview with John Lindsay, 12 Mar. 1992.

139. Cannato, *The Ungovernable City*, p. 379.

140. Interview with Vernon Jordan, 9 Jan. 2001.

141. Coffin, *Once to Every Man*, p. 277; Brewster, Letter on William Sloane Coffin's Reappointment as Chaplain, 25 Apr. 1968. Brewster Personal Papers I-11:22.

142. Interview with Cyrus Vance, 13 Aug. 1993.

143. R. Thomas Hermann, "The Inscrutable King of Yale" (unpublished paper, 7 Aug. 1968), p. 4. Brewster Presidential Records RU 11 I-47:14.

144. "Honorary Degree Citations," *YAM*, July 1968, p. 35.

145. Hermann, "The Inscrutable King of Yale," pp. 4–5.

146. Lyndon Johnson to Cyrus Vance, 15 Apr. 1968. Vance Papers I-5:63.

147. Interview with Nicholas Katzenbach, 4 June 2003.

148. Notes of a meeting, 25 Apr. 1968. *Foreign Relations of the United States, 1964–1968*, vol. 6 (Washington: Government Printing Office, 2002), p. 602.

149. Notes of the president's meeting with foreign policy advisors, 28 May 1968. *Foreign Relations of the United States, 1964–1968*, vol. 6 (Washington: Government Printing Office, 2002), p. 724.

150. Notes of bi-partisan Congressional leadership meeting with Cyrus Vance, 28 May 1968. *Foreign Relations of the United States, 1964–1968*, vol. 6 (Washington: Government Printing Office, 2002), p. 730.

151. Interview with Mary Bundy, 15 Jan. 2002.

152. Max Frankel, "Johnson Chooses 'Think Tank' Panel on Urban Issues," *NYT*, 7 Dec. 1967, p. 1.

153. Interview with Joseph A. Califano Jr., 16 Jan. 2003.

154. *Urban Institute Annual Report, 1998*.

155. Interview with Joseph A. Califano Jr., 16 Jan. 2003.

156. Nicholas Katzenbach to Lyndon Johnson, 4 Apr. 1968. *Foreign Relations of the United States, 1964–1968*, vol. 20 (Washington: Government Printing Office, 2001), pp. 259–60.

157. Bromley Smith to Lyndon Johnson, 4 July 1968. *Foreign Relations of the United States, 1964–1968*, vol. 20 (Washington: Government Printing Office, 2001), pp. 404–06.

158. Embassy in Jordan to the Department of State, 20 July 1968. *Foreign Relations of the United States, 1964–1968*, vol. 20 (Washington: Government Printing Office, 2001), p. 436.

159. Interview with Robert McNamara, 5 July 2001.

160. Cyrus Vance, LBJ Library oral history interview, 9 Mar. 1970, p. 18.

161. Averell Harriman and Cyrus Vance to the Department of State, 29 July 1968. *Foreign Relations of the United States, 1964–1968,* vol. 6 (Washington: Government Printing Office, 2002), p. 913.

162. William Bundy, LBJ Library oral history interview, 2 June 1969, p. 44.

163. Warren I. Cohen, *Dean Rusk* (Totowa, N.J.: Cooper Square, 1980), p. 313.

164. Interview with William Scranton, 16 July 1992.

165. Elliot Richardson to David Martin, 2 Apr. 1968. Richardson Papers I:60, "Martin, David B. H."

166. Elliot Richardson to members of the Massachusetts delegation, 29 July 1968. Richardson Papers I:66, "Republican Convention 1968—Platform materials."

167. "Periscope," *Newsweek,* 14 Oct. 1968.

168. Brewster, "An Institution for University Women at Yale," 13 May 1968. Brewster Presidential Records RU 11 I-222:15.

169. Henry Chauncey Jr. to Kingman Brewster Jr., 19 July 1968. Brewster Presidential Records RU 11 I-222:15.

170. Brewster, "Admission to Yale: Objectives and Myths," *YAM,* Oct. 1966, p. 31.

171. Richard B. Freeman, *The Overeducated American* (New York: Academic Press, 1976), pp. 163–64.

172. John Coots, "Faculty View Coeds with Mixed Feelings," *YDN,* 8 Nov. 1968, p. 7.

173. Yale Students for a Democratic Society, "Coeducation at Yale" [nd]. Brewster Presidential Records RU 11 I-61:1.

174. Gardner Patterson et al., "Report on the Desirability and Feasibility of Princeton Entering Significantly into the Education of Women at the Undergraduate Level," *Princeton Alumni Weekly,* 24 Sep. 1968.

175. "Women and the University," 1 Mar. 1969. Brewster Personal Papers I-14:8.

176. Interview with Mark Zanger, 7 Apr. 1992.

177. Kingman Brewster Jr. to John Hay Whitney, 3 Apr. 1969. Brewster Presidential Records RU 11 I-221:11.

178. Interview with Mark Zanger, 7 Apr. 1992.

179. Timothy Bates, "SDS Proclaims Girls Next Year," *YDN,* 16 Oct. 1968, p. 1; Yale Students for a Democratic Society, "Coeducation at Yale" [nd]. Brewster Presidential Records RU 11 I-61:1.

180. Interview with Mark Zanger, 7 Apr. 1992.

181. Interview with Aviam Soifer, 6 Sep. 1991.

182. Reed Hundt, "Self-Coeducation," *YDN,* 24 Oct. 68, p. 2.

183. Interview with Charles Taylor, 2 Mar. 1992.

184. Jeffrey M. Stern, "Coed Rally Meets 'Brewster at Home,'" *YDN,* 7 Nov. 1968, p. 1.

185. Transcript of Kingman Brewster Jr. remarks at Yale Development Board Convocation, 15 Nov. 1968. Brewster Presidential Records RU 11 I-78:3.

186. Jonathan Lear, "Yale Has Waited for Girls Too Long," *NJ,* 20 Oct. 1968, p. 4.

187. Jeffrey Gordon, "Class History," in *History of the Yale College Class of 1971* (New Haven: Yale University, 1971), p. 275.

188. Brewster, Address at Yale Development Board Convocation, 15 Nov. 1968. Brewster Personal Papers 13:12.

189. Peter Jacobi to Henry Chauncey Jr., 25 Mar. 1970. Brewster Presidential Records RU 11 I-150:14.

190. Morris, *The Cost of Good Intentions,* p. 71.

191. Larry L. King, "Lindsay of New York," *Harper's,* Aug. 1968, p. 41.

192. Martin Mayer, "The Full and Sometimes Very Surprising Story of Ocean Hill, the Teachers' Union and the Teacher Strikes of 1968," *NYTM,* 2 Feb. 1969, p. 18.

193. "On Running New York," *Time,* 1 Nov. 1968, p. 23.
194. Richard Armstrong, "McGeorge Bundy Confronts the Teachers," *NYTM,* 20 Apr. 1969, p. 124.
195. McGeorge Bundy on WNBC-TV *Speaking Freely,* 12 Feb. 1969. Ford Foundation Archives, box 41835.
196. Armstrong, "McGeorge Bundy Confronts the Teachers," p. 122.
197. McGeorge Bundy, Address at DePauw University, 12 Oct. 1968, in Richard Falk (ed.), *The Vietnam War and International Law,* vol. 2 (Princeton: Princeton University Press, 1969), pp. 965–66.
198. Cyrus Vance, LBJ Library oral history interview, 9 Mar. 1970, p. 20.

10: INTO THE STORM

1. Interview with John Lindsay, 12 Mar. 1992.
2. Interview with William Bundy, 24 Apr. 1992.
3. Interview with Paul Moore Jr., 30 Nov. 2000.
4. Interview with William Scranton, 16 July 1992.
5. Brooks M. Kelley, *Yale: A History* (New Haven: Yale University Press, 1974), p. 350.
6. "ROTC I—Does the Uniform Fit?" *YDN,* 29 Mar. 1940, p. 2.
7. "ROTC—II," *YDN,* 30 Mar. 1940, p. 2.
8. "Future of the University," Channel 13, 12 Mar. 1969. Brewster Personal Papers I-14:9.
9. Brewster, Address to the Yale Club of Philadelphia, 14 Feb. 1969. Brewster Personal Papers I-14:4.
10. David Todd and Stephen Schechter, "ROTC to Lose Credit; War Issue Sidestepped," *YDN,* 30 Jan. 1969, p. 1.
11. Brewster, Address to the Cincinnati Yale Forum, 19 Oct. 1970. Brewster Personal Papers I-24:5.
12. Julien Dedman, "Letter to the Editor," *YAM,* Oct. 1968, p. 9; Dedman, *The Rape of Yale* (Southport, Conn.: Southport Productions, 1969), p. 17.
13. Kingman Brewster Jr. to Elmore Jackson, 15 Jan. 1969. Brewster Presidential Records RU 11 I-206:1.
14. Kingman Brewster Jr. et al., *Controlling Conflict in the 1970s* (New York: United Nations Association of the United States of America, 1969).
15. Elliot Richardson, memo of conversation with Cyrus Vance, 1 May 1969. Richardson Papers I:97, "Memcons April–May 1969."
16. Elliot Richardson to Charles Wyzanski, 9 Jan. 1969. Richardson Papers I:81, "Wyzanski, Charles E., Jr."
17. "Richardson's Driving Record Holds Up Senate Approval," *Berkshire Eagle,* 16 Jan. 1969.
18. Peter Janssen, "Is Elliot Richardson Really Clark Kent?" [ns, nd]. Richardson Papers I:110, "News clippings."
19. Christopher Lydon, "Richardson and Justice," *NYTM,* 20 May 1973, p. 94.
20. Elliot Richardson, memo of conversation with Nick Katzenbach, 16 Feb. 1969. Richardson Papers I:96, "Memcons Dec. 1968–Feb. 1969."
21. Interview with Elliot Richardson, 22 June 1997.
22. "Richardson: 'Nixon's Brahmin,'" *Newsweek,* 11 Dec. 1972.
23. Interview with Elliot Richardson, 22 June 1997.
24. Elliot Richardson to O. W. Haussermann Jr., 29 Oct. 1969. Richardson Papers I:95, "H–Ha."

25. Charles L. Whipple, "The Administration's Side on Vietnam: An Interview with Undersecretary of State Richardson," *BG*, 15 Oct. 1969, p. 23.
26. John P. Leacacas, "Undersecretary May Be World Champion Doodler," *Cleveland Plain Dealer*, 25 Jan. 1970, p. 28.
27. Interview with Mark Zanger, 7 Apr. 1992.
28. Richard Norton Smith, *The Harvard Century: The Making of a University to a Nation* (New York: Simon & Schuster 1986), pp. 248-54.
29. Seth Singleton to Georges May, 17 June 1969. Brewster Presidential Records RU 11 I-67:14.
30. Edward B. Benjamin to C. Douglas Dillon, Apr. 1969. Richardson Papers I:95, "Harvard—Rioting etc.—1969."
31. Gerald Aston, "Henry Kissinger: Strategist in the White House Basement," *Look*, 12 Aug. 1969, p. 53.
32. Interview with Archibald Cox, 13 Nov. 1991.
33. Greg Craig to Kingman Brewster Jr., 21 Apr. 1969. Brewster Presidential Records RU 11 I-68:2.
34. "Statement from the Board of Overseers," 14 Apr. 1969. Richardson Papers I:95, "Harvard—Rioting etc.—1969."
35. "Harvard's Ruling Class Reacts to the Strain," *BG*, 12 Oct. 1969; Smith, *The Harvard Century*, p. 269.
36. Elliot Richardson, Memo of conversation with Mac Bundy, 16 Apr. 1969. Richardson Papers I:97, "Memcons April–May 1969."
37. Interview with James Perkins, 20 May 1992.
38. Donald Alexander Downs, *Cornell '69: Liberalism and the Crisis of the American University* (Ithaca, N.Y.: Cornell University Press, 1999), p. 240.
39. Homer Bigart, "Cornell Faculty Reverses Itself on Negroes," *NYT*, 24 Apr. 1969, p. 1.
40. Homer Bigart, "Perkins Requests Cornell Trustees to Find Successor," *NYT*, 1 June 1969, p. 1.
41. Brewster, Address to the Eastern Fairfield County Alumni Association Dinner, 5 Feb. 1970. Brewster Personal Papers I-20:1.
42. Interview with James Perkins, 20 May 1992.
43. Homer Bigart, "Cornell Bears Scars of Conflict; Faculty Is Divided over Perkins," *NYT*, 28 May 1969, p. 1.
44. "The Preoccupations of the Last Six Weeks: Is Harvard's Way the Only Way?" *YAM*, May 1969, p. 14.
45. Paul Moore Jr. to Kingman Brewster Jr., 11 Mar. 1969. Brewster Presidential Records RU 11 I-67:14.
46. "Brewster Plans Stern Action; Briefs Faculty on Disorder Policy," *NHJC*, 17 Apr. 1969; Kingman Brewster Jr. to John Perry Miller, 2 Apr. 1969. Brewster Personal Papers I-14:11; John Perry Miller, *Creating Academic Settings: High Craft and Low Cunning* (New Haven: J. Simeon Press, 1991), pp. 154-57; "Scenario," *The Nation*, 12 May 1969, p. 588.
47. Brewster, Address to Yale National Alumni Meeting in Chicago, 10 May 1969. Brewster Personal Papers I-16:1.
48. Interview with Mark Zanger, 7 Apr. 1992.
49. Alan Barth, "'Bright College Years with Pleasure Rife,'" *WP*, 5 May 1969, p. A26.
50. Interview with Mark Zanger, 7 Apr. 1992.
51. Interview with Aviam Soifer, 6 Sep. 1991; George Kannar, "Whose Movement?" *YDN*, 29 Apr. 1969, p. 1.
52. Tom Anderson, "University Asks for Meetings on ROTC, Yale Governance; Gives Reply to Faculty," *YDN*, 28 Apr. 1969, p. 1.

53. Interview with Gregory Craig, 9 Apr. 1991.

54. Charles W. Sprague, "Concerning ROTC and American Foreign Policy at Yale" (unpublished Political Science 31a paper, Yale College, 9 Jan. 1970), p. 8. Source courtesy of H. Bradford Westerfield.

55. Paul Moore Jr., *Presences: A Bishop's Life in the City* (New York: Farrar, Straus and Giroux, 1997), p. 197.

56. Interview with Gregory Craig, 9 Apr. 1991.

57. Sprague, "Concerning ROTC and American Foreign Policy at Yale," p. 9.

58. Interview with Gregory Craig, 9 Apr. 1991.

59. Interview with Stephen B. Cohen, 5 Aug. 2003.

60. Interview with William Bundy, 24 Apr. 1992.

61. Brewster, Address at the Ingalls Rink Meeting on ROTC, 1 May 1969. Brewster Personal Papers I-15:3.

62. Stewart Alsop, "Yale Revisited," *Newsweek,* 19 May 1969, p. 120.

63. Brewster, Address at the Ingalls Rink Meeting on ROTC, 1 May 1969. Brewster Personal Papers I-15:3.

64. Phil Casey, "Brewster Keeping His, Yale's 'Cool'; Once a Rebel Himself," *Louisville Courier-Journal,* 5 May 1969.

65. George Kannar, "Mass Meeting Splits Evenly on ROTC," *YDN,* 2 May 1969, p. 1.

66. Moore, *Presences,* p. 198.

67. Interview with Gary Johnson, 7 Jan. 2000.

68. Barth, "'Bright College Years with Pleasure Rife,'" p. A26.

69. A transcript of Seale's address appears with an FBI memo of 23 May 1969. Williams Papers I-1:4.

70. Robert Brustein, *Making Scenes: A Personal History of the Turbulent Years at Yale, 1966–1979* (New York: Limelight Editions, 1984), p. 92.

71. William Sloane Coffin Jr., *Once to Every Man: A Memoir* (New York: Atheneum, 1977), p. 299.

72. Kingman Brewster Jr. to Reuben A. Holden, 23 May 1969. Brewster Presidential Records RU 11 I-184:27.

73. Brewster, Commencement Address at Johns Hopkins University, 6 June 1969. Brewster Personal Papers I-16:10.

74. Claire Simon, "Flames of Controversy," *New Haven Advocate,* 11 June 1998, p. 17.

75. Alsop, "Yale Revisited," p. 120.

76. *YDN,* 22 Jan. 1969.

77. "Class Day," *YAM,* July 1969, p. 32.

78. Interview with Stephen B. Cohen, 5 Aug. 2003.

79. William McIlwaine Thompson, "Commencement Address," 9 June 1969. Reprinted in Yale Class of 1969, *25th Reunion Class Book* (New Haven: Yale University, 1994), pp. 22–23.

80. John Lindsay, Address to the Yale Law School Association, *YAM,* July 1969, p. 19.

81. John R. Coyne Jr., *The Impudent Snobs: Agnew vs. the Intellectual Establishment* (New Rochelle, N.Y.: Arlington House, 1972), p. 37.

82. Jonathan Lear to Kingman Brewster Jr., 9 June 1968. Brewster Presidential Records RU 11 I-133:12.

83. Interview with Robert S. McNamara, 5 July 2001.

84. Kingman Brewster Jr., letter to *Harper's,* Oct. 1969, p. 6.

85. Interview with Donald Kagan, 9 June 1992.

86. Interview with Elga Wasserman, 7 May 1992.

87. Paul Taylor, "Five Reasons Yale Did Not Blow," *YDN,* 17 Sep. 1969, p. 2.

88. Interview with Stephen B. Cohen, 5 Aug. 2003.
89. Jeffrey Gordon, "50,000 Mass at Convocation on Green; Brewster, Lee, Udall Denounce Viet War," *YDN,* 16 Oct. 1969, p. 1.
90. Interview with William Farley Jr., 16 Dec. 1991.
91. Brewster, Address at the New Haven Moratorium Day, 15 Oct. 1969. Brewster Personal Papers I-17:8.
92. Anthony Lewis, "A Thoughtful Answer to Hard Questions," *NYT,* 17 Oct. 1969.
93. Tony Lewis to Elliot Richardson, 16 Oct. 1969. Richardson Papers I:96, "'L' miscellaneous."
94. Interview with Gregory Craig, 9 Apr. 1991.
95. Statement of the New Haven moratorium committee, 19 Oct. 1969. Brewster Presidential Records RU 11 I-219:2.
96. William Sloane Coffin Jr., *Once to Every Man,* p. 297.
97. Kingman Brewster Jr. to John Mitchell, 28 Nov. 1969. Mitchell wrote back: "Upon a review of the files I saw no reason to disturb, and in fact I strongly endorse, the initial decision that was made in Mr. Mandel's case." John Mitchell to Kingman Brewster Jr., 17 Dec. 1969. Brewster Presidential Records RU 11 I-150:8.
98. Hearings before the House Committee on Ways and Means, 20 Feb. 1969, in United States Congress, House, *Committee Hearings* vol. 2420 (Washington: Government Printing Office, 1969), p. 378.
99. *Ibid.,* p. 383.
100. Lally Weymouth, "Foundation Woes: The Saga of Henry Ford II: Part Two," *NYTM,* 12 Mar. 1978.
101. Roger M. Williams, "What Ford Learned Last Time Around," *Foundation News and Commentary* June 1998, available at http://int1.cof.org/foundationnews/june1998/ford.html, accessed 2 Aug. 2003.
102. "The Interests of Foundations," *NYT,* 3 Mar. 1969, p. 34.
103. Vincent J. Cannato, *The Ungovernable City: John Lindsay and His Struggle to Save New York* (New York: Basic Books, 2001), p. 406.
104. Hurst B. Amyx, "The Ford Foundation Bankrolls the Left," [nd]. Bundy Records II-14:179.
105. McGeorge Bundy to John Cowles, 8 July 1970. Bundy Records II-14:79.
106. Interview with Mark Zanger, 7 Apr. 1992.
107. "45 Suspended after Wright Hall Occupation; Students Block Office for Almost Four Hours, Hold Embersits, Dobie," *YDN,* 4 Nov. 1969, p. 1.
108. Interview with Mark Zanger, 7 Apr. 1992.
109. Robert H. Kilpatrick and Ren Frutkin, "SDS November Offensive: A Tale of Modest Occupations," *YAM,* Dec. 1969, p. 34.
110. Interview with Mark Zanger, 7 Apr. 1992.
111. Interview with John Wilkinson, 19 May 1992.
112. Robert B. Semple Jr., "Access to the President," *NYT,* 14 May 1970, p. 20.
113. Brewster, Statement before the Senate Subcommittee on Administrative Practice and Procedure, 5 Nov. 1969. Brewster Personal Papers I-18:3.
114. Richard H. Stewart, "Brewster's Plea Moves Kennedy to Act on Draft," *BG,* 6 Nov. 1969, p. 1.
115. Kingman Brewster, Response at a Question and Answer Session of the Yale Development Board Convocation, 21 Nov. 1969. Brewster Personal Papers I-18:5.
116. Interview with Mark Zanger, 7 Apr. 1992.
117. Scott Herhold, "Committee Readmits Suspended Students; Students on Probation; Future Violators Will Be Required to Leave Yale," *YDN,* 11 Nov. 1969, p. 1.

118. Interview with Georges May, 22 Apr. 1992.

119. Interview with Mark Zanger, 7 Apr. 1992.

120. Minutes of the General Yale College Faculty, 11 Nov. 1969. See also minutes for the meetings of the General Yale College Faculty, 13 Nov. 1969 and 20 Nov. 1969.

121. John Morton Blum, "Yale Students and Harvard Fellows," *Yale Review*, April 2003, pp. 4–6. The motion was the work of William Kessen, John Blum, Alvin Kernan, Edmund Morgan, Lloyd Reynolds, and James Tobin. When they gathered to craft the motion, Kessen remembered, "I said, 'This may be the last gathering of the mandarins in Yale's history.'" Interview with William Kessen, 2 June 1992.

122. "Man and Woman of the Year: The Middle Americans," *Time*, 5 Jan. 1970.

123. Joseph Kraft, "Middle America Revisited, and Redefined," *Louisville Courier Journal*, 7 Jan. 1970.

124. Robert D. McFadden, "Former New York Mayor Lindsay Dies at 79," *NYT*, 20 Dec. 2000.

125. Cannato, *The Ungovernable City*, p. 414.

126. *New York Times*, 3 Nov. 1969, p. 51.

127. Emmanuel Perlmutter, "Carey Joins Mayoral Race; Lindsay Gains Supporters," *NYT*, 25 June 1969, p. 1.

128. Elliot Richardson to John Lindsay, 15 Nov. 1969. Richardson Papers I:96, "'L' miscellaneous."

129. Charles R. Morris, *The Cost of Good Intentions: New York City and the Liberal Experiment, 1960–1975* (New York: W. W. Norton, 1980), p. 147.

130. Moore, *Presences*, p. 214.

131. *Ibid.*, p. 224.

132. Paul Moore Jr., *Will the Bishop Pray?* (New Haven: Yale University, 1991), p. 6.

133. Moore, *Presences*, p. 214.

134. William R. MacKaye, "N.Y. Diocese Picks Moore for Top Job," *WP*, 13 Dec. 1969, p. A4.

135. Flora Lewis, "They Didn't Get Yale" [nd, ns]. Brewster Presidential Records RU 16 7:64.

136. SAC, New Haven Division to Director, FBI, 27 Jan. 1969. Williams Paper I-1:1; Gail Sheehy, *Panthermania!* (New York: Harper & Row, 1971), pp. 10–15.

137. The literature on the Panthers tends to proceed from political rather than scholarly bases. See G. Louis Heath, *Off the Pigs: The History and Literature of the Black Panther Party* (Metuchen, N.J.: Scarecrow Press, 1976); David Hilliard and Lewis Cole, *This Side of Glory: The Autobiography of David Hilliard and the Story of the Black Panther Party* (Boston: Little, Brown, 1993); Hugh Pearson *The Shadow of the Panther: Huey Newton and the Price of Black Power in America* (Reading, Mass.: Addison-Wesley, 1994); Bobby Seale, *A Lonely Rage: The Autobiography of Bobby Seale* (New York: Times Books, 1978); Bobby Seale, *Seize the Time: The Story of the Black Panther Party and Huey P. Newton* (New York: Random House, 1972); Kathleen Cleaver and George Katsiaficas (eds.), *Liberation, Imagination and the Black Panther Party: A New Look at the Black Panthers and Their Legacy* (New York: Routledge, 2001).

138. Historian David Burner notes that while "in Oakland and other cities the breakfast program for children, often used in justification of the Panthers, was increasingly based on extortion . . . [o]ne breakfast program in New Haven, Connecticut, does seem to have operated without criminality." David Burner, *Making Peace with the 60s* (Princeton, N.J.: Princeton University Press, 1996) p. 71.

139. John Taft, *Mayday at Yale* (Boulder, Colo.: Westview Press, 1976), pp. 5–10.

140. *Ibid.*, pp. 11–12.

141. "The State of Connecticut vs. New Haven 9" [poster, nd, ns]. Brewster Presidential Records RU 16 7:65.

142. Interview with Mark Zanger, 7 Apr. 1992.

143. A Sister for the NHPDC, "New Haven" [poster, nd, ns]. Brewster Presidential Records RU 16 7:65.

144. "Yale to Be Tried by the People" [poster, nd, ns]. Brewster Presidential Records RU 16 7:65.

145. Andrew Kopkind, "Bringing It All Back Home," *Hard Times* 77 (11–18 May 1970), p. 2.

146. James Nuzzo, interview with Kingman Brewster Jr. [nd (1974)]. Brewster Personal Papers I-45:4.

147. David Holahan to Kingman Brewster Jr., 6 Apr. 1970. Brewster Presidential Records RU 16 7:65.

148. Taft, *Mayday at Yale,* p. 16.

149. "Contempt?" [poster, nd, ns]. Brewster Presidential Records RU 16 7:66.

150. David Winn, interview with Kingman Brewster Jr., 18 May 1971. Brewster Personal Papers I-27:4.

151. James Nuzzo, interview with Kingman Brewster Jr. [nd (1974)]. Brewster Personal Papers I-45:4.

152. See James F. Ahern, *Police in Trouble: Our Frightening Crisis in Law Enforcement* (New York: Hawthorn Books, 1972), pp. 30–72.

153. See Archibald Cox et al., *Crisis at Columbia: Report of the Fact-Finding Commission Appointed to Investigate the Disturbances at Columbia University in April and May 1968* (New York: Vintage Books, 1968); Ken Gormley, *Archibald Cox: Conscience of a Nation* (Reading, Mass.: Addison-Wesley, 1997), pp. 199–226.

154. Interview with Archibald Cox, 13 Nov. 1991.

155. David Winn, interview with Kingman Brewster Jr., 18 May 1971. Brewster Personal Papers I-27:4.

156. James Nuzzo, interview with Kingman Brewster Jr. [nd (1974)]. Brewster Personal Papers I-45:4.

157. David Winn, interview with Kingman Brewster Jr., 18 May 1971. Brewster Personal Papers I-27:4.

158. David Todd, "Faculty Debates Action on Trial," *YDN,* 17 Apr. 1970, p. 1.

159. Alvin Kernan, *In Plato's Cave* (New Haven: Yale University Press, 1999), pp. 170–71.

160. Taft, *Mayday at Yale,* p. 87.

161. Interview with Kurt Schmoke, 22 May 1992.

162. Brewster, Statement at the Yale College Faculty Meeting, 23 Apr. 1970. Brewster Personal Papers I-21:4.

163. Taft, *Mayday at Yale,* p. 89.

164. David Winn, interview with Kingman Brewster Jr., 18 May 1971. Brewster Personal Papers I-27:4.

165. Interview with Peter Brooks, 5 Aug. 1992.

166. David Winn, interview with Kingman Brewster Jr., 18 May 1971. Brewster Personal Papers I-27:4.

167. Jeff Greenfield, *No Peace, No Place: Excavations Along the Generational Fault* (Garden City, N.Y.: Doubleday, 1973), p. 203.

168. Roger Kimball, "The Liberal Capitulation," *New Criterion,* Jan. 1998, p. 11. Robert Bork echoed Kimball's charge that Brewster made "serial capitulations" in handling May Day. Robert H. Bork, *Slouching towards Gomorrah: Modern Liberalism and American Decline* (New York: Regan Books, 1996), p. 43.

169. Interview with Mark Zanger, 7 Apr. 1992.

170. Kingman Brewster Jr., interview with James Nuzzo [nd (1974)]. Brewster Personal Papers I-45:4.

171. David Greenberg, *NJ*, 2 Feb. 1990, p. 40.

172. John Hersey, *Letter to the Alumni* (New York: Alfred A. Knopf, 1970), p. 108.

173. Ellen Katz, "May Day—What Happened?" *NJ*, 2 Feb. 1990, p. 9.

174. John K. Jessup, "Yale Proves Dissent Doesn't Have to Turn Out That Way," *Life*, 15 May 1970, p. 38; Thomas R. Linden and Richard T. Cooper, "Yale's New Approach to Protests Pays Off," *Los Angeles Times*, 4 May 1970, p. 14.

175. Kopkind, "Bringing It All Back Home," p. 4.

176. *YDN*, 4 May 1970.

177. See Philip G. Altbach (ed.), *Student Politics and Higher Education in the United States: A Select Bibliography* (Cambridge, Mass.: Harvard University Center for International Affairs, 1968); Bettina Aptheker (ed.), *Higher Education and the Student Rebellion in the United States, 1960–69: A Bibliography* (New York: American Institute for Marxist Studies, 1969); Charles A. Moser (ed.), *Continuity in Crisis* (Washington: University Professors for Academic Order, 1974); Robert C. Christopher, *The Japanese Mind* (New York: Fawcett Columbine, 1983), pp. 94–97.

178. Brewster, Address to the Yale Club of Philadelphia, 14 Feb. 1969. Brewster Personal Papers I-14:4.

179. Interview with Jonathan Fanton, 17 Apr. 1992.

180. Jay Gitlin to Jeremy Weinberg, May 1992. Source courtesy of Jeremy Weinberg.

181. Interview with David Acheson, 4 Oct. 1990.

182. Interview with Gregory Craig, 9 Apr. 1991.

183. Spiro Agnew, Address at the Florida Republican Dinner, Fort Lauderdale, 28 Apr. 1970. In Spiro Agnew, *Collected Speeches of Spiro Agnew* (New York: Audubon Books, 1970), pp. 132–42.

184. Interview with William F. Buckley Jr., 25 Mar. 1991.

185. See Paul Bass, "Panther Frame-Ups," *New Haven Advocate*, 30 Apr. 1990, p. 1.; Ward Churchill and Jim Vander Wall, *Agents of Repression: The FBI's Secret Wars Against the Black Panther Party and the American Indian Movement*, 2nd ed. (Boston: South End Press, 2002); Yohuru Williams, *Black Politics/White Power: Civil Rights, Black Power, and the Black Panthers in New Haven* (St. James, N.Y.: Brandywine Press, 2000).

186. Kingman Brewster Jr. to Herbert S. MacDonald, 25 Apr. 1970. Brewster Presidential Records RU 11 I-141:11.

187. In a handwritten, undated draft of his 25 April 1970 letter to Herbert S. MacDonald, Brewster wrote that "I would have thought it apparent to all but the most wishful thinker . . . that both blacks and revolutionaries would have more difficulty than others in obtaining an unprejudiced jury of their peers. Whether Scottsboro Boys or Sacco & Vanzetti, there is ample precedent for my skepticism. When black and revolutionary are combined, the difficulty is that much greater. When in addition to this the trial occurs in the midst of a [racial] political backlash against blacks and against radicals, my skepticism is compounded." Brewster Presidential Records RU 11 I-141:11.

188. Fred Wacker to Kingman Brewster Jr., 10 Dec. 1970. Brewster Presidential Records RU 11 I-220:10.

189. Kingman Brewster Jr. to Fred Wacker, 21 Dec. 1970. Brewster Presidential Records RU 11 I-220:10.

190. "Black Panthers Go Free," *Chicago Tribune*, 29 May 1970.

191. Kingman Brewster Jr. to Alfred Van Sinderen, 1 June 1970. Brewster Presidential Records RU 16 6:54.

192. *National Review,* 26 May 1970, p. B75.

193. J. Irwin Miller to C. Colburn Hardy, 12 May 1970. Brewster Presidential Records RU 16 3:21.

194. Sue Hestor to Kingman Brewster Jr., 29 Apr. 1970. Brewster Presidential Records RU 16 3:22.

195. J. Otis Cochran to Kingman Brewster Jr., 14 May 1970. Brewster Presidential Records RU 16 2:10.

196. M——[signature illegible] to Kingman Brewster Jr., 24 May 1970. Brewster Presidential Records RU 16 4:32; Genevieve Hicks Coonly to Kingman Brewster Jr., 28 Apr. 1970. Brewster Presidential Records RU 16 2:10.

197. Interview with Jonathan Fanton, 17 Apr. 1992.

198. Paul S. Cutter to Kingman Brewster Jr. [nd (1970)]. Brewster Presidential Records RU 16 2:12.

199. David L. Boren to Kingman Brewster Jr., 30 Apr. 1970. Brewster Presidential Records RU 16 1:4.

200. Greenfield, *No Peace, No Place,* p. 227.

201. Collins Reed to Kingman Brewster Jr., 21 May 1970. Brewster Presidential Records RU 16 5:46.

202. Henry Louis Gates Jr., "Are We Better Off?," available at www.pbs.org/wgbh/pages/frontline/shows/race/etc/gates.html, accessed 12 Sep. 2002.

203. James Nuzzo, interview with Kingman Brewster, Jr. [nd (1974)]. Brewster Personal Papers I-45:4.

204. Nora Sayre, *Sixties Going on Seventies* (New York: Arbor House, 1973), p. 171.

11: NEW BEGINNINGS AND ENDINGS

1. Interview with Mary Louise Brewster, 27 Nov. 1994; L. Douglas Heck, memo 17 May 1980, source courtesy of Mary Louise Brewster.

2. Paul Moore Jr. to Louis Laun, 14 May 1970. Brewster Presidential Records RU 16 4:29; Richard E. Peterson and John A. Bilorusky, *May 1970: The Campus Aftermath of Cambodia and Kent State* (Berkeley, Calif.: Carnegie Foundation for the Advancement of Teaching, 1971), p. 7.

3. Charles DeBenedetti, *An American Ordeal: The Antiwar Movement of the Vietnam Era* (Syracuse, N.Y.: Syracuse University Press, 1990), p. 279.

4. Brewster, Statement 7 May 1970. Brewster Personal Papers I-22:3.

5. Brewster, "Campuses in Crisis: Three College Presidents Speak," CBS 10 May 1970. Brewster Personal Papers I-22:5.

6. Brewster, Statement 7 May 1970. Brewster Personal Papers I-22:3.

7. Brewster, Discussion Session with Alumni in Woolsey Hall, 13 June 1970. Brewster Personal Papers I-23:2.

8. Interview with Gregory Craig, 9 Apr. 1991.

9. Interview with Gregory Craig, 13 Apr. 2001.

10. McGeorge Bundy, Address at International Ex-Students Conference, University of Texas, 15 May 1970. Ford Foundation Archives, box 41835.

11. Interview with George Zeidenstein, 13 Aug. 2001.

12. Gail Spangenberg to McGeorge Bundy, 1 June 1970. Bundy Records II-14:180.

13. McGeorge Bundy, Notes on Ford Foundation Convocation, 27 May 1970. Bundy Records II-14:181.
14. Fred Bohen to McGeorge Bundy, 11 June 1970. Bundy Records II-14:181.
15. Interview with Siobhan Nicolau, 9 Feb. 2001.
16. George Dugan, "Bishop Moore Installed as Episcopal Coadjutor," *NYT,* 10 May 1970, p. 57.
17. Maurice Carroll, "Police Assailed by Mayor on Laxity at Peace Rally," *NYT,* 10 May 1970, p. 1.
18. Vincent J. Cannato, *The Ungovernable City: John Lindsay and His Struggle to Save New York* (New York: Basic Books, 2001), p. 452.
19. James T. Patterson, *Grand Expectations: The United States, 1945–1974* (New York: Oxford University Press, 1996), p. 756.
20. Thomas F. Brady, "1,000 'Establishment' Lawyers Join War Protest," *NYT,* 15 May 1970, p. 21.
21. Spiro Agnew, Address to the American Retail Federation, 4 May 1970. In John R. Coyne Jr., *The Impudent Snobs: Agnew vs. the Intellectual Establishment* (New Rochelle, N.Y.: Arlington House, 1972), pp. 323–24.
22. Spiro Agnew, Address at the Ohio Republican Dinner, Cleveland, 20 June 1970. *WP,* 26 June 1970, p. A14.
23. Interview with Jonathan Moore, 2 Dec. 2002.
24. Peter Grose, "Russians and Americans Here Debate Problems of Peace," *NYT,* 30 Apr. 1970.
25. Flora Lewis, "Nixon Drowns Out Richardson's Plea," *BG,* 8 May 1970.
26. Christopher Lydon to Elliot Richardson, 4 May 1970. Richardson Papers I:96, "'L' miscellaneous."
27. Henry Kissinger, Telephone Conversation with Elliot Richardson, 8 May 1970. Richardson Papers I:106, "Telecons—May 1–14 1970."
28. Mike Kinsley, "'I Think We Have a Very Unhappy Colleague-on-Leave Tonight,'" *Harvard Crimson,* 19 May 1970, p. 5.
29. "M. Nixon a gagné un repit de quelques mois," *Le Monde,* 14 Oct 70, p. 1.
30. J. Anthony Lukas, "The Council on Foreign Relations—Is It a Club? Seminar? Presidium? 'Invisible Government'?" *NYTM,* 21 Nov. 1971, p. 34.
31. Elliot Richardson to Henry Shattuck, 6 June 1970. Richardson Papers I:127, "Telecons—June 1970."
32. Elliot Richardson, Telephone Conversation with Nancy Dickerson, 6 July 1970. Richardson Papers I:127, "Telecons—June 1970."
33. Juan Cameron, "A Boston Brahmin in 'Heartbreak House,'" *Fortune,* Oct. 1971, p. 90.
34. "Richardson at HEW," *Bridgeport Telegram,* 20 June 1970.
35. William Chapman, "Senators Voice Sympathy for New HEW Head," *WP,* 12 June 1970, p. 2.
36. Jim Morse, "Richardson Conquers 'Impossible' Job," *Boston Sunday Advisor,* 20 Sep. 1970.
37. Peter Janssen, "Is Elliot Richardson Really Clark Kent?" [ns, nd]. Richardson Papers I-110, "Clippings."
38. Elliot Richardson, Telephone Conversation with McGeorge Bundy, 8 June 1970. Richardson Papers I:127, "Telecons—June 1970."
39. James W. Singer, "Mankind Bound for 'Near-End' Collision with Self, ABA Told," *Chicago Sun-Times,* 13 Aug. 1970.
40. John Gardner to McGeorge Bundy, 31 May 1972. Bundy Records II-15:192.

41. Jeremy Weinberg, "Long Live the King's Yale: How Kingman Brewster's University Survived and Thrived in the 1960s" (unpublished Yale senior essay, 13 Apr. 1992), p. 48.
42. Kingman Brewster, Address at the American Jewish Committee Human Relations Dinner, 10 Nov. 1970. Brewster Personal Papers I-25:1.
43. Georges May, "Report of the Dean of Yale College, 1969–70," June 1970. Brewster Presidential Records RU 11 I-73:5.
44. Interview with William Bundy, 24 Apr. 1992.
45. "Mr. Brewster Talks Back," *NYT*, 5 Oct. 1970, p. 42.
46. Joseph B. Treaster, "Brewster Is on Tour to Improve Image of University," *NYT*, 2 Oct. 1970, p. 18.
47. Interview with Jonathan Fanton, 18 July 1992.
48. Interview with Kai Erikson, 9 Mar. 1992.
49. Kingman Brewster Jr. to Marge Austin and Deane Laycock, 3 Nov. 1971. Brewster Presidential Records RU 11 I-73:5.
50. Interview with Charles H. Taylor, 12 May 1992.
51. Interview with Charles H. Taylor, 2 Mar. 1992.
52. Interview with Richard N. Cooper, 8 Apr. 1992.
53. Evan Thomas, "The Once and Future Kingman Brewster" (unpublished article, 1 Sep. 1977), p. 24. Source courtesy of Mary Louise Brewster.
54. Interview with Jonathan Fanton, 18 July 1992.
55. Jeremy Weinberg, "Long Live the King's Yale," p. 49.
56. "The Mood at Yale: When Eerie Turns to Dull," *YDN*, 1 Nov. 1972.
57. Christopher Buckley, "A Keening of Weenies," in Diana Dubois (ed.), *My Harvard, My Yale* (New York: Random House, 1982), p. 267.
58. Interview with Maynard Mack, 13 July 1992.
59. Interview with Jonathan Fanton, 18 July 1992.
60. Leonard Silk and Mark Silk, *The American Establishment* (New York: Basic Books, 1980), p. 135.
61. Interview with Patricia Wald, 31 July 2001. By 1972, Ford provided 86 percent of the grants to environmental and consumer public interest law firms. See Waldemar Nielsen, *The Golden Donors* (New York, Dutton 1985), p. 69.
62. Sandy Jaffe, interview with Tom Hilbink, 11 Nov. 1999. Source provided by Sandy Jaffe.
63. *Ford Foundation Annual Report 1970*, p. 12.
64. M. A. Farber, "$100-Million Ford Grant to Aid Minority Education," *NYT*, 10 Oct. 1971, p. 1.
65. Kingman Brewster Jr. to McGeorge Bundy, 19 Mar. 1970. Brewster Presidential Records RU 11 I-100:3.
66. McGeorge Bundy to Kingman Brewster Jr., 6 July 1970. Brewster Presidential Records RU 11 I-99:2.
67. Interview with Hanna Holborn Gray, 17 Dec. 1991.
68. Nan Robertson, "Aides to Robert Kennedy and Dr. King Are Married in a Virginia Ceremony," *NYT*, 15 July 1968.
69. Ralph Blumenthal, "Saigon Police Halt Protest Including U.S. Marchers," *NYT*, 12 July 1970, p. 3.
70. Paul Moore Jr., *Presences: A Bishop's Life in the City* (New York: Farrar, Straus and Giroux, 1997), p. 272.
71. Jervis Anderson, "Standing Out There on the Issues," *New Yorker*, 28 Apr. 1986, p. 85.
72. "An Activist Bishop Faces Life," *Newsweek*, 25 Dec. 1972, p. 57.
73. Edward B. Fiske, "Bishop Moore Is Enthroned in 8¼ Hour Celebration," *NYT*, 24 Sep. 1972, p. 1.

74. "An Activist Bishop Faces Life," pp. 56–57.
75. Godfrey Hodgson, *America in Our Time* (New York: Vintage 1976), p. 111.
76. Interview with Cyrus Vance, 13 Aug. 1993.
77. Barbara Davidson, "The Knapp Commission Didn't Know It Couldn't Be Done," *NYTM,* 9 Jan. 1972.
78. John Lindsay to Kingman Brewster Jr., 9 July 1970. Brewster Presidential Records RU 11 I-134:14.
79. "3 Rob Bishop Moore in Park," *NYT,* 23 Nov. 1972.
80. Cannato, *The Ungovernable City,* p. 500.
81. "A Mayor of Vision," *NYT,* 31 Dec. 1973, p. 16; "Lindsay in Retrospect: An Eloquent Spokesman for the Cities," *NYT,* 31 Dec. 1973, p. 7.
82. Juan Cameron, "A Boston Brahmin in 'Heartbreak House,'" p. 90.
83. H. R. Haldeman, *The Haldeman Diaries: Inside the Nixon White House* (New York: G. P. Putnam's Sons, 1984), p. 181.
84. *Congressional Record, Senate,* 12 Jan. 1973, p. 1021.
85. William Beecher, "Pentagon to Push for Minority Jobs," *NYT,* 13 Mar. 1973.
86. Elliot Richardson, *The Creative Balance: Government, Politics, and the Individual in America's Third Century* (New York: Holt, Rinehart & Winston, 1976), pp. 4–5.
87. Michael Getler, "Moderation, Pragmatism Emphasized by Richardson," *WP,* 2 May 1973.
88. CHR comments, 7 May 1973. Richardson Papers I:230, "Watergate—Special Prosecutor—Search for Special Prosecutor—Candidates."
89. Elliot Richardson to Cyrus Vance, 18 June 1973. Richardson Papers I:199, "Chronological reading file."
90. Ken Gormley, *Archibald Cox: Conscience of a Nation* (Reading, Mass.: Addison-Wesley, 1997), p. 235.
91. Richard Nixon, *The Memoirs of Richard Nixon,* vol. 2 (New York: Warner Books, 1979), p. 461.
92. Kirkpatrick Sale, *Power Shift: The Rise of the Southern Rim and Its Challenge to the Eastern Establishment* (New York: Random House, 1975), p. 4.
93. William Scranton et al., *The Report of the President's Commission on Campus Unrest* (New York: Avon, 1971), p. 289; Thomas Powers, "The Truth about Kent State," *NYT,* 2 Sep. 1973, p. 213.
94. Anthony Lewis, "Watergate Aftermath," *NYT,* 28 Nov. 1974, p. 33.
95. "The Agnew Connection," *NYTM,* 13 Jan. 1974, pp. 30–31.
96. Tom Huston to George Bell, 25 Jan. 1971. Nixon Presidential Materials, Colson Files, box 38, "Black List."
97. John Dean to H. R. Haldeman. Nixon Presidential Materials, Haldeman Files, box 270.
98. Interview with Richard N. Cooper, 8 Apr. 1992.
99. Brewster, "Excerpt from an Uncompleted Book," in *Kingman Brewster: Remembrances* (New Haven: Yale University, 1997), p. 81.
100. Brewster, Yale Baccalaureate Address, 18 May 1974. Brewster Personal Papers I:34:3. See, for example, Charles W. Colson's directive to George Bull concerning Democratic lawyer Lloyd Cutler: "have him assassinated." Nixon Presidential Materials, Colson Files, box 38, "Black List."
101. Richardson, *The Creative Balance,* p. 44.
102. Gormley, *Archibald Cox,* p. 357.
103. James Bennett, "The Longest Day," *NYTM,* 7 Jan. 2001.
104. Frank Melton, "Hundreds Petition for Impeachment," *YDN,* 22 Oct. 1973, p. 1.

105. Maurice Carroll, "Public Reacts Strongly to Cox Ouster," *NYT,* 22 Oct. 1973, p. 24.
106. John Morton Blum, *Years of Discord: American Politics and Society, 1961–1974* (New York: W. W. Norton, 1991), pp. 451–52.
107. Thomas Oliphant, "Richardson's Specialness," *BG,* 4 Jan. 2000, p. A15.
108. Mary McGrory, "Richardson Maintained His Bearing during Watergate Tempest," *Charleston Gazette,* 11 Jan. 2000, p. A4.
109. Bart Barnes, "Elliot Richardson Dies at 79; 1973 Resignation as Attorney General Shocked the Nation," *WP,* 1 Jan. 2000, p. B7.
110. Brewster, Address at Dinner for Frank Altschul, 17 May 1973. Brewster Personal Papers I-31:12.
111. James Bennett, "The Longest Day."
112. Richardson, *The Creative Balance,* p. 116.
113. Dan Rubock, "Richardson Blasts 'Training of Bulls,'" *YDN,* 2 Apr. 1974, p. 1. Buckley, "A Keening of Weenies," p. 272; background interview.
114. "Cyrus Vance for State," *NYT,* 4 Dec. 1976, p. 19.
115. "Vance and Lance: The Selection Begins," *Time,* 13 Dec. 1976, p. 12.
116. Gaddis Smith, *Morality, Reason and Power: American Diplomacy in the Carter Years* (New York: Hill and Wang, 1986), pp. 40–41.
117. Cyrus Vance, *Hard Choices: Critical Years in American Foreign Policy* (New York: Simon & Schuster, 1983), p. 446.
118. Interview with Joseph A. Califano Jr., 16 Jan. 2003.
119. Suetonius, "Everybody's Man," *The New Republic,* 18 Dec. 1976, pp. 14–15.
120. Bernard Gwertzman, "Vance Says U.S. Erred in Joining War in Vietnam," *WP,* 12 Jan. 1977, p. A1.
121. Interview with Terry Saario, 28 Oct. 2002.
122. McGeorge Bundy, "A Memorandum on the Common Cause Statement of February 23 on Laos," 24 Mar. 1971. Bundy Records II-15:192.
123. Interview with Theodore Hesburgh, 4 Dec. 2000.
124. Elliot Richardson, CUOHA, "US Diplomats at the UN" project.
125. Thomas Vance, "Elliot Richardson: Man of Principle," available at http://www.trustingov.org/research/books/richardson/chap10.htm, accessed 11 Feb. 2002.
126. Elliot Richardson, *Reflections of a Radical Moderate* (New York: Pantheon Books, 1996), p. 218.
127. Martin Mayer, *The Diplomats* (Garden City, N.Y.: Doubleday, 1983), p. 293.
128. Interview with Cyrus Vance, 13 Aug. 1993.
129. John Bainbridge, "Our Far-Flung Correspondents: Excellency," *New Yorker,* 12 Dec. 1977, p. 144.
130. Randy Mastro, "Coffin Asks Students to 'Sound Off' Again," *YDN,* 4 Dec. 1975, p. 10.
131. Mead Treadwell, "Entrenchment," *YDN,* 28 Mar. 1977, p. 2.
132. Interview with Paul Moore Jr., 15 Jan. 2002.
133. "Brewster's Farewell," *YDN,* 8 Apr. 1977, p. 2.
134. Interview with John Blum, 28 Apr. 1992.
135. Brewster, Yale Baccalaureate Address, 15 May 1977. Brewster Personal Papers I-45:1.
136. James Reston, "How to Exit Smiling," *NYT,* 18 May 1977, p. 25.
137. Diane Henry, "Yale Salutes Ford with an LL.D. Degree," *NYT,* 17 May 1977, p. 36.
138. Michael Davies, "Meet Carter's Man in London," *Observer Review,* 3 July 1977.
139. Raymond Seitz, *Over Here* (London: Phoenix, 1998), pp. 64–65.
140. Alan Road, "The Quiet American," *Observer Magazine,* 10 June 1979, p. 65.

141. Brewster, Saint George's House Lecture, 5 May 1978. Brewster Personal Papers I-50:14.

142. R. W. Apple Jr., "Brewster Quietly Follows Own Road as Envoy to Britain," *NYT,* 19 Mar. 1979, p. A12.

143. McGeorge Bundy, marginal notation on Kingman Brewster Jr.'s Address to the Council on Foreign Relations, 23 Apr. 1980. Brewster Personal Papers I-53:8.

144. Bainbridge, "Our Far-Flung Correspondents," pp. 147–48.

145. Kingman Brewster Jr. to Robert Bowie, 17 Sep. 1957. Brewster Personal Papers II-1, "Bowie–Harvard Center for International Affairs."

146. Thomas Simons to Geoffrey Kabaservice, 4 May 1999.

147. Brewster, interview on "Open Air New England," 1981. Source courtesy of Stanley Flink.

148. David R. Francis, "Whatever Became of the British Commonwealth?" *Christian Science Monitor,* 4 Sep. 1985, p. 18.

149. Interview with Edward Streator, 25 July 1999.

150. Patrick Marnham, "The King in England," *The New Republic,* 6 and 13 Sep. 1980, p. 16.

151. "U.S. Ambassador on Veteran Car Run," *Farnham Herald,* 10 Nov. 1978.

152. Brewster, "Excerpt from an Uncompleted Book," pp. 84–85.

153. Interview with Raymond Seitz, 12 July 1999.

154. Brewster, "Excerpt from an Uncompleted Book," p. 85.

155. Brian Connell, "The Civilizing Influences on Mr Brewster," [London] *Times,* 14 July 1980, p. 11.

156. Interview with Edward Streator, 20 June 1991.

157. Quoted in Smith, *Morality, Reason and Power,* p. 42.

158. Hodding Carter III, "Life inside the Carter State Department," *Playboy,* Feb. 1981, p. 214.

159. Marilyn Berger, "Cyrus R. Vance, a Confidant to Presidents, Is Dead at 84," *NYT,* 13 Jan. 2002.

160. Smith, *Morality, Reason and Power,* p. 42.

161. Walter Isaacson and Evan Thomas, *The Wise Men: Six Friends and the World They Made* (New York: Simon & Schuster, 1986), p. 727.

162. T. R. Fehrenbach, "Cyrus Vance: One of the Last of the 'Gentlemen' in Government," *San Antonio Light,* 4 May 1980.

163. John M. Goshko, "Vance Formally Resigns, Citing Raid Opposition; Carter to Name Successor Soon," *WP,* 29 Apr. 1980, p. A1.

164. "The Vance Resignation," *WP,* 29 Apr. 1980, p. A16.

165. Interview with Lloyd Cutler, 10 Apr. 1991.

166. Interview with Edward Streator, 20 June 1991.

167. "An Ambassador Looks Back at the British," *Sunday Telegraph,* 11 Jan. 1981, p. 6.

168. Brewster, "Excerpt from an Uncompleted Book," p. 85.

169. Joseph Lelyveld, "New Yank at Oxford Is Kingman Brewster," *NYT,* 30 Oct. 1986, p. A1.

170. Peter Osnos, "At Least Our New Envoy to Britain Gives Good Parties," *WP,* 2 Jan. 1983, p. B1.

171. John Harris, "Alums Seek True Blue President," *YDN,* 29 Mar. 1977, p. 1.

172. Interview with Henry Chauncey Jr., 22 July 1993.

173. Interview with Jonathan Fanton, 18 July 1992.

174. Lelyveld, "New Yank at Oxford Is Kingman Brewster," p. A1.

175. Cathleen McGuigan with Diane Weathers, "A Yale Man Comes Home Again," *Newsweek,* 27 Apr. 1981, p. 9.

176. Interview with John G. Simon, 22 June 1992.
177. Interview with Peter Solbert, 25 Feb. 1992.
178. Interview with John G. Simon, 22 June 1992.
179. "Ex-President of Yale Gets London Law Post," *NYT,* 24 Jan. 1984, p. D2.
180. "Kingman Brewster, Jr., 69; U.K. Envoy, Yale President," *Los Angeles Times,* 9 Nov. 1988, p. 36.
181. Joseph Soares, *The Decline of Privilege: The Modernization of Oxford University* (Stanford, Calif.: Stanford University Press, 1999), pp. 207–263.
182. Interview with Frank Norall, 20 June 1991.
183. Lesley Hazleton, *England, Bloody England: An Expatriate's Return* (New York: Atlantic Monthly Press, 1990), pp. 126–30.
184. McGeorge Bundy to Kingman Brewster Jr., 14 Apr. 1987. Source courtesy of Mary Louise Brewster.
185. Interview with Frank Norall, 20 June 1991.
186. Stanley E. Flink, "The Passing of a President," *YAM,* Feb. 1989, p. 37.

EPILOGUE

1. Interview with Francis Bator, 19 June 2002.
2. Francis Bator, "Glimpses of Mac," 8 Nov. 1996. Source courtesy of Francis Bator.
3. Interview with Jonathan Moore, 2 Dec. 2002.
4. Ann Kramer, quoted in David Nyhan, "Elliot Richardson: A Winner Where It Truly Counted," *BG,* 16 Jan. 2000, p. C4.
5. Elliot Richardson, *Reflections of a Radical Moderate* (New York: Pantheon Books, 1996), p. 270.
6. Spencer S. Hsu, "Washington Honors Richardson; Admirers Commemorate 'a Great Public Servant,'" *WP,* 16 Jan. 2000, p. C3.
7. Vincent J. Cannato, *The Ungovernable City: John Lindsay and His Struggle to Save New York* (New York: Basic Books, 2001), p. 565.
8. Robert D. McFadden, "Former New York Mayor Lindsay Dies at 79," *NYT,* 20 Dec. 2000.
9. Elisabeth Bumiller, "Thousands Pay Tribute to Lindsay," *NYT,* 27 Jan. 2001, p. A12.
10. Interview with Paul Moore Jr., 15 Jan. 2002.
11. "Vance Remembered as Peacemaker, Old-Fashioned Patriot," *Miami Herald,* 20 Jan. 2002, p. A30.
12. Myra Oliver, "Cyrus R. Vance, 84; 'Superb Statesman,'" *Los Angeles Times,* 13 Jan. 2002, p. B16.
13. Interview with Paul Moore Jr., 15 Jan. 2002.
14. Episcopal Diocese of New York, "Rest in Peace: Bishop Paul Moore; Funeral on May 10," available at www.dioceseny.org/index.cfm?Action=News, accessed 7 May 2003.
15. Interview with Cyrus Vance, 13 Aug. 1993.
16. William H. Honan, "At the Top of the Ivory Tower the Watchword Is Silence," *NYT,* 24 July 1994, p. E5.
17. Interview with Theodore Hesburgh, 4 Dec. 2000.
18. David Halberstam, *The Best and the Brightest* (New York: Random House, 1972), p. 657.
19. John J. Judis, *The Paradox of American Democracy: Elites, Special Interests, and the Betrayal of Public Trust* (New York: Pantheon Books, 2000), p. 255.

20. McGeorge Bundy, "Visions & Revisions," *YDN,* 3 June 1938, p. 2.
21. McGeorge Bundy, Address at the Associated Press Managing Editors Convention in Honolulu, 20 Nov. 1970. Ford Foundation Archives, box 41835.
22. Tom Wicker, "The Guardian Critics," *NYT,* 23 May 1972, p. 41.
23. William Rees-Mogg, "Last of the Brahmins," *Times of London,* 19 Sep. 1996.
24. Interview with Nicholas Katzenbach, 4 June 2003.
25. Elliot L. Richardson, "Beyond the Marlboro Man," *Ripon Forum,* May 1967, p. 1.
26. Quoted in Godfrey Hodgson, *America in Our Time* (New York: Vintage, 1976), p. 498.
27. Theodore H. White, "The Action Intellectuals," *Life,* 23 June 1967, p. 85.
28. Interview with Elliot Richardson, 22 June 1997.
29. Interview with William Sloane Coffin Jr., 9 Dec. 1991
30. Interview with William Sloane Coffin Jr., 26 June, 2000.
31. Garry Wills, "Washington Is Not Where It's At," *NYTM,* 25 Jan. 1998, p. 57.
32. Gordon S. Wood, *The Radicalism of the American Revolution* (New York: Alfred A. Knopf, 1992), p. 369.

ACKNOWLEDGMENTS

I never met Kingman Brewster—never even saw him from a distance. In writing about Brewster and his circle, I depended heavily on the recollections of people who had known them. This book has been a long time in the making, and many of those I talked to are now dead. I am grateful to all who spoke with me.

Most of the interview transcripts on which this book is based are on deposit in two oral history collections, at the Manuscripts and Archives Library in Yale University's Sterling Memorial Library and at the John F. Kennedy Presidential Library in Boston. I worked for two and a half years in the early 1990s on the Griswold-Brewster History Project, conducting interviews with people who had ties to Brewster and his Yale presidential predecessor, A. Whitney Griswold. My deepest thanks go to the members of the committee that oversaw my work and continued to give me guidance over the years: John Morton Blum, Sam Chauncey, Eli Clark, Radley Daly, Kai Erikson, and Stanley Flink. Thanks, too, to Charlotte Pavia and Sandra Radizeski for providing the administrative backbone for the project, and to university archivist Richard Szary for handling the collection's integration into Yale's holdings. I conducted a separate series of interviews on McGeorge Bundy, which I never could have done without the help of Peter Bell, Stephen Bundy, Sandy Jaffe, Richard Magat, and especially the late Doc Howe. Megan Desnoyers helped create an institutional home for these interviews at the Kennedy Library.

The idea for this book grew out of the doctoral dissertation in history I completed at Yale University in 1999. I owe a great deal to the suggestions of several of my fellow graduate students, notably Stacey Davis and David Koistinen, and of my dissertation committee, professors Kai Erikson, Gaddis

Smith, and Cynthia Russett. I'm also in debt to Carter Wiseman, the former editor of the *Yale Alumni Magazine,* who published part of the dissertation's chapter on undergraduate admissions in the magazine in January 2000 and stirred up a hornet's nest of spirited debate. William S. Beinecke kept me from subsisting on roots and grubs during my graduate school years by hiring me to help with his memoir, *Through Mem'ry's Haze,* and has continued to provide friendship and wise advice.

I received incalculable assistance from librarians, archivists, and staff at Yale's Manuscripts and Archives Library, the Beinecke Library at Yale, the Ford Foundation Archives, the Nathan Pusey Library at Harvard University, the Harvard Law School Archives, the Lyndon B. Johnson Presidential Library, the John F. Kennedy Presidential Library, the Jimmy Carter Presidential Library, the Columbia University Oral History Project, the National Archives, the Library of Congress, the Boston Atheneum, the British Library, the University Library at Cambridge University, the Bodleian Library at Oxford University, the Firestone Library at Princeton University, and the Gelman Library at George Washington University. I am particularly thankful for the help of Bruce Kirby at the Library of Congress, and of Chris Connolly and Sandra Staton at Yale's Manuscripts and Archives Library; they uncomplainingly lugged thousands upon thousands of boxes of materials up from the bowels of the collection.

Many thanks also to those people who provided me with archival access or materials otherwise unavailable, particularly Francis Bator, William S. Beinecke, Mary Louise Brewster, William F. Buckley Jr., Stanley Flink, Mary Griswold, Harold Howe II, Sandy Jaffe, Mary Kennedy, Richard C. Lee, Richard Magat, Paul Moore Jr., Claire and John Simon, William Simpich, Jeremy Weinberg, H. Brad Westerfield, Jodi Lynn Wilgoren, and Peter Viereck.

Donald Lamm and Michael Carlisle made the business of finding a publisher as painless as possible for a first-time author, and life would have been very difficult without them. My peerless and long-suffering editor, George Hodgman, provided encouragement and periodic pleas for progress, and improved every aspect of the manuscript. Vanessa Mobley also went through the manuscript with a sharp eye and offered many useful revisions.

A number of people read chapters of the book at different states of gestation, including Sam Chauncey, Eli Clark, William Sloane Coffin, Sarah Hammond, and Jim Sleeper. I very much appreciate the feedback and suggestions they offered. I also received helpful advice from David Cannadine,

Linda Colley, David Fieldhouse, Catherine Holmes, John Judis, and Sam Tanenhaus.

I wrote this book while working full time (and often more than full time) for the Advisory Board Company in Washington, D.C. I am grateful to Chris Denby and Josh Gray for allowing me to take two brief leaves of absence to finish a book that had no connection whatsoever to my job. I doubt many other employers would be as tolerant and enlightened.

A number of people, too many to thank individually, helped keep me afloat through the grueling process of completing the manuscript. I particularly appreciate the support of Catherine Humphries, Bryan Lawrence, Deborah Jo Miller, Carolyn Stephenson, my sister, Marah, and my brothers, Jesse and Ted.

First and last, my thanks go to my parents, who made everything possible. This book is dedicated to them.

INDEX

ABOUT THE AUTHOR

GEOFFREY KABASERVICE received a B.A. from Yale in 1988, an M. Phil from Cambridge University in 1989, and a Ph.D. from Yale in 1999, where he received the university's prize teaching fellowship and award for best dissertation on U.S. history. He is a former lecturer in the Yale History Department and has written for several national publications. He is a Woodrow Wilson Postdoctoral Career Fellow and a project manager at the Advisory Board Company in Washington, D.C.